AMERICA'S PREMIERE TESTING READINESS PROGRAM

Victory
for the
GRE® Test

S T U D E N T   T E X T

Our Mission: Progress Through Partnership
Cambridge Educational Services partners with educators who share the significant mission of educational advancement for all students. By partnering together, we can best achieve our common goals: to build skills, raise test scores, enhance curriculum, and support instruction. A leading innovator in education for twenty years, Cambridge is the nation's premier provider of school-based test preparation and supplemental curriculum services.

Cambridge Publishing, Inc.
www.CambridgeEd.com

© 1991, 1993, 1996, 1998, 1999, 2001, 2002, 2003, 2008, 2010, 2011, 2013 by Cambridge Publishing, Inc.
All rights reserved. First edition 1991
Tenth edition 2013

Printed in the United States of America
18 17 16 15   2 3 4 5

ISBN-13: 978-1-58894-176-3

Why You Must Have This Book

Dear Student,

Congratulations on your decision to pursue a graduate degree. Now, your focus turns to the best possible way to prepare—and that is why you must have this book.

As you realize, your GRE test score is a critical component of your graduate school application. If it is too low, your application will not even be considered. If it is mediocre, your application will receive some (but probably not serious) consideration. You need to achieve the highest possible score you can in order to maximize your chances of admission, and only an expert resource can connect you to the most efficient test prep strategies and the most fruitful areas for review.

The carefully crafted drills, exercises, and tests found in the *Cambridge Victory for the GRE® Student Text, 10th Edition,* fit this bill. The diagnostic pre- and post-assessments quickly identify your specific areas of weakness. The lessons focus on efficiently improving your knowledge in each tested area. The four full-length practice tests give you plenty of opportunities to improve your test-taking skills. The supplemental skills sections provide support for the test-taker who needs a quick review. And bonus sections on preparing your graduate school application will give you an edge even beyond the test.

Graduate school admission is a very competitive arena, and you'll need every possible advantage you can get. So, make the *Cambridge Victory for the GRE® Student Text, 10th Edition,* the foundation of your test prep toolkit.

Best wishes for a successful graduate career,

The Cambridge Curriculum Committee

TABLE OF CONTENTS

Basic Skills Supplement

COURSE OVERVIEW

By enrolling in a Cambridge GRE course, you have selected a test preparation program that will maximize your results while minimizing the required time investment. Your course will include some or all of the elements of this Victory for the GRE Test program, outlined below:

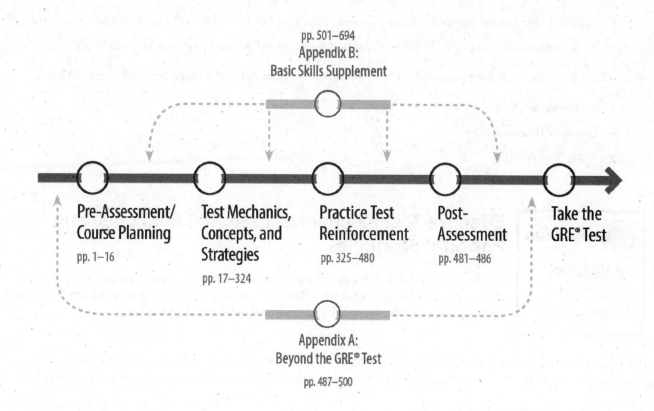

The following introduction briefly explains how to use each part of this book.

Pre-Assessment/Course Planning

Most locations utilizing the Cambridge Victory for the GRE Test program include a pre-assessment at the start of the course. Taking a pre-assessment helps you find out what you already do well and what you could learn to do better. The Pre-Assessment/Course Planning segment of this book contains four sections that explain pre-assessment administration and help you use your results to improve your test score:

- "Pre-Assessment Administration" explains the logistics of taking the pre-assessment.

- "How to Use the Pre-Assessment Reports" helps you make connections between your performance on the pre-assessment and the items in this book that you most need to study.

- "Setting a Test Score Target" helps you understand the graduate school admission process and aids you in setting goals as to where you should apply.

- "Planning a Schedule for the Course" helps you develop a study schedule that will contribute to your success in the course.

Basic Skills Supplement (Appendix B)

You should review some or all of the Basic Skills areas if:

- Your pre-assessment shows a disproportionate number of wrong answers in a particular subject area.
- Your total score is significantly below the target score for the schools to which you will apply.

Appendix B contains three supplemental skills sections that correspond to the three sections of the GRE test:

- Verbal Reasoning
- Quantitative Reasoning
- Analytical Writing

Test Mechanics, Concepts and Strategies

Effective Test Mechanics, Essential Concepts, and Powerful Strategies

This is the heart of the course. When compared with items on the real test, the items in this section have similar content, represent the same difficulty levels, and can be solved by using the same problem-solving skills and test-taking strategies.

The Test Mechanics, Concepts, and Strategies section includes seven chapters, each of which represents a component of the GRE test. The following list includes examples of concepts and strategies in each chapter:

- Verbal Reasoning: Completions
  - Concepts: thought extension, thought reversal, combined reasoning, etc.
  - Strategies: "Anticipate and Test," "Go to Pieces," "Hard Cases," etc.

- Verbal Reasoning: Reading
  - Concepts: implied idea, specific detail, further application, etc.
  - Strategies: eliminate incorrect answers, develop effective pacing, employ careful reading techniques, etc.

- Quantitative Reasoning: Discrete Quantitative
  - Concepts: arithmetic, algebra, geometry, data analysis, etc.
  - Strategies: look for shortcuts, "Test-the-Test," "Plug-and-Chug," etc.

- Quantitative Reasoning: Numeric Entry
  - Concepts: watch for units of measure, features of the on-screen calculator, etc.
  - Strategies: pay attention to thought reversers, etc.

- Quantitative Reasoning: Comparisons

  o Concepts: arithmetic comparison, algebra comparison, geometry comparison, data analysis comparison, etc.
  o Strategies: "Good Enough" principle, simplifying comparisons, "Test-the-Test," etc.

- Quantitative Reasoning: Data Interpretation

  o Concepts: table charts, bar graphs, line graphs, scatterplots, frequency distributions, etc.
  o Strategies: make the picture do the work, learn the types of graphs, etc.

- Analytical Writing

  o Concepts: a clearly articulated position, clear and concise writing, etc.
  o Strategies: read the prompts thoroughly, look to prompts for main points, follow an essay template, etc.

A "Course Concept Outline" at the beginning of each chapter lists the lesson components and tested concepts. Each chapter also includes "Test Mechanics," "Lesson," and "Quizzes" sections. Finally, a "Strategy Summary" at the end of each chapter offers a quick review of the most valuable test prep strategies for that chapter.

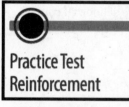

Practice Test Reinforcement

Four full-length GRE practice tests will help you further apply the strategies you have learned and test your knowledge of each concept. The items on these tests mimic those on the real test in content and difficulty level. You may complete some of these tests in class and others at home. The first practice test is a Directed Study Practice Test in which the correct answer and a detailed explanation are provided with each item to guide you through the test. There is no time limit for this exercise. The other three tests are timed exams. If you are taking these four tests on your own, you should complete the Directed Study Practice Test *without* time restrictions and full-length Practice Tests I–III *with* time restrictions. Taking the test without time restrictions will help you get a sense of how long it would take for you to comfortably and accurately solve an item. Applying time pressure then forces you to learn to pace yourself.

Score Booster Supplement

Cambridge's online Score Booster Supplement provides additional practice in a computer-based environment featuring the various question types on the official test. Questions are sorted by difficulty level, allowing you to practice easier questions and challenge yourself with the most difficult questions. As you complete each test section, you will receive performance reports that allow you to evaluate your progress and target your study time. The Score Booster includes the equivalent of three full-length GRE tests.

Post-Assessment

Most locations utilizing the Cambridge *Victory for the GRE® Test* program include a post-assessment at the end of the course. After all of the focused studying you have been doing, your GRE scores are bound to go up. At the close of the course, you will take a post-assessment under actual testing conditions to see how far you have come. This stage of the course also allows you to identify any remaining areas you need to brush up on before the actual exam.

The Post-Assessment contains three sections to help you see how far you've come:

- "Post-Assessment Administration" explains the logistics of taking the post-assessment.

- "How to Use the Post-Assessment Reports" shows you how to use the Student Summary report you will receive to best plan your final days or weeks of studying to prepare for the real test. The report will help you identify areas of study, as well as particular items in your textbook upon which to focus, as you continue to prepare.

- "Post-Assessment Action Plan" provides a short guide to help you design an action plan for the days or weeks between the end of the course and the real test. At this stage of the course, you will put into action everything that you have learned to make the most of your remaining study time.

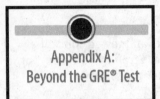

Appendix A:
Beyond the GRE® Test

Beyond the GRE® Test (Appendix A)

After you have reached the score you targeted at the beginning of the program and have successfully taken the official GRE test, you deserve congratulations. However, your work to gain graduate school admission is not over. You must now begin or continue the application process. This section of our book teaches you how to highlight your unique qualities to maximize your chances of admission into your first-choice school. Of course, your GRE test score will also aid in that process, thanks to all the work you have invested to prepare for the test.

Pre-Assessment/ Course Planning

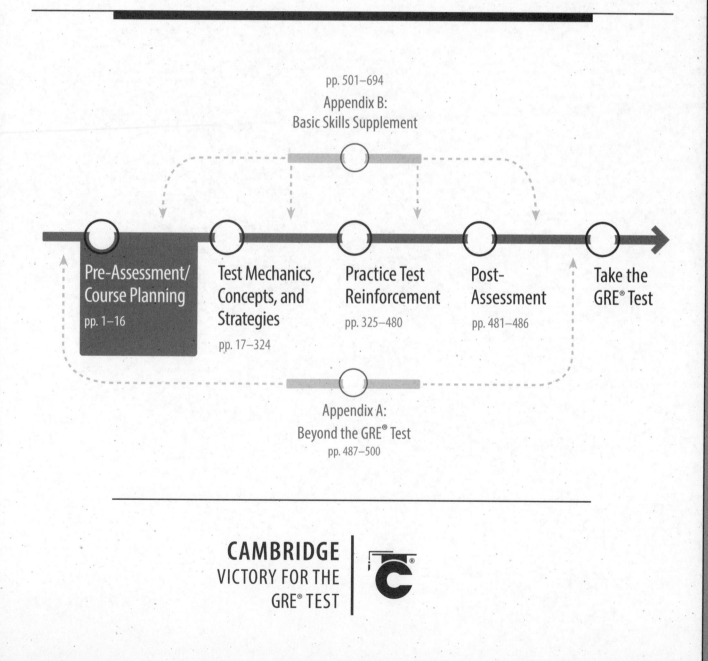

pp. 501–694
Appendix B:
Basic Skills Supplement

Pre-Assessment/
Course Planning
pp. 1–16

Test Mechanics,
Concepts, and
Strategies
pp. 17–324

Practice Test
Reinforcement
pp. 325–480

Post-
Assessment
pp. 481–486

Take the
GRE® Test

Appendix A:
Beyond the GRE® Test
pp. 487–500

CAMBRIDGE
VICTORY FOR THE
GRE® TEST

PRE-ASSESSMENT
ADMINISTRATION

At the beginning of the course, you will take a pre-assessment. When you take the pre-assessment, you should bring sharpened, soft-lead No. 2 pencils, a calculator, and a watch to pace yourself as you work through each test section, in addition to anything else your instructor tells you to bring. For a complete listing of items both permitted and prohibited at GRE testing centers, visit www.ets.org/gre/revised_general/test_day/.

HOW TO USE THE
PRE-ASSESSMENT REPORTS

If your program is using the Cambridge Assessment Service, you will receive the results of your pre-assessment in the form of a Student Summary and a Student Item Analysis approximately 6 days after taking the test. These reports provide details about your performance and will help you to determine where to focus your efforts during the course by strategically targeting those skills that will help you to improve in your areas of weakness. Review the details of the sample reports so that you are familiar with their contents.

Sample Reports

On the following pages are sample Cambridge reports for the GRE test.

Student Summary

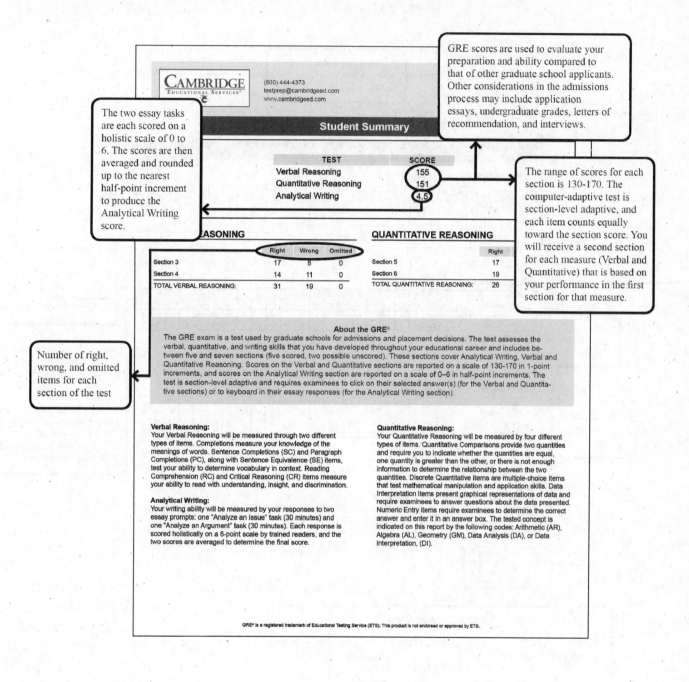

The two essay tasks are each scored on a holistic scale of 0 to 6. The scores are then averaged and rounded up to the nearest half-point increment to produce the Analytical Writing score.

GRE scores are used to evaluate your preparation and ability compared to that of other graduate school applicants. Other considerations in the admissions process may include application essays, undergraduate grades, letters of recommendation, and interviews.

The range of scores for each section is 130-170. The computer-adaptive test is section-level adaptive, and each item counts equally toward the section score. You will receive a second section for each measure (Verbal and Quantitative) that is based on your performance in the first section for that measure.

Number of right, wrong, and omitted items for each section of the test

CAMBRIDGE
EDUCATIONAL SERVICES
(800) 444-4373
testprep@cambridgeed.com
www.cambridgeed.com

Student Summary

TEST	SCORE
Verbal Reasoning	155
Quantitative Reasoning	151
Analytical Writing	4.5

VERBAL REASONING

	Right	Wrong	Omitted
Section 3	17	8	0
Section 4	14	11	0
TOTAL VERBAL REASONING:	31	19	0

QUANTITATIVE REASONING

	Right
Section 5	17
Section 6	19
TOTAL QUANTITATIVE REASONING:	26

About the GRE®

The GRE exam is a test used by graduate schools for admissions and placement decisions. The test assesses the verbal, quantitative, and writing skills that you have developed throughout your educational career and includes between five and seven sections (five scored, two possible unscored). These sections cover Analytical Writing, Verbal and Quantitative Reasoning. Scores on the Verbal and Quantitative sections are reported on a scale of 130-170 in 1-point increments, and scores on the Analytical Writing section are reported on a scale of 0–6 in half-point increments. The test is section-level adaptive and requires examinees to click on their selected answer(s) (for the Verbal and Quantitative sections) or to keyboard in their essay responses (for the Analytical Writing section).

Verbal Reasoning:
Your Verbal Reasoning will be measured through two different types of items. Completions measure your knowledge of the meanings of words. Sentence Completions (SC) and Paragraph Completions (PC), along with Sentence Equivalence (SE) items, test your ability to determine vocabulary in context. Reading Comprehension (RC) and Critical Reasoning (CR) items measure your ability to read with understanding, insight, and discrimination.

Analytical Writing:
Your writing ability will be measured by your responses to two essay prompts: one "Analyze an Issue" task (30 minutes) and one "Analyze an Argument" task (30 minutes). Each response is scored holistically on a 6-point scale by trained readers, and the two scores are averaged to determine the final score.

Quantitative Reasoning:
Your Quantitative Reasoning will be measured by four different types of items. Quantitative Comparisons provide two quantities and require you to indicate whether the quantities are equal, one quantity is greater than the other, or there is not enough information to determine the relationship between the two quantities. Discrete Quantitative items are multiple-choice items that test mathematical manipulation and application skills. Data Interpretation items present graphical representations of data and require examinees to answer questions about the data presented. Numeric Entry items require examinees to determine the correct answer and enter it in an answer box. The tested concept is indicated on this report by the following codes: Arithmetic (AR), Algebra (AL), Geometry (GM), Data Analysis (DA), or Data Interpretation, (DI).

Student Item Analysis

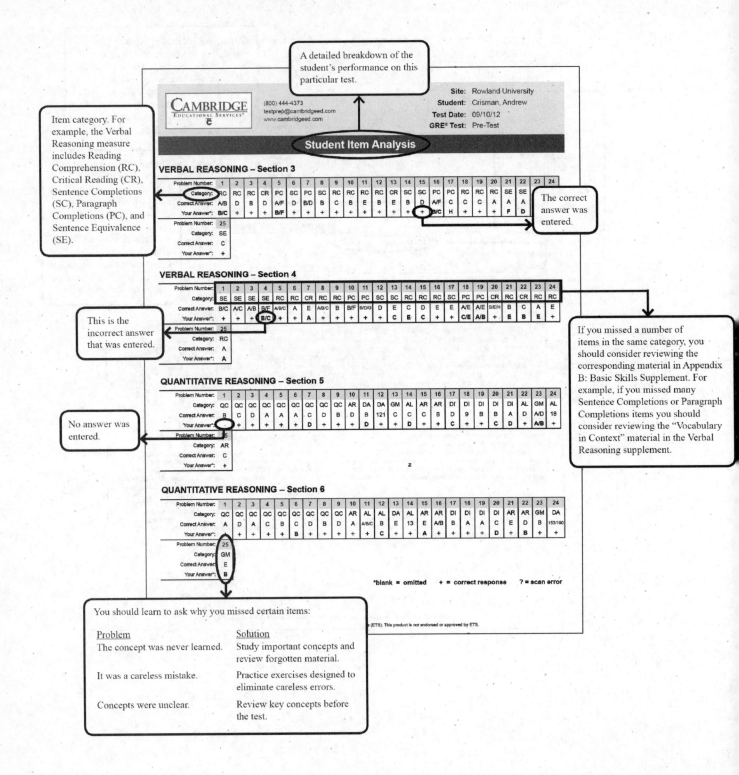

A detailed breakdown of the student's performance on this particular test.

Item category. For example, the Verbal Reasoning measure includes Reading Comprehension (RC), Critical Reading (CR), Sentence Completions (SC), Paragraph Completions (PC), and Sentence Equivalence (SE).

The correct answer was entered.

This is the incorrect answer that was entered.

No answer was entered.

If you missed a number of items in the same category, you should consider reviewing the corresponding material in Appendix B: Basic Skills Supplement. For example, if you missed many Sentence Completions or Paragraph Completions items you should consider reviewing the "Vocabulary in Context" material in the Verbal Reasoning supplement.

You should learn to ask why you missed certain items:

Problem	Solution
The concept was never learned.	Study important concepts and review forgotten material.
It was a careless mistake.	Practice exercises designed to eliminate careless errors.
Concepts were unclear.	Review key concepts before the test.

Using Pre-Assessment Reports to Target Weaknesses

Once you have received your pre-assessment Student Summary and Student Item Analysis, you will be able to make connections between the reports and the specific material in this book that you need to study.

Based on your performance on the Pre-Assessment, consider working through one or more of the supplements provided in Appendix B. For example, if you missed several Reading Comprehension items, a review of the Reading Comprehension Supplement will help you build the core skills you need to improve your Verbal Reasoning score. The table below outlines the supplements available in Appendix B. Consult with your instructor before you begin working on these supplements, because he or she may choose to cover this material in class.

ITEM CATEGORY	SUPPLEMENTAL MATERIAL	PAGE
Completions (CO)	Building Vocabulary Through Context	505
	Exercise 1: Vocabulary in Context	506
	Exercise 2: Vocabulary Completions	513
	Vocabulary List	516
Reading Comprehension (RC)	Honing Your Reading Skills	530
	Exercise 4: Determine the Main Idea	541
	Exercise 5: Outline Passages	543
	Exercise 6: Locate Verbal Signs	545
	Exercise 7: Locate Specific Details	546
	Exercise 9: Consider the Author's Point of View	551
	Exercise 10: Probe the Mood of the Passage	553
	Exercise 11: Bonus Passages	554
Critical Reading (CR)	Exercise 3: Identify Parts of Arguments	537
	Exercise 8: Analyze the Arguments	548
Arithmetic (AR)	Numbers	574
	Percents	582
	Ratios and Proportions	595
	Exponents and Radicals	599
Algebra (AL)	Algebraic Operations	607
	Algebraic Equations and Inequalities	623
	Coordinate Geometry	655
	Story Problems	672
Geometry (GM)	Geometry	639
Data Analysis (DA)	Statistical Measures	589
Analytical Writing	Planning an Essay	679
	Composition	681
	Revision	686

SETTING A TEST SCORE TARGET

One of the most important things you can do at the start of your GRE course is to set a goal for where you want to end up. After all, taking the GRE test is only a means to an end—getting accepted into your first-choice school. Before you can do this, you need to understand how the graduate admission process works, review the schools available to you, narrow down the list of schools that you are interested in, and then define how you will reach your goal.

Learn How the Admission Process Works

GPA and GRE Score

The first thing to understand is that there is no single admission process used by every graduate school. Each school possesses a unique approach. For example, at some schools faculty committees may be required to make the decisions by majority vote or unanimous agreement before an applicant is accepted. In other schools, professional admissions officers or a Dean of Admissions may make the decisions. Alternatively, a committee of members drawn from both administration and faculty might make the call.

Indeed, almost all schools regard the mechanics of the decision-making process as a highly sensitive matter, and they do not readily share the details of that process with outsiders. In any event, you cannot exercise any control over the way a graduate school makes its decisions. And as you will see, you do not need "inside" information to create an effective application.

Despite the variety of formal structures, one generalization is possible:

> *Every graduate school relies to some extent on the applicant's Grade Point Average (GPA) and GRE scores, but there are few (if any) graduate schools that rely only on these quantitative factors.*

This statement contains two ideas. Let us look at each.

The first idea is that every graduate school uses the GPA and GRE scores. While different graduate schools approach these numbers in unique ways, we can use a mathematical model to understand one way in which schools might take these factors into account. This sample formula is designed to weight the numbers approximately equally to give admissions officers some idea of how the applicant stacks up against other applicants. The following is a specific example:

The GRE is scored on a scale from 130 (the minimum) to 170 (the maximum) for the verbal and quantitative exam areas. The 130 to 170 point scale has a relation to the 0 to 4 grading system used by schools: 170 equals 42.5 times 4. This permits the use of a formula to combine the two measures. For example:

$$(\text{Average GRE}) + (42.5 \cdot \text{GPA}) = \text{Index}$$

Let's look at an example: a student with a 3.5 grade point average and GRE scores of 160 (Quantitative Reasoning) and 150 (Verbal Reasoning):

$$\frac{160+150}{2} + (42.5 \cdot 3.5) = 303.75$$

What does the index signify? That brings us to the second idea, as the answer varies from school to school. Some schools have a fairly mechanical admission process that emphasizes the index (or some variation on it). The school may set a minimum index below which applications receive little or no consideration. An application with an index below the minimum is simply rejected. Such schools may also have a second, higher minimum that triggers an automatic acceptance. Students with indices that exceed the higher minimum are accepted unless there is some glaring weakness in the application that otherwise disqualifies them.

At the opposite extreme are schools that claim to minimize the importance of the GRE and the GPA. They claim that the GRE is the very last factor at which they look. Such schools have a very flexible admission process.

Clearly, schools have a variety of GPA and GRE score ranges and requirements. Some schools emphasize these factors more and others less. Typically, these factors are used as a screening device to aid admissions officers in determining how much attention will be given to an application. This often works as follows.

The Competitive Middle

Applications with very low test scores and grades will receive little attention. School officials reason that unless there is something obvious and compelling in the application to offset the low numbers, then the applicant should be rejected. Applications with very high test scores and grades will also receive little attention. The reasoning is that unless there is something obvious and compelling in the application to reject it, it should be accepted. On this theory, the applications with test scores and grades in the middle receive the greatest attention. These are applications from candidates who are at least competitive for the school but who do not command an automatic acceptance. It is in this pool that competition is the most severe.

Here is a table that illustrates this principle:

GPA	GRE SCORE (Percentile)			
	61–70%	71–80%	81–90%	91–100%
3.75+	$\frac{2}{19}$	$\frac{49}{101}$	$\frac{102}{116}$	$\frac{72}{79}$
3.50–3.74	$\frac{6}{112}$	$\frac{75}{275}$	$\frac{301}{361}$	$\frac{120}{129}$
0–3.49	$\frac{10}{160}$	$\frac{90}{601}$	$\frac{375}{666}$	$\frac{201}{250}$

The fractions represent the total number of accepted applicants divided by the total number of applicants.

The categories in the table show what this graduate school did with applications with certain GRE scores (shown in percentile terms) and grade point averages. In the category in the upper right-hand corner are candidates with scores above the 90th percentile and GPAs above 3.75. The table shows that 72 of the 79 were accepted and seven were rejected.

What is obvious from the table is that some candidates with higher indices were rejected in favor of candidates with lower numbers. For example, of those candidates with scores between the 81st and 90th percentiles, 74 more candidates were accepted with a GPA below 3.50 than were students with a higher GPA between 3.50 and 3.74.

Why would a graduate school reject an applicant with higher numbers for one with lower numbers? The answer lies in our analysis of the admission process. Apparently, there were factors in the applications of those who were accepted that suggested to the admissions committee that those applicants would better meet the social and economic goals of the institution. Those factors are unquantifiable ones, such as motivation, commitment, leadership, experience, and so on. While this is good news in some ways—a lower GRE score and/or GPA does not necessarily disqualify you from the schools you want to attend—the safest bet is to maximize all factors. This includes raising your GRE scores.

When to Apply

There are a couple of important factors to consider as you determine when to send in your applications: rolling admissions and early decision programs.

Rolling Admissions

Rolling admissions is a device used by many graduate schools that regulates the release of acceptances. A typical school application season opens in October and may close as early as December or as late as June. Applications are received throughout the application season, and decisions are made on an ongoing basis; this is achieved by targeting an entering class. Based on its admission history, a school will estimate the expected range of GRE scores and GPAs of the students it will accept in the upcoming year. Then, as it receives applications (say, month by month), it will act on them. Students with very strong applications compared with the target group will receive acceptances; students with weak ones will receive rejections. Applications in the middle are carried over, and the applicants receive either no notification or notification that the application is still pending.

The rolling admissions process has advantages for both the graduate school and the applicant. From the applicant's point of view, the earlier the notification of the disposition of an application, the better. That is, you know whether you were accepted or rejected and you can go on from there. From the graduate school's viewpoint, the entering class and, therefore, the stability of the budget begin to take shape as early as possible.

The rolling admissions process is also a tool you can use to your advantage: apply early. Obviously, schools have greater flexibility and there are more seats available earlier in the admission season than later. We do not mean to imply that if you apply late in the season you will be rejected. In fact, it is impossible to quantify exactly the advantage that early applications enjoy. Still, if you want to maximize your chances of acceptance, apply early.

Early Action and Early Decision

Another important factor to consider is early action and early decision programs. Under these program guidelines, students who chose to utilize this option and apply by the program deadline will receive advance notice of their acceptance. If the option is binding, admitted students may not enroll at any other school. Also, these programs may establish more rigorous standards for applicants because they do not know who else will apply under a traditional registration timeline. These factors make research important in your graduate school search process. Make sure you ask about early decision and early action options, whether they are binding or nonbinding, and what deadlines they involve.

Research Graduate Schools and Make Preliminary Application Decisions

Given the economic commitment that you will be making, one of the obvious questions on your mind will be, "Where should I apply?" You probably already have an idea of some graduate schools you would like to attend based on factors like program strength, location, schedule, or specialty. If you don't yet have an idea, sit down and make a list of several schools in which you are interested.

Among other factors, you may be asking, "What are the top graduate schools in the country?" Since there is no single criterion for "best graduate school" that would be accepted by everyone, it is arguable that this question simply cannot be given a meaningful answer. Nevertheless, it is possible to get an approximate answer. The *U.S. News & World Report* survey of graduate schools lists the following as the top schools for 2014 (note that entries on the list may change each year, as may the rankings):[1]

---

[1] "Best Graduate Schools 2014." U.S. News & World Report.
http://grad-schools.usnews.rankingsandreviews.com/best-graduate-schools (accessed May 2, 2013).

BUSINESS	EDUCATION	ENGLISH
1. Harvard University (MA) 1. Stanford University (CA) 3. University of Pennsylvania (Wharton) 4. Mass. Institute of Technology (Sloan) 4. Northwestern University (Kellogg) (IL)	1. Vanderbilt University (Peabody) (TN) 2. Johns Hopkins University (MD) 3. Harvard University (MA) 4. University of Texas—Austin 5. Stanford University (CA)	1. University of California—Berkeley 2. Harvard University (MA) 2. Stanford University (CA) 4. Columbia University (NY) 4. Princeton University (NJ) 4. University of Pennsylvania 4. Yale University (CT)
ENGINEERING	HISTORY	PHYSICS
1. Mass. Institute of Technology 2. Stanford University (CA) 3. University of California—Berkeley 4. California Institute of Technology 5. Carnegie Mellon University (PA) 5. Georgia Institute of Technology 5. University of Illinois—Urbana-Champaign	1. Princeton University (NJ) 1. University of California—Berkeley 1. Yale University (CT) 4. Harvard University (MA) 4. Stanford University (CA) 4. University of Chicago (IL)	1. California Institute of Technology 1. Harvard University (MA) 1. Mass. Institute of Technology 1. Stanford University (CA) 5. Princeton University (NJ) 5. University of California—Berkeley
POLITICAL SCIENCE	PSYCHOLOGY	SOCIOLOGY
1. Harvard University (MA) 2. Princeton University (NJ) 2. Stanford University (CA) 4. University of Michigan—Ann Arbor 4. Yale University (CT)	1. Stanford University (CA) 2. University of California—Berkeley 2. University of California—Los Angeles 4. Harvard University (MA) 4. University of Michigan—Ann Arbor 4. Yale University (CT)	1. Princeton University (NJ) 1. University of California—Berkeley 1. University of Wisconsin—Madison 4. Stanford University (CA) 4. University of Michigan—Ann Arbor

Once you have an idea of some programs you are interested in, begin to consider the range of schools to which you will actually apply. You should apply to a group of schools such that, given your economic resources, you maximize your chances of gaining admission to the schools of your choice.

To apply to a graduate school, you may be required to remit a non-refundable application fee. This means that you are, to speak crudely, gambling with your money. You pay the fee, but you do not know in advance whether you will win or lose. So, hedge your bets. In a gambling situation, a bettor will have several choices. Some will be long shots, others will be almost sure things, and the rest will lie somewhere in the middle. The long shots will pay handsome dividends and the sure things a reasonable return, while the others will pay in between.

Given these considerations, you should select two or perhaps three "long shot" schools. As the term "long shot" implies, the odds of your being accepted to these schools are not very good, but the potential payoff justifies the gamble. On the other hand, you should also select one or two "sure thing" schools. To do this, you may have to apply to a school in your geographical area that does not enjoy a particularly good reputation or to a school that is located in another part of the country. The rest of your applications should go to your "good bet" schools— schools for which the chances for acceptance are 40 percent to 75 percent.

How do you determine which schools are "long shots," "safe schools," and "good bets"? Take a look at the index formulation that we described above. How do your GRE score (use the pre-test to get an idea) and GPA compare to the school's requirements and to the figures for its student population? Do the necessary research and you will be able to make an informed decision with regard to these factors.

Let's assume that you have the resources to apply to ten schools and that you have an above average GPA and GRE score. Depending on the exact numbers, you may very well have a chance at one of the top graduate schools. However, those are your "long shot" schools. You are almost guaranteed acceptance at many schools (your "safe schools"). Finally, there is a long list of "good bet" schools in the middle. At each of these schools, your application will likely receive serious consideration, but it is not guaranteed for acceptance.

This strategy of "stacking" your applications will maximize your chances of acceptance at a school you want, while minimizing the chance that you will not get into any school. Of course, the way the strategy is implemented will vary from person to person. For people who are fortunate enough to have a high GPA and a top GRE score, the middle and bottom tier schools collapse into a single tier. At the other extreme, those who are unfortunate enough to have a GPA and GRE score that are below what most schools accept will have to work with the second and third tiers.

As you prepare to implement this strategy, make a realistic assessment of your chances. Candidates unfortunately tend to overestimate the importance of what they believe to be their own interesting or unique factors. For example, we often hear candidates make statements such as, "Well sure my GPA is a little low, but I had to work part-time while I was in school"; and "I know my GRE scores are not that good, but I was a member of the university Student Council." These are valid points and are usually taken into consideration by admissions officers. However, the question is how much weight they will be given, for they (or some similar point) are true of most people applying to graduate school. For example, if you are thinking of applying to Yale University with a GPA of 3.25 and a GRE score in the 75th percentile, then there had better be something really special in your background, such as an Olympic medal or Nobel Peace Prize. Yale has been known to receive more than one hundred applicants with such numbers and accept none.

Another way of evaluating graduate schools is to think of them as falling into one of two groups: national schools and regional schools. National schools are those with substantial academic reputations, such as those highlighted in *U.S. News & World Report*. Regional schools have a substantial regional reputation but are not known nationally as "top" schools.

At this point, we should say a word about accreditation. Thus far, we have been referring only to accredited graduate schools. There are numerous accreditors of graduate schools and their programs, and some are more reputable than others. At a minimum, verify the accreditation status of schools that you plan to apply to at the Council for Higher Education Accreditation's online accreditation database (www.chea.org).

Define Your GRE Target Score

Now that you have researched the schools you are interested in and have some idea of what schools qualify as "long shots," "sure things," and "good bets" for you, you have a better idea of the GRE score that you need to shoot for. Review the following ways of making sure you know where you stand, and then complete the action steps.

Test

Your first step is to take the GRE pre-assessment that is part of your Cambridge course. After you take this test, you will receive a score that gives you a very accurate measure of where you stand. This knowledge is power. If you receive a score report, this report will let you know the specific areas that you need to focus on to achieve a higher score. To begin the process of setting a test score goal, fill in your pre-test score:

Pre-Test Date: _____	Score: _____

As you use these scores to make a plan for improvement throughout this course, remember that if you had a bad test day (for example, if you were ill or distracted by personal problems), your scores may not be reflective of your true abilities. Be sure to take this into account as you set a goal for your post-test and your real GRE test.

Research

Now, make a list of schools that you are interested in attending and get started on some research. Find out what scores these schools require. Contact the schools on your list if you have questions. Also research the average scores of admitted students so that you can get an idea of how you stack up. After a bit of research, fill in the score that you estimate you need for each school. Compare that to your pre-test score, and you've got an idea of how many more points you need in order to get into your target schools. Keep in mind that schools will consider more than your test scores for admission.

School: _____	Minimum Required GRE Score: _____ Average GRE Score of Admitted Students: _____ My Estimated GRE Score Needed for Admission: _____ Additional Points Needed for Admission: _____
School: _____	Minimum Required GRE Score: _____ Average GRE Score of Admitted Students: _____ My Estimated GRE Score Needed for Admission: _____ Additional Points Needed for Admission: _____
School: _____	Minimum Required GRE Score: _____ Average GRE Score of Admitted Students: _____ My Estimated GRE Score Needed for Admission: _____ Additional Points Needed for Admission: _____
School: _____	Minimum Required GRE Score: _____ Average GRE Score of Admitted Students: _____ My Estimated GRE Score Needed for Admission: _____ Additional Points Needed for Admission: _____

Once you have this chart filled in for several schools, you should have a good idea of the difference between your pre-test score and the score you will need to get into your schools of interest. Fill in this information below:

> **Pre-Test Score:** _____
>
> **Target Score:** _____

Action

How do you translate these numbers into an action plan? See your Student Item Analysis report. The Item Analysis gives you valuable information for every question on the pre-test. You'll see your answer, the correct answer, and the type of question that was asked. With a little analysis, you can see exactly where your weaknesses are and make a plan to address them. The "Using Pre-Assessment Reports to Target Weaknesses" section earlier in this book (p. 7) gives you specific ideas on using the score reports to maximum advantage in targeting a higher score.

Now that you have a better understanding of how the admissions process works, what scores are required for your top schools, and where your weaknesses lie, it's time to take a look at your schedule and make sure you make the necessary adjustments to make time for your GRE preparations.

PLANNING A COURSE SCHEDULE

The **PLAN** method presents four elements for maximizing your time:

> **PRIORITIZE** tasks according to their long-term benefit.
> **LIST** those tasks according to their priority.
> **ARRANGE** those tasks on a schedule.
> **NEGOTIATE** your schedule if those tasks become overwhelming.

P...Prioritize

Though involvement in many activities is important, it is necessary to determine which of these activities are the most important. Students who **prioritize** their tasks arrange them in an optimum order that is based on level of importance: more important tasks take precedence over less important tasks. So, in order to prioritize, you need to identify activities that will benefit you most in the long run. In order to effectively prioritize your tasks, you must first identify your own long-term goals. With a better understanding of your goals for the future, you can more effectively prioritize your activities in the present.

Ask yourself the following questions in order to better determine your long-term goals:

- What type of impact would I like to have on my community?
- What special accomplishments do I want to achieve?
- What types of positive things do I want people to say about me?
- Whom do I want to impress? How will I impress them?
- What will make me a happy and fulfilled person?
- In what additional ways can I prepare for the career I would like to pursue?

L...List

Every week, make a **list** of tasks to accomplish, placing the most important tasks at the top of your list.

A...Arrange

Each day, **arrange** all of your tasks on a daily schedule, prioritizing the most important tasks over tasks that are less important. The key to prioritization is to maintain a clear understanding of what is most important so that you can remain focused on the most significant tasks at hand.

N...Negotiate

In any given term, there are weeks that are especially busy and may prove to be overwhelming. Typically, chapter tests and final exams require considerable amounts of study time. The following are seven tips on how to better **negotiate** the details of your schedule in accordance with the potential added pressures of exam time.

1. Anticipate weeks with heavy workloads and note them on your schedule.
2. Meet with professors to discuss any problems that you might have with completing class work.
3. Get plenty of rest; you will need rest and energy during stressful times.
4. Do not wait until the last minute to complete major projects; procrastination is unproductive.
5. Attempt to get time off from your job during the most hectic times.
6. Say no to distractions such as watching television and reading books or magazines.

Manage Your Time by Using Pyramid Scheduling

A pyramid consists of a large base, or foundation, which transitions into progressively narrower levels until finally reaching a small point at the top. In a similar fashion, pyramid scheduling begins with organizing your long-term projects and then moves on to your more immediate tasks until finally reaching your daily schedule.

Schedule the Entire Term

During the first week of each term, organize all of your major assignments and responsibilities on the calendar. Reference all important dates that coincide with any of the following:

- Class assignments, tests, and exams
- Holidays and vacations
- Personal commitments, such as birthdays and family gatherings
- Employment commitments

Schedule Each Month

Two days before each month begins, review your monthly assignments and test dates. Then, reference any important dates for monthly activities that do not already appear on your calendar, such as:

- Additional assignments and study times for major projects, exams, tests, or quizzes
- Sporting events or concerts that you plan to attend
- Personal commitments, such as work schedule and social engagements

Schedule Each Week

Before beginning each week, review your weekly commitments. Create a weekly schedule that is divided up into mornings, afternoons, and evenings and references the most important times for certain daily activities, such as:

- Classes
- Class assignments, study sessions, tests, and exams
- Personal commitments, such as work schedule and social engagements
- Employment commitments

Schedule Each Day

Each night, create a schedule for the next day that outlines important times for the following daily activities:

- Class schedule and study times
- Job schedule
- Free time
- Additional appointments, tasks, or responsibilities

Remember to Stick to Your Schedule

Unless emergencies arise, stick to your schedule. Do not change your schedule unless it is absolutely necessary to accommodate and prioritize new activities. Remember that time management is really about self-management. So, remain disciplined so that you can follow your schedule without falling prey to distractions. Always remember to schedule your work and work your schedule!

Test Mechanics, Concepts, and Strategies

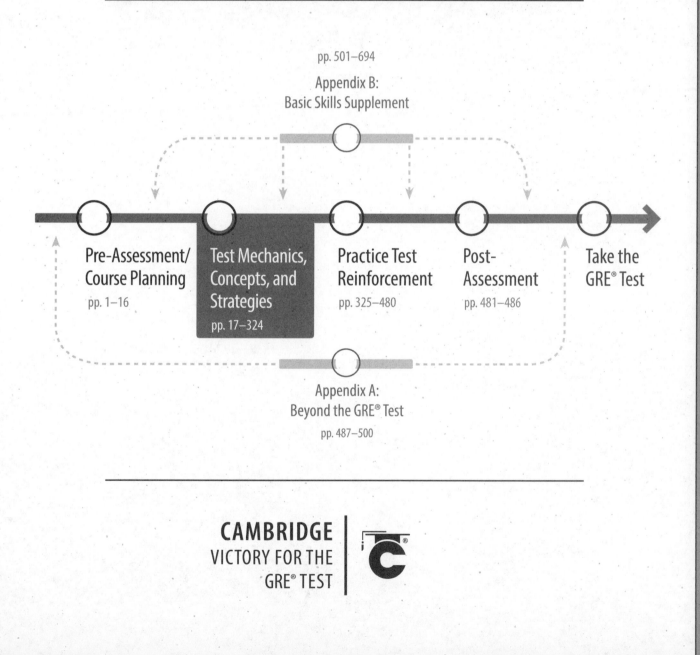

pp. 501–694

Appendix B:
Basic Skills Supplement

Pre-Assessment/
Course Planning
pp. 1–16

Test Mechanics,
Concepts, and
Strategies
pp. 17–324

Practice Test
Reinforcement
pp. 325–480

Post-
Assessment
pp. 481–486

Take the
GRE® Test

Appendix A:
Beyond the GRE® Test
pp. 487–500

CAMBRIDGE
VICTORY FOR THE
GRE® TEST

Verbal Reasoning: Completions

Course Concept Outline

---

[1] Some concepts in this Course Concept Outline are not illustrated through examples in your student text but may be covered by your instructor in class. They are included here to provide a complete outline of your course.

TEST MECHANICS

Overview

The Verbal Reasoning sections of the GRE test include three types of Completions items: sentence completions, paragraph completions, and sentence equivalence completions. **Sentence Completions** are single sentences with one missing element or blank indicated by an empty underlined space. The answer choices are a list of five words or phrases that might complete the sentence, and examinees must choose the one that best fits the meaning of the sentence. **Paragraph Completions** are similar to sentence completions except that the stimulus material (material to be completed) consists of a short paragraph of one to five sentences with two or three blanks. Three choices are offered for each blank. **Sentence Equivalence Completions** consist of a single sentence with one blank and six choices. For this type of Completions item, you must pick *two* choices that complete the sentence *and* that have similar meanings.

Don't worry about memorizing these variations; you'll become familiar with them as you work through the sample items in this chapter and the practice materials that follow later in this book. For ease of reference, your instructor may collectively refer to all three completion types as "completions" or "fill-in-the-blanks," but you'll understand that this general phrase covers three different variations.

The number of Completions items in a test section varies, but generally you can expect to see a total of 10 Completions items per section (on the computer-based test). You shouldn't worry about this insignificant lack of precision because slight variations in the test format occur frequently and because you have to answer the questions presented regardless of whether the exact number meets your expectations.

The items will not be presented in a particular order. A verbal section could begin with Sentence Completions or with Paragraph Completions or Sentence Equivalences or even Reading Comprehension. Also, the items of each variation are not necessarily grouped together. They can be interspersed throughout the section.

Completions items do not involve a lot of reading. Here are some rough approximations of the reading load for each variation:

TYPE	WORD COUNT PER ITEM
Sentence Completions	30
Paragraph Completions	75
Sentence Equivalences	30

Although Completions items do not involve a lot of reading, this does not mean that they are necessarily easy. Some are, but others aren't. In many cases, the item will be about a topic with which you are not familiar. The test-writers sometimes choose unusual topics just to make the item more difficult. The topic itself is just window-dressing and not really a part of the question. Some Completions items are difficult because they test difficult vocabulary words, and others are hard because the logical structure of the sentence to be completed is complicated.

Anatomy

DIRECTIONS: Select one answer choice for each blank from the corresponding column of choices. Fill all blanks in a way that best completes the text.

1. Although the two students seem to have been longtime friends, in reality they met only _____.

   (A) spontaneously
   (B) ethically
   (C) quietly
   (D) recently
   (E) emotionally

2. The diva's autobiography was largely (i)_____; when she wasn't saying wonderful things about herself, she (ii)_____ her mother, who said them for her.

Blank (i)	Blank (ii)
(A) confidential	(D) repudiated
(B) anecdotal	(E) quoted
(C) self-congratulatory	(F) flouted

DIRECTIONS: Select the two words that, when used independently in the sentence, produce logical sentences and produce sentences that are alike in meaning.

3. After enjoying a brief _____, the cockaded wood spackle is once again endangered and even facing extinction.

   (A) reawakening
   (B) reconnoitering
   (C) revivification
   (D) resurgence
   (E) redundancy
   (F) remonstrance

These items are fairly straightforward; read the sentence and fill in the blank(s). For sentences with more than one blank, consider the answers for each blank independently.

1. **(D)** *Often, as you will learn in the lesson, sentence completion items include key words like "although," which indicates a reversal of thought. The idea that follows the comma must reverse the idea that precedes the comma. What precedes the comma is the idea that the students have been longtime friends. Therefore, rather than meeting a long time ago, the friends must have met only "recently," (D).*

2. **(C, E)** *Paragraph completions will include two or three blanks. Remember to note the directions for these items and select answers for each blank that, when used together, create a meaningful sentence. The correct answers could be in the same row or they could be in different rows, as is the case here, where (C) and (E) are the correct choices. "Self-congratulatory" is an extension of "saying wonderful things about herself," and "quoted" extends "said them for her."*

The important difference between items #3–5 and items #1–2 is the new requirement that you pick two answer choices. Do not pick two words or phrases just because they arguably have similar meanings. First, establish that they are suitable completions; then, ask whether the meanings are similar.

3. **(C, D)** *The sentence is characterized by a thought reversal: after a brief _____, more bad news. So, the blank needs to be filled with a word or phrase reporting good news for the bird: a brief "revivification" or "resurgence." Although this type of completion requires words or phrases that are approximately synonymous, the threshold inquiry is the same as that for single or double completions: Does the substitution make sense? Then worry about the issue of synonymy.*

4. While Patton relished battle and delighted in the _____ of his authority, Eisenhower took little or no pleasure in warfare and was impervious to the outward trappings of military leadership.

    (A) manifestations
    (B) perquisites
    (C) conditions
    (D) vindications
    (E) privileges
    (F) absoluteness

4. (B, E) *This sentence is characterized by both a contrast of thought and a continuation. The "while" creates a contrast between Patton and Eisenhower, but there is also a parallelism at work: battle, authority, battle, authority. So the blank is parallel to the "outward trappings" of authority, and "perquisites" and "privileges" are two pretty good synonyms that mean "outward trappings."*

5. Thomas successfully narrates a vexingly complicated story, _____ tracing the influence of gambling, drugs, and even spiritualism on the nation's most popular sport.

    (A) exultantly
    (B) haphazardly
    (C) scrupulously
    (D) punctiliously
    (E) intermittently
    (F) presumptuously

5. (C, D) *The phrase following the comma here provides additional information about and clarification of the main clause by explaining how Thomas "successfully" tells the story. "Scrupulously" and "punctiliously" both mean extremely carefully.*

DIRECTIONS: Select <u>one</u> answer choice for each blank from the corresponding column of choices. Fill all blanks in a way that best completes the text.

Item #6 requires you to follow the same directions you used to answer items #1–2. Similarly, on the GRE test, item-types are interspersed throughout the test section.

6. The Prisoner's Dilemma is a logical (i)_____ involving two accomplices arrested for a crime, interrogated separately, and offered deals. If one prisoner incriminates the other while the second remains silent, the prisoner who talks will be given a sentence of one year, while the other accomplice gets four. If both remain silent, they will be sentenced to only two years; but if both talk, they will receive three years. The rational choice for each prisoner alone is to talk, with the outcome being three years each—even though if both remain silent, they would both be out in two. The dilemma proves that in the absence of trust, self-interest can be (ii)_____.

Blank (i)		Blank (ii)	
(A)	conundrum	(D)	self-defeating
(B)	resolution	(E)	self-contained
(C)	injunction	(F)	self-referential

6. (A, D) *Even though this item stem is much longer than a sentence completion, use the same approach. The dilemma produces paradoxical results and is quite a puzzle, and that is what "conundrum" means. Then, the point of the puzzle is that selfishness can, in some cases, be contrary to one's own interests, so "self-defeating" is a good second choice. Remember, you have to get all the components right to get any credit for the item. There is no partial credit.*

7. It is not entirely clear that the transfer of the Elgin Marbles from Greece to England did not better protect the sculptures than leaving them in place. The Turks, who occupied Greece at the time, (i)_____ the little temple of Athena Nike on the Acropolis in order to make room for their artillery. They used the Parthenon as an ammunition dump, which exploded, doing irreparable damage. They allowed tourists to pick through the ruins. Lord Elgin saved the sculptures from further (ii)_____.

Blank (i)	Blank (ii)
(A) razed	(D) depredation
(B) erected	(E) abnegation
(C) restored	(F) sequestration

7. (A, D) *The main point of the paragraph is that Elgin's theft of the sculptures actually helped to preserve them. So, the final sentence must state that Elgin saved the sculptures from further destruction, and "depredation" is a good fit. As for the first blank, the phrase "in order to" signals a thought extension in the form of a cause and effect connection. To make room for something, it is necessary to remove the existing objects or structures, and "raze" means to destroy completely.*

Pacing

A good rule of thumb is that you should take an average of 90 seconds per Completions item—and less for some. Therefore, 10 completions should take no more than 15 minutes.

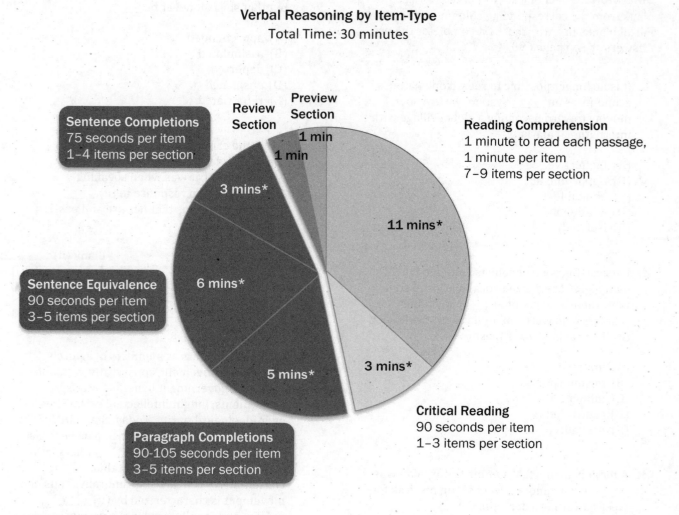

Verbal Reasoning by Item-Type
Total Time: 30 minutes

Sentence Completions
75 seconds per item
1–4 items per section

Review Section
1 min

Preview Section
1 min

Reading Comprehension
1 minute to read each passage,
1 minute per item
7–9 items per section

3 mins*

11 mins*

Sentence Equivalence
90 seconds per item
3–5 items per section

6 mins*

5 mins*

3 mins*

Paragraph Completions
90-105 seconds per item
3–5 items per section

Critical Reading
90 seconds per item
1–3 items per section

*Times are approximate

Since the section-level adaptive format of the GRE allows you to do items in any order that you wish, you might decide to do all of the completions before tackling the reading comprehension questions. This is a matter of personal preference. There is no particular advantage to doing completions first, no weakness in the scoring algorithm to be exploited to gain an edge. Instead, the pacing guideline is fairly straight-forward: plan to do all of the items in the Verbal section and budget your time accordingly.

Time Trial

(10 items; 14 minutes)

> **DIRECTIONS:** Select <u>one</u> answer choice for each blank from the corresponding column of choices. Fill all blanks in a way that best completes the text. Answers are on page 699.

1. It is no longer possible to regard one nation's economy as an _____ system; we are now moving toward becoming a global village with international markets.

    (A) ineffective
    (B) opportunistic
    (C) equitable
    (D) irrational
    (E) isolated

2. Because Deconstructionists employed their own highly specialized vocabulary and style, their theories were often _____ by other scholars who were unfamiliar with the French tradition of literary criticism.

    (A) imitated
    (B) misinterpreted
    (C) influenced
    (D) captivated
    (E) prefigured

3. A terribly ineffectual administrator, Alan was _____: even minor matters sat on his desk for weeks awaiting a decision.

    (A) phlegmatic
    (B) opinionated
    (C) penurious
    (D) duplicitous
    (E) spurious

4. The main character of the book plaintively decries the Immigrant's Dilemma, a conviction that she does not belong in her adopted home but that she can never be _____.

    (A) apprehended
    (B) assimilated
    (C) deported
    (D) enshrined
    (E) repatriated

5. While the candidate delivered the (i)_____ speech flawlessly at every stop on the campaign trail, it was when speaking spontaneously in response to (ii)_____ audience questions that her fire and passion were most evident.

Blank (i)	Blank (ii)
(A) acceptance	(D) unrehearsed
(B) prepared	(E) persuasive
(C) nomination	(F) prearranged

6. During their years as members of a purely opposition movement, conservatives, unable to deliver government benefits to satisfy constituents, fought intellectual skirmishes over ideological purity. Today, they satisfy that need by fighting one another, in part because liberalism, in its current (i)_____, offers less satisfying intellectual combat than conservatives can have intramurally. Thus, the movement is characterized by (ii)_____ conflict and is splintered into a variety of factions and sects.

Blank (i)	Blank (ii)
(A) flaccidness	(D) preemptive
(B) moroseness	(E) internecine
(C) ascendancy	(F) unsavory

7. Early on in his exegesis of the mathematical writings of Copernicus, Vollman offers readers the overly frank admission that he fears that much of the detail of the subject is beyond the competence of a(n) (i)_____ such as he. It turns out he was right to voice (ii)_____, for the self-taught mathematician soon founders among Copernicus' theorems, tables and demonstrations. Vollmann's own (iii)_____seems to have made him forget that, whatever he may think of himself, Copernicus endures as a great mathematical thinker.

Blank (i)		Blank (ii)	
(A)	bibliophile	(D)	contumacy
(B)	autodidact	(E)	trepidation
(C)	parvenu	(F)	dyspepsia

Blank (iii)	
(G)	self-abnegation
(H)	self-determination
(I)	self-aggrandizement

DIRECTIONS: Select the <u>two</u> words that, when used independently in the sentence, produce logical sentences <u>and</u> produce sentences that are alike in meaning.

8. In the witches of *Macbeth*, there is just enough of the popular conception of supernatural creatures of evil to titillate the interest of the ordinary Elizabethan theatergoer, though Shakespeare informed this _____ superstition with a moral significance applicable to all times.

(A) elemental
(B) fortuitous
(C) temporal
(D) common
(E) pastoral
(F) vulgar

9. Overinterpreted correlations between parental behavior and child behavior, such as violence, provide misleading evidence for the effects of parenting, ignoring the possibility that these traits are _____.

(A) irremediable
(B) genetic
(C) benign
(D) inconsequential
(E) hereditary
(F) intractable

10. Howells, in his 1895 novel about new money, incorrectly suggested as the likely source for the manly ideal the middle-class, self-made businessman like Silas Lapham, but the Davy Crockett almanacs were already contrasting the manliness of the low-born against the _____ gentleman in the 1830s.

(A) tendentious
(B) effete
(C) spurious
(D) overweening
(E) whimsical
(F) effeminate

Game Plan

Build Foundational Completion Skills

This course includes a Verbal Reasoning Supplement in Appendix B (p. 503). If you found the Completions items on your pre-assessment challenging, review the supplemental material to enhance your basic vocabulary and sentence completion skills. (Your instructor may also choose to cover this material in class.)

Quickly Preview the Test Section, but Skip the Directions

Last-minute adjustments to the test format are theoretically (but not practically) possible, so check the test section before you start to work, especially the total number of items of each type and the time limit. And yes, the test-writers always tell you to "read the directions carefully." But they don't tell you that you have to read them during the test. Instead, become familiar with them *before* test day. That way, you won't waste 30 seconds or more (enough time to answer an item) re-reading directions with which you are already familiar.

The section-level adaptive format of the GRE test allows you to move forward through the section and move back to the beginning. So, you can take an overview of the material before you begin to work. If you have decided (in advance) that you are going to do the items in a specific order (other than that used by the test writer), then you'll know where to begin.

Be Aware of Item Requirements

The test developers have made the GRE revised General Test as user-friendly as possible, indicating Sentence and Paragraph Completion items with answer choices in ovals and Sentence Equivalence items with answer choices in boxes. However, make sure you pay attention to the item requirements. For example, it is possible to mark as many answers as you like on a Sentence Equivalence item—you could even mark all six answers. However, only one combination of two answer choices yields the correct answer. Avoid careless mistakes by paying attention to the item requirements.

Use Your Completion Sense

Since Sentence and Paragraph Completions items are essentially "fill-in-the-blanks," one or more possible answers may occur to you. Give your "completion sense" a chance to work before you start analyzing the sentence in detail. Read the sentence and try to anticipate a possible answer. Check the answer choices to see if you get a match. This sets up the following basic approach:

Step 1: Read through the sentence for meaning. Read the sentence to yourself at normal speed (as though someone were speaking to you).

Step 2: Formulate a possible completion.

Step 3: Choose the matching answer.

Example:

After his novel was rejected by six publishers, John became embittered and _____, so much so that his friends feared for his sanity.

(A) gentle
(B) wary
(C) morose
(D) pacified
(E) prudent

The correct answer is (C). A reading of the item stem tells you that John was affected negatively and became embittered as well as something else that is like embittered; that is, another negative emotion. Possible completions are words such as "disappointed," "angry," "depressed," or "sullen." The best match is found in (C): "morose."

This basic technique is all you need for many Sentence Completions items, and it should always be your first approach. If your "completion sense" fails you, then you can move on to the more elaborate techniques.

Get Rid of Excess Baggage

Many Completions items are cluttered up by arcane details. This additional information is not needed to find the correct answer, but it does make things more difficult. A good approach to this "static" is just to tune it out.

Example:

By and large, Wittgenstein's treatment of language in *Tractatus Logico-Philosophicus* will be (i)_____ to the lay person, but the more (ii)_____ elements will be grasped only by specialists in the philosophy of language.

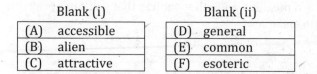

	Blank (i)		Blank (ii)
(A)	accessible	(D)	general
(B)	alien	(E)	common
(C)	attractive	(F)	esoteric

You don't have to know anything about Wittgenstein to solve this problem, so eliminate the unnecessary detail:

> By and large, ~~Wittgenstein's treatment of language in *Tractatus Logico-Philosophicus*~~ [the book] will be _____ to the lay person, but the more _____ elements will be grasped only by specialists ~~in the philosophy of language~~.

Now, you can see that you need a pair of contrasting words to express the idea that the obvious points are fairly easy to understand but the difficult ones are hard to get. The correct answer choices are (A) and (F).

Look for Logical and Grammatical Clues

If your "completion sense" doesn't get you an answer, then you'll need to analyze the text. The test-writers plant a variety of logical and grammatical clues in the sentences for you to find.

Example:

Given the rapidly changing nature of today's technological society, schools should not teach eternal principles, for by tomorrow, today's knowledge is _____.

(A) enriched
(B) reproduced
(C) adequate
(D) precarious
(E) obsolete

The correct answer is (E). The sentence sets up a logical contrast between eternal principles and knowledge that is not eternal. So, you need a word that is the opposite of "eternal," something like "temporary," "outdated," or "transient." (E) provides the best match: "obsolete."

Example:

Retiring by nature and _____ even in private, Eleanor hardly ever spoke in public.

(A) confident
(B) reticent
(C) preoccupied
(D) untamed
(E) courageous

The correct answer is (B). Here, the clue is a grammatical structure. The introductory phrase "retiring...private" modifies "Eleanor." So, Eleanor was unwilling to speak. Some possible completions are "quiet" and "silent." The best match is "reticent."

Use the Process of Elimination

As you know, the process of elimination is a powerful tool for taking the GRE test. The odds are in your favor if you can eliminate even one wrong choice. Because Completions items are in part a test of vocabulary, you may find choices that you know to be wrong as a matter of word meaning and other choices that you can't evaluate because you don't know the word meanings. So, eliminate and guess.

Example:

The ornament was extremely _____, and it broke into thousands of pieces when it dropped on the floor.

(A) durable
(B) tinfilandulate
(C) prascobituant
(D) wrantofulpact
(E) contagprolistic

In this item, four of the five choices are uncommon words. More precisely, (B) through (E) are made-up words, so you're never going to understand them. Still, you know that (A) has to be wrong because a durable object would not break. And once you have eliminated (A), you have to take a guess—even though you don't know what those other words mean.

For Equivalences, Check Sense then Synonymy

The Sentence Equivalence variation includes the additional requirement that the two correct choices will have meanings that are very similar. But this is a secondary consideration.

Example:

His extensive reading and exhaustive archival research yielded a _____ of case histories compiled into an encyclopedic treatment of the topic.

(A) babel
(B) chatter
(C) kaleidoscope
(D) phantasmagoria
(E) plethora
(F) cornucopia

This example is a bit contrived, as we've included three pairs of synonyms just to make the point. (A) and (B), (C) and (D), and (E) and (F) are similar pairs, but only (E) and (F) satisfy the sense of the sentence. So synonymy is a secondary consideration, required but subordinate to sentence sense.

Check Your Answers

Once you've found your answer choice, read the sentence a final time with your completion in place. If the result is a smooth-reading sentence that makes sense to you, then the problem yielded the correct answer. Enter your choice and move on to the next item.

Stay on Schedule

You know that it is important to stick to your time schedule, but Completions items can be a real time trap. You're working on the Completions items, and you keep spending more and more time on the harder Completions items. That's the trap. Instead, when the going gets tough, the tough get going—on to the next item or the next part of the section.

LESSON

The items in this section accompany the Verbal Reasoning: Completions Lesson. You will work through the items with your instructor in class.

DIRECTIONS: Select <u>one</u> answer choice for each blank from the corresponding column of choices. Fill all blanks in a way that best completes the text. Answers are on page 699.

Three Item-Types

Thought Extension

1. Prior to the formation of the Central Intelligence Agency, intelligence-gathering functions were _____, with several departments of the executive branch independently engaged in such activities and refusing to share information with each other.

   (A) reliable
   (B) constricted
   (C) fragmented
   (D) precarious
   (E) indigenous

Thought Reversal

2. Although Barbara argues strongly that current policies are unjust, she does not _____ any particular changes.

   (A) reject
   (B) presume
   (C) advocate
   (D) remember
   (E) oppose

Combined Reasoning

3. Marxist revolution directly challenged the bourgeois order, and Communism explicitly endeavored to destroy traditional religion and to _____ itself as an alternative faith.

   (A) repudiate
   (B) enshrine
   (C) undermine
   (D) illuminate
   (E) placate

Thought Extension Concepts and Strategies

Coordinate Conjunctions

4. The terms "toad" and "frog" refer to two different animals belonging to different genera, and careful students _____ between the two.

   (A) intermingle
   (B) ignore
   (C) distinguish
   (D) confuse
   (E) dispute

5. The delicate aroma and (i)_____ flavor of this fine wine need a sensitive nose and (ii)_____ palate to be appreciated.

Blank (i)		Blank (ii)	
(A)	subtle	(D)	discriminating
(B)	pungent	(E)	calloused
(C)	acrid	(F)	untutored

Subordinate Conjunctions

6. Since the evidence of the manuscript's (i)_____ is (ii)_____, its publication will be postponed until a team of scholars has examined it and declared it to be genuine.

Blank (i)		Blank (ii)	
(A)	authenticity	(D)	infallible
(B)	location	(E)	inconclusive
(C)	legibility	(F)	indubitable

7. If we continue to consume our fossil fuel supply without restraint, then someday it will be _____.

(A) replenished
(B) limited
(C) useless
(D) available
(E) exhausted

8. The critics must have detested the play, for the reviews were not merely (i)_____, they were (ii)_____.

Blank (i)		Blank (ii)	
(A)	laudatory	(D)	interminable
(B)	critical	(E)	prohibitive
(C)	appreciative	(F)	scathing

9. Because it preaches total abstinence from almost all of life's pleasures, this fundamentalist sect finds it difficult to _____ its membership in today's climate of self-indulgence.

(A) admonish
(B) forgive
(C) increase
(D) deride
(E) accept

10. Lars decided to _____ his vacation since he had not yet finished all of the work he had been assigned.

(A) schedule
(B) enjoy
(C) pursue
(D) expand
(E) postpone

11. You must act with _____ if you want to buy your airline ticket before tomorrow's price increase.

(A) celerity
(B) clemency
(C) facility
(D) lassitude
(E) laxity

Key Adjectives and Adverbs

12. The judge, after ruling that the article had unjustly (i)_____ the reputation of the architect, ordered the magazine to (ii)_____ its libelous statements in print.

Blank (i)		Blank (ii)	
(A)	praised	(D)	retract
(B)	injured	(E)	publicize
(C)	extolled	(F)	disseminate

13. The angry parent _____ the children for their behavior in the restaurant.

(A) scolded
(B) prepared
(C) imitated
(D) delighted
(E) praised

14. The proud parent _____ the children for their behavior in the restaurant.

(A) scolded
(B) prepared
(C) imitated
(D) delighted
(E) praised

15. The textbook is a _____ treatment of medieval European history from 800 to 1453 that includes every possible topic.

(A) dramatic
(B) sketchy
(C) inventive
(D) confused
(E) comprehensive

16. The _____ structure of the novel was justified by the author's choice of subject: spies, double spies, and triple spies, all operating for and against various governments and one another.

(A) torpid
(B) alien
(C) insipid
(D) byzantine
(E) humdrum

Punctuation

17. People who use their desktop computers for writing can become almost hypnotized by the unbroken succession of letters and text; in such cases, a computer video game can supply a welcome _____.

(A) burden
(B) diversion
(C) handicap
(D) predicament
(E) insight

18. There is no necessary connection between a dollar and what can be purchased for a dollar: the value of money is (i)_____ and can be (ii)_____ by supply and demand.

Blank (i)		Blank (ii)	
(A)	arbitrary	(D)	inspired
(B)	unconventional	(E)	altered
(C)	lackluster	(F)	prevented

19. The consulting engineer enjoyed the _____ life that she led while visiting projects around the world; she never remained in any one city long enough to get bored.

(A) secretive
(B) mundane
(C) nomadic
(D) rustic
(E) structured

20. Since the actor who played the lead was somewhat _____, the property manager had to let out the costumes and have the furniture used in the production reinforced.

(A) winsome
(B) virulent
(C) fragile
(D) corpulent
(E) flirtatious

21. The hearing of the white tail deer is remarkably _____, capable of detecting even the slightest rustling of a hunter's clothing.

(A) keen
(B) valid
(C) immune
(D) intact
(E) controlled

22. A skillful negotiator, the Dean adopted a posture of patience and _____ toward the protestors, rather than rejecting their demands outright.

(A) arrogance
(B) compromise
(C) insincerity
(D) promiscuity
(E) intransigence

23. The junta's promise of free elections was _____, a mere sop to world opinion.

(A) spurious
(B) contentious
(C) unctuous
(D) lucid
(E) presumptuous

Phrases

24. His _____ should not be confused with cowardice; during the war, I saw him on several occasions risk his own life while rescuing members of his unit.

    (A) heroism
    (B) indifference
    (C) caution
    (D) notoriety
    (E) confidence

25. Her acceptance speech was _____, eliciting thunderous applause at several points.

    (A) tedious
    (B) well-received
    (C) cowardly
    (D) uninteresting
    (E) poorly written

26. The public debates were often _____, finally deteriorating into mudslinging contests.

    (A) informative
    (B) bitter
    (C) theoretical
    (D) inspiring
    (E) insightful

27. The _____ background music hinted of the dangers threatening the movie's heroine.

    (A) trenchant
    (B) ebullient
    (C) sardonic
    (D) portentous
    (E) precocious

28. The Eighteenth Amendment, often called the Prohibition Act, _____ the sale of alcoholic beverages.

    (A) prolonged
    (B) preempted
    (C) sanctioned
    (D) proscribed
    (E) encouraged

29. The Parks Department claims that there is a _____ of wildlife in the New York City area, and that species that have not lived in the area for most of the century are once again being sighted.

    (A) resurgence
    (B) paucity
    (C) superstructure
    (D) prototype
    (E) compendium

30. The city _____ to the advancing invaders without firing a single shot.

    (A) extolled
    (B) regressed
    (C) equivocated
    (D) dissembled
    (E) capitulated

31. If you find peeling potatoes to be _____, perhaps you would prefer to scrub the floors?

    (A) felicitous
    (B) remunerative
    (C) onerous
    (D) vilifying
    (E) redundant

32. To strengthen her client's case, the lawyer sought to put the _____ of the witness in doubt.

    (A) laxity
    (B) posterity
    (C) probity
    (D) onus
    (E) sensitivity

33. His _____ music collection included everything from Bach to rock.

    (A) divisive
    (B) effusive
    (C) eclectic
    (D) intrinsic
    (E) laconic

34. The star of the show is a _____ performer who acts, sings, and dances with equal facility.

    (A) capricious
    (B) pretentious
    (C) versatile
    (D) myopic
    (E) quixotic

35. The film was _____, completely lacking in plot, just a series of beautiful images with no particular connection.

    (A) incoherent
    (B) morbid
    (C) moral
    (D) romantic
    (E) fictitious

Thought Reversal Concepts and Strategies

Coordinate Conjunctions

36. The ease with which the candidate answers difficult questions creates the impression that she has been a public servant for years, but in reality she entered politics only _____.

    (A) securely
    (B) enthusiastically
    (C) frequently
    (D) needfully
    (E) recently

37. The ascent of the mountain is _____, but anyone who makes it to the top is rewarded by a spectacular view.

    (A) helpful
    (B) calculated
    (C) unique
    (D) unpleasant
    (E) automatic

38. The public quite naturally expects that the Picassos and Rembrandts of the museum's painting collection will be on display at all times, but the lack of well-known masterpieces in the photographic collection gives the curator uncommon _____ in deciding which works to exhibit.

    (A) leeway
    (B) guidance
    (C) confidence
    (D) sensitivity
    (E) flair

39. The image of the Indian brave on his pinto pony is so common that most people don't realize that horses are not _____ North America but were introduced by the Europeans.

    (A) exclusive to
    (B) indigenous to
    (C) supplemented to
    (D) inherited in
    (E) predominant in

40. She accepted her own misfortune with perfect _____, but was outraged at any abuse or mistreatment of others.

    (A) equanimity
    (B) reluctance
    (C) sincerity
    (D) rabidity
    (E) pulchritude

Subordinate Conjunctions

41. Although the terms "toad" and "frog" refer to two different animals belonging to different genera, some students _____ the two.

    (A) distinguish
    (B) confuse
    (C) respect
    (D) observe
    (E) mention

42. While Barbara argues strongly that current policies are unjust, she does not _____ any particular changes.

(A) reject
(B) presume
(C) advocate ✓
(D) remember
(E) oppose

43. Although there are more female students at the college than male students, the women seem to have a(n) _____ influence on the student government.

(A) enormous
(B) negligible ✓
(C) provocative
(D) venerable
(E) active

44. Unless we _____ our water resources, there may come a time when our supplies of clean water are completely depleted.

(A) predict
(B) use
(C) conserve ✓
(D) replace
(E) tap

45. Although his dress is _____, in all other ways he appears to be perfectly normal.

(A) ordinary
(B) mellifluous
(C) eccentric ✓
(D) nondescript
(E) recalcitrant

46. John's parents could not comprehend why he was doing so poorly in school since his diagnostic test scores indicated a high degree of _____ which his grades did not reflect.

(A) laziness
(B) aptitude ✓
(C) agility
(D) experience
(E) volition

Key Adjectives and Adverbs

47. For Thomas Aquinas, the Scholastic thinker and author of the *Summa Theologica*, the question of angels dancing on a pinhead was not (i)_____ but a (ii)_____ issue of vital import to his project of reconciling Aristotelian metaphysics with medieval Church doctrine.

Blank (i)		Blank (ii)	
(A)	unanswerable	(D)	fanciful
(B)	comical ✓	(E)	superficial
(C)	capricious	(F)	profound ✓

48. Paradoxically, this world-renowned performer is sometimes outgoing and at other times _____.

(A) discourteous
(B) inventive
(C) sociable
(D) reclusive ✓
(E) passionate

Phrases

49. Despite the fact that they had clinched the divisional title long before the end of regular season play, the team continued to play every game as though it were _____.

(A) superfluous
(B) irrational
(C) lengthy
(D) hopeless
(E) vital ✓

50. In contrast with the early architecture of the Northeast, which was basically utilitarian, the Georgian homes of the early South were far more _____.

(A) supine
(B) inconsequential
(C) grandiose ✓
(D) acrimonious
(E) crude

51. Nutritionists have found that certain elements long known to be lethal in large quantities are _____ to life in small amounts.

    (A) essential ✓
    (B) painful
    (C) pleasurable
    (D) unbearable
    (E) unimportant

52. A long illness can _____ even the strongest constitution.

    (A) obviate
    (B) inculcate
    (C) bolster
    (D) enervate
    (E) disparage

53. As a professor he was a disaster, for his students rarely understood his lectures, yet he was a _____ scholar.

    (A) banal
    (B) failed
    (C) formidable ✓
    (D) second-rate
    (E) contemptuous

Combined Reasoning Concepts and Strategies

54. Though afflicted by headaches, nausea, and respiratory difficulties, Nietzsche (i)_____ to let his (ii)_____ problems prevent him from writing.

Blank (i)		Blank (ii)	
(A)	hoped	(D)	emotional
(B)	failed	(E)	physical ✓
(C)	refused	(F)	financial

55. Although critics denounced the film as silly and inane, people flocked to the theater to see it, guaranteeing its _____ success.

    (A) scholarly
    (B) hypothetical
    (C) critical
    (D) financial ✓
    (E) eventual

56. Elementary school children, who have not yet been repeatedly disappointed by other people, are much more _____ than older and more cynical high school students.

    (A) inquisitive ✓
    (B) relaxed
    (C) enjoyable
    (D) trusting
    (E) enlightened

57. Even the most arbitrary and (i)_____ corporation today must be aware of the attitudes of its employees; management may at times be more or less (ii)_____, but all must respect the power of an organized workforce.

Blank (i)		Blank (ii)	
(A)	authoritarian	(D)	responsive
(B)	susceptible	(E)	permanent
(C)	flexible	(F)	patronizing

58. Although he had inherited a substantial amount of money, his _____ soon led to his filing for bankruptcy.

    (A) prodigality
    (B) volubility
    (C) tenacity
    (D) fastidiousness ✓
    (E) animosity

59. Cultural weightlessness is a defining characteristic of Los Angeles, and each new fashion trend or food fad that emanates from its environs causes its _____ to despair of ever hearing Easterners retract their sneering view of the place as nothing more than a disordered set of clogged freeways.

   (A) detractors
   (B) designers
   (C) loyalists
   (D) expatriates
   (E) imitators

60. Joyce's novel *Finnegan's Wake* continues to (i)_____ critics, including those who find it incomprehensible and call it (ii)_____.

Blank (i)		Blank (ii)	
(A)	appall	(D)	nonsensical
(B)	captivate	(E)	transparent
(C)	engender	(F)	compelling

General Strategies

"Anticipate and Test"

61. The university should _____ the function of the alumni fund so that its importance will be better appreciated by the school's graduates who are asked to contribute to it.

   (A) revoke
   (B) elucidate
   (C) ascertain
   (D) prescribe
   (E) entice

62. According to recent studies, prices in supermarkets are considerably higher in the inner city, thus _____ the poor who receive assistance to buy the food.

   (A) reprimanding
   (B) intimidating
   (C) alleviating
   (D) assuaging
   (E) exploiting

63. Although this disease threatens the lives of several thousand people every year, the scarcity of supplies and equipment has _____ the progress of medical research for a cure.

   (A) ensured
   (B) hampered
   (C) enhanced
   (D) facilitated
   (E) neglected

64. In spite of the (i)_____ of the minister's sermon, when it was finished, most of the congregation was (ii)_____.

Blank (i)		Blank (ii)	
(A)	passion	(D)	fidgety
(B)	understanding	(E)	merciful
(C)	veracity	(F)	inspired

"Simplify Your Life"

65. The passage of the mass transit bill over the Governor's veto, despite opposition by key leaders in the legislature, was a devastating _____ for the party machinery and suggests that other, much-needed legislation may receive similar treatment in the future.

   (A) victory
   (B) optimism
   (C) compromise
   (D) slap
   (E) setback

66. The rocket scientists had fully expected the thermothrockle to hydrolyze under the intense ionizing radiation requiring the mission to be aborted; but the astronauts _____ the problem by tekelating the suborbital flexion, and the mission continued.

   (A) recreated
   (B) transmitted
   (C) misjudged
   (D) circumvented
   (E) proscribed

Hard Cases

"Go to Pieces"

67. It is highly characteristic of business' (i)_____ attitude that little or no interest was evinced in urban renewal until similar undertakings elsewhere proved that such projects could be (ii)_____.

Blank (i)		Blank (ii)	
(A)	prestigious	(D)	profitable ✓
(B)	degrading	(E)	rigid
(C)	pragmatic ✓	(F)	insensitive

68. George Bernard Shaw expressed his (i)_____ for technological progress when he said that the human race is just interested in finding more (ii)_____ ways of exterminating itself.

Blank (i)		Blank (ii)	
(A)	hope	(D)	impartial
(B)	preference	(E)	remote
(C)	contempt ✓	(F)	efficient ✓

Difficult Answers

69. The committee's report is not as valuable as it might have been because it addresses only the symptoms and not the _____ causes of the problem.

(A) unimpeachable
(B) ephemeral
(C) underlying ✓
(D) incipient
(E) superficial

70. Calvin had long been known for his disingenuousness, but even those who knew him well were surprised at the _____ explanation he gave for the shortage of funds.

(A) elegant
(B) mendacious ✓
(C) sincere
(D) dogmatic
(E) bitter

Additional Paragraph Completion Items

71. A good mystery writer knows how to lose the reader in a (i)_____ from which there is no easy exit by anticipating and encouraging seemingly plausible theories only to show, at the appropriate juncture, that these are dead ends; to truly enjoy the book, you have to accept this (ii)_____ and admire the architecture of the twists and turns and cul-de-sacs.

Blank (i)		Blank (ii)	
(A)	chamber	(D)	manipulation ✓
(B)	prison	(E)	inequity
(C)	labyrinth ✓	(F)	clarification

72. Economic protectionism is seductive, but countries that succumb to its allure soon find that it makes (i)_____ promises; conversely, countries that commit to economic (ii)_____ ensure a brighter economic future for their citizens.

Blank (i)		Blank (ii)	
(A)	false ✓	(D)	sanctity ✓
(B)	sincere	(E)	competition
(C)	intrepid	(F)	rigidity

73. The book's treatment of vegetarianism reveals immense learning, the advantage of having read obscure pamphlets alongside literary masterworks, (i)_____ mystical treatises alongside widely distributed political manifestos, and the theories of crackpots alongside the meditations of respected scholars. It traces the origins of vegetarianism to (ii)_____ times: the ancient Greek Pythagoras eschewed meat and is often mentioned as (iii)_____ a vegetarian diet. By the middle of the eighteenth century, vegetarianism had become a secular religion, and by the mid-nineteenth century, it was associated with French revolutionaries, British nudists, and Romantics from across Europe.

Blank (i)		Blank (ii)	
(A)	arcane	(D)	unsettled
(B)	inflamed	(E)	classical
(C)	precocious	(F)	contemporary

Blank (iii)	
(G)	placating
(H)	advocating
(I)	reviling

74. As the human body ages, the brain shrinks, the distance between neurons increases, and connections become (i)_____. Still, a surprising number of mental functions not only remain (ii)_____, they actually improve with age. More mature brains store more expert knowledge. As a consequence, older professionals can more readily distinguish what is important from what is not. This helps to explain why a senior partner in a law firm is better able to handle (iii)_____ litigation involving boxes and boxes of documents, only a few of which are relevant.

Blank (i)		Blank (ii)	
(A)	compressed	(D)	compromised
(B)	attenuated	(E)	insubstantial
(C)	inelastic	(F)	unimpaired

Blank (iii)	
(G)	complex
(H)	hostile
(I)	worrisome

75. The received wisdom that the Spanish Inquisition was an all-powerful, torture-mad institution is largely a nineteenth century (i)_____. In reality, the institution was underfunded and understaffed with scattered tribunals of only (ii)_____ reach and methods more humane than those of most secular courts. Death by fire was the exception, not the rule. The failure of the Reformation in Spain had less to do with the Inquisition than with the populace's (iii)_____ to Protestantism. In virtually every area of action, the Inquisition was ineffective.

Blank (i)		Blank (ii)	
(A)	discovery	(D)	penurious
(B)	invention	(E)	circumscribed
(C)	misnomer	(F)	desperate

Blank (iii)	
(G)	consanguinity
(H)	indifference
(I)	inoculation

76. Sometimes the present culture of argumentation seems to be inspired by malice or a (i)_____ desire to boost ratings, but more often it's the product of a strong belief that trial by combat, or in this case argument, is the best way to get at truth. On this theory, if we had the facts in front of us and were prepared to be rational, we'd all agree upon the truth. The trouble is that (ii)_____ debates rarely generate sufficient facts, and they almost never resolve underlying differences in philosophical (iii)_____. So while we argue much, we seldom reach agreement.

Blank (i)		Blank (ii)	
(A)	ludicrous	(D)	polarized
(B)	whimsical	(E)	verbal
(C)	cynical	(F)	unstructured

Blank (iii)	
(G)	enigmas
(H)	commitments
(I)	pleasantries

77. Elihu's realism was situational rather than theoretical, pragmatic rather than (i)_____. It was characterized as much by reservation as by assertion, (ii)_____ in the expression of its convictions.

Blank (i)		Blank (ii)	
(A)	scientific	(D)	intemperate
(B)	tenuous	(E)	modest
(C)	dogmatic	(F)	innocuous

78. We think that what we do is largely under our (i)_____ control. We believe that we should try to increase this control by reasoning and will power, but this is all wrong. Non-deliberate emotion and intuition are much more important in shaping our lives than reason and will. Knowledge of our actions comes not primarily from (ii)_____ but from systematic external observation.

Blank (i)		Blank (ii)	
(A)	impartial	(D)	introspection
(B)	conscious	(E)	confession
(C)	dubious	(F)	indecision

79. It has been said that Fielding lacked the imaginative faculty. It would be more correct to say that he (i)_____ the fantastic and preposterous parts of invention. His stories are remarkable for the clarity of their (ii)_____.

Blank (i)		Blank (ii)	
(A)	incorporated	(D)	realism
(B)	envisioned	(E)	individualism
(C)	distrusted	(F)	histrionics

80. Gilbert and Sullivan's Grand Inquisitor wails, "When everyone is somebody, then no one's anybody." Indeed, what sense is there in a college course on "Pop Culture"? A century ago, a university don would have been (i)_____ to teach literature in English, not Greek or Latin, let alone build a career out of discursive commentary on everyday life. But (ii)_____ has changed. Soon there will be entire departments devoted to the subject.

Blank (i)		Blank (ii)	
(A)	eager	(D)	academe
(B)	embarrassed	(E)	morality
(C)	compelled	(F)	entertainment

81. McCarthyism was a reckless assault upon the American left. Some bureaucrats seemed above all interested in power. Politicians were concerned primarily with votes. Professional anti-Communist witnesses and blacklisters, (i)_____ artists who demanded a price for clearing one's name, had a financial stake. And there was no (ii)_____ of true believers, including Senator Joseph R. McCarthy, who, though misguided, seemed to be at least genuinely concerned for the welfare of the country.

Blank (i)		Blank (ii)	
(A)	shakedown	(D)	paucity
(B)	renown	(E)	confusion
(C)	dangerous	(F)	insurrection

82. Pharmaceutical companies are not required to determine whether their products have special effects on women as a group. While researching, these companies might discover something that would suppress the demand for a new drug, and this financial (i)_____ means that little unmandated research is done on the workings of drugs in women. The Physicians' Desk Reference is far from being an (ii)_____ guide to drugs because it is a compilation of package inserts provided by drug companies.

Blank (i)		Blank (ii)	
(A)	disincentive	(D)	independent
(B)	placation	(E)	inconsequential
(C)	curiosity	(F)	undocumented

83. Maxwell moved easily through the (i)_____ of the corporate structure of the huge company, actually delighting in the (ii)_____ of the various organization complexities that sometimes included intersecting and even inconsistent lines of authority.

Blank (i)		Blank (ii)	
(A)	boulevards	(D)	certainties
(B)	stairwell	(E)	intricacies
(C)	labyrinth	(F)	pastimes

84. Prior to World War II, the magazine had been notorious for its (i)_____ wit, most especially the sarcasms contributed by Dorothy Parker. Coinciding with the start of the Cold War, however, the managers of the country's literary affairs favored a more (ii)_____ turn of phrase.

Blank (i)		Blank (ii)	
(A)	raffish	(D)	vulgar
(B)	gentile	(E)	cautious
(C)	practiced	(F)	noxious

85. The practice of law too often involves the (i)_____ worship of rationality. Society has somehow persuaded itself that insoluble social problems can be fobbed off on the courts, which solve them if judges (ii)_____ the Constitution and statute books long enough. And judges and lawyers enable this disfunctionality by tacitly encouraging the belief that this end-around is feasible. The technical obscurity of its language and procedure provides vague (iii)_____ that, surely, these experts must know what they are talking about. It's a form of self-delusion and madness.

Blank (i)		Blank (ii)	
(A)	irrational	(D)	pore over
(B)	sudden	(E)	side step
(C)	incurable	(F)	enlighten

Blank (iii)	
(G)	recollection
(H)	assurance
(I)	protestation

Sentence Equivalence Items

DIRECTIONS: Select the <u>two</u> words that, when used independently in the sentence, produce logical sentences <u>and</u> produce sentences that are alike in meaning.

86. Originally derived from the French word for gypsy, "bohemian" came to mean a youthful period of _____ tolerated in the development of a bourgeois citizen.

(A) uncertainty
(B) indulgence
(C) familiarity
(D) grace
(E) languor
(F) preparation

87. The announcement came as no great surprise to anyone familiar with the case, as the details had already been widely _____.

(A) disseminated
(B) disparaged
(C) infiltrated
(D) controverted
(E) consummated
(F) published

88. If at all possible, students avoid Gilbert's introductory course, for his _____ with grades above C is legendary.

(A) unfamiliarity
(B) strategy
(C) parsimony
(D) ebullience
(E) tactfulness
(F) stinginess

89. Farm products are sold for the most part in highly competitive markets, so prices rise and fall _____, while retail prices of industrial goods hold more nearly to a constant level.

(A) precipitously
(B) gradually
(C) incrementally
(D) steeply
(E) tentatively
(F) recursively

90. Gossip is most memorable, but not necessarily most damaging, when it is believable, because it only confirms what people already _____.

(A) reject
(B) encounter
(C) suspect
(D) assume
(E) dismiss
(F) reclaim

91. Japan's mores have been changing for decades, as an extremely formal country has become steadily more _____.

(A) industrialized
(B) casual
(C) accessible
(D) relaxed
(E) educated
(F) predictable

92. If they were indeed more than just friends, theirs was a relationship made in heaven, a blessing rarely offered to _____ lovers.

(A) carnal
(B) amiable
(C) collateral
(D) insensitive
(E) sublunary
(F) secretive

93. Matthew enjoys high risk and unorthodox actions and fancies himself a maverick and a buccaneer, someone who _____ convention.

(A) embraces
(B) defies
(C) glorifies
(D) establishes
(E) flouts
(F) adopts

94. Outstanding private collections that have been donated to museums demonstrate that business acumen and great wealth are not incompatible with artistic discrimination and _____ art.

(A) casualness about
(B) munificence toward
(C) indifference to
(D) charity for
(E) acceptance by
(F) production of

95. All composers have admirers, but Mahler inspires a fanatical enthusiasm in his veritable army of _____.

(A) resisters
(B) instrumentalists
(C) collaborators
(D) amateurs
(E) critics
(F) devotees

96. Heinrich predicted that the end of the Soviet empire would trigger the _____ of art in Russia, but the total lack of any viable new movement proved him dead wrong.

(A) stagnation
(B) efflorescence
(C) blossoming
(D) stasis
(E) demise
(F) decline

97. As a once generous definition of literature gave way to hierarchies that excluded juvenile and domestic fiction, the male authors were _____, while the female authors were deemed unworthy of serious study.

(A) criticized
(B) canonized
(C) infantilized
(D) sanitized
(E) improvised
(F) lionized

98. His paintings are unusual in depicting not momentous events but scenes of _____ life, which, in that day, were still unhackneyed.

(A) quotidian
(B) reproachable
(C) iniquitous
(D) distilled
(E) routine
(F) ubiquitous

99. The richness and the variety of the instrumentation of *The Flying Dutchman* _____ Wagner's greatness, but the opera itself is a work of promise, not attainment.

(A) intimate
(B) portend
(C) inspire
(D) recapitulate
(E) underscore
(F) animate

100. The essential function of political theory at the present time is to recall to liberalism the _____ concrete tasks remaining to be completed.

(A) peripatetic
(B) monolithic
(C) elastic
(D) multifarious
(E) unperfected
(F) manifold

QUIZZES

Complete each of the three Completions quizzes while being timed. Answers are on page 700.

Quiz I
(15 items; 22 minutes)

> **DIRECTIONS:** Select <u>one</u> answer choice for each blank from the corresponding column of choices. Fill all blanks in a way that best completes the text.

1. The merchant _____ a small neighborhood business into a citywide chain of stores.

   (A) appraised
   (B) transferred
   (C) parlayed
   (D) redeemed
   (E) instilled

2. With the evidence _____ from numerous x-ray studies, scientists are beginning to form a picture of the atomic structure of the cell.

   (A) remanded
   (B) gleaned
   (C) pilfered
   (D) atrophied
   (E) implored

3. Although a gala performance, the conducting was _____, and the orchestra less than enthusiastic, but the audience seemed oblivious to the defects and was enthralled.

   (A) auspicious
   (B) perfunctory
   (C) decimated
   (D) voracious
   (E) animated

4. The critic thought the film was completely unrealistic; he termed the plot (i)_____ and the acting (ii)_____.

Blank (i)	Blank (ii)
(A) contrived	(D) unbelievable
(B) absorbing	(E) unparalleled
(C) imaginative	(F) uninspiring

5. Dedicated wildlife photographers willingly travel great distances and gladly endure considerable hardship to share with audiences their _____ for the natural world.

   (A) distaste
   (B) contempt
   (C) preference
   (D) expectations
   (E) enthusiasm

6. The term "Indian," introduced by Columbus and _____ by historians, is a misnomer for the Native American.

   (A) eradicated
   (B) arbitrated
   (C) infiltrated
   (D) perpetuated
   (E) coerced

7. Because the poet was restless and uneasy in society, he sought a (i)_____ existence and a life of (ii)_____.

Blank (i)	Blank (ii)
(A) materialistic	(D) frivolity
(B) stable	(E) solitude
(C) nomadic	(F) urbanity

8. Because he was (i)_____ and the life of the party, his friends thought that he was happy, but his wife was (ii)_____ and shy and was thought to be unhappy.

Blank (i)		Blank (ii)	
(A)	vitriolic	(D)	sophomoric
(B)	garrulous	(E)	taciturn
(C)	inimical	(F)	gregarious

9. The experienced ambassador was generally an (i)_____ person who regained her composure quickly even on those (ii)_____ occasions when she was close to losing her temper.

Blank (i)		Blank (ii)	
(A)	imperturbable	(D)	trivial
(B)	articulate	(E)	momentous
(C)	idealistic	(F)	infrequent

10. As the heir of the Samurai, the Japanese soldier had a worthy heritage, but the Allies initially underestimated the capabilities of the Japanese armed forces. Then, following early Japanese victories, the Allies overestimated them. Thus was born the myth of the Japanese super-soldier, a myth nurtured by Japanese propaganda and spread by (i)_____ war correspondents who wrote about their (ii)_____.

Blank (i)		Blank (ii)	
(A)	persistent	(D)	genealogy
(B)	credulous	(E)	invincibility
(C)	patriotic	(F)	tactics

11. In the nineteenth century, the popular imagination transformed the West into a land of adventure where cowboys (i)_____ the bravery and strength of the rugged individual. Movies, television, and popular fiction continue to promote the (ii)_____ nature of the West.

Blank (i)		Blank (ii)	
(A)	discounted	(D)	feral
(B)	epitomized	(E)	mythical
(C)	actualized	(F)	transitory

DIRECTIONS: Select the two words that, when used independently in the sentence, produce logical sentences and produce sentences that are alike in meaning.

12. The _____ scandals reported almost daily by the media tend to obscure our vision of genuine corruption.

(A) ersatz
(B) factitious
(C) epigrammatic
(D) sedulous
(E) nascent
(F) irresponsible

13. Whistle-blowers need encouragement and protection because they too often end up suffering far more than the _____ they expose.

(A) sentinels
(B) malefactors
(C) evildoers
(D) supernumeraries
(E) troglodytes
(F) freebooters

14. Hentoff is positively giddy about his mentors, and his _____ of them often borders on reverence.

(A) adulation
(B) analysis
(C) worship
(D) discussion
(E) denigration
(F) belittling

15. These small groups of people living peaceably on the land and supporting themselves by _____ resented the distant, centralized authority of the city.

(A) regular conquests
(B) animal husbandry
(C) trading alliances
(D) pastoral activities
(E) arts and crafts
(F) commercial enterprise

Quiz II

(15 items; 22 minutes)

DIRECTIONS: Select <u>one</u> answer choice for each blank from the corresponding column of choices. Fill all blanks in a way that best completes the text.

1. Unlike gold, paper money has no _____ value; it is merely a representation of wealth.

(A) financial
(B) inveterate
(C) economic
(D) intrinsic
(E) fiscal

2. As science progresses, observations that at one time seemed to conflict with one another can sometimes be _____ by a more advanced theory.

(A) established
(B) inferred
(C) detected
(D) reconciled
(E) delimited

3. Carling, a political appointee who was not really able to run the agency, tended to promote others even less _____ than himself who would not question his authority.

(A) competent
(B) likable
(C) honest
(D) wholesome
(E) envied

4. Because the orchestra's conductor is an intensely private person, he _____ making the appearances at fund-raising functions that are part of the job.

(A) loathes
(B) anticipates
(C) excuses
(D) prepares
(E) convenes

5. Although for centuries literature was considered something that would instruct as well as entertain, many modern readers have little patience with (i)_____ works and seek only to be (ii)_____.

Blank (i)	Blank (ii)
(A) didactic	(D) distracted
(B) epic	(E) misled
(C) bawdy	(F) enlightened

6. Recent studies demonstrate that personal memory is actually quite (i)_____, subject to contamination and reshaping so that aspects of a person's memory are apt to be (ii)_____ or erroneous.

Blank (i)	Blank (ii)
(A) implausible	(D) recalcitrant
(B) inhibited	(E) subjective
(C) volatile	(F) reflective

7. Karen was (i)_____ in her vindictiveness, frequently feigning disarming warmth while (ii)_____ waiting for an opportunity to strike back.

Blank (i)	Blank (ii)
(A) confident	(D) overtly
(B) withdrawn	(E) secretly
(C) ruthless	(F) immodestly

8. The sonatas of Beethoven represent the (i)_____ of classicism, but they also contain the seeds of its destruction, romanticism, which (ii)_____ the sonata form by allowing emotion rather than tradition to shape the music.

Blank (i)	Blank (ii)
(A) denigration	(D) shatters
(B) pinnacle	(E) perpetuates
(C) ignorance	(F) restores

9. His offhand, rather (i)_____ remarks (ii)_____ a character that was really rather serious and not at all superficial.

Blank (i)	Blank (ii)
(A) flippant	(D) betrayed
(B) bellicose	(E) masked
(C) pernicious	(F) belied

10. American audiences have assumed that opera in English is a poor substitute for the real thing because it was opera's foreignness that originally made it suitable for (i)_____ consumption by the rich and famous. In every other country where opera is popular, (ii)_____ performances are the norm. As a consequence of this attitude, American opera singers were forced to sing in other languages, rehashing a repertory that has remained more or less (iii)_____ for nearly 100 years.

Blank (i)	Blank (ii)
(A) prosperous	(D) vernacular
(B) auditory	(E) impromptu
(C) conspicuous	(F) extravagant

Blank (iii)
(G) incomprehensible
(H) elastic
(I) static

11. Fermat's last theorem is undoubtedly the most famous (i)_____ in mathematics: the equation $x^n + y^n = z^n$ has no solution in positive whole numbers, when n is a whole number greater than 2. To a non-mathematician, this may seem a(n) (ii)_____ and uninteresting claim. Yet Fermat's tantalizing assertion held a tremendous fascination for many great mathematicians, none of whom has devised a proof of the theorem.

Blank (i)	Blank (ii)
(A) conundrum	(D) jejune
(B) topiary	(E) unvarnished
(C) rejoinder	(F) exhilarating

DIRECTIONS: Select the two words that, when used independently in the sentence, produce logical sentences and produce sentences that are alike in meaning.

12. Before the eighteenth century, European artists and writers had been more or less creatures of the court, and their survival depended largely on aristocratic _____.

(A) patronage
(B) umbrage
(C) sponsorship
(D) collaboration
(E) investiture
(F) depredation

13. Her most severe critics have argued that Kerinski's _____ style was intentionally obscure and that her psychological analyses were a bunch of perfumed platitudes.

(A) belletristic
(B) florid
(C) incomprehensible
(D) turgid
(E) hackneyed
(F) fulsome

14. The tabloids understand that sexual scandal sells newspapers: the more _____ the story, the larger its headline.

(A) invidious
(B) lascivious
(C) salacious
(D) propitious
(E) salubrious
(F) illustrious

15. The idea that a generation of young Americans arose in moral outrage at an unjust war and forced a corrupt, oppressive Establishment to change course is to a great extent inaccurate, but the story is a useful _____ for inspiring idealism.

(A) saga
(B) fable
(C) apologue
(D) history
(E) chronicle
(F) commentary

Quiz III

(15 items; 22 minutes)

> **DIRECTIONS:** Select <u>one</u> answer choice for each blank from the corresponding column of choices. Fill all blanks in a way that best completes the text.

1. The football team was _____ by injuries: of the 53 members, only 40 were fit to play.

(A) truncated
(B) decimated
(C) invaded
(D) ostracized
(E) reviled

2. In the Middle Ages, scientists and clergymen thought the universe was well-ordered and (i)_____; today scientists are more likely to see the world as (ii)_____.

Blank (i)		Blank (ii)	
(A)	transient	(D)	chaotic
(B)	divergent	(E)	dogmatic
(C)	harmonious	(F)	galling

3. The actress owed her reputation to her (i)_____ public and not to the (ii)_____ reviews that bordered on being cruel.

Blank (i)		Blank (ii)	
(A)	diffident	(D)	approbatory
(B)	congenial	(E)	scathing
(C)	adoring	(F)	deferential

4. Since the city cannot ticket their cars, the diplomats can park anywhere with _____.

(A) penury
(B) impunity
(C) precision
(D) languor
(E) ignominy

5. If a person ignores false accusations instead of (i)_____ them, people may conclude that the person is guilty; but any response to a false accusation merely gives it additional (ii)_____.

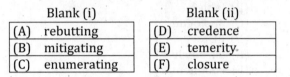

Blank (i)		Blank (ii)	
(A)	rebutting	(D)	credence
(B)	mitigating	(E)	temerity
(C)	enumerating	(F)	closure

6. Although scientists have sought to measure time, only writers and poets have truly (i)_____ its quality and our (ii)_____ experience of it.

Blank (i)		Blank (ii)	
(A)	neglected	(D)	benign
(B)	belied	(E)	ephemeral
(C)	captured	(F)	fractious

7. Although her acting was _____, she looked so good on stage that the audience applauded anyway.

(A) dynamic
(B) laudable
(C) implacable
(D) execrable
(E) intrepid

8. Philosophical differences _____ the unification of the two parties into one.

(A) delegated
(B) legislated
(C) impeded
(D) enacted
(E) entrusted

9. In his private life he was quite (i)_____, but he gave large sums of money to charities, so most people thought of him as a (ii)_____.

Blank (i)		Blank (ii)	
(A)	pusillanimous	(D)	charlatan
(B)	miserly	(E)	savant
(C)	immodest	(F)	philanthropist

10. Rosa Ponselle was blessed with a voice beautiful enough to (i)_____ her total lack of operatic experience. Within a few years of her spectacular debut, it settled into the lower tessitura of a mezzo-soprano. Trained singers cope with the changes that the human voice undergoes as middle age approaches, but the self-taught Ponselle lacked the (ii)_____ to adjust.

Blank (i)

(A)	illuminate
(B)	compensate for
(C)	generate

Blank (ii)

(D)	intellectual horsepower
(E)	technical savvy
(F)	raw musical talent

11. Some people are destroyed precisely because they cannot force themselves into taking unequivocal ideological stances and cannot assess human situations in (i)_____ terms. Camus' emotional and intellectual (ii)_____ led to exile from all of the communities to which he belonged because he refused to endorse simplistic solutions.

Blank (i)		Blank (ii)	
(A)	relativistic	(D)	inconsistencies
(B)	humanistic	(E)	shortcomings
(C)	Manichaean	(F)	vices

DIRECTIONS: Select the <u>two</u> words that, when used independently in the sentence, produce logical sentences <u>and</u> produce sentences that are alike in meaning.

12. Stalin believed that history was fiction, an infinitely _____ text to be shaped to the needs of the State.

(A) transferable
(B) malleable
(C) plastic
(D) divisible
(E) expandable
(F) productive

13. The long-term consequence of the slavish _____ of earlier composers was a bland, stifling uniformity that for years characterized musical theater.

(A) veneration
(B) emulation
(C) contemplation
(D) dissection
(E) imitation
(F) resurrection

14. Saratoga was the turning point of America's Revolutionary War because with that victory the American cause seemed sufficiently _____ for France to conclude an alliance with the Americans.

(A) important
(B) remote
(C) novel
(D) viable
(E) grievous
(F) sustainable

15. Deer are now more numerous than when the first European settlers arrived to this continent, and their _____ forms are often seen at dusk gliding like spirits into the roadside brush.

(A) characteristic
(B) illustrious
(C) phantasmal
(D) predatory
(E) strident
(F) chimerical

STRATEGY SUMMARY

Completions items measure your understanding of both reading comprehension and vocabulary. Completions items come in three forms:

- Sentence Completion: One blank with five answer choices; one correct answer

- Paragraph Completion: Two or three blanks with three answer choices per blank; correct answer includes an answer for each blank, selected independently

- Sentence Equivalence: One blank with six answer choices; correct answer includes two of the six answer choices

Virtually any subject area may be covered, but no special outside knowledge is required. Complex vocabulary and sentence structure increase item difficulty. Answer choices are incorrect when the resulting sentences are not idiomatically valid or when the overall meaning becomes illogical. While an answer choice may be eliminated because the completed sentence fails to make sense, you must not discard an alternative on the basis of grammatical syntax because such syntax will always be correct.

General Strategies

There are also a variety of general strategies that can be used to solve Completions items: "Anticipate and Test," "Simplify Your Life," and Hard Cases ("Go to Pieces" and Difficult Answers). With Paragraph Completions items, read through the text completely to get an overall sense of the material, identifying any of the above reasoning clues that are indicative of the logical structure (e.g., conjunction clues, punctuation, etc.).

"Anticipate and Test"

You should read the sentence(s) through for understanding, trying to *anticipate* what word or words would effectively complete the sentence(s). Then, you should look at the answer choices to find the one that comes closest to your initial prediction. Occasionally, you will find the very word or words that you anticipated, but most of the time the answer choices will include words that are similar to those that came to mind when you initially read the sentence. After picking the answer choice that matches your anticipated guesses, insert the selection into the sentence to *test* it and then read the sentence through to make sure that the answer choice reads smoothly and correctly. Upon reading it, you should be convinced that this is the correct answer choice. If that does not work, test the remaining answer choices. The anticipation part of this strategy does not apply when sentences are open-ended, that is, when they allow for multiple possible completion scenarios. In this event, you should directly substitute the various answer choices into the blank(s) and test for validity.

"Simplify Your Life"

The difficulty of Sentence Completions items is based on the number of details that are included. In general, the more details there are in a sentence, the harder the item is to answer. You can eliminate unnecessary details to make the item easier.

Hard Cases

There are Completions items on the test that are very difficult due to complex logical structures and difficult vocabulary. While the strategies presented above will still be helpful, these items often require a more sophisticated approach. Here are two strategies for handling these "hard cases." The first strategy is for handling sentences with complex logical structures; the second strategy is for handling sentences with difficult vocabulary.

- *"Go to Pieces"*: When approaching Completions items with complex logical structures, you should try to simplify the task by breaking the sentence into pieces and isolating a small part of the sentence that you understand; this part of the sentence must contain an omitted word. Then, test the answer choices, eliminating as many of them as possible. Remember that an answer choice may be incorrect because it does not create an idiomatic construction.

- *Difficult Answers*: Remember that difficult items have difficult answers. The more difficult Completions items can be anywhere, and the relative difficulty of an item will depend on your vocabulary skills. In fact, you may know all of the words in a more difficult item but not all of the words in an easier item. If forced to guess, you should not choose an easy answer choice. Instead, choose the answer choice with the most difficult vocabulary word(s).

Item-Type Strategies

For Completions items, it is quite useful to analyze the logical pattern of the sentence. While a countless number of sentences are possible, logical structure falls into two basic categories (Thought Extension and Thought Reversal) that are often signaled via key words or punctuation. More complex sentences may not contain pure extensions or reversals of thought but may have a mixture of both elements (Combined Reasoning). There are a variety of strategies that can be used to solve each of the three types of Completions items: Thought Extension (Coordinate Conjunctions, Subordinate Conjunctions, Key Adjectives and Adverbs, Punctuation, and Phrases), Thought Reversal (Coordinate Conjunctions, Subordinate Conjunctions, Key Adjectives and Adverbs, and Phrases), and Combined Reasoning (various elements of Thought Extension and Thought Reversal).

Thought Extension

In Thought Extension items, missing words may parallel or serve to extend another thought in the sentence. The following are the most important thought extension clues:

- *Coordinate Conjunctions*: Conjunctions are words that join together words, phrases, clauses, or sentences. They indicate to the reader how the joined elements are related to each other. With Thought Extension items, coordinate conjunction clues continue or reinforce/strengthen the underlying logic (e.g., "and," "or").

- *Subordinate Conjunctions*: A subordinate conjunction joins together two ideas in a sentence and indicates that one idea is subordinate to, or dependent upon, the other idea. Since they have to indicate the way in which the subordinate clause depends upon the main clause, subordinate conjunctions serve as important verbal clues. With Thought Extension items, subordinate conjunction clues continue or reinforce/strengthen the underlying logic (e.g., "since," "if," "for," "because," "so").

- *Key Adjectives and Adverbs*: In many cases, the elements of the sentence that provide descriptive detail (adjectives and adverbs) are important clues. With Thought Extension items, look for terminology that continues or reinforces/strengthens the underlying logic.

- *Punctuation*: Sometimes, a punctuation mark will serve as an important clue. Commas, semicolons, and colons indicate the continuation of a thought.

- *Phrases*: With Thought Extension items, phrase clues consist of any additional information that serves to continue or reinforce/strengthen the underlying logic.

Thought Reversal

In Thought Reversal items, missing word(s) are the reverse, or opposite, of ideas that are presented elsewhere in the sentence. The following are the most important thought reversal clues:

- *Coordinate Conjunctions*: Coordinate conjunction clues set up a contrast with or diminish/weaken the underlying logic (e.g., "but," "or," "yet").

- *Subordinate Conjunctions*: Subordinate conjunction clues set up a contrast with or diminish/weaken the underlying logic (e.g., "although," "while," "unless").

- *Key Adjectives and Adverbs*: Key adjectives and adverbs set up a contrast with or diminish/weaken the underlying logic (e.g., "however," "instead," "not," "large/small").

- *Phrases*: Phrases include any additional information that serves to set up a contrast with or diminish/weaken the underlying logic.

Combined Reasoning

Sometimes, a single strand of reasoning may not be sufficient to dispose of an item. Combined Reasoning items consist of complex sentences that contain a mixture of extensions and reversals of thought. To correctly answer these items, it is important to first understand the overall logical structure of the sentence, identifying the ideas and thoughts that are extended and those that are reversed.

Verbal Reasoning: Reading

Course Concept Outline

I. Test Mechanics (p. 61)

    A. Overview (p. 61)

    B. Anatomy (Items #1–3, pp. 62–64)

    C. Pacing (p. 65)

    D. Time Trial (Items #1–4, pp. 66–67)

    E. Game Plan (p. 68)

        1. Build Foundational Reading Skills (p. 68)
        2. Quickly Preview the Test (p. 68)
        3. Personalize the Passage Order (p. 68)
        4. Preview the Item Stems (p. 68)
        5. Preview the Passage (p. 69)
        6. Read the Passage (p. 70)
        7. Answer the Items (p. 71)
        8. Eliminate Choices, Guess (If Necessary), Enter Selection, and Confirm (p. 71)

II. Lesson (p. 73)

    A. Reading Preliminaries[1]

    B. The Reading Passages

        1. Passages Can Treat Any Subject
          a) Material Is Taken Out of Context
          b) Passages Are Edited
          c) Passages Test Comprehension and Critical Reading, Not Speed Reading
          d) Careful Reading Is Required

---

[1] Some concepts in this Course Concept Outline are not illustrated through examples in your student text but may be covered by your instructor in class. They are included here to provide a complete outline of your course.

TEST MECHANICS

Overview

The computer-based GRE test includes two Verbal Reasoning sections with 20 items each. These sections each include approximately ten Reading items. Some of these items test Reading Comprehension. These items measure the ability to read complex materials with insight and understanding. The Reading Comprehension section includes several passage sets, each set consisting of between one and six items. Passages are between 100 and 450 words long.

Reading Comprehension items fall into clearly defined patterns. In fact, there are only seven different item-types, using three different answer choice formats. When you've learned to recognize these different types based on what's asked and become familiar with the test-writer's strategies for creating right and wrong answers, you'll be in a position to achieve your maximum score on Reading Comprehension—and that is the objective of the first part of the Verbal Reasoning: Reading Lesson.

Other Reading items test Critical Reading. These items ask you to demonstrate skills such as identifying the conclusion of a line of reasoning, uncovering hidden presuppositions of an argument, and evaluating the strength of inferences. These items test the ability to read carefully and think critically—skills learned and refined by way of your school, job, and personal experiences. Each section includes between one and three Critical Reading items, and each item is based on a passage between 50 and 150 words long.

Passages for Reading Comprehension and Critical Reading items may be based on any topic. They are usually drawn from previously published material from the general areas of humanities, social sciences, natural sciences, and even everyday topics. In most cases, the passage will be about a topic with which you are *not* familiar. Indeed, the test-writers choose unusual topics so that items will be a test of reading skill, not subject knowledge. If the passage treats a familiar topic, it will usually include details with which you will not have any prior familiarity.

Reading Comprehension presents a challenge to complete the Verbal Reasoning section within the allotted time. However, it is important to remember that Reading items do not test "speed-reading." Instead, these items test reading *comprehension* and *critical* reading.

Anatomy

DIRECTIONS: For items #1–3, select <u>one</u> answer unless otherwise directed.

Items #1–2 are based on the following passage.

Folklore holds that Atlantic salmon were once so abundant in New England rivers that early colonists walked across the backs of the fish as they ran up the rivers in spring. Then, according to the
5 received wisdom, at the turn of the nineteenth century, increasing pollution in the rivers and the construction of large main stem dams across rivers caused salmon to become severely depleted. For this reason, restoration programs to "bring back the
10 salmon" have been, and continue to be, an extensive and ongoing effort supported by a variety of lobbying groups.

If the theory were accurate, then there should be considerable archaeological evidence that
15 salmon played a significant role in the diets of the aboriginal peoples of New England. But in site after site, although bones of numerous other fish species have been recovered, no salmon bones have been found. It's more likely that the accounts of salmon
20 were intentionally embellished by early writers, who were in reality promoters with strong motives for presenting to the folks back in the old country a favorable image of New England as a place of natural abundance. Since salmon was a much
25 esteemed fish at home, its inclusion and description was important.

In fact, salmon did not begin to colonize New England streams until a period of climatic cooling known as the Little Ice Age (C.E. 1550–1800). At the
30 end of this period, the climatic warming created less favorable environmental conditions for salmon, and hence their range retracted. The idea that initial colonization did not occur until this time, and then only as a temporary range expansion, explains the
35 lack of salmon in prehistoric sites and the depletion of the fish at the end of the eighteenth century.

The directions remind you that some items my ask you to select more than one answer. Remember to check each item for additional directions.

Typically, reading passages discuss an unfamiliar topic. Even if you know something about the depletion of salmon in New England rivers, that information may or may not be helpful since you'll be asked about this particular passage.

The first paragraph introduces a history of salmon in New England, as well as the current depletion in the same rivers and the "received wisdom" that pollution and dams caused this depletion.

The second paragraph briefly traces the evidence that discounts this claim that pollution and dams caused salmon depletion and offers an alternative explanation: the salmon were not as abundant as historic records claim.

The third paragraph further explains this alternative solution, offering a scientific explanation for the expansion and subsequent depletion of the fish.

1. The primary purpose of the passage is to

    (A) propose a long-term plan for restoring
        salmon runs to the rivers of New England
    (B) undermine the theory that particular
        human activities caused the depletion of
        salmon runs in New England rivers
    (C) demonstrate that anthropogenic factors
        are often more powerful than natural ones
        in shaping the environment
    (D) provide evidence that the disappearance
        of salmon was caused by the damming and
        pollution of the rivers
    (E) refute the contention that climatological
        factors play a part in defining the range of
        indigenous species.

2. Identify the sentence that contains
    archaeological evidence to disprove the
    "received wisdom" summarized in the first
    paragraph.

    (A) Lines 8–12 ("For this reason...lobbying
        groups.")
    (B) Lines 13–16 ("If the theory...New England.")
    (C) Lines 16–19 ("But in site...found.")
    (D) Lines 24–26 ("Since salmon...important.")
    (E) Lines 29–32 ("At the end...retracted.")

1. **(B)** *This is a common type of Reading
    Comprehension item: it asks you to identify the
    main idea of the passage. The burden of the
    argument is that it was not pollution or dams
    that caused the salmon to disappear but a
    change in climate.*

2. **(C)** *This item asks about the use of
    archeological evidence in the passage to
    support the author's argument. In (C), the
    author notes that salmon bones are not found
    among the fish bones at sites where aboriginal
    peoples lived. This is evidence, the author says,
    that aboriginal peoples did not eat salmon.*

Item #3 is based on the following passage.

The Consumer Price Index (CPI) is a statistic that measures changes in the prices of goods and services purchased by consumers. It is based on a "basket of goods and services" divided into seven categories, such as housing, food, and transportation, with each category weighted according to its relative impact on a typical budget. Although the CPI is a fairly precise measure of inflation, consumers almost always imagine that prices are rising faster than this measure would indicate.

3. Which one of the following most helps to explain the phenomenon described above?

(A) Typical consumers purchase large ticket items, such as a major appliance or car, so infrequently that even given a low rate of inflation the price of the new purchase will be noticeably higher than that of the previous one.

(B) In recent years, advances in technology have caused the price of electronics, such as computers and stereo equipment, to decline even as new products are introduced that have more extensive capabilities.

(C) Because of long-term pressure in the health care sector, such as the push for higher wages for the lowest-paid health care workers, the cost of medical care has risen faster than the Consumer Price Index.

(D) The Consumer Price Index is compiled by the Bureau of Labor Statistics and is intended primarily as a measure of the effect of rising prices on a typical urban family.

(E) The prices paid for food commodities, which are dependent upon weather conditions, are usually more volatile than those determined by long-term market conditions.

This passage is brief and only relates to one item. Check the item stem to confirm that this is a Critical Reading item. Here, the passage describes a surprising result: consumers believe that prices rise faster than the Consumer Price Index, which is an accurate measure of those prices.

The item stem tells you to find an explanation to account for the apparent paradox that consumers think prices rise faster than the Consumer Price Index would indicate.

3. (A) *Because of the large periods of time between expensive purchases, consumers misinterpret the relatively large jump in the price of a big ticket item as typical of prices in general.*

Pacing

The computer-based GRE Verbal Reasoning section has 20 items and a 30-minute time limit. The section includes about 10 Completions items and 10 Reading items. The number and length of passages will vary, but if you plan to spend thirty seconds to one minute reading each passage and one minute answering each item, you can pace yourself throughout the Verbal Reasoning section. The following chart summarizes the timing for this approach.

Verbal Reasoning by Item-Type
Total Time: 30 minutes

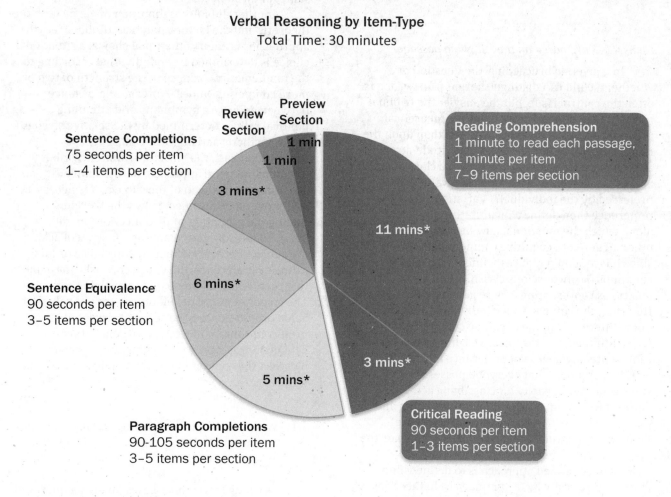

Review Section
1 min

Preview Section
1 min

Sentence Completions
75 seconds per item
1–4 items per section

3 mins*

Reading Comprehension
1 minute to read each passage,
1 minute per item
7–9 items per section

11 mins*

Sentence Equivalence
90 seconds per item
3–5 items per section

6 mins*

3 mins*

5 mins*

Paragraph Completions
90-105 seconds per item
3–5 items per section

Critical Reading
90 seconds per item
1–3 items per section

*Times are approximate

Note that the chart above is representative of a Verbal section but is not an exact replica of what you will see on test day. Each section will contain ABOUT five reading passages, and the length of each passage and number of items associated with each passage will vary. In general, spend 30 seconds to one minute reading each passage and one minute answering each item.

Time Trial

(4 items; 5.5 minutes)

> **DIRECTIONS:** For items #1–4, select <u>one</u> answer unless otherwise directed. Answers are on page 700.

Items #1–3 are based on the following passage.

In a juvenile proceeding, the question of whether a child can distinguish right from wrong is often the central issue, but the answer the tribunal receives may depend more upon the theoretical
5 presuppositions of an expert witness than upon the moral culpability of the child. The attitude-strength approach to the question starts with a class of acts and asks, "How strongly is this class valued or preferred by the individual?" Variations in
10 preference then define a quantitative dimension along which the individual may be compared with others. There is a cognitive component involved, since it is assumed that respondents make a conscious or unconscious classification of concrete
15 objects as representing a more general value-class. However, the comparison of individuals focuses not upon differences in the cognitive component but upon differences in the affective component represented by degree of preference for the class of
20 acts. It is assumed that everyone possesses the same cognitive capacity for classifying acts as authoritarian-democratic or being-becoming and that the critical differences between them are differences in strength of preferences for one or the
25 other class of objects.

A more refined approach is to define value classes empirically by factor analysis. In these cases individuals are asked to choose between concrete acts. Correlations between preferences for each pair
30 of acts are then resolved into factors. The factors are assumed to represent classes or dimensions of objects such that if one object in the class is preferred, so is another, and such that preference for one class of objects or one dimension is
35 independent of another class of objects.

From the point of view of assigning moral and legal blame, this factor-analytic approach is safer than the theoretical approach since it does not simply assume that value organizations known to
40 the theorist exist in the head of the subject but tries to find out what organizations exist in the head of the subject. It shares, however, a questionable assumption of the theoretical attitude-strength approach, the assumption that the classes or
45 dimensions used to organize value objects are the same for all subjects.

Another dubious assumption made by both the theoretic and the factor-analytic attitude-strength approaches is about situational choice: a situational
50 choice is determined by an individual according to the mathematical balance of the strength of two or more competing values. For example, a choice between going to a symphony and attending a political rally is determined by the relative strength
55 of the aesthetic and political values.

By contrast, the structural approach takes a phenomenological approach. Rather than postulate structures in the head of the subject, it is necessary to discover how a subject views the world by
60 finding the groupings and connections made between one object and another. Instead of asking the subject for a predefined action choice or for a rating or preference, the researcher asks the subject to structure the dilemma and to explain the choice.
65 The stages of moral development are not values or value orientations in the sense of classes of preferred content of what is chosen. Rather, to explain moral capacity, a distinction is drawn between the content of the value judgment and the
70 structure.

1. With which of the following statements would the author of the passage be most likely to agree?

(A) Judges who hear cases involving questions of the moral culpability of children should be experts in developmental psychology.
(B) A structuralist approach to the question of moral culpability is preferable to either a theoretical or a factor analysis approach.
(C) Factor analysis is more likely to produce reliable conclusions about moral responsibility than theoretical analysis.
(D) The phenomenological approach to psychology is not suitable for investigating whether a child understands right from wrong.
(E) Only psychologists who employ the phenomenological approach should be permitted to testify in court as expert witnesses.

2. Which of the following investigative techniques is most similar to the factor analysis approach?

    (A) using chemical markers to diagnose disease

    (B) having an eyewitness identify a person

    (C) employing a measuring rod to find length

    (D) taking photographs of a crime scene

    (E) separating a substance into its chemical components

For the following item, consider each answer individually and select all that apply.

3. According to the author, an attitude-strength analysis

    (A) measures only the cognitive decision-making capacity of individuals

    (B) is better suited to the study of populations than of individual subjects

    (C) treats the cognitive component of decisions only indirectly

Item #4 is based on the following passage.

In a newspaper article, the mystery writer Edgar Allen Poe, who was also an amateur cryptographer, invited readers to submit encrypted messages that, he boasted, he would decode. In a later article, Poe wrote, "Out of perhaps 100 ciphers altogether received, there was only one that we did not immediately succeed in resolving. This one was an imposition, that is to say, a jargon of random characters, having no meaning whatever." Perhaps if the cipher had been preserved for posterity, Poe's conclusion could have been tested. As it is, for proof of the claim, we have only his assertion that he was not able to decipher the message.

4. The speaker above implies that Poe's reasoning was faulty because he

    (A) failed to consider that the source of the unsolved message hoped to create a message that could not be decoded

    (B) acknowledged that it is theoretically possible to create an encrypted message that cannot be decoded

    (C) destroyed the mysterious message, making it impossible for others to verify his claim that it was indecipherable

    (D) presupposed that a reader truly interested in answering the challenge would not submit a message in principle indecipherable

    (E) assumed without proof that his failure to discover the meaning of the message proved that the message had no meaning

Game Plan

Build Foundational Reading Skills

This course includes a Verbal Reasoning Supplement in Appendix B (p. 503). If you found the Reading portion of your pre-assessment challenging, review the supplemental material to enhance your basic Reading skills. (Your instructor may also choose to cover this material in class.)

Quickly Preview the Test

The computer-based test allows you to move through all the test items in a particular section before you answer any items. Quickly preview the section, noting the number of reading passages as you go.

Personalize the Passage Order

You don't have to do the items in the order in which they are presented. You can use the "Review" feature to skip from one group of items to another and from item to item within a group.

What factors should you consider? First, you may find a passage topic that seems familiar to you. Of course, you can't expect that you'll already know the answers to the items, but familiarity is a definite advantage. Note passage length and the number of items associated with each passage as well.

When you choose your passage order, write it on the scratch paper provided by your test administrator. However, do not spend too much time personalizing the passage order. You want to save plenty of time for reading the passages and answering each item. Also, remember to use the "Review" feature provided on the GRE test to ensure that you have answered each test item before the end of each Verbal section.

Preview the Item Stems

Before reading a passage, you may find it helpful to preview the item stems, which are presented either as questions or as incomplete statements. If a stem mentions a key word or phrase, make a mental note and look for it as you read the selection.

Also, note any "thought-reverser" signal words, such as "EXCEPT," "LEAST," and "NOT." These signal words turn an item inside-out (or, if you prefer, upside-down): answers ordinarily right are wrong, and answers ordinarily wrong are right. You'll see many examples of this type of item throughout your study of the student materials.

See what you would learn from the following items, in which only the item stems are visible.

Items #1–2 are based on the following passage.

[Passage Omitted]

1. According to the passage, the most important disadvantage of nuclear energy is

(A)
(B)
(C)
(D)
(E)

Previewing would tell you to look for certain information in your reading. The first stem uses the phrase "most important disadvantage of nuclear energy." So, you know that the passage will discuss disadvantages of nuclear energy. When you find the "most important" one, mark that reference so that you can answer this item.

2. According to the author, shifting climate patterns will have all of the following effects EXCEPT:

(A)
(B)
(C)
(D)
(E)

The second stem tells you that the author discusses "shifting climate patterns," probably in some detail since the passage mentions multiple effects. Each time you find one of the effects, mark it so that when you answer this item you can eliminate those choices that mention such effects. ("EXCEPT" means to look for the one NOT mentioned in the passage.)

Item #3 is based on the following passage.

[Passage Omitted]

3. Which of the following, if true, most seriously weakens the argument?

(A)
(B)
(C)
(D)
(E)

Finally, the third stem tells you to look for the answer that weakens the argument. This item requires Critical Reading, and you will find it helpful to identify the assumptions in the passage as you read, then locate the answer choice that points out a flaw in that assumption.

Note that some students may not find this technique useful. Try it, and use it if you believe it works for you. Otherwise, do not preview the item stems.

Preview the Passage

This technique is not necessary when you encounter short passages. However, before you begin reading longer passages, take a few seconds to preview key sentences. Key sentences are the first and last sentences of the passage and the first sentence of each paragraph. Why preview? First sentences are often topic sentences, so reading a series of topic sentences will tell you what the author is trying to say, and it can give you an outline of the development of the passage. Sometimes, though not always, the last sentence is a conclusion.

To see how this can work, preview the following passage about solar energy, in which only the key sentences are visible.

At the present time, 98 percent of world energy consumption comes from sources such as fossil fuels.

5

Our energy consumption amounts to about one ten-thousandth of the energy we receive from the sun.

15

20 It is often stated that the growth rate will decline or that energy conservation measures will preclude any long-range problem.

25

The only practical means of avoiding the problem
30 of thermal pollution is the use of solar energy.

35

To see what you can learn from just a few sentences, think about these questions:

What's the passage about?

- Gas mileage.
- Space exploration.
- Solar energy.

What is a common attitude about energy conservation?

- It doesn't work.
- It might work.
- It does work.

What's the author's view on solar energy?

- It is unnecessary.
- It could be necessary.
- It is absolutely essential.

And the answers are that the passage is about solar energy, which the author believes to be necessary, even though a lot of people think conservation could solve all our problems.

Read the Passage

Keep the following points in mind when reading a passage:

- Read the passage quickly but carefully.

- Read the passage for important themes. Many of the items will ask about important themes of the passage, such as the main point, the purpose of a particular paragraph, or the author's intention.

- Do not try to memorize details. If you need detailed information, you can always go back to the passage to find it. The passage will always appear next to the items.

- Pause at the end to summarize your reading. One of the most helpful reading techniques is to summarize in your own words what you have just read. What is the main point? What did the author do in the first paragraph? In the second paragraph? What did the author prove?

Answer the Items

Keep the following points in mind when answering the accompanying items:

- Identify the type of question being asked. Reading items that test comprehension fall into one of seven categories, such as "Main Idea," "Specific Detail," and "Attitude-Tone." Reading items that test critical reading may ask about an argument's conclusion, assumptions, or inference. If you identify an item's category first, it will be easier to find the right answer. You'll learn more about the Reading item-types later in the "Verbal Reasoning: Reading" Lesson.

- Answer the question being asked. One of the most common mistakes made by examinees is to read the item stem carelessly and then answer the "wrong" question. That is, they respond to what they think they read rather than the question that is actually on the page. Since wrong answers often sound plausible, making this mistake means you're probably going to find a good answer—to the wrong question.

- Read the answer choices carefully. You'll learn how to recognize the Reading item-types and what the correct answer to each should look like. Make sure to read all of the answer choices before selecting the correct answer. A favorite strategy of test-writers is to create an "attractive distractor," that is, to create an answer choice that uses wording highly suggestive of ideas developed in the passage but then disqualify it by including a word or phrase that makes it wrong. For example:

  The deregulation of the regional market promotes healthy competition between rival industries.

  versus:

  The deregulation of the regional market encourages the growth of related industries.

The two choices differ in the use of "competition" and "growth" and in the use of "rival" and "related." Otherwise, they sound very similar. But such distinctions make all the difference in the world. So, read the choices very carefully.

Eliminate Choices, Guess (If Necessary), Enter Selection, and Confirm

Your experience with other exams has already taught you that at some point, if you aren't making any progress on a particular item, you must eliminate as many choices as possible and make an educated guess. While you continue to work on an item in the middle of the series, say item #15 out of 20 items, time continues to tick away, and you run the risk of wasting five minutes or more on an item that is supposed to take, on average, only 90 seconds. So, submit to the discipline of the clock and, as distasteful as it seems, make an educated guess and move on.

LESSON

The items in this section accompany the in-class review of the skills and concepts necessary for success on the Verbal Reasoning: Reading section of the GRE. You will work through the items with your instructor in class. Answers are on page 700.

> **DIRECTIONS:** For each item, indicate the best answer using the directions given. Select <u>one</u> answer unless otherwise directed. Read the directions for each item carefully.

Reading Comprehension: The Item Stems

Seven Item-Types

Items #1–14 refer to the following passage.

To broaden their voting appeal in the Presidential election of 1796, the Federalists selected Thomas Pinckney, a leading South Carolinian, as running mate for the New Englander
5 John Adams. But Pinckney's Southern friends chose to ignore their party's intentions and regarded Pinckney as a Presidential candidate, creating a political situation that Alexander Hamilton was determined to exploit. Hamilton had long been wary
10 of Adams' stubbornly independent brand of politics and preferred to see his running mate, who was more pliant and over whom he could exert more control, in the President's chair.

The election was held under the system
15 originally established by the Constitution. At that time there was but a single tally, with the candidate receiving the largest number of electoral votes declared President and the candidate with the second largest number declared Vice President.
20 Hamilton anticipated that all the Federalists in the North would vote for Adams and Pinckney equally in an attempt to ensure that Jefferson would not be either first or second in the voting. Pinckney would be solidly supported in the South while Adams
25 would not. Hamilton concluded if it were possible to divert a few electoral votes from Adams to Pinckney, Pinckney would receive more than Adams, yet both Federalists would outpoll Jefferson.

Various methods were used to persuade the
30 electors to vote as Hamilton wished. In the press, anonymous articles were published attacking Adams for his monarchical tendencies and Jefferson for being overly democratic, while pushing

Pinckney as the only suitable candidate. In private
35 correspondence with state party leaders the Hamiltonians encouraged the idea that Adams' popularity was slipping, that he could not win the election, and that the Federalists could defeat Jefferson only by supporting Pinckney.

40 Had sectional pride and loyalty not run as high in New England as in the deep South, Pinckney might well have become Washington's successor. New Englanders, however, realized that equal votes for Adams and Pinckney in their states would defeat
45 Adams; therefore, eighteen electors scratched Pinckney's name from their ballots and deliberately threw away their second votes to men who were not even running. It was fortunate for Adams that they did, for the electors from South Carolina
50 completely abandoned him, giving eight votes to Pinckney and eight to Jefferson.

In the end, Hamilton's interference in Pinckney's candidacy lost him even the Vice Presidency. Without New England's support,
55 Pinckney received only 59 electoral votes, finishing third to Adams and Jefferson. He might have been President in 1797, or as Vice President a serious contender for the Presidency in 1800; instead, stigmatized by a plot he had not devised, he served
60 a brief term in the United States Senate and then dropped from sight as a national influence.

Main Idea

1. The main purpose of the passage is to

(A) propose reforms of the procedures for electing the President and Vice President
(B) condemn Alexander Hamilton for interfering in the election of 1796
(C) describe the political events that lead to John Adams' victory in the 1796 Presidential election
(D) contrast the political philosophy of the Federalists to that of Thomas Jefferson
(E) praise Thomas Pinckney for his refusal to participate in Hamilton's scheme to have him elected President

2. Which of the following titles best describes the content of the passage?

(A) The Failure of Alexander Hamilton's Plan for Thomas Pinckney to Win the 1796 Presidential Election
(B) The Roots of Alexander Hamilton's Distrust of John Adams and New England's Politics
(C) Important Issues in the 1796 Presidential Campaign as Presented by the Federalist Candidates
(D) The Political Careers of Alexander Hamilton, John Adams, and Thomas Pinckney
(E) Political and Sectional Differences between New England and the South in the Late 1700s

Specific Detail

3. According to the passage, which of the following was true of the Presidential election of 1796?

(A) Thomas Jefferson received more electoral votes than did Thomas Pinckney.
(B) John Adams received strong support from the electors of South Carolina.
(C) Alexander Hamilton received most of the electoral votes of New England.
(D) Thomas Pinckney was selected by Federalist party leaders to be the party's Presidential candidate.
(E) Thomas Pinckney received all 16 of South Carolina's electoral votes.

4. According to the passage, Hamilton's plan included all BUT which of the following?

(A) articles published in newspapers to create opposition to John Adams
(B) South Carolina's loyalty to Thomas Pinckney
(C) private contact with state officials urging them to support Thomas Pinckney
(D) John Adams' reputation as a stubborn and independent New Englander
(E) support that the New England states would give to John Adams

Vocabulary

5. In line 12, the word "pliant" most nearly means

(A) assertive
(B) public
(C) national
(D) yielding
(E) controlling

Logical Structure

6. Why does the author refer to the election procedure established by the original Constitution?

(A) to prove to the reader that New England as a whole had more electoral votes than the state of South Carolina
(B) to persuade the reader that Thomas Pinckney's defeat could have been avoided
(C) to alert the reader that the procedure used in 1796 was unlike that presently used
(D) to encourage the reader to study Constitutional history
(E) to remind the reader that the President and Vice President of the United States are chosen democratically

7. The overall development of the passage can best be described as

   (A) refuting possible explanations for certain phenomena
   (B) documenting a thesis with specific examples
   (C) offering an explanation of a series of events
   (D) making particular proposals to solve a problem
   (E) attacking the assumption of an argument

Implied Idea

8. The passage implies that some electors voted for John Adams because they were

   (A) in favor of a monarchy
   (B) persuaded to do so by Hamilton
   (C) afraid South Carolina would not vote for Pinckney
   (D) concerned about New England's influence over the South
   (E) anxious to have a President from their geographical region

For the following item, consider each answer individually and select all that apply.

9. Which of the following can be inferred from the passage?

   (A) Thomas Pinckney had a personal dislike for Jefferson's politics.
   (B) Electors were likely to vote for candidates from their own geographical region.
   (C) New England states cast more electoral votes for Jefferson than did the South.

10. It can be inferred that had South Carolina not cast any electoral votes for Jefferson, the outcome of the 1796 election would have been a

    (A) larger margin of victory for John Adams
    (B) victory for Thomas Jefferson
    (C) Federalist defeat in the Senate
    (D) victory for Thomas Pinckney
    (E) defeat of the Federalist Presidential candidate

Further Application

11. The electors who scratched Pinckney's name from their ballots behaved most like which of the following people?

    (A) a newspaper publisher who adds a special section to the Sunday edition to review the week's political events
    (B) a member of the clergy who encourages members of other faiths to meet to discuss solutions to the community's problems
    (C) an artist who saves preliminary sketches of an important work even after the work is finally completed
    (D) a general who orders his retreating troops to destroy supplies they must leave behind so the enemy cannot use the supplies
    (E) a runner who sets too fast a pace during the early stages of a race and has no energy left for the finish

12. Hamilton's strategy can best be summarized as

    (A) divide and conquer *the vote*
    (B) retreat and regroup
    (C) feint and counterattack
    (D) hit and run
    (E) camouflage and conceal

Attitude-Tone

13. The tone of the passage can best be described as

    (A) witty
    (B) comical
    (C) scholarly
    (D) frivolous
    (E) morose

14. The author's attitude toward Hamilton's plan can be described as

    (A) angry
    (B) approving
    (C) analytical
    (D) regretful
    (E) disinterested

Reading Comprehension: The Answer Choices

Items #15–26 refer to the following passage.

The Aleuts, residing on several islands of the Aleutian Chain, the Pribilof Islands, and the Alaskan Peninsula, have possessed a written language since 1825, when the Russian missionary Ivan
5 Veniaminov selected appropriate characters of the Cyrillic alphabet to represent Aleut speech sounds, recorded the main body of Aleut vocabulary, and formulated grammatical rules. The Czarist Russian conquest of the proud, independent sea hunters was
10 so devastatingly thorough that tribal traditions, even tribal memories, were almost obliterated. The slaughter of the majority of an adult generation was sufficient to destroy the continuity of tribal knowledge, which was dependent upon oral
15 transmission. As a consequence, the Aleuts developed a fanatical devotion to their language as their only cultural heritage.

The Russian occupation placed a heavy linguistic burden on the Aleuts. Not only were they
20 compelled to learn Russian to converse with their overseers and governors, but they had to learn Old Slavonic to take an active part in church services as well as to master the skill of reading and writing their own tongue. In 1867, when the United States
25 purchased Alaska, the Aleuts were unable to break sharply with their immediate past and substitute English for any one of their three languages.

To communicants of the Russian Orthodox Church, knowledge of Slavonic remained vital, as
30 did Russian, the language in which one conversed with the clergy. The Aleuts came to regard English education as a device to wean them from their religious faith. The introduction of compulsory English schooling caused a minor renaissance of
35 Russian culture as the Aleut parents sought to counteract the influence of the schoolroom. The harsh life of the Russian colonial rule began to appear more happy and beautiful in retrospect.

Regulations forbidding instruction in any
40 language other than English increased its unpopularity. The superficial alphabetical resemblance of Russian and Aleut linked the two tongues so closely that every restriction against teaching Russian was interpreted as an attempt to
45 eradicate the Aleut tongue. From the wording of many regulations, it appears that American administrators often had not the slightest idea that the Aleuts were clandestinely reading and writing their own tongue or even had a written language of

50 their own. To too many officials, anything in Cyrillic letters was Russian and something to be stamped out. Bitterness bred by abuses and the exploitations the Aleuts suffered from predatory American traders and adventurers kept alive the Aleut
55 resentment against the language spoken by Americans.

Gradually, despite the failure to emancipate the Aleuts from a sterile past by relating the Aleut and English languages more closely, the passage of
60 years has assuaged the bitter misunderstandings and caused an orientation away from Russian toward English as the Aleuts' second language. Even so, Aleut continues to be the language that molds their thought and expression.

Main Idea Item Choices

15. The author is primarily concerned with describing

(A) the Aleuts' loyalty to their language and American failure to understand it
(B) Russian and American treatment of Alaskan inhabitants both before and after 1867
√(C) how the Czarist Russian occupation of Alaska created a written language for the Aleuts
(D) United States government attempts to persuade the Aleuts to use English as a second language
(E) the atrocities committed by Russia against the Aleuts during the Czarist Russian occupation

16. The author is primarily concerned with

√(A) describing the Aleuts' loyalty to their language and American failure to understand it
(B) criticizing Russia and the United States for their mistreatment of the Aleuts
(C) praising the Russians for creating a written language for the Aleuts
(D) condemning Russia for its mistreatment of the Aleuts during the Czarist Russian occupation
(E) ridiculing American efforts to persuade the Aleuts to adopt English as a second language

17. Which of the following titles best fits the passage?

    (A) Aleut Loyalty to Their Language: An American Misunderstanding

    (B) Failure of Russian and American Policies in Alaska

    (C) Russia's Gift to the Aleuts: A Written Language

    (D) Mistreatment of Aleuts During Russian Occupation

    (E) The Folly of American Attempts to Teach Aleuts English

Specific Detail Item Choices

18. According to the passage, which of the following was the most important reason for the Aleuts' devotion to their language?

    (A) invention of a written version of their language

    (B) introduction of Old Slavonic for worship

    (C) disruption of oral transmission of tribal knowledge

    (D) institution of compulsory English education

    (E) prohibition against writing or reading Russian

For the following item, consider each answer individually and select all that apply.

19. According to the passage, which of the following factors caused the Aleuts to resist adopting English as a second language?

    (A) Government regulations prohibiting teaching in any language other than English

    (B) Threats by members of the clergy of the Russian Orthodox Church to excommunicate Aleuts who learned English

    (C) Abuse suffered by the Aleuts at the hands of English speakers such as traders and adventurers

Vocabulary Item Choices

20. In line 48, the word "clandestinely" most nearly means

    (A) secretly

    (B) reliably

    (C) openly

    (D) casually

    (E) definitively

Logical Structure Item Choices

21. Why does the author mention that the Russians killed the majority of adult Aleuts?

    (A) to call attention to the immorality of foreign conquest

    (B) to urge Russia to make restitution to the children of those killed

    (C) to stir up outrage against the Russians for committing such atrocities

    (D) to explain the extreme loyalty Aleuts feel to their language

    (E) to prove that the Aleuts have a written language

22. Select the sentence in the passage that explains the Aleuts' strong attachment to their written language.

    (A) Lines 11–15 ("The slaughter of...transmission.")

    (B) Lines 15–17 ("As a consequence...heritage.")

    (C) Lines 24–27 ("In 1867...languages.")

    (D) Lines 31–33 ("The Aleuts came to regard...faith.")

    (E) Lines 41–45 ("The superficial...Aleut tongue.")

Implied Idea Item Choices

For the following item, consider each answer individually and select all that apply.

23. Which of the following statements about the religious beliefs of the Aleuts can be inferred from the passage?

(A) Prior to the Russian occupation they had no religious beliefs.
(B) American traders and adventurers forced them to abandon all religious beliefs.
(C) The Russians forced Aleuts to become members of the Russian Orthodox Church.

24. The passage implies that

(A) the Cyrillic alphabet was invented for the Aleut language
(B) all of the Cyrillic characters were used in writing the Aleut language
(C) Russian and the Aleut language have some similar speech sounds
(D) English is also written using the Cyrillic alphabet
(E) the Cyrillic alphabet displaced the original Aleut alphabet

Further Application Item Choices

25. Distributing which of the following publications would be most likely to encourage Aleuts to make more use of English?

(A) Russian translations of English novels
(B) English translations of Russian novels
(C) an English-Russian bilingual text devoted to important aspects of Aleutian culture
(D) an Aleut-English bilingual text devoted to important aspects of Aleutian culture
(E) a treatise about religions other than the Russian Orthodox Church written in English

Attitude-Tone Item Choices

26. The author's attitude toward the Aleuts can best be described as one of

(A) understanding and sympathy
(B) callousness and indifference
(C) condemnation and reproof
(D) ridicule and disparagement
(E) awe and admiration

Further Use of Reading Comprehension Strategies

Items #27–34 refer to the following passage.

Many critics of the current welfare system argue that existing welfare regulations foster family instability. They maintain that those regulations, which exclude most poor husband-and-wife families
5 from Aid to Families with Dependent Children assistance grants, contribute to the problem of family dissolution. Thus, they conclude that expanding the set of families eligible for family assistance plans or guaranteed income measures
10 would result in a marked strengthening of the low-income family structure.

If all poor families could receive welfare, would the incidence of instability change markedly? The answer to this question depends on the relative
15 importance of three categories of potential welfare recipients. The first is the "cheater"—the husband who is reported to have abandoned his family, but in fact disappears only when the social caseworker is in the neighborhood. The second consists of a
20 loving husband and devoted father who, sensing his own inadequacy as a provider, leaves so that his wife and children may enjoy the relative benefit provided by public assistance. There is very little evidence that these categories are significant.
25 The third category is the unhappily married couple, who remain together out of a sense of economic responsibility for their children, because of the high costs of separation, or because of the consumption benefits of marriage. This group is
30 large. The formation, maintenance, and dissolution of the family is in large part a function of the relative balance between the benefits and costs of marriage as seen by the individual members of the marriage. The major benefit generated by the
35 creation of a family is the expansion of the set of consumption possibilities. The benefits from such a partnership depend largely on the relative dissimilarity of the resources or basic endowments each partner brings to the marriage. Persons with
40 similar productive capacities have less economic "cement" holding their marriage together. Since the family performs certain functions society regards as vital, a complex network of social and legal buttresses has evolved to reinforce marriage. Much
45 of the variation in marital stability across income classes can be explained by the variation in costs of dissolution imposed by society, e.g., division of property, alimony, child support and the social stigma attached to divorce.

50   Marital stability is related to the costs of achieving an acceptable agreement on family consumption and production and to the prevailing social price of instability in the marriage partners' social-economic group.

55   Expected AFDC income exerts pressures on family instability by reducing the cost of dissolution. To the extent that welfare is a form of government subsidized alimony payments, it reduces the institutional costs of separation and guarantees a
60 minimal standard of living for wife and children. So welfare opportunities are a significant determinant of family instability in poor neighborhoods, but this is not the result of AFDC regulations that exclude most intact families from coverage. Rather, welfare
65 related instability occurs because public assistance lowers both the benefits of marriage and the costs of its disruption by providing a system of government subsidized alimony payments.

27. The author is primarily concerned with

    (A) interpreting the results of a survey
    (B) discussing the role of the father in low-income families
    (C) analyzing the causes of a phenomenon
    (D) recommending reforms to the welfare system
    (E) changing public attitudes toward welfare recipients

28. All of the following are mentioned by the author as factors tending to perpetuate a marriage EXCEPT:

    (A) the stigma attached to divorce
    (B) the social class of the partners
    (C) the cost of alimony and child support
    (D) the loss of property upon divorce
    (E) the greater consumption possibilities of married people

29. Which of the following would provide the most logical continuation of the final paragraph?

    (A) Paradoxically, any liberalization of AFDC eligibility restrictions is likely to intensify rather than mitigate pressures on family stability.
    (B) Actually, concern for the individual recipients should not be allowed to override considerations of sound fiscal policy.
    (C) In reality, there is virtually no evidence that AFDC payments have any relationship at all to problems of family instability in low-income marriages.
    (D) In the final analysis, it appears that government welfare payments, to the extent that the cost of marriage is lowered, encourage the formation of low-income families.
    (E) Ultimately, the problem of low-income family instability can be eliminated by reducing welfare benefits to the point where the cost of dissolution equals the cost of staying married.

30. Which of the following best summarizes the main idea of the passage?

    (A) Welfare restrictions limiting the eligibility of families for benefits do not contribute to low-income family instability.
    (B) Contrary to popular opinion, the most significant category of welfare recipients is not the "cheating" father.
    (C) The incidence of family dissolution among low-income families is directly related to the inability of families with fathers to get welfare benefits.
    (D) Very little of the divorce rate among low-income families can be attributed to fathers deserting their families so that they can qualify for welfare.
    (E) Government welfare payments are at present excessively high and must be reduced in order to slow the growing divorce rate among low-income families.

31. The tone of the passage can best be described as

(A) confident and optimistic
(B) scientific and detached
(C) discouraged and alarmed
(D) polite and sensitive
(E) calloused and indifferent

32. With which of the following statements about marriage would the author most likely agree?

(A) Marriage is an institution which is largely shaped by powerful but impersonal economic and social forces.
(B) Marriage has a greater value to persons in higher income brackets than to persons in lower income brackets.
(C) Society has no legitimate interest in encouraging people to remain married to one another.
(D) Marriage as an institution is no longer economically viable and will gradually give way to other forms of social organization.
(E) The rising divorce rate across all income brackets indicates that people are more self-centered and less concerned about others than before.

33. The passage would most likely be found in a

(A) pamphlet on civil rights
(B) basic economics text
(C) book on the history of welfare
(D) religious tract on the importance of marriage
(E) scholarly journal devoted to public policy questions

34. Select the sentence in the last paragraph that answers a question posed earlier in the passage.

(A) Lines 55–56 ("Expected AFDC...dissolution.")
(B) Lines 57–60 ("To the extent...children.")
(C) Lines 60–64 ("So welfare...coverage.")
(D) Lines 64–68 ("Rather, welfare...payments.")

Items #35–43 refer to the following passage.

President Roosevelt's administration suffered a devastating defeat when, on January 6, 1936, the Agricultural Adjustment Act of 1933 was declared unconstitutional. New Deal planners quickly pushed
5 through Congress the Soil Conservation and Domestic Allotment Act of 1935, one purpose of which was conservation, but which also aimed at controlling surpluses by retiring land from production. The law was intended as a stopgap
10 measure until the administration could formulate a permanent farm program that would satisfy both the nation's farmers and the Supreme Court. Roosevelt's landslide victory over Landon in 1936 obscured the ambivalent nature of his support in
15 the farm states. Despite extensive government propaganda, many farmers still refused to participate in the Agricultural Adjustment Administration's voluntary production control programs, and the burdensome surpluses of 1933
20 were gone not as the result of the AAA, but as a consequence of great droughts.

In February of 1937, Secretary of Agriculture Wallace convened a meeting of farm leaders to promote the concept of the ever normal granary, a
25 policy that would encourage farmers to store crop surpluses (rather than dump them on the market) until grain was needed in years of small harvests. The Commodity Credit Corporation would grant loans to be repaid when the grain was later sold for
30 a reasonable profit. The conference chose a Committee of Eighteen, which drafted a bill, but the major farm organizations were divided. Since ten of the eighteen members were also members of the American Farm Bureau Federation, the measure
35 was quickly labeled a Farm Bureau bill, and there were protests from the small, but highly vocal, Farmer's Holiday Association. When debate on the bill began, Roosevelt himself was vague and elusive and didn't move the proposed legislation into the
40 "desirable" category until midsummer. In addition, there were demands that the New Deal's deficit spending be curtailed, and opponents of the bill charged that the AAA was wasteful and primarily benefited corporations and large scale farmers.
45 The Soil Conservation and Domestic Allotment Act had failed to limit agricultural production as the administration had hoped. Farm prices and consumer demand were high, and many farmers, convinced that the drought had ended the need for
50 crop controls, refused to participate in the AAA's soil conservation program. Without direct crop controls, agricultural production skyrocketed in

1937, and by late summer there was panic in the farm belt that prices would again be driven down to
55 disastrously low levels. Congressmen began to pressure Roosevelt to place a floor under farm prices by making loans through the CCC, but Roosevelt made such loans contingent upon the willingness of Congress to support the
60 administration's plan for a new system of crop controls. When the price of cotton began to drop, Roosevelt's adroit political maneuver finally forced congressional representatives from the South to agree to support a bill providing for crop controls
65 and the ever normal granary. The following year Congress passed the Agricultural Adjustment Act of 1938.

35. The primary purpose of the passage is to

(A) analyze the connection between changes in weather conditions and the movement of agricultural prices
(B) call attention to the economic hardship suffered by farmers during the 1930s
(C) discuss the reasoning that led the Supreme Court to declare the Agricultural Adjustment Act of 1933 unconstitutional
(D) describe the events that led to the passage of the Agricultural Adjustment Act of 1938
(E) pinpoint the weaknesses of the agricultural policies of Roosevelt's New Deal

36. Which of the following is NOT a statement made by the author about the Soil Conservation and Domestic Allotment Act?

(A) It was intended to be a temporary measure.
(B) It aimed at reducing agricultural production.
(C) It aimed at soil conservation.
(D) It was largely ineffective.
(E) It was drafted primarily by the Farm Bureau.

37. According to the passage, the Roosevelt administration wanted agricultural legislation with all of the following characteristics EXCEPT:

(A) It would not be declared unconstitutional by the Supreme Court.
(B) It would be acceptable to the nation's farmers.
(C) It would dismantle the Agricultural Adjustment Administration.
(D) It would provide loans to help farmers store surplus grain.
(E) It would provide for direct control of agricultural production.

38. According to the passage, all of the following were impediments to the passage of the Agricultural Adjustment Act of 1938 EXCEPT:

(A) initial lack of clear Presidential support
(B) prosperity enjoyed by the nation's farmers
(C) opposition to the idea of a Farm Bureau bill
(D) doubts about the constitutionality of the bill
(E) lack of clear support for the bill in farm states

39. The author implies which of the following conclusions?

(A) Roosevelt's ability to gain passage of the Agricultural Adjustment Act of 1938 depended on the large harvests of 1937.
(B) Secretary of Agriculture Wallace alienated members of the American Farm Bureau Federation by proposing an ever normal granary.
(C) The Agricultural Adjustment Act of 1933 was declared unconstitutional because it was written by the Farm Bureau.
(D) The Commodity Credit Corporation was created to offer farmers incentives for taking land out of production.
(E) The compulsory production controls of the Agricultural Adjustment Act 1933 were effective in eliminating surpluses.

40. It can be inferred from the passage that the Farmer's Holiday Association opposed the bill drafted by the Committee of Eighteen because

(A) the bill was not strongly supported by President Roosevelt
(B) the Farmer's Holiday Association opposed the American Farm Bureau Federation
(C) the Roosevelt administration had incurred excessive debt to finance its New Deal
(D) its membership consisted primarily of large-scale farmers
(E) none of its members had been invited to participate in the meeting convened by Wallace

41. Select the sentence in the final paragraph that identifies the key factor that differentiated the Agricultural Adjustment Act of 1938 from previous farm legislation.

(A) Lines 45–47 ("The Soil Conservation...hoped.")
(B) Lines 47–51 ("Farm prices...program.")
(C) Lines 51–55 ("Without direct...levels.")
(D) Lines 55–61 ("Congressmen began...controls.")
(E) Lines 61–65 ("When the price...granary.")

For the following item, consider each answer individually and select all that apply.

42. The passage provides information that would help answer which of the following questions?

(A) Who was Secretary of Agriculture during Roosevelt's second term?
(B) Who was Roosevelt's major opponent in the 1936 Presidential election?
(C) Who was President of the American Farm Bureau Federation in 1937?

43. Which of the following best describes the author's treatment of Roosevelt's farm policies?

(A) scholarly but appreciative
(B) objective but critical
(C) analytical but abrasive
(D) biased and condemnatory
(E) noncommittal and indifferent

Items #44–50 refer to the following passage.

At Nuremberg, 210 individuals were tried before thirteen military tribunals. The International Military Tribunal (IMT) tried the major German war criminals, including Hermann Goering, Rudolph
5   Hess, and Joachim von Ribbentrop, from November 1945 to October 1946. Subsequently, another 185 defendants, grouped by organization or by type of crime, were tried before twelve United States military tribunals. Robert H. Jackson, the United
10 States chief of counsel and an associate justice of the United States Supreme Court, decided for the IMT that in order to obtain convictions of the officials who gave the orders but did not themselves execute them, the prosecution would rely heavily upon
15 documentary evidence. Such evidence was presumably more persuasive than affidavits and direct testimony of witnesses who might easily be brought by defense lawyers to waver in their statements.
20   In the course of the various trials, the prosecution chose from the millions of records available to them about 18,000 records to be presented as evidence. Only 2,500 of these were affidavits or interrogation transcripts. Of the total
25 number of defense exhibits, about one-half were affidavits. The rest of the documentary evidence came from a variety of sources, often from the defendant's personal files, the materials in the tribunal library file, and prosecution records and
30 resources. Heavy reliance on the latter often placed the defense in a position of dependence on the good will of the prosecution.
     The prosecution staff of the IMT established an elaborate system requiring the cooperation of many
35 government agencies for processing documents, and the prosecution at the 12 United States trials at Nuremberg inherited this system. The resources of the defense were, of course, considerably more limited. Though defendants were given the right to
40 present evidence to the tribunal, they were often compelled to engage in a long and often futile struggle to obtain records. Rulings were often affected by factors not directly related to courtroom and document-handling procedures. Some former
45 members of the IMT defense counsel had acquired more expertise than others by defending several of the accused before the various United States tribunals at different times. As the crimes of the Nazis became more remote in time and the
50 differences among the Allies in the cold-war period increased, a strong, rearmed Germany that could serve as an integral part of Western European

defense became desirable. Correspondingly, it became difficult to try German military leaders
55 before United States military tribunals while reestablishing a German military force. Sentences were progressively lightened and procedures softened. Sometimes, however, the nature of the crimes committed precluded the chance of the
60 defendants to receive lighter sentences. Many harsh sentences resulted from the trial of 24 SS Einsatzgruppen for exterminating approximately one million Soviet citizens. In general, SS defendants received severe sentences, often the death penalty,
65 and had greater difficulty in obtaining documents than other defendants.

The judges themselves were also of considerable importance. Judge Toms, from Michigan's third judicial district, Judge Phillips, from
70 North Carolina's thirteenth district, Judge Musamanno, from the Court of Common Pleas in Pennsylvania, and John J. Speight, admitted to the bar of Alabama, adjudicated the Milch and Pohl cases. In addition, judges Musamanno and Speight
75 were on the bench in the Ohlendorf case. Their rulings on document-handling procedures were often more rigid and disadvantageous to defendants than were those of other judges. Among the latter were judges Wennerstrum, Shake, and Christianson
80 of the Supreme Court of Minnesota, who presided over the Weizaecker case.

Although one might say that greater leniency in document procedures might have resulted in better defense, considering the crimes charged,
85 there is no assurance that even the most liberal procedure would have produced exonerating records. The prosecution's greater control of documents in the earlier cases, acting under rules similar to adversary proceedings, tainted the trials.
90 Yet, despite these flaws, the procedures devised at Nuremberg pioneered the massive use of records as court evidence with large groups of defendants. In the face of the terrible hatred engendered by the inhumanities of the Second World War, the
95 tribunals succeeded in dispensing, essentially, justice.

44. The author is primarily concerned with

(A) describing a historical event
(B) developing a theory of jurisprudence
(C) analyzing courtroom procedures
(D) criticizing a government policy
(E) interpreting a legal principle

45. The author's attitude toward the military tribunals can best be described as

(A) restrained contempt
(B) evident awe
(C) uncontrolled rage
(D) profound amusement
(E) qualified endorsement

For the following item, consider each answer individually and select all that apply.

46. Which of the following conclusions can be inferred about the Milch, Pohl, Ohlendorf, and Weizaecker cases?

(A) The Milch, Pohl, and Ohlendorf trials took place before the Weizaecker trial.
(B) The defense attorneys in the Weizaecker case were given more liberal access to documents than in the other cases.
(C) Milch, Pohl, and Ohlendorf were tried by the IMT, but Weizaecker was not.

47. According to the passage, defendants at the Nuremberg trials

(A) were not given the opportunity to present evidence
(B) frequently had difficulty obtaining documents
(C) were not represented by counsel
(D) were tried in absentia
(E) were prosecuted by officers of the United States military

48. It can be inferred from the passage that defendants

(A) called more witnesses than the prosecution
(B) submitted more affidavits than the prosecution
(C) did not have access to the tribunal libraries
(D) were not permitted to testify on their own behalf
(E) relied more heavily on affidavits than the prosecution

49. The author would be most likely to agree with which of the following statements?

(A) Members of the SS were unfairly punished more severely than other war criminals.
(B) The IMT was more effective than the 12 United States military tribunals.
(C) Many war criminals would have received harsher sentences had they been tried earlier.
(D) Counsel who represented the defendants at Nuremberg were often incompetent.
(E) Trial by documentary evidence is inherently prejudicial to the rights of a defendant.

For the following item, consider each answer individually and select all that apply.

50. According to the author, which of the following factors affected the severity of the sentences received by those convicted at Nuremberg?

(A) The nature of the crimes committed
(B) The time elapsed between the trial and the end of the war
(C) The number of documents submitted by the defense

Items #51–57 refer to the following passage.

Two techniques have recently been developed to simplify research and reduce the number of nonhuman primates needed in studies of certain complex hormonal reactions. One technique
5 involves the culturing of primate pituitary cells and the cells of certain human tumors. In the other, animal oviduct tissue is transplanted under the skin of laboratory primates. Both techniques complement existing methods of studying intact
10 animals.

With an *in vitro* culturing technique, researchers are deciphering how biochemical agents regulate the secretion of prolactin, the pituitary hormone that promotes milk production.
15 The cultured cells survive for as long as a month, and they do not require serum, a commonly used culture ingredient that can influence cellular function and confound study results. One primate pituitary gland may yield enough cells for as many
20 as 72 culture dishes, which otherwise would require as many animals.

The other technique allows scientists to monitor cellular differentiation in the reproductive tracts of female monkeys. While falling short of the
25 long-sought goal of developing an *in vitro* model of the female reproductive system, the next best alternative was achieved. The method involves transplanting oviduct tissue to an easily accessible site under the skin, where the grafted cells behave
30 exactly as if they were in their normal environment. In about 80 percent of the grafts, blood vessels in surrounding abdominal skin grow into and begin nourishing the oviduct tissue. Otherwise, the tissue is largely isolated, walled off by the surrounding
35 skin. A cyst forms that shrinks and swells in tandem with stages of the menstrual cycle. With about 80 percent of the grafts reestablishing themselves in the new site, a single monkey may bear as many as 20 miniature oviducts that are easily accessible for
40 study. Because samples are removed with a simple procedure requiring only local anesthesia, scientists can track changes in oviduct cells over short intervals. In contrast, repeated analysis of cellular changes within the oviduct itself would require
45 abdominal surgery every time a sample was taken—a procedure that the animals could not tolerate.

Scientists are using the grafting technique to study chlamydia infections, a leading cause of
50 infertility among women. By infecting oviduct tissues transplanted into the abdominal skin of rhesus monkeys, researchers hope to determine

how the bacteria cause pelvic inflammatory disease and lesions that obstruct the oviduct. Such research
55 could eventually lead to the development of antibodies to the infectious agent and a strategy for producing a chlamydia vaccine.

main idea

51. This passage deals primarily with

(A) reproductive organs of nonhuman primates
(B) diseases of the pituitary glands
(C) *in vitro* studies of pituitary hormones
(D) techniques for studying hormonal reactions
(E) new anesthesia techniques

specific detail

52. According to the passage, the primary benefit of the new research is that

(A) scientists can study the pituitary gland for the first time
(B) the procedures are simpler and require fewer laboratory animals
(C) the study of intact laboratory animals has now been rendered obsolete
(D) researchers were able to discover prolactin
(E) an *in vitro* model of the reproductive system was developed

specific detail

53. All of the following are true of the transplantation technique EXCEPT:

(A) It avoids the need for subjecting a laboratory subject to repeated major surgery.
(B) It permits scientists to monitor changes frequently.
(C) The transplanted cells grow as they would in their normal site.
(D) The transplanted cells can be easily grown *in vitro.*
(E) The transplant operation is usually successful.

specific detail

54. According to the passage, chlamydia causes infertility in women by

(A) causing tissue changes that block the oviduct
(B) shrinking and swelling tissues in conjunction with the menstrual cycle
(C) allowing skin tissue to encyst reproductive tissue
(D) necessitating abdominal surgery to remove damaged tissue
(E) diverting the blood supply from the reproductive organs to the skin

implied idea

55. It can be inferred from the passage that an *in vitro* model of the female reproductive system is

(A) currently available but prohibitively expensive
(B) currently available and widely used
(C) theoretically possible but of no scientific value
(D) theoretically possible but as yet technically impossible
(E) theoretically impossible

specific detail

For the following item, consider each answer individually and select all that apply.

56. Which of the following conclusions about the culturing technique can be inferred from the passage?

(A) It produces more reliable results than research done with cells requiring serum. *15-17*
(B) Cultured cells can be implanted in a living animal several times without harming the animal.
(C) A single pituitary gland may generate sufficient cells for a number of *line 18* experiments.

attitude/tone

57. The author's attitude toward the developments described in the passage is

(A) indifference
(B) concern
(C) enthusiasm
(D) disgust
(E) approval

Items #58–64 refer to the following passage.

Traditional strategies for controlling insect-pests tend to rely on the use of nonselective insecticides that cause extensive ecological disruption. The alternative sterile insect technique, in which members of the target species are irradiated to cause sterility, has enjoyed some modest success. When released into an infested area, the sterile insects mate with normal insects but produce no offspring. Unfortunately, the irradiation weakens the insects, making it less likely that they will mate; and, in any event, sterile insects do not search selectively for non-sterile mates. A third, newly developed strategy is based on parasite release.

Pest hosts and their associated parasites have evolved biological and behavioral characteristics that virtually ensure that the relative numbers of hosts and parasites in the ecosystem they inhabit remain within relatively narrow limits—even though coexisting populations may fluctuate up to 100-fold during a single season. The close numerical relationships are entirely consistent with nature's balancing mechanisms, which permit closely associated organisms to live together in harmony. Thus, in natural populations, the ratios of parasites to hosts are not high enough to result in dependable control. However, it is possible to mass-rear parasites so that they can be released at strategic times and in numbers that result in parasite-to-host ratios sufficient to control host populations.

Biosteres tryoni, for example, has a strong affinity for medfly larvae. Let us assume that a new medfly infestation is discovered. It is likely to have originated from a single female and, even in an area with a good surveillance program, to be in the third reproductive cycle. The rate of population increase is tenfold per generation; so at the time the infestation comes to light, about 1,000 males and 1,000 females are emerging and will produce a total of approximately 80,000 larvae. Reproduction will be concentrated in an area of about one square mile, but scattered reproduction will occur anywhere within a 25-square-mile area. At first glance, the odds of controlling the infestation by parasite release seem low; but with new techniques for mass-producing parasites, it is possible to release one million males and one million females into the infested area. This would mean an average of 62 females per acre, and the average female parasitizes about 30 host larvae during its lifetime. Additionally, the parasites actively search for host habitats by using the kairomone signals emanating from infested fruit. Even assuming that only ten percent of the released females are successful and, further, that they parasitize an average of only ten larvae, they could still parasitize one million larvae. Only 80,000 larvae are available, however; so the actual ratio would be 12.5:1. A ratio as low as 5:1 results in 99 percent parasitism.

This method of pest eradication presents no health or environmental problems and is actually cheaper. The cost of mass-rearing and distributing *B. tryoni* is about $2,000 per million. So, even if six million parasites of both sexes are released during a period corresponding to three medfly reproductive cycles, the total cost of the treatment would be $12,000—compared to $25,000 for a single insecticide spray application to the same 25-square mile area.

58. The author implies that the sterile insect release strategy is not completely effective because

(A) some sterile insects mate with other sterile insects

(B) weakened sterile insects refuse to mate with healthy insects

(C) the cost of producing a sufficient number of sterile insects is prohibitive

(D) sterile insects are incapable of producing offspring

(E) irradiation leaves a radioactive residue offensive to healthy insects

59. According to the passage, *Biosteres tryoni* is effective in controlling medfly infestations because

(A) female *B. tryoni* feed on adult medflies

(B) male and female *B. tryoni* parasitize medfly larvae

(C) male and female *B. tryoni* mate with medflies

(D) male *B. tryoni* prevent male medflies from mating

(E) female *B. tryoni* parasitize medfly larvae

60. It can be inferred that if *B. tryoni* were not attracted by kairomone signals from medfly-infested fruit that the parasite release strategy would be

(A) less effective because some *B. tryoni* would remain in areas not infested
(B) less effective because none of the *B. tryoni* would parasitize medfly larvae
(C) equally as effective because *B. tryoni* do not damage fruit crops
(D) more effective because some *B. tryoni* would fail to reproduce
(E) more effective because the *B. tryoni* would remain more widely dispersed

61. In the development of the passage, the author

(A) explains a scientific theory and then offers evidence to refute it
(B) cites statistics to compare the relative effectiveness of different strategies
(C) speculates on the probable course of scientific developments
(D) states a general principle and then provides an example of its application
(E) poses a question and then provides a detailed answer to it

For the following item, consider each answer individually and select all that apply.

62. Which of the following statements about medfly reproduction can be inferred from the passage?

(A) A new generation of medfly is produced once a year.
(B) A medfly colony will reproduce for only three generations.
(C) Only about 25 percent of larvae reach adulthood.

63. It can be inferred that an insecticide application for the hypothetical infestation would treat a 25-square mile area because

(A) the cost for a single spray application to the area is $25,000
(B) *B. tryoni* would tend to concentrate themselves in infested areas
(C) medfly reproduction might occur anywhere within that region
(D) the spray would repel medflies from fruit not already infested
(E) medflies from another, yet undiscovered infestation might be in the area

64. The author is primarily concerned with

(A) criticizing the use of nonselective insecticides
(B) defending the use of parasite release programs
(C) explaining the workings of a new pest-control method
(D) refuting the suggestion that parasite release is costly
(E) analyzing the reproductive habits of the medfly

Items #65–73 refer to the following passage.

Because some resources must be allocated at the national level, we have created policies that reflect the aggregated attributes of our society. The federal budget determines the proportion of federal
5   resources to be invested in social welfare programs and how these resources are distributed among competing programs. This budget is arrived at through a reiterative aggregative political process which mediates the claims of groups interested in
10 health, education, welfare, and so on, thus socializing the continuing conflict generated by their separate aspirations. The test of whether a policy is "good" under this system is whether it can marshal sufficient legitimacy and consent to provide
15 a basis for cohesion and action. Technical criteria may play a role in the process, but the ultimate criteria are political and social.

Whether a policy that is "good" in the aggregate sense is also "good" for a particular
20 person, however, is a different matter. If everyone had identical attributes, these criteria of goodness would produce identical outcomes. With any degree of complexity or change, however, these criteria will always produce different outcomes. Any policy
25 negotiated to attain an aggregate correctness will be wrong for every individual to whom the policy applies. The less a person conforms to the aggregate, the more wrong it will be.

When a policy is not working, we normally
30 assume that the policy is right in form but wrong in content. It has failed because insufficient intelligence has informed its construction or insufficient energy its implementation. We proceed to replace the old policy by a new one of the same
35 form. This buys time, since some time must elapse before the new policy can fully display the same set of symptoms of failure as the old. We thus continue to invest our time, energy, and other resources as if every new discovery of a nonworking policy is a
40 surprise, and a surprise that can be corrected with some reorganized model. But if policies based on complex, aggregated information are always wrong with respect to the preferences of every person to whom they apply, we should concentrate on
45 limiting such policies to minima or "floors." Rather than trying for better policies, we should try for fewer policies or more limited aggregated ones. Such limitations could be designed to produce policies as spare and minimal as possible, for the
50 resources not consumed in their operation would then be usable in non-aggregative, person-specific ways—that is, in a disaggregated fashion. This will require more than just strengthened "local" capacity; it will require the development of new
55 procedures, institutions, roles, and expectations.

65. Which of the following best states the central theme of the passage?

(A) Policies designed to meet the needs of a large group of people are inherently imperfect and should be scaled down.
(B) Policies created by the democratic process are less effective than policies designed by a single, concentrated body of authority.
(C) The effectiveness of a social policy depends more upon the manner in which the policy is administered than upon its initial design.
(D) Since policies created on the federal level are inherently ineffective, all federal social welfare programs should be discontinued.
(E) Because state, county, and city officials are more knowledgeable about local conditions, responsibility for all social welfare programs should be shifted to the local level.

66. According to the passage, the test of whether a policy is successful in the aggregate sense is whether or not it

(A) applies to a large number of people
(B) satisfies the needs of the people to whom it applies
(C) appeals to a sufficiently large number of people
(D) can be revised periodically in response to changing conditions
(E) can be administered by existing federal agencies

67. Which of the following sentences explains why a common presupposition about aggregate policies is incorrect?

(A) Lines 18–20 ("Whether a policy...matter.")
(B) Lines 20–22 ("If everyone...outcomes.")
(C) Lines 22–24 ("With any degree...outcomes.")
(D) Lines 24–27 ("Any policy...applies.")
(E) Lines 27–28 ("The less a person...be.")

For the following item, consider each answer individually and select all that apply.

68. Which of the following would the author probably agree are examples of a policy based on a process of aggregation?

    (A) A school dietician prepares menus based on a survey of the taste preferences of students.
    (B) A state requires licensed drivers to take an eye examination only once every ten years because most people's eyes do not change radically in a shorter period of time.
    (C) The senate passed a law lowering the legal driving limit to 0.08, based on studies that determined impairment as a function of blood-alcohol levels.

69. In line 18, the author places the word "good" in quotation marks in order to

    (A) emphasize that the word is ambiguous when applied to public policies
    (B) stress that no two people will agree on what is "good" and what is not
    (C) minimize the need to describe public policies in value terms
    (D) point out that the word can be applied to individuals but not to groups
    (E) remind the reader that the word is a technical term

70. Which of the following words, when substituted for the word "aggregate" (line 25), would LEAST change the meaning of the sentence?

    (A) extreme
    (B) group
    (C) average
    (D) quantity
    (E) difference

71. The author regards the use of aggregative policies as

    (A) enlightened but prohibitively expensive
    (B) undesirable but sometimes necessary
    (C) wasteful and open to corruption
    (D) essential and praiseworthy
    (E) ill-conceived and unnecessary

72. Which of the following, if true, would most weaken the author's argument?

    (A) Many aggregative social welfare policies enacted during the 1930s are still in effect even though they have been modified several times.
    (B) A study by the General Services Administration of the federal government concluded that waste and mismanagement in government programs has declined in recent years.
    (C) Many government programs can be made more efficient by applying sophisticated computer models and other advanced technology to the problems they are designed to solve.
    (D) The individuals who are the targets of aggregative policies are not required by law to accept the benefits offered by those programs.
    (E) The resources that would be freed by limiting aggregative policies exist only as tax revenues, which cannot be distributed except through aggregative policies.

73. According to the passage, a policy based on aggregation will be wrong for every person to whom it applies because

    (A) many individuals are unaware of the existence of such programs
    (B) technical criteria aren't given sufficient emphasis
    (C) individuals who have no need for a program may still fit its eligibility criteria
    (D) some administrators may not apply policies uniformly to all
    (E) no individual fits precisely the group profile

Items #74–80 refer to the following passage.

The healthcare economy is replete with unusual and even unique economic relationships. One of the least understood involves the peculiar roles of producer or "provider" and purchaser or
5   "consumer" in the typical doctor-patient relationship. In most sectors of the economy, it is the seller who attempts to attract a potential buyer with various inducements of price, quality, and utility, and it is the buyer who makes the decision.
10   Where circumstances permit the buyer no choice because there is effectively only one seller and the product is relatively essential, the government usually asserts a monopoly and places the industry under price and other regulations. Neither of these
15   conditions prevails in most of the healthcare industry.

In the healthcare industry, the doctor-patient relationship is the mirror image of the ordinary relationship between producer and consumer. Once
20   an individual has chosen to see a physician—and even then there may be no real choice—it is the physician who usually makes all significant purchasing decisions: whether the patient should return "next Wednesday," whether X-rays are
25   needed, whether drugs should be prescribed, etc. It is a rare and sophisticated patient who will challenge such professional decisions or raise in advance questions about price, especially when the ailment is regarded as serious.
30   This is particularly significant in relation to hospital care. The physician must certify the need for hospitalization, determine what procedures will be performed, and announce when the patient may be discharged. The patient may be consulted about
35   some of these decisions, but it is mainly the doctor's judgments that are final. Little wonder, then, that in the eyes of the hospital it is the physician who is the real "consumer." As a consequence, the medical staff, not the administration, represents the "power
40   center" in hospital policy and decision-making.

Although usually there are in this situation four identifiable participants—the physician, the hospital, the patient, and the payer (generally an insurance carrier or government)—the physician
45   makes the essential decisions for all of them. The hospital becomes an extension of the physician; the payer generally meets most of the bona fide bills generated by the physician/hospital; and for the most part the patient plays a passive role. In routine
50   or minor illnesses, or just plain worries, the patient's options are, of course, much greater with respect to use and price. In illnesses that are of

some significance, however, such choices tend to evaporate, and it is for these illnesses that the bulk
55   of the healthcare dollar is spent. We estimate that about 75–80 percent of healthcare expenditures are determined by physicians, not patients. For this reason, economy measures directed at patients or the general public are relatively ineffective.

74. In line 1, the phrase "replete with" most nearly means

(A) filled with
(B) restricted by
(C) enriched by
(D) damaged by
(E) devoid of

75. It can be inferred that doctors are able to determine hospital policies because

(A) it is doctors who generate income for the hospital
(B) most of a patient's bills are paid by his health insurance
(C) hospital administrators lack the expertise to question medical decisions
(D) a doctor is ultimately responsible for a patient's health
(E) some patients might refuse to accept their physician's advice

76. According to the author, when a doctor tells a patient to "return next Wednesday," the doctor is in effect

(A) taking advantage of the patient's concern for his health
(B) instructing the patient to buy more medical services
(C) warning the patient that a hospital stay might be necessary
(D) advising the patient to seek a second opinion
(E) admitting that the initial visit was ineffective

77. The author is most likely leading up to

(A) a proposal to control medical costs
(B) a discussion of a new medical treatment
(C) an analysis of the causes of inflation in the United States
(D) a study of lawsuits against doctors for malpractice
(E) a comparison of hospitals and factories

78. The tone of the passage can best be described as

(A) whimsical
(B) cautious
(C) analytical
(D) inquisitive
(E) defiant

79. With which of the following statements would the author be LEAST likely to agree?

(A) Few patients are willing to object to the course of treatment prescribed by a doctor or to question the cost of the services.
(B) The payer, whether insurance carrier or the government, is likely to acquiesce to demands for payment for services certified as necessary by a physician.
(C) The more serious the illness of a patient, the less likely it is that the patient will object to the course of treatment prescribed or question the cost of services.
(D) An aggressive campaign by health insurers encouraging patients to question doctors' decisions about treatment would significantly curtail healthcare costs.
(E) In the healthcare sector, the typical relationship between the consumer and the seller of service is reversed.

80. The author's primary concern is to

(A) define a term
(B) clarify a misunderstanding
(C) refute a theory
(D) discuss a problem
(E) announce a new discovery

Items #81–88 refer to the following passage.

The present day view of alcoholism as a physical disease was not a scientific discovery; it is a medical thesis that has developed only slowly over the past 200 years and amidst considerable
5 controversy. Historically, the moral perspective of the Judeo Christian tradition has been that excessive use of alcohol is a willful act, one that leads to intoxication and other sinful behavior; but in the early nineteenth century, Benjamin Rush, a
10 founder of American psychiatry, proposed that "The habit of drunkenness is a disease of the will." By the late nineteenth century, physicians generally viewed the habitual use of drugs such as opiates, tobacco, and coffee as a generic disorder stemming
15 from biological vulnerability, either inherited or acquired.

Prohibition represented a triumph of the older morality over a modern medical concept. Where physicians who championed the disease concept of
20 alcoholism emphasized the need for treatment, the Temperance Movement stressed that alcohol itself was the cause of drunkenness and advocated its control and eventually its prohibition. Scientific interest in alcoholism, dampened by Prohibition,
25 revived toward the middle of the twentieth century, not because of any new scientific findings but because of humanitarian efforts to shift the focus from blame and punishment to treatment and concern.

30   The early 1960s witnessed a growing acceptance of the notion that, in certain "vulnerable" people, alcohol use leads to physical addiction—a true disease. Central to this concept of alcoholism as a disease were the twin notions of
35 substance tolerance and physical dependence, both physical phenomena. Substance tolerance occurs when increased doses of a drug are required to produce effects previously attained at lower dosages; physical dependence refers to the
40 occurrence of withdrawal symptoms, such as seizures, following cessation of a drinking bout. In 1972, the National Council on Alcoholism outlined criteria for diagnosing alcoholism. These criteria emphasized alcohol tolerance and physical
45 dependence and treated alcoholism as an independent disorder, not merely a manifestation of a more general and underlying personality disorder.

In 1977, a World Health Organization report challenged this disease model by pointing out that
50 not everyone who develops alcohol related problems exhibits true alcohol dependence. This important distinction between dependence and

other drug related problems that do not involve
dependence was not immediately accepted by the
55 American Psychiatric Association. The early drafts
of the 1980 edition of its *Diagnostic and Statistical
Manual of Mental Disorders* described a dependence
syndrome for alcohol and other drugs in which
tolerance and dependence were important, but not
60 essential, criteria for diagnosis, but at the last
moment, the inertia of history prevailed, and
tolerance and dependence were both included not
as necessary to diagnose dependence but as
sufficient indicators in and of themselves.
65   It was not until 1993 that the American
Psychiatric Association modified this position. In
the fourth edition of the *Manual*, tolerance and
withdrawal symptoms are the first two of seven
criteria listed for diagnosing alcohol and other drug
70 dependence, but the clinician is not required to find
whether either is present or in what degree in order
to make the diagnosis.
        Despite the consensus among health
professionals, we should not forget that the moral
75 perspective on alcoholism is still very much alive. It
perhaps does not surprise us that the Reverend J.E.
Todd wrote an essay entitled "Drunkenness a Vice,
Not a Disease" in 1882, but we should be concerned
that the book *Heavy Drinking: The Myth of
80 Alcoholism as a Disease* was published in 1988. Even
as late as the mid 1970s, sociologists were reporting
that the term "alcoholic" was commonly used in the
United States as a synonym for "drunkard," rather
than as a designation for someone with an illness or
85 a disorder. Apparently, in the mind of
nonprofessionals, the contradictory notions of
alcoholism as a disease and alcoholism as a moral
weakness can coexist quite comfortably.

81. The author's primary concern is to

(A) refute the notion that drunkenness is a serious social problem
(B) argue that alcoholism is less serious than it was 200 years ago
(C) explain the evolution of the idea that alcoholism is a disease
(D) give an example of the way that medical terminology changes over time
(E) propose that the medical community treat alcoholism as a disease

82. According to the passage, members of the Temperance Movement

(A) agreed with doctors that alcohol abuse was a serious problem
(B) agreed with doctors that the solution to alcohol abuse was treatment
(C) agreed with doctors that drunkenness should be treated as a disease
(D) disagreed with doctors that alcoholism was a serious problem
(E) disagreed with doctors that traditional morality proscribed drunkenness

83. The author mentions Benjamin Rush in order to

(A) mark the beginning of the evolution of the disease concept of alcoholism
(B) highlight the seriousness of habitual use of certain drug
(C) discredit a central tenet of the religious view of alcoholism
(D) encourage physicians to treat alcoholism as a physical disease
(E) refute the notion that alcoholism is a moral weakness

84. It can be inferred that the concepts of tolerance and dependence helped to establish the disease model of alcoholism because they

(A) prove that alcoholism is not a manifestation of a fundamental personality disorder
(B) are necessary but not sufficient findings to diagnose alcoholism
(C) demonstrate that alcohol abuse is similar to abuse of opiates and other drugs
(D) are evidence of physical addiction which is an affliction of the body
(E) allow a physician to prescribe specific treatments for alcoholism

85. The author regards the essay "Drunkenness a Vice, Not a Disease" as

(A) misguided and dangerous
(B) incorrect and harmful
(C) insightful and beneficial
(D) outdated but harmless
(E) corrupt but benign

For the following item, consider each answer individually and select all that apply.

86. The author implies that which of the following are true?

(A) Historically, alcoholism has been regarded as a weakness of the will rather than a disease.
(B) In modern times, the medical community has disagreed over the exact definition of alcoholism.
(C) The long held view that alcoholism is a moral problem has finally been totally discredited.

87. According to the fourth paragraph, the draft versions of the 1980 *Diagnostic and Statistical Manual of Mental Disorders* were similar to the final 1993 version in that they

(A) listed tolerance and dependence as both necessary and sufficient conditions for the diagnosis of alcoholism
(B) did not specify tolerance and dependence as essential elements of alcoholism
(C) suggested that alcoholism might be a generic, biological disorder
(D) argued that viewing alcoholism as a disease might actually encourage drunkenness
(E) described alcoholism as a disease that had no fixed set of symptoms

88. With which of the following statements would the author most likely agree?

(A) Shifting public opinion will force physicians to return to the view that alcoholism is a moral weakness.
(B) A physician should not make a finding of alcoholism in a patient in the absence of either tolerance or dependence.
(C) The determination to classify a problem as a disease depends in part on whether it is susceptible to medical treatment.
(D) New scientific findings on the workings of tolerance and dependence warranted a shift to the disease model of alcoholism.
(E) Consensus within the medical community cannot be established in the absence of consensus in the community which it serves.

Items #89–94 refer to the following passage.

Most thinkers have distinguished three political entities: the individual, society, and state. It is normal to begin with the individual and then to consider society as the embodiment of his nature as
5 a social being. Thus, the individual is considered to be both logically and historically prior to society and society both logically and historically prior to the state. But in James Burnham's vision of the future state, the logical priority of the individual
10 over the state is inverted. Burnham changed his mind on many points of detail between one book and the next, primarily because he thought that what was happening in national and world politics at any given moment was decisive. But his general
15 sense of the form political power would take didn't move far from the version of it he gave in *The Managerial Revolution*. In that book he predicted that the weaknesses of capitalism would eventually prove fatal, but the downfall of capitalism would not
20 be the victory of the proletariat followed by a Marxist paradise. Capitalism would be replaced by autocracy even more extreme than that in Stalin's Russia. Under this autocracy, the instruments of production would be controlled by the state, and
25 the state, in turn, would be controlled by a ruling elite of managers.

Burnham argued that managers would control the instruments of production in their own corporate favor and the economy of state
30 ownership would provide the basis for domination and exploitation by a ruling class of an extremity and absoluteness never before known. The masses would be curbed or constantly diverted so that they would, as we say, go along with the managerial
35 arrangements. In Burnham's future state, history has come to an end because existence has removed itself from historical process and become pure essence, its attributes those of official meaning. Perfection is defined as the state of completeness in
40 accordance with the terms prescribed for it by the state, as a proposition in logic or a theorem in mathematics might be faultless.

In *We*, Yevgeny Zamyatin envisaged a one-world state, but Burnham allowed for three states.
45 Three superstates would divide the world between them and would enter into shifting alliances with one another. In 1941, Burnham thought the three would be the United States, Europe, and Japan. The superpowers would wage war over marginal
50 territory. "Ostensibly," Burnham said, "these wars will be directed from each base for the conquest of the other bases. But it does not seem possible for any one of these to conquer the others; and even two of them in coalition could not win a decisive
55 and lasting victory over the third."

By 1947, several of Burnham's predictions had already proved false, a result of his irrepressible tendency to assume that present conditions would persist unchanged indefinitely; but a more damning
60 indictment of his vision is the hypocrisy concealed behind the attack on power. Burnham was infatuated with the image of totalitarianism; he was fascinated by the power he attacked and he despised the democracy he should have defended.
65 Ultimately, Burnham voiced the secret desire of the English intelligentsia to destroy the old, egalitarian version of Socialism and usher in a new hierarchical society in which the intellectual could at last get his hands on the whip.

89. The author's treatment of James Burnham's writing can best be described as

(A) analytical and condemnatory
(B) insightful and neutral
(C) speculative and jaded
(D) cynical and detached
(E) uncertain and hostile

90. The statement that Burnham inverted the logical priority of the individual over the state means that Burnham believed that

(A) the state came into existence before a society of individuals
(B) history culminated in the existence of an all-powerful government
(C) individuals can reach perfection only as social beings
(D) the existence of individuals can be deduced from the existence of a state
(E) people are seen as aspects of the state and not as individuals

91. The author criticizes Burnham for

(A) extrapolating from existing political and social conditions
(B) failing to show how a totalitarian state could evolve from a democracy
(C) thinking that democracy is a form of government superior to oligarchy
(D) reversing the normal relationship between the individual and society
(E) predicting that the world would evolve into a three-world state rather than a one-world state

92. According to Burnham, in the completely autocratic state, history will have come to an end because

(A) the state will define the social forms that individuals must conform to
(B) the means of production will be controlled by a managerial elite
(C) no one superpower will be able to wage war successfully against any other superpower
(D) individuals will be diverted from a study of past events by the state
(E) only the managerial elite will be permitted access to historical records

93. The author's primary concern is to

(A) present his own vision of the future
(B) prove someone else's predictions were wrong
(C) critique a political theory
(D) criticize a literary style
(E) compare two competing theories

For the following item, consider each answer individually and select all that apply.

94. The passage supports which of the following conclusions about the writings of Yevgeny Zamyatin?

(A) They are in large part derivative of the works of James Burnham.
(B) They describe a future society in which the state is all-powerful.
(C) The descriptions they contain are based on conditions that existed at the time they were written.

Items #95–100 refer to the following passage.

Although it is now possible to bring most high blood pressure under control, the causes of essential hypertension remain elusive. Understanding how hypertension begins is at least
5 partly a problem of understanding when in life it begins; and this may be very early—perhaps within the first few months. Since the beginning of the century, physicians have been aware that hypertension may run in families, but before the
10 1970s, studies of the familial aggregation of blood pressure treated only populations 15 years of age or older. Few studies were attempted in younger persons because of a prevailing notion that blood pressures in this age group were difficult to
15 measure or unreliable and because essential hypertension was widely regarded as a disease of adults.

In 1971, a study of 700 children, ages 2 to 14, used a special blood pressure recorder that
20 minimizes observer error and allows for standardization of blood pressure readings. Before then, it had been well established that the blood pressure of adults aggregates familially, that is, the similarities between the blood pressure of an
25 individual and his siblings are generally too great to be explained by chance. The 1971 study showed that familial clustering was measurable in children as well, suggesting that factors responsible for essential hypertension are acquired in childhood.
30 Additional epidemiological studies demonstrated a clear tendency for the children to retain the same blood pressure patterns, relative to their peers, four years later. Thus a child with blood pressure higher or lower than the norm would tend to remain
35 higher or lower with increasing age.

Meanwhile, other investigators uncovered a complex of physiologic roles—including blood pressure—for a vasoactive system called the kallikrein-kinin system. Kallikreins are enzymes in
40 the kidney and blood plasma which act on precursors called kininogens to produce vasoactive peptides called kinins. Several different kinins are produced, at least three of which are powerful blood vessel dilators. Apparently, the kallikrein-
45 kinin system normally tends to offset the elevations in arterial pressure which result from the secretion of salt-conserving hormones such as aldosterone on the one hand and from activation of the sympathetic nervous system (which tends to constrict blood
50 vessels) on the other hand.

It is also known that urinary kallikrein excretion is abnormally low in subjects with essential hypertension. Levels of urinary kallikrein in children are inversely related to the diastolic
55 blood pressures of both children and their mothers. Children with the lowest kallikrein levels are found in the families with the highest blood pressures. In addition, black children tend to show somewhat lower urinary kallikrein levels than white children,
60 and blacks are more likely to have high blood pressure. There is a great deal to be learned about the biochemistry and physiologic roles of the kallikrein-kinin system. But there is the possibility that essential hypertension will prove to have
65 biochemical precursors.

95. The author is primarily concerned with

(A) questioning the assumption behind certain experiments involving children under the age of 15
(B) describing new scientific findings about high blood pressure and suggesting some implications
(C) describing two different methods for studying the causes of high blood pressure
(D) revealing a discrepancy between the findings of epidemiological studies and laboratory studies on essential hypertension
(E) arguing that high blood pressure may be influenced by familial factors

For the following item, consider each answer individually and select all that apply.

96. Which of the following are factors mentioned by the author which discouraged studies of essential hypertension in children?

(A) the belief that children generally did not suffer from essential hypertension
(B) the belief that it was difficult or impossible to measure accurately blood pressure in children
(C) the belief that blood pressure in adults aggregates familially

97. The argument in the passage leads most naturally to which of the following conclusions?

(A) A low output of urinary kallikrein is a likely cause of high blood pressure in children.

(B) The kallikrein-kinin system plays an important role in the regulation of blood pressure.

(C) Essential hypertension may have biochemical precursors which may be useful predictors even in children.

(D) The failure of the body to produce sufficient amounts of kinins is the cause of essential hypertension.

(E) It is now possible to predict high blood pressure by using familial aggregations and urinary kallikrein measurement.

98. The author refers to the somewhat lower urinary kallikrein levels in black children (lines 58–59) in order to

(A) support the thesis that kallikrein levels are inversely related to blood pressure

(B) highlight the special health problems involved in treating populations with high concentrations of black children

(C) offer a causal explanation for the difference in urinary kallikrein levels between black and white children

(D) suggest that further study needs to be done on the problem of high blood pressure among black adults

(E) prove that hypertension can be treated if those persons likely to have high blood pressure can be found

99. The evidence that a child with blood pressure higher or lower than the norm would tend to remain so with increasing age (lines 33–35) is introduced by the author in order to

(A) suggest that essential hypertension may have biochemical causes

(B) show that high blood pressure can be detected in children under the age of 15

(C) provide evidence that factors affecting blood pressure are already present in children

(D) propose that screening of children for high blood pressure should be increased

(E) refute arguments that blood pressure in children cannot be measured reliably

100. The author presents the argument primarily by

(A) contrasting two methods of doing scientific research

(B) providing experimental evidence against a conclusion

(C) presenting new scientific findings for a conclusion

(D) analyzing a new theory and showing its defects

(E) criticizing scientific research on blood pressure done before 1971

Items #101–107 are based on the following passage.

Depletion is a natural phenomenon that characterizes the development of all non-renewable resources and oil in particular. Broadly speaking, depletion is a progressive reduction of the overall
5   stock of a resource as the resource is produced; narrowly, the term refers to the decline of production associated with a particular field, reservoir, or well. Typically, production from a given well increases to a peak and then declines
10   over time until some economic limit is reached and the well is shut in. If it were not for changes in prices, costs, and technology, depletion of the world's resources would resemble the simple decline curve of a single well.
15   Geologists and engineers routinely make estimates of oil resources by field, but the estimates are a "best guess" given the available data, and they are revised as more knowledge becomes available. There is no time frame or probability associated
20   with estimates of total resources in place. In contrast, proved reserves of crude oil are the estimated quantities that, on a particular date, are demonstrated with reasonable certainty to be recoverable in the future from known reservoirs
25   under existing economic and operating conditions. Generally, there is at least a 90 percent probability that, at a minimum, the estimated volume of proved reserves in the reservoir can be recovered under existing economic and operating conditions.
30   Each year, production is taken from proved reserves, reducing both proved reserves and the total resource. Innovative production techniques such as well recompletions, secondary and tertiary enhanced recovery techniques, and expanded
35   production of unconventional resources have reduced net depletion rates at the well and field levels. Advanced exploration and drilling techniques, such as 3-D seismic imaging, directional drilling, and multiple wells from single boreholes,
40   have reduced the cost of finding new pools, reduced the risk of dry holes and dry hole costs, and allowed new pools to be developed and produced more quickly. Lower exploration, drilling, and dry hole costs increase the return on capital by lowering
45   costs. More rapid production of resources from a field increases the return on capital because earnings are realized sooner in the project's life, and therefore, they are discounted less.

Higher returns make some fields that are too
50   expensive to develop under "normal" circumstances economically feasible, because reduced costs allow firms to make profits where they could not before.

On the other hand, more rapid development and production of a field by definition increases the rate
55   of depletion. If an operator produces a field more quickly, the rate of depletion must rise. While the rate of depletion increases with technological progress, the adverse effects of depletion are diminished, and higher levels of production can be
60   maintained for longer periods of time. As depletion leads producers to abandon older fields and develop new ones, the process of developing domestic oil resources leads producers to find and develop the larger, more economical fields first.
65   Later, fields tend to be less desirable, because they are farther away from existing infrastructure or they are smaller in size. Thus, as time progresses, more effort is required to produce the same level of the resource from the same exploration area.
70   While the frontier for new resources is diminishing, increased innovation has, thus far, served to offset depletion at least partially, keeping production stronger than it would have been in the absence of the innovations. Technological progress
75   is expected to continue to enhance exploration, reduce costs, and improve production technology. But eventually, as field sizes decrease, the ultimate recovery from discovered fields will shrink. Thus, despite technological improvements, ultimate
80   recovery from the average field of the future will be smaller than that from the average field today.

101. The passage is primarily concerned with

(A) sketching a plan to prolong production of existing oil resources
(B) warning of the consequences of overexploiting oil resources
(C) discussing economic factors influencing oil production and depletion
(D) describing methods of extracting oil resources more efficiently
(E) proposing alternative energy sources to replace dependence on oil

102. According to the passage, the most important difference between total oil resources and proved reserves is that proved reserves

(A) are determined by geological principles probably found to be present beneath the surface
(B) require the use of advanced production techniques for recovery
(C) cannot be known for certain to exist until their existence has been verified by experts
(D) can be produced at a cost comparable to that required for resources currently being recovered
(E) do not presuppose the existence of advanced technologies for their extractions from the ground

103. Which of the following best explains why the author puts the word "normal" in quotation marks (line 50)?

(A) Baseline conditions are not natural but are artificially defined by economic factors.
(B) Reduced costs make oil production operations more profitable than other economic activities.
(C) Oil is strictly a nonrenewable energy resource in spite of technological advances.
(D) Existing oil production infrastructure eventually wears out and needs to be replaced.
(E) Oil reserves are gradually being depleted, making it more and more difficult to find proved reserves.

104. The passage implies that an oil well is removed from production when

(A) the supply of oil it produces is completely exhausted
(B) the cost of operating the well exceeds the return
(C) new wells have been bored to replace the capacity of the existing well
(D) the cost of capital required to open the well has been recovered
(E) it is no longer possible to accelerate oil production by the well

105. According to the passage, technological innovation offsets natural depletion because it

(A) makes it profitable to locate and extract more oil resources
(B) reduces the ratio of proved reserves to actual oil resources
(C) replenishes oil resources even as it extracts them from the ground
(D) permits the exploitation of more expansive oil fields with large resources
(E) minimizes the need to invest in capital expenditures in order to produce oil

106. Which of the following would be most likely to result in an increase in proved reserves in the United States?

(A) Increased oil production by foreign sources
(B) A significant rise in the price of crude oil
(C) A reduction in estimates of total oil resources
(D) New federal regulations requiring cleaner engines
(E) Discovery of a large field of clean-burning coal

For the following item, consider each answer individually and select all that apply.

107. With which of the following statements would the author of the passage agree?

(A) Rising capital costs associated with the search for new oil fields will cause proved oil reserves to decline sharply in the short-run.
(B) Technological innovation will likely continue to ensure adequate oil resources for use in the foreseeable future.
(C) The cost of recovery of oil resources is in large part irrelevant because of the importance of oil as an energy source.

Items #108–113 are based on the following passage.

Integrating defense technology with commercial technology can reduce fixed costs and result in other significant economic efficiencies by the use of common processes, labor, equipment,
5 material, and facilities. This includes cooperation between government and private facilities in research and development, manufacturing, and maintenance operations; combined production of similar military and commercial items, including
10 components and sub-systems, side-by-side on a single production line or within a single firm or facility; and use of commercial off-the-shelf items directly within military systems. However, several factors determine the extent to which such
15 integration is possible and the ease with which it can be accomplished. It is useful to compare the experience of the United States with its clear separation of the commercial and defense sectors with that of the People's Republic of China (PRC).
20 In the United States, one of the biggest obstacles to integrating civil and military procurement is the body of laws governing military procurement. In large part, due to past accounting and acquisitions scandals, myriad reporting
25 requirements frequently deter commercially successful firms from bidding on military contracts. Additionally, the Department of Defense (DOD) demands extensive rights to technical data to ensure that production of a system continues even
30 in the event of a serious business disruption such as bankruptcy. DOD may request not only data about the system but also information on proprietary manufacturing processes that commercial firms are anxious to protect. The private-public dichotomy
35 that gives rise to these barriers has no parallel in the PRC because the state owns the bulk of the means of production in the first place.
Additionally, the American military emphasizes high performance, even marginal
40 improvements, regardless of cost. Not only is this additional performance not necessarily sought in commercial products (e.g., commercial jetliners have little need for an afterburner), but it also is usually not cost-effective. In the PRC, although
45 operational parameters are set by the People's Liberation Army (PLA), the standards involved in actual production are set by central managers. The latter are far more versed in engineering, whereas the former have generally been capable only of
50 setting out operational requirements without necessarily understanding the industrial demands involved. Thus, production standards have been the

responsibility of the producers rather than the users. Consequently, in the PRC, little effort is made
55 to acquire or develop the very latest state-of-the art weapons technologies.
Yet another obstacle to commercial-military integration involves militarily unique technologies (e.g., ballistic missiles and electronic warfare
60 programming have no civilian applications). In the PRC, military technologies have tended to be rendered "unique" only because certain resources have been in limited supply. That is, the PLA has priority for receiving many of the more advanced
65 and expensive technologies and facilities, but these are in relatively short supply. It is likely, for example, that the Chinese air-defense network has a more advanced set of air-traffic control capabilities than does the Chinese civilian air-traffic net simply
70 because of the scarcity of such equipment.
In general, the PRC appears to have been more successful in integrating military and commercial technology, but it is difficult to assess the extent to which this success is due to the relatively primitive
75 state of technology or to political and economic conditions. It is likely a combination of both. Certainly, replicating in the United States the full degree of integration in the PRC would entail unacceptable political and economic costs. In
80 particular, it is unlikely that the American political system would accept the ambiguity inherent in the commercial use of public facilities and, perhaps more importantly, the conflict of public appropriation of private resources.

108. The primary purpose of the passage is to

(A) compare the integration of military and commercial technology in the United States and the People's Republic of China

(B) use the Chinese political system as the basis for critiquing policies in the United States

(C) criticize the United States for failing to completely integrate military and commercial technology

(D) assess the extent to which military procurement procedures in the People's Republic of China would be useful in the United States

(E) analyze the causes of the failure of the United States to achieve a complete integration of technology between the military and commercial sectors

109. According to the passage, proprietary rights do not present a barrier to integration of commercial and military technology in the People's Republic of China because

(A) the state controls the means of production
(B) commercial and military sectors rely on similar technology
(C) military weapons are not permitted in the commercial sector
(D) the PRC does not pursue state-of-the-art weapons systems
(E) the army of the People's Republic of China does not control defense manufacturing

110. It can be inferred that an increase in the availability of high technology air-traffic control equipment in the People's Republic of China would result in

(A) considerable simplification of the procurement policies for both the civilian and military components of air-traffic control
(B) less effective performance on the part of air-traffic controllers because of unfamiliarity with new technology
(C) increased waste and redundancy as the civilian and military sectors competed for the rights to develop new equipment
(D) cost savings that would be achieved by shifting technicians into lower paying positions
(E) greater disparity between the capabilities of the civilian air-traffic control system and its military counterpart

For the following item, consider each answer individually and select all that apply.

111. The passage mentions which of the following as economic efficiencies that could be achieved by the integration of commercial and military technology?

(A) Production lines creating parts for both the commercial and military sectors
(B) Manufacturing facilities producing sub-systems with civilian and military uses
(C) Research and development facilities working on problems of both commercial and military significance

112. The experience of the People's Republic of China, when compared to that of the United States, most strongly supports which of the following conclusions?

(A) Advanced technologies for weapons systems are adopted more rapidly in countries with planned economies than in nations with capitalistic systems.
(B) Uniquely material applications of advanced technology are less likely to be developed by military forces that are under the close supervision of civilian authorities.
(C) Costs of technologically advanced acquisitions tend to be lower when procurement decisions are made by managers with engineering backgrounds.
(D) Private firms that operate with little or no government oversight prefer to bid on government contracts rather than to produce commercial products for the private sector.
(E) Economies that are controlled by central planners operate less efficiently than economies in which decision-making authority is widely dispersed.

113. Which of the following best states the conclusion of the passage?

(A) Attempts at integrating commercial and military technology in the People's Republic of China have been more successful than those in the United States.

(B) Economic and political differences would make it difficult for the United States to achieve the same integration of commercial and military technology as the People's Republic of China.

(C) Political factors are more important determinants of a nation's ability to integrate its military and commercial technology sectors than economic considerations.

(D) Close integration of technological breakthroughs in the civilian and military sectors frequently results in important economic advantages.

(E) The strength of a country's military posture is in large part determined by the ability of the country's military to incorporate cutting-edge technology into its weapons systems.

Items #114–119 are based on the following passage.

Since 1994, the International Monetary Fund (IMF) has functioned as a quasi-lender of last resort to developing nations. The principles for operating as a lender of last resort were systematically
5 expounded by Henry Thornton in 1802 and reformulated independently by Walter Bagehot in 1873: lend liberally, on good collateral, to the market, for a short term, and at a penalty rate of interest. These recommendations ensure that panic
10 is quelled while the central bank discourages borrowing except by fundamentally solvent parties willing to pay a premium. It is generally accepted that a financial institution other than an aid institution should avoid lending at subsidized
15 (below-market) rates of interest.

It has been a matter of debate whether the IMF honors this important principle. Contributor nations to the IMF do earn interest and can withdraw funds at any time (features that suggest
20 the IMF is like a savings bank), but this ignores the risk involved in IMF loans. Because defaults have been rare, the IMF has not imposed costs in the sense of a nominal operating loss that would reduce the value of the contributions of the members, but a
25 single default by a large borrower would show clearly that the IMF's status does not exclude it from the kinds of risks that the private sector faces when lending to governments. Even in the absence of serious defaults, the U.S. and other contributors
30 have, from time to time, found it necessary to make supplemental contributions to the fund.

Additionally, contributors pay an "opportunity cost." Suppose the IMF pays interest of 2 percent a year for funds it lends to other countries, but a
35 contributor country could earn 6 percent a year lending the funds directly to the same countries. The opportunity cost of the contribution to the IMF is the difference, which amounts to 4 percent a year. Indeed, if participation in the IMF costs nothing at
40 all, contributors would not need to supplement their positions from time to time; the IMF could instead borrow from international financial markets and lend the funds at a suitable mark-up, as banks do.
45 It has been suggested that conditions imposed on loans by the IMF justify lower rates. Typically, the IMF will require that borrowing governments reduce their budget deficits and rate of money growth (inflation); eliminate monopolies, price
50 controls, interest-rate ceilings, and subsidies; and in some cases, devalue their currencies. Often, these conditions are unpopular, but setting aside the

wisdom of the content of conditionality, the important question is regarding the effect on the
55 prospect of repayment. Banks, for example, require mortgage loans to be collateralized by houses. This type of conditionality improves the prospect of repayment and enables banks to make a profit, charging lower interest rates than they otherwise
60 could. The IMF does not require collateral. IMF conditionality, therefore, does not significantly improve the prospects for repayment, and conditionality does not reduce the element of subsidy.
65   Giving a subsidy is undesirable because instead of making borrowers pay penalty rates of interest when they make mistakes, the IMF allows borrowers to pay lower interest rates during crises than they pay to borrow from the private sector in
70 normal, non-crisis periods. Local taxpayers, rather than taxpayers in countries that are net lenders to the IMF, pay most of the cost of a crisis, so the possibility of obtaining loans from the IMF at subsidized rates of interest is not a positive
75 inducement for a crisis; but all things being equal, subsidized interest rates reduce the incentive to take politically painful measures that may prevent a crisis. Subsidized rates also make countries more inclined to turn to the IMF rather than to the private
80 sector for financing. In this sense, the IMF's subsidized loans create a "moral hazard" (reduced vigilance against imprudent behavior because one does not pay its full costs).

114. Which of the following best describes the development of the passage?

(A) The author reviews two different interpretations of a set of facts and rejects one while accepting the other.

(B) The author reviews two different interpretations of a set of facts and concludes that neither is valid.

(C) The author outlines a list of principles and then demonstrates that the principles are outdated.

(D) The author proposes a new economic theory and argues its advantages over the accepted theory.

(E) The author sketches a theory and offers various objections to it without endorsing them.

115. According to the passage, opportunity cost is the difference between the

(A) value received and the cost of pursuing a foregone opportunity

(B) value received and savings realized by not pursuing a foregone opportunity

(C) value received and the value that would have been received from the foregone opportunity

(D) cost of pursuing one option and the cost of pursuing a foregone alternative

(E) cost of pursuing one option and the value that would have been received from a foregone opportunity

116. According to the passage, the IMF sometimes uses conditionality for the purpose that a private bank requires

(A) payment of interest

(B) pledge of collateral

(C) deposits from investors

(D) proof of solvency

(E) repayment of loans

117. The author mentions the possibility of precipitating a financial crisis in order to obtain loans on favorable terms (lines 67–70) in order to

(A) dispose of a weak argument that might otherwise cloud the analysis

(B) isolate one of the hidden assumptions of a possible counterargument

(C) uncover a hidden contradiction in a competing line of analysis

(D) clarify the meaning of a key term used in more than one sense

(E) demonstrate that a line of reasoning leads to an absurd conclusion

118. With which of the following statements would the author of the passage most likely agree?

(A) The IMF could reduce the moral hazard attached to lending at below-market interest by exacting promises from borrowers to improve the efficiency of their markets.

(B) The IMF should lend freely at below-market interest rates because any losses incurred due to default can be offset by supplemental contributions from depositor nations.

(C) The IMF could minimize the danger of default of loans by requiring debtor nations to pledge collateral that is sufficient to secure the value of the loan.

(D) For the IMF to function as a sound financial institution, it must reform its lending practices so that it charges interest that reflects the risk attendant on its loans.

(E) It is immoral for any institution to lend funds to a borrower at below-market interest because the subsidy encourages the borrower to assume excessive risk.

119. The passage suggests that if the IMF charged interest rates that are commensurable with the risks of its loans, then

(A) more borrowers would wish to obtain loans from the IMF

(B) borrowers would be more receptive to conditionality

(C) rates of default on outstanding loans would decline

(D) private lenders would relax conditions imposed on loans

(E) contributors would no longer need to make supplemental contributions

Items #120–125 are based on the following passage.

Meteorite ALH84001 is a member of a family of meteorites, half of which were found in Antarctica, that are believed to have originated on Mars. Oxygen isotopes, as distinctive as fingerprints,
5 link these meteorites and clearly differentiate them from any Earth rock or other kind of meteorite. Another family member, ETA79001, was discovered to contain gas trapped by the impact that ejected it from Mars. Analysis of the trapped gas shows that it
10 is identical to atmosphere analyzed by the spacecraft that landed on Mars in 1976.

The rock of ALH84001 was formed 4.5 billion years ago, and 3.6 billion years ago, it was invaded by water containing mineral salts precipitated out
15 to form small carbonate globules with intricate chemical zoning. These carbonates are between 1 and 2 billion years old. 16 million years ago, an object from space, possibly a small asteroid, impacted Mars and blasted off rocks. One of these
20 rocks traveled in space until it was captured by the Earth's gravity and fell on Antarctica. Carbon-14 dating shows that this rock has been on Earth about 13,000 years.

The carbonate globules contain very small
25 crystals of iron oxide (magnetite) and at least two kinds of iron sulfide (pyrrhotite and another mineral, possibly greigite). Small crystals of these minerals are commonly formed on Earth by bacteria, although inorganic processes can also form
30 them. In addition, manganese is concentrated in the center of each carbonate globule, and most of the larger globules have rims of alternating iron-rich and magnesium-rich carbonates. The compositional variation of these carbonates is not what would be
35 expected from high temperature equilibrium crystallization but is more like low temperature crystallization. It is consistent with formation by non-equilibrium precipitation induced by microorganisms.
40 There are also unusually high concentrations of PAH-type hydrocarbons. These PAHs are unusually simple compared to most PAHs, including PAHs from the burning of coal, oil, or gasoline or the decay of vegetation. Other meteorites contain PAHs,
45 but the pattern and abundances are different. Of course, PAHs can be formed by strictly inorganic reactions, and abundant PAHs were produced in the early solar system and are preserved on some asteroids and comets. Meteorites from these objects
50 fall to Earth and enable us to analyze the PAHs contained within the parent bodies. While some of these are similar to the PAHs in the Martian

meteorite, all show some major differences. One
reasonable interpretation of the PAHs is that they
55 are decay products from bacteria.

Also present are unusual, very small forms that
could be the remains of microorganisms. These
spherical, ovoid, and elongated objects closely
resemble the morphology of known bacteria, but
60 many of them are smaller than any known bacteria
on Earth. Furthermore, microfossil forms from very
old Earth rocks are typically much larger than the
forms that we see in the Mars meteorite. The
microfossil-like forms may really be minerals and
65 artifacts that superficially resemble small bacteria.
Or, perhaps lower gravity and more restricted pore
space in rocks promoted the development of
smaller forms of microorganisms. Or, maybe such
forms exist on Earth in the fossil record but have
70 not yet been found. If the small objects are
microfossils, are they from Mars or from Antarctica?
Studies so far of the abundant microorganisms
found in the rocks, soils, and lakes near the coast of
Antarctica do not show PAHs or microorganisms
75 that closely resemble those found in the Martian
meteorite.

There is considerable evidence in the Martian
meteorite that must be explained by other means if
we are to definitely rule out evidence of past
80 Martian life in this meteorite. So far, we have not
seen a reasonable explanation by others that can
explain all of the data.

120. The main purpose of the passage is to

(A) argue that the available data support the
conclusion that life once existed on Mars
(B) examine various facts to determine what
thesis about ALH84001 is most strongly
supported
(C) answer objections to the contention that
Martian meteorites contain evidence of
primitive life
(D) pose challenges to scientists who hope to
prove that ALH84001 proves that life
exists on Mars
(E) explore different scientific theories as to
the origin of life on Earth

121. According to the passage, what evidence most
strongly establishes that meteorite
ALH84001 originated on Mars?

(A) comparison of trapped gases and the
Martian atmosphere
(B) presence of alternating iron and
magnesium carbonates
(C) evidence of shapes that resemble known
bacteria
(D) pattern of carbonate globules with
unusual zoning
(E) discovery of unusual PAHs in unusual
abundances

**For the following item, consider each answer
individually and select all that apply.**

122. The passage mentions which of the following
as tending to prove that ALH84001 may once
have contained primitive life?

(A) Presence of objects resembling the
morphology of known bacteria
(B) Distinctive oxygen isotopes trapped in
gases
(C) Extraordinarily high concentrations of
unusual PAHs

123. According to the passage, the compositional
variation of the carbonate deposits (lines 24–
27) and the PAH–type hydrocarbons (line 41)
both

(A) result from chemical processes more
likely to occur on Mars than on Earth
(B) might be the product of an organic
reaction or the product of an inorganic
process
(C) tend to occur at relatively cooler
temperatures than other, similar
reactions
(D) are evidence of chemical processes that
occurred during the formation of the
solar system
(E) are byproducts of organic processes and
cannot result from inorganic reactions

124. The author mentions lower gravity and restricted pore space (lines 66–67) in order to explain why

(A) bacteria on Mars might be smaller than ones found on Earth
(B) no microfossil record of bacteria has yet been found in Antarctica
(C) the spherical, ovoid, and elongated shapes in ALH84001 cannot be bacteria
(D) restricted pore space in Martian rocks would hinder bacterial growth
(E) non-equilibrium precipitation is probably not the result of an organic reaction

125. With which of the following conclusions about the possibility of life on Mars would the author most likely agree?

(A) The available evidence strongly suggests that conditions on Mars make it impossible for life to have developed there.
(B) The scientific evidence is ambiguous and supports no conclusion about the possibility of life on Mars.
(C) Scientific evidence cannot, in principle, ever demonstrate that life existed on Mars.
(D) Scientific data derived from ALH84001 is consistent with the proposition that life once existed on Mars.
(E) It is as likely that life developed in a hostile environment such as Antarctica as on Mars.

Items #126–132 are based on the following passage.

In a recent survey, Garber and Holtz concluded that the average half-hour children's television show contains 47 violent acts. When asked about the survey, network television executive Jean Pater
5 responded, "I sure as heck don't think that Bugs Bunny's pouring a glass of milk over a chipmunk's head is violence." Unfortunately, both Garber and Holtz and Pater beg the question. The real issue is whether children view such acts as violence.
10 The violence programming aimed at children almost always appears in the context of fantasy. Cartoon violence generally includes animation, humor, and a remote setting; make-believe violence generally uses only the first two cues; realistic,
15 acted violence, which is not used in programming for children, depends entirely on the viewer's knowledge that the portrayal is fictional. Most children as young as four years can distinguish these three contexts, though there is no support for
20 the idea that children, especially young children, can differentiate types of violence on a cognitive or rational basis—for example, by justification of motives for the violent behavior.
There is no evidence of direct imitation of
25 television violence by children, though there is evidence that fantasy violence can energize previously learned aggressive responses such as a physical attack on another child during play. It is by no means clear, however, that the violence in a
30 portrayal is solely responsible for this energizing effect. Rather, the evidence suggests that any exciting material can trigger subsequent aggressive behavior and that it is the excitation rather than the portrayal of violence that instigates or energizes
35 any subsequent violent behavior. "Cold" imitation of violence by children is extremely rare, and the very occasional evidence of direct, imitative associations between television violence and aggressive behavior has been limited to extremely novel and
40 violent acts by teenagers or adults with already established patterns of deviant behavior. The instigational effect means, in the short term, that exposure to violent portrayals could be dangerous if shortly after the exposure (within 15 to 20
45 minutes), the child happens to be in a situation that calls for interpersonal aggression as an appropriate response—for example, an argument between siblings or among peers. This same instigational effect, however, could be produced by other exciting
50 but nonviolent television content or by any other excitational source, including, ironically enough, a parent's turning off the set.

So, there is no convincing causal evidence of any cumulative instigational effects such as more
55 aggressive or violent dispositions in children. In fact, passivity is a more likely long-term result of heavy viewing of television violence. The evidence does not warrant the strong conclusions advanced by many critics who tend to use television violence
60 as a scapegoat to draw public attention away from the real causes of violence—causes like abusive spouses and parents and a culture that celebrates violence generally.

126. According to the passage, all of the following would deter a child from regarding an incident of television violence as real EXCEPT:

(A) including recognizable cartoon characters
(B) explaining that characters mean no harm
(C) having characters laugh at their misfortunes
(D) using a futuristic setting with spaceships
(E) setting the action in prehistoric times

127. The author implies that a child who has an argument with a sibling two to three hours after watching fantasy violence on television would

(A) surely be more aggressive than usual
(B) tend to act out the fantasy violence on the sibling
(C) probably not be unusually violent or aggressive
(D) likely lapse into a state of total passivity
(E) generally, but not always, be more violent

128. The author mentions the possible effect of a parent's turning off a television (lines 48–52) in order to

(A) demonstrate that children are able to distinguish fantasy violence from real violence
(B) highlight the fact that it is not violence but energy level that stimulates behavior
(C) refute the suggestion that children are able to understand the motive for a violent action
(D) question the evidence for the proposition that television violence causes violent behavior
(E) show that reducing the number of hours a child watches television effectively eliminates passivity

129. The primary purpose of the passage is to

(A) correct a popular misconception
(B) outline the history of a theory
(C) propose a solution to a social problem
(D) criticize the work of earlier researchers
(E) offer a theory of criminal behavior

130. In line 35, "cold" most nearly means

(A) chilling
(B) wrongful
(C) dangerous
(D) exact
(E) craft

131. The author would most likely agree with which of the following statements?

(A) The question of how television affects children cannot be answered by defining or redefining the term "violent," but rather by assessing the effect of programming on behavior.

(B) The lack of direct causal evidence of any long-lasting effect of television viewing on children's behavior proves that children's programs do not contain violence.

(C) The number of violent acts in a television program provides an indication of the cumulative energizing effect that viewing the program is likely to have on behavior.

(D) Adult action programming which features actors engaged in violent behavior is likely to have the same behavioral effects as a cartoon showing similar behavior.

(E) The disagreement between the television industry and its critics over the content of programming for children could be resolved by finding an appropriate definition of "violent."

132. Which of the following best describes the author's attitude about critics who say that television is an important cause of violent behavior in children?

(A) qualified endorsement
(B) contemptuous dismissal
(C) enthusiastic acceptance
(D) moderate skepticism
(E) cautious criticism

Items #133–140 refer to the following passage.

Open government statutes in California have proved both beneficial and harmful. In the energy commission, for example, as in other government commissions, nearly all decisions must be made in
5   public session for which at least seven days' notice must be given. (Two notable exceptions to public participation in commission meetings are meetings that are held to discuss pending litigation and meetings held to discuss staff personnel matters.)
10 The determination of which decisions can be made by the executive director and which are strictly reserved for the commission becomes quite important in this context. If something is a matter for the commission, there must be a public hearing
15 with attendant publicity and preparation of materials for distribution at the meeting. (A formal delegation of authority authorizes the executive director to make purchases of goods and services, including consulting services, costing less than
20 $5,000.)

Furthermore, no more than three of the commission's five commissioners may meet informally with one another or with the executive director or any member of his staff to discuss
25 commission activities. Such behavior would be a violation of open government statutes. Staff briefings must take place commissioner by commissioner or through a commissioner's advisers. More frequently, commissioners or their
30 advisers contact the staff for information, but all such requests must be submitted in writing.

An example of the impact of open government on the operating procedures of a commission is the energy commission's budgetary process. The budget
35 for the commission, unlike that prepared in other state agencies, was prepared in public session by the five commissioners. The session was not simply a "review and comment" session, since the commissioners had not previously discussed the
40 budget. Every item proposed for the budget could be commented on by anyone who attended the hearings. The budget was then forwarded to the governor's office prior to submission to the legislature as part of the executive budget. In a
45 recent case involving development of regulations to ban use of gas pilot lights in new equipment sold in the state, much of the actual development of the regulations was performed by an advisory committee of both environmental and industry
50 representatives in public workshops.

Perhaps open government's effect has been greatest in the promulgation of rules and

regulations. Complaints have arisen from the news media and several legislators about the slowness of
55 the energy commission in setting regulations. In fact, the commission may be unable to meet the original legislatively mandated deadlines for several sets of regulations, including standards for newly constructed nonresidential buildings. If, however, a
60 commission attempts to handle fewer matters without input from state agencies and interested groups in open meetings, it will be criticized for circumventing the open government intentions of the legislation. Thus, if present practices continue,
65 the commission will continue to be criticized for moving too slowly; but if it attempts to move more quickly, the commissioners open themselves up to charges of attempting to circumvent the letter and spirit of the open government law.

133. The author is primarily concerned with discussing the

    (A) disadvantages of California's open government legislation
    (B) effect of an open government statute on California's energy commission
    (C) methods by which California energy commissioners obtain information
    (D) energy policies adopted by the California Energy Commission under the open government statute
    (E) political forces that shape California's energy policies

For the following item, consider each answer individually and select all that apply.

134. The passage implies that the open government statute is intended to accomplish which of the following?

    (A) Minimize the likelihood of secret political deals
    (B) Allow an opportunity for the public to influence government decisions
    (C) Guarantee that a government agency can respond quickly to a problem

135. The passage most strongly supports which of the following conclusions about a decision that is within the authority of the executive director of an agency?

    (A) It would be made more quickly than a decision reserved for a commission.
    (B) It would be made with the assistance of the agency's commissioners.
    (C) It would be a highly publicized event attended by members of the media.
    (D) It would deal with a matter of greater importance than those handled by the commission.
    (E) It would be made only after the director had notified commissioners and their aides in writing.

136. In the final paragraph, the author discusses

    (A) an analogy
    (B) a theory
    (C) a contradiction
    (D) a dilemma
    (E) a counterexample

137. The author makes all of the following points about the rules governing the commission EXCEPT:

    (A) Public sessions can be held only on seven days' notice.
    (B) At a public session, anyone wishing to be heard may comment.
    (C) Meetings to discuss personnel matters do not require a public hearing.
    (D) Requests by a commissioner for information from the staff must be made in writing.
    (E) A meeting of commissioners cannot be held without a quorum of three commissioners.

138. It can be inferred from the passage that the executive director is authorized to make certain purchases costing less than $5,000 in order to

(A) avoid the necessity of holding public hearings on routine matters
(B) take the commission's budget outside the scope of public review
(C) allow commissioners to make their own decisions on matters of staffing
(D) protect the executive director from being sued as an individual
(E) prevent public scrutiny of private work records of staff personnel

139. Which of the following statements about a "review and comment" session can be inferred from the selection?

(A) A "review and comment" session is held to provide members of the legislature with an opportunity to ask commissioners to justify their budget requests.
(B) A "review and comment" session is likely to be much lengthier and more detailed than public sessions required by the open government statute.
(C) A "review and comment" session is held to invite those in attendance to remark on decisions that already have been made.
(D) At a "review and comment" session, the public is given an opportunity to ask specific questions of government officials.
(E) "Review and comment" sessions are held once a year to review the budgetary requests of government agencies.

140. The author's primary concern is to

(A) criticize a government agency
(B) analyze the functioning of a government agency
(C) propose changes in government regulations
(D) respond to criticisms
(E) describe a legal problem

Items #141–146 refer to the following passage.

A single tax is a tax levied upon a single item or a single type of transaction that is intended to meet all or at least the principal revenue needs of a nation or other political jurisdiction. The concept of
5 a single tax on the rent of land was introduced into general economic discussion about the middle of the 18th century by the Physiocrats and was popularized in the late nineteenth century by Henry George, particularly in his *Progress and Poverty* and
10 in his New York mayoralty campaign of 1886. George advocated the abolition of all taxes on industry and its products and the appropriation by taxation of the annual rental value of all the various forms of natural opportunities embraced under the
15 general term "land."

The single tax proposed by Henry George was defended by its supporters as consonant with the theory of natural rights. A human being, they asserted, has an absolute inalienable right to life,
20 equality of opportunity, and the pursuit of property. By virtue of these general rights, a person may claim access to land, which is necessary for the maintenance of life. But land, most of which is privately held, differs in fertility and value. Thus,
25 those who hold poorer land or no land at all are denied their natural rights of life, equality of opportunity, and pursuit of property. These natural rights, argued the supporters of the single tax, give everyone a joint claim to the difference between the
30 value of the worst and the best lands. This differential value, called economic rent, belongs to the community as a whole.

Against this position, it was argued that the theory of natural rights also holds that a person is
35 entitled to the fruits of his or her labor and that the taking of property created by individual effort is confiscatory. Supporters of the single tax argued, however, that any scheme of private ownership was inherently unjust. Because of the scarcity of land
40 and the differences in productivity among various parcels of land, some people are necessarily denied their right of equality of opportunity. Consequently, a single tax on land would not confiscate that which belongs rightly to the landowner but would merely
45 reclaim from the landowner that which by natural right belonged to the entire community.

A second general argument for the single tax on land rested upon the economic theory of distribution. With increases in population, people
50 are forced to bring into cultivation poorer and poorer lands. But as this is done, economic rent— the difference between the productivity of the best

and the worst lands under cultivation—increases.
As a result, wages decrease because wages in
55   general are fixed by the income that can be earned
by occupiers and tillers of freely held land. The
share of capital in the product of industry, George
maintained, follows the same course as wages
(capital being in all essential respects simply labor
60   impressed or congealed into matter). Thus, wages
and interest rates rise and fall together, varying
inversely with rent.

   Not only does rent increase with the increase
in population, according to supporters of the single
65   tax on land, every invention involves a further
demand upon the soil for raw produce, thus
increasing rent. Everything that lowers interest
rates depresses wages and elevates rent; every
increment of capital, being a demand for land, and
70   every additional laborer has the same effect. Under
private ownership of land, increases in population,
science that stimulates invention, frugality that
multiplies capital—in short, material progress
itself—are synonymous with poverty.
75   Finally, advocates of the single tax on land
argued that it would be more expeditious than other
methods of taxation. First, it would eliminate a large
army of tax collectors. Second, it would enormously
increase the production of wealth by removing the
80   taxes upon capital, production, and consumption
which, they theorized, repressed or discouraged
industry and by forcing into use lands held idle for
speculative purposes.

141. The author of the selection is primarily
concerned with

   (A) persuading the reader that a single tax on
land is economically efficient
   (B) encouraging legislators to adopt a single
tax on land in lieu of other taxes
   (C) describing some nineteenth century
arguments in favor of a single tax on land
   (D) discussing the relationship between tax
rates and other economic factors such as
interest rates
   (E) employing the concept of a natural right
to justify government confiscation of
private property

142. According to the passage, Henry George
regarded which of the following as the
primary determinant of the wage level?

   (A) amount of income produced by owners of
freely held land
   (B) number of employers in a geographical
region
   (C) rate of taxation by the government of
wages and salaries
   (D) level of rents paid by renters for the use
of land owned by others
   (E) availability of government jobs as an
alternative to private employment

143. It can be inferred from the passage that
Henry George entitled his work *Progress and
Poverty* because he thought that under the
existing tax structure

   (A) progress would inevitably lead to greater
poverty
   (B) poverty would inevitably lead to more
progress
   (C) progress would inevitably lead to a
reduction in poverty
   (D) higher interest rates would inevitably
lead to lower wages
   (E) higher taxes would inevitably lead to
greater progress and to greater poverty

144. If a government makes previously
unoccupied fertile lands available to the
general population, then economic rent, as
that term was used by the supporters of a
single tax on land, should

   (A) increase
   (B) decrease
   (C) remain unchanged
   (D) become zero
   (E) cause wages to decrease

145. According to the supporters of a single tax on land, an increase in wages should be accompanied by

(A) a decrease in interest rates
(B) an increase in rent
(C) an increase in interest rates
(D) an increase in population
(E) a decrease in capital

146. According to the selection, supporters of a single tax on land claimed that the single tax would do all of the following EXCEPT:

(A) reduce government bureaucracy
(B) discourage land speculation
(C) increase production of wealth
(D) burden poor laborers
(E) stimulate production

Items #147–152 refer to the following passage.

The uniqueness of the Japanese character is the result of two, seemingly contradictory forces: the strength of traditions, and selective receptivity to foreign achievements and inventions. As early as
5   the 1860s, there were counter movements to the traditional orientation. Yukichi Fukuzawa, the most eloquent spokesman of Japan's "Enlightenment," claimed "The Confucian civilization of the East seems to me to lack two things possessed by
10 Western civilization: science in the material sphere and a sense of independence in the spiritual sphere." Fukuzawa's great influence is found in the free and individualistic philosophy of the Education Code of 1872, but he was not able to prevent the
15 government from turning back to the canons of Confucian thought in the Imperial Rescript of 1890. Another interlude of relative liberalism followed World War I, when the democratic idealism of President Woodrow Wilson had an important
20 impact on Japanese intellectuals and, especially, students; but more important was the Leninist ideology of the 1917 Bolshevik Revolution. Again, in the early 1930s, nationalism and militarism became dominant, largely as a result of failing economic
25 conditions.

Following the end of World War II, substantial changes were undertaken in Japan to liberate the individual from authoritarian restraints. The new democratic value system was accepted by many
30 teachers, students, intellectuals, and old liberals, but it was not immediately embraced by the society as a whole. Japanese traditions were dominated by group values, and notions of personal freedom and individual rights were unfamiliar.

35 Today, democratic processes are clearly evident in the widespread participation of the Japanese people in social and political life; yet, there is no universally accepted and stable value system. Values are constantly modified by strong infusions
40 of Western ideas, both democratic and Marxist. School textbooks expound democratic principles, emphasizing equality over hierarchy and rationalism over tradition; but in practice these values are often misinterpreted and distorted,
45 particularly by the youth who translate the individualistic and humanistic goals of democracy into egoistic and materialistic ones.

Most Japanese people have consciously rejected Confucianism, but vestiges of the old order
50 remain. An important feature of relationships in many institutions such as political parties, large corporations, and university faculties is the *oyabun-*

kobun or parent-child relation. A party leader,
supervisor, or professor, in return for loyalty,
55 protects those subordinate to him and takes general
responsibility for their interests throughout their
entire lives, an obligation that sometimes even
extends to arranging marriages. The corresponding
loyalty of the individual to his patron reinforces his
60 allegiance to the group to which they both belong. A
willingness to cooperate with other members of the
group and to support, without qualification, the
interests of the group in all its external relations is
still a widely respected virtue. The *oyabun-kobun*
65 creates ladders of mobility that an individual can
ascend, rising as far as abilities permit, so long as he
maintains successful personal ties with a superior
in the vertical channel, the latter requirement
usually taking precedence over a need for
70 exceptional competence. As a consequence, there is
little horizontal relationship between people even
within the same profession.

147. Which of the following is most like the
oyabun-kobun described in the passage?

(A) a political candidate and the voting
public
(B) a gifted scientist and his protégé
(C) two brothers who are partners in a
business
(D) a judge presiding at the trial of a
criminal defendant
(E) a leader of a musical ensemble who is
also a musician in the group

148. According to the passage, traditional Japanese
attitudes have been reshaped by all of the
following EXCEPT:

(A) the Education Code of 1872
(B) the democratic idealism of Woodrow
Wilson
(C) post-World War II emphasis on
individualism
(D) Leninist ideology
(E) elements of Confucianism

149. It can be inferred that the Imperial Rescript of
1890

(A) was a protest by liberals against the lack
of individual liberty in Japan
(B) marked a return in government policies
to conservative values
(C) implemented the ideals set forth in the
Education Code of 1872
(D) was influenced by the Leninist ideology
of the Bolshevik Revolution
(E) prohibited the teaching of Western ideas
in Japanese school

150. Which of the following is the most accurate
description of the organization of the
passage?

(A) a sequence of inferences in which the
conclusion of each successive step
becomes a premise in the next argument
(B) a list of generalizations, most of which
are supported by only a single example
(C) a chronological analysis of historical
events leading up to a description of the
current situation
(D) a statement of a commonly accepted
theory that is then subjected to a critical
analysis
(E) an introduction of a key term that is then
defined by giving examples

151. Which of the following best states the central thesis of the passage?

(A) The value system of Japan is based upon traditional and conservative values that have, in modern times, been modified by Western and other liberal values.

(B) Students and radicals in Japan have used Leninist ideology to distort the meaning of democratic, Western values.

(C) The notions of personal freedom and individual liberty did not find immediate acceptance in Japan because of the predominance of traditional group values.

(D) Modern Japanese society is characterized by hierarchical relationships in which a personal tie to a superior is often more important than merit.

(E) The influence on Japanese values of the American ideals of personal freedom and individual rights is less important than the influence of Leninist ideology.

152. As used in line 49, the word "vestiges" most nearly means

(A) institutions
(B) superiors
(C) traces
(D) subordinates
(E) virtues

Critical Reading: Preliminaries

Item #153 refers to the following passage.

In her address to the City-Wide Dairy Products Distributors, the mayor cited the success of ABC Farms, which has increased its sales in the city by 23 percent. She encouraged all distributors to make similar efforts, concluding that the overall increase in business would benefit the city.

153. Which of the following, if true, points out a serious weakness in the mayor's reasoning?

(A) Milk and other dairy products contain important nutrients that are vital to the health and well-being of citizens, particularly children.

(B) Redwood Farms achieved the increase in sales by offering discounts to businesses that purchased a complete line of Redwood Farms products.

(C) The mayor made a speech on a previous occasion to the city's chamber of commerce in which she proposed city tax abatements to attract new industry.

(D) During the year cited, Redwood Farms showed only a 15 percent increase in before-tax profits over the previous year.

(E) The size of the market in the city is relatively fixed, so any increase in sales by one firm comes at the expense of sales by other firms.

Critical Reading Items Illustrated

The Conclusion

Item #154 refers to the following passage.

At a recent art auction, a large canvas painted in many colors sold for $100,000. At the same auction, a simple pen-and-ink drawing by the same artist sold for $105,000, because it was more beautiful. Whatever it is that is beauty, that is, whatever it is that we prize so highly, it is not necessarily the product of a lifetime of work but rather the gift of a moment.

154. What is the point of the argument?

(A) Art collectors often do not know the true value of a work of art.

(B) Market forces govern prices for rare art objects.

(C) What one person considers beautiful, another may consider not beautiful.

(D) Artistic achievement requires creative insight and not just technique.

(E) There is a direct correlation between the price of a work of art and the time the artist required to produce the object.

Item #155 refers to the following passage.

Young people who imagine that the life of a writer is one of glamour, riches, or fame soon discover not only the difficulties of the craft but the long odds against achieving any measure of recognition or financial security. Upon being asked, "Aren't most editors failed writers?" T. S. Eliot is said to have remarked, "Yes, but so are most writers."

155. The statement by T. S. Eliot conveys which of the following ideas?

(A) Editing can be just as creative and challenging as writing.

(B) Few writers are fortunate enough to attain real success in their profession.

(C) For a writer, success is measured more by influence exerted than by material gain achieved.

(D) Many writers find that a stint at editorial work is a beneficial apprenticeship for their craft.

(E) There are no clear-cut standards of success and failure for writers, but there are such standards for editors.

Item #156 refers to the following passage.

Personal video recorders that allow viewers to skip commercials have made television network executives worried that the public will stop watching commercials. However, I have noticed that people with such devices watch truly entertaining commercials two or three times because just as it is easy to fast forward past commercials, it is also easy to rewind and view them again.

156. The speaker's statements best support which of the following conclusions?

(A) Television executives need not be concerned that personal video recorders will result in a loss of ad revenue.

(B) People using personal video recorders may watch entertaining commercials more than once.

(C) Entertaining television commercials are more effective at promoting a product than ads that are not entertaining.

(D) Personal video recorders will someday replace traditional television sets as the primary means of viewing telecasts.

(E) Television advertising will become less effective as a means of promoting products than it has been in the past.

Item #157 refers to the following passage.

The earliest vaccines used whole dead viruses or weakened live ones to stimulate the body's immune system. Unfortunately, in a small number of cases, the vaccines caused very serious allergic reactions and in some cases even the disease itself. Vaccines being developed today are much safer because they use only a specific subunit of the viral protein chain.

157. Which of the following conclusions is best supported by the passage?

    (A) The body's immune system responds to a particular part of a virus rather than the virus as a whole.

    (B) The body's immune system is more likely to react to a whole dead virus than a part of a live one.

    (C) Reactions to weakened live viruses are more predictable than reactions to whole dead viruses.

    (D) A vaccine manufactured from a subunit of a virus is more likely to trigger than to prevent a disease.

    (E) The body reacts to a subpart of a virus in the same way it reacts to the virus as a whole.

Item #158 refers to the following passage.

Recently, six Magellanic penguins that were taken from the wild arrived at the San Francisco Zoo. The 46 long-time resident Magellanic penguins, which had spent relatively sedentary lives of grooming and staying in burrows, began to simulate migratory behavior when they watched the new penguins swimming around the 130 feet by 40 feet pool. All 52 birds now swim almost all of the time, resting on the artificial island in the middle of the pool only at night. Indeed, when the pool was drained for cleaning, the penguins refused to leave, walking around it instead of swimming.

158. Which of the following conclusions can be most reliably drawn from the information above?

    (A) Migratory behavior in animals is acquired rather than innate.

    (B) Animals in zoo environments rarely exhibit active behavior.

    (C) Magellanic penguins in the wild spend most of their time swimming.

    (D) The close quarters of a zoo environment suppress animal migratory behavior.

    (E) Animals sometimes mimic the behavior they see in other animals.

Item #159 refers to the following passage.

The cleaning and restoration of Michelangelo's frescoes on the ceiling of the Sistine Chapel were undertaken by some of the world's finest art restorers under the close supervision of an international team of art experts and historians. Nonetheless, the results have produced a storm of controversy. Most modern viewers, it seems, had become accustomed to seeing the frescoes with their colors dulled by layers of yellowing glue and varnish and with the contours of the figures obscured by centuries' accumulation of grime.

159. The argument above implies that Michelangelo's frescoes

(A) have been the subject of intense controversy over their artistic merit
(B) suffered until recently from centuries of obscurity and neglect
(C) should not have been cleaned and restored without more careful planning
(D) have been obscured by dirt during the recent process of restoration
(E) were originally much brighter and more vivid than most modern viewers realize

Item #160 refers to the following passage.

Downsizing is a much-ballyhooed corporate strategy that really doesn't do much to increase profitability. In a large corporation, reducing payroll costs by even 10 percent is likely to result in a reduction in operating costs of at most 1.5 percent.

160. If all the statements above are true, which of the following statements must be true?

(A) Corporate managers who embark on downsizing projects do not really intend to increase profitability.
(B) A downsizing corporation is more likely to lay off junior employees than more experienced employees.
(C) Payroll costs of the typical downsizing corporation are less than the total of non-payroll costs.
(D) Total payroll costs for a typical corporation are approximately 15 percent of overall cost.
(E) Reducing payroll costs by 10 percent is guaranteed to increase a company's profit, if only slightly.

Item #161 refers to the following passage.

In recent years, unions have begun to include in their demands at the collective bargaining table requests for contract provisions that give labor an active voice in determining the goals of a corporation. Although it cannot be denied that labor leaders are highly skilled administrators, it must be recognized that their primary loyalty is and must remain to their membership, not to the corporation. Thus, labor participation in corporate management decisions makes about as much sense as allowing inmates to make decisions about prison security.

161. The reasoning in the argument above leads to the further conclusion that

(A) the authority of corporate managers would be symbolically undermined if labor leaders were allowed to participate in corporate planning
(B) workers have virtually no idea of how to run a large corporation
(C) workers would not derive any benefit from hearing the goals of corporate management explained to them at semiannual meetings
(D) the efficiency of workers would be lowered if they were to divide their time between production line duties and management responsibilities
(E) allowing labor a voice in corporate decisions would involve labor representatives in a conflict of interest

Item #162 refers to the following passage.

French painting during the first half of the nineteenth century was characterized by a lack of imagination. The École des Beaux Arts, the quasi-governmental agency that controlled the dissemination of lucrative government scholarships and commissions, effectively stifled creativity. A student who hoped to achieve any fame or financial success was well advised to paint in the style of the École. It is a small wonder then that the Impressionist painters initially earned only the scorn of their colleagues and empty bellies for their efforts.

162. The statements above imply that

    (A) Impressionist painters did not paint in the style of the École des Beaux Arts

    (B) the Impressionist painters eventually gained control of the École des Beaux Arts

    (C) the École des Beaux Arts promulgated rules defining the permissible subject matter of paintings

    (D) the École des Beaux Arts determined licensing standards for those who wanted to become professional artists

    (E) French painting during the second half of the nineteenth century was less creative than during the first half of the nineteenth century

The Assumptions

Item #163 refers to the following passage.

Superficially, today's problems with the abuse of illegal drugs such as heroin and cocaine resemble the problems of alcohol abuse during the 1920s, when many people kept drinking in spite of Prohibition. There is, however, a significant difference. The use of drugs such as heroin and cocaine has never been a widespread, socially accepted practice among most middle-class, otherwise law-abiding Americans.

163. An underlying assumption of the argument above is that

    (A) during Prohibition, drinking of alcohol was commonly accepted among most Americans

    (B) as long as drugs are available, they will be used despite laws to the contrary

    (C) most Americans consider heroin and cocaine to be in the same category as alcohol

    (D) in a democracy, laws must be based on the fundamental beliefs and values of the majority of citizens

    (E) American popular opinion has always been molded primarily by the values of the middle class

Item #164 refers to the following passage.

It is a truism of military science that "Generals always prepare for the *last* war." In much the same way, public officials generally spend their efforts on problems that were resolved—one way or another—years before. By the time a public issue reaches the consciousness of enough of the citizenry to become a high priority of our elected leaders, the problem is usually past the point at which government efforts can significantly affect it.

164. All of the following are assumed in the argument above EXCEPT:

(A) Most public problems tend to evolve toward a point at which the government can do little to control them.
(B) Political and military leaders are both prone to react tardily to changes in their fields.
(C) Issues attain importance for public officials when large numbers of citizens are concerned about them.
(D) Planning policies solely based on past experiences is likely to be ineffective.
(E) Government officials can generally do little to influence directly the course of public policy.

Item #165 refers to the following passage.

In determining what organisms may morally be used for food, vegetarians are often guided by the principle of "capacity for suffering." If the organism has the capacity for suffering, then it is not morally acceptable to use it for food. Given this rule of thumb, plants are acceptable because they lack even the rudiments of a central nervous system.

165. Which of the following is an assumption required by the argument?

(A) All animals, even the most primitive, have a central nervous system.
(B) Only organisms with a central nervous system have the capacity for suffering.
(C) Primitive animals such as mollusks lack a functioning central nervous system.
(D) Any organism with a central nervous system has the capacity for suffering.
(E) Only organisms that have the capacity for suffering should not be eaten.

Item #166 refers to the following passage.

As the debate on the roots of the so-called obesity epidemic among children rages, it is becoming increasingly clear that public school lunches are not one of the causes. Eighty-six percent of the school lunches prepared on any given day meet the federal nutritional guidelines.

166. All of the following, if true, weaken the argument EXCEPT:

(A) Children are permitted to choose their own food items from several offerings and rarely select the most nutritious items.
(B) Lunchroom administrators find it easier and less costly to heat bland-tasting, prepared vegetables from cans than to cook good-tasting fresh vegetables from scratch.
(C) The number of high school students taking daily physical education classes has dropped to 29 percent from 46 percent in the last 10 years.
(D) School lunches feature surplus commodities that are high in saturated fats and are purchased by the government as a means of supporting farm prices.
(E) Most schools permit children to obtain lunch items from vending machines that dispense sodas and candy.

Item #167 refers to the following passage.

A dog's nose has roughly 200 million olfactory receptors, making it an instrument of remarkable sensitivity, theoretically well suited for detective work; but dogs also return a very high rate of false positives when asked to identify people or substances. Subtle but misleading signals that a trainer can unknowingly communicate to the animal include a glance or step in a certain direction or allowing the dog to spend too much or too little time in a particular spot. A dog that works out of sight of the handler, however, cannot be influenced in these ways, so permitting a dog to work off-leash would eliminate the problem of false positives.

167. Which of the following, if true, most seriously weakens the argument?

(A) Dogs are trained using positive reinforcements such as food treats for finding scents and therefore exhibit behavior calculated to earn rewards.
(B) Dogs are trained to identify basic chemicals but find it difficult to recognize these chemicals when included in a mixture.
(C) Handlers keep logs of all training exercises and review these records periodically for evidence that suggests they are influencing the dog.
(D) Handlers are reluctant to admit that their dogs return false positives and usually claim that the animal reacted to a "trace" of a substance.
(E) Miniature cameras can be attached to a dog's collar to permit a handler to monitor how the dog is working even when out of sight.

Item #168 refers to the following passage.

It is sometimes argued that we are reaching the limits of the earth's capacity to supply our energy needs with fossil fuels. However, in the past 10 years, yields from oil and coal fields have increased tremendously due to technological progress that makes it possible to extract resources from even marginal wells and mines. There is no reason to believe that there is a limit to the earth's capacity to supply our energy needs.

168. Which of the following statements most directly contradicts the conclusion of the passage?

(A) Even if we exhaust our supplies of fossil fuel, the earth can still be mined for uranium for nuclear fuel.
(B) The technology needed to extract fossil fuels from marginal sources is very expensive.
(C) Even given the improvements in technology, oil and coal are not renewable resources, so we will eventually exhaust our supplies of them.
(D) Most of the land under which marginal oil and coal supplies lie is more suitable to cultivation or pasturing than to production of fossil fuels.
(E) The fuels that are yielded by marginal sources tend to be high in sulphur and other undesirable elements that aggravate the air pollution problem.

Item #169 refers to the following passage.

U.S. chemical manufacturers currently export numerous chemicals used in agriculture that are banned here. Now Congress wants to prevent the companies from exporting chemicals. Yet, foreign governments are willing to allow the continued use of the chemicals and may have very good reasons for doing so. It seems to me wrong for the government of this country to substitute its judgment for that of another country about what is best for its citizenry. Therefore, the proposed ban should be voted down.

169. Which of the following, if true, most weakens the argument?

(A) The chemicals that are the subject of the proposed ban greatly enhance agricultural productivity.
(B) The chemicals that are the subject of the proposed ban contaminate produce that is imported into the United States.
(C) The chemicals that are the subject of the proposed ban account for a very small part of the sales of the chemical companies that would be affected.
(D) The U.S. chemical companies that would be affected by the ban are the only ones with the technology to produce the chemicals that would be banned.
(E) Some foreign governments already prohibit the importation and the use of the chemicals that would be the subject of the ban.

Item #170 refers to the following passage.

When the mayor appointed a Hispanic principal to the Board of Education, many Caucasians and African-Americans decried the appointment as political; and when the mayor appointed an African-American businessman as Director of Franchises, many Caucasians and Hispanics made the same charge. They are all correct, but what is wrong with that? The appointments were political acts well within the mayor's rights as defined by the City Charter.

170. Which of the following, if true, most strengthens the argument above?

(A) The principal appointed to the Board of Education and the businessman appointed Director of Franchises were as well qualified as any other candidates for the positions.
(B) Shortly after making the appointments mentioned, the mayor appointed a Caucasian attorney from a powerful law firm to serve as the city's corporation counsel.
(C) African-Americans who opposed the appointment of the Hispanic principal favored the appointment of an African-American who was a school district superintendent.
(D) The actions of an elected official should be judged by how well they serve the needs of the people and not just by whether the actions are legal.
(E) Three of the mayor's key aides were forced to resign when it was discovered that they solicited a bribe from a cable television company seeking a city franchise, and the aides now face criminal indictments.

Item #171 refers to the following passage.

The single greatest weakness of American parties is their inability to achieve cohesion in the legislature. Although there is some measure of party unity, it is not uncommon for the majority party to be unable to implement important legislation. The unity is strongest during election campaigns. After the primary elections, the losing candidates all promise their support to the party nominee. By the time Congress convenes, however, the unity has dissipated. This phenomenon is attributable to the fragmented nature of political parties. The national committees are no more than feudal lords who receive nominal fealty from their vassals. A congressperson builds his or her power upon a local base. Consequently, he or she is likely to be responsive to locally based special-interest groups. Evidence of this is seen in the differences in voting patterns between the upper and lower houses. In the Senate, where terms are longer, there is more party unity.

171. Which of the following, if true, most strengthens the above argument?

(A) On 30 key issues, 18 of the 67 majority party members in the Senate voted against the party leaders.

(B) On 30 key issues, 70 of the 305 majority party members in the House voted against the party leaders.

(C) On 30 key issues, over half of the members of the minority party in both houses voted with the majority party against the leaders of the minority party.

(D) Of 30 key legislative proposals introduced by the President, only eight passed both houses.

(E) Of 30 key legislative proposals introduced by a President whose party controlled a majority in both houses, only four passed both houses.

The Inference

Cause and Effect Situation

Item #172 refers to the following passage.

Foreign-made electronics products gained popularity in the United States during the 1970s primarily because of their low cost. In recent years, changes to the exchange rates of United States currency and other countries' currencies have increased the prices of imported electronics products relative to those produced in the United States. However, sales of imported electronics products have not declined in recent years.

172. Which of the following, if true, would help to explain why sales of imported electronics products remain high?

(A) Trade ministries in foreign nations have pursued policies that prevented prices of electronics products from rising even faster.

(B) The cost of manufacturing electronics products abroad is rising faster than it is in the United States.

(C) A coming shortage in consumer credit in the United States is expected to depress sales of imported products during the next two years.

(D) American consumers now perceive the quality of imports as being high enough to justify the increased prices.

(E) U.S. manufacturers have attempted to persuade Americans to buy electronic products made in the United States.

Item #173 refers to the following passage.

A survey by the economics department of an Ivy League university revealed that increases in the salaries of preachers are accompanied by increases in the nationwide average of rum consumption. From 1965 to 1970, preachers' salaries increased on the average of 15 percent and rum sales grew by 14.5 percent. From 1970 to 1975, average preachers' salaries rose by 17 percent and rum sales by 17.5 percent. From 1975 to 1980, rum sales expanded by only eight percent and average preachers' salaries also grew by only eight percent.

173. Which of the following is the most likely explanation for the findings cited in the argument above?

    (A) When preachers have more disposable income, they tend to allocate that extra money to alcohol.

    (B) When preachers are paid more, they preach longer; and longer sermons tend to drive people to drink.

    (C) Since there were more preachers in the country, there were also more people; and a larger population will consume greater quantities of liquor.

    (D) The general standard of living increased from 1965 to 1980, which accounts for both the increase in rum consumption and preachers' average salaries.

    (E) A consortium of rum importers carefully limited the increases in imports of rum during the test period cited.

Item #174 refers to the following passage.

There has been speculation that the chairman of Global Enterprises will replace the company's CEO next week, but it would be risky for the chairman to make such a change without first consulting formally with the board of directors. There have been no board meetings recently, and no such meeting has been scheduled for the next few weeks. Therefore, the speculation regarding the change in management is probably wrong.

174. Which of the following principles best describes the reasoning found in the argument above?

    (A) If two statements are logically inconsistent and it is known that one is false, the other statement is necessarily true.

    (B) A theory may turn out to be true even though all of the available data initially suggests that the theory is false.

    (C) It cannot be assumed from the fact that event E_2 follows event E_1 in time that event E_1 was therefore the cause of event E_2.

    (D) A hypothesis is weakened when conditions that are normally necessary for an expected result do not exist.

    (E) A cause necessary to ensure a certain outcome may not, in and of itself, be sufficient to guarantee that outcome.

Item #175 refers to the following passage.

In Entonia, where the Parliament chooses the Prime Minister, anyone who supports the majority party in Parliament should also support the Prime Minister because the Prime Minister is chosen by the majority party.

175. Which of the following most closely parallels the pattern of reasoning in the argument above?

(A) People who enjoy watching rugby should also enjoy watching American football because American football, in its patterns of play, its rules, and its structure, is derived from rugby.

(B) People who go to bed before 10:00 p.m. should eat dinner before 6:00 p.m. to ensure that the food that they've eaten is thoroughly digested before they retire for the night.

(C) People who appreciate paintings by Monet should also appreciate paintings by Renoir since both were members of the Impressionist School of painting in late nineteenth-century France.

(D) A person who is able to operate a crane can probably also operate a dredge since the mechanisms and the controls of the two machines are very similar.

(E) A person who reads a daily newspaper will have no reason to read a weekly news magazine since the magazine is just a compilation of the week's news.

Item #176 refers to the following passage.

Between 1960 and 1970, ivory poachers in the African nation of Zinbaku killed over 6,500 elephants. During that period, the total elephant population in Zinbaku fell from about 35,000 to just fewer than 30,000. In 1970, new antipoaching measures were implemented in Zinbaku, and between 1970 and 1980 over 800 poachers were arrested and expelled from the country. Nevertheless, by 1980, the elephant population in Zinbaku had fallen to about 21,000.

176. Which of the following, if true, best helps to explain the apparent paradox presented above?

(A) The poachers arrested in Zinbaku between 1970 and 1980 were usually sentenced to long prison terms.

(B) Because of highly publicized campaigns against the slaughter of elephants, demand for ivory fell between 1970 and 1980.

(C) The elephant population in neighboring Mombassa rose slightly between 1970 and 1980.

(D) Prior to 1970, the antipoaching laws passed by parliament in Zinbaku were rarely enforced.

(E) In Zinbaku, between 1970 and 1980, thousands of acres of forest, the elephant's natural habitat, were cleared for farming.

Item #177 refers to the following passage.

Last year, the number of child abuse cases reported in this city increased by 20 percent. Ironically, children's rights advocates have cited these statistics with approval.

177. Which of the following, if true, logically explains the seemingly paradoxical approval of the children's rights advocates?

    (A) Local judges have begun to deal more harshly with those found guilty of committing child abuse.

    (B) The rate of convictions in child abuse cases in the city has increased steadily over the past three years.

    (C) Child abuse prevention has long been a high priority for leaders of children's rights organizations.

    (D) Most of the increase in reported cases of child abuse occurred in three particularly poorer neighborhoods of the city.

    (E) A new city policy of encouraging people to report child abuse has sharply diminished the number of unreported cases.

Item #178 refers to the following passage.

Concerned about the rough waters in the harbor caused by increasing reliance on commuter ferries, the Port Authority imposed a speed limit on boat traffic because it is well known that modern ferries running at very slow speeds produce little or no wake. Paradoxically, however, during the weeks following the enactment of the speed limit, sensors installed at key monitoring points in the harbor showed that water turbulence actually increased.

178. Which of the following, if true, best explains the paradox described above?

    (A) The sensors showed that the harbor's water is the calmest from midnight to 4:00 a.m. when very few ferries operate.

    (B) Waves produced by ferries propagate outward to the shorelines where they are reflected off bulkheads and other hard surfaces.

    (C) A boat that produces less wake is operating more efficiently than one that is producing a great deal of wake.

    (D) The number of ferry trips made during the period immediately following the imposition of the speed limit did not increase appreciably.

    (E) At faster speeds, modern ferries ride higher, displacing less water and producing less wake, than at moderate speeds.

Item #179 refers to the following passage.

The percentage of family income spent on entertainment has remained almost the same over the past 20 years—about 12 percent. When new forms of entertainment become popular, they do not expand this percentage. Therefore, film exhibitors have observed the video boom with concern, fearing that every dollar spent on rental of videos could mean a dollar less spent on movie theater admissions.

179. Which of the following, if true, most forcefully undermines the conclusion of the argument above?

    (A) The cost of renting a video is generally substantially less than the price of movie theater admission.
    (B) Most film producers receive a portion of the income from the sale of video rights to their movies.
    (C) People with videocassette players watch fewer hours of broadcast television than do people without such machines.
    (D) Since the start of the video boom, money spent on forms of entertainment other than videos and movies has dropped.
    (E) Some movies that were unprofitable when shown in theaters have become successful when released in video form.

Item #180 refers to the following passage.

When a large manufacturing business decides to relocate, the community suffers an economic loss beyond that of the immediate unemployment of those who had been employed at the factory. For example, the automotive service industry in the area may become depressed as well. Unemployed workers would no longer use their cars for the daily commute to and from work, thus reducing the need for fuel and tires and for services to maintain the cars.

180. The point in the above argument is made primarily by

    (A) posing a question and answering it
    (B) appealing to an authority
    (C) attacking the credibility of a source
    (D) presenting an analogy
    (E) analyzing a causal relationship

Item #181 refers to the following passage.

The seasonal increase of influenza has long baffled scientists, but a new study has found that seasonal changes of absolute humidity are the apparent underlying cause of these wintertime peaks. Although somewhat counterintuitive, the study found that the onset of outbreaks might be encouraged by anomalously dry weather conditions, not excessively wet conditions. Outbreaks of influenza typically occur in winter when low absolute humidity conditions strongly favor influenza survival and transmission. The dry period is not a requirement for triggering an influenza outbreak, but it was present in 55 to 60 percent of the outbreaks analyzed. The virus response is almost immediate; transmission and survival rates increase and about 10 days later, the observed influenza mortality rates follow.

181. The reasoning in the argument above primarily

    (A) refutes a possible explanation for a scientific phenomenon
    (B) develops a causal explanation for observed medical facts
    (C) analyzes data to uncover a statistical correlation
    (D) offers an alternative explanation to a commonly accepted myth
    (E) establishes a connection between influenza and a certain virus

Generalization

Item #182 refers to the following passage.

If you take the Defensive Driver's Education Course as I did, you will score high on the exam as I did!

182. The argument relies on a(n)

    (A) ambiguity
    (B) assumption
    (C) appeal to authority
    (D) generalization
    (E) causal analysis

Item #183 refers to the following passage.

There are over 400 species of ladybugs in North America, but more and more, the multi-colored Asian lady beetle predominates. The Asian lady beetle is slightly larger than many native species (about one-third of an inch long); it characteristically has 19 spots on its wing covers, though there may be no spots at all. A black "W" is usually found on the thorax. So, if you find a ladybug without spots and with no black "W" on its thorax, it is definitely a member of a native species.

183. The argument is most vulnerable to criticism on the grounds that it

    (A) presupposes what it is intended to prove
    (B) mistakes a cause of an event for its effect
    (C) fails to consider the possibility that the Asian lady beetle was introduced accidentally
    (D) makes a general claim based on examples that are not fairly representative of the larger population
    (E) interprets evidence that a claim is probably true as establishing the certainty of the conclusion

Item #184 refers to the following passage.

All swans that I have encountered have been white, so it follows that the swans I will see when I visit the Bronx Zoo will also be white.

184. The flawed reasoning in which of the following is most similar to the flawed reasoning in the argument above?

    (A) Some birds are incapable of flight; therefore, swans are probably incapable of flight.
    (B) Every ballet I have attended has failed to interest me; so a theatrical production that fails to interest me must be a ballet.
    (C) All cases of severe depression I have encountered were susceptible to treatment by chlorpromazine, so there must be something in the chlorpromazine that adjusts the patient's brain chemistry.
    (D) Every society has a word for justice, so the concept of fair play must be inherent in the biological makeup of the human species.
    (E) No medicine I have tried for my allergy has ever helped, so this new product will probably not work either.

Item #185 refers to the following passage.

Every household interviewed on this block responded that crime is a serious problem in this area. Therefore, most residents in this neighborhood probably believe that crime is a serious problem here.

185. The argument above depends on which of the following assumptions?

(A) The incidence of crime in the neighborhood surveyed is typical of the incidence of crime nationwide.

(B) The incidence of crime in the neighborhood surveyed is growing.

(C) The households surveyed included at least one person who had been a victim of a crime.

(D) In the neighborhood cited, violent crime is a greater problem than nonviolent crime.

(E) The households surveyed reflect a balanced cross-section of the households in the neighborhood.

Item #186 refers to the following passage.

The existence of flying saucers, unidentified flying objects supposedly piloted by extraterrestrial beings, has been shown to be illusory. Skeptical researchers have demonstrated that a number of photographs purportedly showing flying saucers are either crude forgeries or misinterpreted images of such earthly objects as clouds, birds, weather balloons, or small private planes.

186. If the photographs described above are accurately explained, which of the following most weakens the conclusion drawn?

(A) Some purported unidentified flying objects have proved to be natural phenomena rather than manmade objects.

(B) The fact that a number of photographs of flying saucers are fakes does not generally disprove the phenomenon.

(C) Some of those who claim to have witnessed flying saucers have no apparent motive for lying.

(D) Given the size and complexity of the universe, it seems unreasonable to assume that life exists only on Earth.

(E) Researchers who are skeptical about flying saucers inevitably bring their own biases and preconceptions to their work.

Analogy

Item #187 refers to the following passage.

In nature, only the strong survive to reproduce themselves, thereby ensuring that nature gradually moves closer and closer to perfection. So too war is necessary to eliminate the weak and imperfect nations, for in war only the strong survive. Rather than opposing war, we should support war as the way by which the human species can perfect itself.

187. The reasoning in the argument is flawed because the argument

    (A) makes a hasty generalization
    (B) confuses a cause with an effect
    (C) relies on a false analogy
    (D) appeals to the emotions of the reader
    (E) relies on the use of force to prove its point

Item #188 refers to the following passage.

In an extensive study of the reading habits of magazine subscribers, it was found that an average of between four and five people actually read each copy of the most popular weekly news magazine. On this basis, we estimate that the 12,000 copies of Poets and Poetry that are sold each month are actually read by 48,000 to 60,000 people.

188. The estimate above assumes that

    (A) individual magazine readers generally enjoy more than one type of magazine
    (B) most of the readers of Poets and Poetry subscribe to the magazine
    (C) the ratio of readers to copies is the same for Poets and Poetry as for the most popular weekly news magazine
    (D) the number of readers of the weekly news magazine is similar to the number of readers of Poets and Poetry
    (E) most readers enjoy sharing copies of their favorite magazines with friends and family members

Item #189 refers to the following passage.

Studies have clearly shown that negative commercial advertising tends to alienate consumers. The net result of a particularly nasty ad war between two competing brands of coffee, in which each severely criticized the other, was a sharp drop in the total amount of coffee purchased. Similarly, we should expect that after viewing political attack ads, people's expressed intention to vote would drop sharply. It appears, then, that negative political advertising is self-defeating.

189. The reasoning in the argument above does which of the following?

    (A) draws an analogy
    (B) defines a term
    (C) challenges an authority
    (D) proves a premise
    (E) refutes a theory

Item #190 refers to the following passage.

A Federal lottery would not be a productive revenue raiser. In the 27 states that have lotteries, the lotteries have yielded only two to four percent of total state-raised revenues. At the Federal level, this would mean additional revenues of only $11 billion per year—not a significant figure.

190. Which of the following, if true, most seriously weakens the argument above?

    (A) A Federal lottery would offer larger prizes that would increase participation and thereby generate greater revenues.
    (B) A Federal lottery would discourage participation in state lotteries, so states would lose revenues.
    (C) A lottery is a form of gambling, so a Federal lottery would contribute to the problem of compulsive gambling.
    (D) The proceeds from state lotteries are earmarked for special funds such as education, but proceeds from a Federal lottery would go into general revenues.
    (E) Any money generated by a Federal lottery would not be used to reduce the average tax burden on individuals.

Either-Or Situation

Item #191 refers to the following passage.

Either you will punish your puppy severely when he misbehaves, or the puppy will grow up to be a bad dog. Since your puppy just had an accident on the kitchen floor, you should punish him severely.

191. The argument above is most vulnerable to criticism on the grounds that it relies on

    (A) a false dilemma
    (B) an inappropriate analogy
    (C) a hasty generalization
    (D) a nonrepresentative sampling
    (E) an unproved theory

Item #192 refers to the following passage.

An experienced attorney agreed to take on a law clerk and train her for admission to the bar. According to their agreement, the fee for the training would be due and made payable at the time that the new attorney won her first case. After receiving the training, the new attorney decided not to practice law, and the experienced attorney, tired of waiting for payment, sued for the fee. The new attorney represented herself and claimed that the fee was not owed since she had not won her first case.

192. Which of the following conclusions can be logically inferred from the information above?

    (A) If the younger attorney wins, the fee is then due.
    (B) If the younger attorney wins, the fee is never payable.
    (C) If the younger attorney wins, the fee was due before the suit was filed.
    (D) If the suit is withdrawn, the fee is never payable.
    (E) If the suit is withdrawn, the fee was due before the suit was filed.

Item #193 refers to the following passage.

Chukar partridge chicks can run straight up the side of a tree by flapping their wings. The beating wings do not raise the chicks off the ground but rather serve the same purpose as spoilers on racecars, providing better traction for their feet. Feathered dinosaurs may have done something similar. They flapped their primitive wings to better run up inclines, helping them to catch prey. Thus, the proto-wing offered a survival benefit that was not related to flight and only later did this wing-beating behavior lead to the eventual discovery of the aerial possibilities of wings. This evolutionary path toward flight is different from the two previous models: the arboreal model, in which proto-birds first launched themselves from trees; and the cursorial model, in which they took off from the ground.

193. The reasoning in the argument above does which of the following?

    (A) offers a third alternative to an either-or situation
    (B) provides a counterexample to refute a popular theory
    (C) points out a contradiction in a competing position
    (D) attacks the proponent of a plan rather than its merits
    (E) shifts the burden of proof to an opponent of a plan

Begging the Question

Item #194 refers to the following passage.

To say that humans are moral agents is to imply that they have the capacity to choose one course of action over another, but in reality, humans lack this capacity. When a person seems to choose one course of action, he or she is simply acting on the strongest desire he or she has. And this person must have acted on the strongest of his or her desires, because it finally moved him or her to act. Therefore, human beings cannot be considered moral agents.

194. The argument above is most vulnerable to criticism on the grounds that it

    (A) reaches a general conclusion based on too few examples
    (B) confuses an effect with its cause
    (C) contains a logical contradiction
    (D) relies on questionable authority
    (E) assumes what it tries to prove

Item #195 refers to the following passage.

Recently, the newspaper published a poet's obituary notice that had been written by the deceased in anticipation of the event. The last line of the verse advised the reader that the poet had expired a day earlier and gave as the cause of death "a deprivation of time."

195. The explanation of the cause of the poet's death is

    (A) circular
    (B) speculative
    (C) self-serving
    (D) medically sound
    (E) self-authenticating

Item #196 refers to the following passage.

Ms. Ingres has filed a lawsuit against the firm claiming that she is the victim of gender-based discrimination because she was not promoted to partner. The firm has reviewed her personnel records and concluded that she had an excellent work record that was superior to the records of several men with fewer years of service who were promoted to partner. Additionally, there are no negative entries in her file. Nonetheless, we feel justified in refusing to make her a partner because this lawsuit shows that she is not a team player.

196. The flawed reasoning in which of the following is most similar to the flawed reasoning in the argument above?

    (A) an elected official who is charged with corruption but refuses to resign from office pending a full investigation into the matter
    (B) a contractor who acknowledges that faulty materials were used in a building but who also claims that he was defrauded by a supplier
    (C) a young man who admits killing both of his parents who pleads for a judge to show him mercy because he is an orphan
    (D) a teacher who gives a student a failing mark on a term paper after the student admits plagiarizing the paper
    (E) a soldier who refuses to follow orders from a superior officer and argues that the orders were immoral and therefore invalid

Ambiguity

Item #197 refers to the following passage.

All bushes that bear red roses have thorns. This bush has no thorns. Therefore, this bush cannot bear roses.

197. The flawed reasoning in which of the following is most similar to the flawed reasoning in the argument above?

(A) All Sandarac automobiles have three wheels. This car has three wheels. Therefore, this car is a Sandarac automobile.

(B) All brides wear white. This woman is not wearing white. Therefore, this woman must be the maid of honor.

(C) All professional tennis players use metal rackets. This player does not use a metal racket. Therefore, this player is not a professional tennis player.

(D) All Scottish ivy is heliotropic. This plant is not heliotropic. Therefore, this plant is not ivy.

(E) All pencils have rubber erasers. This eraser is not attached to a pencil. Therefore, this eraser is not made of rubber.

Item #198 refers to the following passage.

Conservatives often boast of the freedoms that U.S. citizens enjoy, yet how much freedom do they really have? Housing, medical care, and other basic needs are increasingly costly, and no one is guaranteed a job. The people living in socialist nations enjoy true freedom because they are free from the fear that the constant threat of poverty brings.

198. The persuasive force of the argument above depends most strongly on the ambiguous use of which of the following pairs of terms?

(A) basic needs and job
(B) poverty and fear
(C) free and freedom
(D) guarantee and poverty
(E) spokespeople and people

Item #199 refers to the following passage.

The new car to buy this year is the Goblin. We had 100 randomly selected motorists drive the Goblin and the other two leading subcompact cars. Seventy-five drivers ranked the Goblin first in handling. Sixty-nine drivers rated the Goblin first in styling. From the responses of these 100 drivers, we can show you that they ranked the Goblin first overall in our composite category.

199. The persuasive appeal of the advertisement's claim is most seriously weakened by its use of the undefined word

(A) randomly
(B) handling
(C) first
(D) responses
(E) composite

Item #200 refers to the following passage.

Advertising for weight-loss products manipulates people by arbitrarily defining key terms in ways that will serve to increase profit. Consider the word "overweight." At what point does a person weighing x pounds become "overweight"—at $x+1$ pounds, or $x+2$ pounds, or $x+3$ pounds? The decision to say that $x+4$ pounds (or any other amount) is overweight is purely arbitrary. The word "overweight" is totally meaningless.

200. The reasoning in the argument above is most similar to that in which of the following?

(A) Laws setting minimum ages for activities such as driving a car are not intended to legislate a distinction between "child" and "adult." Some "children" could begin to drive at 14; others not until 20. But it would be prohibitively expensive to take applications on a case-by-case basis, so the line must be drawn somewhere.

(B) Advertising for the hair-replacement industry doesn't generally use terms like "bald" in an absolute sense. Instead, the ads use phrases like "hair loss." That way, anyone who began with x hairs and now has $x-1$ hairs can seem to be in need of a hair replacement technique.

(C) In the legend, Theseus is adrift in the ocean on a raft. He replaces each of the timbers of the raft one by one until none of the original timbers remain. Since it is impossible to say when the old raft became the new raft, it makes no sense to talk about the raft of Theseus.

(D) The typical school system is divided into grades, the assumption being that a student in a higher grade is more advanced than a student in a lower grade. But we know from experience that sixth-grade work at School X may be taught in fifth grade at School Y. So, grade comparisons should be made only within a school.

(E) The medical practice of triage was developed by Napoleon. It divides battle casualties into three groups: those likely to survive, those not likely to survive, and those in the middle. Surgeons then concentrate on those in the middle. The theory is that those likely to survive don't need immediate medical attention, and those unlikely to survive won't benefit from medical attention.

QUIZZES

This section contains three Reading quizzes. Each item is based on the accompanying passage. Complete each quiz while being timed. Answers are on page 702.

Quiz I

(10 items; 14 minutes)

> **DIRECTIONS:** For items 1–10, select one answer unless otherwise directed.

Items #1–2 refer to the following passage.

Man is the only animal that laughs and weeps, for he is the only animal that is struck with the difference between what things are and what they ought to be. We weep at what exceeds our
5 expectations in serious matters; we laugh at what disappoints our expectations in trifles. We shed tears from sympathy with real and necessary distress; we burst into laughter from want of sympathy with that which is unreasonable and
10 unnecessary. Tears are the natural and involuntary response of the mind overcome by some sudden and violent emotions. Laughter is the same sort of convulsive and involuntary movement, occasioned by mere surprise or contrast.
15 The serious is the stress which the mind lays upon the expectation of a given order of events and the weight attached to them. When this stress is increased beyond its usual intensity and strains the feelings by the violent opposition of good and bad, it
20 becomes the tragic. The ludicrous is the unexpected relaxing of this stress below its usual intensity, by an abrupt transposition of ideas that takes the mind by surprise and startles it into a lively sense of pleasure.

For the following item, consider each answer individually and select all that apply.

1. According to the passage, tears and laughter have which of the following in common?

    (A) They are both involuntary reactions.
    (B) They are both the result of violent emotions.
    (C) They both depend on prior expectations.

2. The author implies that animals lack the ability to

    (A) perceive emotional changes in humans
    (B) feel pain or pleasure
    (C) evoke sorrow or laughter in humans
    (D) respond strongly to external stimuli
    (E) imagine things other than as they are

Items #3–4 refer to the following passage.

The risks of injury and death from motor vehicle accidents involving alcohol have received extraordinary exposure in the United States. Almost one-half of fatally injured drivers have a blood
5 alcohol concentration (BAC) of 0.1 percent or higher. The average adult would have to consume over five ounces of 80 proof spirits over a short time period to attain these levels. Although less than one percent of drivers with BACs of 0.1 percent or
10 more are involved in fatal crashes, the probability of their involvement is 27 times higher than for those without alcohol in their blood.

Laws against driving while alcohol impaired presently target the impaired driver. The law
15 empowers police to request breath tests of drivers cited for any traffic offense, and elevated BAC can be the basis for arrest. The National Highway Traffic Safety Administration estimates, however, that there are about 700 actual violations for every
20 arrest. At this level there is little evidence that laws serve as deterrents to driving while intoxicated.

An alternative approach is to raise the taxes on alcohol. Excessive consumption of alcohol by individuals is strongly correlated with the total
25 alcohol consumption by the population as a whole. Higher taxes on alcohol would reduce total consumption and indirectly have the effect of reducing the incidence of driving while alcohol impaired.

3. The passage is primarily concerned with

(A) interpreting the results of surveys on traffic fatalities
(B) reviewing the effectiveness of attempts to curb drunk driving
(C) suggesting reasons for the prevalence of drunk driving in the United States
(D) analyzing the causes of the large number of annual traffic fatalities
(E) making an international comparison of experience with drunk driving

4. The author implies that a BAC of 0.1 percent

(A) proves a driver has consumed five ounces of 80 proof spirits over a short time
(B) penalizes moderate drinkers but allows heavy drinkers to consume without limit
(C) will effectively deter over 90 percent of the people who might drink and drive
(D) is well below the BAC of most drivers who are involved in fatal collisions
(E) is quite high as a definition of intoxication for purposes of driving

Items #5–7 refer to the following passage.

In order to make truly rational policy decisions, we require a single, generally accepted index of the economic and social welfare of the people of the United States. A glance at it would tell
5   us how much better or worse off we had become each year, and we would judge the desirability of any proposed action by asking whether it would raise or lower this index. The Gross Domestic Product (GDP), while currently insufficient, could be
10 converted into an index of this type.

The output available to satisfy our wants and needs is one important determinant of welfare. We ordinarily can more easily find resources to deal with our wants and needs when output is large and
15 growing than when it is not. GDP measures output fairly well, but to evaluate welfare we need an index of real costs incurred in production, because we are better off if we get the same output at less cost. Use of just hours-worked for welfare evaluation would
20 unreasonably imply that to increase total hours by raising the hours of eight women from 60 to 65 a week imposes no more burden than raising the hours of eight men from 40 to 45 a week, or even than hiring one involuntarily unemployed person
25 for 40 hours a week. A measure of real costs of labor would also have to consider working conditions. Most of us spend almost half our waking hours on the job and our welfare is vitally affected by the circumstances in which we spend those hours.
30 Such calculations are difficult but not impossible. We already survey populations for purposes of determining satisfaction, including product satisfaction, job satisfaction, and even satisfaction with political candidates. With suitable
35 refinements, the same techniques, when coupled with an index of output such as the GDP, could be combined to generate an overall index of general welfare.

5. The author implies that hours worked is not an appropriate measure of real cost because it

    (A) ignores the conditions under which the output is generated
    (B) fails to take into consideration the environmental costs of production
    (C) overemphasizes the output of real goods as opposed to services
    (D) is not an effective method for reducing unemployment
    (E) was never intended to be a general measure of welfare

6. Which of the following sentences explains why a general economic and welfare index would be useful?

    (A) Lines 4–8 ("A glance...index.")
    (B) Lines 11–12 ("The output available...welfare.")
    (C) Lines 12–15 ("We ordinarily...not.")
    (D) Lines 15–18 ("GDP measures...less cost.")
    (E) Lines 34–38 ("With suitable...welfare.")

7. The passage is most likely

    (A) a speech by a university professor to graduating classes
    (B) part of a chapter in a general introduction to statistics
    (C) an element of a pamphlet on government programs to aid the poor
    (D) part of the introduction to a treatise on the foundations of government
    (E) an address to a symposium on public policy decisions

Item #8 refers to the following passage.

The events that occur on some days are more significant than the events that occur on other days. Yet, the evening television news program, which is devoted to the events of the day, is always 30 minutes long.

8. Which of the following is best supported by the information above?

    (A) Every edition of the evening news is forced to cover some events that are not newsworthy.
    (B) Some editions of the evening news cover events that are not as significant as events covered by other editions.
    (C) At least one newsworthy event will be found in every edition of the evening news program.
    (D) Some editions of the evening news cover no events that are truly newsworthy.
    (E) Each day some significant events will not be covered by the evening news.

Item #9 refers to the following passage.

My friend Hector is bilingual, speaking both Spanish and English with equal facility. I do not speak Spanish, so when we are together with Puerto Rican friends who speak Spanish, Hector translates into English for my benefit. One afternoon, judging from the uproarious laughter, a particularly funny joke was told in Spanish. When I asked Hector to translate, he stopped short and said, "I can't."

9. Which of the following, if true, best explains Hector's statement?

(A) Many Spanish words have English cognates, that is, words that are substantially the same in both languages.

(B) Spanish is a romance language derived from Latin, but the basic grammatical forms of English come from German.

(C) In the past, Hector had always been successful in translating jokes into English while preserving their humor.

(D) The joke involved a play on words in Spanish that does not exist when translated into English.

(E) Bilingual people are able to switch from one language to another instantaneously.

Item #10 refers to the following passage.

The average American eats more than 120 pounds of sugar every year. A one-pound box of sugar contains about 113 level teaspoon servings at 116 calories per serving or 13,108 calories per box. So, the average American could save more than one-and-a-half million calories simply by buying and using a sugar substitute.

10. Which of the following, if true, most weakens the argument above?

(A) Some Americans eat more sugar than the average, and some eat less sugar than the average.

(B) Substituting artificial sweetener for sugar for some, even though not all, uses would still save calories.

(C) Replacing sugar with an artificial sweetener would not result in a significant increase in the annual food budget of an average American.

(D) A substantial quantity of the sugar consumed by Americans is as an ingredient in processed foods.

(E) Many Americans are not overweight and therefore do not need to be concerned with the number of calories in sugar.

Quiz II
(10 items; 14 minutes)

DIRECTIONS: For items 1–10, select one answer unless otherwise directed.

Items #1–3 refer to the following passage.

The stars awaken a certain reverence, because though always present, they are inaccessible. In fact, all natural objects make a similar impression— when the mind is open to their influence. Not even
5 the wisest person can extort from Nature all of her secrets nor exhaust his curiosity by finding out all her perfection. Nature never became a toy to a wise spirit.

When we speak of Nature in this manner, we
10 mean the integrity of expression made manifold by natural objects. The charming landscape which I saw this morning is indubitably made up of some twenty or thirty farms. This field is the property of Miller, that one the property of Locke, and that one
15 beyond the wood the property of Manning. But none of them owns the landscape. There is property in the horizon which no man has, but it belongs only to him whose eyes can integrate all the parts. This is the best part of these men's farms, yet to this their
20 warranty gives no title. The power to produce this delight does not reside in Nature but in humans, or in the harmony of both, for Nature is not always decked out in holiday attire. The same scene that yesterday breathed perfume and glittered is
25 overspread with melancholy today. Nature always wears the color of the spirit.

1. The phrase "Nature never became a toy to the wise spirit" means which of the following?

(A) Educated people do not treat nature as children do.
(B) Nature will always conquer even the most learned person.
(C) Nature is unpredictable and human beings cannot understand it.
(D) A truly wise person does not lose his appreciation of nature.
(E) The best things in nature are unattainable.

2. The author implies that the difference between farms and the landscape is primarily a matter of

(A) cultivation
(B) perception
(C) ownership
(D) allegiance
(E) inheritance

3. The author uses the word property in the phrase "property in the horizon" (lines 16–17) to express

(A) melancholy
(B) reverence
(C) disbelief
(D) irony
(E) foolishness

Items #4–5 refer to the following passage.

As Carl Hempel demonstrates in his seminal essay "The Function of General Laws in History," a general law plays the same role in both history and the natural sciences. According to Hempel's
5   deductive-nomological model, proper scientific explanation—whether for history or the natural sciences—includes three sorts of statements:
(A) A set of statements about conditions (that can be designated as C1, C2, and so on) that
10   are true at a particular place and time.
(B) A set of universal hypotheses connecting events of type C with events of type E.
(C) A statement asserting that E is logically deducible from the statements of A and B.
15   The "C" events are, of course, causes, while the "E" events are effects. Given a sufficiently precise description of background conditions by Set A and an adequately articulated set of empirical laws in Set B, a conclusion such as "A popular uprising
20   overthrew the government" can be logically deduced with as much certainty as that of a syllogism.
The notion that a historian cannot study past events in the same way that a chemist studies
25   reactions or a physicist studies falling objects is due to a misunderstanding. Historical explanations intentionally omit from Set A statements about human nature that are well known to the sciences of psychology and sociology because they are too
30   numerous to mention. Further, many of the general laws used by historians do not seem susceptible to easy confirmation in the way that laboratory experiments are. It is difficult to find a sufficiently large number of revolutions to assess the validity of
35   the assertion that a drop of a certain magnitude in a population's standard of living will inevitably be followed by revolution.
Thus, we should more accurately speak not of scientific explanations of historical events but of
40   "sketches" of history. This terminology would call attention to the incompleteness and the imprecision in historical explanation, while at the same time reminding us that the form of explanation is the same as that of the natural sciences.

4. As used in line 5, the word "nomological" most nearly means

(A) law-like
(B) historical
(C) accurate
(D) logical
(E) scientific

For the following item, consider each answer individually and select all that apply.

5. According to the passage, scientific explanations of historical events differ from sketches of history in which of the following ways?

(A) Historical events are not easily replicated in laboratory-type conditions to determine whether the outcome can be replicated.
(B) A historical sketch implicitly relies upon the findings of other social sciences for information about human behavior.
(C) A historical event can never be fully described scientifically because the inner thoughts of key participants cannot be determined.

Items #6–7 refer to the following passage.

The genius of the U.S. Constitution is that it establishes a set of forces and counterforces, like the forces in Newtonian physics. An action in one direction necessarily produces an equal reaction in
5 the opposite direction, creating legal stability. Essential to the scheme is the fact that the forces are self-generated. The Constitution confers power and imposes limitations on power on the institutions themselves, rather than imposing it from without.
10 Suppose a pie is to be divided into two equal pieces for a brother and sister using the same scheme. Rather than setting up a system of judicial review under an equal protection clause—a device that might not work until the pie has become stale—the
15 system simply lets one sibling cut the pie and the other choose a piece.

The intricate system of checks and balances, however, does not necessarily lead to a static legal structure. Each branch's capacity to act is
20 commensurate with its authority to act and to improve its ability to discharge its constitutional responsibilities. For example, Congress may rationalize the legislative process to improve its capability to formulate and carry through a
25 coherent and technically proficient legislative program. Other devices might alleviate the overburdened executive branch, such as a strengthened Cabinet, with a smaller, executive Cabinet of respected statesmen to serve as a link
30 between the White House and the departments, and between the president and Congress.

In a Newtonian constitution, there is always the danger that extraordinary force in one direction is likely to produce extraordinary, and sometimes
35 excessive, force in another direction. In the early years of the New Deal, the Supreme Court, generally over the dissent of its most respected members, engaged in a series of judicial vetoes that reflected an unjudicial approach to the function of judging.
40 The president, on his part, countered with the Court reorganization plan, which seriously threatened the independence of the judiciary. A Newtonian system demands constitutional morality. Without constitutional morality, the system breaks down.

6. With which of the following statements would the author most likely agree?

(A) Congress is more important than either the executive branch or the judiciary.
(B) The branches of government may have more constitutional authority than they use.
(C) The earliest Supreme Court justices were more sincere than today's justices are.
(D) The Constitution sets up a very simple system for governmental decisions.
(E) Constitutionally created hurdles block needed improvements in governmental efficiency.

7. The author regards the president's attempt to reorganize the Supreme Court as

(A) understandable but wrong
(B) ineffective but correct
(C) impractical but well intentioned
(D) necessary but misguided
(E) half-hearted but moral

Item #8 refers to the following passage.

Contrary to popular opinion, a dog doesn't eat grass because it has a stomach ailment. Rather, it eats grass because it is looking for nutrients that are missing from its diet. These nutrients are as essential to your dog's diet today as they were to its ancestors in the wild.

8. Which of the following is most strongly supported by the above statements?

(A) A dog that is eating grass does not have a stomach ailment.
(B) Ancestors of today's dogs ate grass in the wild.
(C) Dogs today have the same nutritional requirements as their ancestors in the wild did.
(D) A dog that eats grass is missing some essential nutrients in its diet.
(E) Grass supplies nutrients that are essential to a dog's health.

Item #9 refers to the following passage.

It has long been regarded as a financial fact that the single most common cause for the failure of new small businesses is lack of capital. But that may no longer be true. A survey of 100 start-up franchise businesses with approximately $10,000 in capital showed that 35 of the 47 that paid an initial franchise fee in excess of $1,000 were still in business after 12 months while only eight of the 53 that paid an initial franchise fee of less than $500 were still operating. Paradoxically, the greater capital available after payment of the initial franchise fee seems to have doomed some businesses.

9. Which of the following, if true, most helps to explain the survey's findings?

(A) Of new franchise businesses that fail, most cease operations within twelve months of beginning operations.
(B) Franchisers who charge more than $500 as an initial fee must give prospective franchisees a detailed prospectus.
(C) The failure rate for new franchise businesses that begin by investing more than $10,000 in an initial fee is about five percent.
(D) The average franchise fee as a fraction of total capital for the 43 businesses that succeeded was approximately 12 percent.
(E) The number of years of business experience for the franchisees who failed was comparable to that of those who succeeded.

Item #10 refers to the following passage.

In pari-mutuel horserace gambling, the bettors are playing against one another, not the house. The track is merely the stakes-holder. After a race is declared official, the track deducts a percentage from the pools—called the take-out—and returns the remainder to holders of winning tickets. The take-out, which ranges from 15 to 28 percent, is then divided amongst the track for operations, purses, and governmental units for taxes; and, of course, there is always pressure, particularly from the government, to increase the take-out percentage. Paradoxically, however, studies have shown that the total of the take-out would actually increase if the percentage were decreased.

10. Which of the following, if true, best explains the studies' findings?

(A) Expansion of off-track betting opportunities and wagering on simulcast races have greatly expanded the total amount bet on races in recent years.
(B) In most jurisdictions, proceeds from the take-out are divided according to a formula that is established by the state legislature.
(C) An increase in the percentage of the take-out has been shown to depress the total number of fans who attend live races at tracks.
(D) The percentage of the take-out is higher on so-called exotic wagers such as the daily double than on straight win, place, and show wagers.
(E) A lower take-out returns more money into the hands of bettors who in turn tend to make even larger wagers that are again subject to the take-out.

Quiz III

(10 items; 14 minutes)

> **DIRECTIONS:** For items 1–10, select one answer unless otherwise directed.

Items #1–4 refer to the following passage.

An assumption that underlies most discussions of electric facility siting is that the initial selection of a site is the responsibility of the utility—subject to governmental review and approval only after the
5 site has been chosen. This assumption must be changed so that site selection becomes a joint responsibility of the utilities and the appropriate governmental authorities from the outset. Siting decisions could be made in accordance with either
10 of two strategies.

The metropolitan strategy takes the existing distribution of population and supporting facilities as given. An attempt is then made to choose between dispersed or concentrated siting and to
15 locate generating facilities in accordance with some economic principle. For example, the economic objectives of least-cost construction and rapid startup may be achieved, in part, by a metropolitan strategy that takes advantage of existing elements
20 of social and physical infrastructure in large cities.

Under the frontier strategy, the energy park may be taken as an independent variable, subject to manipulation by policymakers as a means of achieving desired demographic or social goals, e.g.,
25 rural-town-city mix. Thus, population distribution is taken as a goal of national social policy, not as a given of a national energy policy. In the frontier strategy, the option of dispersed siting does not include as a factor community impact because there
30 is no preexisting community of any size.

For the following item, consider each answer individually and select all that apply.

1. Which of the following are mentioned by the author as characteristics of energy parks?

   (A) energy parks will be built upon previously undeveloped sites
   (B) energy parks will be built in areas remote from major population centers
   (C) energy parks may have considerable effects on population distribution

2. According to the passage, which of the following is a characteristic of past siting decisions for electric facilities?

   (A) Government authorities primarily exercised a review function over decisions made by utilities.
   (B) Decisions were made without regard to the effect the facility would have on people.
   (C) Sites selected by utilities were often opposed by environmentalist groups.
   (D) Future siting decisions will coordinate energy park placement with natural resources.
   (E) America's oldest cities generally have less than adequate energy supplies.

3. Which of the following, if true, most seriously WEAKENS the argument in the passage?

   (A) The first settlements in America were established in order to provide trading posts with Native Americans.
   (B) The cost of constructing an electric power plant in an urban area is not significantly greater than that for a rural area.
   (C) An energy park will be so large that it will be impossible to predict the demographic consequences of its construction.
   (D) Cities in European countries grew up in response to political pressures during the feudal period rather than economic pressures.
   (E) The United States is presently in a period of population migration that will change the rural-town-city mix.

4. The author's attitude toward energy parks can best be described as

   (A) cautious uncertainty
   (B) circumspect skepticism
   (C) studied indifference
   (D) unqualified endorsement
   (E) unrestrained zeal

Items #5–7 refer to the following passage.

The number of aged in Sweden is one of the largest in the world, close to 14 percent of the total population, and the need for health and social support for them has been intensified by
5 improvements in the standard of living. Life expectancy has increased as the willingness of adult offspring to care for aged parents living in their households has decreased. The percentage of aged persons living with their children a decade ago was
10 approximately 10 in Sweden (3 in Stockholm), contrasted with 20 in Denmark, 30 in the United States, 40 in England, 70 in Poland, and 90 in Russia. Sweden placed a moratorium on the construction of new acute beds in favor of long-term beds, but that
15 has foundered because care in a long-stay facility, if done correctly, while less costly than an acute facility, may still be prohibitively expensive.

Payroll is the single most important budgetary component in all branches of hospital service,
20 accounting for over 60 percent of total costs; and the staff-to-bed ratio requirements for the chronic aged are higher than for acute patients, especially with respect to nursing and rehabilitation personnel. Payroll expenditures have grown sizably
25 as the result of advancing standards of industrial justice that challenge the validity of the traditional idea that health workers other than doctors should work for lower wages than persons doing comparable work elsewhere in the economy
30 because of the eleemosynary and humanitarian ethic of patient care.

5. Which of the following, if true, most strengthens the contention that improvements in the standard of living increase the reluctance of adults to care for aged parents?

(A) The United States has a higher standard of living than Sweden.
(B) Stockholm has a substantially higher standard of living than the rest of Sweden.
(C) The number of long-term care beds in England has not increased appreciably in the past five years.
(D) Sweden has fewer aged persons than Denmark.
(E) Sweden has a higher acute to long-term beds ratio than Russia.

6. It can be inferred from the passage that the increasing number of aged requiring care prompted Sweden to

(A) shift funds from construction of facilities for care of the acutely ill to projects to build facilities for long-term care
(B) restructure its tax laws to penalize families who refused to provide in-house care for their aging relatives
(C) attempt to reduce long-term care costs by depressing salaries of hospital workers and delaying wage increases
(D) crowd four or five patients into a room designed for only one patient in order to reduce payroll costs
(E) discontinue construction of long-term hospitals for the psychogeriatric care of the aged

7. It can be inferred from the passage that pay rates in the health field have historically been lower than those for manufacturing and industry because

(A) jobs in the health field have a lower status
(B) service in the health field was considered charitable work
(C) doctors insisted on receiving higher salaries than other workers received
(D) labor costs are the greatest category of expenditures for hospitals
(E) aged people are not able to pay high fees for long-term care

Item #8 refers to the following passage.

Although big stars and movie studios make plenty of money on blockbuster films, the lesser actors, writers, animators, and other participants generally realize nothing from the "net profits" provisions in their contracts, though they are paid a fee or a salary. The reason is the "Hollywood accounting system," in which a conventional set of books is used to show revenues, costs, and profit to shareholders and management and a second set of records called the "contractual books" is used to calculate profits for distribution to participants other than the studios or big names.

8. Which of the following conclusions can be drawn from the statements above?

(A) Participants other than studios or big stars are being underpaid for the work that they do on films.

(B) Movie studios manipulate the financial records to ensure that no film ever shows a "contractual" profit.

(C) The profit calculated using the "contractual" method is less than that calculated by conventional accounting methods.

(D) Movies always show a profit when the accounting is done using conventional methods rather than the "contractual books."

(E) "Contractual books" eliminate any profit by understating the gross revenues earned by a film.

Item #9 refers to the following passage.

The used-car trade is the fastest-growing segment of the automobile market. Nowadays, about six out of every 10 cars and trucks sold are secondhand. This was bound to happen. Evidently, consumers are finally saying no to the ridiculously high and constantly rising new-car prices and are choosing instead to purchase used vehicles.

9. Which of the following, if true, most weakens the argument above?

(A) Last year, sales of used vehicles totaled just over $18 million while sales of new vehicles totaled just under $16 million.

(B) Leasing a new vehicle for just two to four years has become very popular, so the number of available used vehicles is growing.

(C) A car dealer usually makes a profit of about $300 to $500 on a used car but only $100 or even less on a new vehicle.

(D) High-priced luxury import vehicles are significantly less likely to be found in the used-car market than less expensive vehicles.

(E) Many states have so-called "lemon laws" that require used-vehicle dealers to warrant vehicles that they sell for one to three months.

Item #10 refers to the following passage.

The National Centers for Disease Control and Prevention looked at death certificates from 1980 to 1992 and found a 58 percent increase in infectious disease deaths. Yet, the United States gets new drugs to market more slowly than any other major industrial nation. Total drug approval times have jumped from eight years in 1960 to more than 15 years today. If the United States seriously wants to reverse the rising trend of infectious disease deaths, it should reform the procedures used by the Food and Drug Administration to approve drugs.

10. Which of the following additional facts provides the LEAST support for the plan described above?

(A) There was no overall increase in the number of noninfectious disease deaths from 1980 to 1992.

(B) The cost of drugs in the United States is increased considerably by the lengthy delays preceding government approval.

(C) Several drugs awaiting approval by the Food and Drug Administration appear to be highly effective against common deadly infections.

(D) An eight-year drug-approval time by the Food and Drug Administration optimizes the trade-off between safety and speed of approval.

(E) Accelerating Food and Drug Administration approvals would not impair the agency's effectiveness in reviewing applications for approval.

STRATEGY SUMMARY

General Strategies:

Personalize the Passage Order

Take a minute before you begin answering any items to quickly preview the section. Note any passages with topics that are familiar to you, and select those passages to complete first. You might not know the answers to the items, but familiarity is a definite advantage.

Preview the Item Stems

Be sure to read the items carefully, watching for non-standard item stems and thought-reversers. Preview the item stems first. This will enable you to focus on what is being asked when you read the passage.

Preview the Passage

Take a few seconds to preview key sentences, including the first and last sentences of each paragraph. These sentences will give you an outline of the development of the passage.

Reading Comprehension Strategies

Understanding the three levels of reading comprehension and how they relate to the seven Reading Comprehension item-types will help you to identify quickly the type of question that is being asked by a particular item.

General Theme

Main Idea items ask about the overall development of the selection:

- *Which of the following is the main point of the passage?*
- *The primary purpose of the passage is to....*

The first sentence of a paragraph—often the topic sentence—may provide a summary of the content of that paragraph. Also, the last sentence of a paragraph usually provides concluding material that may also be helpful in understanding the central theme that unifies the passage.

Specific Points

Specific Detail items ask about details that are explicitly mentioned in the passage. Specific Detail items often provide line numbers and "locator words" that identify the required information in the passage. For example:

- *The author mentions which of the following?*
- *According to the passage,...?*

Vocabulary items ask about the meaning of a specific word or phrase as it appears in the passage. For example:

- *In line ##, "——" most nearly means....*
- *The author uses the phrase "..." in line ## to mean ...*

Logical Structure items ask about the overall structure of the passage or the logical role played by a specific part of the passage. For example:

- *The author develops the passage primarily by....*
- *The author mentions...in order to....*

Evaluation

Implied Idea items do not ask about what is specifically stated in the passage. Rather, these items ask about what can be logically inferred from what is stated in the passage. For example:

- *The passage implies that....*
- *The author uses the phrase "..." to mean....*
- *It can be inferred from the passage that...*
- *Which of the following can be inferred from the passage?*

Further Application items are similar to Implied Idea items, but they go one step further: you must apply what you have learned from the passage to a new situation. For example:

- *With which of the following statements would the author most likely agree?*
- *The passage is most probably taken from which of the following sources?*

Attitude-Tone items ask about the author's attitude toward a specific detail or the overall voice of the passage. For example:

- *The tone of the passage can best be described as....*
- *The author regards...as....*

Critical Reading Strategies

Critical Reading items test the reader's understanding of parts of an argument and the ability to draw logical conclusions. Remember that an argument consists of a conclusion and premises, as well as the inference that links them. Items can ask about any of these elements.

The Conclusion

To answer items of this type, you must know how to identify the conclusion of an argument. Here are some strategies for identifying the conclusion of an argument:

- Sometimes the conclusion is the last statement of a paragraph. However, the conclusion can appear anywhere.

- Transitional words or phrases may be used to signal the conclusion.

- When you cannot easily identify the conclusion, ask yourself: "What is the author attempting to prove?" or "What is the main point?"

- In some instances, a chain of reasoning may be presented. While there will be one final conclusion, there can be sub-arguments in which an intermediate conclusion from the initial premises is used to assert the ultimate result.

The Assumptions

To answer items of this type, you must know how to identify hidden assumptions. Here are some strategies for identifying hidden assumptions:

- Sometimes premises are stated and signaled using such words as "since," "because," "for," "inasmuch as," and "insofar as." More than one premise may be required to support a conclusion. While some premises may be explicitly stated, others may be partially or completely hidden (implicit or suppressed).

- You may also be asked to identify statements that weaken or strengthen an argument. To do this, you must find answer choices that either identify and rebut a hidden assumption or identify and prove a hidden assumption.

The Inference

Critical Reading items may ask you to identify or critique the use of any of the following types of arguments:

- *Cause and Effect Situation.* Cause and effect items often ask you to find an answer choice that strengthens or weakens a causal explanation. These items may point to unexpected causal factors or require you to explain a paradox. Other items simply talk about an effect and possible causes.

- *Generalization.* These arguments reach broad conclusions based on limited data. To answer items of this type, you will typically need to determine whether the sampling is or is not representative of the group as a whole.

- *Analogy.* An argument from analogy is one in which the writer draws a conclusion about one set of circumstances based upon the similarity of those circumstances to another set of circumstances. Most analogy-based item stems will ask you to weaken or strengthen the argument, and the correct choice will be the one that points to a dissimilarity or similarity between the analogized situations.

- *Either-Or Situation.* An either-or situation is a dilemma, or a situation that requires an individual to choose one of a limited group of possible outcomes. In some cases, either-or situations are not truly exhaustive of the possibilities—this is called a false dilemma.

- *Begging the Question.* This is a type of argument that attempts to prove a conclusion by using the conclusion itself as one of the premises of the argument. This is always wrong because it contains a logical fallacy.

- *Ambiguity.* This results when an argument uses a term in more than one way without defining each use of the term separately.

Quantitative Reasoning:
Discrete Quantitative

Course Concept Outline

---

[1] Some concepts in this Course Concept Outline are not illustrated through examples in your student text but may be covered by your instructor in class. They are included here to provide a complete outline of your course.

TEST MECHANICS

Overview

Each of the two Quantitative Reasoning sections of the GRE test consists of 20 items to be answered in 35 minutes. The items are of four different formats: Discrete Quantitative, Quantitative Comparison, Numeric Entry, and Data Interpretation (Graphs). Discrete Quantitative items are the multiple-choice items that you're accustomed to seeing on standardized exams, plus multiple-choice items that require you to "select all that apply," and these two item-types will be the focus of the Quantitative Reasoning: Discrete Quantitative Lesson. The other three item-types will be addressed later in the course.

The GRE math items presuppose knowledge of arithmetic, algebra (up to a second year of high school algebra) and coordinate geometry, and plane geometry (including basic solids), plus a few elementary statistical concepts like standard deviation. These are the conceptual building blocks of the Quantitative Reasoning sections. While the building blocks are familiar, many of the math items are not exactly what you would expect to see on a graduate school entrance exam.

Example:

How many prime numbers between 1 and 100 are factors of 9,350?

(A) 1
(B) 2
(C) 3
(D) 4
(E) 5

By the eighth grade, you learned everything needed to answer this item: the definitions of "prime" and "factor," and how to count to 9,350. Yet this item could prove difficult because it requires putting together math concepts in a way that you're not ordinarily asked to do. The prime factorization of 9,350 is $9,350 = (10)(935) = (2)(5)(5)(187) = (2)(5)(5)(11)(17)$, so it has four prime factors, (D): 2, 5, 11, and 17.

Superficially, GRE Discrete Quantitative items seem to be the same kind of questions that you'd see on a regular test, even if, as in the example above, they don't look like the sort of thing you'll be doing in graduate school. But as you'll learn, many of these items have a special GRE test "flavor." To help you achieve your goal of doing well on the Quantitative Reasoning section of the test, later in the Quantitative Reasoning: Discrete Quantitative Lesson, you will review these special features and how to use them to your benefit.

Anatomy

DIRECTIONS: Solve each problem and choose the correct answer, using the given directions.

NOTES: Unless otherwise indicated, all figures lie in a plane.

Geometric diagrams and figures ARE NOT NECESSARILY drawn to scale. Coordinate systems and graphic data presentations ARE drawn to scale.

You can assume that lines shown as straight are straight and that the positions of points, angles, regions, etc. exist in the order shown.

All numbers used are real numbers.

You really do not need these general directions at all. Discrete Quantitative items follow two multiple-choice formats: work the problem, choose one answer, or work the problem, choose all answers that apply. Pay attention to the number of answer choices and the directions for each item. Note that the directions used throughout this book are similar to the version used for the printed format of the GRE test. The directions for the actual test and for the Cambridge computer application are very similar to the printed format version except that you indicate your answer by clicking on an oval or square next to the correct statement—where the letters are now.

1. Melissa made two deposits to her bank account totaling $1,500. If the second deposit was $300 more than twice the first deposit, how much, in dollars, was the second deposit?

    (A) $400
    (B) $600
    (C) $900
    (D) $1,050
    (E) $1,100

1. **(E)** *Let d_1 and d_2 be the two deposits:*
    $d_1 + d_2 = \$1,500$ *and* $d_2 = 2d_1 + \$300$.
    Substitute the second equation for d_2 in the first equation and solve for d_1:
    $d_1 + (2d_1 + \$300) = \$1,500 \Rightarrow d_1 = \$400$.
    Substitute this value into either equation and solve for d_2. Using the first equation:
    $d_2 = \$1,500 - \$400 = \$1,100$.

2. At a certain college, there are x more juniors than seniors, and the total number of juniors and seniors is y. Which of the following represents the number of juniors?

    (A) $\dfrac{y-x}{2}$

    (B) $\dfrac{x-y}{x}$

    (C) $\dfrac{x+y}{2}$

    (D) $2y + x$

    (E) $y - 2x$

2. **(C)** *This item tests the use of algebraic expressions and equations to represent the relationships described rather than specific quantities. Create two equations: $J = S + x$ and $J + S = y$. The first can be rewritten and the two combined to eliminate S:*

    $$J - S = x$$
    $$\underline{+\ \ J + S = y}$$
    $$2J = x + y \Rightarrow J = \frac{x+y}{2}$$

3. A navigation beacon is located 8,000 meters from the base of an airport control tower. If radar shows that a plane is located 6,000 meters directly above the beacon, what is the straight line distance, in meters, from the plane to the base of the control tower?

    (A) 2,000
    (B) 7,500
    (C) 10,000
    (D) 14,000
    (E) 32,000

3. **(C)** *This is a geometry item that uses the Pythagorean theorem. Since the plane is directly over the beacon, the plane, the beacon, and the base of the tower are the vertices of a right triangle:*

$$d^2 = 6{,}000^2 + 8{,}000^2$$
$$d = \sqrt{6{,}000^2 + 8{,}000^2} = 10{,}000$$

4. A computer is programmed to randomly position each of three switches in either the "ON" or the "OFF" position. If the probability that any one switch will be set to the "ON" position is $\frac{1}{2}$, what is the probability that at least one of the three switches will be set to the "OFF" position?

    (A) $\frac{1}{8}$

    (B) $\frac{1}{2}$

    (C) $\frac{3}{4}$

    (D) $\frac{7}{8}$

    (E) $\frac{15}{16}$

4. **(D)** *This item tests probability. The probability of at least one switch being set to "OFF" is the sum of the probabilities of all distributions, 1, minus the probability of all three switches being set to "ON":*

$$1 - \left(\frac{1}{2} \cdot \frac{1}{2} \cdot \frac{1}{2} \right) = 1 - \frac{1}{8} = \frac{7}{8}$$

For the following item, consider the answers separately and select all that apply.

5. If $p > q$ and $r < 0$, which of the following is (are) true?

Indicate <u>all</u> such statements.

    (A) $pr < qr$
    (B) $p + r > q + r$
    (C) $p - r < q - r$

5. **(A, B)** *This is an algebra item. Note that the item stem instructs you to indicate <u>all</u> true statements. "Select all" items might instruct you to select a certain number of answer choices, so make sure to read these directions carefully. To solve the item, note that if $p > q$ and $r < 0$, multiplying both sides by the negative number r reverses the inequality, so $pr < qr$, as in (A). Therefore, (A) is true. Conversely, adding or subtracting any number, negative or positive, to both sides of an inequality will leave the direction of the inequality unchanged. Therefore, (B) is true because the inequality should not be reversed, while (C) is false because the inequality should not be reversed.*

There are three other features of Discrete Quantitative items to note:

- ***Answer choices are usually arranged in order.*** For most Discrete Quantitative items, answer choices are arranged from largest to smallest or vice versa. However, there are some exceptions. Choices that consist entirely of variables do not follow the rule, and items that ask, "Which of the following is the biggest?", or some variation, obviously do not follow the rule. That the answer choices are usually arranged in order makes it easier for you to find your choice in the list. It also sets up an important test-taking strategy of starting with (C) when applying the "test-the-test" strategy, which you'll learn about later in the Quantitative Reasoning: Discrete Quantitative Lesson.

- ***Values and answer choices are well-defined.*** The choices are not created so that you have to do "donkey math." Item #1 in the Anatomy feature illustrates this point. The correct answer is $1,100, but you are not given choices like $1,099 and $1,101. The GRE test-writers are not particularly interested in whether you're good at long division. In fact, most, if not all, of the math calculations needed for this problem can be done in your head.

- ***Wrong choices usually correspond to errors in thinking—not errors in arithmetic.*** This feature is important because it is the basis for time-saving strategies that you'll learn later in the Quantitative Reasoning: Discrete Quantitative Lesson. Again, consider item #1 in the Anatomy feature. Choice (A) is the amount of the *first* deposit, not the *second,* and is included as an attractive distractor for those who haven't read the item stem carefully. And, in item #2, a mistake in setting up the first equation ($J + x = S$) leads incorrectly to choice (A).

Pacing

The time limit for the 20 math items (Discrete Quantitative, Quantitative Comparison, Numeric Entry, and Data Interpretation) in each of the two Quantitative Reasoning sections is 35 minutes, so you can afford to spend, on average, about 100 seconds per item. Three rules guide pacing on this section of the exam:

RULE #1: Confirm the answer to item #20 (the last item) just as time expires.
RULE #2: Spend no more than 100 seconds per item.
RULE #3: In case of a violation of rule #2, go faster.

It would be nice to offer some words of wisdom about difficulty levels, order of problem presentation, and timing, but this is not possible. Remember that the difficulty of the second Quantitative Reasoning section you complete will depend on your performance on the first section, so each item may require more time, if you receive a more difficult section, or less time, if you receive a less difficult section.

Realistically, however, you are not going to spend exactly 100 seconds answering each item—trying to do so would be distracting and counterproductive. Plus, some items will not require a full 100 seconds. Instead, glance at the clock every 10 minutes: a quick comparison of the remaining time with the item number you're working on (both of which are displayed for you) will tell you whether you're on schedule or falling behind.

Quantitative Reasoning by Item-Type
Total Time: 35 minutes

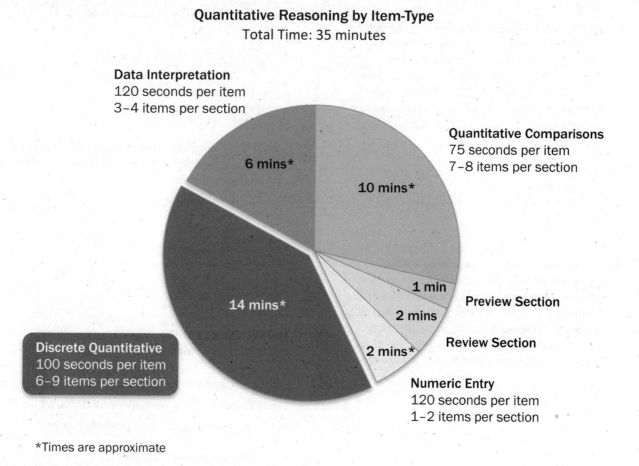

Data Interpretation
120 seconds per item
3–4 items per section

6 mins*

Quantitative Comparisons
75 seconds per item
7–8 items per section

10 mins*

14 mins*

1 min

Preview Section

2 mins

Review Section

2 mins*

Discrete Quantitative
100 seconds per item
6–9 items per section

Numeric Entry
120 seconds per item
1–2 items per section

*Times are approximate

Despite the seeming precision suggested by the numbers, pacing is not an exact science. The following "Time Trial" is designed to give you a better idea of what you'll be up against with timing during the actual exam.

Time Trial

(5 items; 8.5 minutes)

> **DIRECTIONS:** Solve each problem and choose the correct answer, using the given directions. Answers are on page 703.

NOTES: Unless otherwise indicated, all figures lie in a plane.

Geometric diagrams and figures ARE NOT NECESSARILY drawn to scale. Coordinate systems and graphic data presentations ARE drawn to scale.

You can assume that lines shown as straight are straight and that the positions of points, angles, regions, etc. exist in the order shown.

All numbers used are real numbers.

1. The value of a share of Stock P and the value of a share of Stock Q each increased by 16 percent. If the value of a share of Stock P increases by 16 cents, and the value of a share of Stock Q increases by $1.68, what is the difference in the value of the two stocks after the increase?

   (A) $1.48
   (B) $9.50
   (C) $11.02
   (D) $11.50
   (E) $13.34

2. In a certain company, 54 percent of the employees are in the Services Division. If 30 percent of the employees are under the age of 35 and 60 percent of those under the age of 35 are not employed in the Services Division, what percentage of the employees age 35 or older are employees in the Services Division?

   (A) 12%

   (B) 40%

   (C) 60%

   (D) $66\frac{2}{3}$%

   (E) $77\frac{7}{9}$%

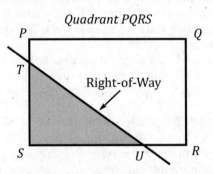

Quadrant PQRS

3. The figure above shows a utility right-of-way that will cut across a rectangular quadrant of land isolating a portion of the property as shown. If the area of the shaded portion is 54 square miles and $\overline{SU}$ is 3 miles longer than $\overline{ST}$, what is the length, in miles, of $\overline{TU}$?

   (A)   9
   (B) 12
   (C) 15
   (D) 17
   (E) 18

4. John is now three times Pat's age. Four years from now, John will be x years old. In terms of x, how old is Pat now?

   (A) $\frac{x+4}{3}$

   (B) $3x$

   (C) $x+4$

   (D) $x-4$

   (E) $\frac{x-4}{3}$

For the following item, consider the answers separately and select all that apply.

5. If s, t, and u are different positive integers and $\frac{s}{t}$ and $\frac{t}{u}$ are also positive integers, which of the following can be a positive integer?

   Indicate **all** such equations.

   (A) $s \cdot t$

   (B) $\frac{u}{s}$

   (C) $(s+t)u$

Game Plan

Build Foundational Quantitative Reasoning Skills

This course includes a Quantitative Reasoning Supplement in Appendix B (p. 563). If you found the Quantitative Reasoning sections of your pre-assessment challenging, review the supplemental material to enhance your basic quantitative reasoning skills. (Your instructor may also choose to cover this material in class.)

Answer the Question That Is Being Asked

Read the Directions Carefully

Multiple-choice items that ask you to select more than one answer may instruct you to select a specific number of answer choices. Don't forget to read the directions for these items carefully. You will be able to select all the answer choices, but you will receive credit if you select *only* the correct answers. Use the "Review" feature to confirm that you have followed the directions for each item; any items you have not answered will be labeled "Not answered," and items you have answered with the incorrect number of answer choices will be marked "Incomplete." Make sure, before time runs out, that each item is labeled "Answered."

Read the Question Carefully

Questions can ask about money spent or amount remaining, the number of odd or even integers, the area of the shaded or unshaded parts of a figure, and countless variations on these themes. The more complex the item stem, the easier it is to misread it and set off on the wrong track. If an item stem is very long, you may want to make a note on scratch paper of what is being asked for.

> **Example:**
>
> In a certain company, the ratio of management to non-management employees is 1 to 15. If the number of management employees is increased by 4 and the number of non-management employees is decreased by 20, the ratio of management to non-management employees would be 1 to 11. How many management employees would the company have after the changes?
>
> (A)   4
> (B)   12
> (C)   16
> (D)   20
> (E)   24
>
> From the given information, it is possible to create a system of equations: $\frac{M}{N} = \frac{1}{15}$ and $\frac{M+4}{N-20} = \frac{1}{11}$. From the
>
> first equation, $N = 15M$. Substitute this into the second equation and solve for M: $\frac{M+4}{15M-20} = \frac{1}{11} \Rightarrow$
>
> $11(M+4) = 15M - 20 \Rightarrow 4M = 64 \Rightarrow M = 16$. But that does not mean that the answer to the item is (C). Instead, the question asks about the number of managers <u>after</u> the changes: $16 + 4 = 20$, (D). You'll avoid this kind of error if you read carefully.

Pay Attention to Units

Some items require that you convert units (for example, feet to inches or hours to minutes). The item stem will tell you which units to use, and if the test-writers sense any possible confusion, the units will be emphasized by being underlined, in bold face, or capitalized.

Example:

Traveling at approximately 186,000 miles per second, approximately how many miles will a beam of light travel in 10 <u>hours</u>?

(A) $1.86 \cdot 10^6$
(B) $1.11 \cdot 10^7$
(C) $6.70 \cdot 10^8$
(D) $1.11 \cdot 10^9$
(E) $6.70 \cdot 10^9$

The correct answer is (E): $d = \dfrac{186{,}000 \text{ miles}}{\text{second}} \cdot \dfrac{60 \text{ second}}{\text{minute}} \cdot \dfrac{60 \text{ minute}}{\text{hour}} \cdot 10 \text{ hours} \approx 6.69 \times 10^9 \text{ miles}$.

This is not to say that the test belabors this issue. There's not much point in asking an examinee to convert "miles per second" to "miles per hour" just to demonstrate the ability to do conversion. Rather, unit conversion ordinarily is necessary as an adjunct to another, more important aspect of the item, as here, where the tested concept is the use of scientific notation.

Pay Attention to Thought-Reversers

A thought-reverser is any word, such as "not," "except," or "but," that turns a question inside out. As with emphasized units, make sure that you pay attention to any thought-reversers.

Example:

How many integers in the set of integers from 1 to 144, inclusive, are <u>not</u> a square of an integer?

(A)   0
(B)   2
(C)   12
(D) 132
(E) 144

Since 1 is the square of 1, and 144 is the square of 12, there are a total of 12 integers in the set of integers from 1 to 144, inclusive, that are a square of an integer (1^2, 2^2, 3^2, 4^2, 5^2, 6^2, 7^2, 8^2, 9^2, 10^2, 11^2, 12^2). Therefore, there are a total of $144 - 12 = 132$ integers in the set that are <u>not</u> a square of an integer, (D).

Use the Answer Choices

Later in the Quantitative Reasoning: Discrete Quantitative Lesson, you will learn some very powerful test-taking strategies that use the answer choices. For now, there are three procedural points to consider regarding answer choices.

Eliminate Answer Choices That Cannot Be Correct

Sometimes, the array of answer choices will include ones that, when taken at face value, seem plausible, but when examined more carefully, must be wrong.

Example:

In the figure above, a circle with center O and a radius of 2 is inscribed in a square. What is the area of the shaded portion of the figure?

(A) $2 - \pi$
(B) $4 - 2\pi$
(C) $16 - 2\pi$
(D) $16 - 4\pi$
(E) $16 - 6\pi$

The shaded area is equal to the area of the square minus the area of the circle. Since the radius of the circle is 2, the side of the square is 4 and its area is $4 \cdot 4 = 16$. The area of the circle is $\pi(2)^2 = 4\pi$. Therefore, the shaded area is $16 - 4\pi$, (D).

Notice that without even solving the item, you can eliminate answer choices. Take a closer look at (A), (B), and (E). Since π is approximately 3.14, (A), (B), and (E) are negative. Area, however, cannot be a negative number, so (A), (B), and (E) must be wrong, and you can eliminate them without doing any other work, Now, if you had to, you can make an educated guess from the remaining choices and the chance of guessing correctly is 50-50.

Use the Answer Choices to Check Your Math

One of the fundamental rules of math in school is to "check your work." On the GRE test, however, this is generally a waste of time for the multiple-choice math items. Let's say that you do a calculation (with or without the on-screen calculator) and the result is $23.10. If one of the choices is $23.10, pick it, confirm your answer, and move on to the next item. Do NOT check your arithmetic. Assuming you have made no <u>conceptual</u> errors, the possibility that you did the arithmetic or entered the formula on the calculator, made a mistake, and still got a value like $23.10 is too remote to consider. On the other hand, if you do not find a choice that matches your calculation, then you'd better check both your set-up of the problem and your arithmetic to find the error. In this way, the answer choices function as a feedback loop on the accuracy of your calculations.

Look for Shortcuts

One of the biggest advantages of the test preparation you're doing right now is the shortcuts that you'll learn.

Example:

The water pouring from a hose at a constant rate can fill a swimming pool in 5 hours. The water pouring from a second hose at a constant rate can fill the pool in 7 hours. If both hoses are used together, how long will it take to fill the pool?

(A) 1 hour
(B) 2 hours
(C) 2 hours and 55 minutes
(D) 6 hours
(E) 12 hours

Of course, you can solve this problem algebraically, or you can devise a shortcut using the strategy of "plug-and-chug" by assuming some numbers. Make a convenient assumption about the volume of the pool: since $5 \cdot 7 = 35$, assume that the capacity of the pool is 35 gallons. The larger hose fills the pool at $\frac{35 \text{ gallons}}{5 \text{ hours}} = 7$ gallons per hour and the smaller hose fills the pool at $\frac{35 \text{ gallons}}{7 \text{ hours}} = 5$ gallons per hour. So, both hoses together fill the pool at 12 gallons per hour. And the time it will take with both working together is $\frac{35 \text{ gallons}}{\frac{12 \text{ gallons}}{\text{hour}}} = 2\frac{11}{12}$ hours $= 2$ hours and 55 minutes, (C).

As you will learn later in the Quantitative Reasoning: Discrete Quantitative Lesson, there are several variations on the theme of shortcuts.

Don't Go Calculator Crazy

Simply because there is an on-screen calculator available for each item in the Quantitative Reasoning section does not mean that you should try to solve every item with the calculator. In fact, for most items, the calculator is the less efficient method of arriving at a solution.

Assume, for example, that you have to do the following arithmetic to get your answer: $\left(\frac{2}{3}\right)\left(\frac{7}{4}\right)\left(\frac{1}{6}\right)$. Since this problem involves single digit multiplication, it's going to be easier to do the arithmetic using your scratch paper than using the on-screen calculator: $\left(\frac{2}{3}\right)\left(\frac{7}{4}\right)\left(\frac{1}{6}\right) = \frac{2 \cdot 7 \cdot 1}{3 \cdot 4 \cdot 6} = \frac{14}{72} = \frac{7}{36}$.

By all means, use the calculator when it will be a definite advantage, but don't automatically assume that every item requires its use.

LESSON

The items in this section accompany the Quantitative Reasoning: Discrete Quantitative Lesson. You will work through the items with your instructor in class.

DIRECTIONS: Solve each problem and choose the correct answer, using the given directions.

NOTES: Some items require a single answer. Other items require one or more answer choices. Carefully read the directions for each item.

All numbers used are real numbers.

Unless otherwise indicated, all figures lie in a plane.

Geometric diagrams and figures **are not necessarily** drawn to scale, so do **not** assume lengths, angle measures, or other quantities are as they appear in a given figure. You should assume that lines shown as straight are straight and that the positions of points, and geometric objects in general, exist in the order shown. Base your answers to questions with geometric figures on reasoning, not visual estimation or measurement.

Coordinate systems and graphic data presentations **are** drawn to scale, so you can answer items based on visual estimation or measurement. Answers are on page 703.

Four Main Categories of Item-Types

Arithmetic

1. Of the following, which number is the greatest?

(A) 0.08
(B) 0.17
(C) 0.171
(D) 0.1077
(E) 0.10771

2. If the price of fertilizer has been decreased from 3 pounds for \$2 to 5 pounds for \$2, how many more pounds of fertilizer can be purchased for \$10 than could have been purchased before?

(A) 2
(B) 8
(C) 10
(D) 12
(E) 15

Algebra

3. If $\frac{2x-5}{3} = -4x$, then $x =$

(A) -1
(B) $-\frac{5}{14}$
(C) 0
(D) $\frac{5}{14}$
(E) 1

4. The oil-fired boiler in the basement of a school building consumes fuel at a rate of g gallons every h hours. Which of the following expressions can be used to calculate the amount of fuel consumed during m minutes of uninterrupted operation?

(A) ghm

(B) $\frac{g}{hm}$

(C) $\frac{60g}{hm}$

(D) $\frac{g}{60hm}$

(E) $\frac{gm}{60h}$

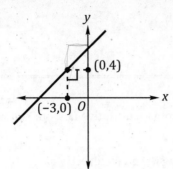

5. In the figure above, the line has a slope of 1. What is the y-intercept of the line?

(A) −5
(B) −3
(C) 0
(D) 3
(E) 7

Geometry

6. If a circle has a radius of 1, what is its area?

(A) $\frac{\pi}{2}$
(B) π
(C) 2π
(D) 4π
(E) π^2

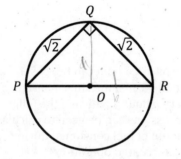

7. In the figure above, a triangle is inscribed in a circle with center O. What is the area of the circle?

(A) $\frac{\pi}{2}$
(B) $\frac{\pi}{\sqrt{2}}$
(C) π
(D) $\pi\sqrt{2}$
(E) 2π

Data Analysis

8. The average weight of the eight packages in a certain shipment is 6 pounds. If the heaviest package is removed, the average weight of the remaining packages is 5 pounds. What is the weight, in pounds, of the heaviest package?

(A) 6
(B) 8
(C) 10
(D) 13
(E) 15

9. If a jar contains r red marbles, b blue marbles, and g green marbles, which of the following expresses the probability that a marble drawn at random will NOT be red?

(A) $\frac{-r}{r+b+g}$
(B) $\frac{r}{r+b+g}$
(C) $\frac{b+g-r}{b+g+r}$
(D) $\frac{r}{b+g}$
(E) $\frac{b+g}{b+g+r}$

General Strategies

A Note about Figures

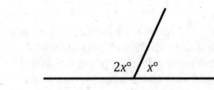

10. In the figure above, $x =$

(A) 15
(B) 30
(C) 45
(D) 60
(E) 120

Items #11–12 refer to the following figure.

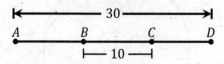

11. In the figure above, $\overline{AB} =$

(A) 5
(B) 10
(C) 15
(D) 20
(E) It cannot be determined from the information given.

12. In the figure above, $\overline{AB} + \overline{CD} =$

(A) 5
(B) 10
(C) 15
(D) 20
(E) It cannot be determined from the information given.

For the following item, consider the answers separately and select all that apply.

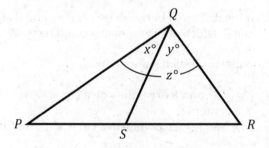

13. Which of the following must be true?

Indicate <u>all</u> such statements.

(A) $\overline{PR} > \overline{PS}$
(B) $z > x$
(C) $x + y = z$

Important Facts about the Answer Choices

Answer Choices Arranged in Order

14. Of the 2,400 students at John Jay High School, $\frac{1}{4}$ are seniors. If, due to overcrowding, $\frac{1}{3}$ of the seniors are transferred to other schools, what fraction of the remaining students at John Jay High School would be seniors?

(A) $\frac{1}{12}$

(B) $\frac{1}{8}$

(C) $\frac{1}{6}$

(D) $\frac{2}{11}$

(E) $\frac{3}{7}$

15. Metal X costs twice as much as Metal Y. If a certain amalgam is $\frac{1}{4}$ Metal X and $\frac{3}{4}$ Metal Y, what fraction of the cost of the amalgam is attributable to the cost of Metal X?

(A) $\frac{1}{8}$

(B) $\frac{1}{5}$

(C) $\frac{1}{4}$

(D) $\frac{2}{5}$

(E) $\frac{3}{5}$

16. Which of the following fractions is the largest?

(A) $\frac{111}{221}$

(B) $\frac{75}{151}$

(C) $\frac{333}{998}$

(D) $\frac{113}{225}$

(E) $\frac{101}{301}$

Wrong Answer Choices Correspond to Conceptual Errors

17. In a certain year, the number of girls who graduated from City High School was twice the number of boys. If $\frac{3}{4}$ of the girls and $\frac{5}{6}$ of the boys went to college immediately after graduation, what fraction of the graduates that year went to college immediately after graduation?

(A) $\frac{5}{36}$

(B) $\frac{16}{27}$

(C) $\frac{7}{9}$

(D) $\frac{29}{36}$

(E) $\frac{31}{36}$

18. A manager has been instructed to reduce the cost of a manufacturing process by 40 percent. Materials account for $\frac{2}{5}$ of the cost, and labor accounts for $\frac{3}{5}$ of the cost. If it is possible to cut materials costs by $\frac{1}{2}$, by what percent must labor costs be reduced in order to achieve the goal?

(A) 20%

(B) 25%

(C) $33\frac{1}{3}\%$

(D) 50%

(E) $66\frac{2}{3}\%$

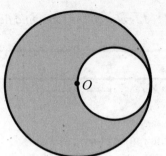

19. In the figure above, O is the center of the larger circle. If the radius of the larger circle is r, what is the area of the shaded portion of the figure?

(A) πr

(B) $\frac{3\pi r}{4}$

(C) $\frac{\pi r}{2}$

(D) $\frac{\pi r^2}{4}$

(E) $\frac{3\pi r^2}{4}$

Emphasized Words Require Special Attention

For the following item, consider the answers separately and select all that apply.

20. If the distances between points P, Q, and R are equal, which of the following could be true?

Indicate <u>all</u> such statements.

(A) P, Q, and R are points on a circle with center O.

(B) P and Q are points on a circle with center R.

(C) P, Q, and R are vertices of an equilateral triangle.

21. A jar contains black and white marbles. If there are 10 marbles in the jar, which of the following could <u>not</u> be the ratio of black to white marbles?

(A) 9:1

(B) 7:3

(C) 1:1

(D) 1:4

(E) 1:10

22. If n is a negative number, which of the following is the <u>least</u>?

(A) $-n$

(B) $n - n$

(C) $n + n$

(D) n^2

(E) n^4

23. If a machine produces 240 thingamabobs per hour, how many <u>minutes</u> are needed for the machine to produce 30 thingamabobs?

(A) 6
(B) 7.5
(C) 8
(D) 12
(E) 12.5

24. Of the 120 people in a room, $\frac{3}{5}$ are women. If $\frac{2}{3}$ of the people are married, what is the maximum number of women in the room who could be <u>unmarried</u>?

(A) 80
(B) 72
(C) 48
(D) 40
(E) 32

Answer the Question Being Asked

25. Three friends are playing a game in which each person simultaneously displays one of three hand signs: a clenched fist, an open palm, or two extended fingers. How many different combinations of the signs are possible?

(A) 3
(B) 9
(C) 10
(D) 12
(E) 27

26. Peter walked from point P to point Q and back again, a total distance of 2 miles. If he averaged 4 miles per hour on the trip from Point P to Point Q and 5 miles per hour on the return trip, what was his average walking speed for the entire trip?

(A) 4

(B) $4\frac{2}{9}$

(C) $4\frac{4}{9}$

(D) $4\frac{1}{2}$

(E) $4\frac{4}{5}$

27. After a 20 percent decrease in price, the cost of an item is D dollars. What was the price of the item before the decrease?

(A) $0.75D$
(B) $0.80D$
(C) $1.20D$
(D) $1.25D$
(E) $1.5D$

28. What is the largest number of non-overlapping sections that can be created when a circle is crossed by three straight lines?

(A) 3
(B) 4
(C) 5
(D) 6
(E) 7

Water Usage in Cubic Feet

29. The water meter at a factory displays the reading above. What is the <u>minimum</u> number of cubic feet of water the factory must use before four of the five digits on the meter are again the same?

(A) 10,000
(B) 1,000
(C) 999
(D) 666
(E) 9

30. If $\frac{1}{3}$ of the girls at a school equals $\frac{1}{5}$ of the total number of students, then what is the ratio of girls to boys at the school?

(A) 5:3
(B) 3:2
(C) 2:5
(D) 1:3
(E) 1:5

31. In a list of the first 100 positive integers, the digit 9 appears how many times?

(A) 9
(B) 10
(C) 11
(D) 19
(E) 20

32. A telephone call from City X to City Y costs $1.00 for the first 3 minutes and $0.25 for every minute thereafter. What is the maximum length of time (in minutes) that a caller could talk for $3.00?

(A) 8
(B) 10
(C) 11
(D) 12
(E) 13

33. If the radius of circle O is 20 percent less than the radius of circle P, the area of circle O is what percent of the area of circle P?

(A) 60%
(B) 64%
(C) 72%
(D) 80%
(E) 120%

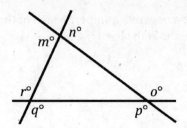

34. In the figure above, $m+n+o+p+q+r =$

(A) 360
(B) 540
(C) 720
(D) 900
(E) It cannot be determined from the information given.

Arithmetic Review and Strategies

Simple Arithmetic Manipulation—Just Do It

35. $\frac{8}{9} - \frac{7}{8} =$

(A) $\frac{1}{72}$

(B) $\frac{1}{8}$

(C) $\frac{1}{7}$

(D) $\frac{15}{72}$

(E) $\frac{15}{7}$

36. $\sqrt{1-\left(\frac{2}{9}+\frac{1}{36}+\frac{1}{18}\right)} =$

(A) $\frac{1}{5}$

(B) $\sqrt{\frac{2}{3}}$

(C) $\frac{5}{6}$

(D) 1

(E) $\sqrt{3}$

Complicated Arithmetic Manipulations—Look for Shortcuts

Simplifying

37. $\frac{1}{2} \cdot \frac{2}{3} \cdot \frac{3}{4} \cdot \frac{4}{5} \cdot \frac{5}{6} \cdot \frac{6}{7} \cdot \frac{7}{8} =$

(A) $\frac{1}{56}$

(B) $\frac{1}{8}$

(C) $\frac{28}{37}$

(D) $\frac{41}{43}$

(E) $\frac{55}{56}$

Factoring

38. $86(37) - 37(85) =$

(A) 0
(B) 1
(C) 37
(D) 85
(E) 86

39. Which of the following is the prime factorization of 120?

(A) (2)(2)(3)(10)
(B) (2)(3)(4)(5)
(C) (2)(2)(2)(3)(5)
(D) (2)(2)(2)(3)(6)
(E) (2)(3)(3)(3)(5)

Approximation

40. $\frac{0.2521 \cdot 8.012}{1.014}$ is approximately equal to

(A) 0.25
(B) 0.5
(C) 1.0
(D) 1.5
(E) 2.0

The "Flying–X" Method

41. Cars are entering the parking lot of a suburban shopping mall at the rate of one car every 3 seconds and leaving at the rate of one car every 7 seconds. The parking lot is filling at a rate of approximately one car every

(A) 6 seconds
(B) $5\frac{1}{3}$ seconds
(C) $5\frac{1}{4}$ seconds
(D) $3\frac{3}{7}$ seconds
(E) $2\frac{1}{10}$ seconds

Decimal-Fraction Equivalents

42. Which of the following is a pair of numbers that are not equal?

(A) $\frac{63}{6}$, $\frac{21}{2}$

(B) 0.3%, 0.003

(C) $\frac{44}{77}$, $\frac{4}{7}$

(D) $\frac{3}{8}$, 0.375

(E) $\sqrt{3^2}$, 9

Complicated Arithmetic Application Problems—Bridge the Gap

43. If the senior class has 360 students, of whom $\frac{5}{12}$ are women, and the junior class has 350 students, of whom $\frac{4}{7}$ are women, how many more women are there in the junior class than in the senior class?

(A) $(360-350)\left(\frac{4}{7}-\frac{5}{12}\right)$

(B) $\dfrac{(360-350)\left(\frac{4}{7}-\frac{5}{12}\right)}{2}$

(C) $\left(\frac{4}{7} \cdot \frac{5}{12}\right)(360-350)$

(D) $\left(\frac{4}{7} \cdot 350\right) - \left(\frac{5}{12} \cdot 360\right)$

(E) $\left(\frac{5}{12} \cdot 360\right) - \left(\frac{4}{7} \cdot 350\right)$

44. If the price of candy increases from 5 pounds for $7 to 3 pounds for $7, how much less candy (in pounds) can be purchased for $3.50 at the new price than at the old price?

(A) $\frac{2}{7}$

(B) 1

(C) $1\frac{17}{35}$

(D) 2

(E) $3\frac{34}{35}$

45. Charles spent $\frac{2}{5}$ of the money that he had saved to start a new business on renovating a store and $\frac{2}{3}$ of what remained on inventory. If he still had $2,000, how much had Charles saved to start the new business?

(A) $10,000

(B) $8,000

(C) $7,500

(D) $5,000

(E) $4,000

46. Diana spent $\frac{1}{2}$ of her allowance on a book and another $3 on lunch. If she still had $\frac{1}{6}$ of her original allowance, how much is Diana's allowance?

(A) $24

(B) $18

(C) $15

(D) $12

(E) $9

47. A company bought a load of water-damaged copy paper, estimating that $\frac{2}{3}$ of the reams could be salvaged, in which case the cost per salvageable ream would be $0.72. If it later turned out that $\frac{3}{4}$ of the reams were salvageable, then what was the actual cost per salvageable ream?

(A) $0.56

(B) $0.60

(C) $0.64

(D) $0.68

(E) $0.80

48. During a three-hour rush, the average number (arithmetic mean) of vehicles passing through a particular toll plaza was 3,000 vehicles per hour. The number of cars passing through the toll plaza during the second hour of the rush was 1.5 times that of the number passing through the toll plaza during the first hour, and the number during the third hour was 2.5 times that of the number of the first hour. How many vehicles passed through the toll plaza during the second hour?

(A) 1,500

(B) 2,700

(C) 3,000

(D) 3,600

(E) 4,500

Common Arithmetic Problems

Properties of Numbers

49. If $0 < x < 1$, which of the following is the largest?

(A) x

(B) $2x$

(C) x^2

(D) x^3

(E) $x+1$

For the following item, consider the answers separately and select all that apply.

50. When the integer n is divided by 4, the remainder is 2. Which of the following is a multiple of 4?

Indicate <u>all</u> such numbers.

(A) $n-2$
(B) $n+2$
(C) $2n$
(D) $3n$
(E) $4n$

Absolute Value

51. $|-2|+3-|-4|=?$

(A) -5
(B) -4
(C) -1
(D) 1
(E) 9

52. $|5|-|-5|+|-3|=?$

(A) -8
(B) -3
(C) 3
(D) 8
(E) 13

Percents

53. A dealer sold two used boats for $3,600 each, making a profit of 25 percent on one and taking a loss of 20 percent on the other. What was the dealer's net gain or loss on the two transactions?

(A) $540 loss
(B) $180 loss
(C) $90 loss
(D) $120 gain
(E) $360 gain

54. At a certain college, 25 percent of the students pay out-of-state tuition while the other 75 percent pay in-state tuition. Half of the students are enrolled in the College of Arts and Sciences while the other half are enrolled in technical schools. If 10 percent of the students enrolled in technical schools pay out-of-state tuition, what percent of the students enrolled in the College of Arts and Sciences pay in-state tuition?

(A) 15%
(B) 30%
(C) 40%
(D) 50%
(E) 60%

55. A pound of water is evaporated from 6 pounds of seawater containing 4 percent salt. The percentage of salt in the remaining solution is

(A) 3.6%
(B) 4%
(C) 4.8%
(D) 5.2%
(E) 6%

Ratios

56. A groom must divide 12 quarts of oats between two horses. If Dobbin is to receive twice as much as Pegasus, how many quarts of oats should the groom give to Dobbin?

(A) 4
(B) 6
(C) 8
(D) 9
(E) 10

57. If the ratio of John's allowance to Lucy's allowance is 3:2, and the ratio of Lucy's allowance to Bob's allowance is 3:4, what is the ratio of John's allowance to Bob's allowance?

(A) $1:6$
(B) $2:5$
(C) $1:2$
(D) $3:4$
(E) $9:8$

58. The Adams Gift Company sold 4,800 deluxe castings of a bronze statue of Pegasus before offering collectors the regular edition. After its release, the regular edition outsold the deluxe edition by a ratio of $4:1$. If a total of 17,400 statues were sold, how many of the deluxe editions were sold?

(A) 2,520
(B) 7,320
(C) 10,080
(D) 12,600
(E) 13,180

Rates

59. Doreen can wash her car in 15 minutes, while her younger brother Dave takes twice as long to do the same job. If they work together, how many minutes will the job take them?

(A) 5
(B) $7\frac{1}{2}$
(C) 10
(D) $22\frac{1}{2}$
(E) 30

60. Pipe P can drain the liquid from a tank in $\frac{3}{4}$ the time that it takes Pipe Q to drain it and in $\frac{2}{3}$ the time that it takes Pipe R to drain it. If all three pipes operating simultaneously but independently are used to drain liquid from the tank, then Pipe Q drains what portion of the liquid from the tank?

(A) $\frac{9}{29}$
(B) $\frac{8}{23}$
(C) $\frac{3}{8}$
(D) $\frac{17}{29}$
(E) $\frac{3}{4}$

Proportions and Direct-Inverse Variation

61. If 4.5 pounds of chocolate cost $10, how many pounds of chocolate can be purchased for $12?

(A) $4\frac{3}{4}$
(B) $5\frac{2}{5}$
(C) $5\frac{1}{2}$
(D) $5\frac{3}{4}$
(E) 6

62. At a certain school, 45 percent of the students bought a yearbook. If 540 students bought yearbooks, how many students did not buy yearbooks?

(A) 243
(B) 540
(C) 575
(D) 660
(E) 957

63. Walking at a constant rate of 4 miles per hour, it takes Jill exactly 1 hour to walk home from school. If she walks at a constant rate of 5 miles per hour, how many <u>minutes</u> will the trip take?

(A) 48
(B) 54
(C) 56
(D) 72
(E) 112

Arithmetic Alternative Strategies

"Test-the-Test"

64. Which of the following is the larger of two numbers, the product of which is 600 and the sum of which is five times the difference between the two?

(A) 10
(B) 15
(C) 20
(D) 30
(E) 50

65. If $\frac{1}{3}$ of a number is 3 more than $\frac{1}{4}$ of the number, then what is the number?

(A) 18
(B) 24
(C) 30
(D) 36
(E) 48

66. If $\frac{3}{5}$ of a number is 4 more than $\frac{1}{2}$ of the number, then what is the number?

(A) 20
(B) 28
(C) 35
(D) 40
(E) 56

67. When both 16 and 9 are divided by n, the remainder is 2. What is n?

(A) 3
(B) 4
(C) 5
(D) 6
(E) 7

68. The sum of the digits of a three-digit number is 16. If the tens digit of the number is 3 times the units digit, and the units digit is $\frac{1}{4}$ of the hundreds digit, then what is the number?

(A) 446
(B) 561
(C) 682
(D) 862
(E) 914

69. If the sum of five consecutive integers is 40, what is the smallest of the five integers?

(A) 4
(B) 5
(C) 6
(D) 7
(E) 8

"Plug-and-Chug"

70. If n is any integer, which of the following is always an odd integer?

(A) $n-1$
(B) $n+1$
(C) $n+2$
(D) $2n+1$
(E) $2n+2$

71. In a clinical trial of an experimental drug, four out of five patients were given the drug while the other one out of five was given a placebo. Of the patients given the drug, 95 percent showed significant improvement; the other 5 percent did not show significant improvement. Of the patients given the placebo, 20 percent showed significant improvement; the others did not. What percent of the patients who showed significant improvement were given the placebo?

(A) 4%
(B) 5%
(C) 8%
(D) 16%
(E) 25%

Algebra Review and Strategies

Simple Algebra Manipulation— Just Do It

72. If $a^3 + b = 3 + a^3$, then $b =$

(A) 3^3
(B) $3\sqrt{3}$
(C) 3
(D) $\sqrt[3]{3}$
(E) $-\sqrt{3}$

73. If $n+1+n+2+n+3 = 1+2+3$, then $n =$

(A) −3
(B) −1
(C) 0
(D) 1
(E) 3

Manipulation of Algebraic Expressions

Evaluating Expressions

74. If $x = 2$, what is the value of $x^2 + 2x - 2$?

    (A) -2
    (B) 0
    (C) 2
    (D) 4
    (E) 6

Manipulating Expressions Involving Exponents

75. $\dfrac{9(x^2 y^3)^6}{(3x^6 y^9)^2} =$

    (A) 1
    (B) 3
    (C) $x^2 y^3$
    (D) $3x^2 y^3$
    (E) $x^{12} y^{12}$

Factoring Expressions

76. $\dfrac{x^2 - y^2}{x + y} =$

    (A) $x^2 - y^2$
    (B) $x^2 + y^2$
    (C) $x^2 + y$
    (D) $x + y^2$
    (E) $x - y$

77. $\dfrac{x^2 - x - 6}{x + 2} =$

    (A) $x^2 - \frac{x}{2} - 3$
    (B) $x^2 - 2$
    (C) $x - 2$
    (D) $x - 3$
    (E) x

Creating Algebraic Expressions

78. If the cost of x meters of wire is d dollars, what is the cost, in dollars, of y meters of wires at the same rate?

    (A) dy
    (B) $\dfrac{dy}{x}$
    (C) $\dfrac{dx}{y}$
    (D) dx
    (E) $\dfrac{xy}{d}$

79. A music store purchased c copies of a particular CD for d dollars per copy. If the store gave away p copies for promotional purposes and sold the remaining copies for k dollars each, which of the following represents the gross profit on the sale of the CDs?

    (A) $k(c - p) - cd$
    (B) $d(c - p) - kc$
    (C) $c(k - p) - cd$
    (D) $p(k - c) - d$
    (E) $p(k - cd)$

80. In a game, special cards are printed with one of three symbols—a star, a circle, or a rectangle. A star is worth 3 points more than a circle and a circle is worth 3 points more than a rectangle. If 3 rectangles are worth x points, a player holding 5 circles and 4 stars has how many points?

    (A) $3x + 12$
    (B) $3x + 39$
    (C) $3x + 42$
    (D) $7x + 39$
    (E) $7x + 42$

81. Originally, an order consisting of T units was to have been shipped in N crates with x units in each crate. If new shipping regulations require the use of an additional S crates, and the order will be shipped with y units in each crate, which of the following represents the difference between x and y?

(A) $\frac{N}{T}$

(B) $\frac{S}{T}$

(C) $\frac{N+S}{T}$

(D) $\frac{TS}{N(N+S)}$

(E) $\frac{TS}{N(N-S)}$

Functions

82. If $[x] = x^2 - x$ for all integers. then $[[3]] = ?$

(A) 27
(B) 30
(C) 58
(D) 72
(E) 121

83. For all numbers $x, y,$ and z, the operation $x * y = x - xy$. What is $x * (y * z)$?

(A) $x - xy + xyz$

(B) $x - xy - xz - xyz$

(C) $x + xy - xz + xyz$

(D) $x^2 - xy^2 - xyz$

(E) $x^2 - xy^2 - x^2yz$

Solving Equations

One Equation with One Variable

84. If $(2+3)(1+x) = 25$, then $x =$

(A) $\frac{1}{5}$

(B) $\frac{1}{4}$

(C) 1

(D) 4

(E) 5

85. A train running between two towns arrives at its destination 10 minutes late when it goes 40 miles per hour and 16 minutes late when it goes 30 miles per hour. The distance in miles between the towns is

(A) $8\frac{6}{7}$
(B) 12
(C) 192
(D) 560
(E) 720

One Equation with Two Variables

86. If $x + y = 3$, then $2x + 2y =$

(A) $\frac{1}{3}$

(B) $\frac{1}{2}$

(C) $\frac{2}{3}$

(D) 6

(E) It cannot be determined from the information given.

Two Equations with Two Variables

87. If $2x + y = 8$ and $x - y = 1$, then $x =$

(A) −2
(B) −1
(C) 0
(D) 1
(E) 3

Quadratic Equations and Relations

For the following item, consider the answers separately and select all that apply.

88. If $x^2 - 3x = 4$, then what are the possible values of x?

Indicate <u>all</u> such values.

(A) −4
(B) −1
(C) 1
(D) 4

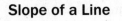

Coordinate Geometry

Slope of a Line

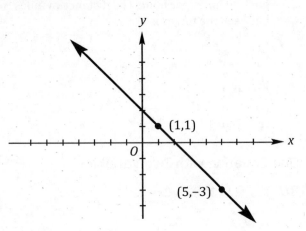

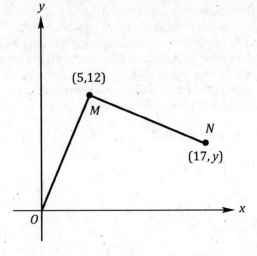

89. In the figure above, what is the slope of the line?

(A) −3
(B) −2
(C) −1
(D) 1
(E) 2

92. In the coordinate plane above, $\overline{MO} \cong \overline{MN}$ and $\overline{MO} \perp \overline{MN}$. What is the value of y?

(A) 5
(B) 7
(C) 12
(D) 13
(E) 17

Slope-Intercept Form of a Linear Equation

90. A line includes the points (2,3) and (3,6). What is the equation of the line?

(A) $y = 2x - 3$
(B) $y = 3x - 3$

(C) $y = \dfrac{3x - 3}{2}$

(D) $y = 3x + 3$
(E) $y = x - 3$

Distance Formula

91. What is the distance between the points (−3,−2) and (3,3)?

(A) $\sqrt{3}$
(B) $2\sqrt{3}$
(C) 5
(D) $\sqrt{29}$
(E) $\sqrt{61}$

Graphs of Linear Equations

93. A school rented a hotel ballroom for a dance. The cost of the rental is $1500 plus $5.00 per person who attends. Each person who attends will pay an admission charge of $12.50. If x represents the number of people who attend, which of the graphs can be used to determine how many people must attend for the admission charges to cover exactly the cost of renting the ballroom?

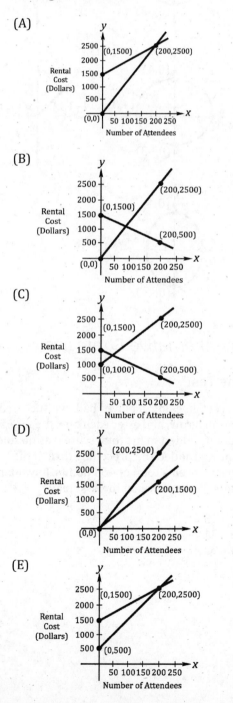

Graphs of First-Degree Inequalities

94. Which of the following is the graph of the inequality $y \geq 2x$?

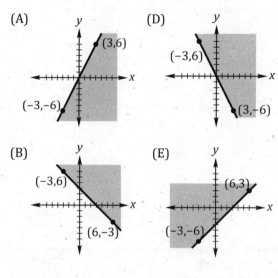

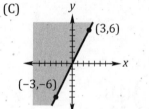

Graphs of Quadratic Equations and Relations

95. Which of the following is the graph of the equation $(x-1)^2 + y^2 = 4$?

(A)

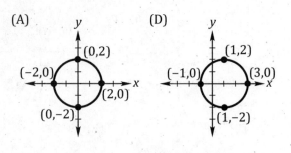

(D)

(B)

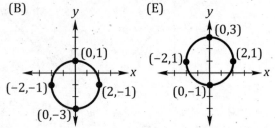

(E)

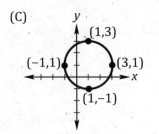

(C)

96. Which of the following is the graph of the equation $\dfrac{x^2}{9} + \dfrac{y^2}{16} = 1$?

(A)

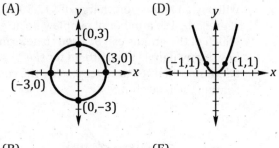

(D)

(B)

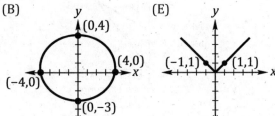

(E)

(C)

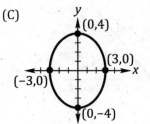

Algebra Alternative Strategies

"Test-the-Test"

97. In a certain game, a player had five successful turns in a row, and after each one, the number of points added to his total score was double what was added the preceding turn. If the player scored a total of 465 points, how many points did he score on the first play?

(A) 15
(B) 31
(C) 93
(D) 155
(E) 270

98. Harold is twice as old as Jack, who is 3 years older than Dan. If Harold's age is 5 times Dan's age, how old in years is Jack?

(A) 2
(B) 4
(C) 5
(D) 8
(E) 10

99. Which of the following is the equation for the line with a slope of 2 that includes point $(0,2)$?

(A) $y = x - 1$
(B) $y = 2x - 1$
(C) $y = 2x - 2$
(D) $y = 2x + 2$
(E) $y = x + 1$

100. On a playground, there are x seesaws. If 50 children are all riding on seesaws, two to a seesaw, and five seesaws are not in use, what is x?

(A) 15
(B) 20
(C) 25
(D) 30
(E) 35

"Plug-and-Chug"

101. At a certain firm, d gallons of fuel are needed per day for each truck. At this rate, g gallons of fuel will supply t trucks for how many days?

(A) $\frac{dt}{g}$

(B) $\frac{gt}{d}$

(C) dgt

(D) $\frac{t}{dg}$

(E) $\frac{g}{dt}$

102. Y years ago, Paul was twice as old as Bob. If Bob is now 18 years old, how old is Paul in terms of Y?

(A) $36 + Y$
(B) $18 + Y$
(C) $18 - Y$
(D) $36 - Y$
(E) $36 - 2Y$

103. If pencils cost x cents each, how many pencils can be purchased for y dollars?

(A) $\frac{100}{xy}$

(B) $\frac{xy}{100}$

(C) $\frac{100y}{x}$

(D) $\frac{y}{100x}$

(E) $100xy$

104. A tank with capacity t gallons is empty. If water flows into the tank from Pipe A at the rate of x gallons per minute, and water is pumped out by Pipe B at the rate of y gallons per minute, and x is greater than y, in how many minutes will the tank be filled?

(A) $\frac{t}{y - x}$

(B) $\frac{t}{x - y}$

(C) $\frac{t - x}{y}$

(D) $\frac{x - y}{60t}$

(E) $\frac{60t}{xy}$

105. If a train travels m miles in h hours and 45 minutes, what is its average speed in miles per hour?

(A) $\frac{m}{h + \frac{3}{4}}$

(B) $\frac{m}{1\frac{3}{4}h}$

(C) $m\left(h + \frac{3}{4}\right)$

(D) $\frac{m + 45}{h}$

(E) $\frac{h}{m + 45}$

106. A merchant increased the original price of an item by 10 percent. If she then reduces the new price by 10 percent, the final result in terms of the original price is

(A) a decrease of 11 percent
(B) a decrease of 1 percent
(C) no net change
(D) an increase of 1 percent
(E) an increase of 11 percent

107. Machine X produces w widgets in 5 minutes. Machine X and Machine Y, working at the same time, produce w widgets in 2 minutes. How long will it take Machine Y working alone to produce w widgets?

(A) 2 minutes, 30 seconds
(B) 2 minutes, 40 seconds
(C) 3 minutes, 20 seconds
(D) 3 minutes, 30 seconds
(E) 3 minutes, 40 seconds

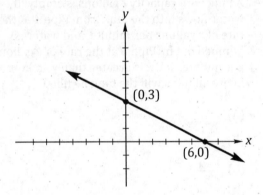

108. The figure above is the graph of which of the following equations?

(A) $x + 2y = 6$
(B) $2x + y = 6$
(C) $x + \frac{y}{2} = 6$
(D) $\frac{x}{2} + y = 2$
(E) $x - 3y = 2$

Geometry Review and Strategies

Complex Figures

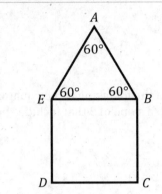

109. If $BCDE$ is a square with an area of 4, what is the perimeter of $\triangle ABE$?

(A) 3
(B) 4
(C) 6
(D) 8
(E) 12

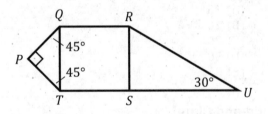

110. In the figure above, if $QRST$ is a square and $\overline{PQ} = \sqrt{2}$, what is the length of $\overline{RU}$?

(A) $\sqrt{2}$
(B) $\sqrt{6}$
(C) $2\sqrt{2}$
(D) 4
(E) $4\sqrt{3}$

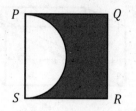

111. In the figure above, *PQRS* is a square, and $\overline{PS}$ is the diameter of a semicircle. If $\overline{PQ} = 2$, what is the area of the shaded portion of the diagram?

(A) $4 - 2\pi$
(B) $4 - \pi$
(C) $4 - \frac{\pi}{2}$
(D) $8 - \pi$
(E) $8 - \frac{\pi}{2}$

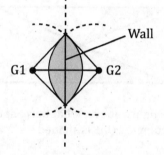

112. In the figure above, two guard stations, G1 and G2, are both 80 yards from the wall on either side, as shown. The line segment between the two guard stations is perpendicular to the wall. Each station has a spotlight projected onto the wall that illuminates a circular region with a radius of 100 yards. What is the length, in yards, of the portion of the wall that is illuminated by both security lights?

(A) 120
(B) 90
(C) 75
(D) 60
(E) 45

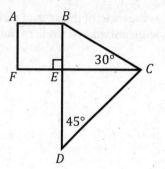

113. In the figure above, square *ABEF* has an area of 9. What is the area of $\triangle ECD$?

(A) $3\sqrt{2}$
(B) $3\sqrt{3}$
(C) 6
(D) $\frac{9\sqrt{3}}{2}$
(E) $\frac{27}{2}$

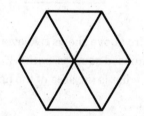

114. In the figure above, if each line segment has a length of 1, what is the area of the hexagonal region?

(A) $\frac{\sqrt{3}}{2}$
(B) $\sqrt{3}$
(C) $\frac{3\sqrt{3}}{2}$
(D) $2\sqrt{3}$
(E) $6\sqrt{3}$

115. What is the ratio of the area of an equilateral triangle inscribed in a circle to the area of the circle?

(A) $\pi\sqrt{3}$

(B) $\frac{\pi\sqrt{3}}{2}$

(C) $\frac{\sqrt{3}}{2}$

(D) $\frac{\sqrt{3}}{4\pi}$

(E) $\frac{3\sqrt{3}}{4\pi}$

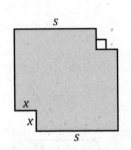

116. The figure above shows two overlapping and superimposed squares, both with side s. If $x = \frac{1}{4}s$, what is the area of the figure?

(A) $\frac{23s^2}{16}$

(B) s^2

(C) $\frac{3s^2}{4}$

(D) $\frac{5s^2}{8}$

(E) $\frac{9s^2}{16}$

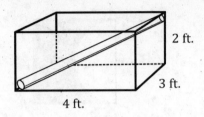

117. A glass tube used in scientific experiments is packed in a crate of dimensions shown. Which of the following measurements, in feet, most closely approximates the length of the tube?

(A) $\sqrt{13}$

(B) $\sqrt{29}$

(C) $\sqrt{41}$

(D) $2\sqrt{13}$

(E) 24

118. In the figure above, what percent of the area of rectangle *PQRS* is shaded?

(A) 20

(B) 25

(C) 30

(D) $33\frac{1}{3}$

(E) 35

Geometry Alternative Strategies

"Test-the-Test"

119. What is the width of a rectangle with an area of $48x^2$ and a length of $24x$?

(A) 2

(B) $2x$

(C) $24x$

(D) $2x^2$

(E) $2x^3$

For the following item, consider the answers separately and select all that apply.

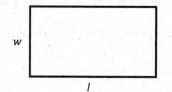

120. In the figure above, three lines intersect as shown. Which of the following must be true?

Indicate <u>all</u> such statements.

(A) $a = x$

(B) $y + z = b + c$

(C) $x + a = y + b$

"Plug-and-Chug"

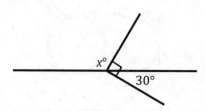

121. The figure above is a rectangle. If the width is increased by 20 percent, and the length is decreased by 10 percent, expressed in terms of w and l, what is the new area of the rectangle?

(A) $0.09wl$

(B) $0.92wl$

(C) $1.1wl$

(D) $1.08wl$

(E) $1.3wl$

122. If each of the dimensions of a rectangle is increased 100 percent, the area is increased by

(A) 100%

(B) 200%

(C) 300%

(D) 400%

(E) 500%

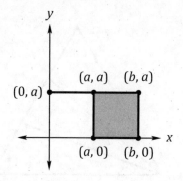

123. What is the area of the shaded portion of the figure above, expressed in terms of a and b?

(A) $a(b-a)$

(B) $a(a-b)$

(C) $b(a-b)$

(D) $b(b-a)$

(E) ab

"Guesstimate"

124. In the figure above, what is the value of x?

(A) 30

(B) 65

(C) 120

(D) 150

(E) 170

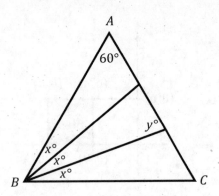

125. In the figure above, $\overline{AB} = \overline{BC} = \overline{CA}$. What is the value of y?

(A) 20
(B) 60
(C) 80
(D) 100
(E) 120

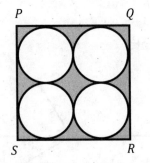

126. In the figure above, $PQRS$ is a square and each of the four circles has a radius of r. What fractional part of the area of the square is shaded?

(A) $\dfrac{\pi - 4}{2}$

(B) $\dfrac{4 - \pi}{4}$

(C) $\dfrac{\pi}{4}$

(D) $\dfrac{4}{\pi}$

(E) π

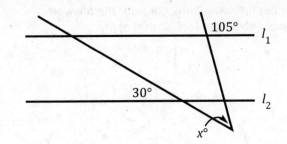

127. In the figure above, if $l_1 \parallel l_2$, then $x =$

(A) 20
(B) 30
(C) 45
(D) 65
(E) 130

Measure

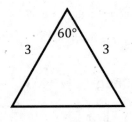

128. The perimeter of the triangle shown above is

(A) $3\sqrt{2}$
(B) 6
(C) 7.5
(D) 9
(E) $9\sqrt{2}$

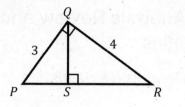

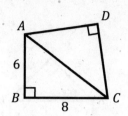

129. In the figure above, what is the length of $\overline{QS}$?

(A) $\frac{25}{3}$

(B) $\frac{20}{3}$

(C) $\frac{15}{4}$

(D) $\frac{12}{5}$

(E) $\frac{7}{5}$

131. In the figure above, $\overline{AD} = \overline{DC}$. What is $\overline{AD} + \overline{DC}$?

(A) $18\sqrt{2}$

(B) 18

(C) $10\sqrt{2}$

(D) 10

(E) $6\sqrt{2}$

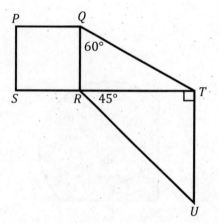

130. In the figure above, $\overline{AC} =$

(A) $30\sqrt{2}$

(B) 50

(C) 75

(D) $60\sqrt{2}$

(E) 100

132. In the figure above, if SRT is a straight line and $PQRS$ is a square with the area of 4, what is the area of triangle RTU?

(A) 2

(B) $2\sqrt{3}$

(C) 4

(D) $3\sqrt{3}$

(E) 6

"Meastimate"

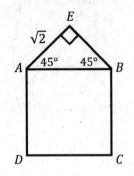

133. In the figure above, what is the area of square *ABCD*?

(A) 2
(B) $2\sqrt{2}$
(C) 4
(D) $4\sqrt{2}$
(E) 8

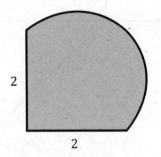

134. If the figure above is composed of a semicircle and a right triangle, what is the area of the shaded region?

(A) $\pi + \sqrt{2}$
(B) $\pi + 2$
(C) $2\pi + 1$
(D) $\sqrt{2\pi} + 1$
(E) $\sqrt{2\pi} + \sqrt{2}$

Data Analysis Review and Strategies

Basic Descriptive Statistics

Mean

135. For a certain student, the average of ten test scores is 80. If the high and low scores are dropped, the average is 81. What is the average of the high and low scores?

(A) 76
(B) 78
(C) 80
(D) 81
(E) 82

136. The average of eight numbers is 6; the average of six other numbers is 8. What is the average of all 14 numbers?

(A) 6
(B) $6\frac{6}{7}$
(C) 7
(D) $7\frac{2}{7}$
(E) $8\frac{1}{7}$

137. In a certain course, a student's final exam grade is weighted twice as heavily as his midterm grade. If a student receives a score of 84 on his final exam and 90 on his midterm, what is his average for the course?

(A) 88
(B) 87.5
(C) 86
(D) 85.5
(E) 85

Median

138. The number of employment applications received by a certain firm per month during 1994 was:

$$8, 3, 5, 3, 4, 3, 1, 0, 3, 4, 0, 7$$

What is the median number of applications?

(A) 3
(B) 4
(C) 5
(D) 6
(E) 7

Mode

139. The monthly electric bills for a given year were as follows: $40, 38, 36, 38, 34, 34, 30, 32, 34, 37, 39, and 40. What is the mode?

(A) $33
(B) $34
(C) $35
(D) $36
(E) $37

Range

140. During Jennifer's drive to work, she notices that gas prices vary. She sees prices of $3.28, $3.46, $3.16, $3.89, and $3.57. What is the range of the gas prices she saw?

(A) 0.18
(B) 0.29
(C) 0.61
(D) 0.73
(E) 0.89

Standard Deviation

141. The salary scale for players in a certain sports league is determined statistically by reference to a curve with a normal distribution. In 1960, the mean salary for players in the league was $10,000 with a standard deviation of $1000. That year, rookie players were paid $8,000. In 2010, the mean salary for players in the league was $1,175,000 with a standard deviation of $300,000. Rookies in 2010 were paid salaries in a dollar amount equal to a position on the normal curve for 2010 that rookie players were paid in the year 1960. What was the salary for rookie players in 2010?

(A) $1,475,000
(B) $1,175,000
(C) $875,000
(D) $575,000
(E) $275,000

Quartiles and Interquartile Range

142. During the last two weeks of January, Billy recorded the following outside temperatures (in °F) for each day: 24, 22, 7, 6, 10, 9, 9, 5, 1, 8, 14, 16, 9, 14. Which of the following is the interquartile range of Billy's data?

(A) 6
(B) 7
(C) 9
(D) 14
(E) 16

Counting Methods

Permutations

143. In how many arrangements can a theater usher seat 4 men and 3 women in a row of 7 seats if the men are to have the first, third, fourth, and seventh seats?

(A) 6
(B) 12
(C) 24
(D) 144
(E) 840

144. Five candidates are running for office. The candidates who come in first, second, and third place will be elected president, vice-president, and treasurer, respectively. How many outcomes for president, vice-president, and treasurer are there?

(A) 15
(B) 24
(C) 30
(D) 60
(E) 120

Combinations

145. Recipes are filed in a recipe box according to at least 12 different color codes. If a combination of three different colors is chosen to represent each color code and if each color code is uniquely represented by that choice of three colors, what is the minimum number of colors needed for the coding? (Assume that the order of the colors in a combination does not matter.)

(A) 3
(B) 4
(C) 5
(D) 6
(E) 10

146. Three students from among a group of five nominees are to be named to a committee. How many different groups of three students are available to be named?

(A) 3
(B) 6
(C) 10
(D) 20
(E) 60

147. If Set $A = \{1, 2, 3, 4, 5, 6\}$ and Set $B = \{1, 2, 3, 4, 5, 6\}$, what is the probability that the sum of one number from Set A and one number from Set B will total 7?

(A) $\frac{1}{12}$

(B) $\frac{5}{36}$

(C) $\frac{1}{6}$

(D) $\frac{1}{5}$

(E) $\frac{1}{3}$

Probability

The Dark Night	History of Canada	RING MORE THAN ONCE	A Bright Morning	Chemistry	George Washington
					C. Adams
		Mary Smith		Victor Brown	
Mary Smith	Carol Kim		T. Jackson		
•Mystery•	•Textbook•	•Mystery•	•Mystery•	•Textbook•	•Biography•

148. If a book is selected at random from the collection shown above, which of the following has the greatest probability of being selected?

(A) A book by Mary Smith
(B) A textbook
(C) A mystery
(D) A book written by either Carol Kim or Victor Brown
(E) A biography

149. A jar originally contains two blue marbles and three red marbles. On a random draw, a red marble is removed and not replaced. On a subsequent random draw, what is the probability of choosing a blue marble?

(A) $\frac{1}{5}$

(B) $\frac{2}{5}$

(C) $\frac{1}{2}$

(D) $\frac{3}{5}$

(E) $\frac{2}{3}$

Venn Diagrams

150. At City High School, the marching band has 48 members and the orchestra has 36 members. If a total of 12 students belong to only one of the two groups and all students belong to at least one group, how many students belong to both groups?

(A) 12
(B) 18
(C) 36
(D) 48
(E) 72

QUIZZES

This section contains three Discrete Quantitative quizzes. Complete each quiz under timed conditions. Answers are on page 704.

Quiz I

(10 items; 15 minutes)

DIRECTIONS: Solve each problem and choose the correct answer, using the given directions.

NOTES: Unless otherwise indicated, all figures lie in a plane.

Geometric diagrams and figures ARE NOT NECESSARILY drawn to scale. Coordinate systems and graphic data presentations ARE drawn to scale.

You can assume that lines shown as straight are straight and that the positions of points, angles, regions, etc. exist in the order shown.

All numbers used are real numbers.

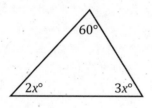

1. In the triangle above, $x =$

(A) 24
(B) 20
(C) 16
(D) 12
(E) 10

2. A normal dozen contains 12 items, and a baker's dozen contains 13 items. If x is the number of items that could be measured either in a whole number of normal dozens or in a whole number of baker's dozens, what is the minimum value of x?

(A) 1
(B) 12
(C) 13
(D) 25
(E) 156

3. A student begins heating a certain substance with a temperature of 50 degrees Celsius over a Bunsen burner. If the temperature of the substance will rise 20 degrees Celsius for each 24 minutes it remains over the burner, what will be the temperature, in degrees Celsius, of the substance after 18 minutes?

(A) 52
(B) 56
(C) 60
(D) 65
(E) 72

4. How many two-element subsets of the set below do <u>not</u> contain the pair red and green?

{red, green, yellow, blue}

(A) 2
(B) 4
(C) 5
(D) 6
(E) 10

5. If the ratio of men to women in a meeting is 8 to 7, what fractional part of the people at the meeting are women?

(A) $\frac{1}{56}$

(B) $\frac{1}{15}$

(C) $\frac{1}{7}$

(D) $\frac{7}{15}$

(E) $\frac{8}{7}$

6. The object of a certain board game is to use clues to identify a suspect and the weapon used to commit a crime. If there are three suspects and six weapons, how many different possible solutions to the game are there?

(A) 2
(B) 3
(C) 9
(D) 12
(E) 18

7. If $x = 6 + y$ and $4x = 3 - 2y$, what is the value of x?

(A) 4

(B) $\frac{13}{11}$

(C) $\frac{5}{2}$

(D) $-\frac{2}{3}$

(E) $-\frac{7}{2}$

8. A jar contains five blue marbles, 25 green marbles, and x red marbles. If the probability of drawing a red marble at random is $\frac{1}{4}$, what is the value of x?

(A) 25
(B) 20
(C) 15
(D) 12
(E) 10

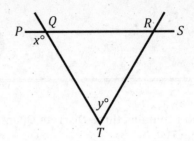

9. In the figure above, $\overline{QT} = \overline{QR}$. If $x = 120$ then $y =$

(A) 30
(B) 60
(C) 75
(D) 90
(E) 120

For the following item, consider the answers separately and select all that apply.

10. If a polygon with all equal sides is inscribed in a circle, then the measure in degrees of the minor arc created by adjacent vertices of the polygon could be which of the following?

Indicate <u>all</u> such measures.

(A) 30
(B) 25
(C) 24
(D) 20
(E) 15

Quiz II

(10 items; 15 minutes)

DIRECTIONS: Solve each problem and choose the correct answer from the choices given.

NOTES: Unless otherwise indicated, all figures lie in a plane.

Geometric diagrams and figures ARE NOT NECESSARILY drawn to scale. Coordinate systems and graphic data presentations ARE drawn to scale.

You can assume that lines shown as straight are straight and that the positions of points, angles, regions, etc. exist in the order shown.

All numbers used are real numbers.

1. A jar contains between 50 and 60 marbles. If the marbles are counted out three at a time, one is left over; if they are counted out four at a time, three are left over. How many marbles are in the jar?

   (A) 52
   (B) 54
   (C) 55
   (D) 58
   (E) 59

2. Starting from points 200 kilometers apart, two trains travel toward each other along two parallel tracks. If one train travels at 70 kilometers per hour and the other at 80 kilometers per hour, how much time, in hours, will elapse before the trains pass each other?

   (A) $\frac{3}{4}$
   (B) 1
   (C) $\frac{4}{3}$
   (D) $\frac{3}{2}$
   (E) 2

3. The average (arithmetic mean) weight of three boxes is $25\frac{1}{3}$ pounds. If each box weighs at least 24 pounds, what is the greatest possible weight, in pounds, of any one of the boxes?

   (A) 25
   (B) 26
   (C) 27
   (D) 28
   (E) 29

4. If n subtracted from $\frac{13}{2}$ is equal to n divided by $\frac{2}{13}$ what is the value of n?

   (A) $\frac{2}{3}$
   (B) $\frac{13}{15}$
   (C) 1
   (D) $\frac{13}{11}$
   (E) 26

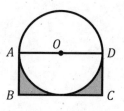

5. In the figure above, $ABCD$ is a rectangle with sides $\overline{AB}$, $\overline{BC}$, and $\overline{CD}$ touching the circle with center O. If the radius of the circle is 2, what is the area of the shaded region?

   (A) $\frac{3\pi}{2}$
   (B) $\frac{3\pi}{4}$
   (C) $8-2\pi$
   (D) $2-\pi$
   (E) $\pi-1$

6. If Yuriko is now twice as old as Lisa was 10 years ago, how old is Lisa today if Yuriko is now n years old?

(A) $\frac{n}{2}+10$

(B) $\frac{n}{2}-10$

(C) $n-10$

(D) $2n+10$

(E) $2n-10$

7. If $2^{x+1}=4^{x-1}$, what is the value of x?

(A) 1

(B) 2

(C) 3

(D) 4

(E) 5

8. What percent of 125 is 100?

(A) 75%

(B) 80%

(C) 120%

(D) 125%

(E) 150%

9. The sum of two integers is 72. If the integers are in a ratio of $4:5$, what is the value of the smaller integer?

(A) 32

(B) 36

(C) 40

(D) 42

(E) 48

For the following item, consider the answers separately and select all that apply.

10. An album contains x black-and-white photographs and y color photographs. If the album contains a total of 24 photographs, then which of the following can be true?

Indicate <u>all</u> such equations.

(A) $x=y$

(B) $x=2y$

(C) $x=3y$

(D) $x=4y$

(E) $x=5y$

Quiz III

(10 items; 15 minutes)

> **DIRECTIONS:** Solve each problem and choose the correct answer from the choices given.

NOTES: Unless otherwise indicated, all figures lie in a plane.

Geometric diagrams and figures ARE NOT NECESSARILY drawn to scale. Coordinate systems and graphic data presentations ARE drawn to scale.

You can assume that lines shown as straight are straight and that the positions of points, angles, regions, etc. exist in the order shown.

All numbers used are real numbers.

1. In a certain direct mail center, each of x computers addresses y letters every z minutes. If every computer works without interruption, how many hours are required for the center to address 100,000 letters?

(A) $\dfrac{100,000z}{60xy}$

(B) $\dfrac{100,000x}{60yz}$

(C) $\dfrac{100,000xy}{60z}$

(D) $\dfrac{60xy}{100,000z}$

(E) $\dfrac{60y}{100,000xz}$

2. $\dfrac{1}{10^{25}} - \dfrac{1}{10^{26}} =$

(A) $\dfrac{9}{10^{25}}$

(B) $\dfrac{9}{10^{26}}$

(C) $\dfrac{1}{10^{25}}$

(D) $-\dfrac{9}{10^{25}}$

(E) $-\dfrac{1}{10}$

3. In a certain community, the property tax is solely a function of the tax rate and the assessed value of the property. If the assessed value of a property is increased by 25 percent while the tax rate is decreased by 25 percent, what is the net effect on the taxes on the property?

(A) An increase of 18.75 percent
(B) An increase of 6.25 percent
(C) No net change
(D) A decrease of 6.25 percent
(E) A decrease of 18.75 percent

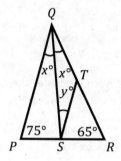

4. In $\triangle PQR$ above, if $\overline{PQ} \parallel \overline{ST}$, then $y =$

(A) 20
(B) 40
(C) 45
(D) 50
(E) 55

5. If $2a = 3b = 4c$, then what is the average (arithmetic mean) of a, b, and c, in terms of a?

(A) $\dfrac{13a}{18}$

(B) $\dfrac{13a}{9}$

(C) $\dfrac{8a}{3}$

(D) $\dfrac{4a}{3}$

(E) $2a$

6. Two circles with radii r and $r+3$ have areas that differ by 15π. What is the radius of the smaller circle?

(A) 4
(B) 3
(C) 2
(D) 1
(E) $\frac{1}{2}$

7. If $p, q, r, s,$ and t are whole numbers and the expression $2[p(q+r)+s]+t$ is even, which of the numbers *must* be even?

(A) p
(B) q
(C) r
(D) s
(E) t

For the following item, consider the answers separately and select all that apply.

8. For all integers, $x \spadesuit y = 2x+3y$. Which of the following must be true?

Indicate <u>all</u> such equations.

(A) $3 \spadesuit 2 = 12$
(B) $x \spadesuit y = y \spadesuit x$
(C) $0 \spadesuit (1 \spadesuit 2) = (0 \spadesuit 1) \spadesuit 2$

9. The sum, the product, and the average (arithmetic mean) of three different integers are equal. If two of the integers are x and $-x$, the third integer is

(A) $\frac{x}{2}$
(B) $2x$
(C) 1
(D) 0
(E) It cannot be determined from the information given.

10. If $\frac{x}{y} = -1$ then $x + y =$

(A) 2
(B) 1
(C) 0
(D) −1
(E) −2

STRATEGY SUMMARY

Discrete Quantitative items are multiple-choice math problems that test arithmetic, algebra, geometry, and data analysis concepts. NO trigonometry or calculus will be on the exam.

Some Discrete Quantitative items will look as though they might have been taken from math textbooks; others will require application of math knowledge to new situations. Therefore, Discrete Quantitative items may be classified according to whether they just test ability to do mathematical manipulations or require some original thinking (application). Methods for attacking a particular item depend on the type of item.

General Strategies

Pay attention to thought-reversers (capitalized and underlined words). When guessing on difficult items, eliminate "simple answer choices" and the "cannot be determined" response, (E). Do not hastily choose an easy answer choice unless you have reasoned to the correct answer. Answering difficult items correctly counts more toward your score than answering easy items correctly, and answering difficult items incorrectly subtracts less from your score than answering easy items incorrectly. So, do not be afraid of working your way into difficult territory. If you can see your way to a quick and elegant solution, solve the problem directly, based on your knowledge of the subject. Translate, use pictures, and substitute useful numbers into story problems. Use the "plug-and-chug" strategy (especially on Algebra items), but look for tricks in difficult problem presentation that allow for easy problem-solving. Since the correct answer is among the answer choices, use the "good enough" principle and approximation to your advantage. Since answer choices are arranged in ascending or descending order, "test-the-test," starting with (C). Remember to guess quickly if you do not understand an item or cannot think of a way to solve the problem.

Arithmetic Concepts

- Simplifying
- Factoring
- Approximation
- The "Flying-X" Method
- Decimal-Fraction Equivalents
- Properties of Numbers: Odd, Even, Negative, Positive, Sequential
- Absolute Value
- Percents
- Ratios: Two-Part, Three-Part, Weighted
- Rates
- Proportions and Direct-Inverse Variation

Algebra Concepts

- Evaluating Expressions
- Manipulating Expressions Involving Exponents
- Factoring Expressions
- Creating Algebraic Expressions
- Solving Equations: Linear, Quadratic, Multiple
- Coordinate Geometry: Slope, Slope-Intercept Form of a Linear Equation, Distance Formula
- Graphs of Linear Equations, First-Degree Inequalities, Quadratic Equations

Geometry Concepts

- Lines and Angles: Perpendicular, Parallel, Intersecting
- Triangles: Equilateral, Isosceles, Acute, Obtuse, Perimeter, Area, Altitude, Pythagorean Theorem
- Quadrilaterals: Squares, Rectangles, Rhombi, Parallelograms, Trapezoids, Perimeter, Area
- Polygons: Sum of Interior Angles
- Circles: Radius, Diameter, Circumference, Area, Chords, Tangents
- Solids (Three-Dimensional): Cubes, Cylinders, Spheres, Volumes, Surface Areas
- Complex Figures

Data Analysis Concepts

- Mean, Median, Mode, Range
- Standard Deviation
- Quartiles and Interquartile Range
- Permutations
- Combinations
- Probability
- Venn Diagrams

Quantitative Reasoning:
Numeric Entry

Course Concept Outline

I. Test Mechanics (p. 203)

II. Lesson (p. 209)

---

[1] Some concepts in this Course Concept Outline are not illustrated through examples in your student text but may be covered by your instructor in class. They are included here to provide a complete outline of your course.

TEST MECHANICS

Overview

The GRE test Quantitative Reasoning sections on the computer-based test include one or two numeric entry items per section. These items include an answer box or boxes requiring you to enter the correct answer using the keyboard or the "Transfer Display" button on the calculator. These items may appear anywhere in the section.

Like the Discrete Quantitative items, Numeric Entry items presuppose a knowledge of pre-algebra and algebra, intermediate algebra and coordinate geometry, and data analysis. These are the conceptual building blocks of the Quantitative Reasoning test sections, whether the items use a multiple-choice format or require a numeric answer.

In most ways, Numeric Entry items are really Discrete Quantitative items that are simply stripped of the answer choices. The following example is the same item stem that appears in the Quantitative Reasoning: Discrete Quantitative "Overview" feature, but here it appears as a Numeric Entry item lacking the five corresponding lettered answer choices.

Example:

How many prime numbers between 1 and 100 are factors of 9,350?

Of course, the numerical solution is the same as when the item is presented in multiple-choice format. The prime factorization of 9,350 is $9,350 = (10)(935) = (2)(5)(5)(187) = (2)(5)(5)(11)(17)$, so it has four prime factors: 2, 5, 11, and 17. The answer is "4," so you must enter the number "4" in the answer box.

Anatomy

1. An hour-long class included 40 minutes of instruction. What fraction of the hour-long class was NOT instructional?

Give your answer as a fraction.

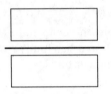

2. Test Car A travels 80 miles and averages 20 miles per gallon of fuel used. If Test Car B travels 30 miles for each gallon of fuel used, how many miles does Test Car B travel on the same amount of fuel used by Test Car A to travel 80 miles?

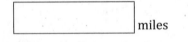 miles

3. If $2(x - y)(x + y) = 24$ and $x - y = 3$, then what is the value of $x + y$?

1. $(\frac{20}{60}, \frac{10}{30}, \frac{5}{15}, \frac{2}{6}, \frac{1}{3})$ *If 40 minutes of the 60 minutes were devoted to instruction, then 20 minutes were not instructional. Therefore, the fraction of the hour-long class that was NOT instructional is $\frac{20}{60}$. Fractions need not be entered in lowest terms, so $\frac{20}{60}, \frac{10}{30}, \frac{5}{15}, \frac{2}{6}$, and $\frac{1}{3}$, as well as any other equivalent fractions, are all acceptable.*

2. **(120)** *This is a story problem that basically tests the concept of proportions. If Test Car A goes 80 miles and averages 20 miles per gallon, then it would use: $\frac{80 \text{ miles}}{20 \text{ miles}/\text{gallon}} = 4 \text{ gallons}$. Thus, if Test Car B gets 30 miles per gallon, on 4 gallons it would travel: $4 \text{ gallons} \cdot \frac{30 \text{ miles}}{\text{gallon}} = 120 \text{ gallons}$.*

3. **(4)** *This is an algebra item with variables, but the answer will necessarily still be a number. Since $x - y = 3$, substitute 3 for $x - y$ in the given expression and solve for $x + y$: $2(x - y)(x + y) = 24 \Rightarrow 2(3)(x + y) = 24 \Rightarrow x + y = 4$.*

4. In a rectangular coordinate system, the center of a circle has coordinates $(3,4)$, and the circle touches the *x*-axis at only one point. What is the radius of the circle?

4. (4) *This item tests coordinate geometry. Since the center has coordinates* $(3,4)$ *and rests on the x-axis, we have:*

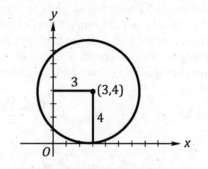

Therefore, $r = 4$.

Pacing

The time limit for the 20 math items (Discrete Quantitative, Quantitative Comparison, Numeric Entry, and Data Interpretation) is 35 minutes, so you can afford to spend, on average, about 100 seconds per item. Numeric Entry items will probably require more time than the other item types, though, because you must work out the problem in its entirety in order to arrive at the correct answer. You cannot use the "Test-the-Test" or "Plug-and-Chug" strategies. Plan to spend, on average, two minutes answering each Numeric Entry item. Each section will include, on average, one or two Numeric Entry items.

Quantitative Reasoning by Item-Type
Total Time: 35 minutes

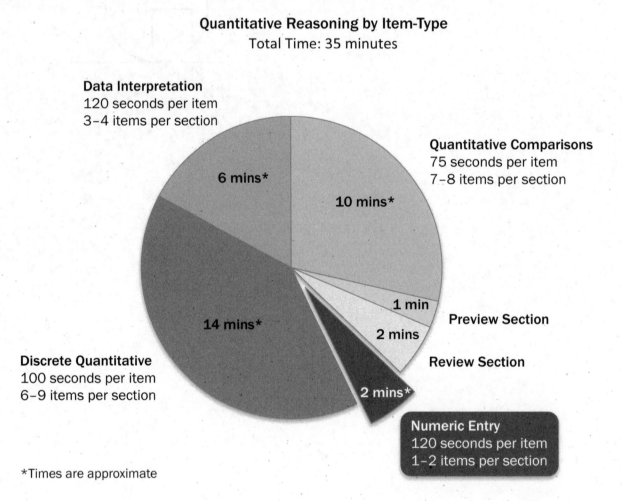

Data Interpretation
120 seconds per item
3–4 items per section

6 mins*

Quantitative Comparisons
75 seconds per item
7–8 items per section

10 mins*

1 min

Preview Section

2 mins

Review Section

14 mins*

Discrete Quantitative
100 seconds per item
6–9 items per section

2 mins*

Numeric Entry
120 seconds per item
1–2 items per section

*Times are approximate

Time Trial

(5 items; 8 minutes)

DIRECTIONS: Solve each problem and choose the correct answer, using the given directions. Answers are on page 704.

NOTES: Some items require a single answer. Other items require one or more answers. Carefully read the directions for each item.

All numbers used are real numbers.

Unless otherwise indicated, all figures lie in a plane.

Geometric diagrams and figures **are not necessarily** drawn to scale, so do **not** assume lengths, angle measures, or other quantities are as they appear in a given figure. You should assume that lines shown as straight are straight and that the positions of points, and geometric objects in general, exist in the order shown. Base your answers to questions with geometric figures on reasoning, not visual estimation or measurement.

Coordinate systems and graphic data presentations **are** drawn to scale, so you can answer items based on visual estimation or measurement.

NUMERIC ENTRY DIRECTIONS: Answers may be integers, decimals, or fractions. Answers may be negative.

Items requiring a fraction will include two answer boxes—one for the numerator and one for the denominator.

Equivalent forms of the answer are also correct (e.g., 9 and 9.0 are both correct forms of 9). Fractions do not need to be expressed in lowest terms.

Enter the exact answer unless the item stem indicates that the answer should be rounded.

1. A recipe for spaghetti sauce uses 4 gallons of tomatoes to make 32 servings. At this rate, how many gallons of tomatoes are needed to make 144 servings of spaghetti sauce?

    gallons

2. The perimeter of a rectangular garden is 280 feet. If the length of one side of the garden is 60 feet, what is the area of the garden, in square feet?

    square feet

3. If $2^{3x} = 4^{x+1}$, what is the value of x?

4. If $f(x) = x^2 + 32$, what is the positive number n such that $2[f(n)] = f(2n)$?

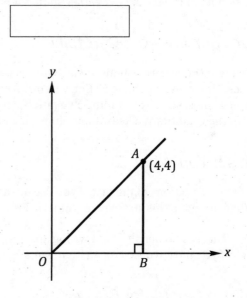

5. Line l (not shown) passes through O and intersects $\overline{AB}$ between A and B at point (x, y). If y is an integer, what is one possible value of the slope of line l?

    Give your answer as a fraction.

Game Plan

Quickly Preview the Test Section, but Skip the Directions

As you get started, take a few seconds to preview the Quantitative Reasoning section. Note where the Numeric Entry items appear. Do NOT, however, read the directions. Remind yourself of your pacing plan and then get to work.

Answer the Question That Is Being Asked

Read the Question Carefully

Some problems are fairly simple, but others are more complex, particularly practical word problems and more difficult geometry problems. The more complex the question, the easier it is to misread and set off down the wrong track. If the question is very long, then note the key part(s) of the question.

Pay Attention to Units

Some items require you to convert units (e.g., feet to inches or hours to minutes). The item stem will indicate the units to use, and if the test-writer senses any possible confusion, the units will be printed after the answer box.

Pay Attention to Thought-Reversers

A thought-reverser is any word, such as "not," "except," or "but," that turns a question inside out. Make sure that you take note of the thought-reverser so that it is staring you in the face as you work the problem.

Enter Your Answers Carefully

For Discrete Quantitative items, identifying the answer choice is a simple process: locate the oval or square(s) and click. However, for Numeric Entry items, you must enter your answer in the provided answer box according to specific rules, such as including a negative sign or decimal, or you won't receive credit for your response. Later, in the Quantitative Reasoning: Numeric Entry Lesson, you'll review the rules for entering the information.

Guess If You Want To

As with other sections of the test, if you are unsure of an answer, you should make an educated guess and move on. When applying this strategy to Numeric Entry items, consider the following:

- There is no penalty for a wrong answer, so a wrong answer will not hurt your score.
- If you have worked on an item, but are not sure of your method or your answer, it's still worth guessing.

Don't Go Calculator Crazy

Simply because there is an on-screen calculator available for each item in the Quantitative Reasoning section does not mean that you should try to solve every item with the calculator. In fact, for most items, the calculator is the least efficient method for arriving at a solution.

Assume, for example, that you have to do the following arithmetic to get your answer: $\left(\frac{2}{3}\right)\left(\frac{7}{4}\right)\left(\frac{1}{6}\right)$. Since this problem involves single digit multiplication, it's going to be easier to do the arithmetic using your scratch paper than using the on-screen calculator: $\left(\frac{2}{3}\right)\left(\frac{7}{4}\right)\left(\frac{1}{6}\right) = \frac{2 \cdot 7 \cdot 1}{3 \cdot 4 \cdot 6} = \frac{14}{72} = \frac{7}{36}$.

By all means, use the calculator when it will be a definite advantage, but don't automatically assume that every item requires its use.

LESSON

The items in this section accompany the in-class review of the skills and concepts tested by the Numeric Entry items in the Quantitative Reasoning test sections. You will work through the items with your instructor in class. Answers are on page 704.

DIRECTIONS: Solve each problem and choose the correct answer, using the given directions.

NOTES: Some items require a single answer. Other items require one or more answer choices. Carefully read the directions for each item.

All numbers used are real numbers.

Unless otherwise indicated, all figures lie in a plane.

Geometric diagrams and figures **are not necessarily** drawn to scale, so do **not** assume lengths, angle measures, or other quantities are as they appear in a given figure. You should assume that lines shown as straight are straight and that the positions of points, and geometric objects in general, exist in the order shown. Base your answers to questions with geometric figures on reasoning, not visual estimation or measurement.

Coordinate systems and graphic data presentations **are** drawn to scale, so you can answer items based on visual estimation or measurement.

NUMERIC ENTRY DIRECTIONS: Answers may be integers, decimals, or fractions. Answers may be negative.

Items requiring a fraction will include two answer boxes—one for the numerator and one for the denominator.

Equivalent forms of the answer are also correct (e.g., 9 and 9.0 are both correct forms of 9). Fractions do not need to be expressed in lowest terms.

Enter the exact answer unless the item stem indicates that the answer should be rounded.

Answer Situations Illustrated

Answer Is a Whole Number

1. What number increased by 25 equals twice the number?

[ ]

2. A car travels from Town A to Town B, a distance of 360 miles, in 9 hours. How many hours would the same trip have taken had the car traveled 5 mph faster?

[ ] hours

Answer Is a Decimal

3. A fence runs along the entire perimeter of a rectangular area 2.8 yards by 4 yards. What is the length, in yards, of the fence?

[ ] yards

Answer Is a Fraction

4. At State College, one-fourth of the students are from abroad. Of those from abroad, one-eighth are from China. What fraction of the student body is from China?

Give your answer as a fraction.

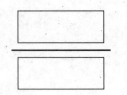

5. A jar contains 15 pennies and 25 nickels. What fraction of the coins are pennies?

Give your answer as a fraction.

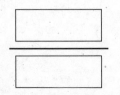

Features of the On-Screen Calculator

6. For all numbers, $x \blacktriangle y = 2xy$. What is $1.5 \blacktriangle 2.5$?

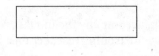

Numeric Entry Items Illustrated

7. What is the value of $\frac{2}{3} - \frac{5}{8}$?

Give your answer as a fraction.

8. What is the value of $65(1) - 65(2) - 65(3) - 65(4)$?

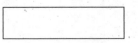

9. Matinee ticket prices are $1.50 for children and $3.50 for adults. Regular ticket prices are $4.50 for children and $6.50 for adults. If 3 adults and 1 child attend a matinee, what percentage of the regular price will they pay?

[ ] %

10. If the average of 8, 10, 15, 20, and x is 11, what is x?

[ ]

11. If $x = 14$, what is the value of $2x - (2 + x)$?

[ ]

12. If $3x + y = 33$ and $x + y = 17$, then what is the value of x?

$x =$ _____

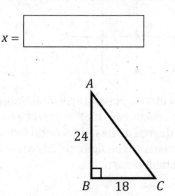

13. In the figure above, what is the length of $\overline{AC}$?

_____

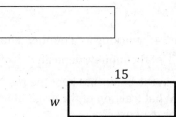

14. In the figure above, if the perimeter of the rectangle is 40, what is the area of the rectangle?

_____

15. If a circle with radius 0.25 is inscribed in a square, what is the area of the square?

_____

16. If the price of a book increases from $10.00 to $12.50, what is the percent increase in price?

_____ %

17. Boys and girls belong to the chess club. There are 36 people in the club, 15 of whom are girls. What fraction of the club is boys?

Give your answer as a fraction.

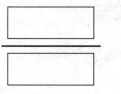

18. Jason built a fence around the perimeter of his rectangular garden. The width of the garden is 2.8 yards, and the length is twice the width. How many yards of fencing did Jason use?

_____ yards

19. If $x = 9$, what is the value of $x^2 + 2x - 9$?

_____

20. If $x = 3y - 1$ and $x + y = -13$, what is the value of x?

_____

21. Jane and Hector have the same birthday. When Hector was 36, Jane was 30. How old was Jane when Hector was twice her age?

_____ years old

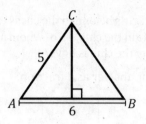

22. In the figure above, what is the area of isosceles △ABC?

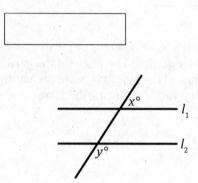

23. In the figure above, if l_1 and l_2 are parallel, what is $x + y$?

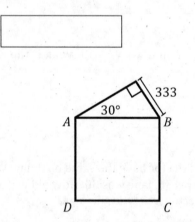

24. In the figure above, what is the perimeter of square ABCD?

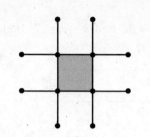

25. In the figure above, equally spaced points are joined by line segments that intersect each other at 90 degree angles. If the total length of all line segments in the figure is 24, what is the area of the shaded part?

26. Su Li made $45 working as a mother's helper. She spent $\frac{1}{5}$ of the money, deposited $\frac{1}{3}$ of the remainder in the bank, and kept the rest for expenses. What fraction of the original $45 did she keep for expenses?

Give your answer as a fraction.

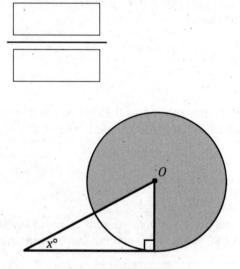

27. In the figure above, the circle with center O has a radius of 6. If the area of the shaded region is 30π, what is the value of x?

$x =$

28. If the sum of two consecutive integers is 29, what is the smaller of these integers?

29. A jar contains 300 marbles, each black or white. If the jar contains 156 white marbles, what percent of the marbles is black?

 %

30. Mr. Wahl spends $\frac{1}{3}$ of his day in meetings, $\frac{1}{6}$ of his day on the phone, and $\frac{1}{8}$ of his day answering questions. What fraction of his day can be devoted to other things?

Give your answer as a fraction.

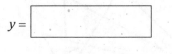

31. Line l, with a slope of $\frac{1}{2}$, passes through the points $\left(0,\frac{1}{4}\right)$ and $(2, y)$. What is the value of y?

$y =$

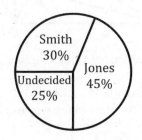

Smith
30%

Jones
45%

Undecided
25%

32. A total of 400 voters responded to the survey represented by the pie chart above. How many more respondents were in favor of Jones than Smith?

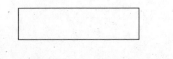

33. In a three-hour examination of 350 questions, there are 50 mathematical problems. If twice as much time should be allowed for each mathematical problem as for each of the other questions, how many minutes should be spent on the mathematical problems?

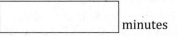 minutes

34. In a pantry, there are 28 cans of vegetables. Each can has a label with lettering that is white, green, or both white and green. 8 cans have labels with only white lettering, and 18 have labels with only green lettering. How many cans have both white and green lettering?

cans

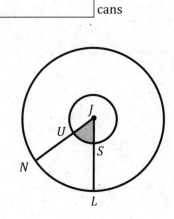

35. Given the circles above, if radius $\overline{JN}$ is 3 times the length of $\overline{JU}$, then the ratio of the shaded area to the area of sector NJL is $1:b$. What is the value of b?

$b =$

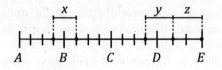

36. In the figure above, points B, C, and D divide $\overline{AE}$ into 4 equal parts. $\overline{AB}$, $\overline{BC}$, and $\overline{CD}$ are divided into 4 equal parts as shown above. $\overline{DE}$ is divided into 3 equal parts as shown. What does $\dfrac{x+z}{y}$ equal?

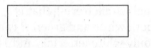

37. The shortest distance from the center of a circle to a chord is 5. If the length of the chord is 24, what is the length of the radius of the circle?

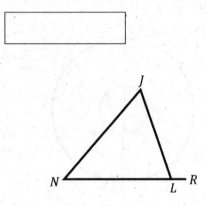

38. In the figure above, $\angle N = (9x - 40)°$, $\angle J = (4x + 30)°$, and $\angle JLR = (8x + 40)°$. What is the measure of $\angle J$?

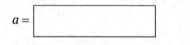 degrees

39. In the figure above, two circles are tangent to each other and each is tangent to 3 sides of the rectangle. If the radius of each circle is 3, then the area of the shaded portion is $a - 18\pi$. What is the value of a?

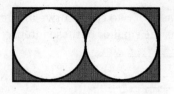

$a = $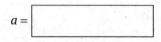

40. In the (x, y) coordinate plane, the length of the line segment with endpoints $(3, -2)$ and $(-4, 5)$ is $b\sqrt{2}$. What is the value of b?

$b = $

41. The area of a circle that is inscribed in a square with a diagonal of 8 is $a\pi$. What is the value of a?

$a = $

42. In the figure above, $\angle DMC = 80°$ and $\angle ENC = 60°$. How many degrees is $\angle BAC$?

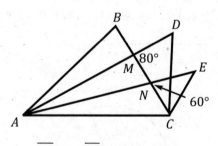

$\overline{DA}$ and $\overline{EA}$ trisect $\angle BAC$.

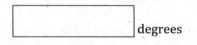 degrees

43. Mrs. Smith has a total of x dollars to donate to various charities. If Mrs. Smith gives $73 to each charity, she will be $4 short; if she gives $70 to each charity, she will have $56 left over. What is the value of x?

$x =$

44. $a - b = b - c = c - a$, $a \neq 0$, $b \neq 0$, and $c \neq 0$.
What is the value of $\frac{2a + 3b}{c}$?

45. If 0.129914 is rounded off to the nearest hundredth, what is the value of the hundredths digit?

46. The average of 4, 5, x, and y is 6, and the average of x, z, 8, and 9 is 8. What is the value of $z - y$?

47. Copy Machine X produces 20 copies per minute, and Copy Machine Y produces 30 copies per minute. If Y is started 1 minute after X, how many minutes after X is started will Y have produced the same number of copies as X?

minutes

48. A triangle has sides of x, 4, and 5. If x is an integer, what is the maximum value of x?

$x =$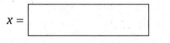

49. Ray is now 10 years older than Cindy. In 8 years, Ray will be twice as old as Cindy is then. How old is Cindy now?

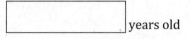 years old

50. Theresa's test grades in Economics this semester were rather inconsistent: 100, 85, 55, 95, 75, 100. For this data, how many scores are within one standard deviation of the mean?

scores

QUIZZES

This section contains three Quantitative Reasoning: Numeric Entry quizzes. Complete each quiz under timed conditions. Use any available space in the section for scratch work. Answers are on page 705.

Quiz I
(5 items; 8 minutes)

DIRECTIONS: Solve each problem and choose the correct answer, using the given directions.

NOTES: Some items require a single answer. Other items require one or more answer choices. Carefully read the directions for each item.

All numbers used are real numbers.

Unless otherwise indicated, all figures lie in a plane.

Geometric diagrams and figures **are not necessarily** drawn to scale, so do **not** assume lengths, angle measures, or other quantities are as they appear in a given figure. You should assume that lines shown as straight are straight and that the positions of points, and geometric objects in general, exist in the order shown. Base your answers to questions with geometric figures on reasoning, not visual estimation or measurement.

Coordinate systems and graphic data presentations **are** drawn to scale, so you can answer items based on visual estimation or measurement.

NUMERIC ENTRY DIRECTIONS: Answers may be integers, decimals, or fractions. Answers may be negative.

Items requiring a fraction will include two answer boxes—one for the numerator and one for the denominator.

Equivalent forms of the answer are also correct (e.g., 9 and 9.0 are both correct forms of 9). Fractions do not need to be expressed in lowest terms.

Enter the exact answer unless the item stem indicates that the answer should be rounded.

1. The difference between x and $3x$ is greater than 7 but less than 11. If x is an integer, what is one possible value of x?

2. If p and q are integers such that $p > q > 0$ and $p + q = 12$, what is the least possible value of $p - q$?

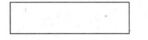

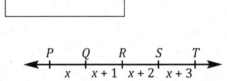

3. In the figure above, if $\overline{PT}$ has a length of 12, then what is the value of x?

Give your answer as a fraction.

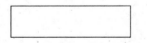

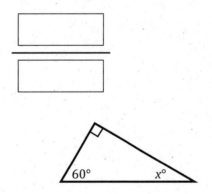

4. In the figure above, what is the value of x?

5. As part of an orienteering exercise, a hiker walks due north from point P for 3 miles to point Q and then due east for 4 miles to point R. What is the straight-line distance (in miles) from point R to point P?

miles

Quiz II

(5 items; 8 minutes)

DIRECTIONS: Solve each problem and choose the correct answer, using the given directions.

NOTES: Some items require a single answer. Other items require one or more answer choices. Carefully read the directions for each item.

All numbers used are real numbers.

Unless otherwise indicated, all figures lie in a plane.

Geometric diagrams and figures **are not necessarily** drawn to scale, so do **not** assume lengths, angle measures, or other quantities are as they appear in a given figure. You should assume that lines shown as straight are straight and that the positions of points, and geometric objects in general, exist in the order shown. Base your answers to questions with geometric figures on reasoning, not visual estimation or measurement.

Coordinate systems and graphic data presentations **are** drawn to scale, so you can answer items based on visual estimation or measurement.

NUMERIC ENTRY DIRECTIONS: Answers may be integers, decimals, or fractions. Answers may be negative.

Items requiring a fraction will include two answer boxes—one for the numerator and one for the denominator.

Equivalent forms of the answer are also correct (e.g., 9 and 9.0 are both correct forms of 9). Fractions do not need to be expressed in lowest terms.

Enter the exact answer unless the item stem indicates that the answer should be rounded.

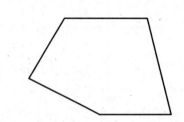

1. In the figure above, what is the maximum number of different diagonals that can be drawn in the pentagon?

2. If $4x = 2(2 + x)$ and $6y = 3(2 + y)$, then what is the value of $2x + 3y$?

3. Let the "JOSH" of a number be defined as 3 less than 3 times the number. What number is equal to its "JOSH"?

   Give your answer as a fraction.

4. Machine A produces flue covers at a uniform rate of 2,000 per hour. Machine B produces flue covers at a uniform rate of 5,000 in $2\frac{1}{2}$ hours. After $7\frac{1}{4}$ hours, Machine A has produced how many more flue covers than Machine B?

   _____ flue covers

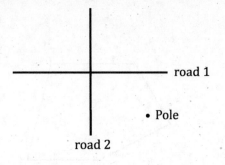

5. In the figure above, two roads intersect at right angles. A pole is 30 meters from one road and 40 meters from the other road. How far (in meters) is the pole from the point where the roads intersect?

| | meters

Quiz III

(5 items; 8 minutes)

> **DIRECTIONS:** Solve each problem and choose the correct answer, using the given directions.

NOTES: Some items require a single answer. Other items require one or more answer choices. Carefully read the directions for each item.

All numbers used are real numbers.

Unless otherwise indicated, all figures lie in a plane.

Geometric diagrams and figures **are not necessarily** drawn to scale, so do **not** assume lengths, angle measures, or other quantities are as they appear in a given figure. You should assume that lines shown as straight are straight and that the positions of points, and geometric objects in general, exist in the order shown. Base your answers to questions with geometric figures on reasoning, not visual estimation or measurement.

Coordinate systems and graphic data presentations **are** drawn to scale, so you can answer items based on visual estimation or measurement.

> **NUMERIC ENTRY DIRECTIONS:** Answers may be integers, decimals, or fractions. Answers may be negative.
>
> Items requiring a fraction will include two answer boxes—one for the numerator and one for the denominator.
>
> Equivalent forms of the answer are also correct (e.g., 9 and 9.0 are both correct forms of 9). Fractions do not need to be expressed in lowest terms.
>
> Enter the exact answer unless the item stem indicates that the answer should be rounded.

1. What is the value of $\left(2a^2 - a^3\right)^2$ when $a = -1$?

2. A jar contains 2 red marbles, 3 green marbles, and 4 orange marbles. If a marble is picked at random, what is the probability that the marble is not orange?

Give your answer as a fraction.

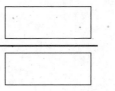

3. In the country of Glup, 1 glop is 3 glips, and 4 glips are 5 globs. How many globs are 2 glops?

Give your answer as a fraction.

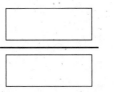

4. If $\frac{k}{3} + \frac{k}{4} = 1$, then what is the value of k?

Give your answer as a fraction.

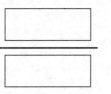

5. If the area of a square with side x is 5, what is the area of a square with side $3x$?

STRATEGY SUMMARY

General Strategies

Even though these items do not provide answer choices, they follow certain guidelines:

- Numbers can be whole numbers, decimals, or fractions.

- Whole numbers and decimals cannot have more than eight digits. Fractions cannot have more than four digits in the numerator and four digits in the denominator.

- Decimal signs should be entered by typing a period.

- Numbers may be negative. The negative sign should be entered by typing a hyphen. To make a number positive, simply press the hyphen key again and the negative sign will disappear.

- Erase using the Backspace key.

- When using the calculator, pressing the "Transfer Display" button will transfer the value displayed on the calculator to the answer box.

- Equivalent forms of an answer are all correct. (9 and 9.0 are both correct forms of the correct answer 9.)

Remember that the computer automatically does the following, as applicable to any given item: converts your answer into a scoreable form (e.g., converts a fraction to a decimal number to determine the credited value), checks to determine whether the value of your answer falls within the credited range, or compares your answer with each of several values considered correct. Do not duplicate these functions, as they each waste time. Instead, do the following:

- Use any form of a fraction (and do not reduce to lowest terms).

- Enter the first occurring acceptable value without searching for others that might also be correct (e.g., if $\frac{1}{4}$, $\frac{1}{2}$, and $\frac{3}{4}$ are within the range, use your first answer).

Enter any number of proper forms within the acceptable range (e.g., whole numbers such that $3 < x < 9$ would be 4, 5, 6, 7, or 8, so pick one and enter it).

Quantitative Reasoning:
Comparisons

Course Concept Outline

---

[1] Some concepts in this Course Concept Outline are not illustrated through examples in your student text but may be covered by your instructor in class. They are included here to provide a complete outline of your course.

TEST MECHANICS

Overview

As you know, the GRE Quantitative Reasoning sections test math from arithmetic up through algebra with a few assorted topics such as basic statistics and probability thrown in for good measure, as well as data interpretation, a topic covered in another chapter. The math ranges from basic middle school manipulations up through some fairly difficult conceptual items that defy classification by grade level. But still, math is just math—until you get to Quantitative Comparisons, and then the rules change.

Quantitative Comparisons are a question type that you will not encounter in real life, only on the GRE test. QCs are governed by a special set of directions. There are some technical issues about the figures that will be covered later in the chapter, and the interactive nature of the computer-based test (as opposed to the book page) will make things easier. But for now, Quantitative Comparisons can be summarized as:

Pick (A) if Quantity A is larger.
Pick (B) if Quantity B is larger.
Pick (C) if the two quantities are equal.
Pick (D) if the relationship cannot be determined from the information given.

Of the 20 items in a math section, 6 to 8 of those will likely be QCs. The Quantitative Comparisons will likely be presented as a group because of their special instructions, but the group or groups can appear anywhere in the section.

Anatomy

DIRECTIONS: Each of the items below consists of two quantities, Quantity A and Quantity B. Compare the two quantities, using the information presented. Choose:

(A) if Quantity A is greater.
(B) if Quantity B is greater.
(C) if the two quantities are equal.
(D) if the relationship cannot be determined from the information given.

NOTES: All numbers used are real numbers.

Unless otherwise indicated, all figures lie in a plane.

Geometric diagrams and figures **are not necessarily** drawn to scale, so do **not** assume lengths, angle measures, or other quantities are as they appear in a given figure. You should assume that lines shown as straight are straight and that the positions of points, and geometric objects in general, exist in the order shown. Base your answers to questions with geometric figures on reasoning, not visual estimation or measurement.

Coordinate systems and graphic data presentations **are** drawn to scale, so you can answer items based on visual estimation or measurement. A symbol that appears more than once in an item has the same meaning throughout the item.

You're probably thinking that Quantitative Comparisons are just ordinary math problems retrofitted with some exotic directions and that you can still solve them by using conventional math techniques. If you think that, you're wrong.

Quantitative Comparisons require an entirely different way of thinking. Sure, you'll be using concepts and formulas reviewed in other math classes, but you'll be using them in a different way. To do really well on Quantitative Comparisons, you have to learn the "QC Mentality" of considering all the possibilities.

$$x < 0$$

Quantity A	Quantity B
1. $3x$	$-3x$

a and *b* are both greater than 1

Quantity A	Quantity B
2. $(2a)(2b)$	$2ab$

1. **(B)** *The centered statement ($x < 0$) provides information about both quantities, and the x in Quantity A represents the same thing as the x in Quantity B. A negative number times a positive number will yield a negative number, while a negative number times a negative number will yield a positive number. Since x is negative, Quantity B is greater than Quantity A, (B).*

2. **(A)** *Quantity A is equivalent to 4ab. Since ab is positive, 4ab is twice as great as 2ab. Therefore, Quantity A is greater than Quantity B, (A).*

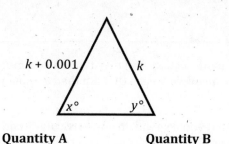

Quantity A	Quantity B
3. x	y

3. (B) *You've learned that, when forced to guess, you can solve some discrete quantitative math items by estimating or measuring a figure.* **Do not use this strategy on Quantitative Comparisons.** *When you look at the triangle, the angles appear to be the same size. So, you might think that the right answer must be (C). Wrong! You have just been had by the GRE. The correct answer is (B), and here's why. The side opposite y is slightly longer than the side opposite x (k + 0.001 is more than k), so y must be larger than x, because in a triangle the angle opposite the longer side of the triangle must be larger than the angle opposite the smaller side of the triangle. Therefore, Quantity B is greater than Quantity A, (B).*

$$4,500 > k > 2,250$$

Quantity A	Quantity B
4. $4,500 - k$	$k - 2,250$

4. (D) *Check the range of each quantity. Quantity A must fall between 0 and 2,250. Quantity B must fall between 2,250 and 0. If $k = 4,499$, then Quantity B will be larger. If $k = 2,251$, then Quantity A will be larger. Therefore, the relationship between the two quantities cannot be determined, (D).*

$$3x + 4y = 12$$
$$2x + 3y = 8$$

Quantity A	Quantity B
5. $x + y$	4

5. (C) *Solve the centered system of equations for $x + y$. Subtract the second equation from the first:*

$$3x + 4y = 12$$
$$- (2x + 3y = 8)$$
$$\overline{ x + y = 4}$$

Therefore, Quantity A is equal to Quantity B, (C).

Pacing

Quantitative Comparisons are one of four types of items in the math section, and they tend to be simpler than the other three types. Therefore, you should aim to spend less time answering each QC item than you plan to spend answering items of the other three types.

It's really not possible to project with great accuracy the time that you'll spend on any particular item. Too much depends on your individual perception of the difficulty of an item. The twist of reasoning required to solve the item could be immediately apparent to you, or it could escape you and require more time.

However, the following should give you an idea of how much time you should spend on the group as a whole and how that translates into "time per item."

Quantitative Reasoning by Item-Type
Total Time: 35 minutes

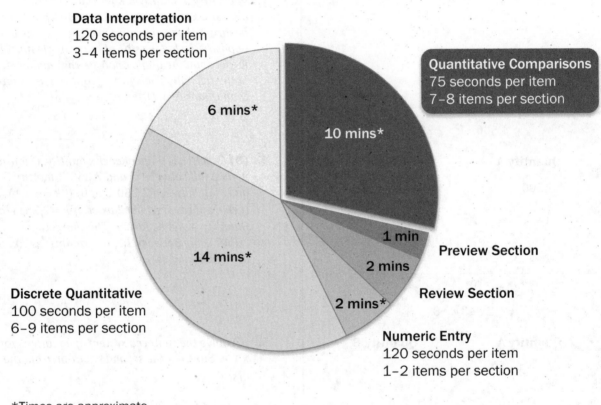

Data Interpretation
120 seconds per item
3–4 items per section

Quantitative Comparisons
75 seconds per item
7–8 items per section

6 mins*

10 mins*

1 min

2 mins

Preview Section

14 mins*

2 mins*

Review Section

Discrete Quantitative
100 seconds per item
6–9 items per section

Numeric Entry
120 seconds per item
1–2 items per section

*Times are approximate

Time Trial

(10 items; 8 minutes)

DIRECTIONS: Each of the items below consists of two quantities, Quantity A and Quantity B. Compare the two quantities, using the information presented. Choose:

(A) if Quantity A is greater.
(B) if Quantity B is greater.
(C) if the two quantities are equal.
(D) if the relationship cannot be determined from the information given.

Answers are on page 705.

	Quantity A	**Quantity B**
1.	0.333	$\frac{1}{3}$

	Quantity A	**Quantity B**
2.	$0.64x + 0.65y$	$0.64(x + y)$

	Quantity A	**Quantity B**
3.	The number of different duos that can be formed from a group of five singers	The number of different trios that can be formed from a group of five singers

Bill's house is four miles from Eva's house, and Eva's house is six miles from Ann's house.

	Quantity A	**Quantity B**
4.	The distance from Bill's house to Ann's house	10 miles

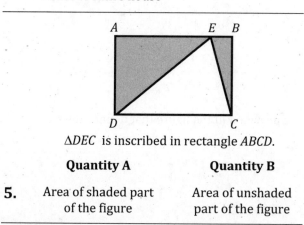

$\triangle DEC$ is inscribed in rectangle $ABCD$.

	Quantity A	**Quantity B**
5.	Area of shaded part of the figure	Area of unshaded part of the figure

$\triangle ABC$ is isosceles and $\angle ABC = 30°$.

	Quantity A	**Quantity B**
6.	The sum of the measures of the two angles of $\triangle ABC$ that have equal measures.	60

	Quantity A	**Quantity B**
7.	7	$\dfrac{7^{23} - 7^{22}}{7^{22}}$

The initial bid by Company B was 28 percent higher than that of Company A. Company B reduced its bid by 28 percent.

	Quantity A	**Quantity B**
8.	The bid of Company A.	The new bid of Company B.

The figure below shows the (x, y) coordinate plane.

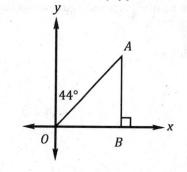

	Quantity A	**Quantity B**
9.	$\overline{OB}$	$\overline{AB}$

	Quantity A	**Quantity B**
10.	$\sqrt{x^4 + 4x^2 + 4}$	$x^2 + 2$

Game Plan

Don't Trust the Geometric Figures

You learned to be wary of geometric figures in the Discrete Quantitative Lesson. This is even more important in the Quantitative Comparisons section. In fact, by drawing a figure as accurately as possible, the GRE can actually trick you into picking the wrong answer.

Example:

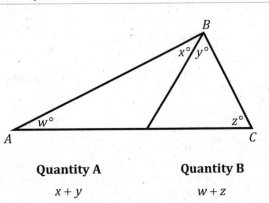

Quantity A	Quantity B
$x + y$	$w + z$

$\angle ABC$ looks like a right angle; if it really is, then $x + y$ would be equal to $w + z$. But don't assume that the angle is 90°; it could be 90°, but it could also be more or less. Therefore, the relationship between Quantity A and Quantity B cannot be determined, (D).

Distort the Figures

Since you cannot trust the figures, you may be able to determine the answer to Quantitative Comparisons by distorting them.

Example:

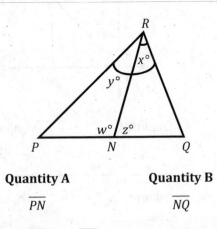

Quantity A	Quantity B
$\overline{PN}$	$\overline{NQ}$

Although $\overline{PN}$ and $\overline{NQ}$ appear to be equal, there is nothing provided in the figure that defines them as mathematically equal. Distort the figure:

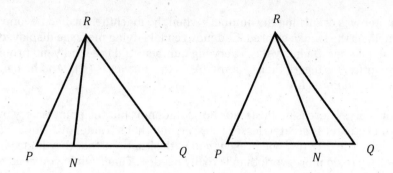

Therefore, a comparison of $\overline{PN}$ and $\overline{NQ}$ is not possible, and the relationship between the two quantities cannot be determined, (D).

Pick (D) Only If You Have a Good Reason

You choose answer (D) when the relationship between the quantities cannot be determined. But don't make the mistake of confusing this idea with "I give up." Choice (D) does not mean "none of the above." Teachers sometimes use "none of the above" when they get tired and can't think of another answer, but the people who write the GRE test never get tired. Compare the following examples:

Examples:

1. If $x = 6 + 7$, then what is the value of x?

    (A) −10
    (B)   1
    (C)   23
    (D) None of the above

$$xy = 0$$

2. | **Quantity A** | **Quantity B** |
   |:---:|:---:|
   | x | y |

The correct answer to the first example is (D) because 6 plus 7 is 13 and none of the answers is 13. The answer to the second example is also (D), but for a different reason. If $xy = 0$, then either x, y, or both x and y are equal to 0, but you don't know which of these scenarios is true. Therefore, the answer is "cannot be determined" (for a good reason) rather than "none of the above."

You have to treat choice (D) as a category in its own right. For every correct answer (D), there is a good reason why the information given is not sufficient to determine the relationship between the two quantities. Don't pick (D) because you are giving up.

Use the "Boris Gudenov" Principle

Perhaps the most important difference between Quantitative Comparisons and ordinary math questions was first identified by the distinguished Cambridge teacher Professor Boris Gudenov of Moscow Polyprep. Professor Gudenov was analyzing the following Quantitative Comparison:

Quantity A	**Quantity B**
$\dfrac{(0.000023)^{23}}{1}$	$\dfrac{1}{(0.000023)^{23}}$

Gudenov's laptop computer was crunching the numbers when the machine, pushed beyond the limits of its hard drive, crashed and burned. As the smoke cleared, Gudenov read its dying message displayed on the monitor: Quantity A is a very small number. Quantity B is a very big number. And the kindly old professor said to himself, "That's good enough; Quantity B is bigger than Quantity A, so the answer is (B)." And he named this principle after himself. (Gudenov = Good Enough)

Okay, so we made up the story. There is no Professor Boris Gudenov, but the point is very important. This is the "Boris Gudenov" Principle: greater is greater, lesser is lesser, and that's "Gudenov." Don't worry about how much greater or how much lesser. The GRE test will present you with situations that they hope will confuse you— situations in which you'll try to do more work than is really needed. That's when you need to remember kindly old Professor Gudenov.

Remember the Two Rules for Guessing

There are two special rules for guessing on Quantitative Comparisons.

Rule 1: If a problem contains nothing but numbers—no geometry figure and no variables—then the correct answer definitely cannot be (D). Consider the following example:

Example:

Quantity A	Quantity B
$\dfrac{(\pi^{23} - 0.62745)^2}{(\sqrt{555} - 0.12)^{10}}$	$\dfrac{(\pi^{23} - 0.62744)^2}{(\sqrt{522} - 0.01)^{10}}$

The GRE test would never ask a question like this because it is just plain silly. We're using it only to make the point that you shouldn't guess (D) to a problem like this. It might take you a week of Sundays to work out the final solution, but you know that eventually you would find that either Quantity A is greater, Quantity B is greater, or that the two quantities are equal. There is no way that the answer could be (D).

Rule 2: If a problem includes a figure that can be manipulated, the answer may well be (D). Earlier, you learned not to trust the figures accompanying Quantitative Comparisons. Now let's take this one step further and turn this feature of the exam to your advantage. The shape that's shown may not be the only possible one for the dimensions specified. If you can think of a way to manipulate the shape shown without violating any of the information given, you may be able to find out something interesting. Consider the following example:

Example:

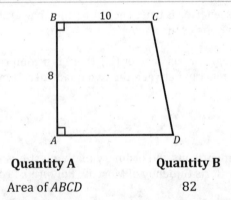

Quantity A	Quantity B
Area of $ABCD$	82

The lengths of $\overline{AD}$ and $\overline{CD}$ aren't specified, so the figure could be a lot of different shapes, including a rectangle. In that case, the area of $ABCD$ would be $8(10) = 80$. But if $\overline{AD}$ were lengthened by extending D to the right, the area of $ABCD$ would increase. Therefore, the area of the figure cannot be determined, so the relationship between the two quantities cannot be determined, (D).

LESSON

The items in this section accompany the Quantitative Reasoning: Comparisons Lesson. You will work through the items with your instructor in class.

DIRECTIONS: Each of the items consists of two quantities, Quantity A and Quantity B. Compare the two quantities, using the information presented. Choose:

> **(A)** if Quantity A is greater.
> **(B)** if Quantity B is greater.
> **(C)** if the two quantities are equal.
> **(D)** if the relationship cannot be determined from the information given.

NOTES: All numbers used are real numbers.

Unless otherwise indicated, all figures lie in a plane.

Geometric diagrams and figures **are not necessarily** drawn to scale, so do **not** assume lengths, angle measures, or other quantities are as they appear in a given figure. You should assume that lines shown as straight are straight and that the positions of points, and geometric objects in general, exist in the order shown. Base your answers to questions with geometric figures on reasoning, not visual estimation or measurement.

Coordinate systems and graphic data presentations **are** drawn to scale, so you can answer items based on visual estimation or measurement.

A symbol that appears more than once in an item has the same meaning throughout the item.

Answers are on page 705.

Examples of What Is Tested

Arithmetic

	Quantity A	Quantity B
1.	2 dozen	23

	Quantity A	Quantity B
2.	$0.5 \cdot 0.2$	$0.5 + 0.2$

	Quantity A	Quantity B
3.	$48^2 + 2(48)(52) + 52^2$	$(100)(100)$

Algebra

	Quantity A	Quantity B
4.	$x + 1$	x

$p > 0$

	Quantity A	Quantity B
5.	p	$2p$

$2x - 4 = 10$

	Quantity A	Quantity B
6.	x	7

	Quantity A	Quantity B
7.	x^3	x^4

(A) if Quantity A is greater.
(B) if Quantity B is greater.
(C) if the two quantities are equal.
(D) if the relationship cannot be determined from the information given.

Geometry

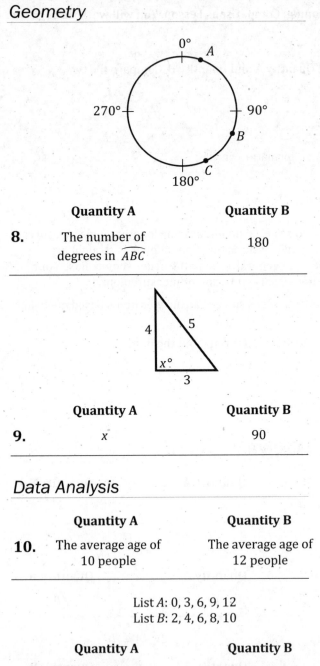

Quantity A	Quantity B
8. The number of degrees in $\overset{\frown}{ABC}$	180

Quantity A	Quantity B
9. x	90

Data Analysis

Quantity A	Quantity B
10. The average age of 10 people	The average age of 12 people

List A: 0, 3, 6, 9, 12
List B: 2, 4, 6, 8, 10

Quantity A	Quantity B
11. Standard deviation of the numbers in List A	Mean of the numbers in List B

The Top Quartile of Difficulty

Quantity A	Quantity B
12. $\frac{2}{3}+\frac{5}{6}$	$\frac{2+5}{3+6}$

Hector is x years old, and Maria is y years younger than Hector.

Quantity A	Quantity B
13. x	y

x is positive.

Quantity A	Quantity B
14. x	x^2

John's birthday is separated from Pat's birthday by three days and Pat's birthday is separated from Ellen's birthday by six days.

Quantity A	Quantity B
15. The number of days separating John's birthday from Ellen's	10

$<x>$ denotes the greatest integer less than or equal to x.

Quantity A	Quantity B
16. $<3\frac{1}{16}>+<-3\frac{1}{16}>$	0

(A) if Quantity A is greater.
(B) if Quantity B is greater.
(C) if the two quantities are equal.
(D) if the relationship cannot be determined from the information given.

Arithmetic and Algebra Comparisons Strategies

Use Your Number Sense

$$\frac{a}{b}=1 \qquad \frac{b}{a}=1$$

	Quantity A	Quantity B
17.	a	1

	Quantity A	Quantity B
18.	$(x^2-y^2)^2$	$(y^2-x^2)^2$

$$x(y+z)=0$$
$$y=-z$$

	Quantity A	Quantity B
19.	x	$y+z$

n is a positive integer.

	Quantity A	Quantity B
20.	Remainder when $2n+1$ is divided by 2	Remainder when $3n+1$ is divided by 2

x and y are positive integers.

	Quantity A	Quantity B
21.	$\dfrac{x}{y}$	$\dfrac{x+1}{y+1}$

$$S_1=\{1,3,5,7,9\}$$
$$S_2=\{2,4,6,8\}$$

	Quantity A	Quantity B
22.	The sum of any 3 different numbers from S_1	The sum of any 2 different numbers from S_2

$$x \cdot 1 = \frac{1}{x}$$

	Quantity A	Quantity B
23.	x	1

x is not equal to 0.

	Quantity A	Quantity B
24.	$\dfrac{|x|}{x}$	1

Simple Operations and Expressions— Just Do It!

	Quantity A	Quantity B
25.	The number of prime numbers between 1 and 25	9

	Quantity A	Quantity B
26.	$-3 \cdot -4 \cdot 3$	$2 \cdot 0 \cdot 5$

	Quantity A	Quantity B
27.	$2{,}000 \cdot 0.05$	$20 \cdot 5$

	Quantity A	Quantity B
28.	$100-0.009$	$99+0.0001$

Medium eggs cost $0.80 per dozen, and large eggs cost $0.90 per dozen.

	Quantity A	Quantity B
29.	The cost of nine dozen medium eggs	The cost of eight dozen large eggs

	Quantity A	Quantity B
30.	The distance traveled in 7 hours and 30 minutes by a train moving at a constant speed of 115 miles per hour	The distance traveled in 5 hours and 30 minutes by a train moving at a constant speed of 150 miles per hour

x is a 2-digit number divisible by 2, 3, and 5.

	Quantity A	Quantity B
31.	x	60

$$5^{m-n} = 5$$

	Quantity A	Quantity B
32.	m	n

$$x = \frac{1}{y}$$

	Quantity A	Quantity B
33.	$x^2 + x^3 + x^4$	$y^2 + y^3 + y^4$

	Quantity A	Quantity B
34.	$(a-b)(a+c)$	$a(a+c) - b(a+c)$

	Quantity A	Quantity B
35.	$3(x+3)$	$3x+3$

	Quantity A	Quantity B
36.	$2(x+2)$	$2x+4$

	Quantity A	Quantity B
37.	$t+t+t$	$3t$

	Quantity A	Quantity B
38.	$x+x+x$	x^3

	Quantity A	Quantity B
39.	$(x^2 y^3)^4$	$(x^4 y^6)^2$

$$xy = 0$$

	Quantity A	Quantity B
40.	$(x+y)^2$	$x^2 + y^2$

$$xy = 2$$

	Quantity A	Quantity B
41.	$(x+y)^2$	$x^2 + y^2 + 2$

	Quantity A	Quantity B
42.	$(x+2)(y+3)$	$(x+3)(y+2)$

	Quantity A	Quantity B
43.	Combined weight of p packages weighing k kilograms each	Combined weight of k packages weighing p kilograms each

$$a > b > 0$$

	Quantity A	Quantity B
44.	(60% of a) + (40% of b)	50%$(a+b)$

(A) if Quantity A is greater.
(B) if Quantity B is greater.
(C) if the two quantities are equal.
(D) if the relationship cannot be determined from the information given.

A dress originally priced at $120 is reduced by 10 percent. The price of the dress is then increased by 10 percent to x dollars.

	Quantity A	Quantity B
45.	x	120

	Quantity A	Quantity B
46.	The cost of x copies of a book at y dollars per copy	The cost of y gallons of fuel at x dollars per gallon

$$\frac{2}{x} + \frac{1}{5} = \frac{1}{3x}$$

	Quantity A	Quantity B
47.	x	-8

$$x > 0$$
$$y > 0$$

	Quantity A	Quantity B
48.	The time required to travel x kilometers at y kilometers per hour	The time required to travel $\frac{x}{2}$ kilometers at $2y$ kilometers per hour

Weather station L recorded at least some precipitation for every day in July. x is the number of days during July for which L recorded more than 0.0 inches but less than 0.15 inches of precipitation, and y is the number of days for which L recorded 0.15 inches or more of precipitation.

	Quantity A	Quantity B
49.	$31 - (x + y)$	Number of days during July for which L recorded no precipitation

In 1999, University U first enrolled part-time students. In 2000, and again in 2001, the number of part-time students enrolled at University U increased by 1,250.

	Quantity A	Quantity B
50.	Percent increase in the number of part-time students from 1999 to 2000	Percent increase in the number of part-time students from 2000 to 2001

$$2^{3x} = 64$$
$$3^{2y} = 81$$

	Quantity A	Quantity B
51.	x	y

The ratio of blue marbles to red marbles in a box is $1 : 2$. After two more red marbles and one more blue marble are added to the box, the ratio of blue marbles to red marbles is $x : y$.

	Quantity A	Quantity B
52.	x	y

In a taste-test matching soft drink P against soft drink Q, each participant chose either P or Q. P was chosen by $\frac{2}{5}$ more people than those who chose Q.

	Quantity A	Quantity B
53.	The fraction of test participants who chose P	$\frac{7}{12}$

(A) if Quantity A is greater.
(B) if Quantity B is greater.
(C) if the two quantities are equal.
(D) if the relationship cannot be determined from the information given.

$$x^2 + 3x - 4 = 0$$

Quantity A	Quantity B
54. Three times the sum of the roots of the equation	-9

$$\frac{1}{x} \div \frac{1}{y} = \frac{2}{7}$$

Quantity A	Quantity B
55. $\frac{x}{y}$	$\frac{y}{x}$

Approximate—That's Good Enough!

Quantity A	Quantity B
56. $\frac{111}{221}$	$\frac{222}{445}$

Quantity A	Quantity B
57. $\left(-\frac{1}{2}\right)^{23}$	$\left(\frac{1}{2}\right)^{23}$

Quantity A	Quantity B
58. $0.123 \div 123$	$123 \div 0.123$

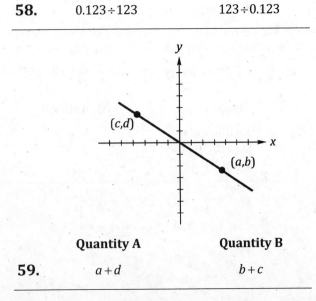

Quantity A	Quantity B
59. $a + d$	$b + c$

Strategy of Number Substitution

Quantity A	Quantity B
60. x^2	x^3

$$x \neq 0$$

Quantity A	Quantity B
61. x^2	x^3

$$x \neq 0$$
$$x \neq 1$$

Quantity A	Quantity B
62. x^2	x^3

$$x > 0$$
$$x \neq 1$$

Quantity A	Quantity B
63. x^2	x^3

$$x > 1$$

Quantity A	Quantity B
64. x^2	x^3

Quantity A	Quantity B
65. $\frac{k}{10^{22}}$	$\frac{k}{10^{21}}$

$$s > t$$

Quantity A	Quantity B
66. s^2	t^2

(A) if Quantity A is greater.
(B) if Quantity B is greater.
(C) if the two quantities are equal.
(D) if the relationship cannot be determined from the information given.

	Quantity A	Quantity B
67.	x^2	$2x$

$$x^2 = y^2$$

	Quantity A	Quantity B
68.	x^2	xy

x and y are positive integers.
x is greater than y.

	Quantity A	Quantity B
69.	x^y	y^x

$$w > 1$$

	Quantity A	Quantity B
70.	The number of widgets produced in an hour if the average rate of production is w widgets per hour	The number of widgets produced in an hour if the average rate of production is 1 widget per w hours

After Diana spent $\frac{1}{2}$ of her allowance on a book and another \$3 on lunch, $\frac{1}{6}$ of her allowance remained.

	Quantity A	Quantity B
71.	Diana's allowance	\$18

Simplify Comparisons

	Quantity A	Quantity B
72.	The sum of all the integers from 33 to 91, inclusive	The sum of all the integers from 34 to 92, inclusive

	Quantity A	Quantity B
73.	$5 \cdot 6 \cdot 7 \cdot 8 \cdot 9 \cdot 10$	$50 \cdot 54 \cdot 56$

	Quantity A	Quantity B
74.	$\frac{13}{14}$	$\frac{14}{15}$

	Quantity A	Quantity B
75.	$(n-1)(n)(n+1)$	n^3

	Quantity A	Quantity B
76.	$\frac{9}{11}$	$\sqrt{\frac{9}{11}}$

	Quantity A	Quantity B
77.	$10^{11} - 10^{10}$	10^{10}

	Quantity A	Quantity B
78.	$\frac{1}{\sqrt{3}}$	$\sqrt{3}$

	Quantity A	Quantity B
79.	$\frac{101}{102} \cdot \frac{102}{103} \cdot \frac{103}{104} \cdot \frac{104}{105} \cdot \frac{105}{106}$	$\frac{101}{106}$

	Quantity A	Quantity B
80.	$3x + 2x + 2$	$2x + 3$

$$m > 1$$

	Quantity A	Quantity B
81.	$\frac{m + m + m + m}{m \cdot m}$	$\frac{4}{m^2}$

(A) if Quantity A is greater.
(B) if Quantity B is greater.
(C) if the two quantities are equal.
(D) if the relationship cannot be determined from the information given.

	Quantity A	Quantity B
82.	$2x$	x

	Quantity A	Quantity B
83.	$\dfrac{x+2}{2}$	$\dfrac{x+4}{5}$

	Quantity A	Quantity B
84.	$25(1)+25(2)+$ $25(3)+25(4)$	250

	Quantity A	Quantity B
85.	$36(437)$	$37(436)$

	Quantity A	Quantity B
86.	$3{,}250^2 - 3{,}249^2$	$7{,}000$

$$x - 1 < 0$$

	Quantity A	Quantity B
87.	$\dfrac{x^2-1}{x-1}$	$x+1$

$$x + 1 \neq 0$$

	Quantity A	Quantity B
88.	$\dfrac{x^2-1}{x+1}$	$x-1$

	Quantity A	Quantity B
89.	$(x+2)^2$	$(x-2)^2$

	Quantity A	Quantity B
90.	0.9	$\sqrt{0.9}$

Method of Simultaneous Equations

$$2x + y = 7$$
$$x + y = 4$$

	Quantity A	Quantity B
91.	x	y

$$x + y = 5$$
$$x - y = 1$$

	Quantity A	Quantity B
92.	x	y

$$3x = 4y$$

	Quantity A	Quantity B
93.	0	$4y - 3x$

An investor bought two CDs. CD X paid 4% interest, and CD Y paid 6% interest. Let a = amount deposited at 4%, and let b = amount deposited at 6%. The total amount of money invested in the two CDs was $60,000. Combined interest from the two CDs was $2,960.

	Quantity A	Quantity B
94.	Amount invested in CD X	Amount invested in CD Y

$$x + y = 7$$
$$xy = 6$$
x and y are integers.

	Quantity A	Quantity B
95.	x	y

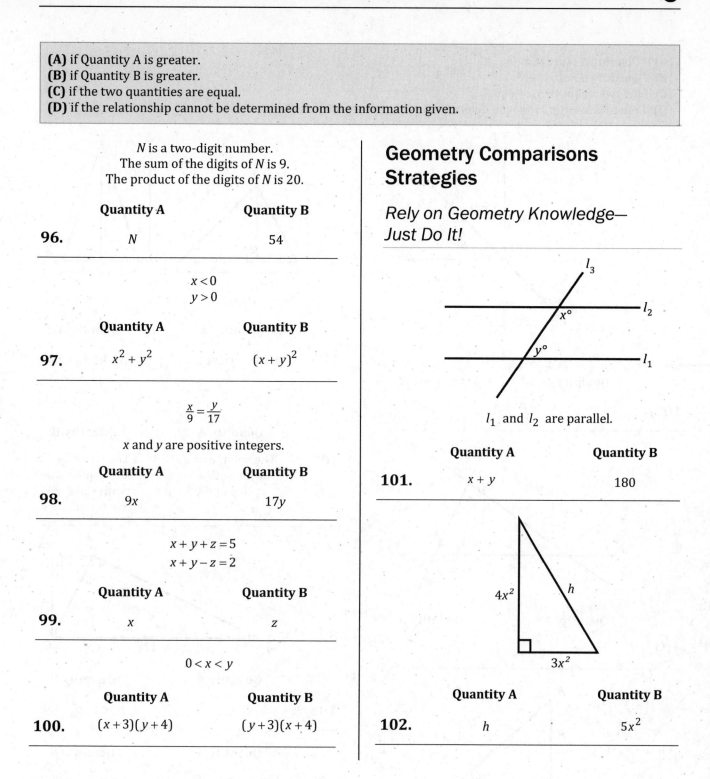

N is a two-digit number.
The sum of the digits of N is 9.
The product of the digits of N is 20.

	Quantity A	Quantity B
96.	N	54

$x < 0$
$y > 0$

	Quantity A	Quantity B
97.	$x^2 + y^2$	$(x + y)^2$

$$\frac{x}{9} = \frac{y}{17}$$

x and y are positive integers.

	Quantity A	Quantity B
98.	$9x$	$17y$

$x + y + z = 5$
$x + y - z = 2$

	Quantity A	Quantity B
99.	x	z

$0 < x < y$

	Quantity A	Quantity B
100.	$(x + 3)(y + 4)$	$(y + 3)(x + 4)$

Geometry Comparisons Strategies

Rely on Geometry Knowledge— Just Do It!

l_1 and l_2 are parallel.

	Quantity A	Quantity B
101.	$x + y$	180

	Quantity A	Quantity B
102.	h	$5x^2$

(A) if Quantity A is greater.
(B) if Quantity B is greater.
(C) if the two quantities are equal.
(D) if the relationship cannot be determined from the information given.

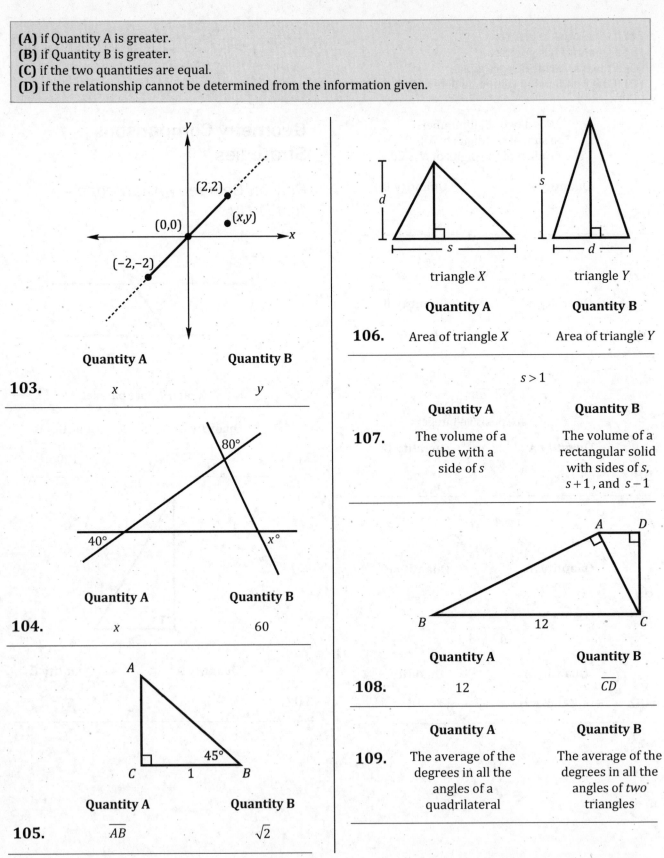

	Quantity A	**Quantity B**
103.	x	y

	Quantity A	**Quantity B**
104.	x	60

	Quantity A	**Quantity B**
105.	$\overline{AB}$	$\sqrt{2}$

triangle X | triangle Y

	Quantity A	**Quantity B**
106.	Area of triangle X	Area of triangle Y

$$s > 1$$

	Quantity A	**Quantity B**
107.	The volume of a cube with a side of s	The volume of a rectangular solid with sides of s, $s+1$, and $s-1$

	Quantity A	**Quantity B**
108.	12	$\overline{CD}$

	Quantity A	**Quantity B**
109.	The average of the degrees in all the angles of a quadrilateral	The average of the degrees in all the angles of *two* triangles

(A) if Quantity A is greater.
(B) if Quantity B is greater.
(C) if the two quantities are equal.
(D) if the relationship cannot be determined from the information given.

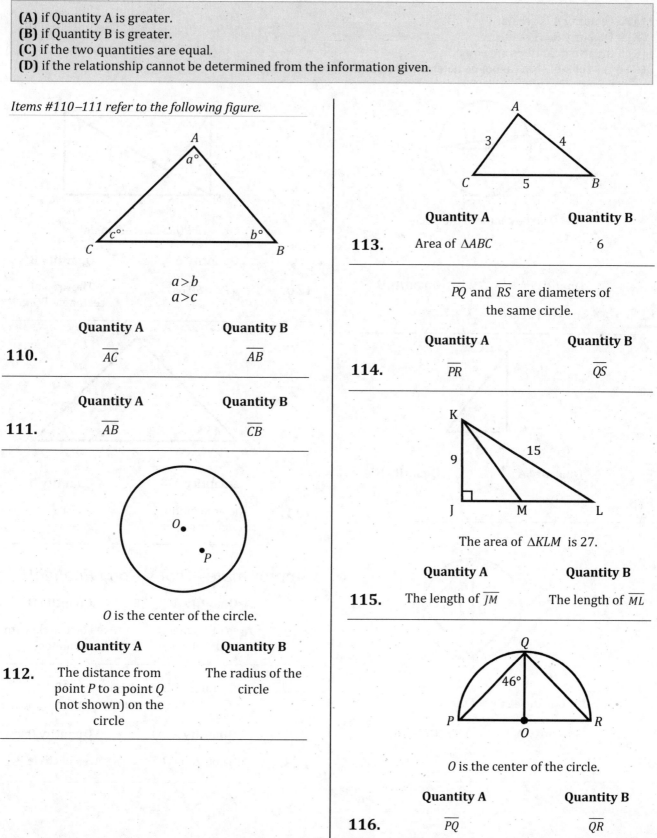

Items #110–111 refer to the following figure.

$$a > b$$
$$a > c$$

	Quantity A	Quantity B
110.	$\overline{AC}$	$\overline{AB}$

	Quantity A	Quantity B
111.	$\overline{AB}$	$\overline{CB}$

O is the center of the circle.

	Quantity A	Quantity B
112.	The distance from point *P* to a point *Q* (not shown) on the circle	The radius of the circle

	Quantity A	Quantity B
113.	Area of $\triangle ABC$	6

$\overline{PQ}$ and $\overline{RS}$ are diameters of the same circle.

	Quantity A	Quantity B
114.	$\overline{PR}$	$\overline{QS}$

The area of $\triangle KLM$ is 27.

	Quantity A	Quantity B
115.	The length of $\overline{JM}$	The length of $\overline{ML}$

O is the center of the circle.

	Quantity A	Quantity B
116.	$\overline{PQ}$	$\overline{QR}$

(A) if Quantity A is greater.
(B) if Quantity B is greater.
(C) if the two quantities are equal.
(D) if the relationship cannot be determined from the information given.

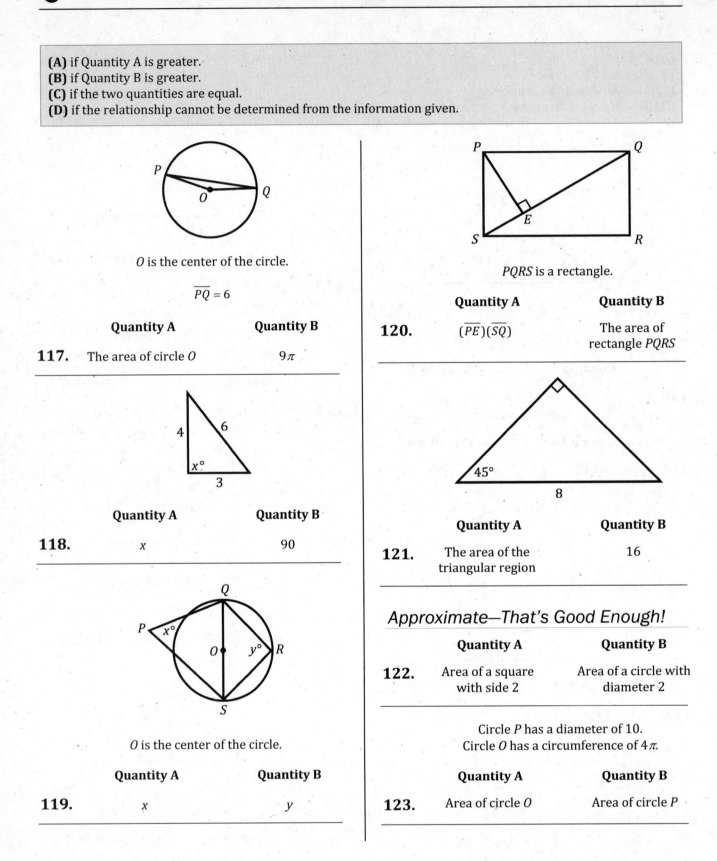

O is the center of the circle.

$$\overline{PQ} = 6$$

	Quantity A	Quantity B
117.	The area of circle *O*	9π

	Quantity A	Quantity B
118.	*x*	90

O is the center of the circle.

	Quantity A	Quantity B
119.	*x*	*y*

PQRS is a rectangle.

	Quantity A	Quantity B
120.	$(\overline{PE})(\overline{SQ})$	The area of rectangle *PQRS*

	Quantity A	Quantity B
121.	The area of the triangular region	16

Approximate—That's Good Enough!

	Quantity A	Quantity B
122.	Area of a square with side 2	Area of a circle with diameter 2

Circle *P* has a diameter of 10.
Circle *O* has a circumference of 4π.

	Quantity A	Quantity B
123.	Area of circle *O*	Area of circle *P*

(A) if Quantity A is greater.
(B) if Quantity B is greater.
(C) if the two quantities are equal.
(D) if the relationship cannot be determined from the information given.

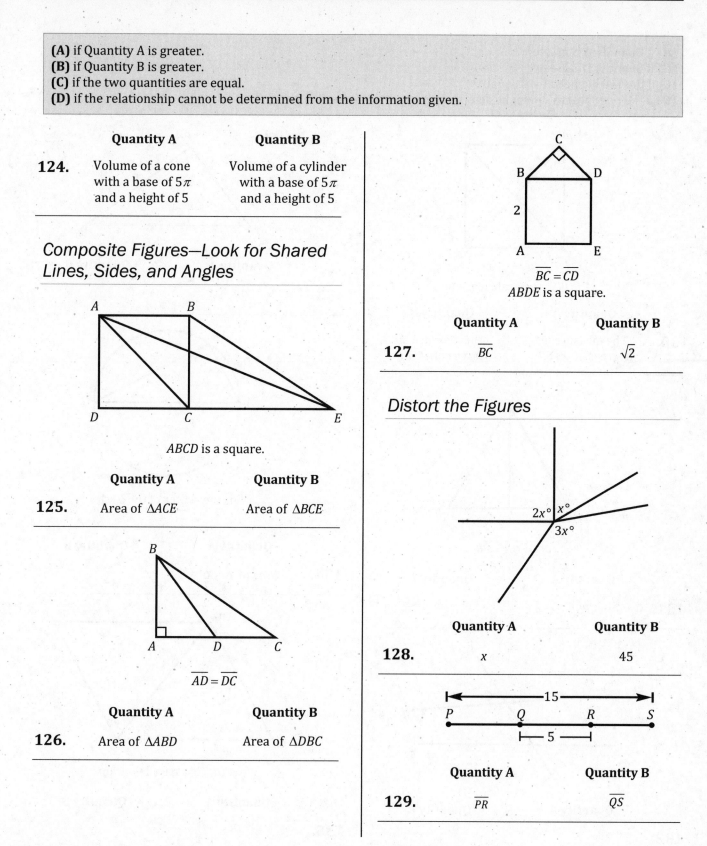

	Quantity A	Quantity B
124.	Volume of a cone with a base of 5π and a height of 5	Volume of a cylinder with a base of 5π and a height of 5

Composite Figures—Look for Shared Lines, Sides, and Angles

ABCD is a square.

	Quantity A	Quantity B
125.	Area of $\triangle ACE$	Area of $\triangle BCE$

$\overline{AD} = \overline{DC}$

	Quantity A	Quantity B
126.	Area of $\triangle ABD$	Area of $\triangle DBC$

$\overline{BC} = \overline{CD}$
ABDE is a square.

	Quantity A	Quantity B
127.	$\overline{BC}$	$\sqrt{2}$

Distort the Figures

	Quantity A	Quantity B
128.	x	45

	Quantity A	Quantity B
129.	$\overline{PR}$	$\overline{QS}$

(A) if Quantity A is greater.
(B) if Quantity B is greater.
(C) if the two quantities are equal.
(D) if the relationship cannot be determined from the information given.

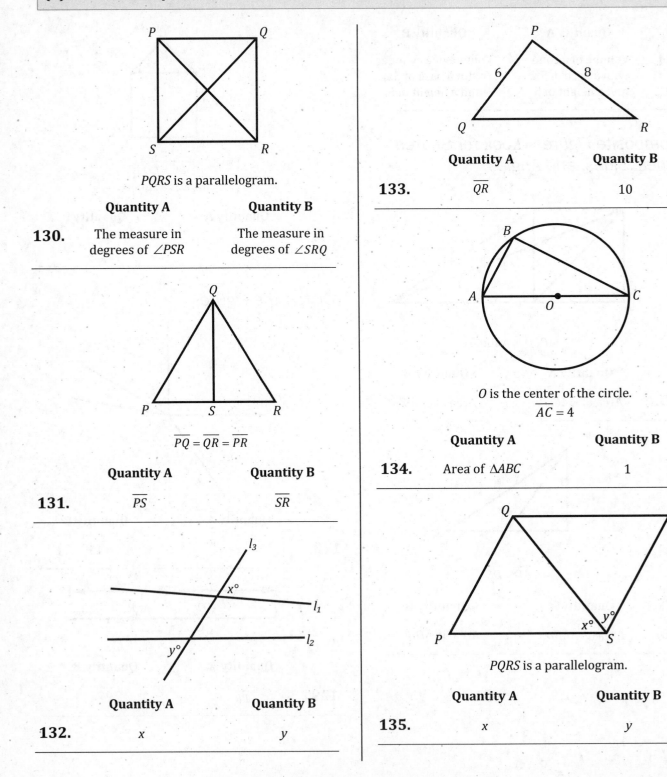

PQRS is a parallelogram.

	Quantity A	Quantity B
130.	The measure in degrees of ∠PSR	The measure in degrees of ∠SRQ

$\overline{PQ} = \overline{QR} = \overline{PR}$

	Quantity A	Quantity B
131.	$\overline{PS}$	$\overline{SR}$

	Quantity A	Quantity B
132.	x	y

	Quantity A	Quantity B
133.	$\overline{QR}$	10

O is the center of the circle.
$\overline{AC} = 4$

	Quantity A	Quantity B
134.	Area of △ABC	1

PQRS is a parallelogram.

	Quantity A	Quantity B
135.	x	y

Comparisons Based on Shaded Figures

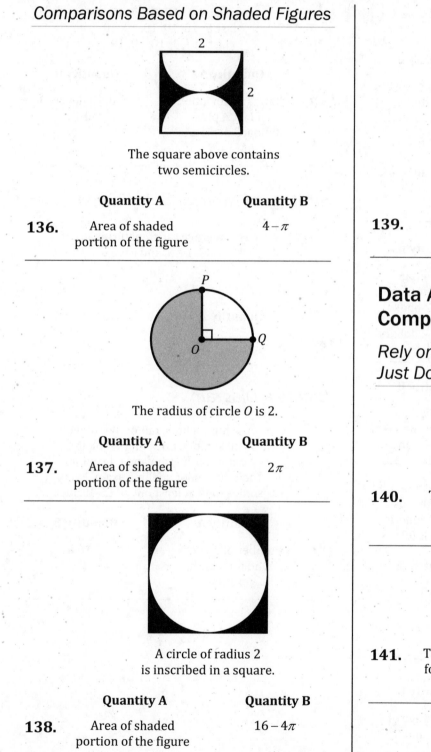

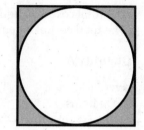

The square above contains
two semicircles.

Quantity A	Quantity B
136. Area of shaded portion of the figure	$4-\pi$

The radius of circle O is 2.

Quantity A	Quantity B
137. Area of shaded portion of the figure	2π

A circle of radius 2
is inscribed in a square.

Quantity A	Quantity B
138. Area of shaded portion of the figure	$16-4\pi$

A circle is inscribed in a square, and
the area of the circle is 36π.

Quantity A	Quantity B
139. Perimeter of the square	48

Data Analysis Comparisons Strategies

Rely on Data Analysis Knowledge—Just Do It!

Three pounds of Brand X laundry powder cost $12.33. Four pounds of Brand Y laundry powder cost $16.44.

Quantity A	Quantity B
140. The average cost per pound of Brand X	The average cost per pound of Brand Y

On a certain test, the average (arithmetic mean) of the scores was 85 for juniors and 89 for seniors.

Quantity A	Quantity B
141. The average score for all juniors and seniors	87

(A) if Quantity A is greater.
(B) if Quantity B is greater.
(C) if the two quantities are equal.
(D) if the relationship cannot be determined from the information given.

The total cost of m items is $21.
The total cost of n items is $25.

	Quantity A	Quantity B
142.	The average cost of the m items	The average cost of the n items

	Quantity A	Quantity B
143.	The average (arithmetic mean) of 23, 19, and 12	The median of 23, 19, and 13

	Quantity A	Quantity B
144.	The average (arithmetic mean) cost of 24 books costing $3x$ dollars	The average (arithmetic mean) cost of 2 books costing $\dfrac{x}{4}$ dollars

	Quantity A	Quantity B
145.	The average (arithmetic mean) of −11, 8, −8, and 11	The average (arithmetic mean) of 1, 2, −1, −2, and 0

The average (arithmetic mean) of a student's 10 test scores is 88. When one of the test scores is dropped, the average (arithmetic mean) of the other 9 test scores is 90.

	Quantity A	Quantity B
146.	The dropped test score	70

Approximate—That's Good Enough!

	Quantity A	Quantity B
147.	The average of 7, 8, and 6	The average of 7, 8, 6, and 0

List A: 9, 10, 11, 7, 13
List B: 10, 10, 10, 10, 10
List C: 1, 1, 10, 19, 19

	Quantity A	Quantity B
148.	Standard deviation of List A plus standard deviation of List B	Standard deviation of List C

Strategy of Number Substitution

The average (arithmetic mean) of 26, 14, x, and y is 10.

$$y > 0$$

	Quantity A	Quantity B
149.	x	0

Create a Diagram

At a high school, out of the total of 120 seniors, 80 seniors took the senior math exam and 64 seniors took the senior spelling exam. Every senior took at least one of the exams.

	Quantity A	Quantity B
150.	Number of seniors who took both exams	16

QUIZZES

This section contains three Quantitative Comparisons quizzes. Complete each quiz while being timed.

DIRECTIONS: Each of the items consists of two quantities, Quantity A and Quantity B. Compare the two quantities, using the information presented. Choose:

    (A) if Quantity A is greater.
    (B) if Quantity B is greater.
    (C) if the two quantities are equal.
    (D) if the relationship cannot be determined from the information given.

NOTES: All numbers used are real numbers.

Unless otherwise indicated, all figures lie in a plane.

Geometric diagrams and figures **are not necessarily** drawn to scale, so do **not** assume lengths, angle measures, or other quantities are as they appear in a given figure. You should assume that lines shown as straight are straight and that the positions of points, and geometric objects in general, exist in the order shown. Base your answers to questions with geometric figures on reasoning, not visual estimation or measurement.

Coordinate systems and graphic data presentations **are** drawn to scale, so you can answer items based on visual estimation or measurement.

A symbol that appears more than once in an item has the same meaning throughout the item.
Answers are on page 706.

Quiz I
(10 items; 16 minutes)

	Quantity A	Quantity B
1.	$\frac{6}{7} - \frac{1}{7}$	$\frac{3}{2} - \frac{1}{2}$

$$\overset{P}{\underset{}{+}} \quad \overset{Q}{\underset{}{+}} \quad \overset{R}{\underset{}{+}} \quad \overset{S}{\underset{}{+}} \quad \overset{T}{\underset{}{+}}$$

	Quantity A	Quantity B
2.	$\overline{PR} + \overline{QT} - \overline{QR}$	$\overline{PT}$

	Quantity A	Quantity B
3.	17.5% of 123	12.3% of 175

$$5 + r + s < 6$$
$$r > 0, s > 0$$

	Quantity A	Quantity B
4.	r	1

	Quantity A	Quantity B
5.	0.3	$\sqrt{0.9}$

$$x^2 = y^3$$

	Quantity A	Quantity B
6.	x^4	y^6

(A) if Quantity A is greater.
(B) if Quantity B is greater.
(C) if the two quantities are equal.
(D) if the relationship cannot be determined from the information given.

Point P with coordinates (x, y)
is exactly 3 units from the origin.

	Quantity A	**Quantity B**
7.	x	3

The perimeter of square $PQRS$ is $12\sqrt{3}$.

	Quantity A	**Quantity B**
8.	Length of a side of square $PQRS$	$4\sqrt{3}$

n is a positive integer.

	Quantity A	**Quantity B**
9.	Remainder when $3n + 4$ is divided by 3	0

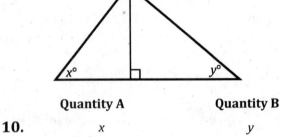

	Quantity A	**Quantity B**
10.	x	y

Quiz II

(10 items; 16 minutes)

DIRECTIONS: Each of the items consists of two quantities, Quantity A and Quantity B. Compare the two quantities, using the information presented. Choose:

(A) if Quantity A is greater.
(B) if Quantity B is greater.
(C) if the two quantities are equal.
(D) if the relationship cannot be determined from the information given.

$$s > t$$

	Quantity A	Quantity B
1.	$s - t$	$t - s$

The cost of three apples and two pears is $2.50.

	Quantity A	Quantity B
2.	The cost of one apple	The cost of one pear

The regular price of a CD is *x* dollars, but it has been discounted by *y* percent.

	Quantity A	Quantity B
3.	x	y

$$p > 0$$
$$q < 0$$

	Quantity A	Quantity B
4.	$p + q$	$p - q$

The distance from City A to City B is 12 miles.
The distance from City A to City C is 10 miles.

	Quantity A	Quantity B
5.	Distance from City A to City B	Distance from City B to City C

The seating capacity of the Red Room is less than the seating capacity of the Blue Room. The seating capacity of the Blue Room is greater than the seating capacity of the Green Room.

	Quantity A	Quantity B
6.	The seating capacity of the Red Room	The seating capacity of the Green Room

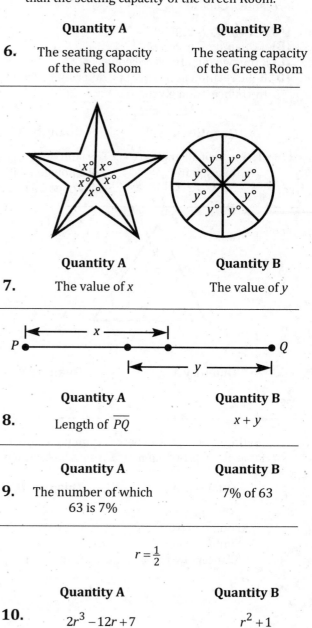

	Quantity A	Quantity B
7.	The value of *x*	The value of *y*

	Quantity A	Quantity B
8.	Length of $\overline{PQ}$	$x + y$

	Quantity A	Quantity B
9.	The number of which 63 is 7%	7% of 63

$$r = \frac{1}{2}$$

	Quantity A	Quantity B
10.	$2r^3 - 12r + 7$	$r^2 + 1$

Quiz III

(10 items; 16 minutes)

DIRECTIONS: Each of the items consists of two quantities, Quantity A and Quantity B. Compare the two quantities, using the information presented. Choose:

(A) if Quantity A is greater.
(B) if Quantity B is greater.
(C) if the two quantities are equal.
(D) if the relationship cannot be determined from the information given.

	Quantity A	Quantity B
1.	The sum of all angles of a square	The sum of all angles of a polygon with sides of equal length

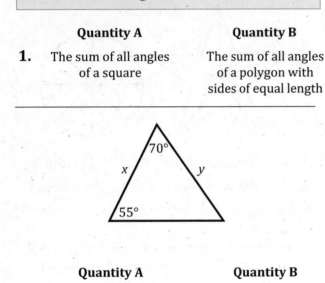

	Quantity A	Quantity B
2.	x	y

Smithtown is 20 kilometers from Jamestown. Jamestown is 50 kilometers from Charlestown.

	Quantity A	Quantity B
3.	Distance in kilometers from Smithtown to Charlestown	70

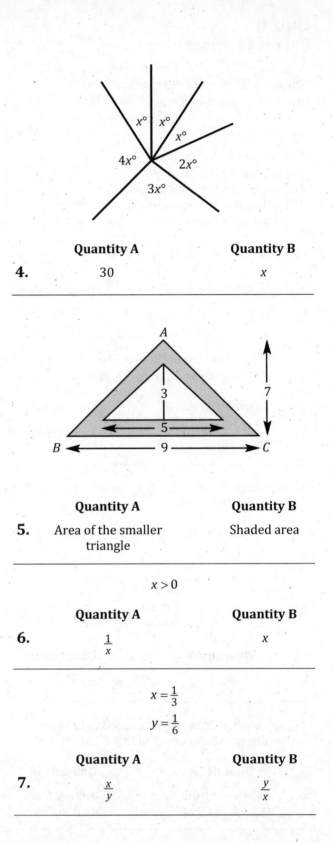

	Quantity A	Quantity B
4.	30	x

	Quantity A	Quantity B
5.	Area of the smaller triangle	Shaded area

$$x > 0$$

	Quantity A	Quantity B
6.	$\dfrac{1}{x}$	x

$$x = \frac{1}{3}$$

$$y = \frac{1}{6}$$

	Quantity A	Quantity B
7.	$\dfrac{x}{y}$	$\dfrac{y}{x}$

(A) if Quantity A is greater.
(B) if Quantity B is greater.
(C) if the two quantities are equal.
(D) if the relationship cannot be determined from the information given.

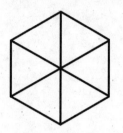

The two-dimensional figure above consists of six equilateral triangles, each with a perimeter of 6.

Quantity A	Quantity B
8. 36	The sum of the lengths of all the line segments in the figure

Quantity A	Quantity B
9. $(a+3)(a-4)$	$a^2 - 7a + 12$

Quantity A	Quantity B
10. Circumference of circle with radius $2r$	Perimeter of square with side πr

STRATEGY SUMMARY

General Strategies

Never guess answer choice (D) to an item that will have numerical solutions.

"Good Enough" Principle: Do only as much work as needed to conserve time.

Simplifying Comparisons: You may add or subtract the same thing to both sides to simplify a comparison; you may also multiply or divide by the same *positive* value.

"Test-the-Test" Strategy: If the problem involves an unknown, you may benefit by substituting numbers. One or two substitutions can eliminate two of the four answer choices.

Different Types of Comparisons

Arithmetic Comparison Strategies

Perform the arithmetic operations if they are manageable, that is, not too time-consuming or complicated (e.g., division and averages).

If the manipulations would take too long, look for one of the shortcuts (e.g., simplifying expressions, factoring, approximations).

Algebra Comparison Strategies

When dealing with variables, remember that negative numbers and fractions sometimes exhibit peculiar behavior. Pay particular attention to the seven ranges on the number line, some of which may be excluded from consideration when the problem's additional information so stipulates: $x < -1$, $x = -1$, $-1 < x < 0$, $x = 0$, $0 < x < 1$, $x = 1$, $x > 1$.

If the item uses algebraic expressions, do whatever operations are indicated, if possible (e.g., distributive law).

If equation(s) are involved, solve for the unknown(s). For example, addition/subtraction or substitution may be used to solve a system of two linear equations with two unknowns.

Employ techniques based on the premise that "it must be one of the guilty suspects." By substituting meaningful numbers for variables, you may gain insight into the appropriate answer or at least eliminate some of the impossible ones. If one of the columns has numerical data, while the other column has a variable, substitute the numerical values for the variable into the scenario presented.

Geometry Comparison Strategies

Use knowledge of geometry principles, such as parallel lines or the Pythagorean theorem.

Quantitative Comparisons items also employ composite figures and figures with shaded areas. So, combine strategies.

Do NOT trust the figures. Do NOT assume that sides are equal, parallel, or at right angles to one another simply because of their appearance. You *are* entitled, however, to assume that lines drawn as straight are straight and that points, angles, and regions are in the relative positions shown.

Data Analysis Comparison Strategies

Use knowledge of data analysis principles, such as calculating an average.

Remember to approximate or substitute numbers when the test allows you to do so.

Create a diagram using your scratch paper if a visual representation of the item will help you determine the answer.

Quantitative Reasoning:
Data Interpretation

Course Concept Outline

---

[1] Some concepts in this Course Concept Outline are not illustrated through examples in your student text but may be covered by your instructor in class. They are included here to provide a complete outline of your course.

TEST MECHANICS

Overview

Each GRE Quantitative Reasoning section contains one or two graphs with two, three, or four corresponding items. This is not written in stone, but, as a generalization, it is pretty reliable.

The graphs are included on the test because many academic disciplines rely heavily on data and use graphs to present the data. Although many people have an initially adverse reaction to graphs, you'll soon find that graphs are not that mysterious. In fact, in many ways, Data Interpretation items are easier than other Quantitative Reasoning items. Frequently, for example, you can solve an item without having to do a calculation—either with the calculator, on paper, or in your head—simply by relying on the data itself.

Anatomy

DIRECTIONS: Solve each problem and choose the correct answer, using the given directions.

Client Lunch Expenses (by partner)					
	Mon	**Tues**	**Wed**	**Thurs**	**Fri**
Anne	$10	$20	$40	$30	$60
Bob	$20	$10	$30	$50	$40
Cathy	$40	$20	$30	$20	$10

1. The total Client Lunch Expenses was greatest on which of the following days?

   (A) Monday
   (B) Tuesday
   (C) Wednesday
   (D) Thursday
   (E) Friday

For the following item, consider the answers separately and select all that apply.

2. The total Client Lunch Expenses was less than $100 for which of the following days?

   Indicate <u>all</u> such days.

   (A) Monday
   (B) Tuesday
   (C) Wednesday

3. On Tuesday, Bob's Client Lunch Expenses accounted for what percent of the total Client Lunch Expenses for that day?

   (A) 10%
   (B) 20%
   (C) 25%
   (D) $33\frac{1}{3}$%
   (E) 40%

This is, technically speaking, not a graph, as it doesn't have an x- and y-axis. But it is data presentation of the most basic format. And it is possible that you could encounter a table like this one on the GRE test.

1. **(E)** *Add up the three Client Lunch Expenses for each of the five days and compare. The largest total is for Friday: $60 + 40 + $10 = $110, (E).*

2. **(A, B)** *On Monday, the total Client Lunch Expenses was $10 + $20 + $40 = $70, on Tuesday $20 + $10 + $20 = $50, and on Wednesday $40 + $30 + $30 = $100. Therefore, the total was less than $100 on Monday, (A), and Tuesday, (B).*

3. **(B)** *The total Client Lunch Expenses on Tuesday was $20 + $10 + $20 = $50, of which Bob's accounted for $10. Therefore, $\frac{\$10}{\$50} = \frac{1}{5} = 20\%$, (B).*

Pacing

The time limit for the 20 math items (Discrete Quantitative, Quantitative Comparison, Numeric Entry, and Data Interpretation) is 35 minutes, so you can afford to spend, on average, about 100 seconds per item. Data Interpretation items have a heavier reading load because of the accompanying data, so plan to spend two minutes answering each of the three or four data interpretation items in each section.

Quantitative Reasoning by Item-Type
Total Time: 35 minutes

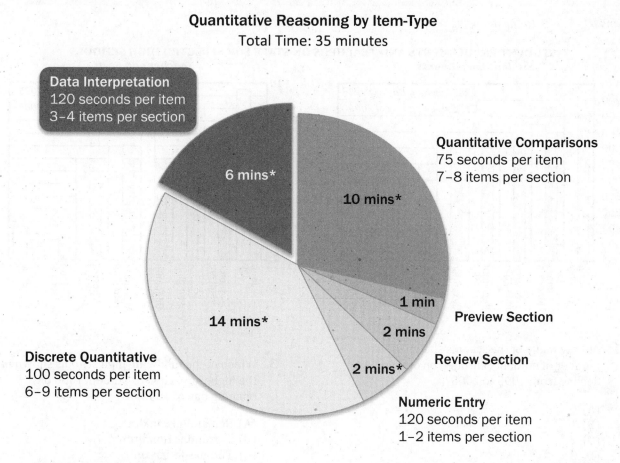

Data Interpretation
120 seconds per item
3–4 items per section

6 mins*

Quantitative Comparisons
75 seconds per item
7–8 items per section

10 mins*

1 min

Preview Section

2 mins

Review Section

14 mins*

2 mins*

Discrete Quantitative
100 seconds per item
6–9 items per section

Numeric Entry
120 seconds per item
1–2 items per section

*Times are approximate

Time Trial

(5 items; 10 minutes)

DIRECTIONS: Each of the following data presentations is accompanied by a series of items. Select the best of the available answer choices or enter your answer. Answers are on page 707.

Items #1–5 refer to the following graphs.

STUDENT ENROLLMENTS AND TEACHERS ON STAFF FOR SELECTED HIGH SCHOOLS

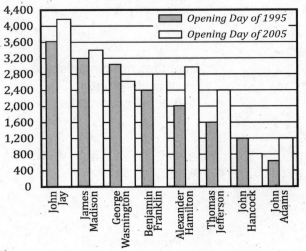

Student Enrollments

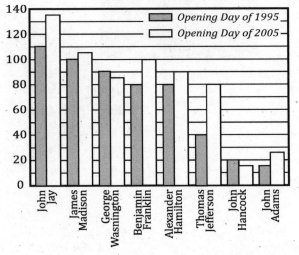

Teachers on Staff

1. At how many of the schools shown did the number of students enrolled on opening day decline from 1995 to 2005?

(A) 0
(B) 1
(C) 2
(D) 3
(E) 4

2. From 1995 to 2005, what was the largest increase in the number of students enrolled on opening day at any high school shown?

(A)   250
(B)   500
(C)   600
(D)   800
(E) 1,000

3. Which of the following high schools shown had the highest teacher-to-student ratio on opening day of 1995?

(A) Benjamin Franklin
(B) Alexander Hamilton
(C) Thomas Jefferson
(D) John Hancock
(E) John Adams

4. Which of the high schools shown had the greatest percent increase in the number of students enrolled on opening day from 1995 to 2005?

   (A) John Jay
   (B) Alexander Hamilton
   (C) Thomas Jefferson
   (D) John Hancock
   (E) John Adams

5. For the school that had the greatest percent increase in the number of teachers on staff on opening day from 1995 to 2005, the number of students enrolled on opening day increased by what percent?

   (A) 20%
   (B) 25%
   (C) $33\frac{1}{3}$%
   (D) 50%
   (E) 60%

Game Plan

Cambridge's GRE Game Plan includes four strategies to help you do your best on Data Interpretation items. Let's look at each strategy in turn.

Learn What Kinds of Data Presentations You Will See

A graph is nothing more than a picture that tells a numerical story. Look again at the table from the "Anatomy" section:

Client Lunch Expenses (by partner)					
	Mon	*Tues*	*Wed*	*Thurs*	*Fri*
Anne	$10	$20	$40	$30	$60
Bob	$20	$10	$30	$50	$40
Cathy	$40	$20	$30	$20	$10

There's nothing wrong with this table, but the information can be presented in many different ways. The following are some examples:

Bar Graph

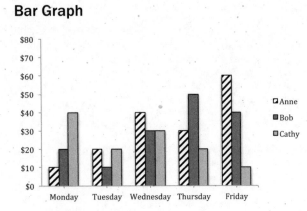

Stacked Bar Graph

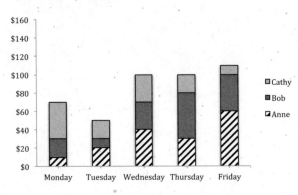

Line Graph

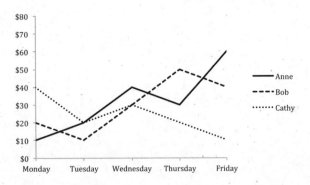

Pie Chart

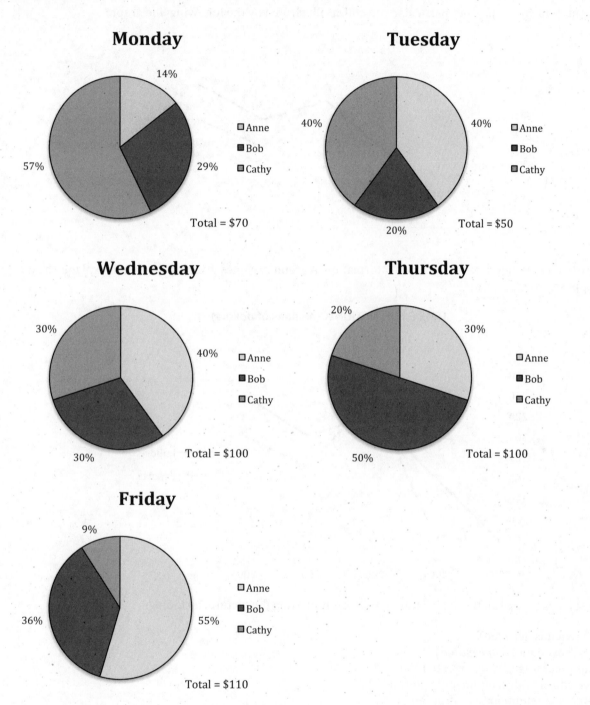

This is only a quick overview of some important types of graphs. Later, you will review data presentations in greater detail.

Read the Graph Before Trying the Items

A data presentation, by itself, is not particularly useful, as illustrated by the following line graph:

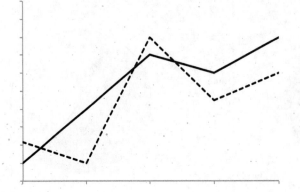

This is a pretty picture, but it doesn't provide information. A graph becomes useful only when it explains the data that it is supposed to represent:

TRADE FOR NATION X (millions of dollars)

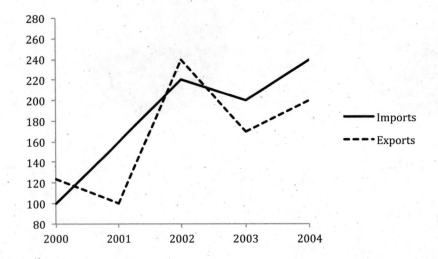

So, your first job is to read all the explanatory notes accompanying the picture, including:

- Title (what is depicted)
- Units (how data are measured)
- *X*-axis (years, ages, category, etc.)
- *Y*-axis (dollar value, number of voters, etc.)
- Footnotes (definitions, clarifications, etc.)

And in the case of pie charts, you know that you will be dealing with percentages. Admittedly, reading all explanatory notes is an investment of time, but if you don't make the investment, then the rest of the time you spend on items is likely to be wasted.

Make the Picture Do the Work

The beauty of graphs is that they do present a picture, and as you know, a picture can be worth a thousand words. Often, you can answer items simply by using the picture.

Examples:

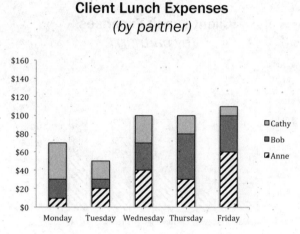

Client Lunch Expenses
(by partner)

1. The partners spent the least amount of money on what day?

   (A) Monday
   (B) Tuesday
   (C) Wednesday
   (D) Thursday
   (E) Friday

The shortest bar shows when the least money was spent, (B).

2. For how many days did the partners' Client Lunch Expenses exceed $60?

   (A) one
   (B) two
   (C) three
   (D) four
   (E) five

As the picture clearly shows, expenses exceeded $60 on Monday, Wednesday, Thursday, and Friday, (D).

Don't Mix Up Percentages and Numbers

The GRE test-writers love to throw curveballs and off-speed pitches, and Data Interpretation items are no exception. A favorite trick of the test-writers is to ask about percentages instead of numbers. The following is an example based on the graph in the previous strategy:

Example:

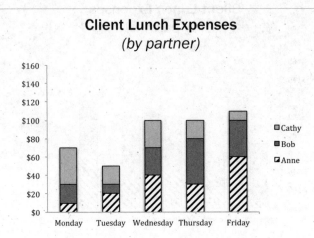

Client Lunch Expenses
(by partner)

The greatest one-day percent increase in Client Lunch Expenses was for which of the following?

(A) Bob: Monday to Tuesday
(B) Cathy: Monday to Tuesday
(C) Bob: Tuesday to Wednesday
(D) Anne: Thursday to Friday
(E) Cathy: Thursday to Friday

The largest percent increase was Bob's $10 to $30 jump from Tuesday to Wednesday, (C): $\dfrac{\text{Change}}{\text{Original}} =$

$\dfrac{\$30-\$10}{\$10} = \dfrac{2}{1} = 200\%$. Note that (D) is an attractive distractor. However, while Anne's increase from Thursday to Friday shows a larger increase in amount ($30), it is a smaller percent increase

$(\dfrac{\text{Change}}{\text{Original}} = \dfrac{\$60-\$30}{\$30} = \dfrac{3}{3} = 100\%)$.

LESSON

The items in this section accompany the Quantitative Reasoning: Data Interpretation Lesson. You will work through the items with your instructor in class.

DIRECTIONS: Each of the following data presentations is accompanied by a series of items. Select the best of the available answer choices or enter your answer. Answers are on page 707.

Facts about Data Interpretation Items

Data Interpretation Figures Are Drawn to Scale

Items #1–4 refer to the following graph.

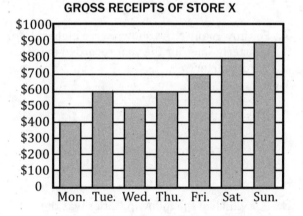

GROSS RECEIPTS OF STORE X

1. During the week shown, what was the greatest increase in sales from one day to the next?

    (A) $50
    (B) $100
    (C) $150
    (D) $200
    (E) $250

2. What was the difference between Tuesday's sales and Wednesday's sales?

    (A) $10
    (B) $50
    (C) $100
    (D) $200
    (E) $500

3. Average daily sales for the week were approximately

    (A) $275
    (B) $400
    (C) $550
    (D) $650
    (E) $850

4. Monday's sales were what percent of Saturday's sales?

    (A) 20%
    (B) $33\frac{1}{3}$%
    (C) 40%
    (D) 50%
    (E) 60%

Different Types of Graphs

Table Charts

Items #5–9 refer to the following graph.

SALES OF COMPANY Z BY CITY
(Thousands of Dollars)

	1st Quarter		2nd Quarter		3rd Quarter		4th Quarter	
	Total	High Week	Total	High Week	Total	High Week	Total	High Week
Atlanta	90.1	10.5	100.3	23.4	60.4	10.6	84.5	12.3
Boston	100.2	14.9	84.7	16.3	120.3	20.7	110.2	23.4
Chicago	151.0	30.1	120.2	33.2	110.7	15.4	118.0	16.3
Detroit	66.2	12.4	48.2	9.5	56.7	8.2	60.2	12.4
Houston	48.9	6.5	40.3	5.4	36.3	6.5	22.1	3.4
Los Angeles	123.7	22.5	116.7	23.4	140.2	22.2	110.4	20.0
Miami	89.2	18.1	76.3	11.1	56.5	8.1	48.2	7.1
New York	220.1	35.2	198.7	26.4	178.3	18.4	199.2	17.6
Seattle	43.2	6.0	38.2	4.5	33.5	3.8	40.1	6.5
Washington, D.C.	76.3	18.1	56.2	8.8	64.2	9.2	53.1	6.6

5. For the first quarter, what was the ratio of the high week to total sales for Chicago?

(A) 1:7
(B) 1:6
(C) 1:5
(D) 1:4
(E) 1:3

6. For the three cities with the highest total sales for the third quarter, approximately what was the average (arithmetic mean) of the total third-quarter sales of those three cities in thousands of dollars?

(A) 110
(B) 128
(C) 135
(D) 146
(E) 158

7. For how many cities shown were highest total quarterly sales for the year recorded in the third quarter?

(A) 2
(B) 3
(C) 4
(D) 5
(E) 6

8. For which of the following cities was the difference in dollar value of total sales recorded between the first quarter and the fourth quarter the least?

(A) Atlanta
(B) Boston
(C) Detroit
(D) Houston
(E) Seattle

For the following item, consider the answers separately and select all that apply.

9. Which of the following conclusions can be inferred from the data?

   Indicate <u>all</u> such conclusions.

   (A) The lowest high week for the entire year was recorded in Seattle.
   (B) The difference between Atlanta's highest quarterly total for the year and its lowest quarterly total was less than that for Washington, D.C.
   (C) For Houston, the lowest ratio of total quarterly sales to high week was recorded in the third quarter.

Item #10 refers to the following table.

HAPPY RIDE AMUSEMENT PARK VISITORS

Day	Number of Visitors
Monday	2,534
Tuesday	2,899
Wednesday	*w*
Thursday	2,219
Friday	2,733

For the following item, enter your answer in the space provided.

10. The table above shows the number of visitors at the Happy Ride Amusement Park from Monday through Friday. If the median number of visitors for the week was 2,534, and no two days had the same number of visitors, what is the greatest possible value for *w*?

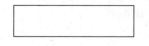

Bar Graphs

Items #11–15 refer to the following graphs.

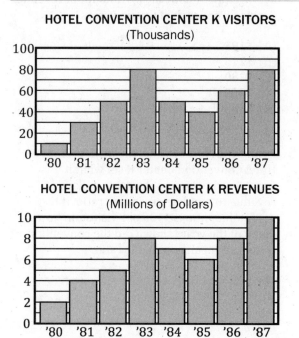

11. For the entire period, what was the greatest increase in visitors from one year to the next?

   (A) 10,000
   (B) 20,000
   (C) 30,000
   (D) 70,000
   (E) 80,000

12. For the period of 1982–86 inclusive, what was the average (mean) number of visitors per year?

   (A) 48,000
   (B) 56,000
   (C) 59,250
   (D) 75,000
   (E) 84,000

13. From 1981 to 1985, which year showed the greatest percentage increase in visitors over the previous year?

   (A) 1981
   (B) 1982
   (C) 1983
   (D) 1984
   (E) 1985

14. If, in 1984, 20 percent of all visitors accounted for 50 percent of the revenues, what was the average (arithmetic mean) amount of revenue derived from each of those visitors?

(A) $185
(B) $215
(C) $280
(D) $350
(E) $385

15. Before the start of 1980, the management of Hotel Convention Center K set what it considered to be an acceptable dollars-of-revenue to number-of-visitors ratio. If the acceptable ratio is $135 per visitor, in how many of the years shown did the convention center attain an acceptable ratio?

(A) 5
(B) 4
(C) 3
(D) 2
(E) 1

Items #16–18 refer to the following graph.

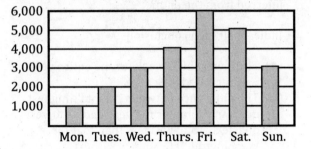

NUMBER OF VEHICLES CROSSING BAY BRIDGE FOR A SELECTED WEEK

16. How many more vehicles crossed Bay Bridge on Saturday than on Sunday?

(A) 1,000
(B) 1,500
(C) 2,000
(D) 2,500
(E) 3,000

17. During the week shown, the average number of vehicles crossing Bay Bridge each day was approximately

(A) 2,100
(B) 2,400
(C) 2,800
(D) 3,000
(E) 3,500

18. The greatest percent increase in the number of vehicles crossing Bay Bridge occurred between

(A) Monday and Tuesday
(B) Tuesday and Wednesday
(C) Wednesday and Thursday
(D) Thursday and Friday
(E) Friday and Saturday

Items #19–21 refer to the following graph.

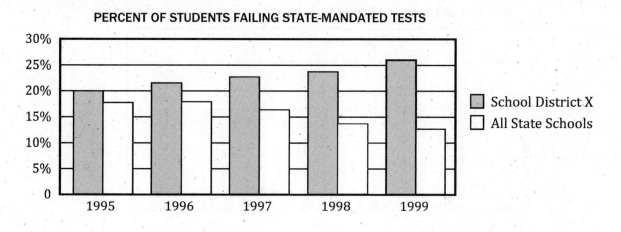

PERCENT OF STUDENTS FAILING STATE-MANDATED TESTS

■ School District X
□ All State Schools

19. If School District X had 1,000 students in 1995, then how many students in District X failed state-mandated tests in that year?

(A) 220
(B) 200
(C) 180
(D) 80
(E) 20

20. If the state classifies as "failing" any school district in which the percent of students failing state-mandated tests exceeds that of all state schools by 50%, in which year was School District X first classified as "failing"?

(A) 1995
(B) 1996
(C) 1997
(D) 1998
(E) 1999

21. Which of the following statements is supported by the data in the graph?

(A) The percent of students in School District X failing state-mandated tests increased by more than 25% from 1995 to 1999.
(B) The number of students in all state schools failing state-mandated tests fell by 50% from 1995 to 1999.
(C) The number of students in all state schools failing state-mandated tests dropped from 1996 to 1999.
(D) The number of students failing state-mandated tests in School District X increased in each of the years between 1996 and 1999.
(E) The number of schools in District X with students failing state-mandated tests exceeded the number of schools statewide in each year shown.

Items #22–24 refer to the following graph.

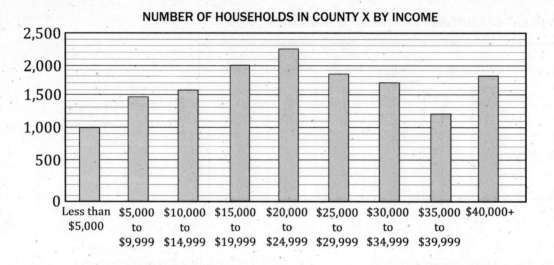

NUMBER OF HOUSEHOLDS IN COUNTY X BY INCOME

22. How many households in County X had incomes between $20,000 and $29,999?

   (A) 1,850
   (B) 2,250
   (C) 4,100
   (D) 4,500
   (E) 4,800

23. By approximately what percent did the number of households in County X with incomes between $15,000 and $19,999 exceed the number with incomes between $10,000 and $14,999?

   (A) 5%
   (B) 10%
   (C) 15%
   (D) 25%
   (E) 40%

24. According to the graph, which of the following statements must be true?

   (A) The number of people living in County X in households with incomes greater than $30,000 but less than $34,999 is 1,750.
   (B) The median income for households in County X is between $20,000 and $24,999.
   (C) The total income of all households in County X with incomes below $5,000 is less than $25,000.
   (D) More households in County X earned between $15,000 and $19,999 than earned between $5,000 and $14,999.
   (E) Total household income for those households in County X with incomes between $35,000 and $39,999 was greater than for those households with incomes between $30,000 and $34,999.

Line Graphs

Items #25–29 refer to the following graph.

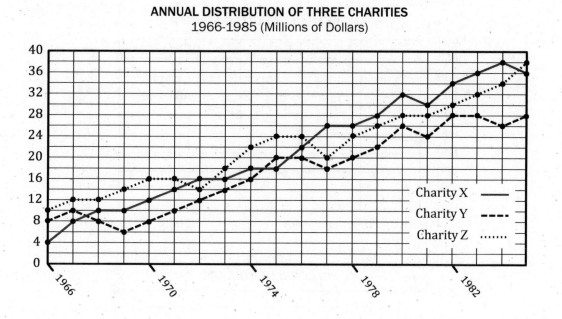

ANNUAL DISTRIBUTION OF THREE CHARITIES
1966-1985 (Millions of Dollars)

25. For how many years was the annual distribution of Charity X greater than those of both Charity Y and Charity Z?

(A) 4
(B) 9
(C) 11
(D) 14
(E) 15

26. From 1971 to 1982, by how many millions of dollars did the annual distribution of Charity Z increase?

(A) 8
(B) 12
(C) 14
(D) 16
(E) 18

27. From 1970 to 1981, by what percent did the annual distribution of Charity X increase?

(A) 100%
(B) 150%
(C) 200%
(D) 250%
(E) 300%

28. In 1977, what were the combined annual distributions of Charity X and Z (in millions)?

(A) 38
(B) 44
(C) 46
(D) 52
(E) 64

For the following item, consider the answers separately and select all that apply.

29. Which of the following statements can be inferred from the information given?

Indicate <u>all</u> such statements.

(A) Between 1969 and 1979, total annual distributions by all three charities combined increased by more than 150%.
(B) For each year after the first year shown, annual distributions by Charity Y failed to increase.
(C) For the years 1978 and 1979 combined, Charity X accounted for greater than one-third of all monies distributed by all charities.

Items #30–32 refer to the following graphs.

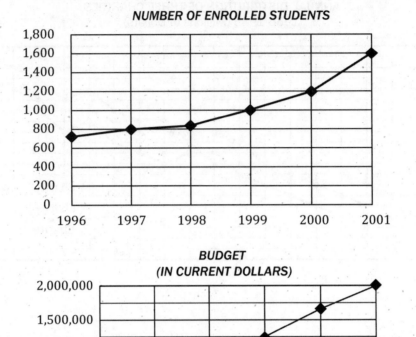

ENROLLMENTS AND BUDGET EXPENDITURES FOR COLLEGE X

NUMBER OF ENROLLED STUDENTS

BUDGET
(IN CURRENT DOLLARS)

30. The average annual increase in the budget (in current dollars) from 1996 to 2001 was approximately

(A) $1,200,000
(B) $750,000
(C) $500,000
(D) $240,000
(E) $25,000

31. For which year did the budget show the greatest percent increase over the previous year?

(A) 1997
(B) 1998
(C) 1999
(D) 2000
(E) 2001

32. The average per student expenditure (in current dollars) was greatest in which year?

(A) 1997
(B) 1998
(C) 1999
(D) 2000
(E) 2001

Items #33–35 refer to the following graph.

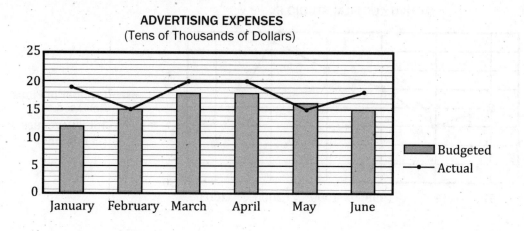

ADVERTISING EXPENSES
(Tens of Thousands of Dollars)

33. For how many of the months shown did actual advertising expenses exceed budgeted advertising expenses?

(A) 2
(B) 3
(C) 4
(D) 5
(E) 6

34. In which of the following months was the ratio of actual advertising expenses to budgeted expenses the highest?

(A) January
(B) February
(C) March
(D) May
(E) June

35. For the entire six-month period shown, total actual advertising expenses exceeded budgeted advertising expenses by

(A) $13,000
(B) $94,000
(C) $107,000
(D) $130,000
(E) $1,007,000

Items #36–38 refer to the following graph.

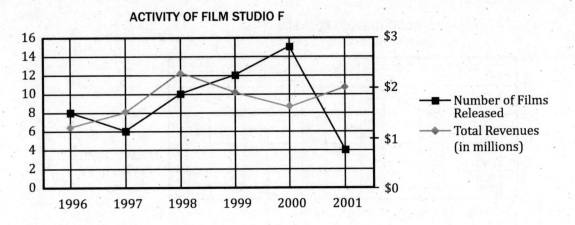

ACTIVITY OF FILM STUDIO F

36. For the period between 1996 and 2001, Film Studio F released how many films?

(A) 40
(B) 46
(C) 49
(D) 52
(E) 55

37. In which year did the films released by Film Studio F generate the greatest revenues per film?

(A) 1997
(B) 1998
(C) 1999
(D) 2000
(E) 2001

38. In how many of the years shown was the average revenue per film released greater than $200,000?

(A) 0
(B) 1
(C) 2
(D) 3
(E) 4

Cumulating Bar Graphs

Items #39–43 refer to the following graphs.

CORPORATION W WORKERS EMPLOYED AND UNITS SHIPPED

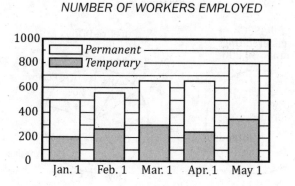

*CORPORATION W
NUMBER OF WORKERS EMPLOYED*

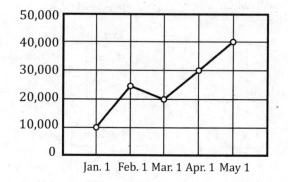

*CORPORATION W
NUMBER OF UNITS SHIPPED*
(Monthly Totals)

39. What was the total number of workers employed by Corporation W on February 1?

(A) 500
(B) 550
(C) 600
(D) 650
(E) 700

40. By what percent did the number of temporary workers employed by Corporation W increase from April 1 to May 1?

(A) 12%
(B) 20%
(C) 25%
(D) $33\frac{1}{3}$%
(E) 40%

41. What was the difference, if any, between the number of permanent workers employed by Corporation W on March 1 and on April 1?

(A) 0
(B) 50
(C) 100
(D) 150
(E) 200

42. Approximately what was the total number of units shipped by Corporation W for the months of January, February, and March, inclusive?

(A) 40,000
(B) 55,000
(C) 60,000
(D) 70,000
(E) 85,000

43. If, on May 1, 60 percent of the permanent workers and 40 percent of the temporary workers employed by Corporation W were women, how many of the workers employed by Corporation W at that time were women?

(A) 180
(B) 200
(C) 260
(D) 410
(E) 800

Circle Graphs

Items #44–48 refer to the following graphs.

**DISTRIBUTION OF ASPCA REGISTERED
DOGS BY BREEDING FOR TWO COUNTIES**

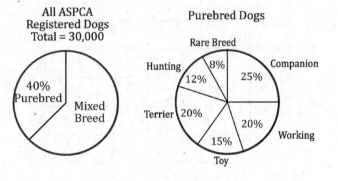

GREEN COUNTY

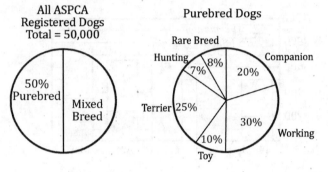

POPE COUNTY

44. How many more purebred dogs are registered with the ASPCA in Pope County than in Green County?

(A) 6,000
(B) 7,500
(C) 10,400
(D) 13,000
(E) 15,500

45. How many more of the purebred dogs registered with the ASPCA in Green County are registered as companion dogs than as working dogs?

(A) 600
(B) 800
(C) 1,600
(D) 2,500
(E) 5,000

46. For Green County and Pope County combined, approximately what percent of all dogs registered with the ASPCA are of mixed breed?

(A) 45%
(B) 49%
(C) 54%
(D) 60%
(E) 69%

47. What is the difference between the number of purebred dogs registered with the ASPCA as working dogs in Pope County and the number registered as working dogs in Green County?

(A) 2,600
(B) 5,100
(C) 6,600
(D) 8,300
(E) 9,000

For the following item, consider the answers separately and select all that apply.

48. Which of the following statements can be inferred from the data?

Indicate all such statements.

(A) More mixed breed dogs are registered with the ASPCA in Green County than in Pope County.
(B) More rare breed purebred dogs are registered with the ASPCA in Green County than in Pope County.
(C) In Pope County, twice as many purebred companion dogs are registered with the ASPCA as purebred toy dogs.

Items #49–51 refer to the following graphs.

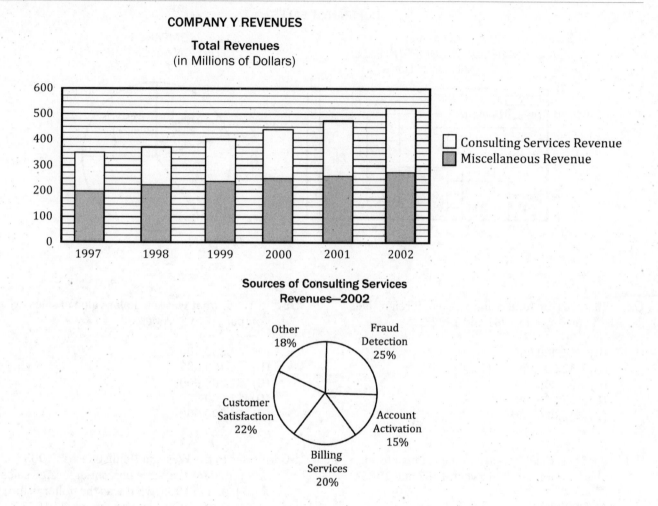

COMPANY Y REVENUES

Total Revenues
(in Millions of Dollars)

**Sources of Consulting Services
Revenues—2002**

49. Total revenues were approximately how much greater in 2001 than in 1998?

(A) $10 million
(B) $40 million
(C) $75 million
(D) $100 million
(E) $125 million

50. From 1998 to 2002, the percent increase in revenues derived from consulting services increased by approximately what percent?

(A) 18%
(B) $33\frac{1}{3}$%
(C) 40%
(D) $66\frac{2}{3}$%
(E) 95%

51. In 2002, the amount of revenue derived from consulting on account activation accounted for what percent of the total revenue for that year?

(A) 3%
(B) 7%
(C) 11%
(D) 18%
(E) 23%

Items #52–56 refer to the following graphs.

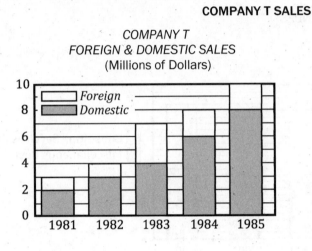

COMPANY T SALES

COMPANY T
FOREIGN & DOMESTIC SALES
(Millions of Dollars)

COMPANY T
FOREIGN SALES (1985)

52. What was the total dollar value of foreign sales by Company T in 1981 and 1982?

(A) $1,000,000
(B) $2,000,000
(C) $3,000,000
(D) $7,000,000
(E) $12,000,000

53. What was the difference in the value of foreign sales by Company T between 1983 and 1985?

(A) $1,000,000
(B) $2,000,000
(C) $3,000,000
(D) $5,000,000
(E) $6,000,000

54. In 1984, foreign sales accounted for what percent of total sales by Company T?

(A) 15%
(B) 20%
(C) 25%
(D) $33\frac{1}{3}$%
(E) 40%

55. In 1985, what was the dollar value of sales by Company T to Europe?

(A) $200,000
(B) $400,000
(C) $1,200,000
(D) $1,600,000
(E) $4,000,000

56. If sales to the Western Hemisphere in 1983 accounted for the same percent of foreign sales as to Japan in 1985, what was the dollar value of sales to the Western Hemisphere in 1983?

(A) $1,050,000
(B) $1,250,000
(C) $1,375,000
(D) $1,425,000
(E) $1,555,000

Items #57–59 refer to the following graphs.

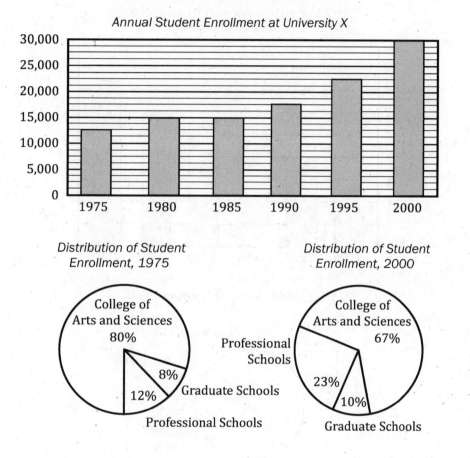

STUDENT ENROLLMENT AT UNIVERSITY X

Annual Student Enrollment at University X

Distribution of Student Enrollment, 1975

Distribution of Student Enrollment, 2000

57. In 1975, the number of students enrolled in professional schools at University X was approximately

(A) 1,000
(B) 1,500
(C) 1,800
(D) 2,400
(E) 10,000

58. Approximately how many more students were enrolled in the College of Arts & Sciences in 2000 than in 1975?

(A) 12,500
(B) 10,000
(C) 8,500
(D) 7,500
(E) 6,000

59. The graphs provide support for which of the following conclusions?

(A) The number of students enrolled in graduate schools increased by $\frac{1}{5}$ from 1975 to 2000.

(B) The number of students enrolled in professional schools almost doubled from 1975 to 2000.

(C) The number of students enrolled in graduate schools increased by approximately the same percentage for each five-year period from 1980 to 2000.

(D) The greatest percent increase in total student enrollment over a five-year period occurred from 1990 to 1995.

(E) The ratio of the number of students enrolled in graduate schools in 2000 to the number enrolled in graduate schools in 1975 was approximately 3 : 1.

Items #60–62 refer to the following graphs.

SALES OF COMPANY X

SALES OF COMPANY X IN THE UNITED STATES
(Billions of Dollars)

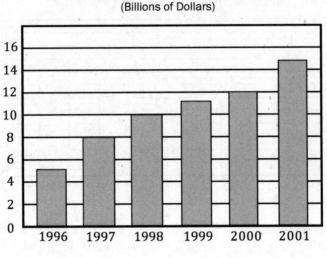

SALES OF COMPANY X BY REGION—2001

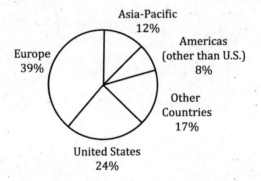

60. Average annual sales by Company X in the United States for the period between 1996 and 2001 was most nearly

(A) $4.5 billion
(B) $6 billion
(C) $7.5 billion
(D) $8.2 billion
(E) $10 billion

61. In which year did the annual sales of Company X in the United States show the greatest percent increase over the previous year?

(A) 1997
(B) 1998
(C) 1999
(D) 2000
(E) 2001

62. Sales of Company X for 2001 in Europe were most nearly

(A) $12 billion
(B) $18 billion
(C) $21 billion
(D) $24 billion
(E) $27 billion

Boxplots

Items #63–64 refer to the following graph.

A professor teaches two classes for Calculus-based Introductory Physics, one class (**1**) of 200 students and the other a class (**2**) of 160 students. The boxplots representing each class's scores on a recent test are shown below.

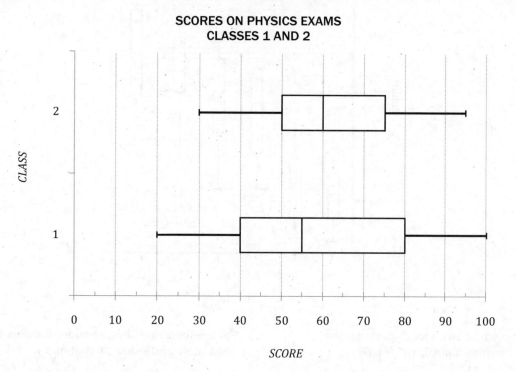

**SCORES ON PHYSICS EXAMS
CLASSES 1 AND 2**

For the following item, consider the answers separately and select all that apply.

63. Which of the following statements can be inferred from the graph?

Indicate all such statements.

(A) The median score for Class 2 was greater than the median score for Class 1.
(B) The range of scores for Class 1 was greater than the range of scores for Class 2.
(C) The number of students in Class 1 who scored below 35 was greater than the number of students in Class 2 who scored below 35.

64. The interquartile range of the scores for Class 1 was how much greater than the interquartile range of the scores for Class 2?

(A) 5
(B) 10
(C) 15
(D) 20
(E) 40

Items #65–66 refer to the following graph.

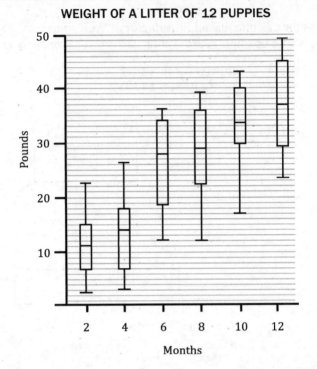

WEIGHT OF A LITTER OF 12 PUPPIES

65. Between which two-month period is the change in third quartile the least?

(A) Between 2 months and 4 months
(B) Between 4 months and 6 months
(C) Between 6 months and 8 months
(D) Between 8 months and 10 months
(E) Between 10 months and 12 months

For the following item, consider the answers separately and select all that apply.

66. Which of the following statements can be inferred from the graphs? Select all that apply.

Indicate <u>all</u> such statements.

(A) The puppies' median weight increased in each successive two-month period.
(B) The median weight of the puppies at 12 months exceeded the third quartile of weights at 10 months.
(C) The range of weights of the puppies was greatest at 8 months.

Scatterplots

Items #67–69 refer to the following graph.

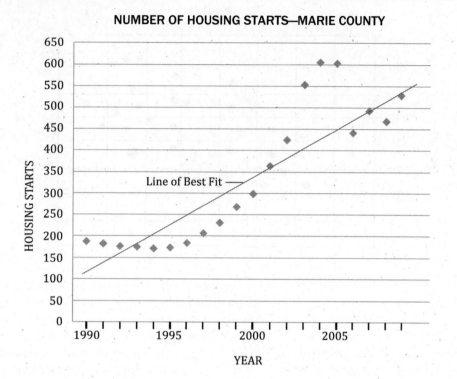

NUMBER OF HOUSING STARTS—MARIE COUNTY

67. In how many of the years shown did the number of housing starts exceed 400?

(A) 3
(B) 4
(C) 5
(D) 7
(E) 8

68. If a year shown on the graph is selected at random, what is the probability that the number of housing starts in that year was greater than 200 but less than 400?

(A) $\frac{1}{4}$

(B) $\frac{3}{10}$

(C) $\frac{2}{5}$

(D) $\frac{1}{2}$

(E) $\frac{7}{10}$

69. The average number of housing starts for the years shown was most nearly

(A) 200
(B) 290
(C) 360
(D) 480
(E) 550

Items #70–72 refer to the following graph.

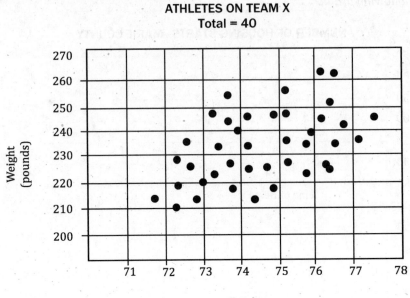

ATHLETES ON TEAM X
Total = 40

70. How many of the athletes are taller than 75 inches but shorter than 77 inches?

(A) 1
(B) 7
(C) 8
(D) 15
(E) 17

72. What percent of the athletes weigh more than 230 pounds or are taller than 74 inches?

(A) 25%
(B) 40%
(C) 50%
(D) 75%
(E) 80%

71. How many of the athletes are shorter than 73 inches and weigh more than 230 pounds?

(A) 1
(B) 7
(C) 8
(D) 13
(E) 14

Frequency Distributions

Item #73 refers to the following graph.

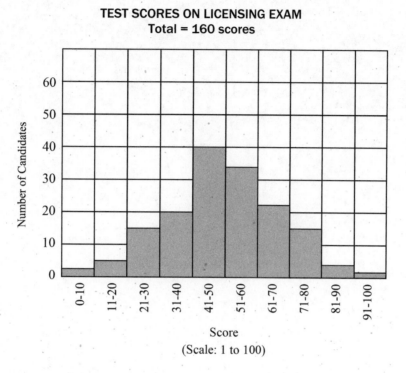

For the following item, consider the answers separately and select all that apply.

73. Which of the following statements can be inferred from the graph?

Indicate <u>all</u> such statements.

(A) More candidates received a score of 50 than received a score of 60.
(B) The lowest score received by any candidate on the exam was 0.
(C) 25 percent of the candidates received scores between 41 and 50 inclusive.

QUIZZES

DIRECTIONS: This section contains three Data Interpretation quizzes. Complete each quiz while being timed. Each of the following questions has five answer choices. Select the best of the available choices. Answers are on page 707.

Quiz I
(5 items; 7 minutes)

Items #1–5 refer to the following graphs.

NEW AND PREVIOUSLY OWNED VEHICLES REGISTERED IN
KING COUNTY AND MEDIAN DECLARED PURCHASED PRICE, 1991-1995

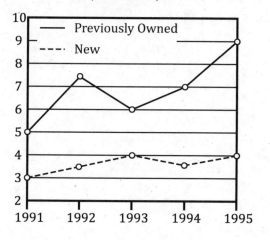

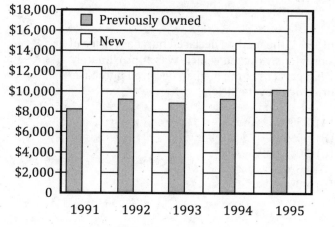

1. According to the information in the graph, the number of new vehicles registered in 1992 was approximately

   (A) 2,500
   (B) 3,500
   (C) 5,000
   (D) 7,500
   (E) 12,500

2. From 1991 to 1995, for how many years was there an increase over the previous year in the number of registrations of both "Previously Owned" vehicles and "New" vehicles?

   (A) 0
   (B) 1
   (C) 2
   (D) 3
   (E) 4

3. From 1993 to 1995, the percent increase in the number of registrations of previously owned vehicles was closest to

(A) 30%
(B) 50%
(C) 60%
(D) 80%
(E) 125%

4. In the year in which the median declared purchase price for previously owned vehicles was closest to that for new vehicles, there were how many registrations of previously owned vehicles?

(A) 5,000
(B) 6,000
(C) 7,500
(D) 8,000
(E) 9,000

5. In 1991, the median declared purchase price of a previously owned vehicle was approximately what percent of the median declared purchase price of a new vehicle?

(A) 25%
(B) 40%
(C) 50%
(D) 65%
(E) 80%

Quiz II

(5 items; 7 minutes)

Items #1–5 refer to the following graphs.

**DISTRIBUTION OF PRIVATE SECTOR WORKFORCE
FOR WASHINGTON AND WARREN COUNTIES**

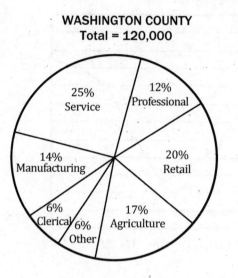

WASHINGTON COUNTY
Total = 120,000

WARREN COUNTY
Total = 160,000

1. In Washington County, how many workers are employed in the professional sector?

   (A) 14,400
   (B) 16,000
   (C) 17,500
   (D) 25,600
   (E) 30,100

2. For Warren County, how many employment categories include more than 24,000 people?

   (A) 1
   (B) 2
   (C) 3
   (D) 4
   (E) 5

3. Warren County has how many more people in the Clerical category than Washington County?

   (A) 8,800
   (B) 7,000
   (C) 5,600
   (D) 4,500
   (E) 3,200

4. The ratio of the number of persons in the Service category in Washington County to the number of persons in the Service category in Warren County is

   (A) 1:2
   (B) 3:4
   (C) 1
   (D) 4:3
   (E) 2

5. For how many of the categories is the number of people employed in Washington County greater than the number of people employed in Warren County?

   (A) 0
   (B) 1
   (C) 2
   (D) 3
   (E) 4

Quiz III

(5 items; 7 minutes)

Items #1–5 refer to the following graphs.

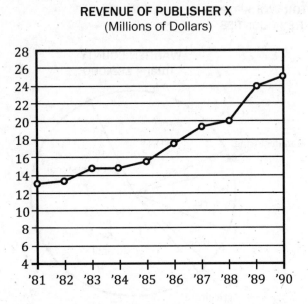

REVENUE OF PUBLISHER X
(Millions of Dollars)

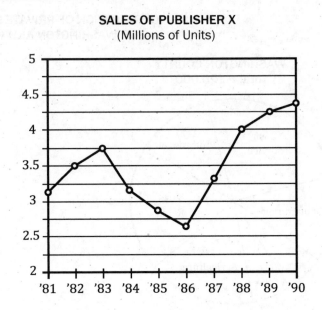

SALES OF PUBLISHER X
(Millions of Units)

1. Revenues of Publisher X were most nearly equal in which of the following years?

   (A) 1981 and 1982
   (B) 1982 and 1983
   (C) 1983 and 1984
   (D) 1984 and 1985
   (E) 1985 and 1986

2. Publisher X sold approximately how many more units in 1988 than in 1984?

   (A)   800,000
   (B) 1,100,000
   (C) 1,400,000
   (D) 1,800,000
   (E) 8,000,000

3. In 1982, Publisher X sold 700,000 units from its fiction line. The fiction line accounted for what percent of the total number of units sold?

   (A)   5%
   (B) 10%
   (C) 15%
   (D) 20%
   (E) 25%

4. How many years after the year 1981 show both an increase in unit sales and an increase in revenues?

   (A) 2
   (B) 3
   (C) 4
   (D) 5
   (E) 6

5. What was the approximate difference between the average revenue per unit generated in 1988 and in 1982?

   (A) $1.20
   (B) $1.70
   (C) $2.50
   (D) $3.25
   (E) $4.10

STRATEGY SUMMARY

General Strategies:

Graphs provide pictorial information accompanied by mathematical problems. Graphs consist not only of lines, bars, or sectors, but also of title(s), legends, scales, and other clarifying information. Understanding data in context takes an investment of time. You may need to calculate minimums/maximums, averages, ratios/percentages, increases/decreases, etc. Get an overview by scanning titles and other verbal cues to understand context. Read the item(s) carefully, and return to the graph(s) to seek needed information. Since graphs are drawn to scale, you can use a sheet of paper as a crude measuring device.

Different Types of Graphs:

Table Charts

Numerical information is presented in matrix form. Rows (records) provide various occurrences (e.g., customers, locations, or accounting transactions). Columns (fields) contain specific attributes pertaining to each record (e.g., purchases, sales, or payments over time). Items may ask for specific information about data within a particular record or field, a group of records or fields, or the entire table.

Bar Graphs

A set of vertical bars denotes comparative numerical values (y-axis values). The horizontal (x-axis) labels, along with graph title(s), indicate the information being tracked (e.g., days of the week, locations of sales, or names of customers). Information may be statistical (histogram or frequency chart). More complicated graphs may contain a group of bars arranged by sets, described via a legend (e.g., sales within specific territories over varying points in time). Alternatively, this type of information could be handled via stacked bar graphs.

Line Graphs

When the horizontal axis is time-related, a series of points may be plotted to denote level of activity over time for various parties. To distinguish the different parties being tracked, the points and/or the lines connecting them will have distinct formats, as indicated by the legend. While discerning trends and intersections is easy, reading values can become somewhat difficult. Using the edge of a piece of paper as a straight-edge may prove valuable.

Cumulating Bar Graphs

Cumulating bar graphs are more complex bar graphs. A set of elements is tracked at each instance along the horizontal axis, as described in the legend. The height/value of the lowest component and the entire bar can be read directly from the vertical scale. Otherwise, specific values can be calculated by subtraction or by using your answer sheet to construct a linear scale.

Pie Graphs

Pie graphs best describe percentages of resource allocation over various parties at a specific point in time. The percentages must total 100%. These graphs are often used in combination with another type of graph, such as a stacked bar graph. In these cases, you need to find the link between the two different graphs (e.g., a particular point in time).

Boxplots

Boxplots, or box-and-whisker plots, provide information about quartiles. The five numbers, L, Q_1, Q_2, Q_3, and G (lowest value, first quartile, second quartile, third quartile, and highest value, respectively), are plotted along a number line (either horizontally or vertically) to indicate the four quartile groups. Remember that Q_2 is simply the median, M.

Frequency Distributions

A histogram showing frequency distribution is simply a variation on the bar graph.

Scatterplots

A scatterplot is exactly what the descriptive title suggests. The picture conveys a rough idea of how the data are distributed (for example, more points above a certain line than below it), but it isn't possible to draw precise conclusions about the distribution. The expectation regarding the types of items associated with scatterplots is that the more complex the presentation (lots of points and little pattern), the more general the questions, and the simpler the presentation (fewer and more clear defined points), the more precise the questions.

Analytical Writing

Course Concept Outline

---

[1] Some concepts in this Course Concept Outline are not illustrated through examples in your student text but may be covered by your instructor in class. They are included here to provide a complete outline of your course.

TEST MECHANICS

Overview

The GRE Analytical Writing section consists of two 30-minute writing tasks: Analyze an Issue and Analyze an Argument. Each writing task is read by at least one human reader who evaluates it on a scale of 0 to 6 in half-point increments, with 6 being the highest possible score. The essay is then evaluated by a computerized scoring system. If the system's score matches the human score, the human score is used as the final score. If the two scores do not match, a second human reader rates the essay, and the average of the two human scores becomes the final score. Once both the Issue and Argument essays are graded, the two scores are averaged to determine the final reported score.

The Analytical Writing section is designed to assess examinees' critical thinking skills and writing abilities, including their reasoning skills, organization, and use of the conventions of standard written English. The best way to prepare for this section of the test is to learn how the topics are structured and how to write effective responses. That's the goal of this part of the program.

The topics are usually called "prompts" by educators. "Prompt" is descriptive of the function of the topic: it prompts you to write something that can be evaluated. (We'll use the terms "prompt" and "topic" interchangeably.) For the Analyze an Issue task, the writing prompt will ask you to take a position and provide evidence supporting your views following a specific format where you evaluate the issue, explore the complexities of the issue, and develop an argument with your point of view supported by reasons and examples. You are expected to demonstrate how well you can develop a compelling argument supporting your point of view and effectively communicate your viewpoint to an academic audience.

For the Analyze an Argument task, the writing prompt asks you to evaluate someone else's argument by assessing its claims and evaluating the evidence it provides. You need to focus on the logical soundness of the argument rather than on whether or not you agree with the position argued. You are expected to demonstrate your ability to understand, analyze, and evaluate arguments.

A word of warning: essays are also reviewed by similarity detection software. ETS may cancel your test scores for the following reasons: substantial similarity to another essay response; inclusion of unattributed quotes, paraphrasing, or ideas; unacknowledged collaboration with others; or borrowed content. If your test scores are cancelled, you forfeit your test fees and are required to pay for and take the entire GRE test again.

Anatomy

Analyze an Issue

Analyze an Issue
30 Minutes

DIRECTIONS: You will be given a brief statement about an issue of general interest and a set of instructions on how to respond to that issue. You will have 30 minutes to plan and write a response following the provided instructions. A response to any other issue will receive a score of zero.

Be sure to follow the specific instructions and support your position with relevant reasons and examples.

Readers will review your essay and grade its overall quality based on the following criteria:

- Follows the specific instructions

- Addresses the complexities of the issue

- Organizes and develops ideas

- Supports ideas with relevant reasons and/or examples

- Controls the elements of standard written English

Take a few minutes to think about the issue and instructions and plan your response before you begin writing. Fully develop your position in a coherent and organized manner. Be sure to leave time to review your essay and make any necessary revisions.

Analyze an Issue
Time—30 minutes

People often complain that manufacturers consciously follow a policy of planned obsolescence and make products that are designed to wear out quickly. Planned obsolescence, consumers insist, wastes both natural and human resources. They fail to recognize, however, that the use of cheaper materials and manufacturing processes keeps costs down for the consumer and stimulates demand.

After the Analyze an Issue writing prompt, you will be presented with one of six sets of instructions:

1. Write an essay in which you discuss the extent to which you agree or disagree with the statement and explain your reasons for the position you take. When developing and supporting your position, consider ways in which the statement may or may not hold true and explain how these considerations shape your position.

2. Write an essay in which you discuss the extent to which you agree or disagree with the recommendation and explain your reasons for the position you take. When developing and supporting your position, describe specific circumstances in which adopting the recommendation could or could not be advantageous and explain how these examples shape your position.

3. Write an essay in which you discuss your views on the policy and explain your reasons for the position you take. When developing and supporting your position, consider the possible consequences of implementing the policy and explain how these consequences shape your position.

4. Write an essay in which you discuss the extent to which you agree or disagree with the claim. When developing and supporting your position, address the most compelling reasons and/or examples that could be used to challenge your position.

5. Write an essay in which you discuss which view more closely aligns with your own position and explain your reasons for the position you take. When developing and supporting your position, address both of the views presented.

6. Write an essay in which you discuss the extent to which you agree or disagree with the claim and the reasons on which that claim is based.

What constitutes a good response? The readers will look at how skillfully you express and support the position you take according to the specified instructions. How well you write is much more important than how much you write. The readers will evaluate your essay's organization, the vocabulary you use, and your writing mechanics and style. Later in the Writing Lesson, you'll learn strategies that will help you create a good impression in each of these areas.

Analyze an Argument

Analyze an Argument
30 Minutes

DIRECTIONS: You will be given a brief passage presenting an argument and a set of instructions on how to respond to that argument. You will have 30 minutes to plan and write a response following the provided instructions. A response to any other argument will receive a score of zero.

Note: You are NOT being asked to present your own views on the subject. Ensure that you follow the specific instructions and support your analysis with relevant reasons and examples.

Readers will review your essay and evaluate its overall quality based on the following criteria:

- Follows the specific instructions

- Identifies and analyzes important features of the argument

- Organizes and develops the evaluation

- Supports the analysis with relevant reasons and/or examples

- Controls the elements of standard written English

Take a few minutes to think about the passage and instructions and plan your response before you begin writing. Fully develop your evaluation in a coherent and organized manner. Be sure to leave time to review your essay and make any necessary revisions.

Analyze an Argument
Time—30 minutes

All commercial airliners operating in the United States should be required to carry a computerized on-board warning system that can receive signals from the transponders of other aircraft. (A transponder is a radio device that signals a plane's course.) The system would be able to alert pilots to the danger of a collision and recommend evasive action. Installation of the system would virtually eliminate the danger of mid-air collisions.

After the writing prompt, you will be presented with one of seven sets of instructions:

1. Write an essay in which you discuss what specific evidence is needed to evaluate the argument and explain how the evidence could weaken or strengthen the argument.

2. Write an essay in which you examine the stated and/or unstated assumptions of the argument. Explain how the argument depends on these assumptions and what the implications are if the assumptions prove unwarranted.

3. Write an essay in which you discuss what questions would need to be answered in order to decide whether the recommendation and the argument on which it is based are reasonable. Explain how the answers to these questions could help to evaluate the recommendation.

4. Write an essay in which you discuss what questions would need to be answered in order to decide whether the advice and the argument on which it is based are reasonable. Explain how the answers to these questions could help to evaluate the advice.

5. Write an essay in which you discuss what questions would need to be answered to decide whether the recommendation is likely to have the predicted result. Explain how the answers to these questions could help to evaluate the recommendation.

6. Write an essay in which you discuss what questions would need to be answered in order to decide whether the prediction and the argument on which it is based are reasonable. Explain how the answers to these questions could help to evaluate the prediction.

7. Write an essay in which you discuss one or more alternatives that could rival the proposed explanation and explain how your explanation(s) can plausibly account for the facts presented in the argument.

A good response will focus on the logic of the writing prompt and not on whether or not you agree with the position presented. The readers will look at your ability to understand, analyze, and evaluate the presented argument according to the specified instructions.

Pacing

Thirty minutes is not a long time to read the topic, consider the specified criteria and provided facts, outline a response, write the response, and then check your work. Consider the following guidelines for pacing on each writing task:

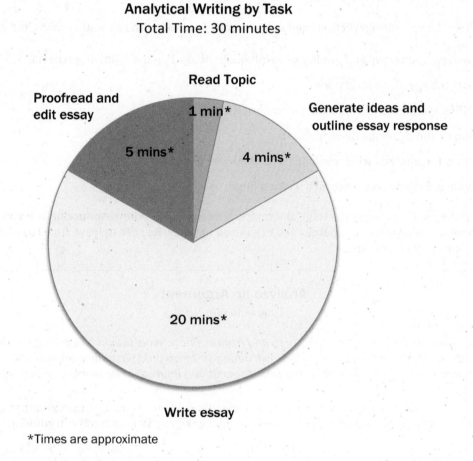

Analytical Writing by Task
Total Time: 30 minutes

Read Topic
1 min*

Proofread and edit essay
5 mins*

Generate ideas and outline essay response
4 mins*

Write essay
20 mins*

*Times are approximate

Each of these four tasks is important and will be discussed in greater detail later in the Writing Lesson. For now, just accept the suggested times for the purpose of discussion. As far as pacing is concerned, you've got to read the topic, generate some ideas, organize your response, write it down, and then proof it to eliminate at least the most egregious of errors. You won't literally spend one minute reading the topic any more than you will spend exactly four minutes thinking and outlining. These are merely suggestions. The main point is that you need a systematic approach: do the steps in this order, and give them the relative importance indicated by the suggested times.

Time Trial

(30 minutes)

DIRECTIONS: You will be given a brief statement about an issue of general interest and a set of instructions on how to respond to that issue. You will have 30 minutes to plan and write a response following the provided instructions. A response to any other issue will receive a score of zero.

Be sure to follow the specific instructions and support your position with relevant reasons and examples.

Readers will review your essay and grade its overall quality based on the following criteria:

- Follows the specific instructions
- Identifies and analyzes important features of the argument
- Organizes and develops the evaluation
- Supports the analysis with relevant reasons and/or examples
- Controls the elements of standard written English

Take a few minutes to think about the issue and instructions and plan your response before you begin writing. Fully develop your evaluation in a coherent and organized manner. Be sure to leave time to review your essay and make any necessary revisions.

> ### Analyze an Argument
> *Time—30 minutes*
>
> All buses used to transport children to and from public schools should be equipped with both lap and harness seat belts. This restraining system would virtually eliminate the danger that a child would be tossed from the seat and injured in the event of an accident.
>
> Write an essay in which you discuss what specific evidence is needed to evaluate the argument and explain how the evidence could weaken or strengthen the argument.

Game Plan

Build Foundational Writing Skills

This course includes a Writing Supplement in Appendix B (p. 677). If you found the Analytical Writing section of your pre-assessment challenging, review the supplemental material to enhance your basic writing skills. (Your instructor may also choose to cover this material in class.)

Respond to the Specific Prompt

Do not write on a topic other than the one specified. Follow the provided instructions. Writing on a topic of your own choice or deviating from the provided instructions is not acceptable.

Don't Copy the Prompt

The readers know the topic, and it is already printed on the screen. If you copy the prompt into your response, it looks like you're simply trying to fill up space.

Be Specific

When writing your essay, be specific. Avoid vague generalizations. For example, here are a few sentences that are weak because they are too vague:

> *"Perfection in house painting is very time-consuming and requires a lot of hard work. You just can't do it in a short time; you've got to invest a lot of effort."*

If you include specific details, the same point can be made much more persuasively. For example, here is the same argument about house painting but made with specific details:

> *"House painting requires attention to details. You have to prepare the surface by scraping away all old and loose paint and carefully washing the surface to be painted. You have to put down dozens of strips of masking tape to protect those areas that should not receive paint, like glass panes, trim to be painted a second color, and fixtures. You have to apply a primer, then a base coat, and then the finishing coat. Finally, you have to apply the second color and clean up all the mistakes. A perfect paint job would take months, and the cost would be prohibitive. That is why when you look closely you will always see imperfections."*

As you can see, the second response is much more compelling because the point of view is supported by specific details. Specific details are frequently the difference between an essay that is successful and one that is not.

LESSON

Grammar Review

DIRECTIONS: The items in this section accompany the in-class review of the concepts and skills, such as grammar, sentence structure, word usage, and punctuation, necessary for success on the GRE Analytical Writing section. Each of the following sentences contains an error of grammar, sentence structure, usage, or punctuation. Circle the letter of the underlined part of the sentence that contains the error. Answers are on page 709.

1. <u>Her</u> and the other members of the team <u>spoke</u>
   A   B
<u>to the press</u> after <u>their</u> final victory.
   C   D

2. In early America, <u>there has been</u> <u>very little</u>
                  A   B
<u>to read</u> except for the books <u>sent</u> from Europe.
  C   D

3. <u>Still remaining</u> in the ancient castle <u>are</u> the
   A   B
Duke's collection of early Dutch paintings,

<u>which</u> <u>will be donated</u> to a museum.
 C   D

4. <u>After having took</u> the entrance examination,
     A
she was <u>absolutely</u> sure that <u>she</u> <u>would be</u>
        B   C   D
<u>admitted</u> to the college.
  D

5. Most students <u>preferred</u> courses in the liberal
         A
arts <u>to</u> courses in science—<u>unless</u> <u>they</u> are
    B   C   D
science majors.

6. The point of the coach's remarks <u>were</u>
                        A
<u>obviously</u> to encourage the team and <u>to restore</u>
  B   C
<u>its</u> competitive spirit.
 D

7. When Mozart <u>wrote</u> "The Marriage of Figaro,"
          A
the Emperor <u>was</u> shocked at <u>him using</u> mere
         B   C
servants <u>as</u> main characters.
    D

8. <u>Since</u> he <u>was called back</u> for a third reading,
  A   B
the actor <u>expected</u> <u>being chosen</u> for the part.
      C   D

9. For a young woman <u>who</u> is ready to join the
              A
work force, there now <u>exists</u> <u>many more</u>
             B   C
opportunities <u>than</u> existed for her mother.
       D

10. Movie fans <u>claim</u> there is <u>no greater</u> director
        A   B
than <u>him</u>, although most critics <u>would mention</u>
   C   D
the names of Bergman or Kurosawa.

11. When the Senate meeting was televised, the
    A   B   C
first issue to be discussed were federal grants
                  D
and loans for higher education.

12. Although the average person watches a news
    A   B
program every day, they do not always
                C
understand the issues discussed.
              D

13. It was said of the noted author Marcel Proust

that he goes out only at night.
A B C   D

14. Most people do not realize that sparkling
              A   B
wines, including champagne, can be made
        C
of red and white grapes.
        D

15. The earliest architecture in the New World

resembled neither that of the European
   A   B
Renaissance or that of the Early Baroque
          C
period, but rather the medieval architecture of
         D
European towns.

16. Like many composers of the period, Debussy
  A
was familiar and admired contemporary poetry
  B   C
and used it as the inspiration for his music.
       D

17. Americans used to go to the movies as often as
                            A
they watched television; however, now that

they can watch movies in their homes, they
 B   C
are doing more of it.
       D

18. After hearing Joan Sutherland perform live at
   A   B
the Metropolitan Opera on December 1, 1984,

I am convinced that she is greater than any prima
                        C
donna of the twentieth century.
 C   D

19. Like Andy Warhol, the pop art of Roy
  A
Lichtenstein is filled with familiar images such as
           B   C   D
cartoon characters.

20. Because the project had been a team effort, we
  A
had divided the bonus equally among the five of
   B   C
us.
D

21. Postponing marriage and having little or no
         A   B
children are not revolutionary choices for
      C
women; they were choices made by the
        D
grandmothers of many postwar women.

22. Being that black bears are large and powerful,
   A   B
most people fear them even though the bears
            C
are really quite shy.
    D

23. Because consumers believe there to be a
       A   B   C
    correlation between price and quality, the cost

    of computer software is steadily raising.
                       D

24. Travel to countries with less than ideal
         A   B
    sanitary conditions increases the amount of
                  C   D
    victims of hepatitis.

25. The fuel truck overturned on the highway,
              A   B
    stopped traffic for over four hours during the
     B   C
    busiest part of the day.
      D

26. Primarily found in the remote mountainous
            A
    regions of the southeastern states, very few
        A
    people die of the bite of the copperhead or
        B
    highland moccasin because very few people
                    C
    come into contact with them.
                 D

27. When Peter started the business in 1982, it
             A
    was hardly nothing more than a one-room
             B
    operation with a single telephone line, but
     B   C
    today Peter has offices in six different states.
           D

28. Unlike in the 1960s when, drugs were used
         A
    primarily by "hippies," cocaine is used today
                       B
    by people from all walks of life, including
     C   D
    lawyers.

29. While the Reagan-Gorbachev summit cannot be
              A
    described as a complete waste of time, nothing
        B   C
    particular significant was accomplished during
         D
    the ten-day meeting.

30. Some people are unusually sensitive
        A   B
    to bee stings and may experience

    allergic reactions including swelling, chills,
               C
    nausea, fever, and they may even become
                  D
    delirious.
      D

31. When Robert introduced the guest speaker he
     A   B
    described his accomplishments in great detail
         C
    but then forgot to mention the speaker's name.
             D

32. The fog was very dense, they were unable
        A   B
    to make out the beacon light on the opposite
     C   D
    shore.
     D

33. Gordon told the clerk that he wanted to order
        A   B
    three bottles of Beaujolais two bottles of port,
             C   D
    three bottles of Merlot, and one bottle of claret.

34. *Guernica*, one of Picasso's many masterpieces
                     A
    was exhibited in the New York Museum of
     A   B
    Modern Art until, as specified in Picasso's will, it
           C
    was returned to Spain once democracy was
        D
    reinstated.

35. <u>Mary Alice who is the dean's choice</u> has
                          A
indicated <u>that she</u> would be willing to serve <u>as</u>
              B   C
chairperson *pro tem* only on the condition that

a search committee <u>be formed</u> within the next
                          D
three weeks.

DIRECTIONS: Your instructor will read through
the following passage in class without and with
the appropriate pauses. Fill in the correct
punctuation.

---

36. On Monday Mark received a letter of
acceptance from State College he immediately
called his mother herself a graduate of State
College to tell her about his acceptance when
he told her he had also been awarded a
scholarship she was very excited after hanging
up Mark's mother decided to throw a surprise
party for Mark she telephoned his brother his
sister and several of his friends because the
party was supposed to be a surprise she made
them all promise not to say anything to Mark
Mark however had a similar idea a party for
his mother to celebrate his acceptance at her
alma mater he telephoned his brother his
sister and several of his parents' friends to
invite them to a party at his house on Saturday
night and he made them all promise to say
nothing to his mother on Saturday night both
Mark and his mother were surprised

Analyze an Issue Essay Concepts and Strategies

This section contains the GRE Analytical Writing Issue prompt that will be used during the in-class lesson to illustrate proper essay development and writing skills. Follow along with your teacher to outline and develop a sample response to the prompt below.

Analyze an Issue
30 Minutes

DIRECTIONS: You will be given a brief statement about an issue of general interest and a set of instructions on how to respond to that issue. You will have 30 minutes to plan and write a response following the provided instructions. A response to any other issue will receive a score of zero.

Be sure to follow the specific instructions and support your position with relevant reasons and examples.

Readers will review your essay and grade its overall quality based on the following criteria:

- Follows the specific instructions
- Addresses the complexities of the issue
- Organizes and develops ideas
- Supports ideas with relevant reasons and/or examples
- Controls the elements of standard written English

Take a few minutes to think about the issue and instructions and plan your response before you begin writing. Fully develop your position in a coherent and organized manner. Be sure to leave time to review your essay and make any necessary revisions.

Analyze an Issue
Time—30 minutes

People often complain that manufacturers consciously follow a policy of planned obsolescence and make products that are designed to wear out quickly. Planned obsolescence, consumers insist, wastes both natural and human resources. They fail to recognize, however, that the use of cheaper materials and manufacturing processes keeps costs down for the consumer and stimulates demand.

Write an essay in which you discuss which view more closely aligns with your own position and explain your reasons for the position you take. When developing and supporting your position, address both of the views presented.

Analyze an Argument Essay Concepts and Strategies

This section contains the GRE Analytical Writing Argument prompt that will be used during the in-class lesson to illustrate proper essay development and writing skills. Follow along with your teacher to outline and develop a sample response to the prompt below.

Analyze an Argument
30 Minutes

DIRECTIONS: You will be given a brief passage presenting an argument and a set of instructions on how to respond to that argument. You will have 30 minutes to plan and write a response following the provided instructions. A response to any other argument will receive a score of zero.

Note: You are NOT being asked to present your own views on the subject. Ensure that you follow the specific instructions and support your analysis with relevant reasons and examples.

Readers will review your essay and evaluate its overall quality based on the following criteria:

- Follows the specific instructions
- Identifies and analyzes important features of the argument
- Organizes and develops the evaluation
- Supports the analysis with relevant reasons and/or examples
- Controls the elements of standard written English

Take a few minutes to think about the passage and instructions and plan your response before you begin writing. Fully develop your evaluation in a coherent and organized manner. Be sure to leave time to review your essay and make any necessary revisions.

Analyze an Argument
Time—30 minutes

All commercial airliners operating in the United States should be required to carry a computerized on-board warning system that can receive signals from the transponders of other aircraft. (A transponder is a radio device that signals a plane's course.) The system would be able to alert pilots to the danger of a collision and recommend evasive action. Installation of the system would virtually eliminate the danger of mid-air collisions.

Write an essay in which you discuss what questions would need to be answered in order to decide whether the recommendation and the argument on which it is based are reasonable. Explain how the answers to these questions could help to evaluate the recommendation.

General Strategies

> **DIRECTIONS:** The sentences below will be used in class to illustrate strategies that will improve the clarity and conciseness of your writing. Read the following sentences and rewrite them to create sentences that are concise, clear, and free of grammatical and mechanical errors. Answers are on page 709–710.

Make Each Sentence Express a Single Thought

37. Although it might be argued that some students will be distracted by windows, but there is no proof of this presented, it is still the case that many students would benefit from the relaxing effect of open scenery, and that could even help them learn.

_____

_____

_____

_____

Plan Each Sentence Before Writing

38. Even if a student is somewhat distracted, they may be even better able to concentrate when their attention returns to the teacher.

_____

_____

_____

Watch for Subject-Verb Agreement

39. This distraction, which occurs in students with more limited attention spans, are easily avoided by arranging desks so that the eyes of a student is directed away from the window.

_____

_____

_____

Watch Pronoun Usage

40. The easiest solution is to have the teacher order each student to keep their eyes directed toward the blackboard.

_____

_____

_____

_____

41. Under this seating arrangement, all of the people in the classroom, except the class monitor and she, will face the blackboard, not the windows.

_____

_____

_____

_____

Avoid Dangling Modifiers

42. While strolling through Central Park, a severe thunderstorm required my companion and me to take shelter in the band shell.

_____

_____

_____

_____

43. Paul told Mary that he would wed her down by the old mill.

_____

_____

_____

_____

Avoid the Passive Voice

44. When the notice was received by me, I immediately reported to the manager's desk.

_____

_____

_____

_____

45. The cake was baked by the chef to please his favorite niece on her wedding day.

_____

_____

_____

_____

Avoid Slang

46. Let the kids do their own thing. It cramps your style to always have the teacher, the man, laying this guilt business on you. Some of the kids would wind up at the shrink's. So, just lay off, and let them be themselves.

_____

_____

_____

_____

QUIZZES

Quiz I – Part A
(Analyze an Issue Essay, 30 minutes)

DIRECTIONS: You will be given a brief statement about an issue of general interest and a set of instructions on how to respond to that issue. You will have 30 minutes to plan and write a response following the provided instructions. A response to any other issue will receive a score of zero.

Be sure to follow the specific instructions and support your position with relevant reasons and examples.

Readers will review your essay and grade its overall quality based on the following criteria:

- Follows the specific instructions
- Addresses the complexities of the issue
- Organizes and develops ideas
- Supports ideas with relevant reasons and/or examples
- Controls the elements of standard written English

Take a few minutes to think about the issue and instructions and plan your response before you begin writing. Fully develop your position in a coherent and organized manner. Be sure to leave time to review your essay and make any necessary revisions.

Analyze an Issue

Time—30 minutes

Many people reminisce about the "good old days," insisting that the quality of life was much better twenty or thirty years ago.

Write an essay in which you discuss the extent to which you agree or disagree with the claim. When developing and supporting your position, address the most compelling reasons and/or examples that could be used to challenge your position.

Quiz I – Part B
(Analyze an Argument Essay, 30 minutes)

DIRECTIONS: You will be given a brief passage presenting an argument and a set of instructions on how to respond to that argument. You will have 30 minutes to plan and write a response following the provided instructions. A response to any other argument will receive a score of zero.

Note: You are NOT being asked to present your own views on the subject. Ensure that you follow the specific instructions and support your analysis with relevant reasons and examples.

Readers will review your essay and evaluate its overall quality based on the following criteria:

- Follows the specific instructions
- Identifies and analyzes important features of the argument
- Organizes and develops the evaluation
- Supports the analysis with relevant reasons and/or examples
- Controls the elements of standard written English

Take a few minutes to think about the passage and instructions and plan your response before you begin writing. Fully develop your evaluation in a coherent and organized manner. Be sure to leave time to review your essay and make any necessary revisions.

Analyze an Argument

Time—30 minutes

The Springwater Regional Library System (SRLS) consists of a main library and twelve branch libraries. In the past, the main library and all but two branches have been open to the public six days a week with the two exceptions open only three days a week. Budget constraints, however, make it impossible to continue this policy. Therefore, in order to ensure that the main library will continue to operate six days a week, some branches should be closed permanently and the operating hours of others should be trimmed as needed.

Write an essay in which you discuss what questions would need to be answered in order to decide whether the recommendation and the argument on which it is based are reasonable. Explain how the answers to these questions could help to evaluate the recommendation.

Quiz II – Part A
(Analyze an Issue Essay, 30 minutes)

DIRECTIONS: You will be given a brief statement about an issue of general interest and a set of instructions on how to respond to that issue. You will have 30 minutes to plan and write a response following the provided instructions. A response to any other issue will receive a score of zero.

Be sure to follow the specific instructions and support your position with relevant reasons and examples.

Readers will review your essay and grade its overall quality based on the following criteria:

- Follows the specific instructions
- Addresses the complexities of the issue
- Organizes and develops ideas
- Supports ideas with relevant reasons and/or examples
- Controls the elements of standard written English

Take a few minutes to think about the issue and instructions and plan your response before you begin writing. Fully develop your position in a coherent and organized manner. Be sure to leave time to review your essay and make any necessary revisions.

Analyze an Issue

Time—30 minutes

Recently, a 98-year-old farmer was asked what he thought was the greatest technological advancement of the past 125 years. He responded, "Electricity, because it made so many chores much easier and faster." A 35-year-old executive was asked the same question, and she responded, "Computers, because they make so many chores much easier and faster."

Write an essay in which you discuss which view more closely aligns with your own position and explain your reasons for the position you take. When developing and supporting your position, address both of the views presented.

Quiz II – Part B
(Analyze an Argument Essay, 30 minutes)

DIRECTIONS: You will be given a brief passage presenting an argument and a set of instructions on how to respond to that argument. You will have 30 minutes to plan and write a response following the provided instructions. A response to any other argument will receive a score of zero.

Note: You are NOT being asked to present your own views on the subject. Ensure that you follow the specific instructions and support your analysis with relevant reasons and examples.

Readers will review your essay and evaluate its overall quality based on the following criteria:

- Follows the specific instructions

- Identifies and analyzes important features of the argument

- Organizes and develops the evaluation

- Supports the analysis with relevant reasons and/or examples

- Controls the elements of standard written English

Take a few minutes to think about the passage and instructions and plan your response before you begin writing. Fully develop your evaluation in a coherent and organized manner. Be sure to leave time to review your essay and make any necessary revisions.

Analyze an Argument
Time—30 minutes

The Village of Twin Forks draws its drinking water directly from Lake Watchakobie. Although the water is filtered to remove solid impurities, it is not treated with chemicals. Many cities, towns, and villages treat water with chlorine and other chemicals to kill bacteria and other organisms that may cause illness and even death. If the Twin Forks filtration plant was reconfigured to include a chemical treatment stage, the health of village residents would be better protected.

Write an essay in which you examine the stated and/or unstated assumptions of the argument. Explain how the argument depends on these assumptions and what the implications are if the assumptions prove unwarranted.

Quiz III – Part A
(Analyze an Issue Essay, 30 minutes)

DIRECTIONS: You will be given a brief statement about an issue of general interest and a set of instructions on how to respond to that issue. You will have 30 minutes to plan and write a response following the provided instructions. A response to any other issue will receive a score of zero.

Be sure to follow the specific instructions and support your position with relevant reasons and examples.

Readers will review your essay and grade its overall quality based on the following criteria:

- Follows the specific instructions
- Addresses the complexities of the issue
- Organizes and develops ideas
- Supports ideas with relevant reasons and/or examples
- Controls the elements of standard written English

Take a few minutes to think about the issue and instructions and plan your response before you begin writing. Fully develop your position in a coherent and organized manner. Be sure to leave time to review your essay and make any necessary revisions.

Analyze an Issue
Time—30 minutes

Many people complain that today's workers no longer take any pride in the work that they do and that, as a result, the products that are made today are not as good as those made years ago.

Write an essay in which you discuss the extent to which you agree or disagree with the statement and explain your reasons for the position you take. When developing and supporting your position, consider ways in which the statement may or may not hold true and explain how these considerations shape your position.

Quiz III – Part B
(Analyze an Argument Essay, 30 minutes)

DIRECTIONS: You will be given a brief passage presenting an argument and a set of instructions on how to respond to that argument. You will have 30 minutes to plan and write a response following the provided instructions. A response to any other argument will receive a score of zero.

Note: You are NOT being asked to present your own views on the subject. Ensure that you follow the specific instructions and support your analysis with relevant reasons and examples.

Readers will review your essay and evaluate its overall quality based on the following criteria:

- Follows the specific instructions
- Identifies and analyzes important features of the argument
- Organizes and develops the evaluation
- Supports the analysis with relevant reasons and/or examples
- Controls the elements of standard written English

Take a few minutes to think about the passage and instructions and plan your response before you begin writing. Fully develop your evaluation in a coherent and organized manner. Be sure to leave time to review your essay and make any necessary revisions.

Analyze an Argument
Time—30 minutes

Central High School has a computer lab. It is available to students Monday through Friday from 8:00 a.m. until 3:00 p.m. Other schools make their computer facilities available during extended hours. If Central High School students are to be able to compete effectively for college admission, scholarships, and jobs, the computer lab must remain open later on weekday afternoons and evenings.

Write an essay in which you examine the stated and/or unstated assumptions of the argument. Explain how the argument depends on these assumptions and what the implications are if the assumptions prove unwarranted.

STRATEGY SUMMARY

Four Testing Areas: Content, Organization, Style, and Mechanics are the four areas tested in the writing assessment. These fall under the task of "how to say it" and are essential to a good essay. The task of "what to say" will become easier with practice.

Strategies for Analyze an Issue Essays:

Position

The first step to developing a strong essay is to take a position. You must decide which position to support, state this position at the start of your essay, and continue to support that position according to the provided instructions.

Instructions

The Analyze an Issue essay will include specific instructions that provide the direction and basis for the development of your essay.

Essay Organization

Because of the 30-minute time limit, essays should be restricted to about four or five paragraphs. The first paragraph should state a position and introduce the main points that support that position. The two or three paragraphs that follow should develop the main points in further detail, following the development outlined in the instructions. The final paragraph should summarize the essay development and may include an optional statement of conclusion.

Writing the Essay

Briefly outline your essay using the provided scratch paper; time spent outlining is included in the 30-minute time limit. When writing the actual essay, do not attempt too much—incomplete essays will receive very low scores. Essays should be concise, avoiding generalities and trite positions. Be sure to save time to proofread your essay.

Strategies for Analyze an Argument Essays:

Content

Chances are that the Argument essay will be a policy topic of some sort. Policy topics cite a problem and propose a solution. The task is to critique the given argument, offering evidence as to why the proposed solution is (or is not) flawed. The answers to the following content questions should make up the heart of the essay:

- **Quantification:** Does the argument establish a serious problem?
- **Inherency:** Is the problem serious enough to warrant radical change?
- **Feasibility:** Are proposed changes possible? Will they work?
- **Disadvantages:** Do the advantages outweigh the disadvantages?

Instructions

The Analyze an Argument essay will include specific instructions that provide the direction and basis for the development of your essay.

Essay Organization

Again, because of the 30-minute time limit, the essay will be no longer than about four or five paragraphs. The first paragraph should state the four reasons why the argument is (or is not) flawed (quantification, inherency, feasibility, and disadvantages). The following four paragraphs should develop each of the four reasons in more detail, giving examples and providing alternative solutions. The last paragraph should summarize the essay's development and provide a statement of conclusion.

Writing the Essay

Again, use the provided scratch paper to briefly outline your essay; time spent outlining is included in the 30-minute time limit. When writing the actual essay, do not attempt too much—incomplete essays will receive very low scores. Essays should be concise; avoid generalities and trite positions. Be sure to save time to proofread your essay.

Practice Test Reinforcement

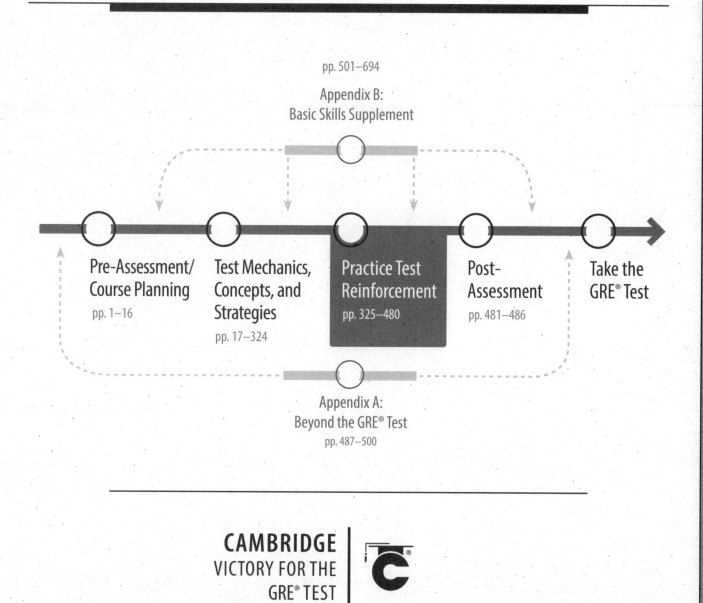

pp. 501–694

Appendix B:
Basic Skills Supplement

Pre-Assessment/
Course Planning
pp. 1–16

Test Mechanics,
Concepts, and
Strategies
pp. 17–324

Practice Test
Reinforcement
pp. 325–480

Post-
Assessment
pp. 481–486

Take the
GRE® Test

Appendix A:
Beyond the GRE® Test
pp. 487–500

CAMBRIDGE
VICTORY FOR THE
GRE® TEST

Directed Study Practice Test

Outline

Section 1–Analytical Writing

Time—30 minutes

Analyze an Issue

DIRECTIONS: You will be given a brief statement about an issue of general interest and a set of instructions on how to respond to that issue. You will have 30 minutes to plan and write a response following the provided instructions. A response to any other issue will receive a score of zero.

Be sure to follow the specific instructions and support your position with relevant reasons and examples.

GRE readers will review your essay and grade its overall quality based on the following criteria:

- Follows the specific instructions
- Addresses the complexities of the issue
- Organizes and develops ideas
- Supports ideas with relevant reasons and/or examples
- Controls the elements of standard written English

Take a few minutes to think about the issue and instructions and plan your response before you begin writing. Fully develop your position in a coherent and organized manner. Be sure to leave time to review your essay and make any necessary revisions.

Issue Topic

> *With improvements in transportation making travel easier and less expensive and advances in technology facilitating communication, individuals increasingly come into contact with more and more people; but as a result, individuals are less likely to form long-lasting and intimate relationships.*
>
> Write an essay in which you discuss the extent to which you agree or disagree with the claim. When developing and supporting your position, address the most compelling reasons and/or examples that could be used to challenge your position.

Analyze an Issue

Sample Essay Response

Because technological advancement has made travel and "virtual travel" easier, people today are better able to form long-lasting and intimate relationships. In the first place, quantity does not necessarily mean a diminution of quality. Second, having access to a wider variety of human experiences makes it more likely that individuals will find other people with whom to share experiences. And third, ease of contact helps people nurture relationships.

First, an increase in the number and variety of people that we know does not necessarily mean that we care less for those with whom we are closest. To be sure, we may meet many more people whom we only get to know casually and with whom we never form lasting bonds. But the fact that we have more casual acquaintances than our parents did does not mean that we cannot have long-lasting and intimate friendships. Indeed, the very fact that many contacts remain superficial means that they cannot possibly overtax our emotional resources. We are still left with a reserve on which to draw to nourish those relations that seem particularly important.

Second, the fact that people today come into contact with so many other people makes it more likely that they will build successful long-lasting and deep relationships—like cross-pollination. For example, 50 years ago, someone who grew up on a farm in Iowa might have had a circle of friends that was limited to people in that immediate area whose experiences were all very similar. Today, the same person might attend a university 1,000 miles away, or spend a summer traveling in other countries, or chat with friends on the internet from around the world. The sheer number of these contacts makes it likely that something will "click" between two people.

Third, if anything, these advances make it easier to nurture long-lasting relationships. The adage "absence makes the heart grow fonder" sounds too much like rationalization: you cannot do anything about separation, so make the best of it. But now if you are away from friends, you can call them on the telephone, exchange e-mail, or even arrange for a special gift over the internet.

Section 2–Analytical Writing

Time—30 minutes

Analyze an Argument

DIRECTIONS: You will be given a brief passage presenting an argument and a set of instructions on how to respond to that argument. You will have 30 minutes to plan and write a response following the provided instructions. A response to any other argument will receive a score of zero.

Note: You are NOT being asked to present your own views on the subject. Ensure that you follow the specific instructions and support your analysis with relevant reasons and examples.

GRE readers will review your essay and evaluate its overall quality, based on the following criteria:

- Follows the specific instructions

- Identifies and analyzes important features of the argument

- Organizes and develops the evaluation

- Supports the analysis with relevant reasons and/or examples

- Controls the elements of standard written English

Take a few minutes to think about the passage and instructions and plan your response before you begin writing. Fully develop your evaluation in a coherent and organized manner. Be sure to leave time to review your essay and make any necessary revisions.

Argument Topic

A recent news article reported that a motorist, angered by the driving of another motorist, rammed the other vehicle, pulled the driver from the car causing serious injury, and then shot a passerby who tried to intervene with a pistol. This is yet another example of road rage, and the best way to combat this rising trend is to require all licensed drivers to attend a one-day clinic on road rage to learn how to recognize its symptoms in themselves and in others and how to control their own rage and avoid becoming the victims of someone else's.

Write an essay in which you examine the stated and/or unstated assumptions of the argument. Explain how the argument depends on these assumptions and what the implications are if the assumptions prove unwarranted.

Analyze an Argument

Sample Essay Response

The argument is an oversimplification in many respects and does not really support the sweeping change called for. First, it fails to quantify the magnitude of the "road rage" problem. Second, it offers no evidence that a one-day clinic will be effective in combating road rage. And third, it may be that such an approach would not be cost-effective and might actually be counterproductive.

First, while "road rage" is a hot topic for the news media, most of what we actually hear is purely anecdotal, like the example included in support of the argument. After all, how many people carry a loaded weapon in their car and are likely to use one? The news media report this or that example of extreme behavior primarily because it is extreme and makes headlines. Before acting on such a suggestion, it would be essential to have some hard data about "road rage": how many incidents occur in a typical period, is the incidence increasing, are encounters really becoming more violent, are the incidents really caused by "road rage" or by some other factor such as job frustration or substance abuse. One just cannot leap from the fact that the incident took place on a roadway to the conclusion that it was caused by driving, any more than one can conclude that a fight caused by too much alcohol was triggered by "bar rage" simply because that is where it occurred.

Second, even assuming that road rage is quantified and documented as a serious syndrome, what reason is there to believe that a one-day workshop would have any beneficial effect? After all, the causes of this sort of violence seem to be deeply rooted, e.g., traumatic childhoods, adult stresses, and many other factors that might respond to long-term professional counseling but probably would not be corrected by a one-day clinic.

Third, the money spent on such clinics might be better spent in other areas. We do not have unlimited resources, and if there is a problem, we need to create policies that will deal with it effectively, for example, perhaps better policing of our highways with more tickets for bad driving would reduce the level of (legitimate) frustration. Additionally, a one-day clinic poorly done might very well trivialize the issue and make already anger-prone people more likely to erupt because they would get the message that the very concept of "road rage" is a joke that no one takes seriously.

Section 3 – Verbal Reasoning

Time—35 minutes

25 Items

For Items #1–4, select <u>one</u> answer choice unless otherwise instructed.

Items #1–4 are based on the following passage.

What we expect of translation is a reasonable facsimile of something that might have been said in our language, but there is involved in this notion a debate between critics as to what constitutes a reasonable facsimile.
5 Most of us at heart belong to the "soft-line" party: a given translation may not be exactly "living language," but the facsimile is generally reasonable. The "hard-line" party aims only for the good translation. The majority of readers never notice the difference, as they
10 read passively, often missing stylistic integrity so long as the story holds them. Additionally, a literature like Japanese may even be treated to an "exoticism handicap."

Whether or not one agrees with Roy A. Miller's
15 postulation of an attitude of mysticism by the Japanese toward their own language, it is true that the Japanese have special feelings toward the possibilities of their language and its relation to life and art, and these feelings have an effect on what Japanese writers write
20 about and how they write. Many of the special language relationships are not immediately available to the non-Japanese.

Even the orthography of written Japanese is a resource not open to us. Tanizaki Jun'ichiro, who
25 elsewhere laments the poverty of "indigenous" Japanese vocabulary, writes in *Bunsho tokuhon* of the contribution to literary effect—to "meaning," if you will—made simply by the way a Japanese author chooses to "spell" a word. In Shiga Naoya's *Kinosaki*
30 *nite*, for example, the onomatopoeic "bu—n" with which a honeybee takes flight has a different feeling for having been written in *hiragana* instead of *katakana*. I read, and I am convinced.

This, of course, is hard to reproduce in translation,
35 although translators labor hard to do so. George Steiner speaks of an "intentional strangeness," a "creative dislocation," that sometimes is invoked in the attempt. He cites Chateaubriand's 1836 translation of Milton's *Paradise Lost*, for which Chateaubriand "created" a
40 Latinate French to approximate Milton's special English as an example of just such a successful act of creation. He also laments what he calls the "'moon in pond like blossom weary' school of instant exotica," with which we are perhaps all too familiar.

1. The author is primarily concerned with

    (A) criticizing translators who do not faithfully reproduce the style of works written in another language

    (B) suggesting that Japanese literature is more complex than English literature

    (C) arguing that no translation can do justice to a work written in another language

    (D) demonstrating that Japanese literature is particularly difficult to translate into English

    (E) discussing some of the problems of translating Japanese literature into English

1. **(E) *Verbal Reasoning/Reading Comprehension/Main Idea***

The author is primarily concerned with discussing some of the problems of translating Japanese literature into English, (E). (A) is wrong because, while the author discusses the difficulty of making a translation, he or she does not criticize translators. (B) is wrong because the author mentions the fact that all languages have their particular difficulties and uses the poetry of Milton—an English poet—as an example of a difficult text to translate. (C) is wrong because, while the author says it is difficult to do justice to a work in another language, he or she refers to some translations that are successful—those that please the "hard-liners," for instance. The author also mentions Chateaubriand's *Paradise Lost* as a successful translation. (D) is wrong because, while the author mentions some of the difficulties of translating Japanese into English, the point of the passage is not that Japanese is particularly difficult but that it is difficult in some particular ways. The passage does not suggest that Japanese is more difficult to translate than are other languages.

2. The author cites Shiga Naoya's *Kinosaki nite* in order to

   (A) illustrate the effect that Japanese orthography has on meaning

   (B) demonstrate the poverty of indigenous Japanese vocabulary

   (C) prove that it is difficult to translate Japanese into English

   (D) acquaint the reader with an important work of Japanese literature

   (E) impress upon the reader the importance of faithfully translating a work from one language to another

2. (A) *Verbal Reasoning/Reading Comprehension/Logical Structure*

The author uses an example taken from *Kinosaki nite* to illustrate the onomatopoeic effect of writing a word in one system of orthography rather than another, (A). (B) is wrong because, while the author mentions the fact that a Japanese writer laments the poverty of indigenous Japanese vocabulary, this is not the point of the example. In fact, the example actually demonstrates a certain richness of the Japanese language. (C) is wrong because the example has nothing to do with translation—it is an example of an effect rendered in Japanese. (D) is wrong because the reader actually learns nothing at all about this work of literature except that this literary device appears in it. Finally, (E) is wrong because, again, the example has nothing to do with translation.

3. In line 23, the word "orthography" means

   (A) poetry
   (B) vocabulary
   (C) spelling
   (D) translation
   (E) literature

3. (E) *Verbal Reasoning/Reading Comprehension/Vocabulary*

In the third paragraph, the author discusses the effect of spelling on Japanese literature, and that is what "orthography" means.

4. It can be inferred that the "exoticism handicap" mentioned by the author is

    (A) the tendency of some translators of Japanese to render Japanese literature in a needlessly awkward style

    (B) the attempt of Japanese writers to create for their readers a world characterized by mysticism

    (C) the lack of literal, word-for-word translational equivalents for Japanese and English vocabulary

    (D) the expectation of many English readers that Japanese literature can only be understood by someone who speaks Japanese

    (E) the difficulty a Japanese reader encounters in trying to penetrate the meaning of difficult Japanese poets

Item #5 is based on the following passage.

Negative consumer reaction to a product is not generated solely by critical negative appraisal of a product's performance. Rather, negative reaction is also the result of a shortfall in product performance in light of consumer expectations. Therefore, businesses should use advertising to adjust consumer expectations to coincide with their products' performances.

5. Which one of the following is implied by the argument above?

    (A) If consumer expectations are sufficiently reduced, then negative consumer reaction to products will disappear.

    (B) If product performances are sufficiently improved, then negative consumer reaction to products will disappear.

    (C) When consumer expectations about product performance are high, negative consumer reaction may persist despite improvements in product performance.

    (D) Performance of consumer products generally is below the level of consumer expectations.

    (E) Consumer expectations often determine the level of performance of consumer products.

4. (A) *Verbal Reasoning/Reading Comprehension/Implied Idea*

The example quoted by the author in the last line of the passage is a translator's attempt to make the English sound exotic because the reader expects the piece to have non-native overtones. Therefore, (A) is the best choice. (B) is wrong because the handicap referred to is the result of translating the poetry, not the result of the Japanese writer's intention. (C) is wrong because, while there may be no word-for-word equivalents, it is a general problem of translation, not merely a problem of translating Japanese into English. (D) is wrong because the handicap is related to translation, not the expectations of the reader. Finally, (E) is wrong because the problem is related to translation, not the problems of a Japanese reader reading in Japanese.

5. (C) *Verbal Reasoning/Critical Reading/ The Conclusion*

With an item such as this that asks for a further conclusion, make sure that the further conclusion is adequately supported by the premises contained in the argument and that it does not go beyond the scope of the argument. The argument states that negative consumer reaction is a function of expectation as well as product performance. Only (C) is implied by the argument: two factors are operating to determine consumer reaction, so adjusting the one but not the other may leave a residuum of dissatisfaction. (A) is wrong because it concludes that expectation is the sole factor in consumer reaction and that product performance is completely irrelevant—(B) is wrong because it concludes that performance is the only relevant factor and that expectations can be ignored—a conclusion that goes beyond the scope of the argument. Furthermore, notice that (A) and (B) both contain extreme language ("disappear"). (D) is wrong because, while the argument discusses negative consumer reaction in light of a product not meeting consumer expectations, it does not suggest that the performance of products is *generally* below the level of those expectations. Finally, (E) is wrong because how well a product performs is not determined by consumer expectations but vice versa.

Items #6–8 are based on the following passage.

For Items #6–8, select <u>one</u> answer choice for each blank from the corresponding column of choices. Fill all blanks in a way that best completes the text.

6. Animal behaviorists theorize that dogs are more (i)_____ than cats because they are pack animals; whereas cats, solitary hunters, are more independent and (ii)_____ and therefore less likely to try to please their owners.

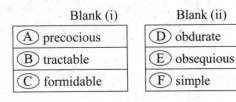

Blank (i)	Blank (ii)
(A) precocious	(D) obdurate
(B) tractable	(E) obsequious
(C) formidable	(F) simple

6. **(B, D)** *Verbal Reasoning/Sentence Completion/Combined Reasoning/Key Adjectives and Adverbs* and *Phrases*

The second blank extends the idea of "solitary" and echoes the idea of independence. On this basis, eliminate (E), "obsequious," and (F), "simple." So, (D) must be the correct choice for the second blank. Indeed, "obdurate," which means "unyielding," extends the idea of independence. The "more _____ than" construction sets up a contrast between some characteristic of dogs and different traits of cats. And the second clause describes cats as independent and unlikely to try to please their owners. So, the first blank must be completed by a word that creates an idea that contrasts with independence, and "tractable," (B), which means "easily managed," works well.

7. On the narrow and _____ mountain road, the truck skidded when it rounded a curve.

(A) pejorative
(B) salutary
(C) propitious
(D) sedulous
(E) torturous

7. **(E)** *Verbal Reasoning/Sentence Completion/Thought Extension/Coordinate Conjunctions*

The coordinate conjunction "and" signals a thought extension: the blank must be filled with a word that extends the idea of a road that is narrow. The phrase that follows the comma ("the truck skidded when it rounded a curve") suggests that the road is dangerous and difficult, and, at the very least, curved. Knowing that "tortuous," (E), means "twisting and winding" answers the question directly. Otherwise, eliminate choices containing words that cannot be correct and make a guess. Note that when the conjunction "and" extends an adjective as part of a pair of adjectives, the second adjective in that pair will not be a synonym of the first adjective. Rather, the missing element will extend the modification.

8. Some concepts, like puberty, have clearly defined biological boundaries. Others, like "adolescence," are (i)_____ umbrellas covering biological moments and their psychological and social consequences. Midlife crisis, with its uncertainty and anxiety, however, has no biological (ii)_____ and is strictly a function of psychology.

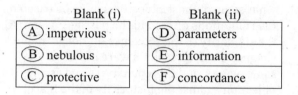

Blank (i)	Blank (ii)
(A) impervious	(D) parameters
(B) nebulous	(E) information
(C) protective	(F) concordance

8. (B, D) *Verbal Reasoning/Paragraph Completion/Combined Reasoning/Phrases*

The first blank must contrast with the "clearly" in the first sentence, and a good opposite is "nebulous," (B). As for the second blank, the paragraph states that "midlife crisis" is defined in psychological terms, not biological terms. So, "parameters," (D), which means "limits or boundaries," is the best choice for the second blank.

For Items #9–13, select <u>one</u> answer choice unless otherwise instructed.

Items #9–12 are based on the following passage.

In the summer of 999, Leif Ericsson voyaged to Norway and spent the following winter with King Olaf Tryggvason. Substantially the same account is given by both the Saga of Eric the Red and the Flat Island Book.
5 Of Leif's return voyage to Greenland the latter says nothing, but according to the former it was during this return voyage that Leif discovered America. The Flat Island Book, however, tells of another and earlier landfall by Biarni, the son of a prominent man named
10 Heriulf, and makes of this Leif's inspiration for the voyage to the new land. In short, like Leif, Biarni, and his companions sight three countries in succession before reaching Greenland, and to come upon each new land takes one "doegr" more than the last until Biarni
15 comes to land directly in front of his father's house in the last mentioned country.

This narrative has been rejected by most later writers, and they may be justified. Possibly, Biarni was a companion of Leif when he voyaged from Norway to
20 Greenland via America, or it may be that the entire tale is but a garbled account of that voyage and Biarni another name for Leif. It should be noted, however, that the stories of Leif's visit to King Olaf and Biarni's to that king's predecessor are in the same narrative in
25 the Flat Island Book, so there is less likelihood of duplication than if they were from different sources.

Additionally, if the two narratives were taken from the same source we should expect a closer resemblance of Helluland. The Saga says of it: "They
30 found there hellus" (large flat stones). According to the Biarni narrative, however, "this land was high and mountainous." The intervals of 1, 2, 3, and 4 "doegr" in both narratives are suggestive, but mythic formulas of this kind may be introduced into narratives without
35 altogether destroying their historicity. It is also held against the Biarni narrative that its hero is made to come upon the coast of Greenland exactly in front of his father's home, but it should be recalled that Heriulfsness lay below two high mountains which
40 served as landmarks for navigators.

I would give up Biarni more readily were it not that the story of Leif's voyage, contained in the supposedly more reliable Saga, is almost as amazing. But Leif's voyage across the entire width of the North
45 Atlantic is said to be "probable" because it is documented in the narrative of a preferred authority, while Biarni's is "improbable" or even "impossible" because the document containing it has been condemned.

For the following item, consider each answer individually and select all that apply.

9. It can be inferred from the passage that scholars who doubt the authenticity of the Biarni narrative make which of the following objections?

   A   Both the Saga of Eric the Red and the Flat Island Book make use of mythical formulas, so it is probable that they were written by the same person.

   B   The historicity of the Saga of Eric the Red is well documented, while the history of the Flat Island Book is very doubtful.

   C   It seems very improbable that a ship, having sailed from America to Greenland, could have found its way to a precise point on the coast of Greenland.

10. The author mentions the two high mountains (line 39) in order to show that it is

   (A) reasonable for Biarni to land precisely at his father's home

   (B) possible to sail from Norway to Greenland without modern navigational equipment

   (C) likely that Biarni landed on America at least 100 years before Leif Ericsson

   (D) probable that Leif Ericsson followed the same course as Biarni

   (E) questionable whether Biarni required the same length of time as Leif Ericsson to complete his voyage

9. (B, C) Verbal Reasoning/Reading Comprehension/Implied Idea

The directions indicate that more than one answer could be correct, so evaluate each answer choice individually. While the author doesn't give a list of the objections to the historicity of the Biarni narrative, it is inferable what some of those objections must be based on the refutations offered in the passage. As for (A), the similarity of the sequence of "doegr" might suggest the two accounts were based on the same events, and this could be raised as an objection against the historicity of the Biarni narrative. But this would not prove the two narratives were written by the same author. Further, someone who rejects the Biarni narrative would surely not want to suggest it has the same source as the saga, the supposedly authentic story. Therefore, (A) is wrong. As for (B), the author specifically attributes this objection to them in the closing sentences. As for (C), in the third paragraph the author argues that it is possible to believe that Biarni could sail directly to his father's house because the house was situated by a known navigational landmark. Therefore, it is inferable that the objectors argue that the event was improbable and that this makes the Biarni narrative less believable. Therefore, (B) and (C) are correct.

10. (A) Verbal Reasoning/Reading Comprehension/Logical Structure

One of the objections to the Biarni narrative is that it would have been difficult for Biarni to navigate so accurately to his father's house. But the author points out that the location of Heriulf's house was clearly indicated by mountains. Therefore, the author mentions the mountains to prove that Biarni could have found the location, (A).

11. It can be inferred that the author regards the historicity of the Biarni narrative as

   (A) conclusively proved
   (B) almost conclusively proved
   (C) possibly true
   (D) highly unlikely
   (E) conclusively disproved

12. Select the sentence in which the author points out the circular reasoning of some authorities.

   (A) Lines 30–32 ("According to the Biarni…mountainous.")
   (B) Lines 32–35 ("The intervals…historicity.")
   (C) Lines 35–40 ("It is also held…navigators.")
   (D) Lines 41–43 ("I would give up…amazing.")
   (E) Lines 44–49 ("But Leif's voyage…condemned.")

11. (C) *Verbal Reasoning/Reading Comprehension/Attitude-Tone*

The answer choices for this item are arranged on a spectrum, ranging from proven to disproven. Use the process of elimination to identify the correct choice. Eliminate (A) and (B) because the author does not claim to have proved his or her case conclusively: in the first sentence of the second paragraph, the author admits that the objectors "may be justified," and in the final paragraph, the phrasing "I would give up…" strongly suggests that the author does not regard the issue as settled. Eliminate (D) and (E) because the author gives several arguments for the historicity of the narrative. Therefore, by the process of elimination, (C) is the correct choice.

12. (E) *Verbal Reasoning/Reading Comprehension/Implied Idea*

In the final paragraph, the author states that the Saga attributes to Leif feats similar to those attributed by the Flat Island Book to Biarni. Yet, most authorities regard Leif's voyage as probable and Biarni's as improbable. Why? Because the Saga is considered authentic and the Flat Island Book inauthentic. But why would the Saga be considered authentic? Because it describes events that are more believable. Hence, the circularity in the argument's reasoning, (E).

Item #13 is based on the following passage.

Production of chlorofluorocarbons (CFCs) is believed to cause the breakdown of fragile ozone molecules in the Earth's atmosphere. During the 1970s, when production of CFCs was high, especially in the United States, scientists found that the quantity of ozone in the atmosphere dropped by an average of about two percent. In 1981, a ban on the manufacture of aerosol spray cans using CFCs went into effect in the United States. In 1986, new measurements showed that ozone quantity levels in the atmosphere had fallen by another one percent as compared to 1981.

For the following item, consider each answer individually and select all that apply.

13. Which of the following, if true, could help provide an explanation for the seeming paradox?

   A   Production of CFCs in Japan and Western Europe rose sharply between 1981 and 1986.

   B   Climatic changes occurring during the early 1980s have contributed to the breakdown of atmospheric ozone.

   C   Other industrialized countries passed similar legislation banning the use of CFCs in aerosol spray cans.

13. (A, B) *Verbal Reasoning/Critical Reading/The Inference/Cause and Effect Situation* and *The Assumptions*

The directions indicate that this item may have more than one correct answer, so consider each answer choice individually. (A) is a possible explanation: even though the United States may have reduced its production of CFCs, it is possible that production increased elsewhere and that this accounted for damage to the ozone layer. (B) is another possible explanation: natural phenomena were at work as well. However, (C) would result in lower CFC levels and therefore higher ozone levels, a result contradictory to that of the passage.

For Items #14–15, select <u>one</u> answer choice for each blank from the corresponding column of choices. Fill all blanks in a way that best completes the text.

14. Modern humans inhabit a sanitized world where disagreeable odors are few and sweet smells abound. The household products aisle in supermarkets offers a (i)_____ of cleansers, deodorants, and air fresheners, all designed to neutralize odors. But sometimes odors are employed to alter behavior. Used cars are sprayed with leather essence to give them the "new car smell" so attractive to car buyers. And a drop of vanilla essence placed on the stove will help create an atmosphere of hominess to (ii)_____ a potential homebuyer. The sense of smell takes us far back in evolutionary time to a more (iii)_____ era when smell was more important than thought.

Blank (i)

(A)	plethora
(B)	paucity
(C)	dearth

Blank (ii)

(D)	entice
(E)	confound
(F)	pacify

Blank (iii)

(G)	primitive
(H)	precious
(I)	corrosive

15. The design of the building was magnificent, but its classical lines seemed almost (i)_____ and out of place in the business district which was (ii)_____ ultramodern steel and glass skyscrapers.

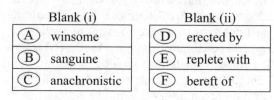

Blank (i)		Blank (ii)	
(A)	winsome	(D)	erected by
(B)	sanguine	(E)	replete with
(C)	anachronistic	(F)	bereft of

14. (A, D, G) *Verbal Reasoning/Paragraph Completion/Combined Reasoning/Phrases* and *Coordinate Conjunctions*

The first blank must describe all of the various products available, so "plethora," (A), which means "abundance," is the best choice. As for the second blank, the sentence states that smells can influence a potential buyer to make a purchase, so "entice," (D), is the best description of the aromas created to attract buyers. Finally, the last sentence refers to a time when smell was more important than thought, and that must have been long ago, so "primitive," (G), is the best choice.

15. (C, E) *Verbal Reasoning/Sentence Completion/Combined Reasoning/Coordinate Conjunctions and Phrases*

In this item, the conjunction "but" signals a thought reversal: the second clause must express an idea that contrasts with the idea that the design of the building is magnificent, which means that the first blank must be completed by a word with negative connotations. Eliminate (A), "winsome," and (B), "sanguine," because these words don't provide the necessary negative contrast to "magnificent." Therefore, (C), "anachronistic," is the correct choice for the first blank. As for the second blank, eliminate (D) because "erected by...skyscrapers" is not logical and eliminate (F) because "bereft of" extends rather than reverses the thought. Therefore, (E), "replete with," is the correct choice for the second blank. Indeed, notice how well (C) and (E) work together: the classical lines belonged to a different time and were therefore out of place in an area filled with modern structures.

For Items #16–20, select <u>one</u> answer choice unless otherwise instructed.

Item #16 is based on the following passage.

The recent 40 percent reduction in airfares represents an attempt by the airlines to boost overall revenues by ensuring that planes fly at or near capacity. The lower fare tickets, which must be purchased within 48 hours of the scheduled time of departure, are intended to encourage impulse travel. The policy, however, is ill-conceived because business travelers, who would normally pay full fare, will now purchase the new discount fare, thus depressing overall revenues.

16. Which one of the following, if true, most weakens the argument above?

   (A) Some people would prefer to pay a higher fare if the additional cost ensured better schedules and service.

   (B) The number of business travelers who will purchase discount tickets is greater than the number of additional passengers who will be attracted by the lower fares.

   (C) An airplane must be operated at or near capacity for the airline to show a profit on a particular flight.

   (D) Impulse travelers are persons whose schedules are highly flexible and who are anxious to find lower fares.

   (E) Most business travelers must arrange their travel schedules more than two days in advance.

16. (E) *Verbal Reasoning/Critical Reading/ The Assumptions*

The correct answer to an item stem asking for the choice that most weakens the argument is often the denial of a hidden assumption of the argument. The conclusion of the argument is that the airlines will lose money. Why? Because business travelers will take advantage of the reduced fares. This argument assumes, however, that business travelers are able to take advantage of the reduced fares. (E) attacks this hidden assumption by noting that business travelers must arrange their schedules in advance, which effectively precludes them from taking advantage of the lower fares. Note that (A) is an attractive distractor. One might argue that some people would avoid using discount fares, preferring better service. The difficulty with this line of thinking is that it attempts to provide a counterexample to a claim that is not universal in the first place. The argument never claims that everyone will take advantage of the lower fares, only that enough people will do so to depress revenues. (B) is wrong because it actually strengthens the argument: in essence, (B) is arguing that revenues will be depressed by the discount fares. (C) is wrong because it doesn't address the logic of the argument: the airlines' cost structure does not necessarily dictate consumer behavior. Finally, (D) is wrong because, while it does provides a definition for "impulse traveler" that is consistent with the argument's usage of the phrase, it does not weaken the argument.

Can computers reason? Reasoning requires the individual to take a given set of facts and draw correct conclusions. Unfortunately, errors frequently occur, and we are not talking about simple carelessness as
5 occurs when two numbers are incorrectly added, nor do we mean errors resulting from simple forgetfulness. Rather, we have in mind errors of a logical nature— those resulting from faulty reasoning. Now, or at least soon, computers will be capable of error-free logical
10 reasoning in a variety of areas. The key to avoiding errors is to use a computer program that relies on the last two decades' research in the field of automated theorem proving. AURA (Automated Reasoning Assistant) is the program that best exemplifies this use
15 of the computer.

AURA solves a problem by drawing conclusions from a given set of facts about the problem. The program does not learn, nor is it self-analytical, but it reaches logical conclusions flawlessly. AURA seldom
20 relies on brute force to find solutions. Instead it solves almost all problems by using sophisticated techniques to find a contradiction. One generally starts with a set of assumptions and adds a statement that the goal is unreachable. For example, if the problem is to test a
25 safety system that automatically shuts down a nuclear reactor when instruments indicate a problem, AURA is told that the system will not shut the reactor down under those circumstances. If AURA finds a contradiction between the statement and the system's
30 design assumptions, then this aspect of the reactor's design has been proved satisfactory. This strategy, known as the set of support strategy, lets AURA concentrate on the problem at hand and avoid the many fruitless steps required to explore the entire theory
35 underlying the problem. The chief use for AURA at this time is for electronic circuit design validation, but a number of other uses will arise. For example, there already exist "expert systems" that include a component for reasoning. These expert programs,
40 unlike human experts, do not die. Such systems continue to improve and have an indefinite life span. Moreover, they can be replicated for pennies.

Will the computer replace the human being? Certainly not. Such programs will assist, rather than
45 replace, humans. Their impact will be felt in design, manufacturing, law, medicine, and other areas. Reasoning assistants will enable human minds to turn to deeper and far more complex ideas.

17. Which of the following titles best describes the content of the passage?

   (A) Scientific Applications of Computers
   (B) Theories of Artificial Intelligence
   (C) Some Suggested Applications for AURA
   (D) Using Computers to Assist Human Reasoning
   (E) The Dangers of Automated Reasoning Assistants

17. (D) *Verbal Reasoning/Reading Comprehension/Main Idea*

The best title to describe the passage will be neither too broad nor too narrow. (A) is too broad: the author is discussing one limited aspect of computer use. (B) is also too broad: though AURA programs may have some implications for theories of artificial intelligence, the author does not discuss them. (C) is too narrow on two counts: AURA is merely an example of how computers might be used to assist human reasoning, and even allowing that AURA is the best example of this possibility, the discussion of AURA is broader than merely possible applications—the author sketches some basic theoretical concepts of AURA as well. (E) is too broad because the author seems to endorse the use of AURA. Therefore, by the process of elimination, (D) is the correct choice.

18. According to the passage, all of the following are advantages of expert programs EXCEPT:

    (A) they have an indefinite life span

    (B) they cost little to reproduce

    (C) many copies can be made available

    (D) they are self-analytical

    (E) more knowledge can be added to them

18. (D) *Verbal Reasoning/Reading Comprehension/Specific Detail*

(A), (B), (C), and (E) are all mentioned as advantages of expert programs in the passage (lines 40–42). As for (D), the only reference to self-analytical programs is in the second paragraph, where the author states that AURA is not self-analytical. Therefore, (D) is the correct choice.

19. If the design of an electronic circuit were tested by AURA, and the conclusion that under certain circumstances a switching device would remain open generated a contradiction, this would lead to the conclusion that

    (A) the circuit was properly designed

    (B) the switch would remain closed under the circumstances

    (C) the switch would remain open under the circumstances

    (D) an error in human reasoning invalidated the design

    (E) the circuit was incorrectly designed

19. (B) *Verbal Reasoning/Reading Comprehension/Further Application*

In the second paragraph, the author describes the theory of the AURA program. The computer is given the design of the system and then told that the goal cannot be reached given the design. Then, if the computer finds a contradiction in that information, this means the goal will be achieved by the design. In other words, we have a sort of indirect proof. We take the set of premises and the negation of the conclusion we hope to prove. If a contradiction can be found in the premises and negation of the conclusion, then the conclusion itself is proved. Therefore, if the assertion that the switch remains open generates a contradiction, then the opposite conclusion is proved: the switch should be closed, (B). (A) is wrong because it is too broad: the contradiction does not prove the system was well designed, only that the result described by (B) will occur—that may or may not be the desired result. (C) is wrong because it is contradicted by the above analysis. Finally, (D) and (E) are both wrong because they make the same error as (A), but in the opposite direction.

20. The author's attitude toward the developments he or she describes can best be described as

    (A) enthusiastic

    (B) reluctant

    (C) cautious

    (D) skeptical

    (E) worried

20. (A) *Verbal Reasoning/Reading Comprehension/Attitude-Tone*

The author obviously thinks very highly of the development he or she is describing. The only adjective in the array of choices consistent with this attitude is "enthusiastic," (A). (B), (C), (D), and (E) all have negative connotations associated with reservations not expressed by the author.

For Items #21–25, select the **two** words that, when used independently in the sentence, produce logical sentences **and** produce sentences that are alike in meaning.

21. Real progress, which has withered or overthrown the barbarous practices and institutions that were the source of infinite suffering and has established more civilized relations and styles of life, has always been achieved through a partial, _____, and deformed application of social theory.

    A | unconventional
    B | meticulous
    C | heterodox
    D | secular
    E | predetermined
    F | antithetical

21. (A, C) *Verbal Reasoning/Sentence Equivalence/Thought Extension/Key Adjectives and Adverbs*

The adjectives "partial" and "deformed" give clues to the word to complete the sentence. A deformed application of theory would not be an application of the pure theory as envisioned by its developers. Instead, it would use some part of the theory and in a way not anticipated by its proponents. Both "unconventional," (A), and "heterodox," (C), which means "having unorthodox views," have a similar meaning.

22. No performance can be judged acceptable if it _____ the score's prescriptions in any detail: metronome markings must be taken as a guide to tempo; crescendos must start and stop as marked.

    A | flaunts
    B | flouts
    C | engages
    D | disregards
    E | informs
    F | brandishes

22. (B, D) *Verbal Reasoning/Sentence Equivalence/Thought Extension/Punctuation*

The information following the colon provides examples of the details the conductor must attend to in order to be faithful to the composer's score. A performance that ignores the score would be one that "flouts," (B), or "disregards," (D), the instructions for the piece. Note that while "flaunts," (A), and "brandishes," (F), have somewhat similar meanings, as do "engages," (C), and "informs," (E), those pairs have meanings that do not make sense in the context here.

23. The artful science of living nature makes the old physics of the law-like motions of inert objects, once believed to be perfect and divine, seem in comparison as uninspired as the movement of a(n) _____.

    A | beast
    B | automaton
    C | robot
    D | planet
    E | pendulum
    F | atom

23. (B, C) *Verbal Reasoning/Sentence Equivalence/Thought Reversal/Phrases*

The sentence contrasts the science of the law-like motion of objects with the art of the life sciences. The blank must be completed by a word that echoes the idea of "inert objects." "Automatons," (B), are "robots," (C), and robots, unlike animals, which react as living creatures, merely execute whatever instructions have been programmed.

24. Although the assertions occasionally smack of
_____, Csikszentmihalyi's message contains a
kernel of truth.

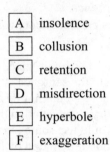

A	insolence
B	collusion
C	retention
D	misdirection
E	hyperbole
F	exaggeration

25. Fuller's sexual lifestyle cannot be documented and
is therefore not subjected to speculation, apart from
an isolated _____ that she may have once made a
pass at Queen Marie of Romania.

A	surmise
B	report
C	insinuation
D	conjecture
E	précis
F	adage

24. (E, F) *Verbal Reasoning/ Sentence Equivalence/Thought Reversal/ Subordinate Conjuctions*

In this item, the "although" sets up a contrast between the statements and a "kernel of truth." Both "hyperbole," (E), and "exaggeration," (F), mean "overstatement," but even in an overstatement, there may be a bit of truth.

25. (A, D) *Verbal Reasoning/Sentence Equivalence/Thought Extension/Phrases*

The sentence specifically says that Fuller's lifestyle is not subjected to speculation save for the one point. This point must be speculative, and "surmise," (A), and "conjecture," (D), both have overtones to suggest uncertainty or speculation. Note that "report," (B), and "insinuation," (C), are attractive distractors. It might be argued that the point was not stated, only insinuated, but the problem with "insinuation" is that it has overtones of trickery or slyness that are not supported by the sentence. And the problem with "report" is that it is too certain in tone to match the clause that follows (that she *may have* once).

Section 4 – Verbal Reasoning

Time—35 minutes

25 Items

For Items #1–4, select the two words that, when used independently in the sentence, produce logical sentences and produce sentences that are alike in meaning.

1. Communism began as an anti-democratic _____ within the Socialist ranks, which was hard to combat and had the further debilitating effect of encouraging the Socialist leaders to cling still more rigidly to the old orthodoxy.

   A   deviationism

   B   rapprochement

   C   reconciliation

   D   heresy

   E   recidivism

   F   recondition

2. The purpose of literature is to incite permanent dissatisfaction in order to keep people in a constant state of _____ against themselves.

   A   rebellion

   B   probity

   C   insurrection

   D   preparedness

   E   incivility

   F   distrust

3. Like the anorexic sculptures of his friend Giacometti, Beckett's work grew ever more _____, halting at the point of disappearance while retaining much of its hypnotic power.

   A   minimal

   B   tangential

   C   austere

   D   robust

   E   insufficient

   F   commercial

1. (A, D) *Verbal Reasoning/Sentence Equivalence/Thought Extension/ Key Adjectives and Adverbs*

The sentence describes a split between the orthodox socialist thinkers and another group. Since the one group is defined as "orthodox," the other would be a "heresy," (D). Then, "deviationism," (A), refers to a split from accepted practices, so "deviationism" and "heresy" are close in meaning. Note that while "rapprochement," (B), and "reconciliation," (C), are also close in meaning, the notion of unification between the two groups does not make sense in the context here.

2. (A, C) *Verbal Reasoning/Sentence Equivalence/Thought Extension/Phrases*

The phrase "against themselves" suggests some kind of conflict, and both "rebellion," (A), and "insurrection," (C), refer to conflict. And both refer to political or military events that are internally directed, for example, the revolting group against the majority.

3. (A, C) *Verbal Reasoning/Sentence Equivalence/Thought Extension/Phrases*

The sentence is controlled by the image of a sculpture of a gaunt figure reduced to utter simplicity, as someone who is severely anorexic. "Minimal," (A), and "austere," (C), describe this sort of appearance or work. Then, this idea is reinforced by the phrase "point of disappearance," which suggests that the work becomes so minimal that it virtually ceases to exist.

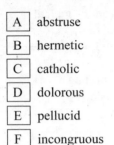

4. Black is largely self-taught, and his unusual selection of obscure readings likely explains why his vocabulary is _____.

    A abstruse

    B hermetic

    C catholic

    D dolorous

    E pellucid

    F incongruous

4. (A, B) Verbal Reasoning/Sentence Equivalence/Thought Extension/ Key Adjectives and Adverbs

The sentence states that Black learned his vocabulary from obscure readings, so it would contain unusual words. And "abstruse," (A), and "hermetic," (B), both mean self-referential and relatively unaffected by outside influence. The result is a set of words that have meanings for insiders but are not likely to be familiar to others.

For Items #5–10, select one answer choice unless otherwise instructed.

Items #5–8 are based on the following passage.

To measure general welfare we would need a measure of changes in the need our output must satisfy. One aspect, population change, is now handled by converting output to a per capita basis on the
5 assumption that, all other things equal, twice as many people need twice as many goods and services to be equally well off. But an index of needs would also account for differences in the requirements for living as the population becomes more urbanized and
10 suburbanized, changes in national defense requirements, and changes in the effect of weather on our needs. The index would have to tell us the cost of meeting our needs in a base year compared with the cost of meeting them equally well under the
15 circumstances prevailing in every other year.

Measures of "needs" shade into measure of the human and physical environment in which we live. We all are enormously affected by the people around us. Can we go where we like without fear of attack? We
20 are also affected by the physical environment—purity of water and air, accessibility of park land and other conditions. To measure this requires accurate data, but such data are generally deficient.

Moreover, weighting is required: robberies and
25 murders should be combined in a crime index; pollution of the Potomac and pollution of Lake Erie should be combined into a water pollution index; and then crime and water pollution should be combined into some general index. But there is no basis for
30 weighting these beyond individual preference. Even if we could construct indexes of output, real costs, needs, and state of the environment, we could not compute a welfare index because we have no system of weights to combine them.

5. The primary concern of the author is with

    (A) refuting arguments for a position
    (B) making a proposal and defending it
    (C) attacking the sincerity of an opponent
    (D) showing defects in a proposal
    (E) reviewing literature relevant to a problem

5. (D) Verbal Reasoning/Reading Comprehension/Main Idea

The author begins by stating the requirements for measuring general welfare and then proceeds to demonstrate why such an index cannot be constructed. Generally, then, the author shows the defects in a proposal for a general index of welfare, and (D) nicely describes this development. (A) is wrong because the author never produces any arguments for the position he or she attacks. And even when the author raises points such as the handling of population change in the first paragraph, arguments are not cited for that position; the author is only mentioning the position to attack it. (B) is wrong because the author is attacking and not defending the proposal discussed. (C) is easily eliminated because the author never attacks the sincerity of those he or she opposes. Finally, (E) is wrong because the author never reviews any literature on the subject he or she is discussing.

6. The author regards the idea of a general index of welfare as

    (A) an unrealistic dream
    (B) a scientific reality
    (C) an important contribution
    (D) a future necessity
    (E) a desirable change

6. (A) *Verbal Reasoning/Reading Comprehension/Attitude-Tone*

The author sees fatal theoretical weaknesses inherent in the idea of an index of welfare. So, it is inferable that the author regards such a notion as an unrealistic, that is, unachievable, dream, (A). (B), (C), and (E) are all wrong because the author does not believe the idea can be implemented. (D) is wrong because there is nothing in the passage to indicate that the author believes the idea of a general index is a necessity.

7. According to the author, an adequate measure of need must take into account all of the following EXCEPT:

    (A) changing size of the population
    (B) changing effects of the weather on people
    (C) differences in needs of urban and suburban populations
    (D) changing requirements for governmental programs such as defense
    (E) accessibility of parkland and other amenities

7. (E) *Verbal Reasoning/Reading Comprehension/Specific Detail*

This item stem includes the thought-reverser "EXCEPT," so the correct choice is NOT explicitly stated in the passage. (A), (B), (C), and (D) are all mentioned in the first paragraph as aspects of a needs index. The second paragraph does not treat the idea of a needs index but the idea of a physical environment index, where the author discusses the items mentioned in (E). Therefore, while the author does mention the items covered by (E), they are not discussed as part of a needs index, so (E) is the correct choice.

8. The passage is most likely

    (A) a speech by a university professor to a graduating class
    (B) part of a chapter in a general introduction to statistics
    (C) an element of a pamphlet on government programs to aid the poor
    (D) part of the introduction to a treatise on the foundations of government
    (E) an address to a symposium on public policy decisions

8. (E) *Verbal Reasoning/Reading Comprehension/ Further Application*

This item stem asks for the *most* likely place for the passage to appear. To be sure, it is possible that the passage *might* appear in any of the five suggested locations, but the *most* likely place is (E): this could easily be an excerpt from a series of papers addressed to a group meeting to discuss public policy decisions. As for (A), while a speech to a graduating glass is an extremely unlikely forum for a discussion about the welfare index, it is to a certain extent plausible. However, (E) is more closely connected to the content of the passage. As for (B), it is not likely that the passage would be an introduction to a general text on statistics: the author is too firmly dedicated to his or her particular ideas, and the use of statistics is in a way subordinate to the author's theoretical discussions. (C) is inappropriate since the discussion bears only remotely on programs to aid the poor. Finally, (D) is even less likely since the passage does not discuss the foundations of government.

Item #9 is based on the following passage.

Dr. Esterhaus is an extremely competent administrator. In the twelve months following her appointment as Chief Executive Officer of the History Department, the number of applications for admission to the program was nearly 150 above that of the previous year.

9. The reasoning in the argument above makes which one of the following assumptions?

   (A) The increase in the number of applications for admissions is not attributable to Dr. Esterhaus' efforts.

   (B) Dr. Esterhaus is well-respected in the academic community as a history scholar.

   (C) The number of applications for admission to a program is a good measure of the effectiveness of the Chief Executive Officer.

   (D) The increase in applicants resulted in an increase in graduation rates.

   (E) The new applicant pool represents a much more culturally diverse student population.

9. **(C)** *Verbal Reasoning/Critical Reading/ The Assumptions*

The argument assumes, as (C) notes, that the number of applications received is a good measure of an administrator's effectiveness. If the number of applications received is not necessarily a good measure of effectiveness, then the conclusion does not follow from the premises. (A) is wrong because the argument actually assumes that the increase *is* attributable to Dr. Esterhaus. As for (B), whether Dr. Esterhaus is a good scholar is irrelevant to the number of applications made to the program or to her effectiveness as an administrator, at least as that term is used in the argument. Finally, while increases in graduation rates, (D), and cultural diversity, (E), might be desirable, they have nothing to do with the assumptions made regarding Dr. Esterhaus' effectiveness.

Item #10 is based on the following passage.

Recently, credit card companies have come under attack by consumer groups who argue that the interest rates charged by these companies are unconscionably high. In fact, the rates are generally several percentage points above those charged by banks for ordinary personal loans. But consumer groups overlook the fact that credit cards afford the user great flexibility. A user can purchase an item while it is on sale. So, the lower cost of the item offsets the extra cost of the credit.

10. The argument above makes which one of the following assumptions?

(A) A credit card application is not rejected unless the applicant has a long history of late payments and other credit problems.

(B) The cost savings of buying an item at a reduced price are at least equal to the excess interest that a consumer pays on purchases made with a credit card.

(C) The prices of items on sale purchased by consumers are still sufficiently high to enable sellers to recoup their costs and make a modest profit.

(D) The consumers who make purchases of sale items with credit cards are people who might not qualify for bank loans with a lower interest rate.

(E) The average outstanding balance of the ordinary credit card user is no greater than the total non-credit card debt of the credit card user.

10. (B) *Verbal Reasoning/Critical Reading/ The Assumptions*

The conclusion of the argument is that despite the comparatively high interest rates charged by credit card companies, on balance consumers are not harmed because they save money by buying items on sale. For this conclusion to be true, it must be the case that the amount of money saved by purchasing items on sale is sufficient to offset the additional cost of the credit. (B) makes this hidden assumption explicit. (A) and (C) are both fairly weak responses. As for (A), the argument claims only that those who have and use credit cards are not disadvantaged by the high interest rates. The argument does not make any claim about the availability of cards. As for (C), the argument claims only that items are offered on sale; it does not have to commit to any position on the wisdom of the seller's marketing strategy. (D) and (E) are somewhat attractive because they both mention the idea of ordinary loans and the idea of credit cards. The difficulty with (D) is that this is a position to which the argument need not commit, and this can be proved by making the opposite assumption. Even if all credit card users could qualify for ordinary bank loans, this does not affect the argument's conclusion that the flexibility afforded by credit cards offsets the additional cost of using them. (E) is wrong for a similar reason; even if (E) is false, the conclusion of the argument is not affected one way or the other.

For Items #11–13, select <u>one</u> answer choice for each blank from the corresponding column of choices. Fill all blanks in a way that best completes the text.

11. Although leprosy is not a highly contagious disease, those who have contracted it have always been pariahs who are _____ by others.

  (A) ostracized
  (B) accepted
  (C) sheltered
  (D) admonished
  (E) lauded

11. (A) *Verbal Reasoning/Sentence Completion/Combined Reasoning/Subordinate Conjunctions and Phrases*

In this item, the word "although" signals a thought reversal: the phrase following the comma ("those who have contradicted...are _____ by others") reverses the idea that leprosy isn't highly contagious. And the blank describes how "pariahs" are treated by others, even though they aren't that contagious—they must be avoided. "Ostracized," (A), which means "excluded," is the best choice.

12. Although the novel was generally boring and awkwardly written, there were (i)_____ passages of power and lyricism that hinted at the author's (ii)_____.

Blank (i)	Blank (ii)
(A) occasional	(D) superficiality
(B) frequent	(E) potential
(C) contrived	(F) malevolence

12. (A, E) *Verbal Reasoning/Sentence Completion/Combined Reasoning/Subordinate Conjunctions and Phrases*

In this item, the word "although" sets up a contrast between "generally boring and awkwardly written" and "_____ passages of power and lyricism," the former a negative judgment and the latter a positive judgment. On this ground, eliminate (B). Eliminate (C) because it does not create a meaningful phrase. Therefore, (A) must be the correct choice for the first blank. Indeed, to create a contrast, the good parts must have been relatively few, or "occasional." As for the second blank, it must be filled by a word that extends the ideas of "power and lyricism," and "potential," (E) is the best choice.

13. The moral status of economic growth is (i)_____.
The plundering of natural resources makes possible
the technological innovations of the Industrial
Revolution and provides the necessary support for
most of this planet's increasingly urban population.
People concerned with global ecology, however,
(ii)_____ the ideology of growth. Unfortunately,
like many other middle-class intellectual
(iii)_____, the debate between ecological
conservatives and economic liberals is too much
about taking sides.

Blank (i)

A	ambiguous
B	unequivocal
C	transitive

Blank (ii)

D	determine
E	decry
F	dissemble

Blank (iii)

G	polarizations
H	rationalizations
I	perorations

13. (A, E, G) *Verbal Reasoning/Paragraph
Completion/Combined Reasoning/Coordinate
Conjunctions and Phrases*

The paragraph describes a debate over
economic growth. One side recognizes the costs
associated with growth but argues that the
advantages outweigh the costs. The other side
emphasizes that the costs are great. The first
sentence, when completed, indicates that the
debate is not concluded and leaves at issue the
moral states of the central issue. "Ambiguous,"
(A), is a good word to describe the failure to
determine finally the moral status of growth.
Then, the "however" in the second sentence sets
up a contrast between those who favor and
those who oppose the ideology of growth that
allows for the plundering of natural resources.
And "decry," (E), is a good match-up for
"oppose." Finally, the last sentence says that the
debate is characterized by taking sides, and
"polarizations," (G), describes this well.

For Items #14–19, select <u>one</u> answer choice unless otherwise instructed.

Items #14–19 are based on the following passage.

The mental health movement in the United States
began with a period of considerable enlightenment.
Dorothea Dix was shocked to find the mentally ill in
jails and alms houses and crusaded for the
5   establishment of asylums in which people could
receive humane care. By the mid 1800s, 20 states had
established asylums; but during the late 1800s and
early 1900s, in the face of economic depression,
legislatures were unable to appropriate sufficient funds.
10 Asylums became overcrowded and prisonlike.
Additionally, patients were more resistant to treatment
than the pioneers in the mental health field had
anticipated. Mental institutions became frightening and
depressing places in which the rights of patients were
15 all but forgotten.
        These conditions continued until after World War
II. At that time, new treatments were discovered for
some major mental illnesses theretofore considered

untreatable (penicillin for syphilis of the brain and
20 insulin treatment for schizophrenia and depressions),
and a succession of books, motion pictures, and
newspaper exposés called attention to the plight of the
mentally ill. Improvements were made, and Dr. David
Vail's Humane Practices Program is a beacon for
25 today. But changes were slow in coming until the early
1960s. At that time, the Civil Rights Movement led
lawyers to investigate America's prisons, which were
disproportionately populated by blacks, and they in
turn followed prisoners into the only institutions that
30 were worse than the prisons, the hospitals for the
criminally insane. The prisons were filled with angry
young men who, encouraged by legal support, were
quick to demand their rights. The hospitals for the
criminally insane, by contrast, were populated with
35 people who were considered "crazy" and who were
often kept obediently in their place through the use of

severe bodily restraints and large doses of major tranquilizers. The young cadre of public interest lawyers found a population that was both passive and
40 easy to champion. Patients' rights groups successfully encouraged reform by lobbying in state legislatures.

Judicial interventions have had some definite positive effects, but there is growing awareness that courts cannot provide the standards and the review
45 mechanisms that assure good patient care. The details of providing day-to-day care simply cannot be

mandated by a court, so it is time to take from the courts the responsibility for delivery of mental health care and assurance of patient rights and return it to the
50 state mental health administrators to whom the mandate was originally given. Though it is a difficult task, administrators must undertake to write rules and standards and to provide the training and surveillance to assure that treatment is given and patients' rights
55 respected.

14. The main purpose of the passage is to

(A) discuss the influence of Dorothea Dix on the mental health movement

(B) provide a historical perspective on problems of mental health care

(C) increase public awareness of the plight of the mentally ill

(D) shock the reader with vivid descriptions of asylums

(E) describe the invention of new treatments for mental illness

For the following item, consider each answer individually and select all that apply.

15. It can be inferred from the passage that which of the following factors contributed to post-war reform of state mental institutions?

A heightened public awareness of the unacceptable conditions in the institutions

B discovery of effective treatments for illnesses previously considered untreatable

C enactment of state legislation to improve conditions in mental institutions

14. (B) *Verbal Reasoning/Reading Comprehension/Main Idea*

The idea is to find a statement that summarizes all of the main points of the passage without going beyond the scope of the passage. The passage summarizes the history of mental health care in the United States, so (B) is the best choice. (A) and (E) are both wrong because they are too narrow: while each is an interesting point made by the author, neither is the main theme of the passage. (C) is wrong because, while a side effect of the passage may be to make some readers aware of a problem, the primary purpose of the passage is to describe, not to increase awareness. Finally, (D) is wrong because of the word "shock": the passage contains no vivid images or anything that would shock the reader.

15. (A, B, C) *Verbal Reasoning/Reading Comprehension/Implied Idea*

This item includes directions that indicate that more than one answer could be correct, so evaluate each answer choice independently. The causes of post-war reform are discussed in the second paragraph, where the author mentions books, motion pictures, and newspaper exposés. Why would these be effective tools of reform? Because each creates a new public awareness of a problem. Thus, (A) is inferable. (B) is also inferable: the author mentions that new treatments had been discovered, so this too must have been one of the factors encouraging reform. As for (C), the author states that patients' rights groups encouraged reform by lobbying, and that these efforts were successful, so it is inferable that the lobbying resulted in some reform legislation.

For the following item, consider each answer individually and select all that apply.

16. The passage provides information that would help answer which of the following questions?

   A   Who are some people who have had an important influence on the public health movement in the United States?

   B   What were some of the most important legal cases that contributed to the new concern for patients' rights?

   C   What were some of the mental illnesses that were considered untreatable until the 1950s?

17. The tone of the final paragraph can best be described as

   (A) stridently contentious
   (B) overly emotional
   (C) cleverly deceptive
   (D) cautiously optimistic
   (E) fiercely independent

16. (A, C) *Verbal Reasoning/Reading Comprehension/Specific Detail*

The directions indicate that this item may have more than one correct answer, so evaluate each answer choice independently. (A) is correct because the passage mentions two people who influenced the public health movement: Dorothea Dix (line 3) and Dr. David Vail (lines 23–24). (B) cannot be answered based on the passage because it doesn't include any specific case names, so (B) is wrong. (C) is correct because lines 19–20 mention some major mental illnesses considered untreatable until after World War II and their new treatments.

17. (D) *Verbal Reasoning/Reading Comprehension/Attitude-Tone*

In the final paragraph, the author makes a specific proposal, which, the author acknowledges, will require effort to implement. Since the author made the proposal, he or she must be optimistic about its chance for success. And, because the author acknowledged that it will not be easy, he or she can be described as cautious as well. Therefore, (D) is the best choice. (A) and (B) are both wrong because, while the author does make an argument in the final paragraph, he or she does so in rather neutral terms—the final paragraph is not contentious, strident, or emotional. (C) is wrong because there is nothing in the passage to suggest that the author is attempting to mislead the reader: one may or may not agree with the author's suggestion in the final paragraph, but there is no reason to conclude that he or she is trying to fool the reader. Finally, (E) is wrong because, while the author evidently does his or her own thinking, the tone of the final paragraph cannot be described as fierce. Be wary of answer choices that contain such extreme language.

18. Which of the following would be the most appropriate topic for the author to address in the next paragraph following the final paragraph of the passage?

- (A) An analysis of landmark cases affecting the civil rights of prisoners and patients in hospitals for the criminally insane
- (B) A discussion of the advantages and disadvantages of treatments that might result in the release of mentally ill persons
- (C) An outline of standards to guide mental health administrators in caring for mentally ill patients while respecting their civil rights
- (D) A proposal to place the administration of mental hospitals directly under the control of the judiciary
- (E) A more detailed description of the conditions in which the patients in mental hospitals lived in the 1960s and early 1970s

18. (C) *Verbal Reasoning/Reading Comprehension/Further Application*

The passage provides a historical perspective on care for the mentally ill, but the author also has a "hidden" agenda—he or she is leading up to something. The point of the historical perspective is contained in the final paragraph: the evolution of the movement has reached the point at which judicial protectionism of patients is no longer critical and professional administrators should reassert their prerogatives. Therefore, (C) is the best choice. (A) is wrong because, while the passage does touch upon the role of judicial activism, judicial activism is seen by the author to be a stage in the evolution of patients' rights. Given the forward-looking development of the passage, the author would probably next discuss a further stage in this development—not return to discuss in detail a prior stage. (B) and (E) are both wrong for the same reason as (A): while the author does touch on these topics, further discussion of them is not consistent with the overall development of the passage. Finally, (D) is wrong because it is directly contradicted by the passage: the author states that it is time for the judiciary to return responsibility for patient care to mental health administrators.

19. It can be inferred from the passage that had the Civil Rights Movement not prompted an investigation of prison conditions,

- (A) states would never have established asylums for the mentally ill
- (B) new treatments for major mental illnesses would likely have remained untested
- (C) the Civil Rights Movement in America would have been politically ineffective
- (D) conditions in mental hospitals might have escaped judicial scrutiny
- (E) many mentally ill prisoners would have been transferred from hospitals back to prisons

19. (D) *Verbal Reasoning/Reading Comprehension/Implied Idea*

The author states that civil rights lawyers who represented black prisoners were drawn naturally into representing patients in mental hospitals, or, X caused Y. The item stem requires the assumption that X did not occur, and on that basis, it is inferable that Y might have not occurred. This logic is used in (D). (A) is wrong because the cause of the establishment of the asylum system was Dorothea Dix's crusade. (B) is wrong because the passage does not state that judicial activism resulted in the discovery of any new treatments (even though it may have resulted in better treatment). (C) is wrong because it goes too far: it is not inferable that a failure in the area of prison reform would have meant complete failure of the Civil Rights Movement. Finally, (E) is wrong because nothing in the passage suggests that judicial activism resulted in the transfer of prisoners to hospitals, so a lack of judicial activism would not necessarily have this effect.

For Items #20–22, select <u>one</u> answer choice for each blank from the corresponding column of choices. Fill all blanks in a way that best completes the text.

20. Portraits painted in Colonial America are quite charming but _____ and demonstrate the isolation of the American painter; they show little or no knowledge of the development of academic painting in Europe.

    Ⓐ grotesque
    Ⓑ refined
    Ⓒ deliberate
    Ⓓ sophisticated
    Ⓔ primitive

20. **(E)** *Verbal Reasoning/Sentence Completion/ Thought Reversal/Coordinate Conjunctions*

The first clause contains a thought reversal: "charming but _____." So, the first word of the correct choice will complete a contrast. (E) is the best choice: American painting was "primitive" because American painters were ignorant of the development of academic European painting. (A) is wrong because, while "grotesque" contrasts with "charming," the fact that American painters were ignorant about European painting does not explain why American painting might have been grotesque. (B), (C), and (D) are all wrong because none provides a contrast to "charming" that makes sense.

21. Although the manager of the corporation was wrong, his stubborn refusal to (i)_____ or even to compromise (ii)_____ an already tense situation.

Blank (i)	Blank (ii)
Ⓐ arbitrate	Ⓓ thwarted
Ⓑ capitulate	Ⓔ exacerbated
Ⓒ censure	Ⓕ rectified

21. **(B, E)** *Verbal Reasoning/Sentence Completion/Combined Reasoning/Phrases*

Two key logical signals are important to understanding the overall structure of the sentence. The first blank sets up a thought extension that is completed by "compromise": the correct choice must be more extreme than compromise. The only choice that sets up this extension is "capitulate," (B). As for the second blank, it must be filled by a word that explains the outcome of the manager's refusal to compromise. A refusal to compromise is most likely to result in an escalation of confrontation or conflict. Thus, "exacerbated," (E), which means "increased the severity of," provides a good completion for the second blank.

22. In his speeches, Havel aims to develop in citizens a(n) (i)_____ their own potential for evil and their obligation to do good. The goal is a careful balance of humility and civic activism. The mystical tone of his speeches will sound strange to ears accustomed to hearing American political (ii)_____, as will the silence about particular government policies. He cares much more about what people feel than how to resolve specific political issues. His rhetoric is characterized by the optimism of someone who has seen the worst of humanity without (iii)_____.

Blank (i)

(A)	cognizance of
(B)	indifference to
(C)	competition between

Blank (ii)

(D)	theory
(E)	gossip
(F)	oratory

Blank (iii)

(G)	promoting instability
(H)	inviting ridicule
(I)	losing faith

22. **(A, F, I)** *Verbal Reasoning/Paragraph Completion/Thought Extension/Phrases*

The paragraph is about Havel's speeches, so the second blank must be completed by a word like "oratory," (F). Then, the content of the speeches aims at making citizens aware of their capacity for evil as well as good, and "cognizance of," (A), nicely expresses this. Finally, the paragraph states that Havel is an optimist, and an optimist is someone who has a positive outlook and doesn't lose faith, (I).

For Items #23–25, select <u>one</u> answer choice unless otherwise instructed.

Items #23–24 are based on the following passage.

Justice Holmes remarked that "the provisions of the Constitution are not mathematical formulas having their essence in their form; they are organic, living institutions." The primary objection to this view seems
5 to be a vague fear that one branch of government will overpower the other two and that the only effective prophylaxis against this malfunction is a blind and unquestioning faith in a strict action-reaction interpretation of the document. To be sure, growth and
10 adaptation have sometimes been seen as mutations, threatening the constitutional order.

It must be admitted that in more recent times we have all too readily assigned responsibility for the Darwinian constitutional evolution to the Supreme
15 Court. Congress has too often either neglected its opportunities and responsibilities or has acted tentatively. When Congress does legislate, it is apt to regard its own constitutional judgment as only provisional, to await as a matter of course a submission
20 to the Supreme Court. A striking example is the recent campaign finance law. But Congress may always reassert its constitutional prerogatives as a coequal branch even before the Supreme Court rules.

The Darwinian model of constitutional
25 interpretation recognizes that the adaptation of living organisms also results in balance. The fluctuating curve of a prey-predator graph illustrates the principle nicely. An imbalance of the numbers of either species in either direction is self-correcting. And if a sense of self-
30 correcting Constitutional morality is an element of the Newtonian model, then is it not equally an element of the Darwinian model? And a keen moral intuition of Constitutional moderation is not the exclusive preserve of the Newtonians.

23. The main purpose of the passage is to

(A) discuss a model of constitutional law
(B) criticize Congress and the executive branch for inaction
(C) suggest a new role for the Supreme Court
(D) challenge the validity of Supreme Court rulings
(E) call for a revised Constitution

23. (A) *Verbal Reasoning/Reading Comprehension/Main Idea*

The passage explores a Darwinian model of the Constitution, (A). (B) is wrong because it is too narrow in scope: the author also criticizes the judiciary; furthermore, the passage is theoretical rather than practical and is focused upon particular government acts—whatever decisions are cited are for illustrative purposes. (C) and (D) are also too narrow in scope: the author does suggest that the Supreme Court has perhaps taken too much responsibility for evolving constitutional doctrine, but that is not the main point of the passage. Finally, (E) is wrong because the author is concerned with how to interpret the existing Constitution.

24. In the final paragraph, the author

(A) proposes an agenda for future research

(B) introduces a new problem of constitutional theory

(C) rejects the Darwinian model

(D) suggests ways for improving governmental efficiency

(E) asks a question and answers it

Items #25 is based on the following passage.

Despite seductive advertisements, so-called low tar and nicotine cigarettes are really no safer than other cigarettes. The seemingly lower levels of tar and nicotine reported by the Federal Trade Commission are attributable to the FTC's use of smoking machines, not human beings, to determine tar and nicotine levels. But people do not smoke like machines. A study of blood samples of smokers found no significant differences among smokers of the various brands and a direct relationship between nicotine intake and the number of cigarettes smoked, regardless of brand.

25. Someone wishing to defend a low tar and nicotine cigarette as a safer smoking alternative could point out that

(A) most people who smoke give little consideration to the health risks involved in smoking

(B) in confined spaces the health of even nonsmokers is endangered by tobacco smoke

(C) a smoker could choose to make his smoking habits similar to the methods of the testing machines

(D) most cigarette companies offer smokers several different brands, including low tar and nicotine cigarettes

(E) cigarette companies are required by law to include tar and nicotine content on the labels of cigarette packages

24. (E) *Verbal Reasoning/Reading Comprehension/Specific Detail*

In the final paragraph, the author uses the idea of constitutional morality to show that there is no real danger in the Darwinian interpretation. Formalistically, this is accomplished by asking "Can't the Darwinian model have the same moral basis as the Newtonian model?" And the answer is provided. Therefore, (E) is the best choice. (A) is wrong because no proposal of any kind is made. (B) is wrong because the problem addressed by the passage was introduced in the first paragraph. (C) is wrong because the author regards the Darwinian model as superior. Finally, (D) is wrong because it is not addressed in the passage.

25. (C) *Verbal Reasoning/Critical Reading/The Inference/Analogy and The Assumptions*

The statement is an attempt to discredit an argument from analogy by pointing out that machines do not smoke like human beings. The claim that low tar and nicotine cigarettes are an improvement over regular cigarettes can be strengthened by repairing the analogy, as (C) attempts to do. (A) is wrong because asserting that smokers simply do not care about their health is not going to do very much to repair the argument for the claim that low tar and nicotine cigarettes have health advantages. (B) is wrong because it fails to address the internal logical structure of the statement. (D) and (E) are both wrong because neither is connected with the question of whether light cigarettes really have any significant advantage in terms of health.

Section 5 – Quantitative Reasoning

40 Minutes
25 Items

Solve each problem and choose the correct answer, using the given directions.

Notes: All numbers used are real numbers.

Unless otherwise indicated, all figures lie in a plane.

Geometric diagrams and figures **are not necessarily** drawn to scale, so do **not** assume lengths, angle measures, or other quantities are as they appear in a given figure. You should assume that lines shown as straight are straight and that the positions of points, and geometric objects in general, exist in the order shown. Base your answers to questions with geometric figures on reasoning, not visual estimation or measurement.

Coordinate systems and graphic data presentations **are** drawn to scale, so you can answer items based on visual estimation or measurement.

Each of the items #1–9 consists of two quantities, Quantity A and Quantity B. Compare the two quantities, using the information presented. Choose:

(A) if Quantity A is greater.
(B) if Quantity B is greater.
(C) if the two quantities are equal.
(D) if the relationship cannot be determined from the information given.

A symbol that appears more than once in an item has the same meaning throughout the item.

$$x = 18 + 19 + 20 + 21 + 22$$
$$y = 22 + 21 + 20 + 19 + 18$$

Quantity A	Quantity B
x	y

1.

1. (C) *Quantitative Reasoning/Arithmetic Comparison/Simple Manipulations*

The trick to solving this item quickly is to recognize that x and y are the sum of the same five numbers, even though those numbers are presented in a different order for x than for y. Therefore, $x = y$ and the two quantities are equal, (C).

$$x = 4$$
$$y = 1$$

Quantity A	Quantity B
$\frac{x+y}{xy}$	$\frac{xy}{x+y}$

2.

2. (A) *Quantitative Reasoning/Algebra Comparison/Manipulation of Algebraic Expressions/Evaluating Expressions*

Substitute $x = 4$ and $y = 1$ into the expressions:

Quantity A equals $\frac{x+y}{xy} = \frac{4+1}{(4)(1)} = \frac{5}{4}$ and Quantity B

equals $\frac{xy}{x+y} = \frac{(4)(1)}{4+1} = \frac{4}{5}$. Therefore, Quantity A is

greater than Quantity B, (A).

Quantity A	Quantity B
3. The number of laps in a 50-mile race if each lap is $\frac{1}{5}$ of a mile	100

$3(x+2) = 7$

Quantity A	Quantity B
4. x	1

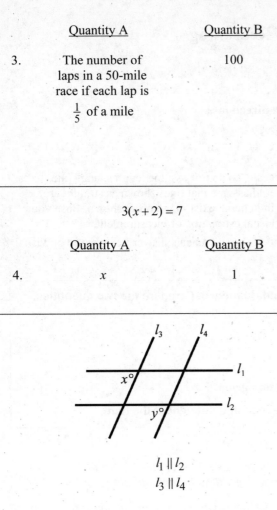

$l_1 \parallel l_2$

$l_3 \parallel l_4$

Quantity A	Quantity B
5. x	y

Cheese costs $4.50 per pound.

Quantity A	Quantity B
6. The amount of cheese that can be purchased for $3.50	$\frac{3}{5}$ pound

3. (A) *Quantitative Reasoning/Arithmetic Comparison/ Common Arithmetic Problems/Proportions and Direct-Inverse Variation*

The number of laps increases as the number of miles increases, so use a direct proportion for

Quantity A: $\dfrac{1\ \text{lap}}{x\ \text{laps}} = \dfrac{\frac{1}{5}\ \text{mile}}{50\ \text{miles}} \Rightarrow x = \dfrac{1\ \text{lap} \cdot 50\ \text{miles}}{\frac{1}{5}\ \text{mile}} =$

250 laps. Therefore, Quantity A is greater than Quantity B, (A).

4. (B) *Quantitative Reasoning/Algebra Comparison/ Solving Equations/One Equation with One Variable*

Solve the centered equation for x: $3(x+2) = 7 \Rightarrow$

$3x + 6 = 7 \Rightarrow 3x = 1 \Rightarrow x = \frac{1}{3}$. Therefore, Quantity B is greater than Quantity A, (B).

5. (C) *Quantitative Reasoning/Geometry Comparison/ Lines and Angles*

Since $l_1 \parallel l_2$ and $l_3 \parallel l_4$, $\angle x$ and $\angle y$ are corresponding angles by definition and the corresponding angles theorem states that corresponding angles are congruent, that is, $x = y$. Therefore, Quantity A is equal to Quantity B, (C).

6. (A) *Quantitative Reasoning/Arithmetic Comparison/ Common Arithmetic Problems/Ratios*

The cost of cheese increases as the amount of cheese increases, so use a direct proportion for Quantity A:

$\dfrac{\$4.50}{\$3.50} = \dfrac{1\ \text{pound}}{x\ \text{pounds}} \Rightarrow x = \dfrac{1\ \text{pound} \cdot \$3.50}{\$4.50} = \dfrac{3.5}{4.5} = \dfrac{7}{9}$ pou

nd. Therefore, Quantity A is greater than Quantity B, (A).

Rectangular solid X has a volume of 24.
Rectangular solid Y has a volume of 20.

Quantity A	Quantity B
7. Area of the base of X	Area of the base of Y

Quantity A	Quantity B
8. $\sqrt{9}$	$\sqrt{6} + \sqrt{3}$

Quantity A	Quantity B
9. Surface area of a sphere with radius 1	Area of a circle with radius 1

7. **(D)** *Quantitative Reasoning/Geometry Comparison/Rectangles and Squares*

Translate the centered information into equations for volume: $\text{volume}_X = \text{height}_X \cdot \text{base area}_X = 24$ and $\text{volume}_Y = \text{height}_Y \cdot \text{base area}_Y = 20$.

However, with two equations and two variables, there is no way to solve for the base of either solid. Do not make the error of assuming that the larger volume has the larger base. Solid X could have a base of 1 by 1 and a height of 24, and Solid Y could have a base of 5 by 4 and a height of 1. Therefore, the relationship between the two quantities cannot be determined, (D).

8. **(B)** *Quantitative Reasoning/Arithmetic Comparison/Simple Manipulations*

Don't be misled into thinking that $\sqrt{6} + \sqrt{3} = \sqrt{9}$. Evaluate the values of both quantities: Quantity A equals $\sqrt{9} = 3$ and Quantity B equals $\sqrt{6} + \sqrt{3} \approx 4.18$. Therefore, Quantity B is greater than Quantity A, (B).

9. **(A)** *Quantitative Reasoning/Geometry Comparison/Circles*

The trick to solving this item quickly is to visualize the figures. Visualize a circle as a two-dimensional section of a sphere—the area of the section of the sphere must be less than the area of the sphere itself. Therefore, Quantity A is greater than Quantity B, (A).

Items #10–25 use several formats. Unless otherwise instructed, select one answer choice. For Numeric Entry items, follow the direction below.

Numeric Entry Directions

- Answers may be integers, decimals, or fractions. Answers may be negative.
- Items requiring a fraction will include two answer boxes—one for the numerator and one for the denominator.
- Equivalent forms of the answer are also correct (e.g., 9 and 9.0 are both correct forms of 9). Fractions do not need to be expressed in lowest terms.

Enter the exact answer unless the item stem indicates that the answer should be rounded.

10. If $\frac{1}{x} + \frac{1}{x} = 8$, then $x =$

    (A) $\frac{1}{4}$

    (B) $\frac{1}{2}$

    (C) 1

    (D) 2

    (E) 4

10. (A) *Quantitative Reasoning/Algebra/Solving Equations/One Equation with One Variable*

Solve the given equation for x: $\frac{1}{x} + \frac{1}{x} = 8 \Rightarrow 2\left(\frac{1}{x}\right) = 8 \Rightarrow x = \frac{2}{8} = \frac{1}{4}$, (A).

11. In a certain school, there are 600 boys and 400 girls. If 20 percent of the boys and 30 percent of the girls are on the honor roll, how many of the students are on the honor roll?

    (A) 120

    (B) 175

    (C) 240

    (D) 250

    (E) 280

11. (C) *Quantitative Reasoning/Arithmetic/Common Arithmetic Problems/Percents*

Translate the given information into "is-over-of" equations for percents ($\frac{is}{of} = \frac{\%}{100}$). The question asks, "What is 20% of 600 plus 30% of 400?", so $\frac{x}{600} = \frac{20}{100} \Rightarrow x = \frac{20 \cdot 600}{100} = 120$ boys on the honor roll and $\frac{y}{400} = \frac{30}{100} \Rightarrow y = \frac{30 \cdot 400}{100} = 120$ girls on the honor roll. Therefore, the total number of students on the honor roll is $120 + 120 = 240$, (C).

For the following item, enter your answer in the space provided.

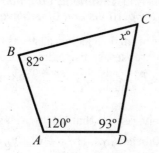

12. In the figure above, $ABCD$ is a quadrilateral. If the measure of $\angle A$ is 120°, the measure of $\angle B$ is 82°, and the measure of $\angle D$ is 93°, what is the value of x?

12. (65) *Quantitative Reasoning/Geometry/ Lines and Angles*

The sum of the measures of the four angles of a quadrilateral is 360°. Thus, $\angle A + \angle B + \angle C + \angle D = 360 \Rightarrow 120 + 82 + x + 93 = 360 \Rightarrow x = 65$.

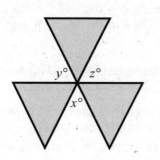

13. In the figure above, three equilateral triangles have a common vertex. $x + y + z =$

   (A)   60
   (B)   90
   (C)   120
   (D)   180
   (E)   240

13. (D) *Quantitative Reasoning/Geometry/ Lines and Angles* and *Triangles/Properties of Triangles* and *Circles*

Begin by labeling the remaining angles:

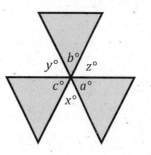

The measure of the degrees in a circle is 360, so $x + y + z + a + b + c = 360$. Since the triangles are equilateral, each of the angles in each triangle is 60°: $a = b = c = 60$. Therefore, $x + y + z + 3(60) = 360 \Rightarrow x + y + z = 180$, (D).

14. If 100 identical bricks weigh p pounds, then in terms of p, 20 of these bricks weigh how many pounds?

(A) $\dfrac{p}{20}$

(B) $\dfrac{p}{5}$

(C) $20p$

(D) $\dfrac{5}{p}$

(E) $\dfrac{20}{p}$

14. **(B)** *Quantitative Reasoning/Algebra/Manipulation of Algebraic Expressions/Creating Algebraic Expressions* and *Arithmetic/Common Arithmetic Problems/Proportions and Direct-Inverse Variation*

The weight of the bricks increases as the number of bricks increases, so use a direct proportion:

$$\frac{100 \text{ bricks}}{20 \text{ bricks}} = \frac{p \text{ pounds}}{x \text{ pounds}} \Rightarrow x = \frac{p \cdot 20}{100} = \frac{p}{5}, \text{ (B)}.$$

Alternatively, reason that if 100 bricks weigh p pounds, 20 bricks, which is $\frac{1}{5}$ of 100, must weigh $\frac{1}{5}$ of p.

15. For any integer n, which of the following represents three consecutive odd integers?

(A) $n,\ n+1,\ n+2$

(B) $n,\ n+1,\ n+3$

(C) $n,\ n+2,\ n+4$

(D) $2n+1,\ 2n+2,\ 2n+3$

(E) $2n+1,\ 2n+3,\ 2n+5$

15. **(E)** *Quantitative Reasoning/Arithmetic/Common Arithmetic Problems/Properties of Numbers*

The trick to solving this item is to recognize that each of the consecutive integers must be odd, regardless of whether n is odd or even. Therefore, immediately eliminate (A), (B), and (C) because n may be odd or even. However, $2n+1$, must be odd ($2n$ is even, so $2n+1$ is odd.), so the next odd integer will be 2 more, or $2n+3$, and the next 2 more than that, or $2n+5$, (E).

16. A group of 15 students took a test that was scored from zero to 100. If exactly 10 students scored 75 or more on the test, what is the *lowest* possible value for the average of the scores of all 15 students?

(A) 25

(B) 50

(C) 70

(D) 75

(E) 90

16. **(B)** *Quantitative Reasoning/Data Analysis/Basic Descriptive Statistics/Mean*

If 10 students have scores of 75 or more, their score total is at minimum $10 \cdot 75 = 750$. Then, even assuming the other 5 students each scored 0, the average for the 15 would be at least $\frac{750}{15} = 50$, (B).

Average Number of Calls Made Daily and Average Cost of Calls for Five Offices of Corporation X

Average Daily Number of Calls

Average Cost Per Call

	Local Domestic	Long Distance	International Long Distance
A	$0.50	$5.80	$19.90
B	$0.80	$7.20	$22.40
C	$0.63	$4.80	$16.40
D	$0.75	$6.20	$18.50
E	$0.40	$6.80	$17.20

17. For which of the five regional offices does the number of international long distance calls account for the greatest proportion of calls of all types?

    (A) Office A
    (B) Office B
    (C) Office C
    (D) Office D
    (E) Office E

17. **(E)** *Quantitative Reasoning/Data Interpretation/ Table Charts* and *Bar Graphs*

To find the office in which international calls accounted for the greatest proportion of all calls, calculate $\frac{\text{international calls}}{\text{total calls}}$ for each office.
According to the bar graph:

Office A: $\frac{80}{280+180+80} = \frac{80}{540} \approx 15\%$

Office B: $\frac{180}{420+360+180} = \frac{180}{960} \approx 19\%$

Office C: $\frac{120}{290+180+120} = \frac{120}{590} \approx 20\%$

Office D: $\frac{90}{180+160+90} = \frac{90}{430} \approx 21\%$

Office E: $\frac{120}{240+120+120} = \frac{120}{480} = 25\%$

Therefore, Office E, (E), had the greatest proportion of international long distance calls.

18. The ratio of the daily cost of calls at Office A to the daily cost of calls at Office D is most nearly

   (A) $\frac{1}{6}$

   (B) $\frac{1}{3}$

   (C) $\frac{4}{7}$

   (D) $\frac{5}{6}$

   (E) 1

18. (E) *Quantitative Reasoning/Data Interpretation/ Table Charts* and *Bar Graphs* and *Arithmetic/ Common Arithmetic Problems/Ratios*

This item requires correlation of data from the two graphs. According to the bar graph, the average number of local, domestic, and international calls for Office A was 280, 180, and 80, respectively; for Office D, the number was 180, 160, and 90, respectively. According to the table chart, the daily cost of calls for Office A was $\$0.50(280) + \$5.80(180) + \$19.90(80) = \$140 + \$1,044 + \$1,592 = \$2,776$; for Office D, the cost was $\$0.75(180) + \$6.20(160) + \$18.50(90) = \$135 + \$992 + \$1,665 = \$2,792$. Therefore, the ratio of the daily cost of calls for Office A to Office D is $\frac{\$2,776}{\$2,792} \approx 1$, (E).

19. If a machine produces x units in t minutes and 30 seconds, what is its average operating speed in units per minute?

   (A) $\frac{t+30}{x}$

   (B) $\frac{x}{t+30}$

   (C) $tx + \frac{x}{2}$

   (D) $\frac{t}{x+\frac{1}{2}}$

   (E) $\frac{x}{t+\frac{1}{2}}$

19. (E) *Quantitative Reasoning/Algebra/Manipulation of Algebraic Expressions/Creating Algebraic Expressions* and *Arithmetic/Common Arithmetic Problems/Rates*

The operating speed is expressed in units per minute. The machine produces x units in t minutes plus $\frac{1}{2}$ minute. So, the average operating speed is $\frac{x}{t+\frac{1}{2}}$, (E).

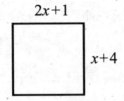

$2x+1$

$x+4$

20. If the figure above is a square, what is the perimeter of the figure?

   (A) 28

   (B) 16

   (C) 12

   (D) 9

   (E) 3

20. (A) *Quantitative Reasoning/Geometry/Rectangles and Squares* and *Algebra/Solving Equations/One Equation with One Variable*

Since the figure is a square, set the two sides equal and solve for x: $2x + 1 = x + 4 \Rightarrow x = 3$. Therefore, each side is $x + 4 = 3 + 4 = 7$, and the perimeter, $4s$, is $4(7) = 28$, (A).

21. If a certain rectangle has a length that is twice its width, what is the ratio of the area of the rectangle to the area of an isosceles right triangle with a hypotenuse equal to the width of the rectangle?

(A) $\frac{1}{8}$

(B) $\frac{1}{4}$

(C) $\frac{1}{2}$

(D) $\frac{4}{1}$

(E) $\frac{8}{1}$

21. **(E)** *Quantitative Reasoning/Geometry/Rectangles and Squares* and *Triangles/45°-45°-90° Triangles.*

Let w be the width of the rectangle, so the length of the rectangle is twice that, or $2w$, and the area of the rectangle $w(2w) = 2w^2$. As for the triangle, since all isosceles right triangles are 45°-45°-90° triangles, w is also the length of the hypotenuse of the 45°-45°-90° triangle. Each of the other two sides (the legs of the right angle) is $\frac{w\sqrt{2}}{2}$. Also, since the two sides form a right angle, they are the altitude and base, so the area of the triangle is

$\frac{ab}{2} = \frac{\left(\frac{w\sqrt{2}}{2}\right)\left(\frac{w\sqrt{2}}{2}\right)}{2} = \frac{w^2}{4}$. Thus, the ratio of the area of the rectangle to that of the triangle is $\frac{2w^2}{\frac{w^2}{4}} = \frac{8}{1}$, (E).

22. For the data in List X, the third quartile is 310 and the first quartile is 120 less than the third quartile. What is the second quartile of the data in List X?

(A) 60
(B) 190
(C) 220
(D) 250
(E) It cannot be determined from the information given.

22. **(E)** *Quantitative Reasoning/Data Analysis/Basic Descriptive Statistics/Quartiles and Interquartile Range*

The first quartile is the median of the lower half of the data, the second quartile is the median of all the data, and the third quartile is the median of the upper half of the data. Therefore, quartiles are not necessarily evenly spaced from one to the next, and there is not enough given information to determine the second quartile, (E).

23. Machine X produces 15 units per minute and Machine Y produces 12 units per minute. In 1 hour, Machine X will produce how many more units than will Machine Y?

(A) 90
(B) 180
(C) 240
(D) 270
(E) 360

23. **(B)** *Quantitative Reasoning/Arithmetic/Common Arithmetic Problems/Rates*

Machine X produces 3 more units per minute than does Machine Y. Therefore, in 1 hour, or 60 minutes, Machine X produces

$\frac{3 \text{ units}}{\text{minute}} \cdot 60 \text{ minutes} = 180$ units, (B), more than Machine Y does.

For the following item, enter your answer in the space provided.

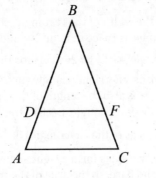

24. In the figure above, $\triangle ABC$ is similar to $\triangle DBF$. If $\overline{DF} = 3$, $\overline{BD} = \overline{BF} = 6$, and $\overline{AC} = 4$, what is the perimeter of $\triangle ABC$?

24. (20) *Quantitative Reasoning/Geometry/ Triangles/Properties of Triangles* and *Arithmetic/Common Arithmetic Problems/Ratios*

The ratio of any two similar sides of similar triangles is equal to the ratio of the perimeters. Therefore,

$$\frac{\text{side of } \triangle DBF}{\text{corresponding side of } \triangle ABC} = \frac{\text{perimeter}_{\triangle DBF}}{\text{perimeter}_{\triangle ABC}} \Rightarrow$$

$$\frac{\overline{DF}}{\overline{AC}} = \frac{\overline{BD} + \overline{DF} + \overline{BF}}{\text{perimeter}_{\triangle ABC}} \Rightarrow P_{\triangle ABC} = \frac{\overline{AC}(\overline{BD} + \overline{DF} + \overline{BF})}{\overline{DF}} =$$

$$\frac{4(6+3+6)}{3} = \frac{4(15)}{3} = 20 .$$

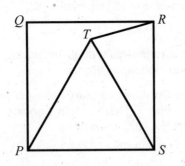

25. In the figure above, $PQRS$ is a square and $\triangle PTS$ is an equilateral triangle. How many degrees are there in $\angle TRS$?

   (A) 60
   (B) 75
   (C) 80
   (D) 90
   (E) It cannot be determined from the information given.

25. (B) *Quantitative Reasoning/Geometry/ Rectangles and Squares* and *Triangles/ Properties of Triangles*

$\triangle PTS$ is an equilateral triangle, so $\angle TSP = 60°$. And $PQRS$ is a square, so $\angle PSR = 90°$. Thus, $\angle TSR = \angle PSR - \angle TSP = 90° - 60° = 30°$. And $\overline{TS} = \overline{PS}$ ($\triangle PTS$ is equilateral) and $\overline{PS} = \overline{RS}$ ($PQRS$ is a square), so $\overline{TS} = \overline{RS}$. Therefore, $\triangle TRS$ must be an isosceles triangle and $\angle RTS = \angle TRS$, so $\angle TRS = \frac{180° - 30°}{2} = 75°$, (B).

Section 6 – Quantitative Reasoning

40 Minutes

25 Items

Solve each problem and choose the correct answer, using the given directions.

Notes: All numbers used are real numbers.

Unless otherwise indicated, all figures lie in a plane.

Geometric diagrams and figures **are not necessarily** drawn to scale, so do **not** assume lengths, angle measures, or other quantities are as they appear in a given figure. You should assume that lines shown as straight are straight and that the positions of points, and geometric objects in general, exist in the order shown. Base your answers to questions with geometric figures on reasoning, not visual estimation or measurement.

Coordinate systems and graphic data presentations **are** drawn to scale, so you can answer items based on visual estimation or measurement.

Each of the items #1–9 consists of two quantities, Quantity A and Quantity B. Compare the two quantities, using the information presented. Choose:

Ⓐ if Quantity A is greater.

Ⓑ if Quantity B is greater.

Ⓒ if the two quantities are equal.

Ⓓ if the relationship cannot be determined from the information given.

A symbol that appears more than once in an item has the same meaning throughout the item.

$$2x^2 + 4x + 3 = 0$$

Quantity A	Quantity B
1. $2x^2 + 4x$	-3

1. **(C)** *Quantitative Reasoning/Algebra Comparison/ Solving Equations/Quadratic Equations and Relations*

Solve the centered equation for the expression in Quantity A: $2x^2 + 4x + 3 = 0 \Rightarrow 2x^2 + 4x = -3$. Therefore, Quantity A is equal to Quantity B, (C).

Quantity A	Quantity B
2. $(111 + 111)^2$	$111^2 + 2(111)^2 + 111^2$

2. **(C)** *Quantitative Reasoning/Arithmetic Comparison/Complicated Manipulations/Factoring* and *Algebra/Solving Equations/Quadratic Equations and Relations*

The trick to solving this item quickly is to recognize that Quantity B, $111^2 + 2(111)^2 + 111^2$, has the general form $x^2 + 2xy + y^2$, which can be factored as $(x + y)(x + y) = (x + y)^2$, or $(111 + 111)^2$. Therefore, the two quantities are equal, (C).

Quantity A	Quantity B
3. The number of integers between 101 and 199 that are squares of integers	The number of integers between 201 and 299 that are squares of integers

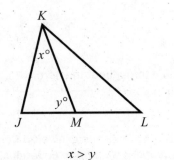

$$x > y$$

Quantity A	Quantity B
4. $\overline{JK} + \overline{LM}$	$\overline{JM} + \overline{KM}$

3. (A) *Quantitative Reasoning/Arithmetic Comparison/Common Arithmetic Problems/ Properties of Numbers*

100 is 10^2, so the next integer, when squared, will be greater than 100:

Quantity A	Quantity B
$11^2 = 121$	$15^2 = 225$
$12^2 = 144$	$16^2 = 256$
$13^2 = 169$	$17^2 = 289$
$14^2 = 196$	

There are more perfect squares between 101 and 199 (4) than between 201 and 299 (3), so Quantity A is greater than Quantity B, (A).

4. (D) *Quantitative Reasoning/Geometry Comparison/Triangles/Properties of Triangles*

Distort the figure. $\overline{LM}$ might be very long, making Quantity A greater:

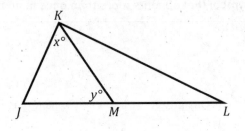

Or $\overline{LM}$ might be very short, in which case, Quantity B would be greater:

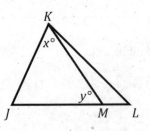

Therefore, the relationship between the two quantities cannot be determined, (D).

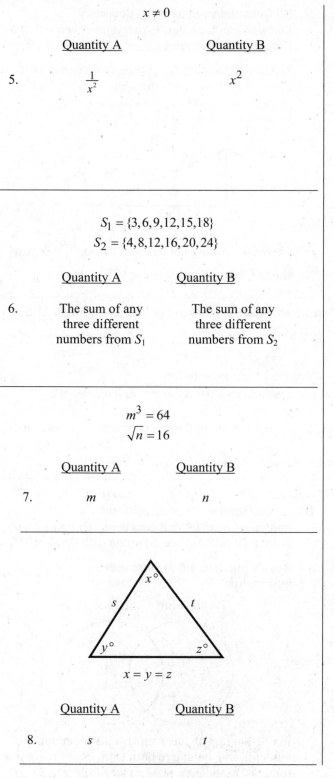

$x \neq 0$

Quantity A	Quantity B
5. $\dfrac{1}{x^2}$	x^2

$S_1 = \{3,6,9,12,15,18\}$
$S_2 = \{4,8,12,16,20,24\}$

Quantity A	Quantity B
6. The sum of any three different numbers from S_1	The sum of any three different numbers from S_2

$m^3 = 64$
$\sqrt{n} = 16$

Quantity A	Quantity B
7. m	n

$x = y = z$

Quantity A	Quantity B
8. s	t

5. **(D)** *Quantitative Reasoning/Algebra Comparison/ Manipulation of Algebraic Expressions/ Manipulating Expressions Involving Exponents*

Test the possible ranges of values for x. If $-1 < x < 1$, then $\dfrac{1}{x^2} > x$. However, if $x > 1$ or $x < -1$, then $x^2 > \dfrac{1}{x^2}$. Therefore, the relationship between the two quantities cannot be determined, (D).

6. **(D)** *Quantitative Reasoning/Arithmetic Comparison/Simple Manipulations*

Determine the ranges of the two quantities. For Quantity A, the minimum value is $3+6+9=18$ and the maximum value is $12+15+18=45$. For Quantity B, the minimum value is $4+8+12=24$ and the maximum value is $16+20+24=60$. The ranges of the two quantities (18–45 and 24–60) overlap in value, so the relationship between the two quantities cannot be determined, (D).

7. **(B)** *Quantitative Reasoning/Algebra Comparison/ Manipulation of Expressions Involving Exponents*

Solve each of the centered equations: $m^3 = 64 \Rightarrow m = \sqrt[3]{64} = 4$ and $\sqrt{n} = 16 \Rightarrow n = (16)^2 = 256$. Therefore, $n > m$, and Quantity B is greater than Quantity A, (B).

8. **(C)** *Quantitative Reasoning/Geometry Comparison/Triangles/Properties of Triangles*

Since the measures of angles x, y, and z are equivalent, the triangle is equilateral, with all three sides equal. Therefore, $s = t$, and Quantity A is equal to Quantity B, (C).

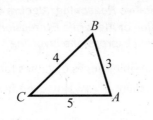

Quantity A	Quantity B
9. Area of region *ABC*	6

9. **(C)** *Quantitative Reasoning/Geometry Comparison/Triangles/Pythagorean Theorem* and *Properties of Triangles*

The trick to solving this item is to recognize that the triangle represents the special case of the Pythagorean theorem in which the lengths of the sides of a right triangle are 3, 4, and 5:

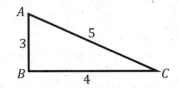

Therefore, the area of triangle *ABC* is $\frac{3(4)}{2} = 6$, and the two quantities are equal, (C).

Items #10–25 use several formats. Unless otherwise instructed, select one answer choice. For Numeric Entry items, follow the direction below.

Numeric Entry Directions

- Answers may be integers, decimals, or fractions. Answers may be negative.
- Items requiring a fraction will include two answer boxes—one for the numerator and one for the denominator.
- Equivalent forms of the answer are also correct (e.g., 9 and 9.0 are both correct forms of 9). Fractions do not need to be expressed in lowest terms.
- Enter the exact answer unless the item stem indicates that the answer should be rounded.

For the following item, enter your answer in the space provided.

10. Of a group of 27 students, 18 belong to the French Club and 15 belong to the Spanish Club. If each student belongs to at least one club, how many students belong to both clubs?

> [   ] students

10. **(6)** *Quantitative Reasoning/Data Analysis/Counting Methods/Venn Diagrams* and *Solving Equations/One Equation with One Variable*

Use a Venn diagram to illustrate the given information:

French Club   Spanish Club

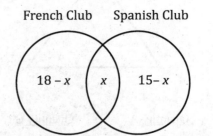

In the diagram above, *x* represents the number of students who belong to both clubs. Since there is a total of 27 students, $(18-x)+x+(15-x)=27$.

Solve the equation for *x*: $(18-x)+x+(15-x)= 27 \Rightarrow 33-x=27 \Rightarrow x=6$.

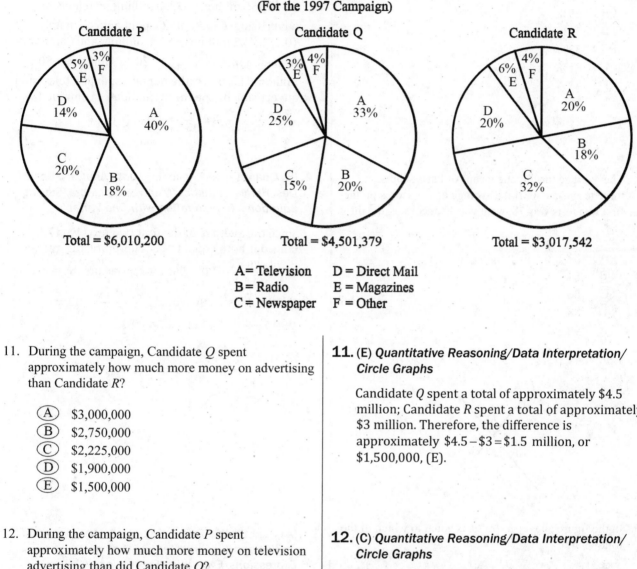

Advertising Expenditures of Three Candidates
(For the 1997 Campaign)

Candidate P
Total = $6,010,200

Candidate Q
Total = $4,501,379

Candidate R
Total = $3,017,542

A = Television   D = Direct Mail
B = Radio   E = Magazines
C = Newspaper   F = Other

11. During the campaign, Candidate *Q* spent approximately how much more money on advertising than Candidate *R*?

(A) $3,000,000
(B) $2,750,000
(C) $2,225,000
(D) $1,900,000
(E) $1,500,000

11. **(E)** *Quantitative Reasoning/Data Interpretation/ Circle Graphs*

Candidate *Q* spent a total of approximately $4.5 million; Candidate *R* spent a total of approximately $3 million. Therefore, the difference is approximately $4.5 – $3 = $1.5 million, or $1,500,000, (E).

12. During the campaign, Candidate *P* spent approximately how much more money on television advertising than did Candidate *Q*?

(A) $1,500,000
(B) $1,100,000
(C) $900,000
(D) $165,000
(E) $125,000

12. **(C)** *Quantitative Reasoning/Data Interpretation/ Circle Graphs*

Candidate *P* spent 40% of the approximately $6 million on television, or (0.40)($6 million) = $2.4 million. Candidate *Q* spent 33% of approximately $4.5 million on television, or (0.33)($4.5 million) ≈ $1.5 million. Therefore, Candidate *P* spent approximately $2.4 – $1.5 = $0.9 million more than Candidate *Q*, or $900,000, (C).

13. Approximately what percentage of the money spent on advertising by the three candidates combined was spent on television advertising?

    (A) 29%
    (B) 31%
    (C) 33%
    (D) 35%
    (E) 37%

13. **(C) Quantitative Reasoning/*Data Interpretation/ Circle Graphs***

Candidate P spent approximately $(0.40)(\$6 \text{ million}) = \$2.4$ million on television advertising; Candidate Q spent approximately $(0.33)(\$4.5 \text{ million}) \approx \$1.5$ million; and Candidate R spent approximately $(0.20)(\$3 \text{ million}) \approx \$0.6$ million. Therefore, the percent spent on television advertising by the three candidates combined was $\frac{\$2.4 + \$1.5 + \$0.6}{\$6 + \$4.5 + \$3} = \frac{4.5}{13.5} \approx 33\%$, (C).

14. The average (arithmetic mean) of Pat's scores on three tests was 80. If the average of her scores on the first two tests was 78, what was her score on the third test?

    (A) 82
    (B) 84
    (C) 86
    (D) 88
    (E) 90

14. **(B) Quantitative Reasoning/*Data Analysis/Basic Descriptive Statistics/Mean* and *Algebra/Solving Equations/One Equation with One Variable***

Since the average of the first two tests was 78, consider both equal to 78. Therefore, the average is $\frac{78 + 78 + x}{3} = 80$, where x represents the score on the third test. Solve for x: $\frac{78 + 78 + x}{3} = 80 \Rightarrow$ $78 + 78 + x = 240 \Rightarrow x = 84$, (B).

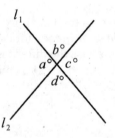

15. In the figure above, $a + c - b$ is equal to which of the following?

    (A) $2a - d$
    (B) $2a + d$
    (C) $2d - a$
    (D) $2a$
    (E) 180

15. **(A) Quantitative Reasoning/*Geometry/Lines and Angles* and *Algebra/Manipulation of Expressions/Evaluating Expressions***

A quick glance at the answer choices indicates that the expression $a + c - b$ needs to be rewritten in terms of a and d. For two intersecting lines, opposite angles are equal, so $a = c$ and $b = d$. Therefore, $a + c - b = a + a - d = 2a - d$, (A).

16. If $3a + 6b = 12$, then $a + 2b =$

   (A) 1
   (B) 2
   (C) 3
   (D) 4
   (E) 6

16. (D) Quantitative Reasoning/*Algebra/*
Manipulation of Algebraic Expressions/Factoring
Expressions

The trick to solving this item is to recognize that $3a + 6b = 3(a + 2b)$, so $3(a + 2b) = 12 \Rightarrow a + 2b = 4$, (D).

17. If x, y, and z are integers, $1 < x < y < z$, and $xyz = 144$, then what is the greatest possible value of z?

   (A) 8
   (B) 12
   (C) 16
   (D) 24
   (E) 36

17. (D) Quantitative Reasoning/*Arithmetic/Common*
Arithmetic Problems/Properties of Numbers and
Complicated Manipulations/Factoring

Begin by factoring 144: $144 = 3 \cdot 3 \cdot 2 \cdot 2 \cdot 2 \cdot 2$. Next, rewrite the factorization in terms of three integers, in which two are as small as possible, without being the same: $3 \cdot 3 \cdot 2 \cdot 2 \cdot 2 \cdot 2 = (2)(3)(3 \cdot 2 \cdot 2 \cdot 2) = (2)(3)(24)$. Therefore, the greatest possible value of z is 24, (D).

18. On the first day after being given an assignment, a student read $\frac{1}{2}$ the number of pages assigned and read three more pages on the second day. If the student still has six more pages to read, how many pages were assigned?

   (A) 15
   (B) 18
   (C) 24
   (D) 30
   (E) 36

18. (B) Quantitative Reasoning/*Arithmetic/*
Complicated Arithmetic Application Problems and
Algebra/Solving Equations/One Equation with One
Variable

If x represents the total number of pages, 6 remain after reading half ($\frac{x}{2}$) plus 3 more, or $x - (\frac{x}{2} + 3) = 6$. Solve for x: $x - (\frac{x}{2} + 3) = 6 \Rightarrow$ $\frac{x}{2} - 3 = 6 \Rightarrow x - 6 = 12 \Rightarrow x = 18$, (B).

19. The sum of two positive consecutive integers is n. In terms of n, what is the value of the larger of the two integers?

   (A) $\frac{n-1}{2}$

   (B) $\frac{n+1}{2}$

   (C) $\frac{n}{2} + 1$

   (D) $\frac{n}{2} - 1$

   (E) $\frac{n}{2}$

19. (B) *Quantitative Reasoning/Arithmetic/Common*
Arithmetic Problems/Properties of Numbers and
Algebra/Solving Equations/One Equation with
One Variable

If the larger of the two integers is m, then the next smaller consecutive integer is $m - 1$. Given that the sum is n, $n = (m - 1) + m$. Solve for m: $n = (m - 1) + m \Rightarrow 2m = n + 1 \Rightarrow m = \frac{n+1}{2}$, (B).

For the following item, enter your answer in the space provided.

20. In a certain population group, 57 percent of the people have characteristic X and 63 percent have characteristic Y. If every person in the group has at least one of the two characteristics, what percentage of the people have both X and Y?

[_____] %

21. List A: 2, 4, 4, 4, 5, 5, 7, 9

What is the difference between the mean and the standard deviation for the data in List A?

(A) 2
(B) 3
(C) 4
(D) 5
(E) 7

20. (20) *Quantitative Reasoning/Data Analysis/ Counting Methods/Venn Diagrams*

Use a Venn diagram to illustrate the given information:

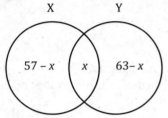

In the diagram above, x represents the number of people who have both characteristics. Since the information is given in terms of percentages, $(57 - x) + x + (63 - x) = 100$. Solve for x:

$(57 - x) + x + (63 - x) = 100 \Rightarrow 120 - x = 100 \Rightarrow$
$x = 20$.

21. (B) *Quantitative Reasoning/Data Analysis/Basic Descriptive Statistics/Mean and Standard Deviation*

The mean (average) of List A is
$\frac{2 + 3(4) + 2(5) + 7 + 9}{8} = 5$. To find the standard
deviation, first sum the squares of the difference between the mean and each data value:

$(5-2)^2 + 3(5-4)^2 + 2(5-5)^2 +$

$(5-7)^2 + (5-9)^2 = (3)^2 + 3(1)^2 + 2(0)^2 + (-2)^2 +$

$(-4)^2 = 9 + 3 + 0 + 4 + 16 = 32$. Next, divide that value by the total number of values in the set and take the square root to get the standard deviation:

$\sqrt{\frac{32}{8}} = \sqrt{4} = 2$. Therefore, the difference between the

mean and the standard deviation is $5 - 2 = 3$, (B).

22. An ice cream truck runs down a certain street 4 times a week. This truck carries 5 different flavors of ice cream bars, each of which comes in 2 different designs. Considering that the truck runs Monday through Thursday, and Monday was the first day of the month, by what day of the month could a person, buying one ice cream bar each truck-run, purchase all of the different varieties of ice cream bars?

 (A) 11th
 (B) 16th
 (C) 21st
 (D) 24th
 (E) 30th

22. (B) *Quantitative Reasoning/Data Analysis/ Counting Methods/Combinations*

There are $5 \cdot 2 = 10$ different varieties of ice cream bars on the truck. Since the truck only runs four times a week, it would take a person 2 weeks + 2 days = 16 days, (B), to purchase all of the different varieties of ice cream bars.

23. If $N! = N(N-1)(N-2)\ldots[N-(N-1)]$, what does $\frac{N!}{(N-2)!}$ equal?

 (A) $N^2 - N$
 (B) $N^5 + N^3 - N^2 + \frac{N}{N^2}$
 (C) $N + 1$
 (D) 1
 (E) 6

23. (A) *Quantitative Reasoning/Algebra/Functions* and *Simple Manipulations*

Do the indicated operations: $\frac{N!}{(N-2)!} =$

$\frac{N(N-1)(N-2)(N-3)(N-4)\ldots[N-(N-1)]}{(N-2)(N-3)(N-4)\ldots[N-(N-1)]}$. Cancel like

factors in the numerator and the denominator:

$\frac{N(N-1)\cancel{(N-2)}\cancel{(N-3)}\cancel{(N-4)}\ldots\cancel{[N-(N-1)]}}{\cancel{(N-2)}\cancel{(N-3)}\cancel{(N-4)}\ldots\cancel{[N-(N-1)]}} = \frac{N(N-1)}{1} =$

$N(N-1) = N^2 - N$, (A).

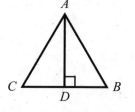

24. In the figure above, $\triangle ABC$ is equilateral and has a perpendicular line drawn from point A to point D. If the triangle is "folded over" on the perpendicular line so that points B and C meet, the perimeter of the new triangle is approximately what percent of the perimeter of the triangle before the fold?

 (A) 100%
 (B) 80%
 (C) 50%
 (D) 32%
 (E) 16%

24. (B) *Quantitative Reasoning/Geometry/Properties of Triangles* and *30°-60°-90° Triangles*

If each side of the original equilateral triangle is labeled x, the original triangle has a perimeter of $3x$. After the triangle is "folded over," the new triangle is a 30°-60°-90° triangle and so has sides in the ratio $\frac{x}{2} : \frac{\sqrt{3}x}{2} : x$, where x is now the hypotenuse of the new triangle. Thus, the perimeter of the new triangle is $\frac{x}{2} + \frac{\sqrt{3}x}{2} + x =$

$\frac{x + \sqrt{3}x + 2x}{2} = \frac{x(3 + \sqrt{3})}{2}$. Therefore,

$\frac{\text{perimeter}_{\text{new triangle}}}{\text{perimeter}_{\text{original triangle}}} = \frac{\frac{x(3+\sqrt{3})}{2}}{3x} = \frac{3+\sqrt{3}}{6} \approx 80\%$, (B).

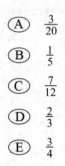

25. Three valves, when opened individually, can drain the water from a certain tank in 3, 4, and 5 minutes, respectively. What is the greatest part of the tank that can be drained in one minute by opening just two of the valves?

(A) $\frac{3}{20}$

(B) $\frac{1}{5}$

(C) $\frac{7}{12}$

(D) $\frac{2}{3}$

(E) $\frac{3}{4}$

25.(C) Quantitative Reasoning/*Arithmetic/Common Arithmetic Problems/Rates*

The question asks for the greatest part of the tank to be drained by only two of the valves, so use the two fastest values. The fastest valve drains the entire tank in 3 minutes, or $\frac{1}{3}$ of the tank in 1 minute. The second fastest valve drains the entire tank in 4 minutes, or $\frac{1}{4}$ of the tank in 1 minute.

Therefore, the two fastest valves drain $\frac{1}{3} + \frac{1}{4}$ of the entire tank in 1 minute, or $\frac{1}{3} + \frac{1}{4} = \frac{4+3}{(3)(4)} = \frac{7}{12}$ of the entire tank, (C).

Practice Test I*:

Outline

*Answers and Explanations begin on page 713.

Section 1–Analytical Writing

Time—30 minutes

Analyze an Issue

DIRECTIONS: You will be given a brief statement about an issue of general interest and a set of instructions on how to respond to that issue. You will have 30 minutes to plan and write a response following the provided instructions. A response to any other issue will receive a score of zero.

Be sure to follow the specific instructions and support your position with relevant reasons and examples.

Readers will review your essay and grade its overall quality based on the following criteria:

- Follows the specific instructions

- Addresses the complexities of the issue

- Organizes and develops ideas

- Supports ideas with relevant reasons and/or examples

- Controls the elements of standard written English

Take a few minutes to think about the issue and instructions and plan your response before you begin writing. Fully develop your position in a coherent and organized manner. Be sure to leave time to review your essay and make any necessary revisions. A sample essay response begins on page 714.

Issue Topic

Great people should be remembered for their accomplishments in their fields—politics, science, art, or business—and not for their shortcomings as human beings.

Write an essay in which you discuss which view more closely aligns with your own position and explain your reasons for the position you take. When developing and supporting your position, address both of the views presented.

Section 2–Analytical Writing

Time—30 minutes

Analyze an Argument

DIRECTIONS: You will be given a brief passage presenting an argument and a set of instructions on how to respond to that argument. You will have 30 minutes to plan and write a response following the provided instructions. A response to any other argument will receive a score of zero.

Note: You are NOT being asked to present your own views on the subject. Ensure that you follow the specific instructions and support your analysis with relevant reasons and examples.

Readers will review your essay and evaluate its overall quality, based on the following criteria:

- Follows the specific instructions

- Identifies and analyzes important features of the argument

- Organizes and develops the evaluation

- Supports the analysis with relevant reasons and/or examples

- Controls the elements of standard written English

Take a few minutes to think about the passage and instructions and plan your response before you begin writing. Fully develop your evaluation in a coherent and organized manner. Be sure to leave time to review your essay and make any necessary revisions. A sample essay response begins on page 714.

Argument Topic

The City Parks Department has authority over all of the City's recreational facilities. The City opens the swimming pools on the Memorial Day Weekend and closes them on Labor Day. During the summer, however, all of the City's indoor facilities are closed. In response to a survey question that asked residents if they wanted children to have the opportunity to play sports such as basketball and handball during the summer, 98 percent of City residents answered yes. It is clear, then, that City residents want all of the City's recreational facilities open during the summer. So, the City should adopt a new policy that keeps the indoor facilities open during the same months the swimming pools are open.

Write an essay in which you discuss what specific evidence is needed to evaluate the argument and explain how the evidence could weaken or strengthen the argument.

Section 3–Verbal Reasoning

Time—35 minutes
25 Items

For Items #1–5, select one answer choice unless otherwise instructed. Answers for Section 3 are on page 713, and explanations are on page 715.

Items #1–4 are based on the following passage.

Considerable advances have been made in the area of healthcare services, including better access to healthcare and improvements in physical plants, but there is mounting criticism of unbridled cost inflation
5 and excessive indulgence in wasteful high-technology "gadgeteering." In recent years, panaceas have proliferated at a feverish pace and disappointments have multiplied at almost the same rate. This has led to an increased pessimism—"everything has been tried
10 and nothing works"—which sometimes borders on cynicism or even nihilism.

The automatic "pass through" of rapidly spiraling costs to government and insurance carriers produced a sense of unlimited resources and encouraged the notion
15 that every practitioner and institution could operate without concern for the "Medical Commons." Full-cost reimbursement encouraged capital investment, and now the industry is overcapitalized. Cities have hundreds of excess hospital beds; hospitals have a
20 superabundance of high-technology equipment; and structural ostentation and luxury have been the order of the day. One-fourth of all beds are vacant; expensive equipment is underused or, worse, used unnecessarily. Capital investment brings rapidly rising operating
25 costs.

Yet, in part, this pessimism derives from expecting too much. Healthcare is usually a painful experience, often accompanied by fear and unwelcome results. Moreover, the capacities of medical science are
30 limited. Humpty Dumpty cannot always be put back together again. Too many physicians are reluctant to admit their limitations to patients; too many patients and families are unwilling to accept such realities. Nor is it true that everything has been tried and nothing
35 works, as shown by prepaid group practice plans. In the main, however, such undertakings have been drowned by a flood of public and private moneys which have supported and encouraged the continuation of conventional practices and subsidized their
40 shortcomings on a massive, almost unrestricted scale. For the most part, there have been no incentives to practice self-restraint or frugality. In this atmosphere, it is not fair to condemn as failures all attempted experiments; it may be more accurate to say many
45 never had a fair trial.

1. The tone of the passage can best be described as

   (A) light-hearted and amused
   (B) objective but concerned
   (C) detached and unconcerned
   (D) cautious but sincere
   (E) enthusiastic and enlightened

For the following item, consider each answer individually and select all that apply.

2. The author mentions which of the following as consequences of full-cost reimbursement?

   A   rising operating costs
   B   underused hospital facilities
   C   lack of essential services

GO ON TO THE NEXT PAGE.

3. According to the author, the "pessimism" mentioned in line 9 is partly attributable to the fact that

(A) there has been little real improvement in healthcare services

(B) expectations about healthcare services are sometimes unrealistic

(C) large segments of the population find it impossible to get access to healthcare services

(D) advances in technology have made healthcare services unaffordable

(E) doctors are now less concerned with patient care

4. The author cites the prepaid plans (line 35) as

(A) counterexamples to the claim that nothing has worked

(B) examples of healthcare plans that were overfunded

(C) evidence that healthcare services are fragmented

(D) proof of the theory that no plan has been successful

(E) experiments that yielded disappointing results

Item #5 is based on the following passage.

Those who deny the existence of miracles say that miraculous events are impossible because they violate the laws of nature. However, we know from personal experience that laws are violated every day; otherwise,
5 there would be no need for police, judges, and prisons. Therefore, there is no reason to believe that the laws of nature may not be violated as well.

5. Which of the following best states the central weakness in the argument?

(A) It places a divine being, who might bring about a miraculous event, on the same moral level as a human criminal.

(B) It misuses the term "law," which, when applied to the laws of nature, has a different meaning than when applied to human laws.

(C) It assumes that miraculous events have taken place without offering substantive proof for their occurrence.

(D) It ignores the fact that under unusual circumstances natural events may occur that appear to violate natural laws without actually doing so.

(E) It attacks the motivations of those who deny the miraculous rather than analyzing the evidence for and against their arguments.

For Items #6–9, select one answer choice for each blank from the corresponding column of choices. Fill all blanks in a way that best completes the text.

6. Execution by lethal injection, although horrifying, is certainly more civilized than the _____ penalty of death by torture or dismemberment.

(A)	pervasive
(B)	viler
(C)	humane
(D)	prolific
(E)	complacent

7. Although vitamins are helpful for maintaining good health, alcohol, caffeine, and other drugs severely (i)_____ their effectiveness, and an (ii)_____ immune system exposes the body to illness.

Blank (i)	Blank (ii)
(A) augment	(D) indelible
(B) inhibit	(E) activated
(C) duplicate	(F) impaired

GO ON TO THE NEXT PAGE.

8. Since there are so few conservative thinkers on the committee, their influence on its recommendations is _____.

(A)	monumental
(B)	negligible
(C)	discriminatory
(D)	impractical
(E)	cathartic

9. Whereas Wilder was well mannered and even a bit (i) _____, Stein was playful and outré. By the time of his meeting with Stein, Wilder was an old hand at stardom. Newer to the game, Stein, who was 60 when they met, was an eager, even (ii)_____, participant, and she spied something unspoiled in the bookish young man, something in need of her own (iii)_____ influence. The two became friends.

Blank (i)	Blank (ii)	Blank (iii)
(A) staid	(D) willing	(G) tonic
(B) inconsiderate	(E) anxious	(H) calming
(C) ambitious	(F) improvident	(I) amicable

For Items #10–13, select one answer choice unless otherwise instructed.

Items #10–11 are based on the following passage.

Art, like words, is a form of communication. Words, spoken and written, render accessible to humans of the latest generations all the knowledge discovered by the experience and reflection both of preceding generations
5   and of the best and foremost minds of their own times. Art renders accessible to people of the latest generations all the feelings experienced by their predecessors and those already felt by their best and foremost contemporaries. Just as the evolution of
10   knowledge proceeds by dislodging and replacing that which is mistaken, so too the evolution of feeling proceeds through art. Feelings less kind and less necessary for the well-being of human kind are replaced by others kinder and more essential to that
15   end. This is the purpose of art, and the more art fulfills that purpose, the better the art; the less it fulfills it, the worse the art.

10. The author develops the passage primarily by

(A) theory and refutation
(B) example and generalization
(C) comparison and contrast
(D) question and answer
(E) inference and deduction

11. The style of the passage can best be described as

(A) speculative
(B) argumentative
(C) expository
(D) poetic
(E) sarcastic

GO ON TO THE NEXT PAGE.

An international conference on the development of the world's undersea resources has proposed that all future use of these resources through undersea mining, harvesting of food in international waters, or other
5 forms of development be subject to an international tax, to be set at a fixed percentage of the profits. The revenues from this tax would be used to support industrial development in the poorest nations of the world. This scheme, if adopted, will probably halt all
10 future development of undersea resources. By removing the profit incentive, the proposed tax will discourage industrial nations from making the investments needed to exploit these valuable but remote undersea resources.

12. Which of the following questions would be most relevant in evaluating the validity of the conclusion of the argument?

(A) What kinds of development projects would be supported by the proposed tax?

(B) What percentage of the profits derived from exploitation of undersea resources would be taken by the proposed tax?

(C) What position has been taken on the issue of the tax by the representatives of the nations that would benefit from the tax?

(D) What definition of "international waters" will be used for purposes of levying the proposed tax?

(E) What international agency would have the responsibility for assessing the tax and redistributing the revenues?

The preeminence of television in modern political campaigns has produced several deleterious effects on our democratic system. Because the attention span of television-trained audiences has been artificially
5 shortened, candidates are forced to encapsulate their programs and ideas in 30- or 60-second summaries—mere slogans embellished with emotionally evocative imagery. And because television commercials are so costly, candidates must spend
10 much of their campaign time raising money rather than delving deeply into the issues confronting our nation and its leaders.

13. The author regards the high cost of television advertising as

(A) a result of the shortened attention span of television-trained audiences

(B) an explanation of the effectiveness of emotionally powerful imagery

(C) one factor explaining why candidates fail to confront serious political issues

(D) the outcome of the deterioration of the democratic political system

(E) a possible cause of the inability of the population to comprehend complex ideas

GO ON TO THE NEXT PAGE.

For Items #14–17, select one answer choice for each blank from the corresponding column of choices. Fill all blanks in a way that best completes the text.

14. Laboratory tests that often maim animals and depend solely on observation to determine results are not only (i)_____ but highly (ii)_____ since no two people see the same thing.

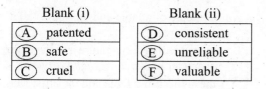

Blank (i)		Blank (ii)	
A	patented	D	consistent
B	safe	E	unreliable
C	cruel	F	valuable

15. The victim confronted his attacker in the courtroom calmly, with (i)_____ and without apparent (ii)_____, although he had been severely traumatized by the incident.

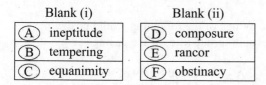

Blank (i)		Blank (ii)	
A	ineptitude	D	composure
B	tempering	E	rancor
C	equanimity	F	obstinacy

16. The politician hungered for power; as a result of this _____, he succeeded in winning the election but in alienating his closest friends and supporters.

A	furtiveness
B	winsomeness
C	malevolence
D	acerbity
E	cupidity

17. The report traces the history of northern New Jersey's beleaguered ecosystem step by step from its industrial (i)_____, through shopping mall construction and suburban development, and, finally, to the stubborn re-emergence of its (ii)_____ wildlife. The story of the region depicts the human potential for both destruction and renewal.

Blank (i)		Blank (ii)	
A	apogee	D	indigenous
B	climax	E	exotic
C	nadir	F	predatory

GO ON TO THE NEXT PAGE.

For Items #18–21, select one answer choice unless otherwise instructed.

Items #18–21 are based on the following passage.

Speaking casually, we call *Nineteen Eighty-Four* a novel; but more exactly, it is a fable. True, the book focuses on Winston Smith, who suffers from a varicose ulcer, and it includes Julia, Mr. Charrington, and
5 O'Brien. They exist, however, mainly in their relation to a political system. In a novel, they would have to be imagined in a far more diverse set of relations. A fable is a narrative relieved of much contingent detail so that it stands forth in an unusual degree of clarity and
10 simplicity. A fable is a structure of types, each simplified lest a sense of difference and heterogeneity reduce the force of the typical.

    Since a fable is predicated upon a typology, the author cannot afford the sense of familiarity that is
15 induced by detail and differentiation. A fable is a caricature, not a photograph. In a political fable there is tension between a political sense, which deals in the multiplicity of social and personal life, and a sense of fable, which is committed to simplicity of form and
20 feature. If the political sense were to prevail, the narrative would be drawn away from fable into the novel, at some cost to its simplicity. If the sense of fable were to prevail, the narrative would appear unmediated, free or bereft of conditions. A reader
25 might feel that the fabulist had lost interest in the variety of human life and fallen back upon an unconditioned sense of its types. The risk is greater still if the fabulist projects the narrative into the future: the reader can't question by appealing to the conditions of
30 life but is asked to believe that the future is another country where "they just do things differently." Thus, *Nineteen Eighty-Four* is a political fable, projected into a near future.

18. In drawing an analogy between a fable and a caricature (lines 15–16), the author would most likely regard which of the following pairs of ideas as also analogous?

  (A) the topic of a fable and the subject of a caricature

  (B) the subject of a caricature and the main character in *Nineteen Eighty-Four*

  (C) the subject of a fable and the artist who draws the caricature

  (D) the artist who draws the caricature and a novelist

  (E) the minor characters in a fable and a photographer

19. Which of the following would be the most appropriate title for the passage?

  (A) A Critical Study of the Use of Characters in *Nineteen Eighty-Four*

  (B) *Nineteen Eighty-Four*: Political Fable Rather Than Novel

  (C) *Nineteen Eighty-Four*: Reflections on the Relationship of the Individual to Society

  (D) The Use of Typology in the Literature of Political Fables

  (E) Distinguishing a Political Fable from a Novel

GO ON TO THE NEXT PAGE.

20. Which of the following best explains why the author mentions that Winston Smith suffers from a varicose ulcer?

(A) to demonstrate that a political fable must emphasize type over detail

(B) to show that Winston Smith has some characteristics that distinguish him as an individual

(C) to argue that Winston Smith is no more important than any other character in *Nineteen Eighty-Four*

(D) to illustrate one of the features of the political situation described in *Nineteen Eighty-Four*

(E) to suggest that *Nineteen Eighty-Four* is too realistic to be considered a work of fiction

21. The author uses the phrase "another country" (lines 30–31) to describe a political fable in which

(A) political events described in a fable occur in a place other than the country of national origin of the author

(B) a lack of detail makes it difficult for a reader to see the connection between his own situation and the one described in the book

(C) too many minor characters create the impression of complete disorganization, leading the reader to believe he is in a foreign country

(D) the author has allowed his personal political convictions to infect his description of the political situation

(E) an overabundance of detail prevents the reader from appreciating the real possibility that such a political situation could develop

---

For Items #22–25, select the <u>two</u> words that, when used independently in the sentence, produce logical sentences and produce sentences that are alike in meaning.

---

22. As a result of DNA testing excluding them as viable suspects, more than 70 persons previously convicted of capital crimes have been _____.

A	exonerated
B	incarcerated
C	absolved
D	indicted
E	liberated
F	identified

23. Crime on the web is a _____ problem as growing numbers of individuals and small gangs are tempted by the extraordinary prospects for illicit gain, and even organized crime is abandoning some of its traditional illegal activities in favor of electronic fraud.

A	petrified
B	preconceived
C	worrisome
D	remunerative
E	proliferating
F	burgeoning

GO ON TO THE NEXT PAGE.

24. Panhandlers dress to look needy but not
    threatening and express appreciation even when
    refused, exhibiting _____ behavior calculated
    to produce the greatest profit in the long run.

    A | judicious
    B | unethical
    C | incoherent
    D | insensitive
    E | prudent
    F | detrimental

25. From childhood, Salinger felt a pronounced sense
    of uniqueness that would later calcify into a
    complete indifference to other people, rendering
    the author totally _____.

    A | misanthropic
    B | solipsistic
    C | alienated
    D | egocentric
    E | irresolute
    F | profligate

STOP. You have reached the end of Section 3.

Section 4–Verbal Reasoning

Time—35 minutes
25 Items

For Items #1–5, select the two words that, when used independently in the sentence, produce logical sentences and produce sentences that are alike in meaning. Answers for Section 4 are on page 713, and explanations are on page 719.

1. All that can be seen of the church _____ by the waters of the reservoir created by the new dam is the top third of the old steeple.

   A | bathed
   B | revealed
   C | inundated
   D | flooded
   E | excavated
   F | eroded

2. The great enthusiasm for journalistic writing that had given birth to more than a thousand newspapers collapsed in just a few years, _____ by long and varied struggles.

   A | enervated
   B | revitalized
   C | invigorated
   D | depleted
   E | compromised
   F | ignored

3. Segismudno's speech in Act II is not original to *Calderon* but is _____ of words and imagery borrowed from several other sources, including Lope de Vega's *Barlán y Josafá*.

   A | a parsimony
   B | an hegemony
   C | a salmagundi
   D | a constabulary
   E | an ossuary
   F | a miscellany

4. The open hearth and electric furnaces for steelmaking produced more refined grades of steel and so required more _____ devices for measuring temperature and controlling the chemical reaction.

   A | sensitive
   B | expensive
   C | delicate
   D | durable
   E | mobile
   F | modern

GO ON TO THE NEXT PAGE.

5. None of the controversial reports of early Finnish history comes from contemporary sources, so it is likely the reports of the savagery of Fenni were exaggerated and perhaps even entirely _____.

A	apocryphal
B	inflammatory
C	sanguinary
D	capricious
E	macabre
F	inauthentic

For Items #6-10, select one answer choice unless otherwise instructed.

Items #6-8 are based on the following passage.

In the first place, it is important to understand that Tibetan is not a language in the way that modern English is a language, with a range of dialects so that speakers easily understand each other in accordance
5 with common vocabulary, grammar, and so forth. There is no standard Tibetan. There is, however, an emergent proto-standard Tibetan that is spoken widely in the diasporic community. This language derives from the Lhasa language, a good basis for a standard
10 Tibetan that could be used across Tibet in addition to regional dialects.

Second, literary Tibetan, typically referred to as classical Tibetan, has a long and distinguished tradition going back at least to the seventh century. Classical
15 Tibetan is remarkably conservative in terms of spelling, grammar usage, and vocabulary. Someone who is conversant in modern classical Tibetan can actually pick up tenth century texts and read them fluently, something that is not at all true of English.
20 Unfortunately, most Tibetan dialects are not equally conservative in pronunciation and vocabulary. As a result, classical Tibetan is dramatically divergent from spoken Tibetan, which makes classical Tibetan unnecessarily difficult to learn. Also, many standard
25 colloquial spoken terms have no standardized spelling or use in literary Tibetan. A modern literary Tibetan language has begun to emerge in creative writing, newspapers, and the like, but this modern literary Tibetan has yet to become a fully transregional
30 vernacular, that is, a literary Tibetan that can be easily understood, easily learned, and used for daily communications.

Third, Tibetans who are fluent in spoken Tibetan often lack specific colloquial competencies not because

35 they are pressured to switch over to Chinese, but because often they are actually unable to use Tibetan in specific professional or intellectual environments. They do not know the vocabulary. When speaking of computer science, mathematics, biology, or certain
40 governmental activities, they literally do not know how to talk. Thus, it is important to promote the use of Tibetan equivalents to Chinese terms in these professional areas.

Why do the Tibetans not give up Tibetan
45 altogether and simply speak Chinese? Everyone could become, in two or three generations, native speakers of Chinese. This shift to Chinese would be damaging because it would create a traumatic rift between the way of life for modern Tibetans and their 1,300-year
50 literary and cultural history. A people's sense of identity, place, and time is inextricably bound up with their language. By losing the Tibetan language, the specifically Tibetan identity and world with its culture, insights, values and behaviors, is essentially consigned
55 to the past.

Within two or three decades, it is possible that the Tibetan language will be all but extinct, surviving only as the province of a few isolated monasteries. There is, however, another possibility in which standard Tibetan
60 could become widely spoken and again become a medium for educational and commercial contexts. A newly generated vernacular Tibetan could become one that is meaningful in educational and personal contexts.

GO ON TO THE NEXT PAGE.

6. As used in this context, the word "conservative" (line 15) means

  (A) illiterate
  (B) limited
  (C) subordinate
  (D) collective
  (E) stable

7. Select the sentence in the first two paragraphs that is included by the author to correct or pre-empt a possible misunderstanding.

  (A) Lines 1–5 ("In the first place…so forth.")
  (B) Lines 6–8 ("There is, however…community.")
  (C) Lines 12–14 ("Second, literary Tibetan…century.")
  (D) Lines 16–19 ("Someone who is…English.")
  (E) Lines 26–32 ("A modern literary…communications.")

For the following item, consider each answer individually and select all that apply.

8. The author provides information to help answer which of the following questions?

  A   What would be the consequences of Tibetans abandoning their language?

  B   What is the significance of Tibetan language and culture?

  C   What events or actions might help preserve Tibetan as a language?

Item #9 is based on the following passage.

A Roman poet wrote, "It is sweet and noble to die for one's country." It is hard to see how any sensation of sweetness could be involved in the experience of dying in battle, in excruciating pain, in a muddy ditch miles
5 from home, hearth, and family. Therefore, we may well doubt that nobility may be said to inhere in the act of dying itself.

9. The main point of the author's argument is that

  (A) it is the consequence of the act of dying in defense of one's country that is important, not the act of dying itself

  (B) the political and military objectives of war may not be evident to each soldier

  (C) the word "sweetness" is ambiguous when it is used to describe actions rather than taste sensations

  (D) the consequences of war have changed little since ancient times

  (E) dying in defense of one's country is an action that may or may not be noble depending on whether the cause of the war is just

GO ON TO THE NEXT PAGE.

Here is news for all coffee drinkers. In 17 cities across the nation, we tested our instant coffee against perked coffee, and we won! In a survey of thousands of coffee drinkers, two out of every five expressed a preference
5   for Flash Instant Coffee over perked coffee. Shouldn't you try Flash, the coffee with the same rich taste as perked coffee?

10. Which of the following, if true, most weakens the claim above?

(A) The 17 cities were concentrated primarily in the Midwest and West.

(B) The survey included 150 people in each of the 17 cities.

(C) The taste tests used a medium-priced brand of perked coffee.

(D) For purposes of the survey, "coffee drinker" was defined as anyone who drinks at least one cup of coffee per day.

(E) Those coffee drinkers who preferred Flash to perked coffee were already instant-coffee drinkers

For Items #11–14, select one answer choice for each blank from the corresponding column of choices. Fill all blanks in a way that best completes the text.

11. The chief interest for us now is in what science fiction writer Jules Verne got right and what he got wrong about the twentieth century. Writing in 1863, he mentions gas-powered cars, the elevator, wind power, and even the computer, all (i)_____ to the world of science and technology. When Verne tries for anything broader, he is hopelessly, ridiculously (ii)_____. He also predicted that war would no longer be possible because all armies would have been disbanded.

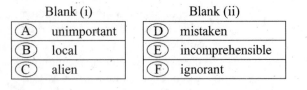

	Blank (i)		Blank (ii)
(A)	unimportant	(D)	mistaken
(B)	local	(E)	incomprehensible
(C)	alien	(F)	ignorant

12. Worshipped by friends, despised by enemies, cryptic, secretive, and opaque, Whittaker Chambers is a(n) (i)_____ figure who at once seemed to (ii)_____ and resent the burdens of history.

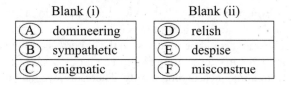

	Blank (i)		Blank (ii)
(A)	domineering	(D)	relish
(B)	sympathetic	(E)	despise
(C)	enigmatic	(F)	misconstrue

GO ON TO THE NEXT PAGE.

13. Contrary to political legend, the peasantry did not play a critical role in the Russian Revolution. Most peasants wanted simply to be left alone by the state and envisioned freedom in a pre-political sense, as the right to live, essentially, an (i)_____ existence. Following the fall of the czar, the peasants seized the gentry's lands and then (ii)_____ resisted all power, whether Red or White. This lack of (iii)_____ rendered them vulnerable to the numerically weaker but better organized Bolsheviks.

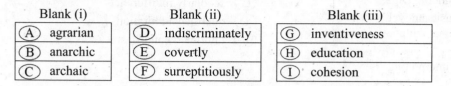

Blank (i)	Blank (ii)	Blank (iii)
(A) agrarian	(D) indiscriminately	(G) inventiveness
(B) anarchic	(E) covertly	(H) education
(C) archaic	(F) surreptitiously	(I) cohesion

14. In Doyle's famous detective stories, Mycroft, the brother of Sherlock Holmes, is described as quite _____, going only from his apartment to his office to his club and back to his apartment.

(A) illustrious
(B) omnivorous
(C) loquacious
(D) spontaneous
(E) sedentary

For Items #15–18, select one answer choice unless otherwise instructed.

Items #15–17 are based on the following passage.

Literary critics are fond of referring to a work as a "musical novel" whenever a writer employs techniques that can be conveniently described in musical terminology, but the notion that all such works are of
5 the same genre is an oversimplification. The writers who have given us the most important "musical novels" have used musical techniques for very different purposes.

In *Moderato Cantabile*, Marguerite Duras follows
10 the form of the first movement of a sonata, developing two contrasting themes in different keys—the first tonic, the second dominant—and finally resolving them in a recapitulation by modulation of the second theme to the key of the first theme, thereby providing
15 resolution and closure. "Moderato" indicates measure and control: Anne's life is structured and boring. "Cantabile" signifies the lyrical impulse: She is stifled by a structured, boring life.

In the second chapter, Anne begins her strange
20 affair with Chauvin. Chauvin, or the second theme, is Anne's quest for the "cantabile." They meet again and again, until the eighth chapter. Then, just as the eighth note of the musical scale is the same as the first—the tonic—but an octave higher, the final resolution comes
25 in a symbolic reenactment of the murder that occurs at the end of the first chapter:

Chauvin: I wish you were dead.
Anne: I already am.

And Anne returns permanently to her boring life.
30 When most literary critics pronounce *Moderato Cantabile* a "musical novel," they overlook what makes *Moderato Cantabile* a truly musical novel: It is actually "heard" by the reader. The novel is mostly dialogue punctuated by background noise, like musical
35 phrases defined by rests.

Ironically, this technique that makes *Moderato Cantabile* a "musical novel" may account for Duras' relative lack of success as a filmmaker. Few of the 19 films that she wrote and directed did well, primarily
40 because words often replaced action entirely.

GO ON TO THE NEXT PAGE.

15. The primary purpose of the passage is to

(A) provide a definition for the phrase "musical novel"

(B) compare the literary works of Virginia Woolf to those of Marguerite Duras

(C) show that the term "musical novel" does not have a clear, unambiguous meaning

(D) provide guidelines for interpreting musical novels

(E) evaluate the relative effectiveness of different literary techniques

16. Which of the following conclusions can be inferred from the passage about the musical structure of Moderato Cantabile?

(A) Chapter two of the novel is intended to represent the recapitulation.

(B) The symbolic reenactment of the murder represents the modulation of the second theme.

(C) Anne corresponds to the tonic theme, and Chauvin corresponds to the dominant theme

(D) Anne's return to her previous life corresponds to the beginning of a sonata.

(E) The murder in the first chapter echoes the "moderato" of the novel's title.

17. The attitude of the author toward Duras' work can best be described as

(A) studied neutrality

(B) muted criticism

(C) scholarly indifference

(D) qualified admiration

(E) unbridled enthusiasm

Item #18 is based on the following passage.

It is sometimes argued that a national lottery would cut into revenues generated by state lotteries. As a consequence, according to the argument, there would be no net increase in the money amount going to
5   government, just a redistribution of funds from the state to the federal level. This argument ignores the fact that federal and state governments share personal and corporate income taxes and certain excise taxes. Similarly, lottery states could piggyback on a federal
10 lottery, increasing the total participation in both.

18. The author argues primarily by

(A) citing an authority

(B) relying on statistics

(C) creating a distinction

(D) drawing an analogy

(E) proposing a change

GO ON TO THE NEXT PAGE.

For Items #19-21, select one answer choice for each blank from the corresponding column of choices. Fill all blanks in a way that best completes the text.

---

19. Population growth creates a demand-driven inflation, and prices eventually exceed the limits within which they fluctuated during the preceding period of (i)_____. People accept inflation as a natural condition and make economic decisions to minimize its effects. Because the rich can better protect themselves against rising prices, economic inequality (ii)_____.

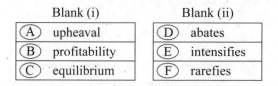

Blank (i)	Blank (ii)
(A) upheaval	(D) abates
(B) profitability	(E) intensifies
(C) equilibrium	(F) rarefies

20. Perhaps the most unfair thing about war is the curse it lays upon the innocent descendants of the (i)_____. Throughout the world, there are vast killing fields of unexploded mines, bombs and shells, military (ii)_____ that cause enormous injury and suffering to children who play on the now silent battlefields.

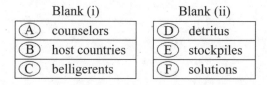

Blank (i)	Blank (ii)
(A) counselors	(D) detritus
(B) host countries	(E) stockpiles
(C) belligerents	(F) solutions

21. At the time the decision was made to extend the rail line to the Pacific Coast, the Milwaukee Road had an unquestioned reputation for (i)_____ business behavior. A more reasonable explanation for the company's failure in eastern Montana than the one that there was some master scheme to defraud everyone is that the railroad simply took its previously successful approach and extended it into an area where physical limitations wore it thin. This (ii)_____ resulted from the fact that the settlement of eastern Montana was not a primary goal of the railroad.

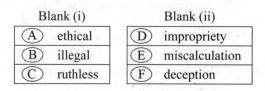

Blank (i)	Blank (ii)
(A) ethical	(D) impropriety
(B) illegal	(E) miscalculation
(C) ruthless	(F) deception

For Items #22-25, select one answer choice unless otherwise instructed.

Items #22-25 are based on the following passage.

The liberal view of democratic citizenship that developed in the seventeenth and eighteenth centuries was fundamentally different from that of the classical Greeks. The pursuit of private interests with as little interference as
5 possible from government was seen as the road to human happiness and progress rather than the public obligations and involvement in the collective community that were emphasized by the Greeks. Freedom was to be realized by limiting the scope of governmental activity and political
10 obligation and not through immersion in the collective life of the *polis*. The basic role of the citizen was to select governmental leaders and keep the powers and scope of public authority in check. In the liberal view, the rights of citizens against the state were the focus of special
15 emphasis.

Over time, the liberal democratic notion of citizenship developed in two directions. First, there was a movement to increase the proportion of members of society who were eligible to participate as citizens—
20 especially through extending the right of suffrage—and to ensure the basic political equality of all. Second, there was a broadening of the legitimate activities of government and a use of governmental power to redress imbalances in social and economic life.
25 Political citizenship became an instrument through which groups and classes with sufficient numbers of votes could use the state's power to enhance their social and economic well-being.

GO ON TO THE NEXT PAGE.

Within the general liberal view of democratic
30 citizenship, tensions have developed over the degree to
which government can and should be used as an
instrument for promoting happiness and well-being.
Political philosopher Martin Diamond has categorized two
views of democracy as follows. On the one hand, there is
35 the "libertarian" perspective that stresses the private
pursuit of happiness and emphasizes the necessity for
restraint on government and protection of individual
liberties. On the other hand, there is the "majoritarian"
view that emphasizes the "task of the government to uplift
40 and aid the common man against the malefactors of great
wealth." The tensions between these two views are very
evident today. Taxpayer revolts and calls for smaller
government and less government regulation clash with
demands for greater government involvement in the
45 economic marketplace and the social sphere.

---

22. According to the passage, all of the following are
characteristics that would distinguish the liberal
idea of government from the Greek idea of
government EXCEPT:

(A) The emphasis on the rights of private
citizens

(B) The activities that government may
legitimately pursue

(C) The obligation of citizens to participate in
government

(D) The size of the geographical area
controlled by a government

(E) The definition of human happiness

23. The author cites Martin Diamond in the last
paragraph because the author

(A) regards Martin Diamond as an authority on
political philosophy

(B) wishes to refute Martin Diamond's views
on citizenship

(C) needs a definition of the term "citizenship"

(D) is unfamiliar with the distinction between
libertarian and majoritarian concepts of
democracy

(E) wants voters to support Martin Diamond as
a candidate for public office

24. It can be inferred from the passage that the Greek
word "*polis*" mentioned in line 11 means

(A) family life
(B) military service
(C) marriage
(D) private club
(E) political community

25. A majoritarian would be most likely to favor
legislation that would

(A) eliminate all restrictions on individual
liberty

(B) cut spending for social welfare programs

(C) provide greater protection for consumers

(D) lower taxes on the wealthy and raise taxes
on the average worker

(E) raise taxes on the average worker and cut
taxes on business

STOP. You have reached the end of Section 4.

Section 5–Quantitative Reasoning

40 Minutes

25 Items

Solve each problem and choose the correct answer, using the given directions. Answers are on page 713, and explanations are on page 722.

Notes: All numbers used are real numbers.

Unless otherwise indicated, all figures lie in a plane.

Geometric diagrams and figures **are not necessarily** drawn to scale, so do **not** assume lengths, angle measures, or other quantities are as they appear in a given figure. You should assume that lines shown as straight are straight and that the positions of points, and geometric objects in general, exist in the order shown. Base your answers to questions with geometric figures on reasoning, not visual estimation or measurement.

Coordinate systems and graphic data presentations **are** drawn to scale, so you can answer items based on visual estimation or measurement.

Each of the items #1–9 consists of two quantities, Quantity A and Quantity B. Compare the two quantities, using the information presented. Choose:

(A) if Quantity A is greater.

(B) if Quantity B is greater.

(C) if the two quantities are equal.

(D) if the relationship cannot be determined from the information given.

A symbol that appears more than once in an item has the same meaning throughout the item.

	Quantity A	Quantity B	
1.	$x + y$	z	(A) (B) (C) (D)

	Quantity A	Quantity B	
2.	$5^7 - 2^4$	$5^7 - 2^5$	(A) (B) (C) (D)

$$x \neq 0$$

	Quantity A	Quantity B	
3.	$\sqrt{x^2}$	$\sqrt{x^2 + 1}$	(A) (B) (C) (D)

GO ON TO THE NEXT PAGE.

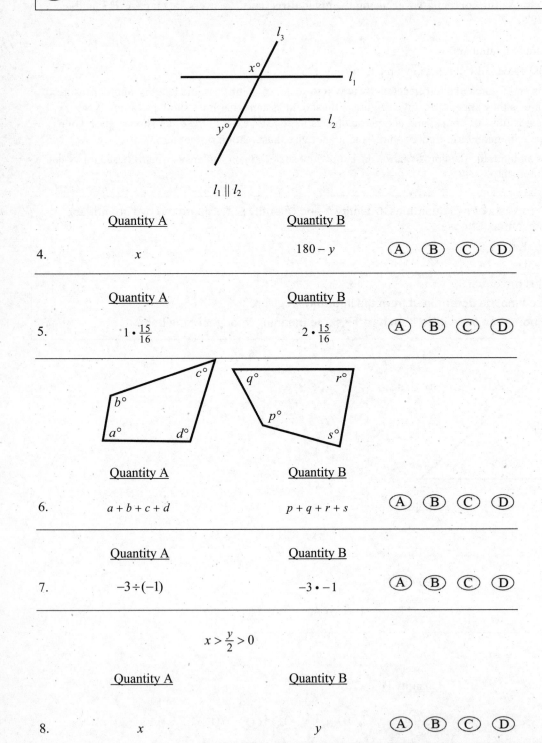

$l_1 \parallel l_2$

Quantity A	Quantity B	
4. x	$180 - y$	(A) (B) (C) (D)

Quantity A	Quantity B	
5. $1 \cdot \frac{15}{16}$	$2 \cdot \frac{15}{16}$	(A) (B) (C) (D)

Quantity A	Quantity B	
6. $a + b + c + d$	$p + q + r + s$	(A) (B) (C) (D)

Quantity A	Quantity B	
7. $-3 \div (-1)$	$-3 \cdot -1$	(A) (B) (C) (D)

$$x > \frac{y}{2} > 0$$

Quantity A	Quantity B	
8. x	y	(A) (B) (C) (D)

GO ON TO THE NEXT PAGE.

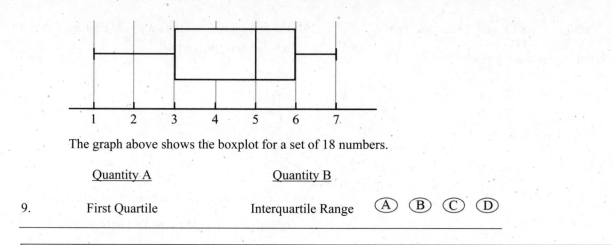

The graph above shows the boxplot for a set of 18 numbers.

Quantity A	Quantity B	
9. First Quartile	Interquartile Range	Ⓐ Ⓑ Ⓒ Ⓓ

Items #10–25 use several formats. Unless otherwise instructed, select one answer choice. For Numeric Entry items, follow the directions below.

Numeric Entry Directions

- Answers may be integers, decimals, or fractions. Answers may be negative.
- Items requiring a fraction will include two answer boxes—one for the numerator and one for the denominator.
- Equivalent forms of the answer are also correct (e.g. 9 and 9.0 are both correct forms of 9). Fractions do not need to be expressed in lowest terms.
- Enter the exact answer unless the item stem indicates that the answer should be rounded.

---

10. If $2^x = 16$ and $x = \frac{y}{2}$, then $y =$

Ⓐ 2
Ⓑ 3
Ⓒ 4
Ⓓ 6
Ⓔ 8

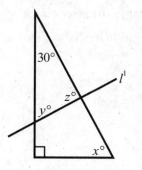

11. In the figure above, if $x = y$, then $z =$

Ⓐ 30
Ⓑ 45
Ⓒ 60
Ⓓ 75
Ⓔ 90

For the following item, enter your answer in the space provided.

12. At Glen Ridge High School, 20 percent of the students are seniors. If all of the seniors attended the school play, and 60 percent of all the students attended the play, what percent of the non-seniors attended the play?

☐ %

GO ON TO THE NEXT PAGE.

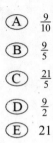

13. If $6 \le x \le 30$, $3 \le y \le 12$, and $2 \le z \le 10$, then what is the least possible value of $\frac{x+y}{z}$?

(A) $\frac{9}{10}$

(B) $\frac{9}{5}$

(C) $\frac{21}{5}$

(D) $\frac{9}{2}$

(E) 21

14. The following data are heights x (in inches) of Margaret's volleyball teammates. Which interval contains the third quartile?

Interval	Frequency
$60 < x \le 65$	2
$65 < x \le 70$	4
$70 < x \le 75$	3
$75 < x \le 80$	1

(A) $60 < x \le 65$

(B) $65 < x \le 70$

(C) $70 < x \le 75$

(D) $75 < x \le 80$

(E) It cannot be determined from the information given.

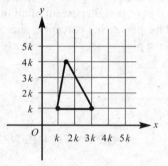

15. If the area of the triangle in the figure above is 12, then $k =$

(A) 1

(B) 2

(C) 3

(D) 4

(E) 6

16. If x and y are two different positive integers and $x^3 y^2 = 200$, then $xy =$

(A) 5

(B) 6

(C) 10

(D) 25

(E) 40

17. After trimming, a sapling has $\frac{9}{10}$ of its original height. If it must grow $\frac{9}{10}$ foot to regain its original height, what was its original height?

(A) 8

(B) 9

(C) 10

(D) 16

(E) 18

18. If $f(-1) = 1$ and $f(2) = 7$, what is the slope of the graph of $f(x)$ in the coordinate system?

(A) -3

(B) $-\frac{1}{2}$

(C) $\frac{1}{2}$

(D) 2

(E) $\frac{5}{2}$

19. If $\frac{2}{3}$ is written as a decimal to 101 places, what is the sum of the first 100 digits to the right of the decimal point?

(A) 66

(B) 595

(C) 599

(D) 600

(E) 601

GO ON TO THE NEXT PAGE.

Sales and Expenditures of Company X

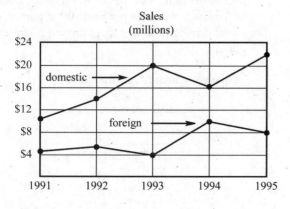

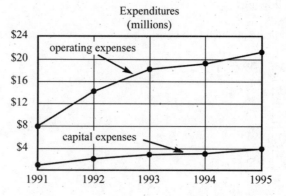

20. Which of the following circle graphs best represents the division of total sales between foreign and domestic sales for 1994?

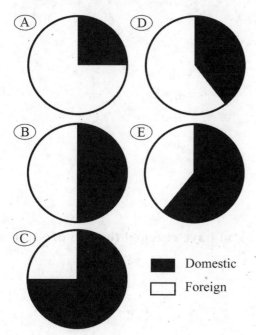

(A)

(D)

(B)

(E)

(C)

■ Domestic
□ Foreign

21. If Company X considers its profit to be the difference between total sales (foreign and domestic) and total expenses (capital and operating), in how many of the years shown were profits more than 20 percent of total sales?

(A) 0
(B) 1
(C) 2
(D) 3
(E) 4

22. A tank contains g gallons of water. Water flows into the tank by one pipe at the rate of m gallons per minute, and water flows out by another pipe at the rate of n gallons per minute. If $n > m$, how many minutes will it take to empty the tank?

(A) $\dfrac{g - m}{n}$

(B) $\dfrac{g}{m - n}$

(C) $\dfrac{n - g}{m}$

(D) $\dfrac{n - m}{g}$

(E) $\dfrac{g}{n - m}$

GO ON TO THE NEXT PAGE.

For the following item, consider the answers separately and select all that apply.

23. If $\frac{13t}{7}$ is an integer, then t could be which of the following?

   Indicate <u>all</u> such numbers.

A	−49
B	−7
C	3
D	91
E	105

24. If $\frac{x+y}{x} = 4$ and $\frac{y+z}{z} = 5$, what is the value of $\frac{x}{z}$?

   (A) $\frac{1}{4}$

   (B) $\frac{1}{3}$

   (C) $\frac{3}{4}$

   (D) $\frac{4}{3}$

   (E) 3

For the following item, enter your answer in the space provided.

25. On a certain trip, a motorist drove 10 miles at 30 miles per hour, 10 miles at 40 miles per hour, and 10 miles at 50 miles per hour. What portion of her total driving time was spent driving 50 miles per hour?

   Give your answer as a fraction.

   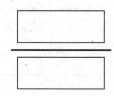

STOP. You have reached the end of Section 5.

Section 6–Quantitative Reasoning

40 Minutes

25 Items

Solve each problem and choose the correct answer, using the given directions. Answers are on page 713, and explanations are on page 726.

Notes: All numbers used are real numbers.

Unless otherwise indicated, all figures lie in a plane.

Geometric diagrams and figures **are not necessarily** drawn to scale, so do **not** assume lengths, angle measures, or other quantities are as they appear in a given figure. You should assume that lines shown as straight are straight and that the positions of points, and geometric objects in general, exist in the order shown. Base your answers to questions with geometric figures on reasoning, not visual estimation or measurement.

Coordinate systems and graphic data presentations **are** drawn to scale, so you can answer items based on visual estimation or measurement.

Each of the items #1–9 consists of two quantities, Quantity A and Quantity B. Compare the two quantities, using the information presented. Choose:

(A) if Quantity A is greater.

(B) if Quantity B is greater.

(C) if the two quantities are equal.

(D) if the relationship cannot be determined from the information given.

A symbol that appears more than once in an item has the same meaning throughout the item.

$$\begin{array}{r} 50M \\ \times\ \ 7 \\ \hline 3,56N \end{array}$$

M and N represent digits.

Quantity A	Quantity B	
1. $\quad M$	N	(A) (B) (C) (D)

For all positive integers f and g, $f \infty g$ is defined by the equation $f \infty g = fg - (f + g)$.

Quantity A	Quantity B	
2. $\quad f \infty g$	$g \infty f$	(A) (B) (C) (D)

---

x is a positive integer.

Quantity A	Quantity B	
3. Remainder when $2x + 2$ is divided by 2	1	(A) (B) (C) (D)

GO ON TO THE NEXT PAGE.

(A) if the quantity in A is greater
(B) if the quantity in B is greater
(C) if the two quantities are equal
(D) if the relationship cannot be determined from the information given

Quantity A	Quantity B	
4. 2 multiplied by the average of x and y	The average of $2x$ and $2y$	(A) (B) (C) (D)

x, y, and z are three consecutive even integers,
and $x < y < z$.

Quantity A	Quantity B	
5. $x + y + 1$	$y + z - 1$	(A) (B) (C) (D)

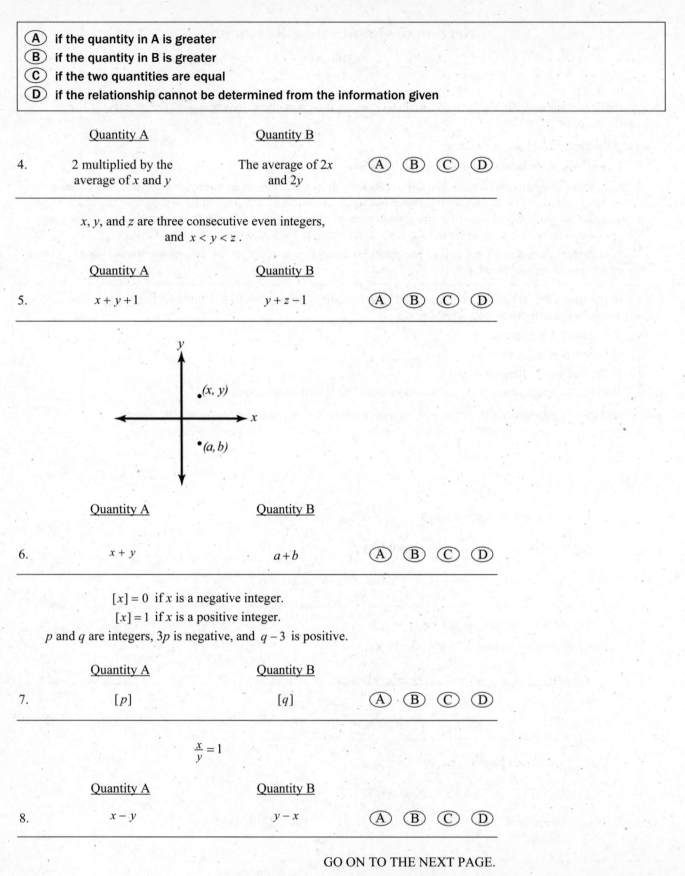

Quantity A	Quantity B	
6. $x + y$	$a + b$	(A) (B) (C) (D)

$[x] = 0$ if x is a negative integer.
$[x] = 1$ if x is a positive integer.
p and q are integers, $3p$ is negative, and $q - 3$ is positive.

Quantity A	Quantity B	
7. $[p]$	$[q]$	(A) (B) (C) (D)

$$\frac{x}{y} = 1$$

Quantity A	Quantity B	
8. $x - y$	$y - x$	(A) (B) (C) (D)

GO ON TO THE NEXT PAGE.

(A)	if the quantity in A is greater
(B)	if the quantity in B is greater
(C)	if the two quantities are equal
(D)	if the relationship cannot be determined from the information given

The volume of a cube is 8 cubic centimeters.

Quantity A	Quantity B	
9.	The number of square centimeters on the surface of the cube.	8	(A) (B) (C) (D)

Items #10–25 use several formats. Unless otherwise instructed, select one answer choice. For Numeric Entry items, follow the directions below.

Numeric Entry Directions

- Answers may be integers, decimals, or fractions. Answers may be negative.
- Items requiring a fraction will include two answer boxes—one for the numerator and one for the denominator.
- Equivalent forms of the answer are also correct (e.g. 9 and 9.0 are both correct forms of 9). Fractions do not need to be expressed in lowest terms.
- Enter the exact answer unless the item stem indicates that the answer should be rounded.

---

10. If $x + 3 = 3 + 12$, what is the value of x?

    (A)   0
    (B)   3
    (C)   6
    (D)   9
    (E)   12

12. If $x + 2y = 3$, what is the value of $2x + 4y$?

    (A)   –3
    (B)   0
    (C)   2
    (D)   6
    (E)   9

For the following item, consider the answers separately and select all that apply.

11. Which of the following can be written as the sum of two negative numbers?

Indicate all such numbers.

A	–5
B	$-3\sqrt{2}$
C	–1
D	0

13. The average (arithmetic mean) of three numbers is 6. If the sum of two of the numbers is 11, then the third number is

    (A)   5
    (B)   6
    (C)   7
    (D)   8
    (E)   9

GO ON TO THE NEXT PAGE.

Items #14–16 refer to the following graphs.

REVENUE/SALES FIGURES FOR THE RED ROSE CAR DEALERSHIP

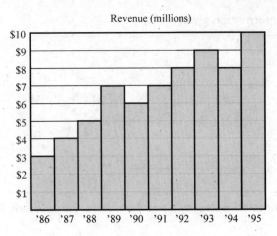

Revenue (millions)

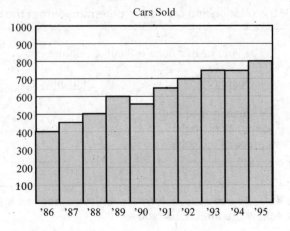

Cars Sold

14. From 1988 to 1992 inclusive, the greatest increase in revenue over the previous year was

   (A) $200,000
   (B) $750,000
   (C) $1,500,000
   (D) $1,750,000
   (E) $2,000,000

15. In 1993, what was the average price of a car sold by the Red Rose Car Dealership?

   (A) $8,500
   (B) $9,250
   (C) $10,250
   (D) $11,500
   (E) $12,000

16. Between the years 1987 and 1992 inclusive, in which year did the number of cars sold increase by the greatest percent over the previous year?

   (A) 1987
   (B) 1988
   (C) 1989
   (D) 1990
   (E) 1991

17. In the xy-coordinate system, $(m, 0)$ is one of the points of intersection of the graphs of $y = x^2 - 4$ and $y = -x^2 + 4$. If $m > 0$, what is the value of m?

   (A) 2
   (B) 4
   (C) 8
   (D) 16
   (E) 32

18. Joan had exactly $9 before Jerry repaid her $6 that he had borrowed. After the debt was repaid, both Joan and Jerry had the same amount of money. How much money did Jerry have before the debt was repaid?

   (A) $3
   (B) $9
   (C) $15
   (D) $21
   (E) $24

GO ON TO THE NEXT PAGE.

19.

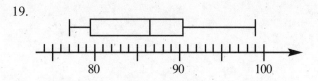

The boxplot above represents the following data: 77, 79, 80, 86.5, 86.5, 87, 94, 99.

What is the interquartile range of the data?

(A) 5
(B) 7.5
(C) 11
(D) 20.5
(E) 22

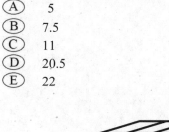

20. The figure above is a plan that shows one view of a solid set of steps to be constructed from concrete blocks of equal size. How many blocks are needed to construct the steps?

(A) 12
(B) 15
(C) 18
(D) 21
(E) 24

For the following item, enter your answer in the space provided.

21. 88, 87, 88, 75, 75, 75, 100, 100, 100, 100, 80, 76, 99, 89, 94

The 15 numbers shown represent the homework grades that Jerry received during the month of February. What is the second quartile of his homework grades?

☐ points

For the following item, consider the answers separately and select all that apply.

22. List A: 2, 4, 5, x, y

List A has a mean of 5 and a standard deviation of 2. Which of the following could be members of List A?

Indicate __all__ such numbers.

A	6
B	8
C	9

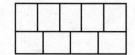

23. Nine playing cards from the same deck are placed as shown in the figure above to form a large rectangle of area 180 sq. in. How many inches are there in the perimeter of this large rectangle?

(A) 29
(B) 58
(C) 64
(D) 116
(E) 210

For the following item, enter your answer in the space provided.

24. The function $[x]$ is defined by $[x] = x^2 - x$ for all integers. What is the value of $[-2]$?

☐

25. What is 10 percent of $\frac{x}{3}$ if $\frac{2x}{3}$ is 10 percent of 60?

(A) 0.1
(B) 0.2
(C) 0.3
(D) 0.4
(E) 0.5

STOP. You have reached the end of Section 6.

Practice Test II*:

Outline

*Answers and Explanations begin on page 731.

Section 1–Analytical Writing

Time—30 minutes

Analyze an Issue

DIRECTIONS: You will be given a brief statement about an issue of general interest and a set of instructions on how to respond to that issue. You will have 30 minutes to plan and write a response following the provided instructions. A response to any other issue will receive a score of zero.

Be sure to follow the specific instructions and support your position with relevant reasons and examples.

Readers will review your essay and grade its overall quality based on the following criteria:

- Follows the specific instructions

- Addresses the complexities of the issue

- Organizes and develops ideas

- Supports ideas with relevant reasons and/or examples

- Controls the elements of standard written English

Take a few minutes to think about the issue and instructions and plan your response before you begin writing. Fully develop your position in a coherent and organized manner. Be sure to leave time to review your essay and make any necessary revisions. A sample essay response begins on page 732.

Issue Topic

In this age of computers, some people complain that our lives are being controlled by machines. But, in reality, computers actually improve the quality of our lives.

Write an essay in which you discuss the extent to which you agree or disagree with the claim. When developing and supporting your position, address the most compelling reasons and/or examples that could be used to challenge your position.

Section 2–Analytical Writing

Time—30 minutes

Analyze an Argument

DIRECTIONS: You will be given a brief passage presenting an argument and a set of instructions on how to respond to that argument. You will have 30 minutes to plan and write a response following the provided instructions. A response to any other argument will receive a score of zero.

Note: You are NOT being asked to present your own views on the subject. Ensure that you follow the specific instructions and support your analysis with relevant reasons and examples.

Readers will review your essay and evaluate its overall quality, based on the following criteria:

- Follows the specific instructions

- Identifies and analyzes important features of the argument

- Organizes and develops the evaluation

- Supports the analysis with relevant reasons and/or examples

- Controls the elements of standard written English

Take a few minutes to think about the passage and instructions and plan your response before you begin writing. Fully develop your evaluation in a coherent and organized manner. Be sure to leave time to review your essay and make any necessary revisions. A sample essay response begins on page 732.

Argument Topic

A recent review of the records of the Putnam Township volunteer rescue squad shows that its average response time is 6 minutes greater than that of the Empire Ambulance Service, a for-profit company operating in the Putnam area. Putnam should disband the rescue squad, sell the equipment, and contract ambulance services out to Empire. We would get much better emergency care for our citizens.

Write an essay in which you discuss what questions would need to be answered in order to decide whether the prediction and the argument on which it is based are reasonable. Explain how the answers to these questions could be used to evaluate the prediction.

Section 3–Verbal Reasoning

Time—35 minutes
25 Items

For Items #1–5, select one answer choice unless otherwise instructed. Answers for Section 3 are on page 731, and explanations are on page 733.

Items #1–4 are based on the following passage.

Conventional echocardiography provides highly detailed, two-dimensional pictures of the heart's anatomy and motion by using high-frequency sound reflected off anatomic surfaces. Cardiologists have
5 even been able to measure the direction and magnitude of blood flow within the heart. But conventional echocardiography provides no direct information about tissue structure or the healing process that follows a heart attack.
10 Recently, it has been learned that the acoustic properties of healthy tissue differ from those of injured tissue, and investigators anticipate that these differences can be diagnostically useful. Research is currently focused on ischemic injury, which occurs
15 when the blood supply to part of the heart is obstructed. Ischemia often occurs when the disease process atherosclerosis causes coronary arteries to become narrowed by fatty plaques, which can eventually cause a myocardial infarction, or heart attack.
20 Ischemia and infarction can be studied in the laboratory by blocking one of the coronary arteries of an animal. Deprived of blood, portions of the myocardium die. As the injured heart heals over a period of weeks, scar tissue forms at the damaged site,
25 or infarct zone.
The degree of attenuation, or loss of signal strength, is different for healthy and damaged tissue and varies according to frequency for damaged tissue. By compiling data associating the quantitative measure
30 of attenuation with the qualitative features of heart tissues, researchers hope to develop a valuable complement to existing echocardiography techniques.

1. The author is primarily concerned with discussing

   (A) the causes of heart disease
   (B) a new technique for studying the heart
   (C) laboratory studies of heart attacks
   (D) procedures of conventional echocardiography
   (E) the process by which the heart heals following myocardial infarction

2. The author mentions that cardiologists have been able to measure the direction and magnitude of the flow of blood in the heart in order to

   (A) prove that atherosclerosis can lead to heart attack
   (B) illustrate a method of doing research with laboratory animals
   (C) acquaint the reader with the functioning of the heart
   (D) demonstrate that conventional echocardiography is very sophisticated
   (E) illustrate for the reader the meanings of some unfamiliar medical terms

3. The passage implies that the use of high frequency sound to characterize the physical condition of tissues is

   (A) widely used
   (B) very reliable
   (C) extremely dangerous
   (D) still experimental
   (E) theoretically impossible

4. According to the passage, data on the relationship between the qualitative features of tissue and attenuation

   (A) will render conventional echocardiography obsolete
   (B) is available in already published materials
   (C) could be used in conjunction with conventional echocardiography
   (D) should be used only in a medical emergency
   (E) will have little clinical value

GO ON TO THE NEXT PAGE.

Item #5 is based on the following passage.

An inventor protects his rights by obtaining a patent; to do this, he or she must exhibit a working model of the invention and demonstrate that the invention is original by showing that it represents a significant departure
5 from other similar devices. The law also protects industrial trade secrets such as the chemical formula for a soft drink, but businesses are not required to register these secrets. As a result, one business could find that it has inadvertently used the trade secret of
10 another business and wind up on the losing end of a lawsuit. It would be better for all if trade secrets were registered with a Trade Secrets Office, so that a business could regularly check to determine that it was not infringing upon another business' trade secrets.

5. The argument is most vulnerable to criticism on the grounds that it

  (A) contains a logical contradiction
  (B) reverses a cause-and-effect connection
  (C) generalizes on the basis of a single example
  (D) relies upon a questionable analogy
  (E) relies upon circular reasoning

For Items #6–8, select one answer choice for each blank from the corresponding column of choices. Fill all blanks in a way that best completes the text.

6. Because of the _____ of acupuncture therapy in China, Western physicians are starting to learn the procedure.

  (A) veracity
  (B) manipulation
  (C) liquidity
  (D) effectiveness
  (E) inflation

7. Black comedy is the combination of that which is humorous with that which would seem antithetical to humor: the _____.

  (A) ignoble
  (B) salacious
  (C) grandiose
  (D) innocuous
  (E) macabre

8. The press conference did not clarify many issues since the President responded with (i)_____ and (ii)_____ rather than clarity and precision.

Blank (i)	Blank (ii)
(A) sincerity	(D) candor
(B) congruity	(E) vagueness
(C) obfuscation	(F) lucidity

GO ON TO THE NEXT PAGE.

For Items #9-12, select one answer choice unless otherwise instructed.

Items #9-12 are based on the following passage.

Synchrotron radiation is the name given to pulses of intense x-rays created by electrons circulating within a large evacuated storage ring at nearly the speed of light. Compared with conventional sources, these
5 electron rings produce a much more intense, highly collimated beam of x-rays. Additionally, synchrotron radiation is tunable. By using a monochromonator, a researcher can select x-rays of specific wavelengths or energies.
10   Synchrotron radiation can decipher structural changes during a reaction such as cellular respiration. Data gathered with an array of time-resolved spectroscopic methods, for example, can provide glimpses of local molecular events—the breaking of
15 chemical bonds and the formation of intermediate compounds—that may transpire within a few millionths of a second.
     The biggest payoff from the gain in beam intensity, however, will be the enhanced sensitivity of
20 measurements that will maintain the high precision in the high-resolution data of atomic distances on the order of 0.02 to 0.05 angstroms. When working with less powerful machines, researchers compensate for deficiencies in beam intensity by preparing samples
25 that contain high concentrations of protein. The high concentration increases the strength of the signals emanating from the sample when it is exposed to a beam. But many macromolecules cannot be highly concentrated; and when extracted proteins can be
30 concentrated, the sample is not likely to represent conditions in the living membranes, where proteins are scattered over a large area.

9. The author is primarily concerned with describing

    (A) a new scientific theory
    (B) the properties of x-rays
    (C) the structure of proteins
    (D) the functioning of cells
    (E) an instrument for scientific research

For the following item, consider each answer individually and select all that apply.

10. In developing the passage, the author utilizes which of the following devices?

    [A] statistics to prove a theory
    [B] a contrast of technique
    [C] an example to illustrate a point

11. According to the passage, researchers using conventional x-ray sources to study proteins use highly concentrated samples in order to

    (A) simulate the conditions in living cells
    (B) obtain a larger picture of the sample
    (C) condense several experiments into a short span of time
    (D) allow for respiration by sample components
    (E) compensate for the inadequacy of the x-ray beam

12. The passage makes all of the following statements about synchrotron radiation EXCEPT:

    (A) The length of the waves that make up the beam can be controlled.
    (B) The beam is more intense than that of conventional x-ray sources.
    (C) It yields more precise data than conventional x-ray sources.
    (D) It is less dangerous to researchers than conventional x-ray sources.
    (E) It is composed of pulsating x-rays.

GO ON TO THE NEXT PAGE.

For Items #13–15, select one answer choice for each blank from the corresponding column of choices. Fill all blanks in a way that best completes the text.

13. Web blogs, television commentators, and talk radio have made this the age of polarizing opinion. There is no lack of (i)_____ assertion, little of it informed by (ii)_____ as opposed to ideological presupposition.

Blank (i)	Blank (ii)
(A) incongruous	(D) confident guesswork
(B) sentimental	(E) genuine knowledge
(C) contentious	(F) arrogant disinformation

15. The conclusion of the program was a modern symphony with passages so discordant that the piece produced a sound similar to the (i)_____ one hears as the individual orchestra members tune their instruments before a concert. The conductor might have been better advised to select a (ii)_____ piece to end the evening.

Blank (i)	Blank (ii)
(A) melody	(D) more radical
(B) harmony	(E) highly focused
(C) cacophony	(F) less demanding

14. It is difficult for a modern audience, accustomed to the (i)_____ of film and television, to appreciate opera with its grand spectacle and (ii)_____ gestures.

Blank (i)	Blank (ii)
(A) irreverence	(D) extravagant
(B) minutiae	(E) subtle
(C) flamboyance	(F) hapless

For Item #16, select one answer choice for each blank from the corresponding column of choices. Fill all blanks in a way that best completes the text.

16. During their years as members of a purely opposition movement, conservatives, unable to deliver government benefits to satisfy constituents, fought vigorous intellectual skirmishes over ideological purity. Today, they satisfy that need by fighting one another, in part because liberalism, in its current (i)_____, offers less satisfying intellectual combat than conservatives can have intramurally. Thus, the movement is characterized by (ii)_____ conflict and (iii)_____, splintered into a variety of factions and sects.

Blank (i)	Blank (ii)	Blank (iii)
(A) flaccidness	(D) preemptive	(G) contumacy
(B) moroseness	(E) internecine	(H) intentionality
(C) ascendancy	(F) unsavory	(I) fractiousness

GO ON TO THE NEXT PAGE.

For Items #17–22, select one answer choice unless otherwise instructed.

Items #17–20 are based on the following passage.

The National Security Act of 1947 created a national military establishment headed by a single Secretary of Defense. The legislation had been a year and a half in the making—the final measure to emerge from
5 Congress was a compromise on various revisions of President Truman's original recommendation of a unified armed service. Most of the opposition to the bill came from the Navy and its numerous civilian spokesmen, including Secretary of the Navy James
10 Forrestal. In support of unification (and a separate air force that was part of the unification package) were the Army Air Forces, the Army, and, most importantly, the President of the United States.

Rather than unify, the act served only to federate
15 the military services. It neither halted the rapid demobilization of the armed forces that followed World War II nor brought to the new national military establishment the loyalties of officers steeped in the traditions of the separate services. At a time when the
20 balance of power in Europe and Asia was rapidly shifting, the services lacked any precise statement of United States foreign policy from the National Security Council on which to base future programs. The services bickered unceasingly over their respective
25 roles and missions, already complicated by the Soviet nuclear capability. Not even the appointment of Forrestal as the first Secretary of Defense allayed the suspicions of naval officers and their supporters that the role of the U.S. Navy was threatened with
30 permanent eclipse.

By 1948, the United States military establishment was forced to make do with a budget approximately 10 percent of what it had been at its wartime peak. Meanwhile, the cost of weapons procurement was
35 rising geometrically as the nation put more and more reliance on the atomic bomb and its delivery systems. These two factors inevitably made adversaries of the Navy and the Air Force, as the battle between advocates of the B-36 and the supercarrier so amply
40 demonstrates. Given severe fiscal restraints on the one hand and the nation's increasing reliance on strategic nuclear deterrence on the other hand, the conflict between these two services over roles and missions was essentially a contest over slices of an ever-
45 diminishing pie.

Yet if in the end neither service was the obvious victor, the principle of civilian dominance over the military clearly was. If there had ever been any danger that the United States military establishment might
50 exploit, to the detriment of civilian control, the goodwill it enjoyed as a result of its victories in World War II, that danger disappeared in the interservice animosities engendered by the battle over unification.

17. It can be inferred from the passage that Forrestal's appointment as Secretary of Defense was expected to

(A) placate members of the Navy
(B) result in decreased levels of defense spending
(C) outrage advocates of the Army Air Forces
(D) win Congressional approval of the unification plan
(E) make Forrestal a Presidential candidate against Truman

18. According to the passage, President Truman supported

(A) the elimination of the Navy as a separate armed force
(B) a unified military service with a separate air force
(C) the continued existence of the Army Air Forces
(D) the creation of a single, unified military academy
(E) the discontinuation of the B-36 and the supercarrier projects

GO ON TO THE NEXT PAGE.

19. With which of the following statements about defense unification would the author most likely agree?

   (A) Unification ultimately undermined United States military capability by inciting interservice rivalry.
   (B) The unification legislation was necessitated by the drastic decline in appropriations for the military services.
   (C) Although the unification was not entirely successful, it had the unexpected result of ensuring civilian control of the military.
   (D) In spite of the attempted unification, each service was still able to pursue its own objectives without interference from the other branches.
   (E) Unification was in the first place unwarranted, and in the second place ineffective.

20. The author is primarily concerned with

   (A) discussing the influence of personalities on political events
   (B) describing the administration of a powerful leader
   (C) criticizing a piece of legislation
   (D) analyzing a political development
   (E) suggesting methods for controlling the military

Item #21 is based on the following passage.

I remember waiting in my mother's classroom after school, swinging my short legs back and forth and gazing at her chalkboard, covered with her slanting penmanship, while she met with students who had
5 homework questions. I remember my father marking up his students' essays with one hand and eating dinner with his other hand. When I went to college, I knew I wanted to be a teacher. My wife is a teacher, too. Because my parents, my wife, and I are all teachers, I
10 know that when my children grow up they will become teachers, too.

21. The argument is most vulnerable to criticism on the grounds that it

   (A) fails to define the term "teacher"
   (B) oversimplifies a causal connection
   (C) does not rely upon statistics
   (D) uses an ambiguous term
   (E) uses circular reasoning

   GO ON TO THE NEXT PAGE.

Item #22 is based on the following passage.

A poll taken 10 days before the election showed that 36 percent of the people surveyed planned to vote for Green and 42 percent planned to vote for his opponent. When the votes were finally tallied, Green received 52 percent of the vote, while his opponent received only 46 percent. Thus, the survey method used for the pre-election poll was flawed.

5

22. Which of the following, if true, most weakens the conclusion of the argument?

(A) A poll taken 21 days before the election showed that 32 percent of the people surveyed planned to vote for Green.

(B) At the time that the pre-election poll was taken, many voters had not yet made up their minds about which candidate to vote for.

(C) During the week just before the election, Green's opponent received an important endorsement from a major newspaper.

(D) The voter turnout for the election in question was extremely light due to inclement weather.

(E) The pre-election survey also questioned voters about their attitudes toward a referendum authorizing the legislature to legalize pari-mutuel gambling.

For Items #23–25, select the <u>two</u> words that, when used independently in the sentence, produce logical sentences and produce sentences that are alike in meaning.

23. Shortly after his appointment as minister-president of Prussia, Bismarck solved a political riddle that had _____ European diplomats for two generations: how to unify Germany.

A	placated
B	survived
C	prefigured
D	stymied
E	retarded
F	confounded

24. No culture has been found that failed to prescribe rituals for the treatment of deceased bodies and their _____ presence in the memory of the descendants.

A	effervescent
B	posthumous
C	indelible
D	perfunctory
E	vindictive
F	postmortem

25. Soon after her election to her first term, the _____ legislator surprised everyone by securing an appointment to one of the most powerful committees in Congress, a position usually reserved for very senior members.

A	implacable
B	resilient
C	accomplished
D	novice
E	neophyte
F	beleaguered

STOP. You have reached the end of Section 3.

Section 4–Verbal Reasoning

Time—35 minutes
25 Items

For Items #1–4, select the <u>two</u> words that, when used independently in the sentence, produce logical sentences and produce sentences that are alike in meaning. Answers for Section 4 are on page 731, and explanations are on page 736.

1. Corruption, nepotism, cheating, and dishonesty are _____ the state house: three of the last four chief executives are currently serving lengthy prison sentences.

   A illustrative of
   B preferable to
   C sacrosanct to
   D endemic to
   E prevalent in
   F preparation for

2. Wilde had been the *enfant terrible* of England, flouting acceptable morals and being notoriously _____ as to manners.

   A unconventional
   B unoriginal
   C capricious
   D outrageous
   E contrarian
   F misanthropic

3. In order to be effective in creating a brand name, the advertising must be _____ and intentionally obtrusive so as to fix as permanently as possible the image and name of the product in the mind of the consumer.

   A ubiquitous
   B entertaining
   C omnipresent
   D deceptive
   E frivolous
   F surreptitious

4. For many years, events were the manifestation of old, deep-rooted conditions such as poverty and lack of development, _____ instability of regimes, and the long-term disparity between the frontiers of the new states and tribal and geographic realities.

   A chronic
   B enduring
   C volatile
   D remediable
   E anachronistic
   F acute

GO ON TO THE NEXT PAGE.

For Items #5–9, select one answer choice unless otherwise instructed.

Items #5–8 are based on the following passage.

The geological story of the Rocky Mountains is a long one, the details of which are lost in the passage of hundreds of millions of years. Scientists have put together some of the story from bits of scattered
5 evidence that strongly indicate a certain chain of events, few of which can be proved to everyone's satisfaction. Most of the rocks in the Colorado region are crystalline and ancient. The gneiss and schist were, in part, once sediments formed in the seas—perhaps a
10 billion years ago. These sediments were buried beneath thousands of feet of other sediments, cemented and hardened into layers of sedimentary rock and later squeezed, crushed, and elevated by slow, ceaselessly working Earth forces that produced mountains. During
15 this period, the sedimentary rocks were changed to harder metamorphic rocks, probably because of deep burial under tremendous pressure and considerable heat. Masses of molten rock welled up into these earlier deposits and hardened under the Earth's surface.
20 This later intrusive material is now exposed granite in many parts of the Rocky Mountains.

These ancient mountains were gradually worn away by wind, rain, and other agents of erosion, which must have attacked the surface of the Earth as
25 vigorously then as now. With the passage of millions of years, these mountains were gradually worn away until a new sea lapped over the land where mountains had been, and once again sediments were dropped in its bottom. This new invasion of the ocean affected the
30 Colorado region during the many millions of years in which dinosaurs dominated the Earth.

In response to little-understood rhythms of the Earth's crust, which have lifted mountains ever so slowly at great intervals all over the world, the seas
35 drained away as the crust rose again, and the rising land once more became subject to the ceaseless attack of erosion. This uplift—which began 60 million years ago—originated the system of mountain ranges and basins that today gives Colorado its spectacular scenery
40 and much of its climate.

5. The passage deals primarily with the

    Ⓐ scenic beauty of Colorado's mountains
    Ⓑ geological history of Colorado's mountains
    Ⓒ classification of rock types
    Ⓓ rhythms of the Earth's crust
    Ⓔ era of the dinosaurs

6. According to the passage, all of the following are true of metamorphic rock EXCEPT:

    Ⓐ It is harder than sedimentary rock.
    Ⓑ It is formed from sedimentary rock.
    Ⓒ It is extremely old.
    Ⓓ It is a preliminary form of granite.
    Ⓔ It is created by extreme temperatures and high pressure.

7. The author regards the explanation he or she gives as

    Ⓐ conclusively proven
    Ⓑ complete fiction
    Ⓒ highly tentative and unsupported by evidence
    Ⓓ speculative but supported by evidence
    Ⓔ certain but unprovable

8. Based on the author's description of the geological process, it can be inferred that the gneiss and schist are

    Ⓐ types of sedimentary rock
    Ⓑ types of granite
    Ⓒ types of metamorphic rock
    Ⓓ types of crystal
    Ⓔ types of igneous rock

GO ON TO THE NEXT PAGE.

Item #9 is based on the following passage.

Amid great fanfare, the Taxi and Limousine Commission announced last June that a new dress code for taxicab drivers would be incorporated into the Commission's rules. After six months, no driver has lost his license or even been fined under the new dress code. Evidently, drivers have chosen to comply with the new dress code.

9. Which of the following, if true, most weakens the argument?

   (A) Prior to the announcement of the new dress code, an average of 16 taxicab drivers each month lost their licenses for various violations of the Commission's rules.

   (B) Inspectors routinely stop taxicab drivers to inspect licenses, the safety and cleanliness of the vehicle, and the driver's record of fares.

   (C) The Commission's lawyers have refused to prosecute drivers cited under the new dress code because they believe that the law is unconstitutional.

   (D) A survey of passengers who say they regularly use taxicabs shows that 45 percent of the riders do not believe that drivers are better dressed.

   (E) During July and August, the number of taxicab drivers available for work is less than it is during the other months of the year.

For Items #10–13, select one answer choice for each blank from the corresponding column of choices. Fill all blanks in a way that best completes the text.

10. The essay starts out as a relaxed (i)_____ along a familiar path with recognizable moral landmarks and reassuring intellectual sights. In the end, however, the reader will feel (ii)_____ by difficult questions, the answers to which are likely to embarrass.

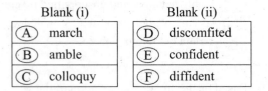

Blank (i)	Blank (ii)
(A) march	(D) discomfited
(B) amble	(E) confident
(C) colloquy	(F) diffident

11. The cartoon strip "Dilbert" voices the mocking contempt that most people who work for large corporations have for their bosses. Each day, the cartoonist (i)_____ fashionable management theories. The no-nonsense comments of Dilbert the engineer expose the fads for what they are: cleverly phrased but intellectually (ii)_____.

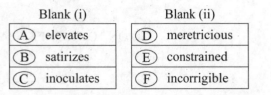

Blank (i)	Blank (ii)
(A) elevates	(D) meretricious
(B) satirizes	(E) constrained
(C) inoculates	(F) incorrigible

12. Though the story is set in a small village in a remote area of South America, the novel's themes are so _____ that its events could have occurred anywhere and involved any of us at any time.

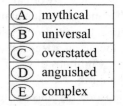

(A) mythical
(B) universal
(C) overstated
(D) anguished
(E) complex

13. Determinist philosophers have argued that our moral intuitions are _____ rather than learned and that they are dictated by genetic makeup.

(A) transcendental
(B) fortuitous
(C) innate
(D) contingent
(E) empirical

GO ON TO THE NEXT PAGE.

For Items #14–18, select one answer choice unless otherwise instructed.

Items #14–16 are based on the following passage.

Traditionally, the resource endowment of a location—and especially its situation relative to the primary industry of the hinterland—has had a special importance in American history. In the early
5 agricultural period, the most valued natural endowment was arable land with good climate and available water. America's oldest cities were mercantile outposts of such agricultural areas. Deepwater ports developed to serve the agricultural hinterlands, which produced
10 staple commodities in demand on the world market. From the 1840s onward, the juxtaposition of coal, iron ore, and markets afforded the impetus for manufacturing growth in the northeastern United States. The American manufacturing heartland
15 developed westward to encompass Lake Superior iron ores, the Pennsylvania coalfields, and the Northeast's financial, entrepreneurial, and manufacturing roles. Subsequent metropolitan growth has been organized around this national core.
20 　　An energy park, though a human construct, would seem every bit as formidable as the natural harbor conditions or coal deposits which underwrote the growth of the great cities of the past. The existing electric power plant at Four Corners in the southwest
25 United States—visible to orbiting astronauts—generates only four thousand megawatts electricity. The smallest energy parks will concentrate five times the thermal energy represented by the Four Corners plant.
30 　　The founders of past settlements could not choose the geographic locations of their natural advantages, but energy parks can theoretically be sited anywhere under the frontier energy siting strategy. The availability of a frontier siting strategy helps explain
35 why some environmentalists perceive the energy park idea as a threat to nature. But the problems of modern society, including siting decisions for energy parks, which are necessary to support the growing energy demand in urban and rural areas, require planning, and
40 that means greater government involvement. With government participation, energy parks can be sited according to the principle of created opportunity, thereby advancing American social history rather than merely responding to power needs in an unplanned, ad
45 hoc manner.

14. With which of the following statements would the author be LEAST likely to agree?

(A) Electric facility siting decisions can be made in ways that advance important societal goals.

(B) Energy parks will have a significant long-term influence on the demographic features of the American population.

(C) Urban growth in the United States has traditionally been the result of economic forces rather than conscientious planning.

(D) Under the frontier siting strategy for energy parks, siting decisions are dictated by the natural features of the land.

(E) America needs larger power production facilities in urban and rural areas to meet the increased demand for energy.

15. With which of the following statements would the author most likely agree?

(A) Decisions about the locations for power plants should be left to the utilities.

(B) Government leaders in the nineteenth century were irresponsible in not supervising urban growth more closely.

(C) Natural features of a region such as cultivatable land and water supply are no longer important to urban growth.

(D) Modern society is so complex that governments must take greater responsibility for decisions such as power plant siting.

(E) The Four Corners plant should not have been built because of its mammoth size.

GO ON TO THE NEXT PAGE.

16. According to the passage, the most important difference between the natural advantages of early cities and the features of an energy park is

  (A) the features of an energy park will be located where the builders choose

  (B) natural advantages are no longer as important as they once were

  (C) natural features cannot be observed from outer space, but energy parks can

  (D) early cities grew up close to agricultural areas while energy parks will be located in mountains

  (E) policy planners have learned to minimize the effects of energy parks on nature

---

Item #17 is based on the following passage.

Our college newspaper recently surveyed 1,000 students, asking them to rate the "Office of Inter-Student Dispositional Appeals" as:

  (1) Very Effective
  (2) Somewhat Effective
  (3) Ineffective
  (4) Very Ineffective
  (5) Not familiar with the agency

Sixty-three students chose (1) or (2); 31 chose (3) or (4); 885 chose (5); and the rest did not respond. However, the "Office of Inter-Student Dispositional Appeals" does not exist; it was a fiction created for the survey.

17. Which of the following general conclusions is most supported by the information?

  (A) Most college students do not have sufficient information to judge whether the school is providing a quality education.

  (B) Most people who decline to respond to a survey do so because they believe that the survey has been poorly drafted.

  (C) Many people who are asked to respond to a survey avoid expressing extreme opinions for fear of alienating the questioner.

  (D) Some people who respond to surveys do so despite not having sufficient knowledge to offer an informed opinion.

  (E) Some college students respond to surveys by selecting answers that do not reflect their actual opinions on the survey subject.

Item #18 is based on the following passage.

Psychology originated in researchers' attempts to record, classify, and explain their own mental impressions, thoughts, and feelings and those of others as they described them verbally. It matured into a
5 science only when the reliance on subjective impressions was gradually abandoned and researchers concentrated on human behavior. Then, psychology truly became a science of mental activity.

18. The argument makes which of the following assumptions?

  (A) It is possible to observe episodes of mental activity directly.

  (B) Early research was unreliable because researchers gave less-than-candid accounts of their mental experiences.

  (C) Research participants intentionally altered their experiences when relaying them to researchers.

  (D) Human behavior is an expression of mental activity.

  (E) All sciences in their infancy deal with subjective mental impressions.

GO ON TO THE NEXT PAGE.

For Items #19–22, select one answer choice for each blank from the corresponding column of choices. Fill all blanks in a way that best completes the text.

19. The age of the Olympian critic as cultural arbiter is concluded. While there remain literary critics and prominent publications that issue (i)_____ rulings on matters of literary taste, their imperious pronouncements no longer matter and merely add to the (ii)_____ of culture.

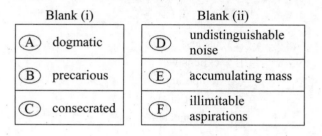

Blank (i)	Blank (ii)
(A) dogmatic	(D) undistinguishable noise
(B) precarious	(E) accumulating mass
(C) consecrated	(F) illimitable aspirations

20. The rescue workers' gnawing sense of _____ developed into concern and ultimately despair as they gradually approached the remote site of the car crash.

(A)	resignation
(B)	foreboding
(C)	anticipation
(D)	urgency
(E)	duplicity

21. The history book, written in 1880, was tremendously_____, unfairly blaming the South for the Civil War.

(A)	biased
(B)	objective
(C)	suppressed
(D)	questionable
(E)	complicated

22. Contrary to popular opinion, bats are not generally aggressive and rabid; most are shy and _____.

(A)	turgid
(B)	disfigured
(C)	punctual
(D)	innocuous
(E)	depraved

GO ON TO THE NEXT PAGE.

For Items #23–25, select one answer choice unless otherwise instructed.

Items #23–25 are based on the following passage.

A fundamental principle of pharmacology is that all drugs have multiple actions. Actions that are desirable in the treatment of disease are considered therapeutic, while those that are undesirable or pose risks to the
5 patient are called "effects." Adverse drug effects range from the trivial to the serious or even lethal. Therefore, an effective system for the detection of adverse drug effects is an important component of the healthcare system of any advanced nation. Much of the research
10 conducted on new drugs aims at maximizing beneficial effects and minimizing the risk of adverse effects.

The current system of drug investigation in the United States has proved very useful and accurate in identifying the common side effects associated with
15 new prescription drugs. By the time a new drug is approved by the Food and Drug Administration, its side effects are usually well described in the package insert for physicians. The investigational process, however, cannot be counted on to detect all adverse
20 effects because of the relatively small number of patients involved in pre-marketing studies and the relatively short duration of the studies. Animal toxicology studies are, of course, done prior to marketing in an attempt to identify any potential for
25 toxicity, but negative results do not guarantee the safety of a drug in humans.

This recognition prompted the establishment in many countries of programs to which physicians report adverse drug effects. The United States and other
30 countries also send reports to an international program operated by the World Health Organization. These programs, however, are voluntary reporting programs and are intended to serve a limited goal: alerting a government or private agency to adverse drug effects
35 detected by physicians in the course of practice. Other approaches must be used to confirm suspected drug reactions and to estimate incidence rates. These other approaches include conducting retrospective control studies, for example, the studies associating
40 endometrial cancer with estrogen use.

Thus, the overall drug surveillance system of the United States is composed of a set of information bases, special studies, and monitoring programs, each contributing in its own way to our knowledge about
45 marketed drugs. The system is decentralized among a number of governmental units and is not administered as a coordinated function. Still, it would be inappropriate at this time to attempt to unite all of the disparate elements into a comprehensive surveillance

50 program. Instead, the challenge is to improve each segment of the system and to take advantage of new computer strategies to improve coordination and communication.

23. In line 49, the word "disparate" most nearly means

(A) useless
(B) expensive
(C) temporary
(D) educational
(E) unconnected

GO ON TO THE NEXT PAGE.

24. It can be inferred that the estrogen study mentioned in the last sentence of the third paragraph

   (A) uncovered long-term side effects of a drug that had already been approved for sale by the Food and Drug Administration

   (B) discovered potential side effects of a drug that was still awaiting approval for sale by the Food and Drug Administration

   (C) revealed possible new applications of a drug that had previously been approved for a different treatment

   (D) is an example of a study that could be more efficiently conducted by a centralized authority

   (E) proved that the use of the drug estrogen was not associated with side effects such as thromboembolism

25. The author is most probably leading up to a discussion of some suggestions about how to

   (A) centralize authority for drug surveillance in the United States

   (B) centralize authority for drug surveillance among international agencies

   (C) coordinate better the sharing of information among the drug surveillance agencies

   (D) eliminate the availability and sale of certain drugs now on the market

   (E) improve drug-testing procedures to detect dangerous effects before drugs are approved

STOP. You have reached the end of Section 4.

Section 5–Quantitative Reasoning

40 Minutes
25 Items

Solve each problem and choose the correct answer, using the given directions. Answers are on page 731, and explanations are on page 740.

Notes: All numbers used are real numbers.

Unless otherwise indicated, all figures lie in a plane.

Geometric diagrams and figures **are not necessarily** drawn to scale, so do **not** assume lengths, angle measures, or other quantities are as they appear in a given figure. You should assume that lines shown as straight are straight and that the positions of points, and geometric objects in general, exist in the order shown. Base your answers to questions with geometric figures on reasoning, not visual estimation or measurement.

Coordinate systems and graphic data presentations **are** drawn to scale, so you can answer items based on visual estimation or measurement.

Each of the items #1–9 consists of two quantities, Quantity A and Quantity B. Compare the two quantities, using the information presented. Choose:

Ⓐ if Quantity A is greater.
Ⓑ if Quantity B is greater.
Ⓒ if the two quantities are equal.
Ⓓ if the relationship cannot be determined from the information given.

A symbol that appears more than once in an item has the same meaning throughout the item.

Quantity A   Quantity B

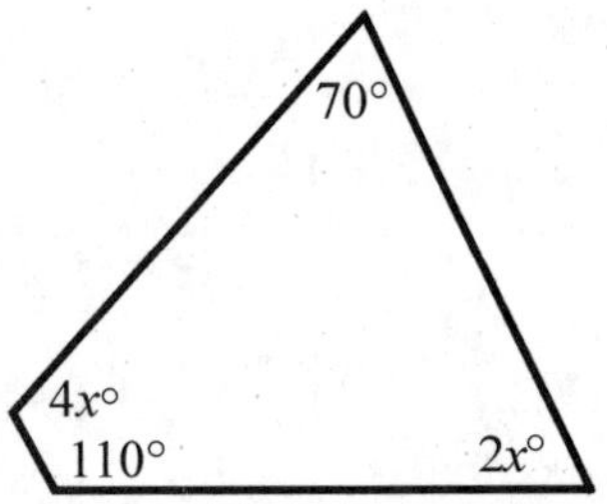

	Quantity A	Quantity B	
1.	x	30	Ⓐ Ⓑ Ⓒ Ⓓ

	Quantity A	Quantity B	
2.	$\sqrt{6} \cdot \sqrt{10}$	$\sqrt{3} \cdot \sqrt{20}$	Ⓐ Ⓑ Ⓒ Ⓓ

$$x < 0$$

	Quantity A	Quantity B	
3.	x^{15}	x^{16}	Ⓐ Ⓑ Ⓒ Ⓓ

GO ON TO THE NEXT PAGE.

$$0 \quad x \quad 50 \qquad 100$$

Quantity A	Quantity B	
4. $50 + x$	100	Ⓐ Ⓑ Ⓒ Ⓓ

The average of x, y, and z is y.

Quantity A	Quantity B	
5. x	z	Ⓐ Ⓑ Ⓒ Ⓓ

Points (x, z) and (z, y) are in
Quadrants I and IV, respectively.

Quantity A	Quantity B	
6. x	y	Ⓐ Ⓑ Ⓒ Ⓓ

Peanuts cost $1.25 per pound and
cashews cost $2.25 per pound.

Quantity A	Quantity B
7. The number of pounds of peanuts in 2 pounds of a mix of peanuts and cashews that costs $1.75 per pound	1

Ⓐ Ⓑ Ⓒ Ⓓ

GO ON TO THE NEXT PAGE.

(A) if the quantity in A is greater
(B) if the quantity in B is greater
(C) if the two quantities are equal
(D) if the relationship cannot be determined from the information given

---

Quantity A	Quantity B

8. The sum of the three greatest odd integers less than 100 | The sum of the three greatest even integers less than 100

(A) (B) (C) (D)

List *A*: 0, 4, 8, 12, 16
List *B*: 4, 8, 12, 16, 20

Quantity A	Quantity B

9. Interquartile range of the numbers in List *A* | Second quartile of the numbers in List *B*

(A) (B) (C) (D)

Items #10–25 use several formats. Unless otherwise instructed, select one answer choice. For Numeric Entry items, follow the directions below.

Numeric Entry Directions

- Answers may be integers, decimals, or fractions. Answers may be negative.
- Items requiring a fraction will include two answer boxes—one for the numerator and one for the denominator.
- Equivalent forms of the answer are also correct (e.g. 9 and 9.0 are both correct forms of 9). Fractions do not need to be expressed in lowest terms.
- Enter the exact answer unless the item stem indicates that the answer should be rounded.

10. $121,212 + (2 \cdot 10^4) =$

(A) 321,212
(B) 141,212
(C) 123,212
(D) 121,412
(E) 121,232

For the following item, enter your answer in the space provided.

11. If $\frac{4}{5}$ is subtracted from its reciprocal, then what value is the result?

Give your answer as a fraction.

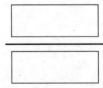

GO ON TO THE NEXT PAGE.

For the following item, consider the answers separately and select all that apply.

12. Jack, Ken, Larry and Mike are j, k, l, and m years old, respectively. If $j < k < l < m$, which of the following <u>could</u> be true?

    Indicate <u>all</u> such statements.

A	$k = j + l$
B	$j = k + l$
C	$j + k = l + m$
D	$j + k + m = l$
E	$j + m = k + l$

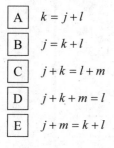

13. What is the perimeter of the rectangle shown above?

    (A) $10a - 6$
    (B) $10a - 3$
    (C) $6a - 2$
    (D) $5a - 6$
    (E) $5a - 3$

For the following item, consider the answers separately and select all that apply.

14. If the standard deviation of a data set is equal to 0, what <u>must</u> be true about the data values in the given set?

    Indicate <u>all</u> such conclusions.

A	All data values in the set are equal.
B	All data values in the set are 0.
C	All data values in the set are equal to the mean.

15. If x is 80 percent of y, then y is what percent of x?

    (A) $133\frac{1}{3}\%$
    (B) 125%
    (C) 120%
    (D) 90%
    (E) 80%

For the following item, consider the answers separately and select all that apply.

16. From which of the following statements can it be deduced that $m > n$?

    Indicate <u>all</u> such statements.

A	$m + 1 = n$
B	$2m = n$
C	$m + n > 0$
D	$m - n > 0$
E	$mn > 0$

17. If for any number n, 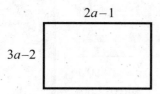 is defined as the least integer that is greater than or equal to n^2,

    then $\overset{\text{-1.1}}{\bigstar}$ =

    (A) -2
    (B) -1
    (C) 0
    (D) 1
    (E) 2

    GO ON TO THE NEXT PAGE.

Items #18–20 refer to the following graph.

ANNUAL EXPENDITURES FOR THE JONES FAMILY
(percent of disposable income)

Category	1995	1996
Rent	23.0%	19.3%
Food	17.6%	18.2%
Clothing	14.2%	15.1%
Automobile	11.3%	12.3%
Utilities	10.9%	10.2%
Savings	6.2%	5.1%
Entertainment	5.2%	5.3%
Medical and Dental Care	4.0%	3.7%
Charitable Contributions	3.2%	3.9%
Household Furnishings	2.9%	3.1%
Other	1.5%	3.8%
	100.0%	100.0%
Total Expenditures:	$34,987.00	$40,012.00

18. Approximately how much money did the Jones family spend on medical and dental care in 1995?

   (A) $1,200
   (B) $1,400
   (C) $1,520
   (D) $2,250
   (E) $4,000

19. By approximately what percent did the Jones family's expenditures increase from 1995 to 1996?

   (A) 8.5%
   (B) 11%
   (C) 14%
   (D) 18%
   (E) 22%

20. If the categories in the table are rank ordered from one to eleven in each year, for how many categories would the rank ordering change from 1995 to 1996?

   (A) 2
   (B) 3
   (C) 4
   (D) 5
   (E) 6

GO ON TO THE NEXT PAGE.

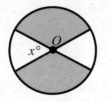

21. The circle with center O has a radius of length 2. If the total area of the shaded regions is 3π, then $x =$

    (A) 270
    (B) 180
    (C) 120
    (D) 90
    (E) 45

22. If a bar of metal alloy consists of 100 grams of tin and 150 grams of lead, what percent of the entire bar, by weight, is tin?

    (A) 10%
    (B) 15%
    (C) $33\frac{1}{3}\%$
    (D) 40%
    (E) $66\frac{2}{3}\%$

Item #23 refers to the following data.

Number of Dogs	Number of Presidents
0	19
1	10
2	6
4	2
5	2
7	2
9	1
10	1
12	1

23. Twenty-five of the first forty-four presidents owned dogs as detailed in the chart above. What is the standard deviation of this population to the nearest tenth?

    (A) 1.9
    (B) 2.1
    (C) 2.5
    (D) 2.9
    (E) 3.2

For the following item, enter your answer in the space provided.

24. After filling the car's fuel tank, a driver drove from P to Q and then to R. She used $\frac{2}{5}$ of the fuel driving from P to Q. If she used another 7 gallons to drive from Q to R and still had $\frac{1}{4}$ of a tank left, how many gallons does the tank hold?

    gallons

25. A local real estate agency sold 40 houses, each of which had a different commission. Judy, a real estate agent for this company, received a commission of $5,400 for one of her home sales. This commission is the second-highest commission in the second quartile of the 40 sales. If the real estate company sells 4 more homes for commissions less than the lowest commission in the second quartile, what would Judy's sale be with respect to the quartiles of the 44 commissions at the company?

    (A) The fourth-highest commission in the second quartile
    (B) The highest commission in the second quartile
    (C) The lowest commission in the third quartile
    (D) The second-lowest commission in the third quartile
    (E) The third-lowest commission in the third quartile

STOP. You have reached the end of Section 5.

Section 6–Quantitative Reasoning

40 Minutes
25 Items

Solve each problem and choose the correct answer, using the given directions. Answers are on page 731, and explanations are on page 744.

Notes: All numbers used are real numbers.

Unless otherwise indicated, all figures lie in a plane.

Geometric diagrams and figures **are not necessarily** drawn to scale, so do **not** assume lengths, angle measures, or other quantities are as they appear in a given figure. You should assume that lines shown as straight are straight and that the positions of points, and geometric objects in general, exist in the order shown. Base your answers to questions with geometric figures on reasoning, not visual estimation or measurement.

Coordinate systems and graphic data presentations **are** drawn to scale, so you can answer items based on visual estimation or measurement.

Each of the items #1–9 consists of two quantities, Quantity A and Quantity B. Compare the two quantities, using the information presented. Choose:

(A) if Quantity A is greater.
(B) if Quantity B is greater.
(C) if the two quantities are equal.
(D) if the relationship cannot be determined from the information given.

A symbol that appears more than once in an item has the same meaning throughout the item.

	Quantity A	Quantity B	
1.	Area of $\triangle ABC$	6	(A) (B) (C) (D)

	Quantity A	Quantity B	
2.	$\dfrac{0.667}{0.166}$	$\dfrac{\frac{2}{3}}{\frac{1}{6}}$	(A) (B) (C) (D)

There are more than 40 but fewer than 50 marbles in a jar. If they are counted out four at a time, three are left over.

	Quantity A	Quantity B	
3.	The number of marbles in the jar	47	(A) (B) (C) (D)

GO ON TO THE NEXT PAGE.

	Quantity A	Quantity B	
4.	Twice the area of a circle with radius r	Half the area of a circle with radius $2r$	Ⓐ Ⓑ Ⓒ Ⓓ

x and y are points on the number line.

	Quantity A	Quantity B	
5.	$\overline{xy}$	0.30	Ⓐ Ⓑ Ⓒ Ⓓ

	Quantity A	Quantity B	
6.	The average of three numbers the greatest of which is 15	The average of three numbers the greatest of which is 46	Ⓐ Ⓑ Ⓒ Ⓓ

$$x + 3y = 6$$

	Quantity A	Quantity B	
7.	$\dfrac{2x + 6y}{5}$	$\dfrac{13}{5}$	Ⓐ Ⓑ Ⓒ Ⓓ

k, x, and y are positive integers,
and $xy = k$.

	Quantity A	Quantity B	
8.	x	k	Ⓐ Ⓑ Ⓒ Ⓓ

	Quantity A	Quantity B	
9.	$x - y$	$w - z$	Ⓐ Ⓑ Ⓒ Ⓓ

GO ON TO THE NEXT PAGE.

Items #10–25 use several formats. Unless otherwise instructed, select one answer choice. For Numeric Entry items, follow the directions below.

Numeric Entry Directions

- Answers may be integers, decimals, or fractions. Answers may be negative.
- Items requiring a fraction will include two answer boxes—one for the numerator and one for the denominator.
- Equivalent forms of the answer are also correct (e.g. 9 and 9.0 are both correct forms of 9). Fractions do not need to be expressed in lowest terms.
- Enter the exact answer unless the item stem indicates that the answer should be rounded.

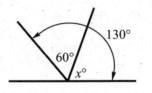

10. In the figure above, what is the value of x?

(A) 70
(B) 60
(C) 50
(D) 40
(E) 30

For the following item, enter your answer in the space provided.

11. 14, 17.5, 13.5, 12, 16, 15.5

The six numbers shown represent the dollar amount spent by six people attending the same movie. What is the first quartile of these numbers?

☐ dollars

12. Of the actors in a certain play, 5 are in Act I, 12 are in Act II, and 13 are in Act III. If 10 of the actors are in exactly two of the three acts and all of the other actors are in just one act, how many actors are in the play?

(A) 17
(B) 20
(C) 24
(D) 30
(E) 38

13. A certain bicycle traveling k meters per second requires $\frac{k^2}{20} + k$ meters to stop. If $k = 10$, how many meters does the bicycle need to stop?

(A) 10
(B) 12
(C) 15
(D) 20
(E) 30

GO ON TO THE NEXT PAGE.

Items #14–15 refer to the following graphs.

SALES AND EARNINGS OF COMPANY K

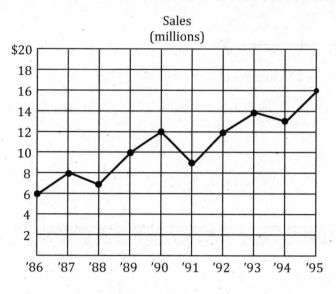

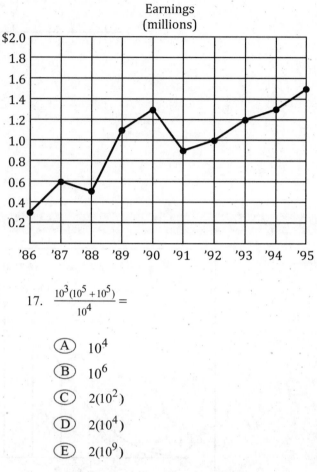

14. From 1986 to 1995, earnings of Company K increased by what percent?

    (A)   150%

    (B)   200%

    (C) $233\frac{1}{3}\%$

    (D)   400%

    (E)   500%

15. In how many of the years shown were earnings equal to or greater than 10 percent of sales?

    (A)   3

    (B)   4

    (C)   5

    (D)   6

    (E)   7

16. If $n = \frac{x}{12} + \frac{x}{12} + \frac{x}{12} + \frac{x}{12}$ and n is a positive integer, then the <u>least</u> possible value of x is

    (A)   2

    (B)   3

    (C)   4

    (D)   5

    (E)   6

17. $\dfrac{10^3(10^5 + 10^5)}{10^4} =$

    (A) 10^4

    (B) 10^6

    (C) $2(10^2)$

    (D) $2(10^4)$

    (E) $2(10^9)$

For the following item, enter your answer in the space provided.

18.    $\frac{1}{100}$ is the ratio of 0.1 to what number?

GO ON TO THE NEXT PAGE.

Items #19–20 refer to the following number line.

The letters in the number line below represent a series of consecutive integers.

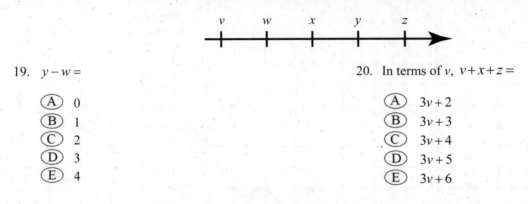

19. $y - w =$

(A) 0
(B) 1
(C) 2
(D) 3
(E) 4

20. In terms of v, $v + x + z =$

(A) $3v + 2$
(B) $3v + 3$
(C) $3v + 4$
(D) $3v + 5$
(E) $3v + 6$

Item #21 refers to the following graph.

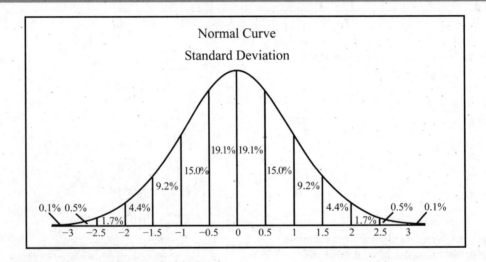

21. Professor Trelawney has 273 students in her college mathematics lecture class. The scores on the midterm exam are normally distributed with a mean of 75.4 and a standard deviation of 8.2. How many students in the class can be expected to receive a score between 80 and 88? Express the answer to the nearest integer.

(A) 37
(B) 41
(C) 52
(D) 66
(E) 78

22. For all positive integers x:

$\clubsuit(x) = x^2$ if x is even

$\clubsuit(x) = \sqrt{x}$ if x is odd

What is the value of $\clubsuit(7 + 1)$?

(A) 64
(B) 50
(C) 25
(D) $2\sqrt{2}$
(E) $\sqrt{7}$

GO ON TO THE NEXT PAGE.

23. If a recipe that will produce 8 servings of a dish uses 2 eggs, then how many eggs are needed to produce 12 servings of the dish?

(A) 12

(B) 8

(C) 6

(D) 4

(E) 3

25. If S is 150 percent of T, then T is what percent of $S + T$?

(A) $33\frac{1}{3}\%$

(B) 40%

(C) 50%

(D) 75%

(E) 80%

For the following item, enter your answer in the space provided.

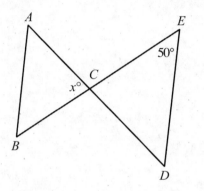

24. In the figure above, $\overline{AB} \parallel \overline{ED}$ and $\overline{AC} = \overline{BC}$. If $\angle BED$ is 50°, then what is the value of x?

STOP. You have reached the end of Section 6.

Practice Test III*:

Outline

*Answers and Explanations begin on page 749.

Section 1–Analytical Writing

Time—30 minutes

Analyze an Issue

DIRECTIONS: You will be given a brief statement about an issue of general interest and a set of instructions on how to respond to that issue. You will have 30 minutes to plan and write a response following the provided instructions. A response to any other issue will receive a score of zero.

Be sure to follow the specific instructions and support your position with relevant reasons and examples.

Readers will review your essay and grade its overall quality based on the following criteria:

- Follows the specific instructions
- Addresses the complexities of the issue
- Organizes and develops ideas
- Supports ideas with relevant reasons and/or examples
- Controls the elements of standard written English

Take a few minutes to think about the issue and instructions and plan your response before you begin writing. Fully develop your position in a coherent and organized manner. Be sure to leave time to review your essay and make any necessary revisions. A sample essay response begins on page 750.

Issue Topic

The sole function of public schools should be to teach academic and practical skills and not to inculcate ethical values.

Write an essay in which you discuss your views on the policy and explain your reasons for the position you take. When developing and supporting your position, consider the possible consequences of implementing the policy and explain how these consequences shape your position.

Section 2–Analytical Writing

Time—30 minutes

Analyze an Argument

DIRECTIONS: You will be given a brief passage presenting an argument and a set of instructions on how to respond to that argument. You will have 30 minutes to plan and write a response following the provided instructions. A response to any other argument will receive a score of zero.

Note: You are NOT being asked to present your own views on the subject. Ensure that you follow the specific instructions and support your analysis with relevant reasons and examples.

Readers will review your essay and evaluate its overall quality, based on the following criteria:

- Follows the specific instructions

- Identifies and analyzes important features of the argument

- Organizes and develops the evaluation

- Supports the analysis with relevant reasons and/or examples

- Controls the elements of standard written English

Take a few minutes to think about the passage and instructions and plan your response before you begin writing. Fully develop your evaluation in a coherent and organized manner. Be sure to leave time to review your essay and make any necessary revisions. A sample essay response begins on page 750.

Argument Topic

Two years ago, the Fort Ann School purchased twelve new computers and implemented a requirement that all students take at least two hours of computer instruction each week. The Hudson Falls School, which is near Fort Ann School and has about the same number of students, does not have such a requirement. Over the past two years, the number of Fort Ann School seniors going on to college has increased by 20 percent while the number of Hudson Falls seniors going on to college has remained constant. Therefore, if Hudson Falls wants to give its students the opportunities they deserve, it should buy new computers and teach students how to use them.

Write an essay in which you examine the stated and/or unstated assumptions of the argument. Explain how the argument depends on these assumptions and what the implications are if the assumptions prove unwarranted.

Section 3–Verbal Reasoning

Time—35 minutes
25 Items

For Items #1–4, select one answer choice unless otherwise instructed. Answers for Section 3 are on page 749, and explanations are on page 751.

Items #1–2 are based on the following passage.

About twice every century, one of the massive stars in our galaxy explodes. The shock waves heat interstellar gas, evaporate small clouds, and compress larger clouds so they collapse under their own gravity to form
5 new stars. The general picture that has been developed for these supernova explosions and their aftermath goes something like this.

Throughout its evolution, a star is like a leaky balloon. It keeps its equilibrium by a balance of
10 internal pressure against the tendency to collapse under its own weight. The pressure is generated by nuclear reactions in the core of the star that supply energy to balance the energy leaking out in the form of radiation. Eventually the nuclear fuel is exhausted and pressure
15 drops in the core. With nothing to hold it up, the matter in the center of the star collapses, creating higher and higher densities and temperatures, until nuclei and electrons are fused into a superdense lump of matter known as a neutron star.
20 As overlying layers rain down on the surface of the neutron star, the temperature rises until, in a blinding flash of radiation, the collapse reverses. A thermonuclear shock wave runs through the now expanding stellar envelope, fusing lighter elements into
25 heavier ones and producing a brilliant burst as intense as the light of 10 billion suns. The exploding shell of matter plows through the surrounding gas, producing an expanding bubble of hot gas with temperatures in the millions of degrees. This gas emits most of its
30 energy at x-ray wavelengths, and more than twenty supernova remnants have now been detected in x-ray studies.

Recent discoveries of meteorites with anomalous concentrations of certain isotopes indicate that a
35 supernova might have precipitated the birth of our solar system more than four and a half billion years ago. Although the cloud that collapsed to form the Sun and the planets was composed primarily of hydrogen and helium, it also contained carbon, nitrogen, and oxygen,
40 elements essential for life as we know it. Elements heavier than helium are manufactured deep in the interior of stars and would, for the most part, remain there if it were not for the cataclysmic supernova explosions that blow giant stars apart. Additionally,
45 supernovas produce clouds of high-energy particles called cosmic rays. These high-energy particles continually bombard the Earth and are responsible for many of the genetic mutations that are the driving force of the evolution of species.

1. According to the passage, all of the following are true of supernovas EXCEPT:

(A) they are extremely bright
(B) they are an explosion of some sort
(C) they emit large quantities of x-rays
(D) they result in the destruction of a neutron star
(E) they are caused by the collision of large galaxies

2. It can be inferred from the passage that the meteorites mentioned by the author in line 33

(A) contain dangerous concentrations of radioactive materials
(B) give off large quantities of x-rays
(C) include material not created in the normal development of our solar system
(D) are larger than the meteors normally found in a solar system like ours
(E) contain pieces of a supernova that occurred several billion years ago

GO ON TO THE NEXT PAGE.

Item #3 is based on the following passage.

A basic social function of the university is to provide a setting within which all points of view may be freely debated, including those whose radical nature may offend some or even most members of the community. Unfortunately, this mandate includes totalitarian views that might themselves threaten the freedom and diversity of expression to which the university is dedicated.

3. The author is most concerned with discussing a(n)

(A) dilemma
(B) contradiction
(C) paradox
(D) analogy
(E) generalization

Item #4 is based on the following passage.

"Channel One" is a 12-minute school news show that includes two minutes of commercials. The show's producers offer high schools $50,000 worth of television equipment to air the program. Many parents and teachers oppose the use of commercial television in schools, arguing that advertisements are tantamount to indoctrination. However, students are already familiar with television commercials and know how to distinguish programming from advertising.

4. The argument assumes that

(A) the effects of an advertisement viewed in a classroom would be similar to those of the same advertisement viewed at home
(B) many educators would be willing to allow the indoctrination of students in exchange for new equipment for their schools
(C) television advertising is a more effective way of promoting a product to high school students than print advertising
(D) high school students are sufficiently interested in world affairs to learn from a television news program
(E) a television news program produced especially for high school students is an effective teaching tool

---

For Items #5–8, select one answer choice for each blank from the corresponding column of choices. Fill all blanks in a way that best completes the text.

---

5. Despite the billions of dollars spent on improvements, the country's telephone system remains (i)_____; it is a major inconvenience to the citizenry, and it (ii)_____ economic progress.

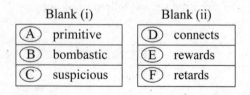

Blank (i)	Blank (ii)
(A) primitive	(D) connects
(B) bombastic	(E) rewards
(C) suspicious	(F) retards

6. Unlike the images in symbolist poetry, which are often vague and (i)_____, the images of surrealist poetry are startlingly (ii)_____ and bold.

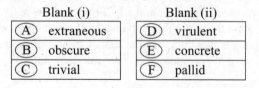

Blank (i)	Blank (ii)
(A) extraneous	(D) virulent
(B) obscure	(E) concrete
(C) trivial	(F) pallid

GO ON TO THE NEXT PAGE.

7. Psychologists and science fiction writers argue that people persist in believing in extraterrestrial life, even though the federal government discourages all such beliefs, because people need to feel a personal sense of _____ in a godless universe.

(A)	morbidity
(B)	despair
(C)	guilt
(D)	spirituality
(E)	alienation

8. Conditions in China seem to offer two equally plausible outcomes for the country, making (i)_____ a risky proposition. No China expert wants to predict stability only to be (ii)_____ by another eruption like the one that occurred in 1989 or to be on record as foreseeing disintegration only to have China endure.

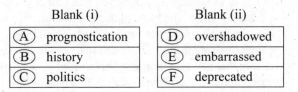

Blank (i)		Blank (ii)	
(A)	prognostication	(D)	overshadowed
(B)	history	(E)	embarrassed
(C)	politics	(F)	deprecated

For Items #9–13, select one answer choice unless otherwise instructed.

Item #9 is based on the following passage.

School dietician: A redesigned layout in the school cafeteria that provides individual food items for purchase would help to promote good nutrition for students. Putting nutritious foods like broccoli at the beginning of the cafeteria line rather than in the middle has been shown to increase the amount students purchased by 10 percent to 15 percent. Giving healthy food choices descriptive names, such as "creamy corn," instead of simply "corn," increases sales by 25 percent to 30 percent. Pulling the salad bar away from the wall and putting it in front of the checkout register nearly triples sales of salads. These simple changes can greatly improve the diets of students.

9. Which one of the following, if true, most seriously weakens the school dietician's argument?

(A) Many students will not eat one or more foods considered nutritious because they object to the taste of those foods.

(B) The cost of redesigning the school cafeteria layout would be small compared to the total dollar value of food sales.

(C) Students who purchase food items on impulse or through enticement are unlikely to eat the food they have purchased.

(D) Statistics on increases of healthy food purchases stimulated by layout redesign range over several percentage points.

(E) Some schools' cafeterias are not spacious enough to permit relocation of a salad bar to a location near the checkout register.

GO ON TO THE NEXT PAGE.

The basic objective of the antitrust laws is to achieve desirable economic performance as measured by such criteria as efficient manufacturing and distributive processes, rapid technological progress, economic
5 growth, and equity in the distribution of the fruits of progress. A society may achieve these objectives in a variety of ways. The basic philosophy of the antitrust laws, however, is to attempt to maintain sufficiently competitive market structure and market conduct to
10 ensure that private enterprise performs in a socially acceptable manner. The assumption is that we can avoid government intervention in the economically and politically hazardous thicket of specifying industrial performance by controlling certain aspects of industrial
15 structure and competitive conduct. Hence, the antitrust approach is not regulation, per se.

Much of the job of antitrust enforcement involves formulating rules that govern the ways in which the competitive game is played. Economic theory suggests,
20 and business experience verifies, that market structure plays a powerful role in determining or conditioning business conduct, and that business conduct, in turn, determines the ultimate quality of industrial performance. This is not to say that an industry's
25 structure and conduct are the only factors determining ultimate performance, but the available empirical evidence indicates that such structural characteristics as the height of entry barriers facing potential competitors, the degree of product differentiation, and
30 the level of market concentration always are of some importance, and often are of decisive importance, in determining industry performance. There is also general agreement that certain forms of business conduct result in undesirable performance. For
35 example, restrictive agreements among competitors may result in monopoly pricing, even in industries that would otherwise generate competitive prices. Other forms of conduct may adversely affect market structure and thereby ultimately industry performance. Predatory
40 pricing is an example. Although in the short run such conduct may give consumers low prices, it may also destroy competitors and result in higher prices in the end.

Antitrust policy does not involve exhaustive
45 investigation or analysis of all the factors that conceivably might have a bearing on industrial performance, nor does it involve direct specification of desired performance. This is both the great strength and the great weakness of the antitrust approach. Its
50 strength derives from the fact that a maximum effect may flow from a minimum of government intervention.

It is not necessary to assemble and maintain a vast bureaucracy that exercises continued intervention in and surveillance of the affairs of business. The
55 Interstate Commerce Commission, whose major responsibilities involve the setting of rates and other performance characteristics, has twice as many employees as the combined employees in antitrust enforcement at the Federal Trade Commission and the
60 Department of Justice—and the ICC is responsible for just a part of the field of transportation.

10. The author cites the Interstate Commerce Commission to prove that

(A) direct government intervention requires a large bureaucracy
(B) antitrust enforcement is not an exact science
(C) controlling market structures is more effective than regulation
(D) antitrust laws can eliminate entry barriers for business
(E) some government agencies intervene directly in the marketplace

11. The author's attitude toward the theory of antitrust policy is best described as

(A) wary acceptance
(B) categorical rejection
(C) cautious skepticism
(D) qualified endorsement
(E) reluctant dismissal

12. The author mentions all of the following as measures of economic performance EXCEPT:

(A) distributional efficiency
(B) manufacturing efficiency
(C) technological progress
(D) high industry profits
(E) distributional equity

GO ON TO THE NEXT PAGE.

For the following item, consider each answer individually and select all that apply.

13. The author mentions which of the following as examples of business behavior that adversely affect performance?

- A | price-fixing
- B | outsourcing
- C | predatory pricing

For Items #14–16, select one answer choice for each blank from the corresponding column of choices. Fill all blanks in a way that best completes the text.

14. Seventy years ago, a generation of Americans in the economic throes of the Great Depression embraced a style called modernism, purchasing Alvar Aalto chairs and Russel Wright dinnerware, or, more often, low-cost alternatives that made their way into the mainstream. Modernism expressed the (i)_____ spirit of the day. Today, a different movement for lean times, knows as the "undecorated movement," offers a (ii)_____ authenticity in opposition to the polished trappings of a design establishment, a "democratization of design."

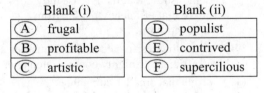

Blank (i)	Blank (ii)
Ⓐ frugal	Ⓓ populist
Ⓑ profitable	Ⓔ contrived
Ⓒ artistic	Ⓕ supercilious

15. Pollen grains and spores that are 200 million years old are now being extracted from shale and are reshaping the theory that the breakup of the continents occurred in stages; in fact, it seems that the breakups occurred almost _____.

Ⓐ longitudinally
Ⓑ simultaneously
Ⓒ imperceptibly
Ⓓ vicariously
Ⓔ cataclysmically

16. A good trial lawyer will argue only what is central to an issue, eliminating (i)_____ information or anything which might (ii)_____ the client.

Blank (i)	Blank (ii)
Ⓐ extraneous	Ⓓ amuse
Ⓑ prodigious	Ⓔ jeopardize
Ⓒ reprehensible	Ⓕ initiate

GO ON TO THE NEXT PAGE.

For Items #17–21, select one answer choice unless otherwise instructed.

Items #17–21 are based on the following passage.

A National Industrial Conference Board study prepared by Bock and Forkas examined the relationship between average productivity measured in terms of labor inputs of the top companies in an industry and other
5 companies in the same industry and the relationship between industry concentration and industry productivity. The study shows that, on average, the top companies in an industry had higher rates of productivity than did the remaining companies in the
10 same industry and that the industries with the highest productivity tended, on average, to have high concentration ratios. This prompted the nation's most sophisticated weekly business magazine to title its story on the NICB study "Bigness Means Efficiency."
15 The NICB study does find that there is a tendency for concentration to be higher in industries with high shipments per employee (or value added per employee) and lower in industries with low shipments per employee. However, this does not establish a causal
20 link. The observed weak association between "productivity" and concentration is due mainly to two factors. First, the reason many industries are relatively unconcentrated is that the capital requirements for entry are very low. Frequently such industries are
25 relatively labor-intensive and therefore have relatively low shipments or value added per employee—the measures of "productivity" used in the NICB study. It is not surprising, therefore, that the study found that of the 35 industries with the lowest productivity, 90
30 percent were located in areas such as textiles and apparel, lumber and wood products, and miscellaneous products such as lampshades and umbrellas. Once these industries are excluded from the analysis, the statistical association between concentration and
35 shipments per employee disappears entirely, and that between concentration and value added per employee very nearly disappears. Additionally, the study's measure of "productivity" includes not only output per employee but also profits and advertising outlay per
40 employee. Hence, the higher productivity observed in the study is partly due to the presence of noncompetitive profits and greater advertising outlays in the more concentrated industries.
The NICB study also found that in 87 percent of
45 the industries studied, the top four companies had greater "productivity" than did other firms in their industries, but the observed association between size and productivity is misleading. Often the smaller companies in a Census industry are actually in a

50 different industry than the leading companies. For example, according to the Census of Manufacturers, there are 158 companies competing with the four largest operators of blast furnaces and steel mills. Many of the smaller companies are actually in
55 different, more labor-intensive industries than the top four. It is more relevant to compare large companies with medium-sized ones. When the top four are compared with the second four companies, their apparent superiority disappears.
60 Finally, if the study's measure of productivity is a meaningful one, then the leading companies have such a decided advantage over their smaller rivals that they should be increasing their market share of the industry. Yet, since 1947, the leading companies have lost
65 ground in most producer goods industries, the very industries where technology is most important. Only in consumer goods have they made net gains, but the reasons for this are not to be found in technology.

17. The primary purpose of the passage is to

(A) demonstrate that the NICB study does not prove that efficiency results from concentration

(B) argue that less concentrated industries are as efficient as highly concentrated ones

(C) prove that smaller companies are as efficient as the largest firms in any given industry

(D) explain why labor-intensive industries are likely to have low shipments per employee

(E) criticize the nation's leading business magazine for printing its story about the NICB study

18. The passage implies all of the following conclusions about the textile and apparel industry EXCEPT:

(A) It is relatively labor intensive.

(B) It is relatively unconcentrated.

(C) It has low shipments per employee.

(D) It is relatively easy for a firm to enter the industry.

(E) It has high profits and advertising expenditures per employee.

GO ON TO THE NEXT PAGE.

For the following item, consider each answer individually and select all that apply.

19. According to the passage, the study's finding that large firms have greater productivity than other firms is misleading for which of the following reasons?

    | A | It failed to include the consumer goods industries. |
    | B | It included small firms not properly belonging to the studied industries. |
    | C | It compared medium-sized firms to the four largest firms in certain industries. |

20. According to the selection, the study tends to overstate shipments per employee in some industries because

    (A) productivity included profits and advertising outlays

    (B) capital requirements for entry are low

    (C) the category "all other" industries is overly inclusive

    (D) top companies, on the average, have higher rates of productivity

    (E) low-productivity industries are relatively unconcentrated

21. The author regards the conclusions of the NICB study as

    (A) open to debate

    (B) conclusively disproved

    (C) probably true

    (D) possibly true

    (E) not subject to verification

For Items #22–25, select the two words that, when used independently in the sentence, produce logical sentences and produce sentences that are alike in meaning.

22. The novel reveals the protagonist's character as a _____ of conflicting and often contradictory desires, being erased and overwritten with each new episode.

    | A | tournament |
    | B | harbinger |
    | C | palimpsest |
    | D | superimposition |
    | E | reconciliation |
    | F | conundrum |

23. Guilt is the self-knowledge of a disturbed moral _____, and the more perfect the balance, the more sensitive it is to slightest disorder.

    | A | equipoise |
    | B | precept |
    | C | clarity |
    | D | stasis |
    | E | collusion |
    | F | profundity |

GO ON TO THE NEXT PAGE.

24. A polyglot, an accomplished musician, and a noted authority on world literature, Professor Scalia seemed supremely confident except among mathematicians and scientists, in whose company he exhibited marked _____.

A superiority

B diffidence

C sophistication

D modesty

E narcissism

F petulance

25. Otto von Bismarck, who always appeared in uniform even though he had never really served, was viewed with _____ by military leaders for what they regarded as excessive moderation.

A admiration

B suspicion

C atonement

D skepticism

E respect

F ardor

STOP. You have reached the end of Section 3.

Section 4–Verbal Reasoning

Time—35 minutes
25 Items

For Items #1–5, select the <u>two</u> words that, when used independently in the sentence, produce logical sentences and produce sentences that are alike in meaning. Answers for Section 4 are on page 749, and explanations are on page 755.

1. The protests reflect student opposition to being programmed into a vast bureaucratic and industrial system aimed at maximizing production and economic expansion but _____ of any human concern.

   A   devoid
   B   remiss
   C   accepting
   D   cautious
   E   accepting
   F   bereft

2. Long a favorite of newspaper writers, the Lion's Head Pub was ruled by a(n) _____ bartender whose formidable temper even regular patrons feared.

   A   garrulous
   B   loquacious
   C   irascible
   D   tenured
   E   choleric
   F   lachrymose

3. Through despotic policies, it is possible for a regime to control some daily activities, but the economic _____ of political activities will not be so constrained as markets, free and black, will spontaneously emerge.

   A   implications
   B   barricades
   C   demands
   D   analog
   E   endeavor
   F   counterpart

4. Snakebites still represent a potentially mortal _____ for rural people in tropical regions, as evidenced by several hundred thousand recorded cases per year, of which perhaps 20,000 prove fatal.

   A   existence
   B   tribulation
   C   encounter
   D   travail
   E   livelihood
   F   combat

GO ON TO THE NEXT PAGE.

5. Although they have much in common in their historical experiences, both remote and recent, the African countries, in their rejection of colonial domination, developed in ____ ways that limit the validity of generalization about events.

- A | divergent
- B | bellicose
- C | tendentious
- D | penurious
- E | salubrious
- F | disparate

For Items #6–10, select one answer choice unless otherwise instructed.

Items #6–9 are based on the following passage.

The founders of the Republic viewed the revolution in political rather than economic or social terms. They spoke of education as essential to the public good—a goal taking precedence over knowledge as
5. occupational training or as a means to self-fulfillment. Both liberals and conservatives felt that the welfare of the Republic rested upon an educated citizenry and that free public schools were the best means of educating the citizenry in civic values and the obligations needed
10. for a republican society. All agreed that the principal ingredients of a civic education were literacy and the inculcation of patriotic and moral virtues.

The founders and their successors were long on rhetoric, but it fell to the textbook writers to distill the
15. essence of those values for school children. The earliest textbook writers were mostly conservatives, more likely Federalist than Jeffersonian, and they almost universally agreed that political virtue rests upon moral and religious precepts. Since most were New
20. Englanders, texts were infused with Protestant and, above all, Puritan outlooks.

In the first half of the Republic, education in the schools emphasized civic values and made little attempt to develop participatory political skills. That
25. task was left to political parties, town meetings, and churches. Additionally, the press did more to disseminate realistic as well as partisan knowledge of government than the schools. The goal of education was to achieve a higher form of *unum* for the new
30. Republic.

In the middle nineteenth century, political values taught in school were not substantially different from those of the first fifty years of the Republic. Their rosy hues if anything became golden. To the resplendent
35. values of liberty, equality, and a benevolent Christian morality were now added the middle-class virtues—especially of New England—of hard work, honesty, integrity, the rewards of individual effort, and obedience to parents and legitimate authority. But of all
40. the political values taught in school, patriotism was preeminent; and whenever teachers explained to school children why they should love their country above all else, the idea of liberty assumed pride of place.

6. According to the passage, the founders of the Republic regarded education primarily as

- (A) a religious obligation
- (B) a private matter
- (C) an unnecessary luxury
- (D) a matter of individual choice
- (E) a political necessity

For the following item, consider each answer individually and select all that apply.

7. It can be inferred that which of the following would likely have been the subject of an early American textbook?

- A | Patriotism and other civic virtues
- B | Vocational education
- C | Principles of American government

GO ON TO THE NEXT PAGE.

8. The author states that textbooks written in the middle part of the nineteenth century

   (A) departed radically in tone and style from earlier textbooks

   (B) mentioned for the first time the value of liberty

   (C) treated traditional civic virtues with even greater reverence

   (D) were commissioned by government agencies

   (E) contained no reference to conservative ideas

9. The author implies that an early American Puritan would likely insist that

   (A) moral and religious values are the foundation of civic virtue

   (B) textbooks should instruct students in political issues of vital concern to the community

   (C) textbooks should give greater emphasis to the value of individual liberty than to the duties of patriotism

   (D) private schools with a particular religious focus are preferable to public schools with no religious instruction

   (E) government and religion are separate institutions and the church should not interfere in political affairs

---

Item #10 is based on the following passage.

Professor Gerald Hawkins conducted one of the most influential studies of the ancient construction known as Stonehenge. Hawkins used computer calculations to compare the locations of stones in Stonehenge with the positions of stars, planets, and the sun at the time the structure was built. He concluded that the stones could have been used to mark viewing angles along which the rising and setting of heavenly bodies could be observed, making Stonehenge a kind of primitive "computer" for predicting astronomical events.

10. Which of the following, if true, most seriously weakens Hawkins' argument?

    (A) There is no reliable scientific evidence that the ancient people who built Stonehenge worshipped heavenly bodies.

    (B) Hawkins' computer calculations, though on their face accurate, have not been independently verified.

    (C) The positions of heavenly bodies have shifted slightly in the thousands of years since Stonehenge was built.

    (D) The fragility of the already-damaged stones of Stonehenge has caused authorities to limit the access of scholars to the site.

    (E) Any structure as complex as that at Stonehenge must inevitably contain some astronomical viewing angles, even if the builders did not intend them.

GO ON TO THE NEXT PAGE.

> **For Items #11–13, select one answer choice for each blank from the corresponding column of choices. Fill all blanks in a way that best completes the text.**

11. The delegates at the socialist convention called for a fair division of wealth and for an end to the cycles of economic panic and depression. They contemplated ambitious schemes of international cooperation to overcome the ancient rancor of (i)_____ nationality. And, in order to carry forward those (ii)_____ ideas, they formed the peaceable organization that, after many twists and turns, would become known as the Socialist International.

Blank (i)		Blank (ii)	
(A)	systematic	(D)	extravagant
(B)	parochial	(E)	antagonistic
(C)	impending	(F)	insipid

12. Hot milk has long been a standard cure for insomnia because of its _____ quality.

(A)	malevolent
(B)	amorphous
(C)	soporific
(D)	plaintive
(E)	desultory

13. His untimely death, at first thought to be due to a debilitating fever, was later _____ to poison.

(A)	relegated
(B)	ascribed
(C)	reduced
(D)	abdicated
(E)	prescribed

> **For Items #14–17, select one answer choice unless otherwise instructed.**

Items #14–17 are based on the following passage.

In the 1950s, the development of antipsychotic drugs called neuroleptics radically changed the clinical outlook for patients in mental institutions who had previously been considered hopelessly psychotic. Daily
5   medication controlled delusions and made psychotherapy possible. Many who otherwise might never have left institutions returned to society. Now, physicians have learned that there is a price to be paid for these benefits. Approximately 10 to 15 percent of
10 patients who undergo long-term treatment with antipsychotic drugs develop a cluster of symptoms called tardive dyskinesia, the most common symptoms of which are involuntary repetitive movement of the tongue, mouth, and face, and sometimes the limbs and
15 trunk.

Neuroleptic drugs interfere with the action of dopamine, an important neurotransmitter in the brain and a prime suspect in the pathophysiology of schizophrenia, by binding to the dopamine receptors of
20 nerve cells. Large doses of drugs such as amphetamines, which stimulate secretion of dopamine, produce a psychosis resembling schizophrenia. Reducing the activity of this neurotransmitter alleviates

the delusions that cause psychotic behavior. Although
25 the inhibition of dopamine activity can control psychotic behavior, researchers now believe that the central nervous systems of some patients adapt to long-term therapy by increasing the number of specific dopamine binding sites. The net result is dopamine
30 hypersensitivity, which is correlated with the subsequent appearance of tardive dyskinesia.

The risk of developing tardive dyskinesia is not so great that doctors have considered abandoning the use of antipsychotic drugs. Patients generally are
35 bothered only slightly by the physical side effects, though the abnormal movements are troubling and may hinder social adjustment. Additionally, early diagnosis and prompt discontinuation of the neuroleptics might decrease the incidence of the movement disorders.
40 Unfortunately, without neuroleptic drugs, psychotic behavior returns. So, researchers have tried to achieve a satisfactory balance between the two effects,

GO ON TO THE NEXT PAGE.

lowering dosages to a level that minimizes movement disorders yet controls psychosis.

45   Research has shown that psychoses can be controlled at the same time that tardive dyskinesia symptoms are reduced. This suggests that a drug more specifically affecting the mechanism of psychoses might not cause movement disorders. Sulpiride, a drug
50 not available in the United States but widely used in Europe, where it was developed, may be one such alternative. The drug selectively blocks D–2 dopamine receptors, perhaps especially those in the limbic area of the brain, which is involved in emotion and behavior. It
55 does not adversely affect the adenylate cyclase-linked D–1 dopamine receptors. Sulpiride has proven effective in the short term, but whether it suppresses tardive dyskinesia over a long period of treatment is not yet known.

14. It can be inferred that the primary danger of tardive dyskinesia is the

(A) psychological effect on the patient
(B) long-term therapeutic use of drugs
(C) addiction of a patient to dopamine
(D) physical injuries caused by violent muscle spasms
(E) inability of the patient to remain in therapy

15. It can be inferred that neuroleptic drugs control psychosis by

(A) suppressing the production of dopamine in the brain
(B) blocking the nerve impulses transmitted to the muscles
(C) preventing the absorption of dopamine by brain cells
(D) creating a hypersensitivity to dopamine
(E) counteracting the effect of other prescription drugs

16. The tone of the final paragraph can be described as

(A) cautiously optimistic
(B) bitterly disappointed
(C) unconcerned
(D) alarmed
(E) outraged

17. Select the sentence in which the author provides empirical evidence of a possible link between dopamine and some psychotic behavior.

(A) Lines 9–15 ("Approximately 10 to 15 percent...trunk.")
(B) Lines 20–22 ("Large doses...schizophrenia.")
(C) Lines 32–34 ("The risk of developing...drugs.")
(D) Lines 34–37 ("Patients generally are...adjustment.")
(E) Lines 37–39 ("Additionally, early diagnosis...disorders.")

GO ON TO THE NEXT PAGE.

For Items #18–20, select one answer choice for each blank from the corresponding column of choices. Fill all blanks in a way that best completes the text.

18. Country music follows a predictable cycle. First, the pure musicians create strong, emotionally true styles. Then, clever imitators and shrewd entrepreneurs (i)_____ these styles to produce a musical product for painless consumption by a larger audience seeking (ii)_____ rather than edification. In time, the gruel becomes so unsatisfying that a (iii)_____ new generation of upstarts moves in, appropriates the musical territory, and builds upon it a new music with vitality and integrity.

Blank (i)	Blank (ii)	Blank (iii)
(A) refine	(D) diversion	(G) rebellious
(B) inflate	(E) passion	(H) talented
(C) adulterate	(F) constancy	(I) predictable

19. Although Mozart's music suggests a composer of great (i)_____ and seriousness, his letters imply that he was naïve and (ii)_____ .

Blank (i)	Blank (ii)
(A) levity	(D) uncouth
(B) fragility	(E) grave
(C) sophistication	(F) macabre

20. Nutritional and herbal supplements can provide significant health benefits when properly integrated into a dietary plan but in certain combinations can have _____ side effects that pose serious health risks.

(A) benign
(B) innocuous
(C) intangible
(D) adverse
(E) natural

For Items #21–25, select one answer choice unless otherwise instructed.

Item #21 is based on the following passage.

A decade ago, "earn your age" was the immediate goal of every recent business school graduate. For example, a 26-year-old MBA expected to earn $26,000 per year. This standard no longer holds true in America—a

5   newly graduated MBA in America would want to earn much more—but it is still the norm in England. It seems, therefore, that a starting MBA in America is economically better off than one in England.

21. Which of the following, if true, most weakens the argument?

(A) Many students from England earn their MBAs in the United States.

(B) Most students in American business schools have had prior work experience.

(C) The British pound is worth almost twice as much as the American dollar.

(D) Graduates from American law schools earn more than graduates from American business schools do.

(E) England produces fewer MBAs each year than the United States.

GO ON TO THE NEXT PAGE.

Item #22 is based on the following passage.

When the military forces of the Soviet Union were compared directly with those of the United States, the two superpowers appeared to be about equal, with each side leading and trailing in several categories of
5 weapons, equipment, and manpower. When the forces of the other Warsaw Pact nations were added to those of the Soviet Union, and the forces of the NATO allies of the United States were added to those of the United States, a substantial advantage for the NATO side in
10 nearly every category was found to exist. We can conclude, therefore, that the United States actually enjoyed military superiority over the Soviet Union.

22. Which of the following can be most reliably inferred from the argument?

(A) In a war between the Warsaw Pact nations and the NATO countries, the NATO countries would prevail.

(B) The military forces of the NATO allies of the United States were greater than those of the Soviet Union's Warsaw Pact allies.

(C) The NATO allies of the United States had combined military forces that were greater than those of the United States itself.

(D) A portion of the military forces of the Soviet Union were deployed for the purpose of deterring an attack by the NATO countries.

(E) There were more member countries in the NATO alliance than there were in the Warsaw Pact.

Items #23–25 are based on the following passage.

Programs intended to reduce the incidence of driving while alcohol impaired face philosophical, constitutional, and practical objections. The approach that most people find philosophically intuitive makes
5 driving while impaired a crime. This approach targets the individual, but its efficacy is questionable. In Britain, motor vehicle fatalities fell 25 percent immediately following implementation of the Road Safety Act in 1967. Then, as British drivers
10 increasingly recognized that they could drink and not be stopped, the effectiveness of the law declined.

In the United States, police are usually empowered to conduct a field sobriety test on a stopped driver if the officer has reason to believe that the driver
15 is alcohol impaired. The officer has the additional authority to ask for an alcohol breath test. A driver who exceeds the legal limit for blood alcohol content, usually 0.08 percent, is subject to arrest, and a driver who refuses to participate in the testing faces automatic
20 licensure suspension. Still, many alcohol impaired drivers escape detection; and while courts have upheld the constitutionality of random traffic stops, more rigorous enforcement practices would surely face additional legal challenges.
25 The alternative approach of taxing alcohol at a higher rate than at present also presents a problem. While the heaviest drinkers would be taxed the most,

anyone who drinks at all would be penalized by this approach.
30 The effectiveness of any approach ultimately depends on the extent to which those who drive with high blood alcohol content are capable of controlling their intake in response to economic or penal threat.

Therapeutic programs constitute another
35 approach, but the few controlled trials that have been reported supplied little evidence that rehabilitation programs for those repeatedly arrested for drunken behavior have reduced either the recidivism or the crash rates, although these trials have improved the
40 general public's knowledge and attitudes greatly. However, one thing is clear: unless we deal with automobile and highway safety and reduce accidents in which alcoholic intoxication plays a role, many people will continue to die needlessly.

GO ON TO THE NEXT PAGE.

23. It can be inferred from the passage that the 1967 Road Safety Act in Britain

    (A) changed an existing law to lower the BAC level defining driving while intoxicated
    (B) made it illegal to drive while intoxicated
    (C) increased drunk driving arrests
    (D) placed a tax on the sale of alcoholic drinks
    (E) required drivers convicted under the law to undergo rehabilitation

24. With which of the following statements about making driving while intoxicated a criminal offense versus increasing taxes on alcohol consumption would the author most likely agree?

    (A) Making driving while intoxicated a criminal offense is preferable to increased taxes on alcohol because the former is aimed only at those who abuse alcohol by driving while intoxicated.
    (B) Increased taxation on alcohol consumption is likely to be more effective in reducing traffic fatalities because taxation covers all consumers and not just those who drive.
    (C) Increased taxation on alcohol will constitute less of an interference with personal liberty because of the necessity of breath alcohol tests to determine blood alcohol levels in drivers suspected of intoxication.
    (D) Since neither increased taxation nor enforcement of criminal laws against drunk drivers is likely to have any significant impact, neither measure is warranted.
    (E) Because arrests of intoxicated drivers have proved to be expensive and administratively cumbersome, increased taxation on alcohol is the most promising means of reducing traffic fatalities.

25. The author cites the British example in order to

    (A) show that the problem of drunk driving is worse in Britain than in the U.S.
    (B) prove that passing of laws against intoxicated drivers would reduce traffic deaths
    (C) prove that a slight increase in the number of arrests of intoxicated drivers will not deter drunk driving
    (D) suggest that taxation of alcohol consumption may be more effective than criminal laws
    (E) demonstrate the need to lower the blood alcohol content level that defines whether a person is driving while alcohol impaired

STOP. You have reached the end of Section 4.

Section 5–Quantitative Reasoning

40 Minutes
25 Items

Solve each problem and choose the correct answer, using the given directions. Answers are on page 749, and explanations are on page 751.

Notes: All numbers used are real numbers.

Unless otherwise indicated, all figures lie in a plane.

Geometric diagrams and figures **are not necessarily** drawn to scale, so do **not** assume lengths, angle measures, or other quantities are as they appear in a given figure. You should assume that lines shown as straight are straight and that the positions of points, and geometric objects in general, exist in the order shown. Base your answers to questions with geometric figures on reasoning, not visual estimation or measurement.

Coordinate systems and graphic data presentations **are** drawn to scale, so you can answer items based on visual estimation or measurement.

Each of the items #1–9 consists of two quantities, Quantity A and Quantity B. Compare the two quantities, using the information presented. Choose:

(A) if Quantity A is greater.
(B) if Quantity B is greater.
(C) if the two quantities are equal.
(D) if the relationship cannot be determined from the information given.

A symbol that appears more than once in an item has the same meaning throughout the item.

Village V assesses each parcel of land for tax purposes at p percent of the fair market value of the land. The fair market value of parcel Q is $240,000, and the assessed value for tax purposes is $6,000.

Quantity A	Quantity B	
1. The assessed value for tax purposes of parcel T in Village V with a fair market value of $300,000.	$7,500	(A) (B) (C) (D)

GO ON TO THE NEXT PAGE.

(A)	if Quantity A is greater.
(B)	if Quantity B is greater.
(C)	if the two quantities are equal.
(D)	if the relationship cannot be determined from the information given.

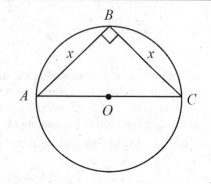

The circumference of circle O is 4π.

Quantity A   Quantity B

2. Area of triangular region ABC.   4   (A) (B) (C) (D)

$$\frac{4}{5}x - 7 = 3$$

Quantity A   Quantity B

3. x 8   (A) (B) (C) (D)

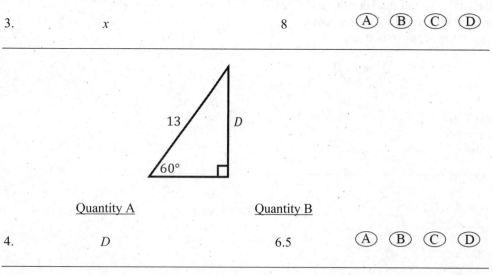

Quantity A   Quantity B

4. D 6.5   (A) (B) (C) (D)

GO ON TO THE NEXT PAGE.

> (A) if Quantity A is greater.
> (B) if Quantity B is greater.
> (C) if the two quantities are equal.
> (D) if the relationship cannot be determined from the information given.

S is the set of all fractions of the form $\dfrac{n}{n+1}$,

where n is a positive integer less than 10.

Quantity A	Quantity B
5. The product of any two different fractions in S.	One-half of the value of the largest fraction in S.	(A) (B) (C) (D)

---

x, y, and z are integers such that $x < y < z < 0$.

Quantity A	Quantity B
6. $x + y + z$	xyz	(A) (B) (C) (D)

Archaeologists divide the Stone Age into periods:

2,000,000 BP to 8300 BCE   Paleolithic
8300 BCE to 4500 BCE   Neolithic
4500 BCE to 3300 BCE   Chalcolithic

Of 1,275 Stone Age artifacts recovered and dated from an archaeological site, P were from the Paleolithic Period and C were from the Chalcolithic Period.

Quantity A	Quantity B
7. Number of artifacts recovered and dated from the site from the Neolithic period	$1{,}275 - P - C$	(A) (B) (C) (D)

$$0 > x > y$$

Quantity A	Quantity B
8. $(xy)^2$	xy	(A) (B) (C) (D)

GO ON TO THE NEXT PAGE.

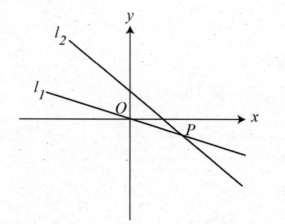

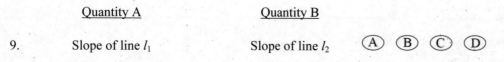

Quantity A	Quantity B	
9. Slope of line l_1	Slope of line l_2	Ⓐ Ⓑ Ⓒ Ⓓ

GO ON TO THE NEXT PAGE.

Items #10–25 use several formats. Unless otherwise instructed, select one answer choice. For Numeric Entry items, follow the direction below.

Numeric Entry Directions

- Answers may be integers, decimals, or fractions. Answers may be negative.
- Items requiring a fraction will include two answer boxes—one for the numerator and one for the denominator.
- Equivalent forms of the answer are also correct (e.g. 9 and 9.0 are both correct forms of 9). Fractions do not need to be expressed in lowest terms.
- Enter the exact answer unless the item stem indicates that the answer should be rounded.

10. From one year to the next, the number of applications for admission received by University U increased from 12,500 to 15,000. What the percent increase in the number of applications?

(A) 10%

(B) $12\frac{1}{2}\%$

(C) $16\frac{2}{3}\%$

(D) 20%

(E) 80%

11. Depending on the value of k, the expression $3k + 4k + 5k + 6k + 7k$ may or may not be divisible by 7. Which of the terms, when eliminated from the expression, guarantees that the resulting expression is divisible by 7 for every positive integer k?

(A) $3k$

(B) $4k$

(C) $5k$

(D) $6k$

(E) $7k$

For the following item, consider the answers separately and select all that apply.

12. If n is a positive integer, which of the following must be an even integer?

Indicate all such statements.

A	$n+1$
B	$3n+1$
C	$3n+2$
D	n^2+1
E	n^2+n

13. A college registrar assigned T students taking introductory economics to classes to be taught by three professors. She assigned x students to Mr. Afar's class. She assigned three fewer students to Dr. Hinderaker's class than to Mr. Afar's class, and she assigned four more students to Ms. Baker's class than to Dr. Hinderaker's class. Which of the following equations gives T in terms of x?

(A) $T = x + 1$

(B) $T = 3x - 2$

(C) $T = 3x + 1$

(D) $T = 3x + 3$

(E) $T = \dfrac{x}{3}$

GO ON TO THE NEXT PAGE.

14. Motorcycle X averages 40 kilometers per liter of gasoline while Motorcycle Y averages 50 kilometers per liter. If the cost of gasoline is $2 per liter, what will be the difference in the cost of operating the two motorcycles for 300 kilometers?

(A) $3
(B) $6
(C) $12
(D) $15
(E) $20

For the following item, enter your answer in the space provided.

15. If the total surface area of a cube is 54 units, what is the volume of the cube?

_____ units^3

16. Tank A and Tank B are similar tanks of the same capacity, each with a drain that completely empties the tank in four hours. The tanks are filled to capacity. If the drain is opened on Tank A at time t, and one hour later the drain is opened on Tank B, and both are permitted to drain until empty, how many hours will have elapsed since t when the quantity of liquid in Tank A is equal to one-half that in Tank B?

(A) t
(B) $t+1$ hour
(C) $t+2$ hours
(D) $t+3$ hours
(E) $t+4$ hours

17. If m is the average (arithmetic mean) of 5, 7, and c, what is the value of c in terms of m?

(A) $\dfrac{12+m}{3}$

(B) $\dfrac{12-m}{3}$

(C) $m+3$
(D) $m+12$
(E) $3m-12$

GO ON TO THE NEXT PAGE.

Items #18–19 refer to the following graphs.

SELECTED DATA ON HANDGUNS FOR THE UNITED STATES

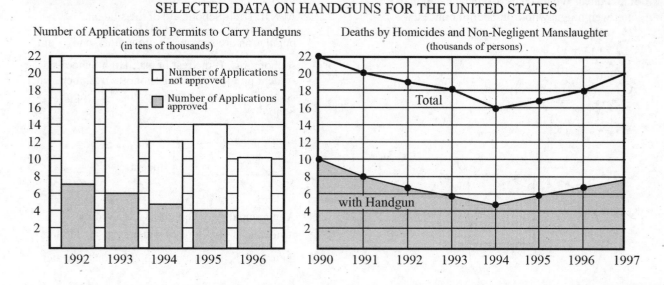

Number of Applications for Permits to Carry Handguns (in tens of thousands)

Deaths by Homicides and Non-Negligent Manslaughter (thousands of persons)

18. In 1993, approximately what percentage of the applications for permits to carry handguns were NOT approved?

(A) 12%

(B) 25%

(C) $33\frac{1}{3}\%$

(D) 50%

(E) $66\frac{2}{3}\%$

19. For the period 1993 through 1996, inclusive, in how many years did both the total number of deaths by homicide and non-negligent manslaughter increase, and the number of applications for permits to carry a handgun increase?

(A) 0

(B) 1

(C) 2

(D) 3

(E) 4

GO ON TO THE NEXT PAGE.

20. To mail a letter costs x cents for the first ounce and y cents for every additional ounce or fraction of an ounce. What is the cost, in cents, to mail a letter weighing a whole number of ounces, w?

   (A) $w(x+y)$

   (B) $x(w-y)$

   (C) $x(w-1)+y(w-1)$

   (D) $x+wy$

   (E) $x+y(w-1)$

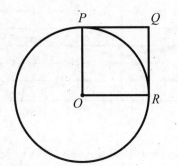

21. In the figure above, if the area of the square $OPQR$ is 2, what is the area of the circle with center O?

   (A) $\frac{\pi}{4}$

   (B) $\pi\sqrt{2}$

   (C) 2π

   (D) $2\sqrt{2}\pi$

   (E) 4π

22. How many positive integers less than 30 are equal to 3 times an odd integer?

   (A) 10

   (B) 7

   (C) 5

   (D) 4

   (E) 3

For the following item, enter your answer in the space provided.

23. At NJL High School, $\frac{1}{4}$ of the student population are seniors, $\frac{1}{5}$ are juniors, and $\frac{1}{3}$ are sophomores. If the rest of NJL High School's student population consists of 390 freshmen, what is the total student population of NJL High School?

                             students

24. A municipality meters the water used by residents. If g gallons of water cost $\frac{d}{100}$ dollars, then what is the cost of 10,000 gallons of water?

   (A) $\frac{gd}{1,000}$

   (B) $\frac{gd}{10,000}$

   (C) $100gd$

   (D) $\frac{100d}{g}$

   (E) $\frac{d}{100g}$

25. The average of a group of 100 numbers is 5 and the standard deviation is x where $x > 0$. Which numbers can be added to the group to ensure that the new standard deviation, y, satisfies $0 < y < x$?

   (A) 0 and -5

   (B) 0 and 0

   (C) 0 and 5

   (D) 5 and 5

   (E) 0 and 10

STOP. You have reached the end of Section 5.

Section 6–Quantitative Reasoning

40 Minutes
25 Items

Solve each problem and choose the correct answer, using the given directions. Answers are on page 749, and explanations are on page 763.

Notes: All numbers used are real numbers.

Unless otherwise indicated, all figures lie in a plane.

Geometric diagrams and figures **are not necessarily** drawn to scale, so do **not** assume lengths, angle measures, or other quantities are as they appear in a given figure. You should assume that lines shown as straight are straight and that the positions of points, and geometric objects in general, exist in the order shown. Base your answers to questions with geometric figures on reasoning, not visual estimation or measurement.

Coordinate systems and graphic data presentations **are** drawn to scale, so you can answer items based on visual estimation or measurement.

Each of the items #1–9 consists of two quantities, Quantity A and Quantity B. Compare the two quantities, using the information presented. Choose:

(A) if Quantity A is greater.
(B) if Quantity B is greater.
(C) if the two quantities are equal.
(D) if the relationship cannot be determined from the information given.

A symbol that appears more than once in an item has the same meaning throughout the item.

Quantity A	Quantity B	
1. $\sqrt{2}$	$\dfrac{2}{\sqrt{2}}$	(A) (B) (C) (D)

$$xy \neq 0$$

Quantity A	Quantity B	
2. $\dfrac{1}{x}+\dfrac{1}{y}$	$x+y$	(A) (B) (C) (D)

r and s are radii of the circles.

Quantity A	Quantity B	
3. Area of the smaller circle of the figure	Area of the shaded portion of the figure	(A) (B) (C) (D)

GO ON TO THE NEXT PAGE.

(A) if Quantity A is greater.
(B) if Quantity B is greater.
(C) if the two quantities are equal.
(D) if the relationship cannot be determined from the information given.

A jar contains 32 red marbles and
16 blue marbles. Seventy-five percent of
the red marbles and 50 percent of the blue
marbles are removed from the jar.

Quantity A	Quantity B

4.

The fraction of
the original number
of marbles still
remaining in the jar

$\frac{2}{3}$

(A) (B) (C) (D)

A student purchased a total of 17 pens and
pencils. The pens cost $0.35 each, and the
pencils cost $0.20 each. The total cost of
the pens and pencils was $4.60.

Quantity A	Quantity B

5.

The number of
pens purchased
by the student

The number of
pencils purchased
by the student

(A) (B) (C) (D)

The figure above is the graph of $y = ax + b$ in the coordinate plane.

Quantity A	Quantity B

6.

a

$-\dfrac{b}{c}$

(A)(B)(C)(D)

GO ON TO THE NEXT PAGE.

(A) if Quantity A is greater.
(B) if Quantity B is greater.
(C) if the two quantities are equal.
(D) if the relationship cannot be determined from the information given.

Percentage of Mouse Population P Infected with Lime Disease

Male	12%
Female	16%
Total	14.1%

	Quantity A	Quantity B	
7.	Number of male mice in Population P	Number of female mice in Population P	(A) (B) (C) (D)

In the coordinate plane, points A, B, and C have coordinates (1,7), (5,4), and (6,7).

	Quantity A	Quantity B	
8.	AB	AC	(A) (B) (C) (D)

---

x is an integer greater than 1.

	Quantity A	Quantity B	
9.	$\dfrac{x^{23} - x^{22}}{x}$	x^{22}	(A) (B) (C) (D)

GO ON TO THE NEXT PAGE.

Items #10–25 use several formats. Unless otherwise instructed, select one answer choice. For Numeric Entry items, follow the direction below.

Numeric Entry Directions

- Answers may be integers, decimals, or fractions. Answers may be negative.
- Items requiring a fraction will include two answer boxes—one for the numerator and one for the denominator.
- Equivalent forms of the answer are also correct (e.g. 9 and 9.0 are both correct forms of 9). Fractions do not need to be expressed in lowest terms.
- Enter the exact answer unless the item stem indicates that the answer should be rounded.

10. Which of the following numbers <u>cannot</u> be expressed as the sum of the squares of two different integers?

   (A) 10
   (B) 13
   (C) 18
   (D) 34
   (E) 41

11. A laboratory technician divided a sample into three different amounts labeled A, B, and C. A weighed half as much as B, and the weight of C was equal to the average of the weights of A and B. The ratio of the weight of C to the weight of A was:

   (A)   2:1
   (B)   3:2
   (C)   1:1
   (D)   1:2
   (E)   1:4

For the following item, enter your answer in the space provided.

12. If $2x + 2y = 6$ and $3x - 3y = 9$, what is the value of $x^2 - y^2$?

$$x^2 - y^2 = \boxed{}$$

GO ON TO THE NEXT PAGE.

Items #13–14 refer to the following graphs.

UNITED STATES CONSUMPTION OF OIL (DAILY AVERAGE)

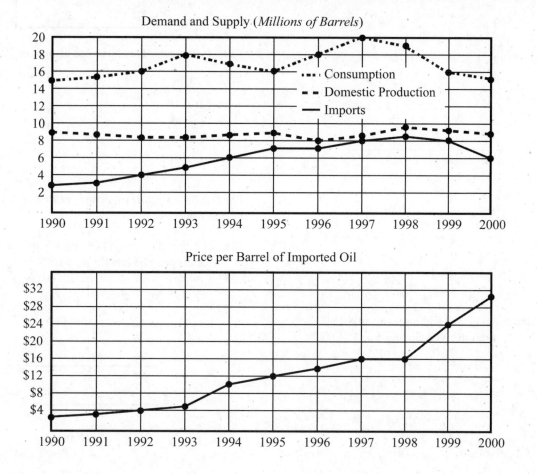

Demand and Supply (*Millions of Barrels*)

Price per Barrel of Imported Oil

13. In 2000, the average (arithmetic mean) cost of oil imported into the United States each day was approximately

(A) $180 million
(B) $150 million
(C) $120 million
(D) $90 million
(E) $50 million

14. From 1991 through 2000, inclusive, in how many years did both the quantity and price of imported oil increase from the previous year?

(A) 4
(B) 5
(C) 6
(D) 7
(E) 8

For the following item, enter your answer in the space provided.

15. At College C, three juniors and two seniors will be named to the Upper Class Honorary Society. If the final list of candidates includes five juniors and six seniors, how many different combinations of individuals could be named to the list? (The order of the list does not matter.)

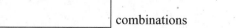 combinations

GO ON TO THE NEXT PAGE.

16. List X is the set of all integers between and including 101 and 500. What is the interquartile range of List X?

   (A) 199
   (B) 200
   (C) 399
   (D) 400
   (E) 500

17. $\sqrt{1+2+3+4+1+2+3+4+1+2+3+4+1+2+3} =$

   (A) $3\sqrt{2}$
   (B) $3\sqrt{3}$
   (C) 4
   (D) 5
   (E) 6

18. What is the average (arithmetic mean) of all integers 6 through 15 (including 6 and 15)?

   (A) 6
   (B) 9
   (C) 10.5
   (D) 11
   (E) 21

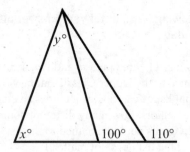

19. In the figure above, if $x = 50$, then $y =$

   (A) 30
   (B) 45
   (C) 50
   (D) 60
   (E) 75

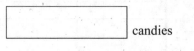

20. If the rectangle above has an area of 72, then $x =$

   (A) 3
   (B) 4
   (C) 6
   (D) 8
   (E) 9

For the following item, enter your answer in the space provided.

21. If 12 candies cost $1.70, how many of these candies can be bought for $10.20?

   [   ] candies

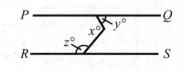

$$y = 60$$
$$z = 130$$

22. In the figure above, $\overline{PQ}$ is parallel to $\overline{RS}$. How many degrees are there in $\angle x$?

   (A) 90
   (B) 100
   (C) 110
   (D) 120
   (E) 130

GO ON TO THE NEXT PAGE.

23. The legislative body of a certain state is comprised of 324 members, 74 of whom are serving a first term and 56 of whom are age 30 or younger. What is the <u>maximum</u> number of members who could be age 30 or younger and serving a first term?

    (A) 26
    (B) 30
    (C) 56
    (D) 74
    (E) 324

24. A motorist drives 60 miles to her destination at an average speed of 40 miles per hour and makes the return trip at an average speed of 30 miles per hour. Her average speed in miles per hour for the entire trip is

    (A) 17
    (B) $34\frac{2}{7}$
    (C) 35
    (D) $43\frac{1}{3}$
    (E) 70

25. If $(x+1)(x-2)$ is positive, then

    (A) $x < -1$ or $x > 2$
    (B) $x > -1$ or $x < 2$
    (C) $-1 < x < 2$
    (D) $-2 < x < 1$
    (E) $x = -1$ or $x = 2$

STOP. You have reached the end of Section 6.

Post-Assessment

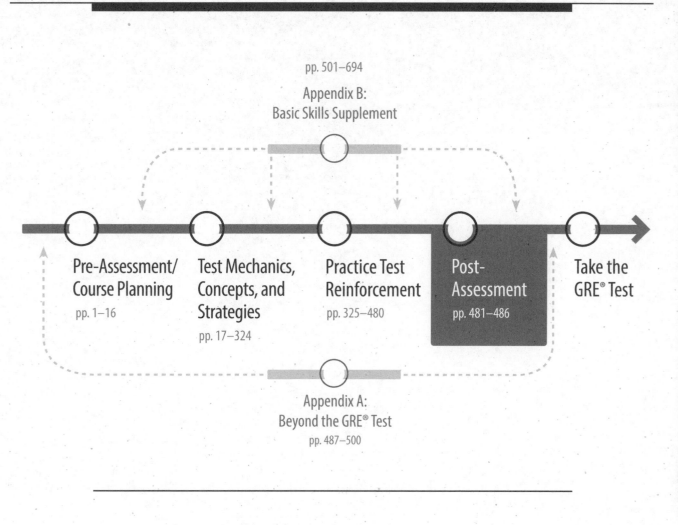

pp. 501–694

Appendix B:
Basic Skills Supplement

Pre-Assessment/
Course Planning
pp. 1–16

Test Mechanics,
Concepts, and
Strategies
pp. 17–324

Practice Test
Reinforcement
pp. 325–480

Post-
Assessment
pp. 481–486

Take the
GRE® Test

Appendix A:
Beyond the GRE® Test
pp. 487–500

CAMBRIDGE
VICTORY FOR THE
GRE® TEST

POST-ASSESSMENT
ADMINISTRATION

At the end of the course, you will take a post-assessment. If your program has ordered post-assessment reports, you will receive these reports with your post-assessment results. These reports will help you determine the areas in which you need continued study. You can then utilize your study time to prepare in those areas so that when you take the real test, you are ready to do your best. Refer to the "How to Use the Pre-Assessment Reports" section of this book (p. 4) to learn more about how to read and use the Student Summary and Item Analysis reports.

HOW TO USE THE POST-ASSESSMENT REPORTS

In the transition from the post-assessment to developing your post-assessment action plan, you and your teacher will use the results of your post-assessment to recognize your individual strengths and weaknesses. Additionally, be sure at this point in the course that you have not only reviewed the "Setting a Test Score Target" section of this book (p. 8), but that you have also followed through on your schedule for the course.

You will receive the results of your post-assessment in the form of Student Summary and Item Analysis reports approximately six days after taking the test. These reports provide details about your performance and will help you to determine where to focus your efforts from now until your official test date by strategically targeting those skills, concepts, and strategies that will help you to improve in your areas of weakness. Just as you did with the pre-assessment, review the details of the sample Student Summary and Item Analysis reports in this book (pp. 5–6) so that you are familiar with their contents.

Once you have received your post-assessment reports, you can make connections between the reports and the specific skills, concepts, and strategies that you need to study. Use these reports to identify which items you answered incorrectly. After identifying the item types you missed, use the Item Index at the back of this book to find similar items to review. Then make a "to do" list using the following page.

TOPIC	START DATE	DATE TO BE COMPLETED	DATE COMPLETED

POST-ASSESSMENT ACTION PLAN

Up until this point, you have spent a great deal of time preparing for the test both in class and on your own. After receiving the results of your post-assessment and finishing the Cambridge GRE program, you will most likely have some time before test day. Below are some tips to maximize your use of this time to reinforce and maintain the skills, concepts and strategies that you have learned throughout the course.

- Use a calendar to develop a plan of action, determining what topics you will study each day and allotting time to study those sections of the book and complete the relevant exercises. Remember that it is not necessary for you to do everything all at once. Instead, picking a few things to focus on each week will help you to better manage your time between now and the real test. After you have designed a basic study plan, ask your instructor for insight. He or she can help you set goals for each core subject and may be able to suggest further strategies or a subtle re-allotment of your time.

- Review the Pre-Assessment/Course Planning section of this book when designing your study plan.

- While it is important to review all subject areas to maintain competency, you should devote a good portion of your remaining study time to areas where you have the most opportunity for improvement. Use your pre- and post-assessment data (see "How to Use the Post-Assessment Reports," p. 4) to identify these areas. For example, if you are satisfied with your Verbal Reasoning score but have not attained your goal for the Quantitative Reasoning test section, you might consider designing a study plan that emphasizes Quantitative Reasoning material. You may also want to review the practice tests in this book. Look out for topics that you know you could improve upon if you had the opportunity to peek at your notes.

- In the final days before the test, you will not be able to learn a great deal of new material. Focus instead on practicing the skills, concepts and strategies that you have already learned.

- Stick with your study schedule and follow your plan. But do not study too much. An hour or two of studying each day will be more productive than a severe study schedule that leaves you physically and mentally exhausted.

Appendix A:
Beyond the GRE® Test

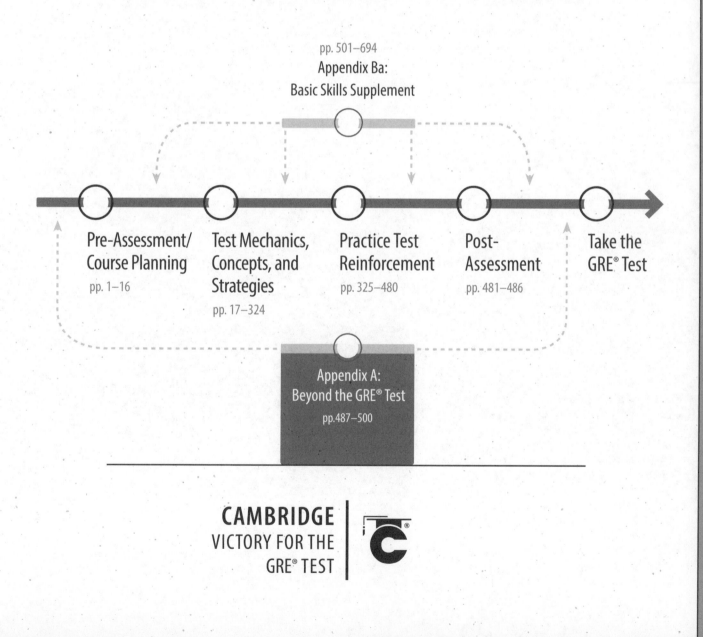

pp. 501–694
Appendix Ba:
Basic Skills Supplement

Pre-Assessment/
Course Planning
pp. 1–16

Test Mechanics,
Concepts, and
Strategies
pp. 17–324

Practice Test
Reinforcement
pp. 325–480

Post-
Assessment
pp. 481–486

Take the
GRE® Test

Appendix A:
Beyond the GRE® Test
pp.487–500

CAMBRIDGE
VICTORY FOR THE
GRE® TEST

APPLICATION PREPARATION

This section echoes our analysis of the admission process in "Setting a Test Score Target" (p. 8). To maximize your chances of success, you must create an admission application that satisfies the needs of the school to which you are applying. This does not mean that you create an application that is fictitious, but it does mean that you organize and present your experiences in a way that depicts you in the most favorable light.

Function of the Admission Process

In order to decide where to apply, you must understand and appreciate the function of the admission process as a social and economic process. Many prospective applicants view the filing of a graduate school application only from their own individual perspective and consider themselves outside spectators who merely benefit from (or are victims of) a bureaucratic juggernaut. This attitude is based on a misinterpretation of the admission process and does not take into consideration the school's social and economic factors. Let us examine this process from two perspectives: yours and that of a graduate school.

First, from your perspective, you must keep in mind that the graduate school admission process is much more than merely answering a few questions about your educational background and employment history. Rather, the application process is just the first step on a career path that will last for most of the rest of your life. Decisions you make at this stage may have implications for your life 30 or 40 years from now.

Additionally, you must appreciate the financial commitment that you are making. In the first instance, the cost of the application process alone could be as much as $1,400. The fee that you pay Educational Testing Services to take the Graduate Record Examination with score reports could be as much as $172 ($160 for general test registration and $12 to receive scores over the phone). You can request up to four schools receive your test results at the time that you take the test with no additional fees. If you need additional score reports, these are available for a fee of $23 per school. Furthermore, the application fees charged by schools run between $50 and $125. If you apply to ten schools, you could easily spend $1,500 or more on application fees and score distribution charges. In addition, you will probably spend at least $100 on administrative details, such as document preparation, copying, postage, and long distance telephone calls. Add another $450 or more for test preparation for the GRE, and you are already committed to $2,500 or more.

On top of application expenses, most schools require that you respond to an acceptance offer by a certain deadline with a non-refundable deposit. You may find yourself in the uncomfortable position of paying such a deposit to ensure that you have a graduate school seat even though you have not yet heard from some other schools. However, these sums pale in comparison to the cost of tuition. In-state tuition at a public school may be $12,000–$35,000 per year, while tuition at a top private school may be as much as $40,000–$55,000 per year. With the expense of room and board taken into consideration, (approximately $7,500–$25,000 per year, depending on the school), the entire expense to obtain your graduate degree could be anywhere from $40,000 to $320,000.

Do not let those numbers frighten you. We are not trying to dissuade you from pursuing a graduate degree. We are trying to dramatize a point: the decision to apply to graduate school has significant social and economic implications for you as an individual.

Graduate schools seek to create a rigorous and fair process that places into their student bodies those students who best serve the interest of the school. With this in mind, during the application process, you may for a time feel like a lab specimen placed under a microscope. Why do graduate programs invest so much time and energy in assessing each and every student who applies? Why do schools ask so many questions, need transcripts and test scores, and require references? Why does it so intensely matter to a graduate school which students are accepted to study in their programs, especially when test scores and undergraduate GPAs are so similar? Why does it seem that some schools open their doors wide for almost anyone to attend while others only allow a select few to study at their institutions? Some answers to these questions are simple, but others are more complex.

First, graduate schools are selective because of their own financial needs. A graduate school connected to a college or university has to be run in the same way as any other business. It has paid employees; it owns or rents property; it operates a library; it buys furniture and office equipment; it pays utility bills; etc. As a student, your tuition and fees pay for many of these expenses. A graduate school, therefore, is absolutely dependent upon a steady flow of tuition income. At the same time, most graduate schools must limit the number of students that they can allow to attend. This limitation may be due to the amount of total spaces available for student housing, the quantity of classrooms on hand, or even the number of students that its board of directors allows based on various college or university rules and regulations. So, admissions directors make decisions about whether you will be accepted in the context of budgetary constraints. The college or university needs you to start paying tuition and to continue paying tuition (or have someone else—parents, a scholarship, state or federal aid, etc.— pay tuition). A graduate school simply cannot afford to have large numbers of students dropping out of school. Therefore, one of the primary concerns of a graduate school admissions officer is to ensure that those applicants who are accepted are committed to completing a course of study.

Second, schools worry about their reputations and how potential students might help or hinder that reputation. Colleges and universities, and their graduate schools, want to accept future alumni who will make their school look good to others. It should not be surprising to learn that as an applicant, if you show considerable professional promise, you would be considered more favorably than others. A school with successful alumni gets a reputation for being a good school, and such a reputation tends to attract highly qualified applicants.

Third, graduate schools also want to show social responsibility to individuals and the wider society. They meet this responsibility in some fairly obvious ways, such as by actively seeking applicants from groups who are under-represented in the professional community and by establishing programs to train professionals for positions of special need.

Regardless of the various filters that schools use to evaluate potential students, the admissions process should benefit both the student and the graduate school. The process is ideally designed to create a positive mutual relationship between students and institutions. Unfortunately, for decades, there have been more students who are interested in spots available at certain accredited graduate schools. For a great number of graduate schools, there are actually far more applicants than available seats. Given the mismatch between the number of available seats and the number of applicants, the application process has turned into a rigorous competition. Thus, you will need to stand out from the crowd of other applicants. To do this, you must make yourself attractive to a graduate school. You must persuade the admissions committee that you will help them satisfy their economic and social needs. That thought must guide you as you create your application.

Creating Your Application

To maximize your chances of success, you must create an application that satisfies the needs of the school to which you are applying. This does not mean that you create an application out of whole cloth, but it does mean that you organize and present your experiences in a way that depicts you in the most favorable light.

As you create your application, keep these two complementary points in mind:

- Quantitative factors such as GRE score, GPA, and class rank are important.
- Quantitative factors are not the whole story.

Creating an application for graduate schools requires the skill to shine light on the most favorable elements that factor into these complementary points.

On a graduate school application, questions will appear that seek to access information about your aptitudes and abilities that are not necessarily reflected in your GRE score or GPA. Some of the questions you will be asked need only short answers. For example:

- What was your employment history while in school?
- In what clubs or extracurricular activities did you participate?
- What honors or awards did you receive?

You do not have much room to maneuver here. However, you should try to communicate as much information as possible in your short answers. Stay focused on the question and don't digress. Communicate with clarity any information or ideas that would compel the graduate school to seriously consider your abilities. For example, compare the following pairs of descriptions and note how the latter description more clearly communicates achievements:

BEFORE	AFTER
• Member of College Orchestra	• Second Violinist of the College Orchestra
• Played Intra-Mural Volleyball	• Co-captain of the Phi Kappa Volleyball Team
• Member of the AD's CSL	• One of three members on the Associate Dean's Committee on Student Life
• Worked at Billy's Burger Barn	• Assistant Manager at Billy's Burger Barn (25 hours per week)

In addition to the short-answer questions, most applications invite you to complete a personal statement. Some applications ask for targeted information. For example:

- In a paragraph, explain to us why you want to go to graduate school.

Other applications are open-ended:

- On a separate sheet of paper, tell us anything else you think we ought to know about you.

The point of the question is for you to give the admissions committee any information that might not be available from your GRE score, GPA, and short-answer questions.

You should consider the personal statement to be the most important part of your application for two reasons. First, the personal statement should make up your argument to the admissions committee for your acceptance. It should give them good reasons to accept you. Second, the personal statement is the one aspect of the application over which you can exercise any real control. Your work experience is established, your GPA is already settled, and your GRE has been scored. These aspects of the application cannot easily be manipulated. The personal statement, however, is under your control.

What should go into a personal statement? You should include arguments that interpret your academic, employment, and personal history in such a way as to indicate that you have the ability to complete graduate school and that you are committed to studying and later to pursuing a graduate career. Most importantly, the information provided in a personal statement must not be a simple restatement of facts already in the application. Imagine, for example, a statement that reads as follows:

I went to State University where I received a 3.5 GPA. I was a member of the Associate Dean's Committee on Student Life, and I worked as the assistant manager on the night shift at Billy's Burger Barn. Then, I took the GRE and scored a 158. I know I will enjoy my future vocation.

This is not very interesting. Furthermore, all of that information is already included in the answers to the standard questions on the application. There is no point in simply repeating it.

Instead, you need to *interpret* the facts of your life to make them *reasons* for accepting you. For instance, if given an open-ended essay about your academic successes, you might start with your GPA. Try to bring out facts that suggest that the GPA is really better than it looks. Did you have one particularly challenging semester, during which you took physics, calculus, and Latin, that pulled your average down? Was there a death in the family or some other difficult time that interfered with your studies? How many hours did you work in an average week, and how did that influence your studies? What extracurricular or family commitments took time away from your studies? Did you follow an unusual course of study, such as an honors program or a double major? Was your college major particularly challenging? Did you participate in any unusual courses, such as field research?

These are the points that the admissions committee wants to hear. For example:

> *The committee will see that my final GPA is 3.5. I should point out that the average would have been higher had I not needed to work 20 hours each week to finance my education. Additionally, my grades in the first semester of my junior year were disappointing because my grandmother, who lived with my family and with whom I was very close, died. Finally, in order to fulfill the requirements for the honors program, I wrote a 50-page honors thesis on the Dutch fishing industry of the eighteenth century. I have included a copy of the introduction to my thesis with this application.*

You should take the same approach to your work experience. For example:

> *During my junior and senior years in college, I worked an average of 20 hours per week at Billy's Burger Barn as the manager on the night shift. I would report to work at midnight and get off at 4 a.m. As night manager, I supervised eight other employees and was responsible for making emergency repairs on kitchen equipment. For example, once I was able to keep the deep fryer in operation by using a length of telephone cable to repair a faulty thermostat. As the night manager, I was also responsible for maintaining order. It is not an easy job to convince intoxicated students who become too rowdy to leave without calling the police. Moreover, we were robbed at gunpoint, not once but twice.*

Of course, if you have considerable work experience, e.g., if you graduated from college several years ago, you will want to go into that experience in more detail than if you had only student work experience. When possible, use your work experience to highlight your most positive traits, such as ambition, innovativeness, creativity, thoroughness, integrity, communication, etc.

As you submit positive information about yourself, can you say anything about the GRE score? Probably not much—the GRE score is straightforward and not usually open to interpretation. However, there are some exceptions. One such exception is a history of poor scores on standardized exams. Consider the following:

> *I believe that my GRE score of 145 understates my real ability, for I have never had much success on aptitude tests. My SAT score was only 925. Yet, I finished college with a 3.6 GPA.*

> *The committee will see that I have two GRE scores: 144 and 160. During the first test, I had the flu and a fever and simply could not concentrate.*

These are the two most common excuses for a disappointing GRE score.

Finally, you must also persuade the admissions committee that you are serious about obtaining your graduate school degree. You must be able to show the committee something in your background that explains why you want to go to graduate school. In addition, it will help your case if you can suggest what you might do with a graduate school degree. For example:

> *As a chemistry major, I joined the Student Environmental Association. Working with private company executives, who had themselves satisfied E.P.A. admissions standards, we convinced the University to stop polluting the Ten-Mile Run Creek. From this experience, I learned how business helps to protect our environment. I plan to make environmental resources my area of study, and I hope to work for the government or a private agency to protect the environment.*

A word of warning is in order here. Your career objectives have to be believable. It is not sufficient to write, "I plan to solve the environmental problems of American industry." That is much too abstract. Nor are graduate school admissions officers interested in a general discourse on the advantages of democracy or the hardship of poverty. If you write, "I want to eliminate damage to the planet and to help private industries help themselves environmentally" then there had better be something in your experience that makes this believable.

Finally, with regard to motivation, do not imagine that there is a preferred political position that you should adopt. Graduate school admissions officers span the political spectrum. To be sure, some are political liberals, but some are conservatives. You do not have to write a "tear-jerker" essay in order to be accepted.

Thus far, we have discussed the issues of ability and motivation. You may also wish to include in your personal statement information that shows that you have something that will help the school create a diverse student body. This additional information can be something dramatic:

> *One morning, a patron choked on a burger and lost consciousness. I used the Heimlich maneuver to dislodge the food and performed CPR until a team of paramedics arrived. The patron recovered fully, in large part, according to her doctors, because of my first aid.*

Conversely, the information may not be dramatic:

> *My parents are Armenian immigrants, so I am fluent in Armenian as well as English. I would enjoy meeting others who share an interest in the politics, legal developments, and culture of that part of the world.*

Do not underestimate the value of this kind of information. It is, so to speak, the "icing on the cake." It makes you a more interesting individual and might tip the scale in your favor when all other things are equal. It will not, however, get you an acceptance at a school for which you are not otherwise competitive in terms of GRE and GPA.

Now, we turn our attention to matters of style. When you marshal your arguments for acceptance, you need to present them in an organized fashion. Your arguments should be well reasoned, your ideas logical, and your presentation grammatically and stylistically based on proper English composition. Avoid the use of slang or abbreviations that are common to email or text messaging communications.

The following is an example of an outline for an essay asking for additional information:

I. I have the ability to succeed in graduate school
    A. My college studies are good
        1. I had one bad semester
        2. I was in the honors program
        3. I wrote a thesis
    B. My work experience is good
        1. I worked while in college
        2. I was promoted to shift leader at my job
II. I want to earn my graduate degree
    A. I worked with PhD students on the pollution problem
    B. I would become a specialist in environmental chemistry
III. There is something interesting about me

The prose that you use should display your own natural style of writing. Do not write something that appears contrived. Admissions officers do not want to read essays that are written as manuscripts, with footnoted "documentary evidence." You should create your outline using as many arguments as possible. Then, you must begin to edit. For most people, the final document should not be more than a page to a page and a half in length— typed, of course! During the editing process, you should strive for an economy of language so that you can convey as much information as possible. Additionally, you will be forced to make considered judgments about the relative importance of various points. You will be forced to delete those ideas that are not really very compelling. In order to compose a really good essay, it may be necessary to reduce five or six pages to a single page, and the process may require more than 20 drafts. Proofread carefully, and seek feedback and editing assistance from qualified persons.

Letters of Recommendation

Perhaps the best advice that we can give you about so-called "letters of recommendation" is that you should think of them as evaluations rather than recommendations. Indeed, many admissions officers refer to letter-writers as evaluators. These letters can be very important factors in an application, so who should actually write them?

Most schools require or at least permit you to submit two or three letters of evaluation. (A handful of schools require a letter from the dean of students [or similar functionary] at your college. The requirement is in essence an inquiry to the school about your behavior.) When you are able to choose your evaluators, who should you ask? First, let us dispose of a common misunderstanding. A letter of evaluation does not have to come from a famous person. How effective is the following letter?

William Hardy, Chief Judge
Chairperson of the Board

To the Admissions Committee:

I am recommending Susan Roberts for graduate school. Her mother is a member of our board of directors. Susan's mother earned her doctorate at the University of Chicago and she regularly makes significant contributions to our corporate meetings. Susan, following her mother's example, will make a fine graduate school candidate.

Sincerely,
William Hardy

The letterhead holds great promise, but the body of the letter is worthless. It is obvious that William Hardy does not really have any basis for his conclusion that Susan Roberts "will make a fine graduate school candidate."

Find people who know you very well to write the very best letters of recommendation (e.g., a professor with whom you took several courses, your immediate supervisor at work, or a business associate with whom you have worked closely). A good evaluation will incorporate personal knowledge into the letter and will make references to specific events and activities. For example:

Mary P. Weiss
White, Weiss, and Blanche

To the Admissions Committee:

White, Weiss, and Blanche is a consulting firm that advises corporations on environmental concerns. Susan Roberts has worked for us for the past two summers. Her work is outstanding, and she is an intelligent and genial person.

Last summer, as my assistant, Susan wrote a 25-page report that outlined a way of altering a client's exhaust stack to reduce sulfur emissions. The report was organized so that it was easy to follow and written in a style that was clear and easy to understand. Additionally, Susan gave a live presentation during a meeting with the client's board of directors and engineers.

She was confident and handled some very difficult questions in an easy manner. I should note that we have used Susan's innovation in several other plants.

Finally, Susan made an important contribution to our company softball team. The team finished in last place, but Susan played in every game. Her batting average was not anything to brag about, but her enthusiasm more than made up for it.

Sincerely,
Mary Weiss

This letter demonstrates that the writer knows the applicant very well. The writer is able to address several aspects of the applicant's character, personality, and work ethic from a position of familiarity. A letter like this one makes for a very meaningful contribution to any graduate school application, so you should strive to receive this type of recommendation as part of your application portfolio.

SUCCEEDING IN GRADUATE SCHOOL

As a successful student, you have invested many years of your life climbing the winding stairway of the academic multi-storied tower. Each step upward elevated you toward a new level of opportunity to learn and develop advanced skills, further knowledge, and deeper analytical abilities. The fact that you have conquered the lower levels of academia and now are ascending to a level known as "graduate school" clearly suggests that you are bright, talented, and motivated.

But be aware that graduate school programs are qualitatively different than undergraduate programs. Faculty throws higher expectations on graduate students' efforts. Papers and exams are graded with a more critical eye. Universities, which often financially subsidize graduate programs and graduate students, anticipate higher levels of personal and professional achievements from graduate school students. And employers who hire students from various graduate school programs demand more knowledge and greater skill for the higher wages that those graduates desire and deserve.

Consider Life Beyond Graduation Right Now

To succeed in graduate school, you must well understand for what ultimate purpose you are attending graduate school. When you consider the following four statements, which one most describes your desire for a graduate program?

- After graduation, I want to immediately pursue a professional vocation in my field of study and will immediately search for employment in my field.
- After graduation, I want to continue with further educational opportunities in a doctoral or post-doctoral program of study in my academic area.
- After graduation, I want to continue my education in a different field (e.g., go on to law school, medical school, or another complementary research area).
- After graduation, I want to pursue an academic career in higher education (e.g., become a professor or work in higher education administration).

Each statement above requires you to take a slightly different approach to a graduate school program. Your end goal should directly influence the classes you take, the professors you seek as mentors, the research projects you request, the internships you approach, and even the other students with whom you network.

In a short statement, can you describe what you want for yourself immediately following your graduation from your graduate program? When you can do this, set up a meeting with your academic advisor or faculty mentor and together begin to plan how your graduate program can help you meet this goal.

Attend and Learn from Orientation

Graduate school orientations provide a wealth of vital information that will help you bridge from life as an undergraduate student to life as a graduate student.

Take note of the following items covered by most graduate school orientations:

- Securing assistantships and internships
- Meeting graduation requirements
- Finding technological resources
- Understanding academic policies and procedures
- Knowing your rights as a student
- Preparing for your thesis, dissertation, or research project
- Exploring the surrounding community
- Meeting key faculty, advisors, and administrators
- Finding housing and transportation
- Obtaining financial support or research funding
- Hearing "inside advice" from previous graduate students
- Paying tuition and fees
- Knowing about health insurance and other university benefits
- Understanding the university calendar, major deadlines, and schedules
- Gaining an overview of the campus layout, parking, and safety factors
- Getting to know other students

Some of this information is more personal in nature while some is more academic. But all of it is important for you to be successful. Invest your time and energy wisely by listening and learning well at your graduate school orientation sessions.

Network Above, Around, and Beyond

Graduate school provides you a unique opportunity to explore and research a particular academic area (e.g., physics, art history, accounting, sociology) at deeper levels. But successful graduate students know that it is not simply *what* they study that pays dividends, but also *with whom* they study. A key connection with the right person or persons can launch your academic or career path forward in untold ways.

Networking is the fine art of establishing and maintaining relationships with others who may provide valuable resources in the future. By building relationships with other people, you plant relational seeds that grow into a valuable harvest of future opportunities.

With whom should you network?

- **Professors**—Seek to find at least two or three professors in your program to serve as mentors to you. Networking with professors is essential since they typically provide a wealth of experience and knowledge both about the academic world (e.g., what class should you take next, how you can find an assistantship, what research will likely get published) and the professional world through their own network of alumni and friends. Ask for their advice on classes, research projects, internships, and career goals.
- **Professionals**—Often, graduate schools offer lectures or seminars presented by "outside" professionals in your particular area of study. Look to build relationships with "outside" presenters since they may serve as a great source for internship or future job contacts.
- **Other Students**—While most graduate students "socialize" with other students, spend time networking with other students in your program. A relationship with a student who graduates a year or two before you may prove a valuable contact later when you are looking for a job.
- **University Administrators**—Though this may be difficult, seek a solid relationship with those who can help you within the university, such as financial aid administrators or academic advisors. A friendly relationship with a "gatekeeper" (a secretary or administrative assistant) to a university administrator may help open the door when others find it shut.
- **Alumni**—Don't forget to build relationships with alumni. These individuals who financially support the university often want to help graduates obtain jobs and further educational opportunities.

How do you network?

- **Attend academic functions**—Go to departmental socials, workshops, or special lectures.
- **Go to conferences**—Attend annual meetings in your field where other faculty and students gather.
- **Never eat lunch alone**—Connect with professors and other students during meals.
- **Send thank you notes**—Show gratitude to those who have helped you.
- **Let people know you are interested**—Listen well and remember names.
- **Take the initiative**—Step out of your comfort zone and make the appointment to talk with a key contact in your area of study.
- **Ask for advice**—Professors and professionals often respond well to graduate students who are seeking genuine advice.
- **Use social media and technology**—connect with peers, professors, and professionals in your field of study through tools such as Facebook, LinkedIn, Twitter, etc.

Go to Seminars Prepared

The staple diet of many undergraduate programs is the lecture. Professors stand before classes and provide a monologue of information and analysis that students record in the form of notes and outlines. Class reading assignments often supplement or support the professor's lecture. Discussion is minimal. Students are assessed on how well they recall and reconstruct the information on tests or exams.

Many graduate students will experience classes where professors lecture using a one-way communication style. But graduate students will also most likely experience a variety of classes that utilize a graduate "seminar" approach. Seminars may vary in exact approach, but generally there is an expectation in a seminar class that students will fully participate in class dialogue both with the professors and other students. In some seminars, the professor may intensively question students on the nuances of assigned reading, arguments, or research findings. In others, students may read and then debate papers they themselves have written. In still others, students may be required to present and defend new research findings or methods. Whatever the particular style of the seminar, graduate students are expected to fully engage in the discussion, explain or debate merits of others' arguments, and present thoughtful questions and answers.

How do you succeed in a seminar class environment?

- Always go to class prepared, since there is little chance of faking your way through the intensity of these dialogues. Don't call attention to yourself if, for some reason, you have not adequately prepared (e.g., don't raise your hand).
- Anticipate what your professor will ask and discuss. Know what types of questions, research areas, or findings your professor typically utilizes.
- Form a study group with peers. Before going to class, ask questions of each other, debate critical material, and anticipate discussion areas. Preview with others the particular theme of the seminar.
- Stay sharp. Get rest the night before these types of classes, which require you to think on your feet.

Learn to Write Well for Your Field

For most programs, especially those that ultimately require a thesis, major final project, or dissertation, excellent writing skills are essential. Each program has a writing style and tone unique to it. Some styles are direct and factual. A few styles call for creativity. Many expect particular vocabulary. Successful students prepare to write well for their particular programs.

- Take a refresher course in writing prior to beginning your graduate program.
- Read the journals or articles written in your field. Learn the unique writing style for your field.
- Learn the accepted methods for citing references and for avoiding plagiarism.

- Get advice from professors if you think your writing is below standard.
- Brush up on your vocabulary. Memorize the words essential to your field.
- Find a tutor or proofreader for your papers who can give recommendations for more acceptable writing.

Read Critically

At the undergraduate level, professors assign reading often for the purposes of passing on foundational information. At the graduate level, it is expected that you already know the foundational content in your area and are now ready to critically assess the merits of an author's findings, arguments, or methodologies.

Here are some foundational questions to ask when reading critically:

Who is the author and with what biases does he or she write?

- What is the author's background and how does this influence his or her arguments or opinions (e.g., nationality, economic status, gender, education)?
- What are the author's credentials and does the author have a vested reason to argue his or her opinion (e.g., certifications, titles, degrees, positions held)?
- What are the author's direct or indirect biases and how do they appear in his or her opinions (e.g., strong likes, dislikes, prejudices)?
- What positive or negative experiences have flavored the author's point of view?

Why did the author write this?

- Is the author attempting to inform or persuade?
- What side of the issues did this author take? Are there other sides?
- What does the author ultimately want you to believe?
- Why is the author passionate about this issue?

Are the author's research findings and arguments valid?

- Are the research methods used by the author generally accepted in his or her field of research?
- Do the conclusions that he or she reached directly support his or her findings or arguments?
- Are there alternative conclusions that he or she could have reached given his or her findings?
- Are the arguments complete or do they lack logical consistency?

The skill of critical reading is necessary in graduate school. If you want to work on this skill, begin by reading broadly from academic journals, journal your thoughts as you deconstruct and reconstruct various authors' work, learn acceptable research methodologies, and review the basics of logical argumentation.

Time Management is Self-Management

Successful graduate learners maintain their forward momentum as students by managing to accomplish a multitude of tasks in an efficient and effective manner. To juggle the many responsibilities that fall to them, they learn that time management is really self-management and using the following steps to self-management:

- **Prioritize**—Always do the most important tasks for your success first.
- **Prime time**—Learn what time of day you enter your peak performance stage and do your most critical work then.
- **Push the non-essentials aside**—Learn to say "no" and mean it.

- **Piece together the puzzle**—Use those ten- to fifteen-minute "open" slots to accomplish smaller but necessary tasks (e.g., review notes, memorize important facts, proofread a paper).
- **Pull away**—Don't forget to find time to rest and relax. Stress is a factor that all graduate students must acknowledge and manage.

Conclusion

No graduate program guarantees that all students who enter their particular program will be successful. Instead, you as a beginning graduate student must take those important and critical steps to help yourself succeed. Be proactive. Take initiative. Be tenacious. Go succeed!

Appendix B:
Basic Skills Supplement

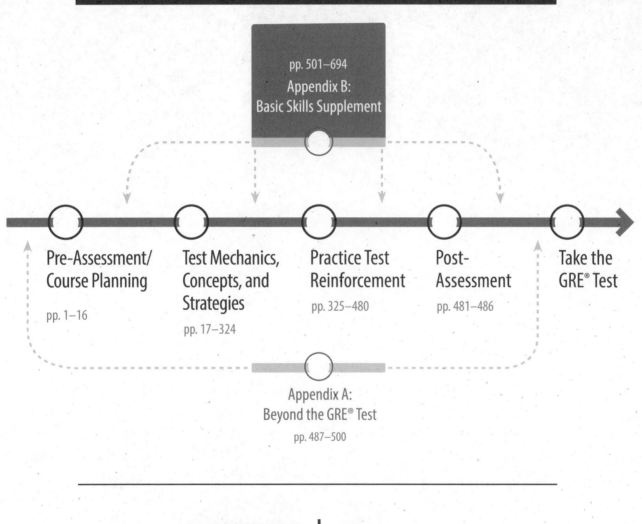

pp. 501–694
Appendix B:
Basic Skills Supplement

Pre-Assessment/
Course Planning

pp. 1–16

Test Mechanics,
Concepts, and
Strategies

pp. 17–324

Practice Test
Reinforcement

pp. 325–480

Post-
Assessment

pp. 481–486

Take the
GRE® Test

Appendix A:
Beyond the GRE® Test

pp. 487–500

Verbal Reasoning
Supplement

Outline

BUILDING VOCABULARY THROUGH CONTEXT

Unlike other vocabulary books that provide random lists of words and their definitions, this program builds vocabulary by helping you to learn the meaning of words in the context of short stories, essays, and other types of reading selections.

Students often believe that if they don't know what a word means, they won't be able to answer correctly an item that includes that word. This is simply not true. This section will help you to recognize word parts, become more familiar with challenging vocabulary words, and use context clues to determine what difficult words mean. This section will also help you to understand the logical structure of a sentence and how to use that understanding to anticipate appropriate words in vocabulary-related items.

The exercises in this section will enrich and build your vocabulary skills. You will work with vocabulary words in the context of a reading selection so you can actually learn them rather than simply memorize them.

Vocabulary in Context
Exercise 1

DIRECTIONS: The following is a vocabulary exercise. After reading the passage, choose the *best* answer to each item. Answer all items on the basis of what is suggested by adjacent material in the passage. Answers are on page 771.

Passage I

This passage is adapted from Edgar Allan Poe's "The Oval Portrait."

The portrait was that of a young girl. It was a mere head and shoulders, done in what is technically termed a vignette manner; much in the style of the favorite heads of Sully. The arms, the
5 bosom, and even the ends of the radiant hair, melted imperceptibly into the vague yet deep shadow, which formed the background of the whole. The metallic yellow frame was a valuable oval, richly gilded and filigreed in exquisitely fine detail.
10 As a thing of art nothing could be more admirable than the painting itself. But it could have been neither the execution of the work nor the immortal beauty of the countenance, which had so suddenly and so vehemently moved me. Least of all could it
15 have been that my fancy, shaken from its half slumber, had mistaken the head for that of a living person. I saw at once that the peculiarities of the design, of the vignetting, and of the frame, must have instantly dispelled such ideas—must have
20 prevented even its momentary entertainment. Thinking earnestly upon these points, I remained, for an hour perhaps, half sitting, half reclining, with my vision riveted upon the portrait. At length, satisfied with the true secret of its effect, I fell back
25 within the bed. I had found the spell of the picture in an absolute *life-likeness* of expression, which at first startling, finally confounded, subdued, and appalled me. With deep and reverent awe, I replaced the candelabrum in its former position. The cause of my
30 deep agitation being thus shut from view, I sought eagerly the volume which discussed the paintings and their histories. Turning to the number which designated the oval portrait, I there read the vague and quaint words which follow:
35 "She was a maiden of rarest beauty, and not more lovely than full of glee. And evil was the hour when she saw, and loved, and wedded the painter. He, passionate, studious, austere, and having already a bride in his Art; she all light and smiles
40 and frolicsome as the young fawn; loving and cherishing all things: hating only the Art which was her rival; dreading only the palette and brushes and other untoward instruments which deprived her of the countenance of her lover. It was thus a terrible
45 thing for this lady to hear the painter speak of his desire to portray even his young bride. But she was humble and obedient, and sat meekly for many weeks in the dark high turret-chamber where the light dripped upon the pale canvas only from
50 overhead. But he, the painter, took glory in his work, which went on from hour to hour from day to day. And he was a passionate and moody man, who became lost in reveries; so that he *would* not see that the light which fell so ghastly in that lone turret
55 withered the health and the spirits of his bride, who pined visibly to all but him. Yet she smiled on and still on, uncomplainingly, because she saw that the painter (who had great renown) took a fervid and burning pleasure in his task, and wrought day and
60 night to depict her who so loved him, yet who grew daily more dispirited and weak. And in sooth some who beheld the portrait spoke of its resemblance in low words, as of a mighty marvel, and a proof not less of the power of the painter than of his deep love
65 for her, whom he depicted so surpassingly well. But at length, as the labor drew nearer to its conclusion, there were admitted none into the turret; for the painter had grown wild with the ardor of his work, and turned his eyes from the canvas rarely, even to
70 regard the countenance of his wife. And he would not see that the tints which he spread on the canvas were drawn from the cheeks of her who sat beside him. And when many weeks had passed, but little remained to do, save one brush upon the mouth and
75 one tint upon the eye, the spirit of the lady again flickered up as the flame within the socket of the lamp. And then the brush was given, and the tint was placed; and for one moment, the painter stood entranced before the work which he had wrought
80 but in the next, while he yet gazed, he grew tremulous and very pallid, and aghast, and crying with a loud voice, 'this is indeed *Life* itself!' turned suddenly to regard his beloved—*She was dead!*"

1. The physical differences between the fraternal twins were so _____ that only their family members were able to tell them apart.

   (A) apparent
   (B) invisible
   (C) detectable
   (D) imperceptible
   (E) noticeable

2. Many Republicans are _____ opposed to fighting climate change with legislation, charging that the Democrats' current bill would drastically raise costs for the average American family.

   (A) impassively
   (B) sarcastically
   (C) vehemently
   (D) ironically
   (E) humbly

3. To help control the rapidly increasing national debt, the Finance Minister recently announced a very _____ set of economic measures that drastically cut government services.

   (A) mysterious
   (B) lackadaisical
   (C) lenient
   (D) inept
   (E) austere

4. The critic wrote in her review of the ballet that the _____ and conviction with which the dancers performed excused any minor imperfections in the overall performance.

   (A) doubt
   (B) ardor
   (C) flawlessness
   (D) indifference
   (E) deliberation

5. When the animal control officer cornered the stray dog in an attempt to catch it, the dog bristled and whined in a low _____ tone.

   (A) tremulous
   (B) confident
   (C) unexpected
   (D) erratic
   (E) passive

6. It can be inferred that the word "vignette," as it is used in line 3, primarily refers to

   (A) a brief incident or scene
   (B) a particular style of brushstroke
   (C) a short musical composition
   (D) a picture with no definite border, shading off gradually at its edges

7. In line 9, "gilded" is best understood to mean

   (A) sponsored
   (B) overlaid with gold
   (C) entangled
   (D) overfilled

8. In line 9, "filigreed" is best understood to mean

   (A) excessive greed or avarice
   (B) characterized by lack of taste
   (C) adorned with delicate ornamentation
   (D) to be unfounded

9. As it is used in line 13, the word "countenance" most nearly means

   (A) facial features
   (B) approval
   (C) pretense
   (D) motif

10. In context, "designated" (line 33) most nearly means

   (A) delegated
   (B) indicated
   (C) appointed
   (D) delivered

11. In line 43, "untoward" most nearly means

   (A) appropriate
   (B) disorderly
   (C) fortunate
   (D) troublesome

12. It can be inferred that the word "reveries," as it is used in line 53, primarily refers to

   (A) indifferences
   (B) daydreams
   (C) certainties
   (D) reverences

13. As it is used in line 56, the word "pined" most nearly means

   (A) longed for
   (B) increased
   (C) wasted away
   (D) imagined

14. In line 58, "renown" is best understood to mean

   (A) fame
   (B) aptitude
   (C) obscurity
   (D) perseverance

15. As it is used in line 59, the word "wrought" most nearly means

   (A) hammered
   (B) wreaked havoc
   (C) worked with great care
   (D) operated carelessly

Passage II

This passage is adapted from a chapter in an agricultural science textbook exploring modern agricultural problems.

Rapid increases in human population have steadily intensified pressures to augment the productivity of existing grazing and agricultural land.

5 Grazing land in the Indian subcontinent and isolated islands in the Philippines have a relatively low carrying capacity and are currently capable of sustaining only marginal levels of subsistence. Over-exploitation has not only decreased their
10 productivity but is continuously destroying the fertility and stability of affected soils. The problem is particularly injurious in areas of Pakistan and Northeast India, where over-grazing is resulting in desertification. In the Luni blocks of Rajasthan, most
15 pastures now have only 10 to 15 percent of their original carrying capacity and the forage deficit is met by expansion into standing vegetation. Within a twenty-year period, infecund sand cover has increased from 25 to 33 percent of the area.
20 In most Asian countries, rice is the principal food crop. Increased cultivation has barely met the demands of the growing populations. In the Philippines, while food production has increased slightly faster than the size of the population, even
25 greater increases in per capita food demand have created new shortfalls. Indonesia, once an important rice exporter, has been dependent on imported rice for several years. Most countries are merely keeping up with their current needs, and
30 gross shortages can be anticipated.

The intensified agricultural production required in these countries has potential adverse side effects on other resources. The disruptive effects of the large-scale reservoirs needed for
35 irrigation of more land are self-evident. Some other problems include waterlogging and salinity, soil erosion, increased populations of pests, and agricultural pollution.

Waterlogging and salinity can be a problem
40 wherever surface water is applied to irrigated land with inadequate underground drainage. Water will rise to within a few feet of the surface, vitiating the growth of deep-rooted crops and allowing a concentration of minerals and salt to build up near
45 the surface. This has been seen in China, India, and Pakistan. Control projects involving the construction of new wells and drainage systems have been successful in reversing some of the deleterious effects, but at prodigious costs.
50 The establishment of broad area monoculture, primarily irrigated riceland, can result in difficult

pest management problems. Recently, Indonesia
has had some destructive and noisome pest
outbreaks that have reduced rice yields up to 60
55 percent in the last two years. Double-cropping does
not allow dry-season pest population enervation,
and their numbers are therefore maintained. An
integrated pest management program is needed to
realize increased productivity. This program must
60 be done assiduously, not on an intermittent
schedule.

    Soil erosion is occurring in hilly and
mountainous areas, which often constitute the only
remaining land available for cultivation. With the
65 monsoon rains, erosion is inevitable unless there is
an extensive terracing system. The rivers of Nepal
annually carry over 240 million cubic meters of soil
to India. This deprivation has been called Nepal's
"most dear export."

16. In the nineteenth century, expanding
European-American settlement of the United
States forced large numbers of Native
Americans onto _____ lands.

  (A) valuable
  (B) sustentative
  (C) precarious
  (D) central
  (E) marginal

17. Michael Pollan argues in "The Botany of
Desire" that while _____ may offer economic
advantages, it invites serious environmental
risks because a field of identical plants will
always be vulnerable to all the forces of
nature.

  (A) agriculture
  (B) monoculture
  (C) nomenclature
  (D) polyculture
  (E) permaculture

18. The neighbors of the confined animal feeding
operation complained about the _____ odors
and groundwater pollution.

  (A) harmless
  (B) noisome
  (C) helpful
  (D) noisy
  (E) benign

19. Donna tended her garden _____, taking care
to weed every other day and to fertilize with
every watering.

  (A) inconsistently
  (B) strenuously
  (C) assiduously
  (D) irreverently
  (E) respectfully

20. Although a ceasefire had been signed, _____
and sporadic gunfire disturbed the silence of
the desert night.

  (A) constant
  (B) incipient
  (C) contented
  (D) intermittent
  (E) deliberate

21. It can be inferred that the word "augment," as
it is used in line 2, means to

  (A) decrease
  (B) increase
  (C) remain constant
  (D) cease

22. In line 8, "subsistence" most nearly means

  (A) extinction
  (B) productivity
  (C) wastefulness
  (D) survival

23. It can be inferred that the word "desertification" (line 14) refers to the process by which

(A) land becomes wet and humid
(B) land becomes dry and arid
(C) air becomes wet and humid
(D) air becomes dry and arid

24. As it is used in line 18, the word "infecund" most nearly means

(A) offensive smelling
(B) infectious
(C) unproductive
(D) fertile

25. In line 32, "adverse" is best understood to mean

(A) unfavorable
(B) constructive
(C) poisonous
(D) beneficial

26. The word "salinity" (line 36) most nearly means

(A) sourness
(B) sweetness
(C) saltiness
(D) bitterness

27. As it is used in line 42, the word "vitiating" most nearly means

(A) assisting or helping
(B) energizing or strengthening
(C) depriving of oxygen
(D) making faulty or defective

28. It can be inferred that the word "deleterious," as it is used in line 49, most nearly means

(A) delicious
(B) harmless
(C) involuntary
(D) destructive

29. In line 49, "prodigious" most nearly means

(A) enormous
(B) marginal
(C) average
(D) luxuriant

30. The word "enervation" (line 56) refers to

(A) weakening
(B) strengthening
(C) extinction
(D) animation

Passage III

This passage is adapted from an essay about La Gioconda, *the painting by Leonardo da Vinci more commonly known as the* Mona Lisa. *The actual person in the painting may have been Lisa, the third wife of Francesco del Giocondo.*

La Gioconda is, in the truest sense, Leonardo's masterpiece; the revealing paradigm of his mode of thought and work. We all know the face and hands of the figure, set in its marble chair, in that circle of
5 fantastic rocks, as in some faint light under the sea. Perhaps of all ancient pictures, time has chilled it least.

As often happens with works in which genius seems to surpass its limit, there is an element in it
10 transmitted by, but not invented by, the master. In that inestimable folio of drawings, once in the possession of Vasari, were certain designs by Verrocchio, faces of such impressive beauty that Leonardo, in his boyhood, copied them many times.
15 It is difficult not to see these designs of the elder master as the germinal principle of that unfathomable smile, with its touch of something sinister, which infects all Leonardo's work.

Besides, the picture is a portrait. From
20 childhood, we see this image defining itself on the fabric of his dreams, and were it not for explicit historical testimony, we might fancy this was his ideal lady, embodied and beheld at last.

What was the relationship of a living
25 Florentine to the creature of his thought? By what strange affinities had the dream and the person grown up so apart, and yet so close? Present from the first incorporeal ideas in Leonardo's brain,

dimly traced in the designs of Verrocchio, she is
30 found present at last in del Giocondo's house.

To be sure, it is a portrait, a painting, and
legend has it that mimes and musicians were used
to protract that smile. Was it in four months or as by
a stroke of magic the image was projected?

35   The presence that rises so strangely beside the
waters is expressive of what after a thousand years
men had come to desire. Hers is the head upon all
"the ends of the world are come," and the eyelids
are a little weary. It is a beauty brought out from
40 within and deposited upon the flesh, bit by bit, cell
by cell—strange thoughts and fantastic reveries and
exquisite passions. Set it for a moment beside one of
those Greek statues of beautiful women of antiquity.
How they would be troubled by this beauty, into
45 which the soul with all of its maladies had been
passed! All the thoughts and experience of the
world are etched and molded there: the animalism
of Greece, the lust of Rome, the mysticism of the
Middle Ages with its spiritual ambition and
50 imaginative loves, the return of the pagan world, the
sins of the Borgias.

She is older than the rocks among which she
sits. Like the vampire, she has been dead many
times, and learned the secrets of the grave; and has
55 submerged herself in deep seas and kept their fallen
day about her; and trafficked for some strange webs
with Easter merchants and as Leda, the mother of
Helen of Troy, and as Saint Anne, the mother of
Mary. All of this has been to her but as the sound of
60 lyres and flutes, and lives only in the delicacy with
which it has molded the changing lineaments and
tinged the eyelids and the hands.

31. The established and successful member-
owned cooperative served as a(n) _____ for
the small, locally-owned food markets that
have recently sprung up in the region.

(A) benefit
(B) substitution
(C) paradigm
(D) affliction
(E) anomaly

32. There is such a strong _____ between new
cars made by rival automakers today that the
casual observer cannot tell them apart.

(A) dissimilarity
(B) competition
(C) deterioration
(D) affinity
(E) variation

33. The notion that there is a(n) _____ realm of
existence that is distinct from the material
universe is fundamental to the belief in a
divine being.

(A) physical
(B) logistical
(C) imaginary
(D) substitute
(E) incorporeal

34. In order to _____ the telephone call long
enough to put a trace on it, the detective kept
the caller engaged in seemingly pointless
conversation.

(A) distract
(B) mitigate
(C) protract
(D) contract
(E) interrupt

35. Katya's memory of the moment was _____
with sorrow; while her voice was firm, it was
obviously touched with grief.

(A) confused
(B) tipped
(C) prolonged
(D) tinged
(E) arranged

36. In line 2, "masterpiece" most nearly refers to
an artist's

(A) most important work
(B) beginning stages of a piece
(C) posthumously published work
(D) rehearsal or practice pieces

37. As it is used in line 2, the word "mode" most nearly refers to a(n)

(A) sound
(B) feeling
(C) asset
(D) method

38. In line 11, "folio" is best understood to refer to a(n)

(A) duplicate
(B) burial
(C) booklet
(D) painting

39. It can be inferred that the word "germinal," as it is used in line 16, refers to the

(A) overriding themes
(B) early stages
(C) destructive elements
(D) tutorial process

40. The word "explicit" (line 21) most nearly means

(A) clearly expressed
(B) involved or entwined
(C) embedded or contained
(D) brought out

41. In line 42, "exquisite" most nearly means characterized by

(A) an even temperament
(B) expensive taste
(C) mind-numbing detail
(D) intense emotions

42. It can be inferred that the word "antiquity," as it is used in line 43, most nearly means

(A) modern culture
(B) ancient times
(C) the future
(D) prehistory

43. In line 45, "maladies" is best understood to refer to

(A) dreams
(B) sicknesses
(C) painful emotions
(D) memories

44. In line 48, "mysticism" refers to

(A) the historical record
(B) exciting curiosities
(C) the beliefs of mystics
(D) a political system

45. It can be inferred that the word "lineaments," as it is used in line 61, refers to

(A) skin ointments
(B) descendants from a common ancestor
(C) facial features
(D) ground plans

Vocabulary Completions
Exercise 2

DIRECTIONS: For items #1–12, select an appropriate completion for each blank in the following paragraph from the corresponding numbered lists provided. Answers are on page 771.

Today, the Surgeon General announced the findings of a new **(1)**_____ that concludes that smoking represents a serious **(2)**_____ to non-smokers as well as to **(3)**_____. According to the Surgeon General, disease risk due to **(4)**_____ of tobacco smoke is not limited to the **(5)**_____ who is smoking, but it can also extend to those who **(6)**_____ tobacco smoke in the same room. Simple **(7)**_____ of smokers and non-smokers within the same airspace may reduce, but does not **(8)**_____, exposure of non-smokers to environmental smoke. A spokesperson for the tobacco industry **(9)**_____ the report, saying the available **(10)**_____ does not support the conclusion that environmental tobacco smoke is a hazard to non-smokers. On the other hand, the Coalition on Smoking OR Health, an anti-smoking organization, **(11)**_____ the report and called for **(12)**_____ government action to ensure a smoke-free environment for all non-smokers.

1. (A) movie
   (B) election
   (C) report
   (D) advertisement
   (E) plan

2. (A) consciousness
   (B) hazard
   (C) remedy
   (D) possibility
   (E) treatment

3. (A) cigarettes
   (B) fumes
   (C) alcoholics
   (D) pipes
   (E) smokers

4. (A) observation
   (B) criticism
   (C) improvement
   (D) inhalation
   (E) cessation

5. (A) individual
   (B) doctor
   (C) campaign
   (D) reporter
   (E) objector

6. (A) create
   (B) breathe
   (C) enjoy
   (D) ban
   (E) control

7. (A) encouragement
   (B) prohibition
   (C) separation
   (D) intermingling
   (E) prosecution

8. (A) imagine
   (B) increase
   (C) prepare
   (D) eliminate
   (E) satisfy

9. (A) purchased
   (B) prepared
   (C) understood
   (D) criticized
   (E) worshipped

10. (A) alibi
    (B) publicity
    (C) evidence
    (D) reaction
    (E) resources

11. (A) praised
    (B) rejected
    (C) prolonged
    (D) denied
    (E) proclaimed

12. (A) minimal
    (B) immediate
    (C) reactionary
    (D) uncontrolled
    (E) theoretical

DIRECTIONS: For items #13–22, write down a few *possible* words that you anticipate could be used to fill in the blank and complete the sentence. Possible answers are on page 771.

13. Stress is the reaction an individual feels when he believes the demands of a situation _____ his ability to meet them.

   _____
   _____
   _____

14. The _____ of his career, capturing the coveted "Most Valuable Player" award, came at a time of deep personal sadness.

   _____
   _____
   _____

15. Martin's opponent is a(n) _____ speaker who is unable to elicit a reaction from a crowd on even the most emotional of issues.

   _____
   _____
   _____

16. The cold weather caused _____ damage to the Florida citrus crop, prompting growers to warn that the reduced yield is likely to result in much higher prices.

   _____
   _____
   _____

17. The report is so _____ that it covers all of the main points in detail and at least touches on everything that is even remotely connected with its topic.

   _____
   _____
   _____

18. The Constitution sets up a system of checks and balances among the executive, the legislative, and the judicial branches to ensure that no one branch can establish _____ control over the government.

   _____
   _____
   _____

19. The females of many common species of birds have dull coloring that _____ them when they are sitting on a nest in a tree or other foliage.

   _____
   _____
   _____

20. She was one of the most _____ criminals of the 1930s, her name a household word and her face in every post office.

   _____
   _____
   _____

21. Although he had not been physically injured by the explosion, the violence of the shock left him temporarily _____.

   _____
   _____
   _____

22. Good teachers know that study habits learned as a youngster stay with a student for life, so they try to find ways to _____ enthusiasm for studies.

   _____
   _____
   _____

DIRECTIONS: For items #23–32, underline a few words or phrases that provide clues for the completion of the sentences. Then, write down a few *possible* words that you anticipate could be used to fill in the blanks and complete the sentences. Possible answers are on page 772.

23. The survivors had been drifting for days in the lifeboat, and in their weakness, they appeared to be _____ rather than living beings.

_____

_____

_____

24. The guillotine was introduced during the French Revolution as a reformatory measure, an alternative to other _____ means of execution.

_____

_____

_____

25. Because of the _____ nature of the chemical, it cannot be used near an open flame.

_____

_____

_____

26. The Mayor's proposal for a new subway line, although a(n) _____, is not a final solution to the city's transportation needs.

_____

_____

_____

27. In a pluralistic society, policies are the result of compromise, so political leaders must be _____ and must accommodate the views of others.

_____

_____

_____

28. The committee report vigorously expounded the bill's strengths but also acknowledged its _____.

_____

_____

_____

29. Because there is always the danger of a power failure and disruption of elevator service, high-rise buildings, while suitable for younger persons, are not recommended for _____.

_____

_____

_____

30. For a child to be happy, his day must be very structured; when his routine is _____, he becomes nervous and irritable.

_____

_____

_____

31. The current spirit of _____ among different religions has led to a number of meetings that their leaders hope will lead to better understanding.

_____

_____

_____

32. Our modern industrialized societies have been responsible for the greatest destruction of nature and life; indeed, it seems that more civilization results in greater _____.

_____

_____

_____

Vocabulary List

Review the following vocabulary list to familiarize yourself with the meanings of words of varied difficulty.

Difficulty *Level 1*

abacus—a frame with beads or balls used for doing or teaching arithmetic

abash—disconcert; to make embarrassed and ill at ease

abate—to deduct; to make less

abduction—to carry off by force

aberration—a deviation from the normal or the typical

abhor—detest; to shrink from in disgust or hatred

abhorrence—loathing; detestation

abide—to stay; stand fast; remain

abominate—loathe; to dislike very much

abrade—to scrape or rub off

abridge—shorten; to reduce in scope or extent

abrogate—cancel; call off

abscond—to go away hastily and secretly

absolve—acquit; to pronounce free from guilt or blame

abstinence—the act of voluntarily doing without pleasures

absurdity—nonsense

abut—adjoin, touch

abysmal—awful or dreadful

abyss—chasm; a deep fissure in the earth; bottomless gulf

acclaim—to greet with loud applause or approval

accretion—growth in size by addition or accumulation

acerbic—sharp, bitter, or harsh in temper and language

acquisition—something or someone acquired or added

acrimony—asperity; bitterness or harshness of temper, manner, or speech

acute—shrewd; keen or quick of mind

adapt—adjust; to make fit or suitable by changing

adjunct—connected or attached in a secondary or subordinate way

adorn—ornament; to put decorations on something

adroit—expert; clever; skillful in a physical or mental way

adulterate—not genuine; to make inferior or impure

adversary—opponent; a person who opposes or fights against another

advocate—a person who pleads another's cause

aesthete—a person who artificially cultivates artistic sensitivity or makes a cult of art and beauty

aesthetic—artistic; sensitive to art and beauty

affable—gentle and kindly

affinity—connection; close relationship

afflict—to cause pain or suffering to; distress very much

affluent—plentiful; abundant; flowing freely

aggrandize—to make seem greater

alias—assumed name

allegiance—loyalty or devotion

alleviate—to reduce or decrease; lighten or relieve

allocate—allot; to distribute in shares or according to a plan

alloy—the relative purity of gold or silver; fineness

allude—to refer in a casual or indirect way

altercation—an angry or heated argument

ambiguous—not clear; having two or more possible meanings

ambivalence—simultaneously conflicting feelings toward a person or thing

amble—to go easily and unhurriedly

amenable—willing to follow advice or suggestion; answerable

amiable—good-natured; having a pleasant and friendly disposition

amicable—peaceable; showing good will

amphibious—can live both on land and in water

anachronism—someone or something incorrectly listed outside of its correct time period

anagram—a word or phrase made from another by rearranging its letters

analogy—partial resemblance; similarity in some respects between things otherwise unlike

anarchy—the complete absence of government

anecdote—a short, entertaining account of some happening

animosity—hostility; a feeling of strong dislike or hatred

annexation—attachment; adding on

anomalous—abnormal; deviating from the regular arrangement, general rule, or usual method

anthology—a collection of poems, stories, songs, or excerpts

antidote—a remedy to counteract a poison

antigen—a protein, toxin, or other substance to which the body reacts by producing antibodies

antipathy—strong or deep-rooted dislike

anvil—an iron or steel block on which metal objects are hammered into shape

apathetic—feeling little or no emotion; unmoved

appease—to satisfy or relieve

appraise—to set a price for; decide the value of

apprehension—an anxious feeling of foreboding; dread

apprentice—novice; any learner or beginner

arbitrary—unreasonable; unregulated; despotic

arbitrate—to decide a dispute

arboreal—of or like a tree

arcane—hidden or secret

ardor—passion; emotional warmth

arduous—difficult to do; laborious; onerous

arid—dry and barren; lacking enough water for things to grow

aromatic—smelling sweet or spicy; fragrant or pungent

arouse—to awaken, as from sleep

arrhythmic—disruption or disturbance in rhythm

articulate—expressing oneself easily and clearly

artisan—craftsman; a worker in a skilled trade

ascertain—to learn indefinitely, to make clear

aspiration—strong desire or ambition

assail—assault; to attack physically and violently

assay—an examination or testing

assert—to state positively; declare; affirm

assimilate—to absorb and incorporate into one's thinking

astound—amaze; to bewilder with sudden surprise

astute—cunning; having or showing a clever or shrewd mind

atrocity—brutality; a very displeasing or tasteless thing

auditor—a hearer or listener

augment—enlarge; to make greater, as in size, quantity, or strength

auspicious—successful; favored by fortune

austere—forbidding; having a severe or stern look or manner

avid—eager and enthusiastic

avow—to declare openly or admit frankly

ballad—a romantic or sentimental song

banal—commonplace; dull or stale because of overuse

bane—ruin; death; deadly harm

barrage—a heavy, prolonged attack of words or blows

barren—empty; devoid

barrio—in Spanish-speaking countries, a district or suburb of a city

bask—to warm oneself pleasantly, as in the sunlight

baste—to sew with long, loose stitches

beacon—any light for warning or guiding

bedazzle—to dazzle thoroughly

belated—tardy; late or too late

belligerent—at war; showing a readiness to fight or quarrel

beneficent—doing good

benevolence—a kindly, charitable act or gift

benign—good-natured; kindly

bequeath—to hand down; pass on

berate—to scold or rebuke severely

bewilder—puzzle; to confuse hopelessly

bias—a mental leaning or inclination; partiality; bent

bilge—the bulge of a barrel or cask

bilk—to cheat or swindle; defraud

blandishment—a flattering act or remark meant to persuade

blatant—disagreeably loud or boisterous

blithe—carefree; showing a gay, cheerful disposition

boisterous—rowdy; noisy and unruly

bolster—a long, narrow cushion or pillow; to support

boon—blessing; welcome benefit

boor—a rude, awkward, or ill-mannered person

bourgeois—a person whose beliefs, attitudes, and practices are conventionally middle-class

boycott—refusal to use, buy, or support; used as a means of coercion

brazen—like brass in color, quality, or hardness; impudent

breach—a breaking or being broken

breadth—width; lack of narrowness

brevity—the quality of being brief

buttress—a projecting structure built against a wall to support or reinforce it

cadet—a student at a military school; younger son or brother

cadge—to beg or get by begging

cajole—to coax with flattery and insincere talk

calk—a part of a horseshoe that projects downward to prevent slipping

callous—unfeeling; lacking pity or mercy

camaraderie—loyal, warm, and friendly feeling among comrades

candid—honest or frank

caprice—whim; a sudden, impulsive change

capricious—erratic; flighty; tending to change abruptly

caption—a heading or title, as of an article

carping—tending to find fault

cartographer—a person whose work is making maps or charts

castigate—to punish or rebuke severely

cataclysm—a violent upheaval, or violent physical event

catalyst—a person or thing acting as the stimulus in bringing about or hastening a result

catapult—a slingshot or type of launcher

catastrophe—any great and sudden disaster or misfortune

caustic—corrosive; that which can destroy tissue by chemical action

cavern—a cave

cerebral—intellectual; appealing to the intellect rather than the emotions

charlatan—a person who pretends to have expert knowledge or skill

chassis—framework and working parts of an automobile

chasten—to punish; to refine; to make purer in style

chide—to scold

chivalrous—gallant; courteous; honorable

circuitous—roundabout; indirect; devious

circumspect—cautious; careful

circumvent—entrap; to surround or encircle with evils

citizenry—all citizens as a group

clairvoyant—having the power to perceive that which is outside of the human senses

clamor—a loud outcry; uproar

clamorous—noisy; loudly demanding or complaining

clandestine—kept secret or hidden

cleave—split; to divide by a blow

cliché—an expression or idea that has become trite

coalesce—to grow together; to unite or merge

coddle—to treat tenderly

coerce—enforce; to bring about by using force

cognizance—perception or knowledge

cognizant—aware or informed

coherent—clearly articulated; capable of logical, intelligible speech and thought

colloquial—conversational; having to do with or like conversation

combustion—the act or process of burning

commend—praise; to express approval of

commensurate—proportionate; corresponding in extent or degree

commingle—intermix; blend; to mingle together

commodity—anything bought and sold

communicable—that which can be communicated

compassion—deep sympathy; sorrow for the sufferings of others

compatible—that which can work well together, get along well together, combine well

compelling—captivating; irresistibly interesting

competent—well qualified; capable; fit

complacency—quiet satisfaction; contentment

complacent—self-satisfied; smug

complaisant—willing to please; obliging

compliance—a tendency to give in readily to others

compliant—yielding; submissive

comprehensive—able to understand fully

comprise—to include; contain

compulsion—that which compels; driving force

computation—calculation; a method of computing

concession—an act or instance of granting or yielding

conciliatory—tending to reconcile

concise—brief and to the point; short and clear

concoct—devise; invent; plan

condemn—censure; disapprove of strongly

condescension—a patronizing manner or behavior

condolence—expression of sympathy with another in grief

condone—forgive; pardon; overlook

conduit—a channel conveying fluids; a tube or protected trough for electric wires

confiscate—to seize by authority

conformity—action in accordance with customs, rules, and prevailing opinion

congeal—to solidify, harden, or set

congregation—a gathering of people or things

congruent—in agreement; corresponding; harmonious

conjoin—to join together; unite; combine

conjunction—a joining together or being joined together

consensus—an opinion held by all or most

conspire—to plan and act together secretly

constituent—component; a necessary part or element

consummate—supreme; complete or perfect in every way

contemn—scorn; to view with contempt

contemporaneous—existing or happening in the same period of time

contemptuous—scornful; disdainful

contentious—always ready to argue; quarrelsome

contentment—the state of being satisfied

context—the whole situation, background, or environment relevant to a particular event, personality, creation, etc.

contrite—penitent; repentant; feeling sorry for sins

conventional—customary; of, sanctioned by, or growing out of custom or usage

conversion—a change from one belief, religion, doctrine, opinion, etc. to another

convey—to make known

conviction—a strong belief

convoluted—extremely involved; intricate; complicated

copious—very plentiful; abundant

coronation—act or ceremony of crowning a sovereign

corpuscle—a very small particle

corroborate—confirm; to make more certain the validity of

countenance—facial expression; composure

coup—a sudden, successful move or action

covert—concealed; hidden; disguised

covet—to want ardently; long for with envy

crass—tasteless; insensitive; coarse

craven—very cowardly; abjectly afraid

credence—belief, especially in the reports or testimony of another

credulity—a tendency to believe too readily

crescendo—any gradual increase in force, intensity

criterion—a standard on which judgment can be based

critique—a critical analysis or evaluation

cryptic—mysterious; having a hidden or ambiguous meaning

culmination—climax; the highest point

cultivate—to promote development or growth

cumulative—accumulated; increasing in effect, size, quantity, etc.

cunning—skillful or clever

curator—a person in charge of a museum, library, etc.

cynical—sarcastic; sneering

daunt—intimidate; to make afraid or discouraged

dawdler—a slacker or lazy person

debacle—an overwhelming defeat

debase—cheapen; to make lower in value, quality, character, or dignity

debilitate—to make weak or feeble

decelerate—to reduce speed; slow down

decipher—decode; to make out the meaning of

decisive—showing determination or firmness

decry—denounce; to speak out against strongly and openly

defer—yield; delay

deference—courteous regard or respect

defiance—open, bold resistance to authority or opposition

defiant—openly and boldly resisting

defunct—no longer living or existing; dead or extinct

defuse—to render harmless

degenerate—having sunk below a former or normal condition

delegate—to send from one place to another; appoint; assign

delineate—describe; to depict in words

delirium—uncontrollably wild excitement or emotion

demise—a ceasing to exist; death

demure—affectedly modest or shy; coy

denounce—to condemn strongly

destitute—living in complete poverty

detonate—to explode violently and noisily

devastate—to make helpless; overwhelm

devious—not straightforward or frank

diction—manner of expression in words

diffuse—to disperse or spread

diminutive—very small; tiny

din—loud confusing noise

disabuse—to rid of false ideas or misconceptions

discern—make out clearly

disconcert—embarrass; confuse

discord—disagreement; conflict

discordant—disagreeing; conflicting

discourteous—impolite; rude; ill-mannered

discrepancy—difference; inconsistency

disparage—show disrespect for; belittle

disparate—basically different; unrelated

dissident—not agreeing

dissonant—lacking in harmony; discordant

distillate—the essence; purified form

distraught—extremely troubled

divergence—separating; branching off

divergent—deviating; different

diverse—different; dissimilar

diversion—distraction of attention

divination—the art of foretelling future events; clever conjecture

divulge—to disclose or unveil

dogma—a doctrine; tenet; belief

dogmatic—adhering to a tenet

dolt—a stupid, slow-witted person; blockhead

dormant—as if asleep; quiet; still

dote—regularly displaying excessive love or affection

drub—to defeat soundly in a fight or contest

dubious—feeling doubt; hesitating; skeptical

duress—constraint by threat; imprisonment

eccentricity—irregularity; oddity

eclectic—selecting from various systems, doctrines, or sources

effluent—runoff or overflow

effusive—expressing excessive emotion

embellish—decorate by adding detail; ornament

embodiment—concrete expression of an idea

eminent—rising above other things or places

emissary—a person sent on a specific mission

emollient—softening; soothing

empathy—ability to share in another's emotions, thoughts, or feelings

emulate—imitate

enamor—fill with love and desire; charm

encroach—trespass or intrude

encumber—hinder

endow—provide with some talent or quality

engender—cause; produce

enigma—riddle; a perplexing and ambiguous statement

enmity—hostility; antagonism

enthrall—captivate; fascinate

enumerate—count; determine the number of

epigram—a short poem with a witty point

epithet—a descriptive name or title

epitome—a person or thing that shows typical qualities of something

equivocal—having two or more meanings

equivocate—to be deliberately ambiguous

eradicate—wipe out; destroy; to get rid of

erroneous—mistaken; wrong

esoteric—hard to understand

espionage—the act of spying

espouse—support or advocate

euphoria—feeling of vigor or well-being

evocation—calling forth

ewe—female sheep

exalt—elevate; to praise; glorify

exasperate—irritate or annoy very much; aggravate

exemplary—serving as a model or example

exhort—urge

exorbitant—extremely excessive, gratuitous

expunge—erase or remove completely

extol—praise highly

extrapolate—arrive at conclusions or results

exuberance—feeling of high spirits

faddish—having the nature of a fad

fallacious—misleading or deceptive

fallacy—false, deceptive, or misleading nature

famine—hunger; a withering away

faultfinder—one who regularly complains or finds fault

feckless—weak; ineffective

feral—untamed; wild

fervent—hot; burning; glowing

fervid—impassioned; fervent

finite—having measurable or definable limits; not infinite

fissure—a long, narrow, deep cleft or crack

flaccid—flabby

fledgling—an inexperienced person or young bird

flippant—frivolous and disrespectful; saucy

flounder—to struggle, or thrash about helplessly

flout—show scorn or contempt

forage—search for food or provisions

forbearance—patience

forbid—not permit; prohibit

forensics—debate or formal argumentation

forge—a furnace for heating metal to be wrought; to advance

forlorn—without hope; desperate

formidable—causing fear or dread

forthright—straightforward; direct; frank

fortify—strengthen

fortuitous—accidental; by chance

fracas—a noisy fight or loud quarrel; brawl

fractious—hard to manage; unruly

fraught—emotional; tense; anxious; distressing

frenetic—frantic; frenzied

futile—ineffectual; trifling or unimportant

genial—cheerful; friendly; sympathetic

germinate—start developing or growing

glib—done in a smooth, offhand fashion

goad—driving impulse; spur

gouge—scrape or hollow out

gourmand—a glutton; one who indulges to excess

gratuitous—given freely; unwarranted

gregarious—fond of the company of others; sociable

gristle—cartilage found in meat

grouse—complain; grumble

grovel—behave humbly or abjectly

hackles—hairs on back and neck

hapless—unfortunate; unlucky; luckless

haste—the act of hurrying; quickness of motion

haughty—proud; arrogant

headlong—rash, without thought

hedonist—one who believes pleasure is sole aim in life

heed—take careful notice of

hence—thereafter; subsequently

herbaceous—like a green leaf in texture, color, shape

heroine—girl or woman of outstanding courage and nobility

hierarchy—an arrangement in order of rank, grade, class

hindsight—ability to see, after the event, what should have been done

homogeneous—of the same race or kind
hone—to perfect; sharpen; yearn
hoodwink—mislead or confuse by trickery
hue—a particular shade or tint of a given color
humble—not proud; not self-assertive; modest
humdrum—lacking variety; dull; monotonous
humility—absence of pride or self-assertion
hybrid—anything of mixed origin; unlike parts
hypocrisy—pretending to be what one is not
hypothesis—unproved theory

idealist—visionary or dreamer
idiosyncrasy—personal peculiarity or mannerism
idol—object of worship; false god
idolatrous—given to idolatry or blind adoration
idolatry—worship of idols
illusory—deceptive, created by an illusion
immaculate—perfectly clean; unsoiled
impart—make known; tell; reveal
impeccable—without defect or error; flawless
impede—obstruct or delay
impinge—to make inroads or encroach
implicate—to involve or concern
imposture—fraud; deception
inadvertent—not attentive or observant; heedless
incantation—chanted words or formula
incarcerate—imprison; confine
incessant—continual; never ceasing
incinerate—burn up; cremate
incisive—sharply expressive
incongruous—lacking harmony or agreement
incontrovertible—not disputable or debatable
incorrigible—unable to be corrected, improved, or
    reformed
incumbent—lying, resting on something; imposed
    as a duty
indignation—righteous anger
indignity—unworthiness or disgrace
indiscernible—imperceptible
indiscriminate—confused; random
indispensable—absolutely necessary or required
indolent—lazy
indomitable—not easily discouraged, defeated, or
    subdued
industrious—diligent; skillful
indigent—poor
infallible—incapable of error; never wrong
infamy—bad reputation; notoriety; disgrace
ingratiate—to achieve one's good graces by
    conscious effort
innate—existing naturally rather than through
    acquisition
innocuous—harmless; not controversial, offensive,
    or stimulating

inquisitor—harsh or prying questioner
intractable—stubborn
insipid—not exciting or interesting; dull
intelligible—clear; comprehensible
interpolate—insert between other things
intersperse—spread, scatter
interstellar—between or among the stars
intrepid—brave
inure—make accustomed to something difficult
irascible—easily angered; quick-tempered
irksome—annoying, irritating, frustrating

jaunty—gay and carefree; sprightly; perky
jubilant—joyful and triumphant; elated; rejoicing
jurisprudence—a part or division of law
juxtapose—place side by side

kernel—the most central part; a grain
knell—tolling of a bell
knoll—little round hill

lackluster—lacking energy or vitality
lambaste—scold or denounce severely
lament—mourn; grieve
languid—without vigor or vitality; drooping; weak
laudable—praiseworthy; commendable
laudatory—expressing praise
legion—a large number; multitude
lethargic—abnormally drowsy or dull; sluggish
limerick—nonsense poem of five anapestic lines
lionize—treat as a celebrity
listless—spiritless; languid
literati—scholarly or learned people
lithe—bending easily; flexible; supple
litigant—a party to a lawsuit
liturgy—ritual for public worship in any of various
    religions or churches
livid—grayish-blue; extremely angry
loquacious—fond of talking
loquacity—talkativeness
lucid—transparent
luminary—someone or something that illuminates
    or inspires

magnanimous—noble in mind
magnitude—greatness; importance or influence
malevolence—malice; spitefulness; ill will
malfeasance—wrongdoing or misconduct
masque—dramatic composition
maverick—a person who takes an independent
    stand
maxim—statement of a general truth
meager—thin; lean; emaciated
medieval—characteristic of the Middle Ages

melee—fight

menace—threaten harm or evil

mercenary—motivated by a desire for money or other gain

merriment—gaiety and fun

metaphor—a figure of speech containing an implied comparison

methodology—system of procedures

meticulous—extremely careful about details

miser—a greedy, stingy person

mitigate—make less rigorous or less painful; moderate

mnemonic—helping, or meant to help, the memory

modicum—small amount

modulate—to adapt, adjust, or alter

mollify—soothe

monarch—hereditary head of a state

morose—ill-tempered; gloomy

myriad—indefinitely large number

mythical—imaginary; fictitious

narcissism—self-love

negate—make ineffective

nexus—a connected group or series

nib—point of a pen

nocturnal—active during the night

noisome—having a bad odor; foul-smelling

nomad—one who has no permanent home, who moves about constantly

nostalgia—longing for things of the past

notoriety—prominence or renown, often unfavorable

novice—apprentice; beginner

nuance—a slight or delicate variation

obliterate—erase; efface

obsolete—no longer in use or practice

obstinate—unreasonably determined to have one's own way; stubborn

obtuse—not sharp or pointed; blunt

occult—secret; esoteric

oligarchy—government by a privileged few

ominous—threatening; sinister

omnipotent—unlimited in power or authority

onerous—burdensome; laborious

opulent—very wealthy or rich

oration—a formal public speech

orator—eloquent public speaker

ornate—heavily ornamented or adorned

orthodox—strictly conforming to the traditional

oscillate—to be indecisive in purpose or opinion; vacillate

ossify—settle or fix rigidly

ostensible—apparent; showing outwardly; professed

ostracism—rejection or exclusion by general consent

overwrought—overworked; fatigued

palliate—relieve without curing; make less severe

pallid—faint in color; pale

palpable—tangible; easily perceived by the senses

pantomime—action or gestures without words as a means of expression

paradigm—example or model

paradox—a statement that seems contradictory

paramount—ranking higher than any other

parch—dry up with heat

pariah—outcast

parody—a poor or weak imitation

pathology—conditions, processes, or results of a particular disease

peccadillo—minor or petty sin; slight fault

penchant—strong liking or fondness

penitent—truly sorry for having sinned and willing to atone

peremptory—intolerantly positive or assured

perfunctory—indifferent; done merely as a duty; superficial

peril—exposure to harm or injury; danger

peripheral—outer; external; lying at the outside

pervade—to become prevalent throughout

petulant—peevish; impatient or irritable

philistine—a person smugly narrow and conventional in views and tastes

piety—devoutness; reverence for God

pithy—essential; brief and to the point

placate—stop from being angry; appease

platitude—commonplace, flat, or dull quality

plethora—overabundance; excess

pliant—flexible, easy to modify

poignant—emotionally touching or moving

ponderous—cumbersome, heavy

poseur—a person who assumes attitudes or manners merely for their effect upon others

postulate—claim; demand; require

pragmatic—busy or active in a meddlesome way; practical

preclude—shut out; prevent

precocious—exhibiting premature development

predilection—preconceived liking; partiality or preference

presage—sign or warning of a future event; omen

prescience—foreknowledge

preside—exercise control or authority

proclivity—natural or habitual inclination

procure—obtain; secure

profane—show disrespect for sacred things; irreverent

profuse—generous, often to excess

proliferate—to reproduce (new parts) in quick succession

prolific—turning out many products of the mind

propagate—reproduce; multiply

propriety—properness; suitability

prosaic—matter of fact; ordinary

prose—ordinary speech; dull

protract—prolong in time or space; extend; lengthen

protuberance—projection; bulge

provocative—stimulating; erotic

prudence—careful management

pundit—actual or self-professed authority

pungent—stinging; sharp in taste; caustic

punitive—inflicting, concerned with, or directed toward punishment

pyre—a combustible heap

quaff—drink deeply in a hearty or thirsty way

quell—crush; subdue; put an end to

querulous—full of complaint; peevish

ramify—divide or spread out into branches

rancor—deep spite or malice

rarefy—to make rare or refined

rasp—rough, grating tone

ratify—approve or confirm

raucous—loud and rowdy

reciprocate—cause to move alternately back and forth

recluse—secluded; solitary

recompense—repay; compensate

regale—delight with something pleasing or amusing

relegate—exile or banish

relinquish—give up; abandon

remedial—providing a remedy

reparation—restoration to good condition

replete—well-filled or plentifully supplied

reprieve—give temporary relief to, as from trouble or pain

reproach—to blame or find fault

reprobate—disapprove of strongly

repugnant—contradictory; inconsistent

requiem—musical service for the dead

resplendent—dazzling; splendid

restitution—return to a former condition or situation

reticent—habitually silent; reserved

rhapsodize—to describe in an extravagantly enthusiastic manner

rogue—a rascal; scoundrel

rubric—a category or section heading, often in red; any rule or explanatory comment

ruffian—brutal, violent, lawless person

ruse—trick or artifice

sacred—holy; of or connected with religion

salutary—healthful; beneficial

salutation—greeting, addressing, or welcoming by gestures or words

salve—balm that soothes or heals

sanctimonious—pretending to be very holy

sanction—support; encouragement; approval

sate—to satisfy or fill

savant—learned person; eminent scholar

scrupulous—having principles; extremely conscientious

scurvy—low; mean; vile; contemptible

seminal—of reproduction; germinal; originative

serene—calm; peaceful; tranquil

servile—humbly yielding or submissive; of a slave or slaves

shroud—covers, protects, or screens; veil; shelter

signatory—joined in the signing of something

sinister—wicked; evil; dishonest

sinuous—not straightforward; devious

slake—make less intense by satisfying

snide—slyly malicious or derisive

sodden—filled with moisture; soaked

solace—comfort; consolation; relief

soluble—able to be dissolved

somber—dark and gloomy or dull

soporific—pertaining to sleep or sleepiness

spectrum—a range or scale

spendthrift—one who spends money extravagantly

sporadic—occasional; not constant or regular

spurious—not true or genuine; false

squalid—foul or unclean

static—showing a lack of motion

stealth—secret, furtive, or artfully sly behavior

stigma—mark or sign indicating something not considered normal or standard

stint—restrict or limit

stringent—vigorous; rigid; binding

subliminal—on the threshold of consciousness; under the surface

submission—resignation; obedience; meekness

suffice—be adequate

sully—soil; stain; tarnish by disgracing

sunder—break apart; separate; split

superfluous—excessive

surreptitious—acting in a secret, stealthy way

symbiosis—relationship of mutual interdependence

syntax—orderly or systematic arrangement of words

tactile—perceived by touch; tangible
tangible—having actual form and substance
tawdry—cheap and showy; gaudy; sleazy
tedium—tediousness
temporal—not lasting forever; limited by time
tempt—persuade; induce; entice
tenacity—holding fast
tenet—principle, doctrine, or belief held as a truth
tenuous—slender or fine; not dense
terrestrial—worldly; earthly
throng—crowd
timorous—subject to fear; timid
tome—large book
toupee—a man's wig
tractable—easily worked; obedient; malleable
tranquil—calm; serene; peaceful
transcend—exceed; surpass; excel
transcendent—exceeding usual limits; incomparable; beyond ordinary existence; peerless
transgress—go beyond a limit
translucent—partially transparent or clear
transmute—transform; convert
treacherous—untrustworthy or insecure
treachery—perfidy; disloyalty; treason
trepidation—fearful uncertainty; anxiety
trite—no longer having originality
troubadour—minstrel or singer
truncate—cut short
tumultuous—wild and noisy; uproarious
turmoil—commotion; uproar; confusion
tyranny—very cruel and unjust use of power or authority

uncanny—inexplicable; preternaturally strange; weird
undergird—to support or secure
underling—one in a subordinate position; inferior
unequivocal—plain; obvious
unfeigned—genuine; real; sincere
unfetter—free from restraint; liberate
unification—state of being unified
unintelligible—unable to be understood; incomprehensible
unity—oneness; singleness
univocal—unambiguous
unscrupulous—not restrained by ideas of right and wrong
untenable—incapable of being occupied
untoward—inappropriate; improper
unwitting—not knowing; unaware

upbraid—rebuke severely or bitterly
uproarious—loud and boisterous
usury—interest at a high rate
utilitarian—stressing usefulness over beauty
utopia—idealized place

vacillate—sway to and fro; waver; totter
vacuum—completely empty space
vagabond—wandering; moving from place to place
vagrant—a person who lives a wandering life
valiant—brave
vapid—tasteless; flavorless; flat
veer—change direction; shift
vehement—acting or moving with great force
venerate—show feelings of deep respect; revere
vengeance—revenge
vestige—a trace of something that once existed
verbose—wordy
veritable—actual; being truly so
vex—distress; afflict; plague
vicarious—serving as a substitute
villainous—evil; wicked
virtuoso—a master of art and music, a scholar
vivacious—full of life and animation; lively
vocation—trade; profession; occupation
volatile—flying or able to fly
voluble—talkative
voluminous—large; bulky; full
voracious—ravenous; gluttonous

waft—float, as on the wind
wane—grow dim or faint
wanton—excessively merry; frolicsome; having no regard for others
wary—cautious; on one's guard
wheedle—coax; influence or persuade by flattery
whet—make keen; stimulate
wile—sly trick
wither—shrivel; wilt
witty—cleverly amusing
wrath—intense anger; rage; fury
wrench—sudden, sharp twist or pull

yacht—small vessel for pleasure cruises or racing
yearn—to have longing or desire
yielding—submissive; obedient

zeal—intense enthusiasm
zenith—highest point; peak

Difficulty Level 2

abeyance—temporary suspension
abjure—recant; to give up (opinions) publicly
abstemious—exercising moderation; self-restraint
abstruse—hard to understand; deep; recondite
aggregation—gathered together; accumulated
alacrity—cheerful promptness; eagerness
amalgamate—unite; combine
ambient—surrounding
ameliorate—improve; to make or become better
amorphous—shapeless; formless
anathema—a thing or person greatly detested
anatomist—a person who analyzes in great detail
anhydrous—without water
antediluvian—before the flood; antiquated
apocryphal—not genuine; spurious; counterfeit; of
        doubtful authorship or authenticity
apostate—fallen from the faith
arabesque—a complex and elaborate decorative
        design
arrogate—to claim or seize as one's own
ascetic—practicing self-denial; austere
ascribe—attribute to a cause
asperity—having a harsh temper; roughness
assuage—lessen; soothe
assiduous—diligent
attenuation—a thinning out
augury—a token or omen
august—great dignity or grandeur
avaricious—greedy; covetous
aver—affirm; declare to be true

bacchanalian—drunken
baleful—menacing; deadly
bedizen—to dress or decorate in a cheap, showy
        way
beguile—to deceive; cheat; charm; coax
beleaguer—besiege or attack; harass
bellicose—belligerent; pugnacious; warlike
belie—misrepresent; be false to
bombastic—pompous; puffed up with conceit; using
        inflated language
bovine—resembling a cow; placid or dull
bucolic—rustic; pastoral
burgeon—grow forth; send out buds

cacophony—harsh or discordant sound; dissonance
calumny—slander
capacious—roomy; spacious
capitulate—surrender
cathartic—purgative; inducing a figurative
        cleansing
cavil—disagree; nit-pick; make frivolous objections

celerity—swiftness
centurion—the commander of a century in an
        ancient Roman army
chary—careful; cautious
chimerical—fantastically improbable; highly
        unrealistic
churlish—rude; surly
circumlocution—an indirect way of expressing
        something
circumscribe—limit
codicil—an appendix or supplement
cogent—convincing
coeval—of the same age or period
collusion—conspiring in a fraudulent scheme
comely—attractive; agreeable
compendium—brief, comprehensive summary
concord—harmony
confluence—flowing or coming together
consecrate—induct into a religious office; declare
        sacred
consonance—agreement; harmony
consternation—great fear or shock that makes one
        feel helpless or bewildered
contiguous—to be near, adjacent
contumacious—stubbornly rebellious; willfully
        disobedient
contumely—insult; contemptuous treatment
conundrum—riddle; difficult problem
cosset—pamper
culpable—deserving blame; blameworthy
cupidity—excessive desire for money; avarice
cursory—hasty; done without care

dearth—any scarcity or lack
decimate—destroy a great number
deleterious—injurious; harmful to health or well-
        being
demagogue—a leader who gains power using
        popular prejudices and false claims; a
        leader of the common people in ancient
        times
demur—to take exception; object
denigrate—blacken someone's reputation or
        character
denouement—the outcome, solution, unraveling, or
        clarification of a plot in a drama, story
deposition—a statement or declaration
derision—ridicule
descry—to detect or discover
despotic—of or like a despot; autocratic; tyrannical
desiccate—dry up; drain
desuetude—disuse; the condition of not being used

desultory—aimless; unmethodical; unfocused
detumescence—a gradual shrinking of a swelling
diaphanous—translucent; see-through
diatribe—speech full of bitterness
didactic—intended primarily to instruct
diffidence—modesty; shyness; lack of confidence
dilatory—given to delay or procrastination
dilettante—aimless follower of the arts; amateur; dabbler
disaffection—lack of trust; to cause discontent
disarming—deprive of resentment; peaceable or friendly; win over
discombobulate—upset the composure of
discomfit—make uneasy
discursive—rambling; passing from one topic to another
disingenuous—deceitful; lacking in candor; not frank
disinter—bring to light
disputatious—argumentative
disquietude—uneasiness; anxiety
dissemble—conceal true motives; pretend
dissolute—loose in morals or conduct
doggerel—trivial, awkward, satirical verse
dolorous—sorrowful; having mental anguish
dross—waste matter; worthless stuff; rubbish
dulcet—sweet-sounding; melodious
duplicity—deception by pretending to feel and act one way while acting another; bad faith; double dealing

ebullient—greatly excited
edify—instruct; correct morally
efface—erase; obliterate as if by rubbing it out
efficacious—having the intended result; effective
efficacy—power to produce desired effect
effrontery—shameless boldness; impudence; temerity
egregious—notorious; shocking
emend—correct or improve
encomium—glowing praise
endemic—prevailing among a specific group
enervate—weaken; debilitate
ensconce—settle in; hide; conceal
ephemeral—fleeting; short-lived
equanimity—calmness; composure
equipoise—state of balance or equilibrium
erudite—learned; scholarly
eschew—shun
etymology—study of word parts
evanescent—tending to vanish like vapor
evince—show clearly
exacerbate—worsen; embitter
excoriate—denounce harshly

exculpate—clear from blame
execrable—detestable
exegesis—explanation, especially of biblical passages
exigency—urgent situation
expatriate—one choosing to live abroad
extant—still existing; not extinct

facile—easily accomplished; ready or fluent
fatuous—foolish or inane
fealty—loyalty; allegiance
feint—a false show; sham
felicitous—well chosen; apt; suitable
ferment—agitation; commotion
fetid—malodorous
filial—pertaining to a son or daughter
florid—highly decorated; gaudy; showy; ornate
foment—stir up; instigate
frieze—ornamental band formed by a series of decorations
froward—not easily controlled; stubbornly willful
fulminate—to thunder; explode
fulsome—offensively flattering
fungible—capable of being used in place of something else

gainsay—contradict; speak or act against
galvanize—stimulate by shock; stir up; revitalize
gambol—romp; to skip about
garrulous—loquacious; wordy; talkative
gossamer—sheer, like cobwebs
guile—slyness and cunning

hackney—make trite by overuse
halcyon—calm; peaceful
harbinger—one that announces or foreshadows what is coming; precursor; portent
hummock—small hill
hegemony—dominance, especially of one nation over another
heinous—atrocious; hatefully bad
hermetic—obscure and mysterious; relating to the occult
hew—chop or cut with an ax or knife; hack; gash
hirsute—hairy; shaggy; bristly
hubris—arrogance; excessive self-conceit
humus—substance formed by decaying vegetable matter

iconoclastic—attacking cherished traditions
ignominious—dishonorable; disgraceful
imbroglio—complicated situation
immolate—offer as a sacrifice
immutable—unchangeable

impalpable—imperceptible; intangible
impecunious—without money; poor
impenitent—without regret, shame, or remorse
impertinent—intrusive or presumptuous; irrelevant
imperturbable—cannot be disconcerted, disturbed, or excited; impassive
impervious—not affected
impetuous—moving with great, sudden energy
impious—lacking respect or dutifulness
implacable—unable to be appeased or pacified; relentless
importune—repeatedly urge
impudent—characterized by impertinence
impuissance—powerlessness; feebleness
impugn—to doubt; to challenge a statement, case, or motive
impunity—freedom from punishment or harm
inchoate—recently begun; rudimentary
incipient—becoming apparent; beginning
inculcate—impress on the mind by admonition
incursion—temporary invasion
indelible—not able to be removed or erased
indemnify—make secure against loss
indite—write; compose
ineffable—too overwhelming to be expressed in words
inefficacious—unable to produce the desired effect
ineluctable—irresistible; not to be escaped
inexorable—not to be moved by entreaty; unyielding; relentless
inimical—hostile; unfriendly
iniquitous—wicked; immoral
insidious—deceitful; treacherous
insouciant—calm and untroubled; carefree
insularity—detachment; isolation
intemperate—lacking restraint; excessive
internecine—mutually destructive
intransigence—refusal to compromise
invective—abuse
inveterate—habitual; of long standing; deep-rooted
inveigh—condemn; censure

jaundice—prejudice; envious; yellow
jettison—throw overboard
jocose—given to joking
jocund—merry
juggernaut—irresistible, crushing force

ken—range of knowledge
kinetic—producing motion
kismet—fate

lachrymose—producing tears
laconic—using few words

largess—liberal giving; generous gift
lascivious—lustful
lassitude—weariness; debility
latent—potential but undeveloped; dormant
laxity—carelessness
legerdemain—sleight of hand
leviathan—a massive and powerful marine animal or ship
licentious—amoral; lewd and lascivious
Lilliputian—extremely small
limn—describe
limpid—clear
lugubrious—mournful, often to an excessive degree
lummox—a clumsy, stupid person

maelstrom—whirlpool
maladroit—clumsy; bungling
malediction—curse
malleable—capable of being shaped
malignant—growing worse
malinger—pretend to be ill to escape duty or work; shirk
maraud—rove in search of plunder
martinet—one who issues orders
masticate—chew
maudlin—effusively sentimental
mazurka—a lively Polish folk dance
megalomania—mania for doing grandiose things
mellifluous—sounding sweet and smooth; honeyed
mendacity—untruthfulness
mendicant—beggar
mercurial—volatile; changeable; fickle
meretricious—flashy; tawdry
metamorphose—transform
miasma—a poisonous atmosphere
minatory—menacing; threatening
misanthrope—a person who hates mankind
miscreant—villain
monolithic—consisting of a single character; uniform; unyielding
mordant—biting; cutting; caustic; sarcastic
moribund—dying
multifarious—numerous, having many different forms or parts
munificent—generous
myopic—nearsighted; lacking foresight

nadir—lowest point
nascent—incipient; coming into being
nebulous—unclear; vague; hazy; cloudy
necromancy—black magic; dealing with the dead
nefarious—wicked
nostrum—questionable medicine
nubile—marriageable

nugatory—futile; worthless

obdurate—stubborn; unyielding
obfuscate—make obscure; confuse
obloquy—slander; disgrace; infamy
obsequious—compliant; dutiful; servile
obstreperous—unruly; boisterous; noisy
obviate—make unnecessary
occlude—shut; close
odious—hateful; vile
odium—disgrace brought on by hateful action
officious—ready to serve; obliging
opprobrious—disgraceful, shameful, appalling
opprobrium—infamy; vilification

paean—a song of joy, triumph, praise
panegyric—haughty or elaborate praise
paragon—model of perfection
parlance—language; idiom
parlay—exploit successfully
parsimonious—stingy
paucity—scarcity
pecuniary—obsessed by money
pedantic—bookish
pejorative—negative in connotation; having a
 tendency to make worse; disparaging
pellucid—transparent or translucent; clear
penurious—marked by penury; stingy
perdition—eternal damnation; complete ruin
perfidy—treacherous; betrayal of trust
pernicious—fatal; very destructive or injurious
perspicacious—having insight; penetrating; astute
perspicuous—plainly expressed
petrous—of or like rock; hard
phlegmatic—calm; not easily disturbed
piebald—of different colors; mottled; spotted
pillory—criticize or ridicule
pinion—confine or shackle
piquancy—something that stimulates taste; tartness
polemic—controversy; argument in support of a
 point of view
polyglot—speaking several languages
portent—sign; omen; something that foreshadows a
 coming event
precipitous—abrupt or hasty
prig—annoyingly pedantic person
probity—honesty; integrity
prodigal—wasteful; reckless with money
prodigious—marvelous; enormous
profligate—dissolute; reckless; loose in morals; wanton
profundity—intellectual depth
prolix—wordy; long-winded
promulgate—proclaim; make public; put into effect
propinquity—nearness of relationship; kinship

propitious—favorable; timely
proscribe—outlaw; ostracize; banish
puerile—childish; lacking in maturity
pugnacious—eager and ready to fight; quarrelsome
pusillanimous—cowardly

quiescence—motionless, at rest
quiescent—at rest; dormant; temporarily inactive
quixotic—idealistic but impractical
quotidian—everyday; usual or ordinary

raconteur—someone who is skilled at telling stories
 or anecdotes
raffish—vulgar; crude
raiment—clothing
rapacious—taking by force; plundering
recalcitrant—stubborn; refractory; reluctant;
 unwilling; refusing to submit
recidivism—habitual return to crime
recondite—abstruse; profound; secret
recumbent—reclining; lying down
redolent—suggestive of an odor; fragrant
redoubtable—formidable; causing fear
refractory—stubborn; obstinate
remand—order back; return to service
remonstrate—object; protest
remunerative—compensating; rewarding for
 service
repine—complain; mourn; fret
ribald—wanton; profane or coarse; joking or
 mocking

sagacious—perceptive; shrewd; having insight
salacious—lustful; lecherous; lascivious
salient—standing out conspicuously; prominent
salubrious—healthful
sanguine—having a ruddy complexion; cheerful;
 hopeful
sardonic—sneering; sarcastic; cynical
sartorial—tailored
saturnine—sullen; sardonic; gloomy
sedition—resistance to authority
sedulous—diligent; persevering
semaphore—system of signaling
sententious—terse; concise; aphoristic
sophistry—seemingly plausible but fallacious
 reasoning
specious—seeming reasonable but incorrect
splenetic—bad-tempered; irritable
stentorian—powerful in sound; extremely loud
stolid—unexcitable; impassive
stymie—situation in which one is obstructed or
 frustrated
succor—aid; assistance; comfort

supine—sluggish; listless; passive
supercilious—contemptuous; arrogant
surfeit—too great an amount or supply; excess
sycophant—one who seeks favor by flattering; a
     parasite

taciturn—quiet; habitually silent
tangential—peripheral; only slightly connected
temerity—foolish or rash boldness
toady—servile flatterer; a "yes man"
torpor—lack of activity; lethargy
tortuous—winding; full of curves
traduce—to speak falsely
trenchant—effective; thorough; cutting; keen
truculent—threatening; aggressively self-assertive;
     savage
turbid—muddy
turgid—swollen; distended
turpitude—depravity

ubiquitous—being everywhere; omnipresent
unctuous—oily; suave
undulating—moving with a wavelike motion

vacuity—emptiness
vainglorious—boastful
vanguard—forerunner; advance forces
variegate—vary; diversify
venal—capable of being bribed
venial—forgivable; trivial
veracious—truthful
verdant—green; lush in vegetation
verisimilitude—appearance of truth
vicissitude—change of fortune
viscid—having a cohesive and sticky fluid
vitiate—spoil; corrupt
vitriolic—corrosive; sarcastic
vituperative—abusive; scolding
vociferous—clamorous; noisy
vouchsafe—bestow condescendingly; guarantee

waggish—mischievous; humorous; tricky
welter—to become soaked; stained; bathed
winnow—sift; separate good parts from bad
winsome—agreeable; gracious
wizen—wither; shrivel

xenophobia—fear or hatred of foreigners

zealous—fervent; enthusiastic
zephyr—gentle breeze; west wind

HONING YOUR READING SKILLS

When you move from reading materials that entertain to reading literature that requires higher levels of critical reading ability and that tests your ability to comprehend complex arguments, you must develop an aptitude for reading carefully and deliberately.

This section includes a series of exercises to help you hone your reading skills and identify a passage's main idea, supporting details, implied ideas, and tone.

To read a densely written passage carefully for comprehension, there are five major reading elements you should consider.

Understand the Five Elements of Reading Passages

Content

The content of a passage is made up of the information, data, images, and descriptions found in the text. The author uses words, phrases, and sentences to build the basic facts, figures, illustrations, and examples of a passage. He or she writes to communicate the basic "who," "what," "where," and "when" of the literary piece.

As a reader, you discover the content by asking, "What is the author attempting to tell, show, or explain to me?"

Case

The case (think of a legal case) of the author establishes the reasoning, arguments, or explanations for the content's purpose. The author is attempting to demonstrate that the main point of the content is meaningful, logical, emotionally moving, or important. Even in fictional works, narratives, or poetic literature, authors regularly point directly or indirectly to some reason or explanation for their views.

You discover the case in the passage by asking, "What evidence, arguments, explanations, or reasons does the author use to prove his or her point?"

Cause

The cause (or the "because") is the point of view or perspective from which the author writes. An author may or may not directly tell you his or her point of view. As a critical reader, you may need to "read between the lines" to discover some experience, perspective, background, personal view, opinion, or set of ideas that influence an author to write about specific content or argue in a certain manner.

You discover the cause by asking, "Why is the author exploring this specific content, arguing in this particular style, or writing in this particular manner?"

Context

The context refers to the time and place from which the author writes. All authors write from particular surroundings that influence their understanding of culture, science, history, social structures, etc. For example, an author writing in Spain during the sixteenth century would have a significantly different context than an author writing in New York City during the twenty-first century.

You discover the context by asking, "From when and where did the author write this passage, and how might it influence his or her point of view?"

Character

The character of the passage is the general mood or feeling that an author attempts to communicate. An author may write logically, emotionally, passionately, humorously, whimsically, sarcastically, or in a variety of other styles that project a particular mood.

You discover the character of a passage by asking, "How does the author use his or her style (words, phrases, sentence structure, paragraph patterns, images, illustrations, etc.) to communicate the general mood or feeling of the passage?"

The following strategies will assist you in reading all the previously described reading passage elements. The chart below illustrates how the reading elements correspond to the reading strategies.

READING ELEMENT	QUESTION TO ASK	READING STRATEGY
Content	"What is the author attempting to tell, show, or explain to me?"	• Clearly identify the main idea. • Determine the outline employed to develop the passage. • Locate the important specific details.
Case	"What evidence, arguments, explanations, or reasons does the author use to prove his or her point?"	• Analyze the arguments or persuasive devices.
Cause	"Why is the author exploring this specific content, arguing in this particular style, or writing in this particular manner?"	• Consider the author's point of view.
Context	"From when and where did the author write this passage and how might it influence his or her point of view?"	• Consider the author's point of view.
Character	"How does the author use his or her style (words, phrases, sentence structure, paragraph patterns, images, illustrations, etc.) to communicate the general mood or feeling of the passage?"	• Probe the mood of the passage.

Use the Six Strategies for Reading Carefully and Comprehensively

In the following section, you will learn the six basic strategies for reading passages more seriously, carefully, and comprehensively.

1. Clearly identify the main idea of the written material.
2. Determine the outline employed to develop the passage.
3. Locate the important specific details.
4. Analyze the arguments or persuasive devices.
5. Consider the author's point of view.
6. Probe the mood of the passage.

Identify the Main Idea (Main Theme) of the Passage

In presenting content, an author typically begins writing with a main idea in mind. This may also be called the main theme or the thesis of the passage. All other ideas, examples, facts, or illustrations in the passage are meant to support the main idea.

You discover the main theme by asking the following types of questions:

- What is the primary purpose of this paragraph or passage?
- What is the principal idea or central concept within this particular passage?
- What one statement or sentence best summarizes this reading material?
- What major idea or theme is the author attempting to communicate?

As you read, be careful not to confuse the arguments, examples, or specific details with the main theme of the passage. The arguments, examples, and details are presented in a passage to support the main theme.

Example:

Though I love planet Earth with her snow-capped mountains, sand blown deserts, and deep blue oceans, as a scientist and a philosopher, I believe that humanity cannot live here forever. Colonization of other planets, like the red planet Mars, will be necessary. With the human population growing so quickly, there will simply not be enough room for all of us on Earth by 2050. By that year, food and water will be extremely scarce for all but the most powerful and wealthy, and many will suffer from drought and famine. Because of the growing population problems, the governments of nations around the world will need to band together soon to support a long-term plan to colonize other planets by sending humans to live in space by 2050. Personally, I am too nervous to be a pioneer on a distant planet, but it will be necessary that some humans undertake this great adventure.

What is the primary purpose of this paragraph?

- The main idea of this passage is that colonization of other planets will be necessary by the year 2050. The writer describes why colonization of other planets will be increasingly necessary by 2050. Though the author provides other arguments about why colonization will become necessary and includes thoughts about his or her own nervousness with space travel, the primary purpose is to communicate the coming need to colonize other planets by 2050.

NOTE: One practical strategy for determining the main idea is to rephrase the passage into a single, concise sentence that summarizes the entire passage.

Determine the Outline Employed to Develop the Passage

Once you identify the main idea, you need to determine how the author develops that theme using logical arguments, examples, illustrations, facts, or details. A good way to understand the development of a passage is to outline the key ideas, statements, or arguments in that passage. A simple outline provides a way to line up the content in a thoughtful, logical, or sequential manner.

When outlining a passage, find the key statements or thoughts the author uses to support his or her main idea. Ask these questions to help determine the outline:

- What is the main idea of the passage?
- What supporting ideas, primary facts, or arguments does the author use to confirm or strengthen the main idea?
- What order of ideas or information does the author use to communicate those facts or arguments?

An author may order his or her writing using, among others, one of the following styles:

- *Temporal:* time ordered (e.g., past to present, morning to evening, hours in a day)
- *Sequential:* ordered intervals (e.g., smallest to largest, simplest to most complex, least to most)
- *Categorical:* parts of a system (e.g., classification of animal kingdom, types of stars)
- *Geographical:* locations (e.g., east to west, floor to ceiling, inside to outside)
- *Logical:* rational order (e.g., *x* to *y* and *y* to *z*, *x* logically follows *y*)
- *Emotional:* feeling related (e.g., least impacting to most impacting, saddest time to happiest time)

Review the following reading passage and outline.

Example:

First-year college students should be required to provide five hours of community service each week. This requirement would greatly benefit the surrounding community. A recent survey shows that communities need more volunteer help. An interview with the mayor demonstrates that her city needs immediate help from more volunteers. This requirement would greatly benefit the student as well. Research demonstrates that students who participate in community service make better grades than those who do not participate in community service. Also, students who participate in community service make more friends than those who do not participate in community service.

Main Idea: First-year college students should be required to provide five hours of community service each week.

1. Fact One: This requirement would greatly benefit the surrounding community.
   a) Argument One: A recent survey shows that communities need more volunteer help.
   b) Argument Two: An interview with the mayor demonstrates that her city needs immediate help from more volunteers.

2. Fact Two: This requirement would greatly benefit the student as well.
   a) Argument One: Research demonstrates that students who participate in community service make better grades than those who do not participate in community service.
   b) Argument Two: Students who participate in community service make more friends than those who do not participate in community service.

Review the following outline that uses a temporal flow (earliest period to latest period).

Example:

Main Idea: A historical overview of book printing

1. Era One: Printing before the invention of movable type
   a) The Egyptian printing methods
   b) The Greco-Roman printing methods
   c) The printing methods of the Middle Ages

2. Era Two: Printing immediately after the invention of movable type
   a) Contemporary practices at the time of Gutenberg's printing press
   b) European printing after Gutenberg's press

3. Era Three: Modern innovations in printing
   a) Innovations before computer technology
   b) Innovations after computer technology

Review the following outline that uses a categorical outline (systems of the human anatomy).

Example:

Introduction to Human Anatomy

1. The Digestive System
2. The Reproductive System
3. The Nervous System
4. The Skeletal System
5. The Muscular System

Locate the Important Specific Details

Authors add specific details to a passage to provide necessary information, define terms, add color, or give examples. To skillfully comprehend reading passages, you must locate the most important specific details in a passage.

NOTE: One way to identify the most important details is to look for verbal signals. Verbal signals are words or phrases that the author uses to draw attention to significant facts or information.

Prompting Words

Authors use prompting words to clue you in that something very important will soon be communicated. Look for words like "significantly," "importantly," "considerably," "vitally," "critically," "notably," or "essentially."

Defining Words

Authors use defining words to introduce a specific meaning of a word, phrase, or idea. A defining word can be as simple as the word "is" (e.g., A totem "is" a Native American religious symbol carved from wood). Other defining words or phrases include "means," "is defined as," or "that is." Regardless of whether an author uses one of these defining words or phrases, you should take special note whenever he or she provides a definition of a word, phrase, or idea.

Similarity Words

Similarity words make comparisons between two or more ideas. "Like" is the most familiar similarity word (e.g., A plant cell is "like" an animal cell since both have cell walls and genetic material inside those cell walls). Other similarity words or phrases include "comparable," "similar," "equal to," or "related to."

Contrast Words

The word "but" is an extremely important verbal signal. It sets up a contrast between two ideas (e.g., The Ohio River traffics many shipping barges "but" not nearly as many as does the Mississippi River). Other similar verbal clues include "in contrast," "as opposed to," "although," or "unlike."

Example Words

The phrase "for example" serves as a verbal signal that a specific illustration or pattern will follow. The author uses one or more illustrations to support the given argument. Other similar verbal clues include "illustration," "for instance," "model," or "lesson."

Specific details may come in a variety of forms. A detail may be a number, a date, a quote, a definition, a color, a time, a location, etc. Again, a specific detail is not the main idea of the passage, but it may play an important supporting role in making the passage more understandable or more readable. Specific details help readers to better understand the meaning of a passage.

Analyze the Arguments or Persuasive Devices

An author may employ a number of persuasive tools or arguments to attempt to prove his or her main ideas. As a critical reader, you will want to note what persuasive tools or arguments are used. In addition, you will want to analyze whether those arguments are valid and truly support the author's ideas.

To discover and analyze the arguments or persuasive devices, ask the following questions:

- How does the author support the main ideas in his or her passage?
- What arguments does the author make for his or her conclusions?
- Is the supporting evidence valid, logical, or reasonable?
- Do the arguments make sense?

The following are various types of evidence or support that an author may use to prove or advance his or her arguments:

- Scientific data or research
- Statistics
- Historical facts
- Quotations from prominent individuals
- Personal experiences
- Logic
- Statements or ideas from other experts
- Emotional statements or stories

NOTE: Authors may give direct cues when persuasive tools are used. Look for key words or phrases like "because," "for this reason," "due to," "in order that," "since," "as an example," or "for instance." When not given direct cues, you will need to infer when and how an author argues for his or her propositions.

Consider the Author's Point of View

When considering an author's point of view in a passage, you determine underlying intentions or assumptions of the author. You uncover the reasons why the author wrote on a particular topic using a particular line of reasoning or style of presentation. The author may directly state some of these reasons within the written materials or the author may leave reasons unstated or hidden. You will need to infer the unstated or hidden reasons from the passage.

An author generally writes from a position of expertise or experience. An author who writes without true expertise in a given area may be writing merely opinion at best or fabrication at worst. This is important to recognize. You should attempt to determine a writer's level of expertise and experience when reading a passage.

Here are some questions to consider in uncovering an author's point of view:

- What is the author's background (e.g., nationality, economic status, education)?
- What are the author's credentials (e.g., certifications, titles, degrees)?
- What are the author's biases (e.g., strong likes, dislikes, prejudices)?

- What positive/negative experiences have flavored the author's point of view?
- Did the author write simply to inform (e.g., a textbook, factual passages, brochure), or did the author write to persuade?
- What side of the issue does the author take?
- What does the author ultimately want you to believe?
- Why is the author passionate about this issue?
- How did the time or period in which the author wrote influence the author?
- How did the place or location of the author influence the writing of the passage?
- To whom was the author writing and how did that influence the passage?
- How did the circumstances of the author's surroundings influence his or her ideas?

Probe the Mood of the Passage

You must take into account the overall mood of a passage. In short, mood is the feeling or tone of a passage. The mood of a passage will provide you with cues about the author's intent in writing the passage. An author's mood can be upbeat, sad, humorous, angry, depressed, analytical, entertaining, informational, academic, confused, scholarly, etc.

Here are some questions you may use to increase awareness of the mood of a passage:

- What is the overall feeling of the passage?
- What ideas does the author use to show he or she is passionate or dispassionate about the topic?
- What does the author want the reader to do after reading the passage (e.g., act in a certain way, think more deeply, understand concepts)?
- What emotional words, images, stories, or examples does the author use?

Identify Parts of Arguments
Exercise 3

DIRECTIONS: Isolate the hidden assumption(s) in each of the following items. Then select the best answer choice given. Answers are on page 773.

1. Students at Duns Scotus High must get a better education than students at Erasmus High because the grade point average of students at Duns Scotus High is higher than that of students at Erasmus High.

   The claim above depends upon which of the following assumptions?

   (A) There are fewer students at Duns Scotus High than at Erasmus High.
   (B) The average grade earned by students is a poor measure of the quality of education that those students receive.
   (C) Extracurricular activities at Duns Scotus High are given more emphasis than at Erasmus High.
   (D) Property taxes are higher in the Duns Scotus High neighborhood than in the Erasmus High neighborhood.
   (E) The grading standards at the two high schools are roughly the same.

2. A government survey released today shows that 80 percent of the people who fly are satisfied with the service they receive from the airlines in this country. Three interviewers stood outside the airport terminal of a major airline and asked people leaving the terminal, "Do you have any complaints about the flight you just got off?" Only 20 percent responded "yes!"

   Which of the following, if true, would most undermine the conclusion of the argument above?

   (A) Sixty percent of the people coming out of the airline terminal were not people who had just gotten off a flight.
   (B) One percent of the people approached by the interviewers refused to respond to their inquiries.
   (C) The interviewers began their inquiries just after passengers were discharged from a flight that was 40 minutes late.
   (D) The interviewers were able to speak to only 70 percent of the people leaving the terminal, but those people were selected at random.
   (E) For six months following the day of the interviews, no passengers filed official complaints with the federal agency that regulated the airlines.

3. An efficiency expert made the following suggestion to the manager of a shirt factory: purchase larger spools of sewing thread. With more thread per spool, your operators will not need to stop production as often to change spools. This will reduce your labor costs.

The efficiency expert apparently assumes that

(A) thread wound on larger spools is not as strong as thread wound on smaller spools
(B) sewing machines do not break down and do not require routine maintenance
(C) workers in the factory are paid by the hour rather than on a piecework basis
(D) machine operators are not allowed to leave their machines during the work period
(E) speeding up production will improve the quality of the shirts made at the factory

4. Colonel Mustard did not commit the murder in the dining room with the candlestick; therefore, Mrs. Peacock committed the murder in the conservatory with the knife.

The argument above depends upon which of the following assumptions?

(A) The murder was committed either with the candlestick or with the knife.
(B) The murder was committed either in the dining room or in the conservatory.
(C) The murder was committed either by Colonel Mustard or by Mrs. Peacock.
(D) The murder was either committed by Colonel Mustard in the dining room with the candlestick or by Mrs. Peacock in the conservatory with the knife.
(E) The murder was not committed by Colonel Mustard in the dining room with the candlestick.

5. A major insurance company reported that approximately 80 percent of all traffic accidents never result in an insurance claim. So, we can conclude that about 80 percent of all losses due to theft also go unreported.

The argument above assumes that

(A) more traffic accidents occur per capita than thefts
(B) traffic accidents represent a more serious danger to the individual than do thefts
(C) the average dollar value of a traffic accident claim is equal to the average dollar value of a theft loss claim
(D) offenders in traffic accidents are as likely to be caught as are those involved in theft
(E) statistics about automobile insurance claims are applicable to claims for theft losses

6. The increasing reliance on computers represents a serious threat to the privacy of the individual. Recently, we have seen numerous examples of hackers breaking the security codes of stores and banks and obtaining sensitive financial information about customers.

The argument above depends upon which of the following assumptions?

(A) People who obtain sensitive financial information about others will not share it.
(B) It is not possible to develop a security system for a computer that cannot be broken.
(C) Computers are not more efficient than other systems of record keeping.
(D) It is much less expensive to maintain computer systems for private businesses than to maintain other systems of record keeping.
(E) Computer hackers are rarely brought to justice.

DIRECTIONS: Underline the conclusion of each of the following arguments. Answers are on page 773.

7. Every winter for the past ten years, I have caught at least one cold. This winter, I will probably catch one or more colds.

8. All members of the Board of Trustees are graduates of the college. Irving, who is a trustee, is a graduate of the college.

9. The company rules require a supervisor to discipline a habitually tardy employee either by docking his pay or by firing him. Since Smith has been late every day this week, either his pay will be docked or he will be fired.

10. The student protest proved very effective. The day after the students first occupied the administration building, the president of the college announced that he would reverse the longstanding policy of requiring certain courses.

11. It is possible to reduce our reliance on foreign energy sources because, despite the fact that the United States relies heavily on imported oil as an energy source, we have a considerable nuclear energy capacity that remains idle.

12. The tuition and other costs of getting a college education continue to soar, and recent cutbacks in government aid for students have made it even more difficult for families of even moderate means to finance their children's education. We may soon see the day when a college education is once again the prerogative of only the very rich.

13. The Federal Reserve Board must have moved last month to slow the growth of the money supply. Following a month in which prices rose more than they did the month before, interest rates rose noticeably and, in similar situations in the past, the Board has moved to counteract inflation.

14. Protectionists argue that an excess of exports over imports is essential to maintaining a favorable balance of trade. The excess can then be "cashed in" as precious metals. This means, however, that the most favorable of all trade balances will occur when a country exports its entire national product and, in turn, imports only gold and silver. Since one cannot eat gold and silver, the protectionists must surely be wrong.

DIRECTIONS: For each of the following items indicate which of the following errors of argument is used:

    (A) False Cause
    (B) Hasty Generalization
    (C) False Analogy
    (D) Either/Or Situation
    (E) Begging the Question
    (F) Ambiguity

Answers are on page 774.

15. The state has banned all smoking in railroad cars because of the threat posed by passive smoking to nonsmoking passengers. The city should learn from this lesson and pass an ordinance banning smoking in all restaurants and public meeting places.

16. Government programs often create problems or intensify problems rather than solve them. In the past five years, all levels of government have stepped up efforts to educate students about the dangers of drugs. And sure enough, the incidence of drug use among students has increased as well.

17. This semester, I am teaching philosophy of law at Bartlett College. On the first day, I asked whether any of the students in the class owned a computer. No one raised a hand. It is clear, therefore, that no one at Bartlett College owns a computer.

---

18. The home team lost the game because its players were unable to score more points than the visiting team.

---

19. A banana is yellow. Yellow is a color. Therefore, a banana is a color.

---

20. Dad: John, I'm afraid we're going to cut your allowance in half.

John: Why?

Dad: Because money is tight, and we have to reduce expenses. If we don't cut somewhere, we'll all wind up living on the street.

Determine the Main Idea
Exercise 4

DIRECTIONS: For each of the following passages, determine what answer best describes the main idea or main theme of the paragraph. Answers are on page 774.

1. College professors are currently facing a major problem in their classes. While their students are studying as hard as students did ten to fifteen years ago, today's students are failing more classes. After forming a special committee to investigate why students were failing, one college arrived at an intriguing conclusion. They discovered that students are using more text messaging to communicate, and thus are less practiced at writing in a formal and grammatically acceptable manner.

   (A) Colleges should use special committees to investigate failing students.
   (B) College professors should teach students proper English grammar.
   (C) College students are failing more classes because they no longer practice using formal English grammar.
   (D) College students should be persuaded not to use text messaging.

2. Twenty years ago, the African elephant population was declining at an alarming rate due primarily to poaching that supplied a large, illegal trade in ivory. Total elephant numbers declined by as much as 50 percent in the 1970s and 1980s. The Convention on International Trade in Endangered Species (CITES) enacted an international moratorium on the buying and selling of ivory, which was quickly followed by significant declines in ivory trading and in the rate of elephant poaching. Elephant populations in many African countries have since stabilized.

   (A) CITES is an organization that helps endangered elephants, especially those who were born prior to 1970.
   (B) Though twenty years ago the African elephant population was declining due to illegal hunting, it has now stabilized.
   (C) Selling elephant ivory is very profitable.
   (D) If trends continue, in twenty years, African elephants will no longer exist.

3. A flood is an overflow of water that covers lands that are normally not covered by water. A flood occurs, for example, when a stream or river overflows its banks. Small streams are subject to flash floods—that is, the very rapid increases in water that may last only a few minutes. In larger streams, floods usually last from several hours to a few days, and a series of storms might keep a river above flood stage for several weeks.

   (A) Floods are natural occurrences that result in negative consequences for people.
   (B) Rivers sometimes flood.
   (C) Small streams are often subject to flash floods that last only a few minutes.
   (D) A flood occurs when an overflow of water covers lands not normally covered by water.

4. If I could change one important thing about my country, it would be to have a mandatory service requirement. I mean that everyone who is able would be required to serve his or her country for a one- or two-year period following high school graduation. People would be given a choice about what kind of service they would do. They could choose to enter the military, to work in a poor area in a city, or to serve in a national park.

   (A) All high school graduates should be required to spend one or two years fulfilling a mandatory service requirement.
   (B) Because my country is not perfect, I would change one thing.
   (C) Military service is more important than working in a city or at a national park.
   (D) People should be given a choice about what kind of mandatory service they would enjoy, whether working in the military, in an urban area, or in a national park.

5. Like Shakespeare's King Richard, the woman had experienced a winter of discontent when life itself felt cold, wind blown, and gray. She longed for spring to come to her soul, when she would experience a warming of her moods. But sadness overtook her, like a blizzard covering a street with racing pillows of snow. No matter how hard she tried, she could not force spring before the proper time, but simply endured this season of sadness.

   (A) Blizzards caused the woman to become sad, much like they did for King Richard.
   (B) The woman experienced a sadness that she could not force to go away.
   (C) In winter, the woman experienced cold wind and clouds.
   (D) The woman desired for her soul to experience the type of winter that Shakespeare experienced.

Outline Passages
Exercise 5

DIRECTIONS: For each of the following passages, write an outline that follows the author's development of the content. Examples of outlines are on page 774.

Passage 1

Speaking unscientifically, we say that lightning strikes an object on the ground; but from a scientific point of view, this language is inaccurate. Cloud-to-ground lightning begins when complex
5   meteorological processes cause a tremendous electrostatic charge to build up within a cloud. Typically, the bottom of the cloud is negatively charged. When the charge reaches 50 to 100 million volts, air is no longer an effective insulator, and
10   lightning occurs within the cloud itself. Approximately 10 to 30 minutes after the onset of intra-cloud lightning, negative charges called stepped leaders emerge from the bottom of the cloud, moving toward the Earth in 50-meter
15   intervals at speeds of 100 to 200 kilometers per second, creating an ionized channel. As the leaders near the Earth, their strong electric field causes streamers of positively charged ions to develop at the tips of pointed objects connected directly or
20   indirectly to the ground. These positively charged streamers flow upward.

When the distance, known as the striking distance, between a stepped leader and one of the streamers reaches 30 to 100 meters, the
25   intervening air breaks down completely and the leader is joined to the Earth via the streamer. Now, a pulse of current known as a return stroke ranging from thousands to hundreds of thousands of amperes moves at one-tenth to one-third the speed
30   of light from the Earth through the object from which the streamer emanated and up the ionized channel to the charge center within the cloud. An ionized channel remains in the air, and additional negative charges called dart leaders will quickly
35   move down this path, resulting in further return strokes. It is this multiplicity that causes the flash to flicker. The entire event typically lasts about one second. The return stroke's extremely high temperature creates the visible lightning and
40   produces thunder by instantly turning moisture into steam.

PASSAGE OUTLINE

Passage 2

Twenty years ago, the African elephant population was declining at an alarming rate due primarily to poaching that supplied a large, illegal trade in ivory. Total elephant numbers declined by
5 as much as 50 percent in the 1970s and 1980s. The Convention on International Trade in Endangered Species (CITES) enacted an international moratorium on the buying and selling of ivory, which was quickly followed by significant declines
10 in ivory trading and in the rate of elephant poaching. Elephant populations in many African countries have since stabilized.

U.S. involvement in African elephant conservation, through both its import control
15 provisions and its grant programs, remains important. One of the earliest projects funded was a cooperative effort with the Central African Republic and the World Wildlife Fund. A cooperative effort was underway to establish a reserve in the
20 southeastern portion of that country. While funds for gating the reserve were anticipated, no funds were available for basic equipment and operations of anti-poaching patrols—hired from local communities—until a cooperative project was
25 implemented using funds provided by the United States. When the first patrols were put into place, the only signs of elephants in a local clearing within the park were the carcasses of several poached animals. Today, more than 2,000 individual
30 elephants, young and old, have been identified as using that clearing.

In Senegal, the westernmost population of elephants in Africa is now secure. Through an African elephant conservation fund grant, an
35 anti-poaching program has provided local community employment and protection for the remaining elephant population. For the first time in years, baby elephants are now seen in this small but genetically valuable population. Similar to the
40 projects described above, funds have been provided to augment anti-poaching and management support in Cameroon, Congo, Eritrea, Gabon, Mali, Tanzania, Zambia, and Zimbabwe.

PASSAGE OUTLINE

Locate Verbal Signs
Exercise 6

DIRECTIONS: In the following passage, underline and then label in the right margin any prompting, defining, similarity, contrast, or example verbal signals. Answers are on page 774.

A flood is an overflow of water that covers lands that are normally not covered by water. A flood occurs, for example, when a stream or river overflows its banks. Small streams are subject to
5   flash floods—that is, the very rapid increases in water that may last only a few minutes. In larger streams, floods usually last from several hours to a few days, and a series of storms might keep a river above flood stage for several weeks.
10   Floods can occur at any time, but weather patterns have a strong influence on when and where floods happen. Cyclones—similar in structure to tornadoes—bring moisture inland from the ocean, causing floods in the spring in the
15   western United States. Thunderstorms are relatively small but intense storms that cause flash floods in smaller streams during the summer in the Southwest. Frontal storms at the edge of large, moist air masses moving across the country cause
20   floods in the northern and eastern parts of the United States during the winter.
The magnitude of a flood is described by a term called the recurrence interval, which is based upon long-term study of flow records for a stream.
25   A five-year flood is one that would occur, on the average, once every five years. Although a 100-year flood is expected to happen only once in a century, it is important to remember that there is a one percent chance that a flood of that size could
30   happen during any given year.
Of course, the frequency and magnitude of floods can be altered if changes are made in the drainage basin of a stream or river. Significantly, harvesting timber or changing land use from
35   farming to housing can cause the runoff to increase, resulting in an increase in the magnitude of flooding. On the other hand, dams can protect against flooding by storing storm runoff. Although the same volume of water must eventually move
40   downstream, the peak flow can be reduced by temporarily storing water and then releasing it when water levels have fallen.

Locate Specific Details
Exercise 7

Items #1–3 are based on the following passage.

Fraktur is a uniquely American folk art rooted in the Pennsylvania Dutch (Pennsylvania German) culture. In German, *fraktur* refers to a particular typeface used by printers. Derived from the Latin
5 *fractura*, "breaking apart," *fraktur* suggests that the letters are broken apart and reassembled into designs. Fraktur as a genre of folk art refers to a text (usually religious) that is decorated with symbolic designs.

1. Pennsylvania Dutch is the same term as which of the following?

   (A) Pennsylvania Irish
   (B) Pennsylvania Scottish
   (C) Pennsylvania German
   (D) Pennsylvania Mennonite

2. The word *"fractura"* in Latin means

   (A) breaking apart
   (B) forging together
   (C) artful lettering
   (D) German lettering

3. Fraktur would generally appear in what type of text?

   (A) Latin
   (B) Dutch
   (C) Broken
   (D) Religious

Items #4–6 are based on the following passage.

Lightning is basically an electrical discharge of immense proportions. Some 80 percent of lightning occurs within clouds; about 20 percent is cloud-to-ground lightning; and an extremely small
5 percentage is cloud-to-sky lightning.

4. According to the passage, lightning is

   (A) an immense proportion
   (B) an electrical discharge
   (C) a natural occurrence for clouds
   (D) always within clouds

5. The percentage of lightning that occurs within clouds is

   (A) 10 percent
   (B) 20 percent
   (C) 80 percent
   (D) 100 percent

6. According to the passage, 20 percent of lightning travels from clouds to

   (A) ground
   (B) sky
   (C) clouds
   (D) electricity

Items #7–10 are based on the following passage.

We are now in the throes of a third
transformation in communications, although when
it began exactly is difficult to say. One might choose
that evening in 1844 when Samuel Morse
5 telegraphed the message "What has God wrought!"
Or possibly one could point to the invention by
Charles Babbage of the "Analytic Engine," a
mechanical device that prefigured the modern
electronic computer. Or perhaps this third
10 transformation began with the ENIAC computer
developed during World War II as the first digital
electronic computer. In any case, it is estimated that
it took about 150,000 years for human knowledge
to first double, then 1,500 years for it to double
15 again, and that it now doubles every 15 years or
less.

7. What computer was developed during World
War II?

(A) ENIAC
(B) Morse Code
(C) The Analytic Engine
(D) The telegraph

8. Who invented the "Analytic Engine"?

(A) Samuel Morse
(B) Charles Babbage
(C) The ENIAC Company
(D) No one can say.

9. How frequently does knowledge currently
double?

(A) Every 150,000 years
(B) Every 1,500 years
(C) Every 15 years or less
(D) All of the above

10. According to the passage, the era in
communications we are currently
experiencing is the

(A) first transformation
(B) digital computer age
(C) doubling of information age
(D) third transformation

Analyze the Arguments
Exercise 8

> **DIRECTIONS:** Read the following passages and then answer the corresponding items. Answers are on page 775.

Items #1–2 are based on the following passage.

Alcohol abuse and dependence are serious problems affecting 10 percent of adult Americans, and the toll is high: 3 out of 100 deaths in the United States can be linked directly to alcohol. In addition
5   to traffic crashes, injuries in the home and on the job, and serious long-term medical consequences, alcohol abuse has been implicated in aggression and crime. The cost of alcohol abuse and alcohol dependence is estimated to be as high as $1 trillion
10 annually.

Items #3–4 are based on the following passage.

Regardless of where the hopeful migrants originated, the months-long trip to the California gold country was perilous. A journey across the continent meant rough conditions and possibly
5   attacks by Indians or by other emigrants. Those coming by sea from Europe and the eastern United States had to travel around stormy Cape Horn. The sea journey could be shortened by going overland through the jungles of the Isthmus of Panama, but it
10 was a region rife with cholera and other diseases. From San Francisco, getting to the mining areas was difficult. There was little housing, disease was rampant, and food prices were astronomically high.

3. According to the author, journey to the California gold country was perilous. What dangers does the author suggest that migrants might have experienced?

(A) Attacks by other emigrants
(B) Jungle diseases
(C) Sea storms
(D) All of the above

1. The author argues that alcohol abuse and dependence are serious problems. Which of the following reasons does he NOT use to support his main idea?

(A) Three out of 100 deaths in the United States can be linked directly to alcohol.
(B) Aggression and crime can be correlated to alcohol abuse.
(C) The cost of alcohol abuse and dependence is as high as $1 trillion annually.
(D) Ten percent of adult Americans experience traffic crashes and injuries in the home and on the job due to alcohol abuse.

2. What type of evidence or support does the author use to prove his or her argument?

(A) Historical quotation
(B) Statistics
(C) A personal story
(D) A statement from an expert

4. The author claims that when emigrants arrived in California gold country, there was little housing, much disease, and high food prices. What does the author imply?

(A) Even upon arrival at their destination, the emigrants continued to experience great peril.
(B) Many emigrants returned home before arriving in California.
(C) Conditions were less difficult in San Francisco.
(D) Travel by sea was less costly than travel over inland trails.

Items #5–8 are based on the following passage.

During the past decade, the problem of gang-related crime has become a significant policy issue in the United States. According to recent estimates, more than 16,000 gangs are active in this country,
5   with at least half a million members who commit more than 600,000 crimes each year.

Gang membership leads to criminal behavior. According to a certain study, 80 percent of individual gang members said that they had stolen
10 cars, but only 10 percent of at-risk youths were not gang members. Gang members were also more involved with selling drugs.

The study reports similar contrasts for violent crimes. About 40 percent of gang members had
15 participated in a drive-by shooting, compared with 2 percent of at-risk youths. Gang members were far likelier to own guns, and the guns they owned were of a larger caliber.

Most gang members join for security and a
20 sense of belonging. As for security, research demonstrates that the benefits of avoiding gang membership far outweigh those of joining. For example, gang members are five times as likely to suffer a violent death as are at-risk youths who are
25 not gang members. As for the sense of belonging, creative prevention that fosters feelings of belonging in the community as a whole might dissuade many of these youths from joining gangs.

5. According to the author, gang membership has become a serious policy issue because

(A) gang members long for a sense of belonging
(B) drive-by shootings are becoming far too frequent
(C) gang members are more likely to be involved in violent crime
(D) gang members are less frequently found to be involved in illegal drug use

6. The author reasons that gang members are wrong in thinking they will be more secure by joining a gang. Which of the following statements best describes the author's argument?

(A) Gang members do not join gangs for security but for a sense of belonging.
(B) A gang member is five times as likely to suffer a violent death as is someone who is not affiliated with a gang.
(C) Research demonstrates that gang members do indeed feel more secure joining a gang.
(D) None of the above

7. The author argues that gang members are more likely to participate in which of the following?

(A) Drive-by shootings
(B) Selling drugs
(C) Gun ownership
(D) All of the above

8. The author suggests that potential gang members may be dissuaded from joining a gang if

(A) they owned their own weapons
(B) they felt more of a sense of belonging in their own communities
(C) the government created new policies that punish violent criminals
(D) gang membership did not lead to criminal behavior

Items #9–10 are based on the following passage.

The Amazon River of South America is the most environmentally important river in the entire world. By pure volume of water, it is the largest river in the world. In fact, by simple calculation of
5 the total flow of water from river to ocean, the Amazon River disperses more water into the ocean than the other ten largest rivers flowing into the ocean combined. By percentage, the Amazon River expels 20 percent of all the freshwater discharge
10 into the oceans. Though officially the Nile River is the longest in the world, by volume of water and the percentage of freshwater discharge, the Amazon persists the queen of the rivers.

The author argues that the Amazon River is the most environmentally important river in the entire world. What statement does he or she use to support his or her position?

(A) The Amazon River discharges 20 percent of all freshwater into the oceans.
(B) The Nile is the longest river in the world.
(C) The Amazon River is in South America.
(D) Scientists can calculate the volume of the Amazon River.

10. What persuasive device does the author use to support his or her opinion?

(A) Famous quotations
(B) Life experiences
(C) Scientific facts
(D) Emotional stories

Consider the Author's Point of View
Exercise 9

DIRECTIONS: Read the following passages and then answer the corresponding questions. Answers are on page 775.

Items #1–6 are based on the following passage.

The history of western medicine can be traced to Hippocrates, a Greek physician who lived on the island of Cos. Few particulars are known about the life of Hippocrates, but the establishment of the
5   school of medicine on Cos is regarded as his most important achievement. The school emphasized reason and observation and regarded disease as having natural, not supernatural, causes. Reason and observation are important elements of modern
10 medicine. In addition to a systematized body of empirical knowledge free of superstition, the school of Hippocrates evolved a tradition of the highest standards of conduct. Today, the Hippocratic Oath, which defines the duties and moral obligations of a
15 physician, is taken by all medical students upon completion of their training.
　　As a physician myself, I believe all medical students must accept and endorse the methodology of Hippocrates—reason and observation—prior to
20 being admitted to medical school. As one of the older professors in a highly prestigious medical school, I have grown tired of students who desire to be doctors only for fame and fortune and fail to understand the rich scientific foundations of the
25 profession.

1. Who is the author?

_____

2. Does the author have expertise or experience regarding this particular subject?

_____

_____

3. What are the author's likes or dislikes?

_____

_____

_____

4. Why did the author write this passage?

_____

_____

_____

5. What does this author want you to believe?

_____

_____

_____

6. What is the passage mainly about?

_____

_____

_____

Items #7–10 are based on the following passage.

After spending 30 years in the American banking industry, I have come to believe strongly that government bailouts of failing banks are harmful because they create incentives that
5 aggravate the underlying economic problems. Indeed, I have seen first-hand how moral hazard incentives are the villains in the recent, unprecedented wave of financial system collapses. Banks willingly and knowingly take on more risks—
10 especially default risks—than they would if they were not protected by government safety nets. In extreme cases, banking collapses lead to the fiscal insolvency of governments that bail out banks and to exchange rate collapse. As one of the first female
15 members of Congress, I wrote legislation that would have kept the government from bailing out failed banks. Unfortunately, few listened to my cogent arguments and instead they foolishly allowed themselves to be deceived by the banks.

7. Who is the author?

_____

_____

_____

8. Does the author have expertise or experience regarding this particular subject?

_____

_____

_____

9. Why did the author write this passage?

_____

_____

_____

10. What does this author want you to believe?

_____

_____

_____

Probe the Mood of the Passage
Exercise 10

DIRECTIONS: Read the following passage and then answer the corresponding questions. Answers are on page 776.

The following is a passage from Jonathan Swift's "A Modest Proposal."

It is a melancholy object to those, who walk through this great town, or travel in the country, when they see the streets, the roads and cabin-doors crowded with beggars of the female sex,
5 followed by three, four, or six children, all in rags, and importuning every passenger for alms. These mothers instead of being able to work for their honest livelihood, are forced to employ all their time in strolling to beg sustenance for their helpless
10 infants who, as they grow up, either turn thieves for want of work, or leave their dear native country, to fight for the Pretender in Spain, or sell themselves to the Barbadoes.

I think it is agreed by all parties, that this
15 prodigious number of children in the arms, or on the backs, or at the heels of their mothers, and frequently of their fathers, is in the present deplorable state of the kingdom, a very great additional grievance; and therefore whoever could
20 find out a fair, cheap and easy method of making these children sound and useful members of the common-wealth, would deserve so well of the public, as to have his statue set up for a preserver of the nation.

25 But my intention is very far from being confined to provide only for the children of professed beggars: it is of a much greater extent, and shall take in the whole number of infants at a certain age, who are born of parents in effect as
30 little able to support them, as those who demand our charity in the streets.

1. What is the mood of the passage?

_____

_____

_____

2. How does the author demonstrate the mood of the passage?

_____

_____

_____

Bonus Passages
Exercise 11

The following bonus passages are provided so that you can comprehensively practice all of the "Honing Your Reading Skills" strategies.

DIRECTIONS: Each passage below is followed by a number of items. Answer each item based upon the content of the passage. Answers are on page 776.

Items #1–10 are based on the following passage.

In 1848, gold was discovered in California, and newspapers quickly spread the word. President James K. Polk confirmed the discovery in his 1848 State of the Union message to Congress. The
5 president's words and the knowledge that taking the precious metal was completely unregulated in California were enough to trigger the greatest national mass migration in U.S. history and a global gold fever. People used their life savings, mortgaged
10 their homes, and sold everything they had to travel to California in hopes of becoming wealthy. At the time gold was discovered, there were approximately 11,000 non-Native Americans living in California. Between the time of the discovery and
15 1852, some 300,000 people, mostly young and male, traveled to California from all quarters.

Regardless of where the hopeful travelers originated, the months-long trip was perilous. A journey across the continent meant rough
20 conditions and possibly attacks by Indians or by other emigrants. Those coming by sea from Europe and the eastern United States had to travel around stormy Cape Horn. The sea journey could be shortened by going overland through the jungles of
25 the Isthmus of Panama, but it was a region rife with cholera and other diseases. From San Francisco, getting to the mining areas was difficult. There was little housing, disease was rampant, and food prices were astronomically high.
30 There were tales of people finding thousands of dollars of gold in only a few weeks, but most miners just encountered hard times. To survive, some left mining or worked for wages in other men's operations. The problem for many was that
35 they couldn't afford to return home, and any news of other people striking it rich would renew hope. Many people lost, but a few lucky ones won. By 1860, approximately $600 million in gold had been mined—gold worth more than $10 billion today.

1. In line 6, the word "precious" most nearly means

   (A) legal
   (B) scarce
   (C) beautiful
   (D) valuable

2. The author mentions that 300,000 people moved to California in order to

   (A) demonstrate that many people became wealthy
   (B) underscore the size of the migration
   (C) show that they came from all over the world
   (D) explain why so many miners failed to find gold

3. It can be inferred that some people mortgaged their homes in order to

   (A) get money to travel to California
   (B) ensure a place to return to
   (C) provide insurance against failure
   (D) purchase gold from California

4. It can be inferred that travelers who crossed the Isthmus of Panama

   (A) generally came from the eastern U.S.
   (B) arrived in California after the Gold Rush
   (C) avoided the trip around Cape Horn
   (D) paid less than others for their trip

5. In line 25, the word "rife" most nearly means

(A) devoid
(B) filled
(C) immune
(D) suspected

6. The author mentions all of the following as difficulties facing travelers when they arrived in San Francisco EXCEPT

(A) high food prices
(B) a housing shortage
(C) widespread disease
(D) lack of work

7. In line 18, the word "perilous" most nearly means

(A) dangerous
(B) lengthy
(C) uneventful
(D) expensive

8. In line 35, "couldn't afford" most nearly means

(A) weren't able to sell their gold
(B) couldn't find transportation
(C) had no money
(D) didn't want

9. According to the selection, why did so many people move to California?

(A) They hoped to become rich by mining gold.
(B) President Polk encouraged them to go.
(C) They wanted to open stores to sell goods to miners.
(D) They had no homes of their own.

10. What is the main focus of the selection?

(A) The conditions in San Francisco during the California Gold Rush
(B) The various modes of transportation available during the mid-1800s
(C) The demographic characteristics of the people who came to California
(D) The California migration triggered by the discovery of gold

Items #11–18 are based on the following passage.

At the peak of its prosperity, Chicago's Black Metropolis was recognized as a model of African American achievement. By 1900, a small South Side black community centered at State and 35ᵗʰ Streets
5 began to take on the characteristics of a "city-within-a-city," which paralleled the growth and expansion of the city of Chicago at large. It grew and prospered until the 1930s, when the Great Depression and associated socio-economic
10 conditions virtually halted its further development.

The established white businesses and social communities of Chicago historically had no interest in the black community; consequently, the black community gradually evolved a complete
15 commercial, social, and political base of its own. A great amount of money was generated within the black community, and Joseph Binga established Chicago's first black-owned bank in 1908. With greater access to financial resources, the
20 commercial and business interests of Black Metropolis greatly diversified into a wide range of professional, commercial, and manufacturing interests. The vicinity of State and 35ᵗʰ Streets was rapidly transformed into the Wall Street of the black
25 community.

In marked contrast to the staid banks, insurance companies, and professional offices which conducted business by day on State Street, the area was magically transformed at night by the
30 bright lights and exciting sounds of the numerous nightclubs and all-night restaurants scattered throughout the business district. These were the popular clubs where such notables as King Oliver, Louis Armstrong, and Jelly Roll Morton played and
35 earned Chicago its reputation as a jazz center with a uniquely Chicago style. It was often said that if a horn were held up at the corner of State and 35ᵗʰ Streets, because of all the music in the air, the horn would play itself.
40 Churches played an important role in the development of Black Metropolis, both from a social as well as a spiritual standpoint. Large congregations such as the Olivet Baptist Church and Pilgrim Baptist Church conducted extensive social
45 programs and were instrumental in securing lodging and employment for the newcomers who arrived from the South during the Great Migration. Similar programs were conducted at the Wabash Avenue Y.M.C.A., which opened in 1914 through the
50 impetus of philanthropist Julius Rosenwald, the President of Sears, Roebuck & Company. Programs

at the Y.M.C.A. included extensive job training programs such as auto repair and manual training.

Organized political alliances gave Black
55 Metropolis increased power in Chicago's city government, beginning with the election of Oscar DePriest as the city's first black alderman in 1915. Initially working in alliance with the white Republican bosses who controlled the political
60 destiny of the Black Metropolis wards, DePriest later built a political organization of his own, forming the "People's Movement Club" with headquarters on South Indiana Avenue. The political voting strength of the Black Metropolis
65 wards was such that, by the 1920s, political control was effectively taken from the white political bosses who formerly controlled them and put into the hands of political figures from within the black community. In 1928, Oscar DePriest had the
70 distinction of being the first black from the North to be elected to a seat in the United States House of Representatives, a seat he held for three consecutive terms.

The growth and prosperity of Black Metropolis
75 was directly tied to the rapid growth of the black population, particularly during the Great Migration. The sharp decline in new arrivals during the 1920s weakened the financial base of the community, adversely affecting the businesses that relied on
80 support from within the black community. When white businessmen, who previously had ignored the black community, began to realize the economic potential of the black community, an alternate business area was created along 47ᵗʰ Street by
85 white developers and store owners who controlled the property to such an extent that black-owned businesses were largely excluded from the area. The introduction of established white chain stores and commercial enterprises along 47ᵗʰ Street siphoned
90 off its energy and self-supporting financial base. The final blow to Black Metropolis came from the Great Depression of 1929, which closed down most of its black-owned banks, insurance companies, and other business interests, while many of the businesses of
95 47ᵗʰ Street, with their broader access to credit and nationwide financial backing, survived. The self-supporting momentum of Black Metropolis, which its backers had hoped would lead to recognition and eventual integration with the downtown business
100 establishment, was thus dealt a serious blow.

11. According to the passage, Joseph Binga was a

(A) banker
(B) musician
(C) politician
(D) minister

12. According to the passage, in what year was Oscar DePriest first elected to the United States House of Representatives?

(A) 1900
(B) 1908
(C) 1915
(D) 1928

13. According to the passage, the event that led to the closing of most black-owned business in Black Metropolis was

(A) the Great Migration
(B) the opening of black-owned banks
(C) the election of a black alderman
(D) the Great Depression

14. The author explains that the black community developed its own businesses because

(A) white-controlled chain stores dominated 47th Street
(B) State and 35th Streets were convenient to all Chicago residents
(C) white businesses were not interested in the black community
(D) the number of people moving into the area declined sharply

15. In lines 5–6, the phrase "city-within-a-city" is used by the author to express the idea that Black Metropolis

(A) had a population larger than that of Chicago
(B) was largely independent of greater Chicago
(C) was an important center for jazz music
(D) had its own city government

16. Which of the following is NOT mentioned in the passage as a program undertaken by churches with large congregations?

(A) Lending money to black-owned business
(B) Finding housing for recent arrivals
(C) Helping newcomers to find jobs
(D) Conducting extensive social programs

17. All of the following people are mentioned in the passage as being musicians EXCEPT

(A) Louis Armstrong
(B) Jelly Roll Morton
(C) Julius Rosenwald
(D) King Oliver

18. The passage states that Oscar DePriest began his political career by first

(A) building a headquarters on South Indiana Avenue
(B) working with the powerful white Republican politicians
(C) forming the People's Movement Club
(D) being elected to the United States House of Representatives

Items #19–26 are based on the following passage.

How jazz is defined depends on whom you talk to. There are many types and styles of jazz: jazz-rock, Latin jazz, acid jazz, fusion, and several other "jazzes." The dictionary itself has several
5 definitions. However, most people agree that jazz developed in the early twentieth century, that it was created mainly by African-Americans, and that it has elements of European and African-American cultures.

10 As for the origin of the word "jazz," one popular story describes a somewhat inebriated customer in Chicago who, in a moment of excitement, leapt to his feet and shouted to the band, "Jass it up boys, jass it up." The story then
15 goes that through a printer's error jass became jazz, and the name stuck. Perhaps the best response to the question, "What is jazz?" was provided by Louis Armstrong, who, when asked that question, said, "If you don't know, don't mess with it."

20 Jazz is basically a style of music. It has a lot of the same characteristics as other music but also treats the basic elements of music in a unique way. Any melody can be played in a jazz fashion by putting triplets behind the basic beat. In fact, one of
25 the common practices of jazz players is to quote melodies from various sources, including classical pieces, in their solos. By putting the triplet feeling in their playing, jazz players achieve a "swinging" effect in the playing of the melody. The triplet
30 feeling contrasts with the more common straight eighth note feel that is found in most music. The triplet feel is much "looser" and has a "swinging feeling" when compared with the eighth note feeling. The ability to play in a swing style is a basic
35 building block for the jazz musician.

More important even than interpretation, in fact the most important element of jazz, is improvisation. This is the jazz player's ability to instantaneously compose, edit, revise, and perform.
40 It is also the most difficult element to master, and this is why most players spend their entire lives working on developing this aspect of their playing. Improvisation is the element by which jazz players are judged and by which they establish their
45 claim to immortality. It is an incredibly complex procedure that encompasses every element of not only jazz but of music itself. It is what makes jazz, jazz. Again, jazz is not the only music to use improvisation, but it uses it to an extent far greater
50 than any other style of music.

Rhythm is also important. In this area, jazz distinguishes itself with a tremendous reliance on syncopation. Syncopation is an accent or emphasis where you least expect it. It can happen on a part of
55 a beat or a part of a measure. It gives the music life and provides a tremendous variety in the rhythm of a given piece. Syncopation also occurs when an expected accent is left out by the musician.

Finally, there is tempo. Tempo is just another
60 name for the speed of a piece of music. In jazz, more often than not, the tempo remains steady from the beginning of the piece to the end. This is not the only music where this occurs, but the tempo variations that characterize other types of music are
65 not found in the majority of jazz performances.

Although any melody or piece can be played in a "jazz" style, the blues holds a special place in every jazz performer's heart. It is a very stylized form almost always consisting of twelve measures of
70 music and only three chords. The improviser needs to play only one scale to sound good when he or she solos over the changes (chords). Though blues has a very important influence on jazz, the blues is itself a separate musical entity from jazz.

75 Is jazz better than classical music? There really is no contest between these two types of music because they have different goals. Jazz is a player's art and classical music is a composer's art. In classical music, for the most part, the performers
80 are trying to re-create what the composer had in mind. If you listen to ten recordings of Beethoven's "Ninth Symphony," they would pretty much sound the same. Listen to ten recordings of Duke Ellington's "In a Sentimental Mood" and even the
85 melody would not be treated the same way by the individual players. Individuality is encouraged, sought after, rewarded, and absolutely necessary for the art of jazz to survive.

19. Which of the following sentences about jazz does NOT make a true statement?

(A) Jazz originated in the early twentieth century.
(B) Jazz has elements of European culture in it.
(C) Jazz is a single type of music that is easily defined.
(D) Jazz was mainly created by African American musicians.

20. The passage explains that the word "jass" became "jazz" because

(A) the dictionary definition changed
(B) composers preferred jazz to jass
(C) musicians could not define jazz
(D) a printer made a spelling error

21. According to the passage, jazz musicians create a swinging effect by using

(A) straight eighth notes
(B) triplets
(C) blues scales
(D) tempo variations

22. In lines 25–26, the phrase "quote melodies from" most nearly means

(A) listen to music from
(B) mention the composers of
(C) play notes from
(D) change the rhythm of

23. The passage mentions all of the following as typical of jazz music EXCEPT

(A) improvisation
(B) syncopation
(C) interpretation
(D) tempo variations

24. In line 68, the word "stylized" most nearly means

(A) unusual
(B) predictable
(C) complicated
(D) serious

25. According to the passage, the blues is characterized by

(A) twelve measures, three chords, and one scale
(B) twelve measures, one chord, and three scales
(C) three measures, one chord, and twelve scales
(D) one measure, twelve chords, and three scales

26. As used in the passage, improvisation means to

(A) create spontaneously
(B) rehearse carefully
(C) prepare beforehand
(D) follow a plan

Items #27–34 are based on the following passage.

The Hawaiian Islands, which are entirely of volcanic origin, have formed in the middle of the Pacific Ocean nearly 2,000 miles from the nearest plate boundary. How do the Hawaiian Islands and
5 other volcanoes form in the interior of plates?

J. Tuzo Wilson, a geophysicist, came up with an ingenious idea that became known as the "hotspot" theory. Wilson noted that in certain locations, such as Hawaii, volcanism has been active for very long
10 periods of time. This could only happen if relatively small, long-lasting, and exceptionally hot regions— called hotspots—existed below the plates to provide localized sources of high heat energy, called thermal plumes, to sustain volcanism.

15 Wilson hypothesized that the distinctive linear shape of the Hawaiian Islands resulted from the Pacific Plate moving over a deep, stationary hotspot in the mantle, located beneath the present-day position of the island of Hawaii. Heat from this
20 hotspot produced a persistent source of magma by partly melting the overriding Pacific Plate. The magma, because it is lighter than the surrounding solid rock, then rises through the mantle and crust to erupt onto the seafloor, forming an active
25 seamount. Over time, countless eruptions cause the seamount to grow until it finally emerges above sea level to form an island volcano.

Wilson suggested that continuing plate movement eventually carries the island beyond the
30 hotspot, cutting it off from the magma source, and volcanism ceases. As one island volcano becomes extinct, another develops over the hotspot, and the cycle is repeated. This process of volcano growth and death, over many millions of years, has left a
35 long trail of volcanic islands and seamounts across the Pacific Ocean floor.

According to Wilson's hotspot theory, the volcanoes of the Hawaiian chain should get progressively older and become more eroded the
40 farther they travel beyond the hotspot. The oldest volcanic rocks on Kauai, the most northwestern inhabited Hawaiian island, are about 5.5 million years old and are deeply eroded. By comparison, on the "Big Island" of Hawaii—the most southeastern
45 in the chain and presumably still positioned over the hotspot—the oldest exposed rocks are less than 0.7 million years old and new volcanic rock is continually being formed.

The possibility that the Hawaiian Islands
50 become younger to the southeast was suspected by the ancient Hawaiians, long before any scientific studies were done. Hawaiians noticed the differences in erosion, soil formation, and vegetation and recognized that the islands to the
55 northwest (Niihau and Kauai) were older than those to the southeast (Maui and Hawaii). This idea was handed down from generation to generation in the legends of Pele, the fiery Goddess of Volcanoes. Pele originally lived on Kauai. When her older sister
60 Namakaokahai, the Goddess of the Sea, attacked her, Pele fled to the Island of Oahu. When she was forced by Namakaokahai to flee again, Pele moved southeast to Maui and finally to Hawaii, where she now lives in the Halemaumau Crater at the summit
65 of Kilauea Volcano. The mythical flight of Pele from Kauai to Hawaii is consistent with geologic evidence that clearly shows the islands become younger from northwest to southeast.

Although Hawaii is perhaps the best known
70 hotspot, others exist beneath the oceans and continents. More than a hundred hotspots beneath the Earth's crust have been active during the past 10 million years.

A few hotspots are thought to exist below the
75 North American Plate. Perhaps the best known is the hotspot in the region of Yellowstone National Park. Here are found several calderas (large craters formed by the ground collapse accompanying explosive volcanism) that were produced by three
80 gigantic eruptions during the past two million years, the most recent of which occurred about 600,000 years ago. Ash deposits from these powerful eruptions have been mapped as far away as Texas. The thermal energy of the Yellowstone hotspot fuels
85 more than 10,000 hot pools and springs, geysers (like Old Faithful), and pools of boiling mud. A large body of magma, capped by a hydrothermal system (a zone of pressurized steam and hot water), still exists beneath the caldera.

27. Which of the following Hawaiian Islands was formed first?

(A) Kauai
(B) Maui
(C) Oahu
(D) Hawaii

28. According to Wilson's theory, what is the first event that occurs in the formation of a volcanic island like Hawaii?

(A) The plate moves away from the heat plume.
(B) Magma spills onto the ocean floor to make a seamount.
(C) Repeated eruptions increase the height of the seamount.
(D) A seamount emerges to form a volcanic island.

29. According to the passage, all of the following are found in Yellowstone Park EXCEPT

(A) calderas
(B) hot springs
(C) pools of boiling mud
(D) seamounts

30. According to Hawaiian legend, after fleeing from Namakaokahai, Pele finally settled on

(A) Niiau
(B) Oahu
(C) Kauai
(D) Hawaii

31. According to the passage, the magma produced by a hotspot rises because it is

(A) lighter than the surrounding rock
(B) influenced by the plate's movement
(C) in the middle of the plate
(D) no longer volcanically active

32. In line 50, the word "younger" most nearly means

(A) volcanically inactive
(B) more thoroughly eroded
(C) more recently formed
(D) lacking vegetation

33. According to the passage, the last major eruption in the Yellowstone Park area occurred

(A) 10 million years ago
(B) 2 million years ago
(C) 600,000 years ago
(D) 10,000 years ago

34. The passage explains that the ash from Yellowstone Park found in Texas was deposited there by

(A) geysers and springs
(B) volcanic eruptions
(C) pressurized steam
(D) collapsing craters

Quantitative Reasoning
Supplement

Outline

NUMBERS

Basic Terms and Operations

For simplicity, we will introduce the terms and operational concepts associated with all numbers using **whole numbers**. **Whole numbers** are the numbers used for counting, plus the number zero: $\{0, 1, 2, 3, 4, \ldots\}$. Later we will return to the other numbers of the real number system, including fractions, signed numbers, and irrational numbers.

Basic Terms

sum (total): The result of adding numbers together. The **sum**, or total, of 2 and 3 is 5: $2+3=5$.

difference: The result of subtracting one number from another. The **difference** between 5 and 2 is 3: $5-2=3$.

product: The result of multiplying numbers together. The **product** of 2 and 3 is 6: $2 \cdot 3 = 6$.

quotient: The result of dividing one number by another. The **quotient** when 6 is divided by 2 is 3: $6 \div 2 = 3$.

remainder: In division, if the quotient is not itself a whole number, the result can be written as a whole number quotient plus a whole number remainder. For example, $7 \div 3 = 2$, plus a **remainder** of 1.

Symbols of Inclusion

Sets of **parentheses**, **brackets**, and **braces** indicate the order in which operations are to be performed. The innermost symbol of inclusion indicates which operation should be executed first. Generally, operations in parentheses are done first, operations in brackets are done second, and operations in braces are done third. Parentheses, brackets, and braces have the same meaning—three different symbols are used for clarity.

Examples:

1. $(2+3) \cdot 4 = 20$

2. $2 + (3 \cdot 4) = 14$

3. $\frac{(2 \cdot 3) \cdot (2+1)}{3 \cdot (5-4)} = \frac{(6) \cdot (3)}{3 \cdot (1)} = \frac{18}{3} = 6$

A particularly complex statement might use parentheses, brackets, and even braces if necessary. With problems such as these, work from the inside out. Start with the operations within parentheses; then do the operations within the brackets; and finally complete the indicated operations.

Example:

$\{[(2 \cdot 3) - 5] \cdot 1\} + [2 \cdot (4-1)] = [(6-5) \cdot 1] + (2 \cdot 3) = (6-5) + 6 = 1 + 6 = 7$

Order of Operations

Parentheses, brackets, and braces eliminate ambiguity, but they do not always dictate the order in which operations must be done. Use this mnemonic to remember the order of operations for simplifying expressions: **Please Excuse My Dear Aunt Sally.**

Please:	**P**arentheses, brackets, braces
Excuse:	**E**xponents, radicals
My:	**M**ultiplication*
Dear:	**D**ivision*
Aunt:	**A**ddition*
Sally:	**S**ubtraction*

*Remember: add/subtract and multiply/divide in expressions as the operations occur from left to right.

Examples:

1. $6 + 4 \cdot 3 - 5 = 6 + 12 - 5 = 18 - 5 = 13$

2. $[2(3+4)](3 \cdot 2) = [2(7)](6) = (14)(6) = 84$

3. $\{(2+7) - [(8 \cdot 6) \div 2] + 25\}\{[2 + 3(2-1)] \div 5\} = [(2+7) - (48 \div 2) + 25]\{[2 + 3(1)] \div 5\} =$
   $[(2+7) - 24 + 25](5 \div 5) = (9 - 24 + 25)(1) = (-15 + 25) = 10$

Factoring and Canceling

An important point to make is that even when multiplication and addition are combined, you have a choice about order of operations. In the following example, most people would probably do the addition first and then the multiplication. It is also permissible, however, to do the multiplication first.

Example:

$5(2+3+4) = 5(9) = 45$
$5(2+3+4) = 5(2) + 5(3) + 5(4) = 10 + 15 + 20 = 45$

Thus, $10 + 15 + 20$ is equal to $5(2) + 5(3) + 5(4)$, which in turn equals $5(2+3+4)$. This reverse multiplication process is called **factoring**. Factoring can be a tremendous labor-saving device. It is almost always more efficient to first simplify expressions by factoring.

Example:

$(723)(34) - (723)(33) = 24,582 - 23,859 = 723$
$(723)(34) - (723)(33) = 723(34 - 33) = 723(1) = 723$

Factoring can be combined with division for even greater simplifying power. Division of factors common to both the numerator and the denominator is called **canceling**.

Example:

$$\frac{24 + 36}{12} = \frac{12(2+3)}{12} = (1)(2+3) = 5$$

- In this case, 12 can be factored from both 24 and 36. It is then possible to divide 12 by 12, which is 1.

Properties of the Integers 0 and 1

The integers 0 and 1 have special properties that differ from other integers. First, the integer 0 is neither positive nor negative. If n is any number, then $n \pm 0 = n$ and $n \cdot 0 = 0$. Also, division by 0 is not defined. Therefore, it is never allowable to divide anything by 0. The integer 1 multiplied by any number n is equal to the original number; that is, $1 \cdot n = n$. Also, for any number $n \neq 0$, $n \cdot \frac{1}{n} = 1$. Note that the number 1 can be expressed in many ways; for example, $\frac{n}{n} = 1$ for any number $n \neq 0$. Finally, multiplying or dividing an expression by 1, in any form, does not change the value of that expression.

Examples:

1. $4 + 0 = 4$

2. $4 - 0 = 4$

3. $3 \cdot 0 = 0$

4. $1 \cdot 5 = 5$

5. $2 \cdot \frac{1}{2} = 1$

6. $\frac{4}{4} = 1$

Factors, Multiples, and Primes

Numbers that evenly divide another number are called the **factors** of that number. If a number is evenly divisible by another number, it is considered a **multiple** of that number. 1, 2, 3, 4, 6, and 12 are all factors of 12: 12 is a multiple of 2, a multiple of 3, and so on. Some numbers are not evenly divisible except by 1 and themselves. A number such as this is called a **prime** number. For example, 13 is evenly divisible by 1 and 13 but not by 2 through 12. **Note:** 1 is NOT considered a prime number even though it is not evenly divisible by any other number. The following are examples of prime numbers: 2, 3, 5, 7, 11, 13, 17, 19, and 23.

Example:

Let $D = 120$. How many positive factors, including 1 and 120, does D have?

- Express 120 using prime factors: $120 = 2(2)(2)(3)(5) = 2^3(3)(5)$. The exponents of the prime factors 2, 3, and 5 are 3, 1, and 1, respectively. Add 1 to each exponent and multiply the results together: $(3+1)(1+1)(1+1) = (4)(2)(2) = 16$.

The **greatest common factor** of two or more whole numbers is the largest whole number that divides evenly into each of the numbers. There are two methods for finding the greatest common factor. The first method is to list all the factors of each number and then choose the largest factor common to both lists. The second method for finding the greatest common factor is to list the prime factors and then multiply the common prime factors. Note that if the numbers do not share any prime factors, than the greatest common factor is 1.

Example:

Find the greatest common factor of 28 and 72.

- *First Method:* The factors of 28 are: 1, 2, 4, 7, 14, and 28. The factors of 72 are: 1, 2, 3, 4, 6, 8, 9, 12, 18, 24, 36, and 72. Therefore, the greatest common factor—the largest number common to each list of factors—is 4.

- *Second Method:* The prime factorization of 28 is: $28 = (2)(14) = (2)(2)(7)$. The prime factorization of 72 is: $72 = (2)(36) = (2)(2)(18) = (2)(2)(2)(9) = (2)(2)(2)(3)(3)$. The prime factorizations of 28 and 72 both have two 2s in common. Therefore, the greatest common factor is: $(2)(2) = 4$.

Odd and Even Numbers

An **odd number** is not evenly divisible by 2; an **even number** is a number that is divisible by 2. Any number with a last digit that is 0, 2, 4, 6, or 8 is divisible by 2 and is even. Any number with a last digit that is 1, 3, 5, 7, or 9 is not evenly divisible by 2 and is odd. Zero is considered an even number. The following are important principles that govern the behavior of odd and even numbers.

PRINCIPLES OF ODD AND EVEN NUMBERS

1. $\text{EVEN} \pm \text{EVEN} = \text{EVEN}$

2. $\text{EVEN} \pm \text{ODD} = \text{ODD}$

3. $\text{ODD} \pm \text{EVEN} = \text{ODD}$

4. $\text{ODD} \pm \text{ODD} = \text{EVEN}$

5. $\text{EVEN} \cdot \text{EVEN} = \text{EVEN}$

6. $\text{EVEN} \cdot \text{ODD} = \text{EVEN}$

7. $\text{ODD} \cdot \text{EVEN} = \text{EVEN}$

8. $\text{ODD} \cdot \text{ODD} = \text{ODD}$

Examples:

1. $2+4=6$; $2-4=-2$

2. $4+3=7$; $4-3=1$

3. $3+4=7$; $3-4=-1$

4. $3+5=8$; $3-5=-2$

5. $2 \cdot 4 = 8$

6. $2 \cdot 3 = 6$

7. $3 \cdot 2 = 6$

8. $3 \cdot 5 = 15$

The rules for multiplication DO NOT apply to division. For example, if you divide the even number 4 by the even number 8, the result is $\frac{1}{2}$. Odd and even are characteristics of whole numbers and negative integers, but not fractions. A fraction is neither odd nor even.

Consecutive Integers

Consecutive integers immediately follow one another. For example, 3, 4, 5, and 6 are consecutive integers, but 3, 7, 21, and 45 are not. In a string of consecutive integers, the next number is always one more than the preceding number. Thus, if n is the first number in a string of consecutive integers, the second number is $n+1$, the third number is $n+2$, the fourth number is $n+3$, and so on.

1st	2nd	3rd	4th
n	$n+1$	$n+2$	$n+3$
3	4	5	6

We can also speak of *consecutive even integers* and *consecutive odd integers*. 2, 4, 6, and 8 are consecutive even integers; 3, 5, 7, and 9 are consecutive odd integers. If n is the first number in a string of consecutive even or odd integers, the second number is $n+2$, the third number is $n+4$, the fourth number is $n+6$, and so on.

1st	2nd	3rd	4th
n	$n+2$	$n+4$	$n+6$
3	5	7	9
4	6	8	10

Do not be confused by the fact that the sequence for consecutive odd integers proceeds as n, $n+2$, $n+4$, etc. Even though 2, 4, etc. are even numbers, $n+2$, $n+4$, etc. will be odd numbers when the starting point, n, is odd.

Working with Signed Numbers

Numbers are just positions in a linear system. Each whole number is one greater than the number to its left and one less than the number to its right. The following number line represents the **integer number system**, which consists of the signed (positive and negative) whole numbers and zero:

$$(-) \longleftarrow \overset{-15 \qquad -10 \qquad -5 \qquad 0 \qquad 5 \qquad 10 \qquad 15}{\underset{}{|\!|\!|\!|\!|\!|\!|\!|\!|\!|\!|\!|\!|\!|\!|\!|\!|\!|\!|\!|\!|\!|\!|\!|\!|\!|\!|\!|\!|\!|}} \longrightarrow (+)$$

A number's **absolute value** is its distance on the number line from the origin, without regard to direction: $|x| = |-x|$.

Examples:

1. $|4| = 4$

2. $|-10| = 10$

3. $|5| - |3| = 5 - 3 = 2$

4. $|-2| + |-3| = 2 + 3 = 5$

PRINCIPLES FOR WORKING WITH NEGATIVE NUMBERS ✓

1. *Subtraction* of a *negative* number is equivalent to *addition* of a *positive* number.

   Example: $10 - (-5) = 10 + |-5| = 10 + 5 = 15$

2. *Addition* of a *negative* number is equivalent to *subtraction* of a *positive* number.

   Example: $10 + (-4) = 10 - |-4| = 10 - 4 = 6$

3. *Multiplication* or *division* involving an *odd* number of *negative* numbers always results in a *negative* number.

   Examples: a. $-1 \cdot -2 \cdot -3 = -6$

   b. $\dfrac{4}{-2} = -2$

4. *Multiplication* or *division* involving an *even* number of *negative* numbers always results in a positive number.

   Examples: a. $\dfrac{(-2)(6)}{-4} = \dfrac{-12}{-4} = 3$

   b. $-1 \cdot -2 = 2$

Numbers
Exercise 1

DIRECTIONS: Choose the correct answer to each of the following items. Answers are on page 777.

1. Subtracting 1 from which digit in the number 12,345 will decrease the value of the number by 1,000?

A. 1 C. 3 E. 5
B. 2 D. 4

2. $(1 \cdot 10,000) + (2 \cdot 1,000) + (3 \cdot 100) + (4 \cdot 10) + (5 \cdot 1) = ?$

A. 5,000 C. 12,345 E. 543,210
B. 15,000 D. 54,321

3. What is the sum of 5, 7, and 8?

A. 12 C. 20 E. 28
B. 15 D. 25

4. What is the difference between 28 and 14?

A. 2 C. 14 E. 392
B. 7 D. 42

5. What is the product of 20 and 50?

A. 70 C. 1,000 E. 100,000
B. 100 D. 10,000

6. What is the product of 12 and 10?

A. 2 C. 120 E. 300
B. 22 D. 240

7. What is the sum of $(5+1)$ and $(2+3)$?

A. 4 C. 24 E. 40
B. 11 D. 33

8. What is the difference between $(5+2)$ and $(3 \cdot 2)$?

A. 0 C. 3 E. 14
B. 1 D. 10

9. What is the difference between the product of 3 and 4 and the product of 2 and 3?

A. 2 C. 6 E. 36
B. 3 D. 12

10. What is the remainder when 15 is divided by 8?

A. 0 C. 4 E. 89
B. 1 D. 7

11. When both 12 and 19 are divided by a certain number, the remainder is 5. What is the number?

A. 3 C. 5 E. 9
B. 4 D. 7

12. $[(36 \div 12) \cdot (24 \div 3)] \div [(1 \cdot 3) - (18 \div 9)] = ?$

A. 3 C. 16 E. 24
B. 8 D. 20

13. $[(12 \cdot 3) - (3 \cdot 12)] + [(8 \div 2) \div 4] = ?$

A. 0 C. 4 E. 16
B. 1 D. 8

14. $12 + 24 + 36 = ?$

A. $3 \cdot 12$ D. $6(2) + 6(3) + 6(4)$
B. $12(1 + 2 + 3)$ E. $12 \cdot 24 \cdot 36$
C. $12(3 + 4 + 5)$

15. $\dfrac{99(121) - 99(120)}{33} = ?$

A. 1 C. 33 E. 120
B. 3 D. 99

16. How many prime numbers are greater than 20 but less than 30?

A. 0 C. 2 E. 4
B. 1 D. 3

17. How many prime numbers are greater than 50 but less than 60?

A. 0 C. 2 E. 4
B. 1 D. 3

18. Which of the following numbers is (are) prime?

I. 11
II. 111
III. 1,111

A. I only D. I and III only
B. II only E. I, II, and III
C. I and II only

19. What is the greatest common factor of 25 and 40?

A. 5   C. 10   E. 25
B. 8   D. 15

20. What is the greatest common factor of 36 and 54?

A. 2   C. 6   E. 36
B. 3   D. 18

21. What is the greatest common factor of 56 and 84?

A. 4   C. 14   E. 36
B. 7   D. 28

22. What is the greatest common factor of 7, 14, and 21?

A. 1   C. 14   E. 35
B. 7   D. 21

23. What is the smallest multiple of both 5 and 2?

A. 7   C. 20   E. 40
B. 10   D. 30

24. What is the smallest multiple of both 12 and 18?

A. 36   C. 72   E. 216
B. 48   D. 128

25. If n is an even number, then which of the following <u>may not</u> be even?

A. $(n \cdot n) + n$ C. $n + 2$ E. $\frac{n}{2}$
B. $n \cdot n - n$ D. $3(n + 2)$

26. If m, n, and o are consecutive whole numbers that total 15, what is the largest of the three numbers?

A. 4   C. 6   E. 17
B. 5   D. 14

27. If $A = 2^2(3)(7) = 84$, how many positive factors, including 1 and 84, does a have?

A. 12   C. 36   E. 84
B. 24   D. 42

28. $5 + 8 + (-2) + (-1) = ?$

A. 3   C. 10   E. 23
B. 7   D. 13

29. $12 - 7 + 6 + (-1) = ?$

A. 2   C. 10   E. 18
B. 6   D. 14

30. $-2 + (-3) + (-4) = ?$

A. −24   C. −6   E. 6
B. −9   D. 0

31. $-2 \cdot -1 \cdot 1 = ?$

A. −3   C. 1   E. 4
B. −2   D. 2

32. $-10 \cdot -10 \cdot -10 = ?$

A. −1,000   C. −1   E. 1,000
B. −30   D. 1

33. $-1 \cdot -1 \cdot -1 \cdot -1 \cdot -1 \cdot -1 \cdot -1 \cdot -1 \cdot -1 \cdot -1 = ?$

A. −10   C. 0   E. 10
B. −1   D. 1

34. $-12 \div -12 = ?$

A. −144   C. 1   E. 144
B. −1   D. 24

35. $[(2 \cdot -1) + (4 \div -2)][(-6 + 6) - (2 - 3)] = ?$

A. 5   C. −2   E. −23
B. 2   D. −4

36. $(2 - 3)(3 - 2)(4 - 3)(3 - 4)(5 - 4)(4 - 5) = ?$

A. −625   C. 1   E. 625
B. −1   D. 50

37. $[2(3 - 4)] + [(125 \div -25)(1 \cdot -2)] = ?$

A. −12   C. 2   E. 125
B. −8   D. 8

38. $-\frac{1}{2} \cdot 2 \cdot -\frac{1}{2} \cdot 2 \cdot -\frac{1}{2} \cdot 2 = ?$

A. −16   C. −1   E. 2
B. −8   D. 1

39. If n is any negative number, which of the following must also be negative?

 I. $n + n$
 II. $n \cdot n$
 III. $n - n$

A. I only   D. II and III only
B. II only   E. I, II, and III
C. I and III only

40. If n is any positive number, which of the following must be positive?

   I. $-n-(-n)$
   II. $-n \cdot -n$
   III. $n \div (-n \cdot -n)$

   A. I only   D. I and III only
   B. II only   E. II and III only
   C. III only

41. In the figure below, what point between A and B is three times as far from A as from B?

$$\begin{array}{cc} A & B \\ \bullet & \bullet \\ -12 & 28 \end{array}$$

   A. 12   C. 20   E. 24
   B. 18   D. 21

42. $|1| + |-2| + |3| + |-4| + |5| + |-6| + |7| + |-8| + |9| + |-10| + |11| + |-12| = ?$

   A. -12 C. 6   E. 78
   B. -6 D. 12

PERCENTS

A *percent* is a special type of fraction that always has a denominator equal to 100. The percent sign, "%," is shorthand for "$\frac{x}{100}$." For example, $67\% = \frac{67}{100}$.

Converting to and from Percents

Since percents are simply a special type of fraction, both fractions and decimals can be converted to percents, and vice versa. The easiest conversion is to change a decimal to a percent: move the decimal point two places to the right and add the percent sign.

Examples:

1. $0.27 = 27\%$

2. $0.50 = 50\%$

3. $0.275 = 27.5\%$

This substitutes "%" for two decimal places—simply a matter of changing things from one form into an equivalent form, which is a process we have already used in several ways. To change a percent back to a decimal, move the decimal point two places to the left and drop the percent sign.

Examples:

1. $27\% = 0.27$

2. $50\% = 0.50$

3. $27.5\% = 0.275$

To convert a fraction to a percent, just convert the fraction to a decimal and follow the rule above.

Examples:

1. $\frac{3}{4} = 0.75 = 75\%$

2. $\frac{5}{8} = 0.625 = 62.5\%$

3. $\frac{1}{10} = 0.10 = 10\%$

To reverse the process, follow the rule given above for turning percentages back into decimals, and then convert the decimal to a fraction.

Examples:

1. $75\% = 0.75 = \frac{75}{100} = \frac{3}{4}$

2. $62.5\% = 0.625 = \frac{625}{1,000} = \frac{5}{8}$

3. $10\% = 0.1 = \frac{1}{10}$

There are two tricky types of percents: those greater than 100% and those less than 1%. First, it is possible to have a percent that is larger than 100. This would be the result of converting a mixed number, such as $2\frac{3}{4}$, to a percent: $2\frac{3}{4} = 2.75 = 275\%$. Second, percents can also be less than 1, in which case they are written with decimals; for example, 0.5%. However, these numbers follow the general rules outlined above. To convert 0.5% to a fraction: $0.5\% = 0.005 = \frac{5}{1,000} = \frac{1}{200}$. Similarly, fractions smaller than $\frac{1}{100}$ will yield a percent less than 1: $\frac{1}{2,500} = 0.0004 = 0.04\%$.

Operations of Percents

Adding and Subtracting Percents

Percents are fractions, so they can be manipulated like other fractions. All percents have 100 as the denominator. It is easy to add and subtract percents because you already have a common denominator.

Examples:

1. Paul originally owned 25 percent of the stock of a certain company. He purchased another 15 percent of the stock privately, and he received a gift of another 10 percent of the stock. What percent of the stock of the company does Paul now own?

   - $25\% + 15\% + 10\% = 50\%$

2. In a certain election, Peter and Mary received 50 percent of all the votes that were cast. If Peter received 20 percent of the votes cast in the election, what percent of the votes did Mary receive?

   - $50\% - 20\% = 30\%$

Multiplying Percents

To multiply percents, first convert them to decimals and then multiply. For example, $60\% \cdot 80\% = 0.60 \cdot 0.80 = 0.48 = 48\%$.

Example:

In a certain group, 80 percent of the people are wearing hats. If 60 percent of those wearing hats are also wearing gloves, what percent of the entire group is wearing both a hat and gloves?

- 60% of $80\% = 60\% \cdot 80\% = 0.60 \cdot 0.80 = 0.48 = 48\%$

Dividing Percents

To divide percents, first convert them to decimals and then divide. For example, $\frac{100\%}{12.5\%} = \frac{1}{0.125} = 8$.

Example:

Peter is purchasing an item on a layaway plan. If he pays weekly installments of 8 percent of the purchase price, how many weeks will it take for Peter to pay off the entire purchase price?

- $100\% \div 8\% = 1 \div 0.08 = 12.5$ weeks

Percent Story Problems

Four basic variations of percent problems appear on the exam as story problems:

- What is x percent of something?
- This is what percent of that?
- This is a given percent of what?
- What is the percent change from this quantity to that quantity?

Notice that in each of the first three question forms, there is the phrase "of that" and the phrase "is this" ("this is"). When you set up a fraction for the percent, always place the "is this" value over the "of that" value. This allows us to write the following equation for percents: $\frac{is}{of} = \frac{\%}{100}$. We call this the "is-over-of" equation.

"What Is X Percent of Some Quantity?"

Percents are fractions, so in the question, "What is x percent of some quantity?", the "of" indicates multiplication.

Examples:

1. A certain class is made up of 125 students. If 60 percent of the students are men, how many men are in the class?

   - 60 percent of $125 = 60\% \cdot 125 = 0.60 \cdot 125 = 75$.

2. If Sam originally had $25 and gave 25 percent of that amount to his friend Samantha, how much money did Sam give to Samantha?

   - 25 percent of $\$25 = 25\% \cdot 25 = 0.25 \cdot 25 = \$6.25$.

3. If Paula had 50 marbles and gave 20 percent of them to her friend Paul, how many marbles did Paula give to Paul?

   - 20 percent of $50 = 20\% \cdot 50 = 0.20 \cdot 50 = 10$.

Noting the slight variation in phrasing, "is this" can be represented by "what number." Therefore, you can use the "is-over-of" equation to solve for the unknown value.

Examples:

1. What number is 20 percent of 25?

   - x is 20% of 25: $\frac{is}{of} = \frac{\%}{100} \Rightarrow \frac{x}{25} = \frac{20}{100} \Rightarrow x = \frac{20 \cdot 25}{100} = \frac{20}{4} = 5$.

2. If Paula had 50 marbles and gave 20 percent of them to her friend Paul, how many marbles did Paula give to Paul?

   - Simplify the item stem: "x is 20% of 50." Thus, $\frac{is}{of} = \frac{\%}{100} \Rightarrow \frac{x}{50} = \frac{20}{100} \Rightarrow x = \frac{20 \cdot 50}{100} = \frac{20}{2} = 10$.

"What Percent Is This of That?"

A second common item involving percents has the form, "What percent is this of that?"

Example:

What percent is 3 of 12?

- Convert $\frac{3}{12}$ to a decimal by dividing 3 by 12 and then change that decimal number to a percent:

  $\frac{3}{12} = \frac{1}{4} = 0.25 = 25\%$.

There are other ways of phrasing the same question:

- 3 is what percent of 12?
- Of 12, what percent is 3?

Note that all three of the above questions are equivalent and represent the three following general forms:

- What percent is this of that?
- This is what percent of that?
- Of that, what percent is this?

Again, you can set up an "is-over-of" equation and solve for the unknown value.

Example:

5 is what percent of 25? Of 25, what percent is 5? What percent is 5 of 25?

- Notice that all three of these questions are equivalent: "5 is $x\%$ of 25." Set up the "is-over-of" equation and solve for the unknown: $\frac{\text{is}}{\text{of}} = \frac{\%}{100} \Rightarrow \frac{5}{25} = \frac{x}{100} \Rightarrow x = \frac{5 \cdot 100}{25} = \frac{100}{5} = 20\%$.

As long as you place the "is this" value in the numerator and the "of that" value in the denominator, you cannot make a mistake.

Examples:

1. What percent is 20 of 50?

   - 20 is $x\%$ of 50: $\frac{\text{is}}{\text{of}} = \frac{\%}{100} \Rightarrow \frac{20}{50} = \frac{x}{100} \Rightarrow x = \frac{20 \cdot 100}{50} = 20 \cdot 2 = 40\%$.

2. Of 125, what percent is 25?

   - 25 is $x\%$ of 125: $\frac{\text{is}}{\text{of}} = \frac{\%}{100} \Rightarrow \frac{25}{125} = \frac{x}{100} \Rightarrow x = \frac{25 \cdot 100}{125} = \frac{100}{5} = 20\%$.

3. 12 is what percent of 6?

   - 12 is $x\%$ of 6: $\frac{\text{is}}{\text{of}} = \frac{\%}{100} \Rightarrow \frac{12}{6} = \frac{x}{100} \Rightarrow x = \frac{12 \cdot 100}{6} = 2 \cdot 100 = 200\%$.

No matter how wordy or otherwise difficult such items get, you can still use the "is-over-of" method by first simplifying the item stem.

Example:

John received a paycheck for $200. Of that amount, he paid Ed $25. What percent of the paycheck did John give Ed?

- Simplify the item stem: "$25 is $x\%$ of $200." Thus, $\frac{\text{is}}{\text{of}} = \frac{\%}{100} \Rightarrow \frac{\$25}{\$200} = \frac{x}{100} \Rightarrow x = \frac{25 \cdot 100}{200} = \frac{25}{2} = 12.5\%$.

"This Is X Percent of What?"

In the third type of percent problem, the task is to manipulate a given value and percent to determine the unknown total value. Again, you can use the "is-over-of" equation for this variation as well—simply solve for the unknown value.

Examples:

1. 5 is 20 percent of what number?

   - 5 is 20% of x: $\frac{\text{is}}{\text{of}} = \frac{\%}{100} \Rightarrow \frac{5}{x} = \frac{20}{100} \Rightarrow x = \frac{5 \cdot 100}{20} = 5 \cdot 5 = 25$.

2. Seven students attended a field trip. If these 7 students were $6\frac{1}{4}$ percent of all the 9th graders, find the total number of 9th graders.

   - Simplify the item stem: "7 is 6.25% of x." Thus, $\frac{\text{is}}{\text{of}} = \frac{\%}{100} \Rightarrow \frac{7}{x} = \frac{6.25\%}{100} \Rightarrow x = \frac{7 \cdot 100}{6.25} = 7 \cdot 16 = 112$.

Percent Change

The fourth percent item involves a quantity change over time. This type of item asks you to express the relationship between the change and the original amount in percent terms. To solve, create a fraction that is then expressed as a percent. Think of this as the "change-over-original" trick, because the fraction places the change over the original amount.

Examples:

1. The price of an item increased from $20 to $25. What was the percent increase in the price?

   - $\frac{\text{Change}}{\text{Original Amount}} = \frac{25 - 20}{20} = \frac{5}{20} = \frac{1}{4} = 0.25 = 25\%$.

2. Mary was earning $16 per hour when she received a raise of $4 per hour. Her hourly wage increased by what percentage?

   - $\frac{\text{Change}}{\text{Original Amount}} = \frac{4}{16} = 0.25 = 25\%$.

The "change-over-original" trick works for decreases as well.

Examples:

1. A stock's value declined from $50 per share to $45 per share. What was the percent decrease in the value of a share?

   - $\frac{\text{Change}}{\text{Original Amount}} = \frac{5}{50} = \frac{1}{10} = 0.10 = 10\%$.

2. Student enrollment at City University dropped from 5,000 students in 1995 to 4,000 students in 2005. What was the percent decrease in the number of students enrolled at City University?

   - $\frac{\text{Change}}{\text{Original Amount}} = \frac{1,000}{5,000} = \frac{1}{5} = 0.20 = 20\%$.

Percents
Exercise 2

DIRECTIONS: Choose the correct answer to each of the following items. Answers are on page 777.

1. What is 0.5555 expressed as a percent?

A. 5,555% C. 55.55% E. 0.555%
B. 555.5% D. 5.555%

2. What is 1.25 expressed as a percent?

A. 125% C. 1.25% E. 0.0125%
B. 12.5% D. 0.125%

3. What is 10 expressed as a percent?

A. 1,000% C. 10% E. 0.1%
B. 100% D. 1%

4. What is 25 percent expressed as a decimal?

A. 25.0 C. 0.25 E. 0.0025
B. 2.5 D. 0.025

5. What is 1,000 percent expressed as a decimal?

A. 1,000.0 C. 10.0 E. 0.01
B. 100.0 D. 1.0

6. What is 0.25 percent expressed as a decimal?

A. 25.0 C. 0.025 E. 0.00025
B. 0.25 D. 0.0025

7. What is 0.099 percent expressed as a decimal?

A. 99 C. 0.099 E. 0.00099
B. 0.99 D. 0.0099

8. What is $\frac{4}{5}$ expressed as a percent?

A. 4.5% C. 45% E. 450%
B. 8% D. 80%

9. What is $9\frac{99}{100}$ expressed as a percent?

A. 999% C. 9.99% E. 0.0999%
B. 99.9% D. 0.999%

10. What is $\frac{13}{5}$ expressed as a percent?

A. 260% C. 2.6% E. 0.026%
B. 26% D. 0.26%

11. Which of the following is equal to 18 percent?

A. $\frac{18}{1}$ C. $\frac{18}{100}$ E. $\frac{18}{10,000}$
B. $\frac{18}{10}$ D. $\frac{18}{1,000}$

12. Which of the following is equal to 10.101 percent?

A. 0.0010101 C. 0.10101 E. 10.101
B. 0.010101 D. 1.0101

13. $37\% + 42\% = ?$

A. 6% C. 106% E. 154%
B. 79% D. 110%

14. $33\% - 25\% = ?$

A. 0.08% C. 8% E. 800%
B. 0.8% D. 80%

15. $100\% - 0.99\% = ?$

A. 1% C. 11% E. 99.99%
B. 9.9% D. 99.01%

16. $222\% - 22.2\% = ?$

A. 221.88% C. 22.188% E. 1.998%
B. 199.8% D. 19.98%

17. If John read 15 percent of the pages in a book on Monday and another 25 percent on Tuesday, what percent of the book did he read on Monday and Tuesday combined?

A. 7.5% C. 55% E. 80%
B. 40% D. 75%

Items #18–19 refer to the following table:

SCHEDULE FOR COMPLETING PROJECT X					
	Mon	Tue	Wed	Thu	Fri
% of work to be completed each day	8%	17%	25%	33%	17%

18. By the end of which day is one-half of the work scheduled to be completed?

A. Monday C. Wednesday E. Friday
B. Tuesday D. Thursday

19. By the end of Tuesday, what percent of the work is scheduled to be completed?

A. 8% C. 25% E. 88%
B. 17% D. 50%

20. If 0.1 percent of the 189,000 names on a certain mailing list have the initials "BD," how many names on the list have the initials "BD"?

A. 1.89 C. 189 E. 189,000
B. 18.9 D. 18,900

21. What percent of 12 is 3?

A. 2.5% C. 25% E. 400%
B. 3.6% D. 36%

22. 50 is what percent of 40?

A. 125% C. 80% E. 8%
B. 90% D. 12.5%

23. If Patty's age is 48 and Al's age is 36, then Al's age is what percent of Patty's age?

A. 7.5% C. 75% E. 175%
B. 25% D. $133\frac{1}{3}$ %

24. If the price of an item increases from $5.00 to $8.00, the new price is what percent of the old price?

A. 20% C. 62.5% E. 160%
B. 60% D. 92.5%

25. If the price of a share of stock drops from $200 to $160, what was the percent decrease in the price?

A. 20% C. 50% E. 125%
B. 25% D. 80%

Items #26–27 refer to the following table:

ENROLLMENTS FOR A ONE-WEEK SEMINAR	
Week Number	Number of Enrollees
1	10
2	25
3	20
4	15
5	30

26. The number of people who enrolled for the seminar in Week 5 was what percent of the number of people who enrolled in Week 4?

A. 15% C. 50% E. 200%
B. 25% D. 100%

27. What was the percent increase in the number of people enrolled for the seminar from Week 1 to Week 2?

A. 40% C. 100% E. 250%
B. 80% D. 150%

28. If a textbook costs $30 plus 8.5 percent sales tax, what is the total cost of one textbook?

A. $3.55 C. $23.55 E. $33.55
B. $12.55 D. $32.55

29. How much is 25 percent of 80?

A. 2 C. 20 E. 45
B. 8 D. 40

30. How much is 2.3 percent of 90?

A. 1.07 C. 2.17 E. 2.3
B. 2.07 D. 2.7

31. On a test that had 50 items, Gertrude got 34 out of the first 40 correct. If she received a grade of 80 percent on the test, how many of the last 10 items did Gertrude have correct?

A. 6 C. 10 E. 34
B. 8 D. 12

32. If the Wildcats won 10 out of 12 games, to the nearest whole percent, what percentage of their games did the Wildcats win?

A. 3% C. 38% E. 94%
B. 8% D. 83%

33. On Thursday, Hui made 86 out of 100 free throws. On Friday, she made 46 out of 50 free throws. What was Hui's free throw percentage for the two days?

   A. 8.8%   C. 28%   E. 88%

   B. 12.8%   D. 82%

34. A stereo was discounted by 20 percent and sold at the discount price of $256. Which of the following equals the price of the stereo before the discount?

   A. less than $300

   B. between $300 and $308

   C. between $308 and $316

   D. between $316 and $324

   E. more than $324

35. A piece of wood weighing 10 ounces is found to have a weight of 8 ounces after drying. Which of the following equals the moisture content?

   A. 80%   C. $33\frac{1}{3}$%   E. 20%

   B. 40%   D. 25%

36. A bag contains 800 coins. Of these, 10 percent are dimes, 30 percent are nickels, and the rest are quarters. Which of the following equals the amount of money in the bag?

   A. less than $150

   B. between $150 and $300

   C. between $301 and $450

   D. between $450 and $800

   E. more than $800

37. The value of Super Company Stock dropped from $25 a share to $21 a share. Find the percent decrease.

   A. 4%   C. 12%   E. 20%

   B. 8%   D. 16%

38. The Rubins bought their home for $30,000 and sold it for $60,000. Find the percent increase.

   A. 100%   C. 200%   E. 150%

   B. 50%   D. 300%

39. During the pre-holiday rush, Martin's Department Store increased its sales staff from 150 to 200 persons. By what percent must it now decrease its sales staff to return to the usual number of salespersons?

   A. 25%   C. 20%   E. 75%

   B. $33\frac{1}{3}$%   D. 40%

40. If enrollment at City University grew from 3,000 to 12,000 in the last 10 years, what was the percent increase in enrollment?

   A. 25%   C. 300%   E. 400%

   B. 125%   D. 330%

STATISTICAL MEASURES

Mean (or average), *median*, *mode*, *range*, *standard deviation*, and *frequency distribution* are types of statistics that can be determined for a given set of numbers. These statistics provide information about a particular set of data.

Mean

Calculating a Mean (Average)

To calculate an *average (arithmetic mean)*, just add the quantities contributing to the average and then divide that sum by the number of quantities involved. For example, the average of 3, 7, and 8 is 6: $3+7+8=18$, and $18 \div 3 = 6$. Typically, on the exam, the term "average" is used instead of "mean" or "arithmetic mean."

> **Example:**
>
> A student's final grade is the average of her scores on five exams. If she receives scores of 78, 83, 82, 88, and 94, what is her final grade?
>
> - To find the average, add the five grades and divide that sum by 5: $\frac{78+83+82+88+94}{5} = \frac{425}{5} = 85$.

It is possible that an easy item might ask that you find the average of a few numbers, as above; however, items about averages can take several other forms. The generalized formula for an average (arithmetic mean) is given by the following equation.

EQUATION FOR FINDING AN AVERAGE ✓
Average (Arithmetic Mean) $= \overline{x} = \dfrac{x_1 + x_2 + x_3 + \ldots + x_n}{n}$

Determining Missing Elements

Some items provide the average of a group of numbers and some—but not all—of the quantities involved. You are then asked to find the *missing element(s)*. For example, if the average of 3, 8, and x is 6, what is the value of x? Since the average of the three numbers is 6, the sum, or total, of the three numbers is $3 \cdot 6 = 18$. The two given numbers are equal to $3+8=11$, so the third number must be $18-11=7$. Check the solution by averaging 3, 8, and 7: $3+8+7=18$, and $18 \div 3 = 6$.

> **Examples:**
>
> 1. For a certain five-day period, the average high temperature (in degrees Fahrenheit) for Chicago was 30°. If the high temperatures recorded for the first four of those days were 26°, 32°, 24°, and 35°, what was the high temperature recorded on the fifth day?
>
>   - The sum of the five numbers is $5 \cdot 30 = 150$. The sum for the four days we know about is: $26+32+24+35=117$. Thus, the fifth day must have had a high temperature of $150-117=33$. Note that this is the same as setting up an equation for the average and solving for the missing element: $\frac{26+32+24+35+x}{5} = 30 \Rightarrow x = (30 \cdot 5) - (26+32+24+35) = 150-117 = 33$.

2. The average of Jose's scores on four tests is 90. If three of those scores are 89, 92, and 94, what is his fourth score?

- The sum of all four scores must be 4 • 90 = 360. The three known scores sum to: $89 + 92 + 94 = 275$. Thus, the remaining score must be $360 - 275 = 85$. Note that this is the same as setting up an equation for the average and solving for the missing element: $\frac{89 + 92 + 94 + x}{4} = 90 \Rightarrow x =$ $(90 \cdot 4) - (89 + 92 + 94) = 360 - 275 = 85$.

3. The average of a group of eight numbers is 9. If one of these numbers is removed from the group, the average of the remaining numbers is 7. What is the value of the number removed?

- The sum of the original numbers is $8 \cdot 9 = 72$. The sum of the remaining numbers is $7 \cdot 7 = 49$, so the value of the number that was removed must be $72 - 49 = 23$.

A variation on this type of an item might ask about more than one missing element.

Example:

In a group of children, three of the children are ages 7, 8, and 10, and the other two are the same age. If the average of the ages of all five children is 7, what is the age of the other two children?

- The total sum of the five ages must be $5 \cdot 7 = 35$. The known ages total only $7 + 8 + 10 = 25$, so the ages of the two other children must total 10. Since there are two of them, each one must be 5 years old.

Calculating Weighted Averages

In the average problems discussed thus far, each element in the average has been given equal weight. Sometimes, averages are created that give greater weight to one element than to another.

Example:

Cody bought 4 books that cost $6.00 each and 2 books that cost $3.00 each. What is the average cost of the 6 books?

- The average cost of the 6 books is not just the average of $6.00 and $3.00, which is $4.50. He bought more of the higher priced books, so the average must reflect that fact. One method is to treat each book as a separate expense: $\frac{6 + 6 + 6 + 6 + 3 + 3}{6} = \frac{30}{6} = 5$. Another method is to "weigh" the two different costs: $6(4) + 3(2) = 30$ and $\frac{30}{6} = 5$.

Median

The *median* of an odd number of data values is the middle value of the data set when it is arranged in ascending or descending order. The median of an even number of data values is the average of the two middle values of the data set when it is arranged in ascending or descending order.

Examples:

1. What is the median of $\{1, 1, 2, 3, 4, 5, 6, 7, 7, 7, 8, 8, 9\}$?

- The set contains an odd number of data values, so the median is the middle value: 6.

2. What is the median of $\{7, 9, 10, 16\}$?

- The set contains an even number of data values, so the median is the average of the two middle values: $\frac{9+10}{2} = 9.5$.

Mode

The **mode** is the value that appears most frequently in a set of data. Some data sets have multiple modes, while other data sets have no modes. Note that if a data set has more than two modes (bimodal) it is said to have no mode.

Examples:

1. The mode of $\{2, 4, 5, 5, 5, 6, 6, 19, 2\}$ is 5.

2. The group of numbers $\{-3, 5, 6, -3, -2, 7, 5, -3, 6, 5, 5, -3\}$ is bimodal since -3 and 5 each occur four times.

Range

There are several ways to measure the degree to which numerical data are spread out or dispersed. The **range** of a set of numbers is the simplest measure of the spread of the data. The range is the difference between the highest and lowest numbers in the set. Note that the range depends on only these two values in the data. The greater the range, the greater the spread in the data.

Example:

The range of $\{5, 10, 3, 24, 11, 4\}$ is $24 - 3 = 21$.

Standard Deviation

Another common measure of dispersion is **standard deviation**. Generally, the greater the spread of the data away from the mean, the greater the standard deviation. The standard deviation of n numbers can be calculated using the following steps.

Step 1: Calculate the arithmetic mean (average) of the n numbers.
Step 2: Calculate the differences between the mean and each of the n numbers.
Step 3: Square each of the differences.
Step 4: Calculate the average of the squared differences.
Step 5: Take the nonnegative square root of the average from Step 4. This is the standard deviation of the n numbers.

Unlike the range of a data set, the standard deviation depends on every data value, though it depends most on values that are farthest from the mean. Therefore, a data set distributed closely around the mean will have a smaller standard deviation than will data spread far from the mean.

Example:

What is the standard deviation of the data set $\{0, 2, 2, 5, 7, 8\}$?

- Calculate the average of the 6 numbers: $\text{average}_{\text{data set}} = \frac{0+2+2+5+7+8}{6} = \frac{24}{6} = 4$. Next, calculate the differences between the average (4) and each of the 6 numbers, and square each of these differences:

$$x = 0: \; 0 - 4 = -4 \Rightarrow (-4)^2 = 16$$
$$x = 2: \; 2 - 4 = -2 \Rightarrow (-2)^2 = 4$$
$$x = 2: \; 2 - 4 = -2 \Rightarrow (-2)^2 = 4$$
$$x = 5: \; 5 - 4 = 1 \Rightarrow 1^2 = 1$$
$$x = 7: \; 7 - 4 = 3 \Rightarrow 3^2 = 9$$
$$x = 8: \; 8 - 4 = 4 \Rightarrow 4^2 = 16$$

Calculate the average of the 6 squared differences: $\text{average}_{\text{squared differences}} = \dfrac{16 + 4 + 4 + 1 + 9 + 16}{6} =$ $\dfrac{50}{6} = \dfrac{25}{3}$. The standard deviation is equal to the nonnegative square root of this average: standard deviation $= \sqrt{\dfrac{25}{3}} \approx 2.9$.

Note that for most standard deviation items on the actual exam, it is unlikely that knowledge of the formula for standard deviation will be tested. Rather, understanding of the concept behind standard deviation—that it is a measure of how the data values vary from the mean—is tested.

Example:

Arrange the following data sets from greatest standard deviation to least standard deviation: $\{12, 13, 14, 15, 16\}$, $\{14, 14, 14, 14, 14\}$, and $\{6, 14, 14, 14, 24\}$.

- The second data set has no variation, so the standard deviation is 0. The first data set has small deviations from the mean of 14, so the standard deviation in this set is greater than in the second set. Because of the extreme values 6 and 24, the variation in the third set is clearly greater than the variation in the first set. Thus, the standard deviation in the third set is greater than the standard deviation in 1.

Frequency Distribution

Finally, a frequency distribution is a simple way of displaying how numerical data are distributed. This method arranges the data according to the varying frequencies with which the data occurs.

Example:

Display the following 16 numbers using a frequency distribution: $\{-2, 0, 2, 0, 1, -1, 2, -1, 4, 0, -2, 0, 2, -1, -1, 1\}$. What is the mean, median, and mode of this data set?

- List the different numerical values, x, in the data set and the frequencies, f, with which they occur:

x	F
−2	2
−1	4
0	4
1	2
2	3
4	1
Total	16

The mean (average) is $\dfrac{-2(2) + -1(4) + 0(4) + 1(2) + 2(3) + 4(1)}{16} = \dfrac{-4 - 4 + 0 + 2 + 6 + 4}{16} = \dfrac{4}{16} = \dfrac{1}{4}$. The set contains an even number of data values, so the median is the average of the two middle values. According to this frequency distribution, the two middle values both occur at 0, so the median is 0. The data set is bimodal since −1 and 0 both occur four times.

Statistical Measures
Exercise 3

DIRECTIONS: Choose the correct answer to each of the following items. Answers are on page 777.

1. What is the average of 25, 28, 21, 30, and 36?

A. 25   C. 29   E. 44
B. 28   D. 34

2. What is the average of $\frac{1}{4}$, $\frac{3}{4}$, $\frac{5}{8}$, $\frac{1}{2}$, and $\frac{3}{8}$?

A. $\frac{3}{32}$ C. $\frac{1}{2}$ E. $\frac{27}{32}$
B. $\frac{5}{16}$ D. $\frac{5}{8}$

3. What is the average of $0.78, $0.45, $0.36, $0.98, $0.55, and $0.54?

A. $0.49   C. $0.56   E. $0.61
B. $0.54   D. $0.60

4. What is the average of 0.03, 0.11, 0.08, and 0.5?

A. 0.18   C. 0.28   E. 1.0
B. 0.25   D. 0.50

5. What is the average of 1,001, 1,002, 1,003, 1,004, and 1,005?

A. 250   C. 1,003   E. 5,000
B. 1,000   D. 2,500

6. What is the average of -8, -6, and -13?

A. -8 C. -13 E. -9
B. -15 D. -12

7. Jordan receives test scores of 79, 85, 90, 76, and 80. What is the average of these test scores?

A. 82   C. 84   E. 86
B. 83   D. 85

8. Mr. Whipple bought five different items costing $4.51, $6.25, $3.32, $4.48, and $2.19. What is the average cost of the five items?

A. $3.40   C. $3.90   E. $4.15
B. $3.80   D. $4.00

9. Nadia received scores of 8.5, 9.3, 8.2, and 9.0 in four different gymnastics events. What is the average of her scores?

A. 8.5   C. 8.9   E. 9.1
B. 8.75   D. 9

10. In a certain government office, if 360 staff hours are needed to process 120 building permit applications, on the average how long (in hours) does it take to process one application?

A. 3   C. 12   E. 36
B. 6   D. 24

11. In a chemical test for Substance X, a sample is divided into five equal parts. If the purity of the five parts is 84 percent, 89 percent, 87 percent, 90 percent, and 80 percent, then what is the overall purity of the sample (expressed as a percent of Substance X)?

A. 83   C. 86   E. 88
B. 84   D. 87

12. The average of three numbers is 24. If two of the numbers are 21 and 23, what is the third number?

A. 20   C. 26   E. 30
B. 24   D. 28

13. The average of the weight of four people is 166 pounds. If three of the people weigh 150 pounds, 200 pounds, and 180 pounds, what is the weight of the fourth person?

A. 134   C. 155   E. 165
B. 140   D. 161

14. Sue bought ten items at an average price of $3.60. The cost of eight of the items totaled $30. If the other two items were the same price, what was the price she paid for each?

A. $15.00   C. $6.00   E. $1.50
B. $7.50   D. $3.00

15. The average of a group of seven test scores is 80. If the lowest and the highest scores are thrown out, the average of the remaining scores is 78. What is the average of the lowest and highest scores?

A. 100 C. 90 E. 85
B. 95   D. 88

16. In a certain group, twelve of the children are age 10, and eight are age 15. What is the average of the ages of all the children in the group?

A. 9.5 C. 11   E. 12
B. 10.5 D. 11.5

17. Robert made the following deposits in a savings account:

Amount	Frequency
$15	4 times
$20	2 times
$25	4 times

What was the average of all the deposits Robert made?

A. $18.50 C. $21.50 E. $22.50
B. $20.00 D. $22.00

18. The average of the weights of six people sitting in a boat is 145 pounds. After a seventh person gets into the boat, the average of the weights of all seven people in the boat is 147 pounds. What is the weight, in pounds, of the seventh person?

A. 160 C. 155 E. 147
B. 159 D. 149

19. Find the mean of the following 5 numbers: 2, 3, 13, 15, and 1.

A. 4.6 C. 6.8 E. 16.8
B. 6.2 D. 8.6

20. If the mean of 6 numbers is 10, what is the sixth number if the five given numbers are -3, 5, 6, 13, and 17?

A. 12 C. 18 E. 22
B. 16 D. 20

21. The average of 5 numbers is 56. If two new numbers are added to the list, the average of the 7 numbers is 58. Which of the following equals the average of the two new numbers?

A. 64 C. 62 E. 60
B. 63 D. 61

22. Arranged in some order, $3x+1$, $2x+4$, and $x+10$ represent 3 consecutive whole numbers. If x represents a whole number and the average of the 3 numbers is 13, then solve for x.

A. 2 C. 6 E. 10
B. 4 D. 8

Items #23–25 refer to the following information:

During the last 14 games, a basketball player scored the following points per game: 42, 35, 29, 42, 33, 37, 26, 38, 42, 47, 51, 33, 30, and 40.

23. What is the median score?

A. 35.4 C. 36 E. 38
B. 35.7 D. 37.5

24. What is the mode?

A. 35.4 C. 38 E. 44
B. 37.5 D. 42

25. If after one more game, the player's average for points per game is exactly 37, how many points did the player score in the fifteenth game?

A. 30 C. 37.5 E. 44
B. 37 D. 42

26. Find the median of the following 5 numbers: 1, 3, 7, 2, and 8.

A. 1 C. 3 E. 7
B. 2 D. 4.2

27. Find the median for the following data set: {2, -3, 8, 4, 9, -16, 12, 0, 4, 2, 1}.

A. 4 C. 2 E. 0
B. 2.1 D. 1

28. Find the mode of the following 5 numbers: 4, 8, 10, 8, and 15.

A. 4 C. 9 E. 15
B. 8 D. 10

29. Find the mode of the following data set: {6, 8, 10, 2, −2, 2, 8, 4, 2}.

A. 6   C. 4   E. 1
B. 4.4   D. 2

30. A set of seven numbers contains the numbers: 1, 4, 5, and 6. The other three numbers are represented by $2x+8$, $x-4$, and $7x-4$. If the mode of these seven numbers is a negative even integer, then what is a possible value for x?

A. 0   C. 2   E. 5
B. 1   D. 4

31. Arthur purchased 75 six-inch rulers costing 15¢ each, 100 one-foot rulers costing 30¢ each, and 50 one-yard rulers costing 72¢ each. What was the average price per ruler?

A. $26\frac{1}{8}$¢   C. 39¢   E. $77\frac{1}{4}$¢

B. $34\frac{1}{3}$¢   D. 42¢

32. What is the average grade for a student who received 90 in English, 84 in algebra, 75 in French, and 76 in music, if the subjects have the following weights: English 4, algebra 3, French 3, and music 1?

A. 81   C. 82   E. 83
B. $81\frac{1}{2}$ D. $82\frac{1}{2}$

Items #33–35 refer to the following information:

A census shows that on a certain neighborhood block the number of children in each family is 3, 4, 4, 0, 1, 2, 0, 2, and 2, respectively.

33. Find the average number of children per family.

A. 4   C. $3\frac{1}{2}$ E. $1\frac{1}{2}$

B. 3   D. 2

34. Find the median number of children.

A. 1   C. 3   E. 5
B. 2   D. 4

35. Find the mode of the number of children.

A. 0   C. 2   E. 4
B. 1   D. 3

36. The diameter of a rod is required to be 1.51 ± 0.015 inches. Which of the following represents the possible range of measurements for the rod's diameter?

A. 1.490 inches to 1.520 inches
B. 1.495 inches to 1.520 inches
C. 1.495 inches to 1.525 inches
D. 1.495 inches to 1.530 inches
E. 1.500 inches to 1.530 inches

37. A is a set containing 5 different numbers, B is a set containing 4 different numbers, all of which are members of A. Which of the following statements CANNOT be true?

A. The mean of A is equal to the mean of B.
B. The median of A is equal to the median of B.
C. The range of A is equal to the range of B.
D. The mean of A is greater than the mean of B.
E. The range of A is less than the range of B.

38. If a set of data values has a mean of 10.0 and a standard deviation of 1.5, which of the following values is less than 1.0 standard deviations from the mean?

A. 8.0   C. 9.5   E. 12.0
B. 8.5   D. 11.5

39. The arithmetic mean and standard deviation of a certain normal distribution are 15.5 and 3.0, respectively. What value is exactly 1.5 standard deviations less than the mean?

A. 10.5   C. 12.5   E. 14
B. 11.0   D. 13.0

40. If the variables A, B, and C take on only the values 1, 2, 3, 4, or 5 with frequencies indicated by the shaded regions below, for which of the frequency distributions is the mean equal to the median?

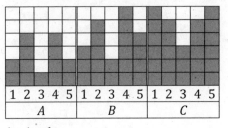

A. A only
B. B only
C. C only
D. A and C only
E. A, B, and C

RATIOS AND PROPORTIONS

A *ratio* is a statement that compares any two quantities. A *proportion* states that two ratios are equivalent and can be written in fractional form as an equation. This is the foundation for the process called cross-multiplication, a process that is useful in solving for an unknown element in a proportion.

Examples:

1. $\frac{2}{3} = \frac{8}{12} \Rightarrow \frac{2}{3} \gtrless \frac{8}{12} \Rightarrow 2 \cdot 12 = 3 \cdot 8$

2. $\frac{6}{9} = \frac{12}{x} \Rightarrow \frac{6}{9} \gtrless \frac{12}{x} \Rightarrow 6x = 108 \Rightarrow x = \frac{108}{6} = 18$

   - After cross-multiplying, divide both sides of the equality by the numerical coefficient of the unknown. Then, check the correctness of this solution by substituting 18 back in to the original proportion:

     $\frac{6}{9} = \frac{12}{18} \Rightarrow \frac{6}{9} \gtrless \frac{12}{18} \Rightarrow 6 \cdot 18 = 9 \cdot 12$.

3. $\frac{3}{15} = \frac{x}{45} \Rightarrow \frac{3}{15} \gtrless \frac{x}{45} \Rightarrow 3 \cdot 45 = 15x \Rightarrow x = \frac{135}{15} = 9$

   - Check the solution by substitution: $\frac{3}{15} = \frac{9}{45} \Rightarrow \frac{3}{15} \gtrless \frac{9}{45} \Rightarrow 3 \cdot 45 = 15 \cdot 9 \Rightarrow 135 = 135$.

Direct Proportions

The use of proportions can be a powerful problem-solving tool. *Direct proportions* equate ratios of two quantities having a direct relationship. The more there is of one quantity, the more there is of the other quantity, and vice versa.

Example:

If the cost of a dozen donuts is $3.60, what is the cost of 4 donuts? Assume there is no discount for buying in bulk.

   - One method for solving this item is to calculate the cost of one donut ($3.60 ÷ 12 = $0.30), and then multiply that cost by four ($0.30 • 4 = $1.20). While this approach is not incorrect, the same result can be reached in a conceptually simpler way. The more donuts being purchased, the greater the total cost, and vice versa. Relate the quantities using a direct proportion: $\frac{\text{Total Cost } X}{\text{Total Cost } Y} = \frac{\text{Number } X}{\text{Number } Y} \Rightarrow \frac{\$3.60}{x} = \frac{12}{4} \Rightarrow$ $12x = \$3.60 \cdot 4 \Rightarrow x = \frac{\$14.40}{12} = \$1.20$.

In the previous example, we set up the proportion by grouping like terms: "cost" is on one side of the proportion and "number" is on the other side. It is equally correct to set up the proportion as $\frac{\text{Total Cost } X}{\text{Number } X} = \frac{\text{Total Cost } Y}{\text{Number } Y}$.

Additionally, it does not matter which quantity is on top or bottom: $\frac{\text{Number } X}{\text{Total Cost } X} = \frac{\text{Number } Y}{\text{Total Cost } Y}$ is equally correct.

However, it is generally a good idea to group like terms to avoid confusion. Consider the following examples of direct proportions:

- The LONGER the travel time, the GREATER the distance traveled (and vice versa), assuming a CONSTANT speed.

  ### Example:

  If a plane moving at a constant speed flies 300 miles in 6 hours, how far will the plane fly in 8 hours?

  - Group like terms and solve for the missing value: $\frac{\text{Time } X}{\text{Time } Y} = \frac{\text{Output } X}{\text{Output } Y} \Rightarrow \frac{6}{8} >=< \frac{300}{x} \Rightarrow x = \frac{300(8)}{6} = 400$ miles.

- The LONGER the time of operation, the GREATER the output (and vice versa).

  ### Example:

  If an uninterrupted stamping machine operating at a constant rate postmarks 320 envelopes in 5 minutes, how long will it take the machine to postmark 480 envelopes?

  - Group like terms and solve for the missing value: $\frac{\text{Time } X}{\text{Time } Y} = \frac{\text{Output } X}{\text{Output } Y} \Rightarrow \frac{5}{x} >=< \frac{320}{480} \Rightarrow x = \frac{5(480)}{320} = 7.5$ minutes.

- The GREATER the number of items, the GREATER the weight (and vice versa).

  ### Example:

  If 20 jars of preserves weigh 25 pounds, how much do 15 jars of preserves weigh?

  - Group like terms and solve for the missing value:
  $\frac{\text{Weight of Jars } X}{\text{Weight of Jars } Y} = \frac{\text{Jars } X}{\text{Jars } Y} \Rightarrow \frac{25}{x} >=< \frac{20}{15} \Rightarrow x = \frac{25(15)}{20} = 18.75$ pounds.

Inverse Proportions

In some situations, quantities are related inversely; that is, an increase in one results in a decrease in the other. For example, the more workers, or machines, doing a job, the less time it takes to finish. In this case, quantities are related inversely to each other. To solve problems involving inverse relationships, use the following procedure to set up an inverse proportion.

Step 1: Set up an ordinary proportion—make sure to group like quantities.
Step 2: Invert the right side of the proportion.
Step 3: Cross-multiply and solve for the unknown.

Example:

Traveling at a constant rate of 150 miles per hour, a plane makes the trip from Phoenix to Grand Junction in 4 hours. How long will the trip take if the plane flies at a constant rate of 200 miles per hour?

- First, set up a direct proportion: $\frac{\text{Speed } X}{\text{Speed } Y} = \frac{\text{Time } X}{\text{Time } Y} \Rightarrow \frac{150}{200} = \frac{4}{x}$. Then, invert the right side of the proportion

  and solve for the missing value: $\frac{150}{200} >=< \frac{x}{4} \Rightarrow x = \frac{150(4)}{200} = 3$ hours.

As mentioned above, it is possible, though not advisable, to set up a direct proportion without grouping like terms. Indirect proportions, though, *must* be set up by grouping like terms. This is sufficient reasoning to always group like terms: you will not make a mistake if the item involves an inverse proportion.

Ratios and Proportions
Exercise 4

DIRECTIONS: Choose the correct answer to each of the following items. Answers are on page 778.

1. If a jar contains 3 blue marbles and 8 red marbles, what is the ratio of blue marbles to red marbles?

   A. 3:11   C. 8:3   E. 4:1
   B. 3:8   D. 11:3

2. If a school has 24 teachers and 480 students, what is the ratio of teachers to students?

   A. $\frac{1}{20}$ C. $\frac{1}{48}$ E. $\frac{1}{200}$

   B. $\frac{1}{24}$ D. $\frac{1}{56}$

3. If an airplane flies 275 miles on 25 gallons of fuel, then what is the average fuel consumption for the entire trip expressed in miles per gallon?

   A. 25   C. 15   E. 7
   B. 18   D. 11

4. If three farkels buy two kirns, and three kirns buy five pucks, then nine farkels buy how many pucks?

   A. 2   C. 8   E. 17
   B. 5   D. 10

5. If 48 marbles are to be divided between Bill and Carl in the ratio of 3:5, how many marbles should Bill get?

   A. 6   C. 18   E. 30
   B. 8   D. 24

6. If $\frac{6}{8} = \frac{x}{4}$, then $x = ?$

   A. 12   C. 4   E. 2
   B. 6   D. 3

7. If $\frac{14}{x} = \frac{2}{7}$, then $x = ?$

   A. 7   C. 28   E. 343
   B. 14   D. 49

8. If $\frac{3}{4} = \frac{4}{x}$, then $x = ?$

   A. $\frac{3}{16}$ C. $\frac{4}{3}$ E. $\frac{16}{3}$

   B. $\frac{3}{4}$ D. $\frac{7}{3}$

9. If 240 widgets cost $36, what is the cost of 180 widgets?

   A. $8   C. $24   E. $32
   B. $16   D. $27

10. If 50 feet of electrical wire cost $4.80, then $10.80 will buy how many feet of the wire?

    A. 60   C. 67.25   E. 112.5
    B. 62.5   D. 75

11. If a certain fundraising project has raised $12,000, which is 20 percent of its goal, how much money will have been raised when 50 percent of the goal has been reached?

    A. $60,000   C. $18,000   E. $4,800
    B. $30,000   D. $15,000

12. If the trip from Soldier Field to Wrigley Field takes two hours walking at a constant rate of four miles per hour, how long (in hours) will the same trip take walking at a constant rate of five miles per hour?

    A. 2.5   C. 1.6   E. 1.25
    B. 1.75   D. 1.5

13. If the space shuttle typically orbits the earth in 90 minutes, how long (in minutes per orbit) will it take the shuttle to orbit the earth if increases its speed by half?

    A. 60   C. 135   E. 180
    B. 90   D. 150

14. If it takes Canopy Tree Care 4 hours to cut down a maple tree with a crew of 5 workers, how long does it take to cut down the same tree with a crew of 4 workers?

    A. 2   C. 4   E. 6
    B. 3   D. 5

15. Annika can solve 10 math problems in 30 minutes. At this rate, how many math problems can she solve in 48 minutes?

A. 8   C. 32   E. 56
B. 16   D. 46

16. If 4 candy bars cost $1.04, how much should 6 candy bars cost?

A. $0.96   C. $1.56   E. $2.06
B. $1.25   D. $1.85

17. In 4 days, a worm grew from 5 centimeters to 12 centimeters. At this rate, how long, in centimeters, will the worm be in another 6 days?

A. 21   C. 22.25   E. 23
B. 22   D. 22.5

18. A snapshot measures $2\frac{1}{2}$ inches by $1\frac{7}{8}$ inches.

If it is enlarged proportionally so that the longer dimension is 4 inches, what is the length, in inches, of the enlarged shorter dimension?

A. $2\frac{1}{2}$ C. $3\frac{3}{8}$ E. 5
B. 3   D. 4

19. Aluminum bronze consists of copper and aluminum, usually in the ratio of $10:1$ by weight. If an object made of this alloy weighs 77 pounds, how many pounds of aluminum does it contain?

A. 0.7   C. 7.7   E. 77.0
B. 7.0   D. 70.7

20. It costs 31 cents per square foot to lay vinyl flooring. How much will it cost to lay 180 square feet of flooring?

A. $16.20   C. $55.80   E. $180.00
B. $18.60   D. $62.00

21. Assuming that on a blueprint $\frac{1}{8}$ inch equals 12 inches of actual length, what is the actual length, in inches, of a steel bar represented on the blueprint by a line $3\frac{3}{4}$ inches long?

A. $3\frac{3}{4}$ C. 36   E. 450
B. 30   D. 360

22. A bug crawls clockwise around the outside rim of a clock from the 12 to the 4 and travels 7 inches. If a second bug crawls around the outside rim from the 6 to the 11, in the same direction, how many inches did the bug travel?

A. 7.75   C. 8.25   E. 8.75
B. 8   D. 8.5

EXPONENTS AND RADICALS

Powers and Exponents

The notation system for designating the power of a number is a superscript following the number. The number being multiplied is the **base,** and the superscript is the **exponent**. The exponent indicates the operation of repeated multiplication.

Example:

1. The third power of 2 is written as 2^3 : base $\rightarrow 2^3 \leftarrow$ exponent $= 2 \cdot 2 \cdot 2$.

There are special rules that apply to operations involving exponents. When you begin working with radicals (fractional exponents) and algebraic expressions, these same rules will apply.

OPERATIONS INVOLVING EXPONENTS ✓

1. $x^1 = x$
2. $x^0 = 1$, if $x \neq 0$
3. $x^m \cdot x^n = x^{m+n}$ and $ax^m \cdot bx^n = abx^{m+n}$
4. $\dfrac{x^m}{x^n} = x^{m-n}$
5. $(x^m)^n = x^{m \cdot n}$
6. $(x^m \cdot y^p)^n = x^{mn} \cdot y^{pn}$
7. $\left(\dfrac{x^m}{y^p}\right)^n = \dfrac{x^{mn}}{y^{pn}}$
8. $x^{-n} = \left(\dfrac{1}{x}\right)^n = \dfrac{1}{x^n}$

Roots and Radicals

A **square root** of a number x is a solution to the equation $\sqrt{x} = b$, in which $x = b^2$. The operation of taking a square root of a number is signaled by the **radical** sign, $\sqrt{}$. **Radical** comes from the Latin word "rad," which means "root." Radicals can be rewritten using **rational (fractional) exponents**. The relationship between a rational exponent and the radical representing a given root is: $\sqrt[n]{x^m} = x^{\frac{m}{n}}$, where m and n are integers, and $n \neq 0$. An easy way to remember which exponent goes where is to say "top in, bottom out."

Example:

1. $\sqrt{4} = 4^{\frac{1}{2}} = 2$

OPERATIONS INVOLVING RADICALS (RATIONAL EXPONENTS) ✓

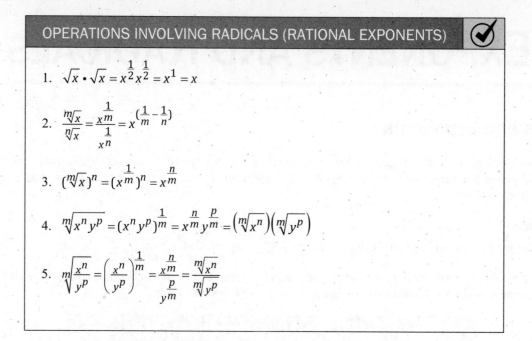

1. $\sqrt{x} \cdot \sqrt{x} = x^{\frac{1}{2}} x^{\frac{1}{2}} = x^1 = x$

2. $\dfrac{\sqrt[m]{x}}{\sqrt[n]{x}} = \dfrac{x^{\frac{1}{m}}}{x^{\frac{1}{n}}} = x^{\left(\frac{1}{m} - \frac{1}{n}\right)}$

3. $\left(\sqrt[m]{x}\right)^n = \left(x^{\frac{1}{m}}\right)^n = x^{\frac{n}{m}}$

4. $\sqrt[m]{x^n y^p} = (x^n y^p)^{\frac{1}{m}} = x^{\frac{n}{m}} y^{\frac{p}{m}} = \left(\sqrt[m]{x^n}\right)\left(\sqrt[m]{y^p}\right)$

5. $\sqrt[m]{\dfrac{x^n}{y^p}} = \left(\dfrac{x^n}{y^p}\right)^{\frac{1}{m}} = \dfrac{x^{\frac{n}{m}}}{y^{\frac{p}{m}}} = \dfrac{\sqrt[m]{x^n}}{\sqrt[m]{y^p}}$

Exponents and Radicals
Exercise 5

DIRECTIONS: Choose the correct answer to each of the following items. Answers are on page 778.

1. What is the fourth power of 2?

   A. 2   C. 8   E. 32
   B. 4   D. 16

2. $2^3 \cdot 2^2 = ?$

   A. 6   C. 2^5 E. 4^6
   B. 8   D. 2^6

3. $2^3 \cdot 2^4 \cdot 2^5 = ?$

   A. 2^{12} C. 8^{12} E. 8^{60}
   B. 2^{60} D. 4^{60}

4. $\dfrac{2^5}{2^3} = ?$

   A. 2^2 C. 2^8 E. 2^{15}
   B. 4^4 D. 4^8

5. $\dfrac{3^2}{3^3} = ?$

   I. 3^{-1}

   II. $\dfrac{1}{3}$

   III. -1

   A. I only   D. I and III only
   B. II only   E. I, II, and III
   C. I and II only

6. $(5^2)^6 = ?$

   A. 5^8 C. 10^4 E. 10^{12}
   B. 5^{12} D. 10^8

7. $(5 \cdot 3)^2 = ?$

   I. 15^2
   II. $5^2 \cdot 3^2$
   III. 8^2

   A. I only   D. I and II only
   B. II only   E. I, II, and III
   C. III only

8. $\left(\dfrac{8}{3}\right)^2 = ?$

   I. $\dfrac{64}{9}$

   II. $\dfrac{8^2}{3^2}$

   III. 11^2

   A. I only   D. I and III only
   B. II only   E. I, II, and III
   C. I and II only

9. $(2 \cdot 2^2 \cdot 2^3)^2 = ?$

   A. 2^8 C. 2^{12} E. 2^{18}
   B. 2^{10} D. 2^{16}

10. $\left(\dfrac{5^{12} \cdot 7^5}{5^{11} \cdot 7^5}\right)^2 = ?$

   A. 25   C. 5^7 E. 7^5
   B. 49   D. 5^{11}

11. $\sqrt{36} = ?$

   I. 6
   II. -6
   III. $3\sqrt{3}$

   A. I only   D. II and III only
   B. I and II only   E. I, II, and III
   C. I and III only

12. $\sqrt{52} = ?$

   A. $\sqrt{5} + \sqrt{2}$ C. $2\sqrt{13}$ E. 13^2
   B. 7   D. $13\sqrt{4}$

13. $\dfrac{\sqrt{81}}{\sqrt{27}} = ?$

A. $\sqrt{3}$ C. $3\sqrt{3}$ E. $9\sqrt{3}$
B. 3   D. 9

14. $\sqrt{12}$ is approximately equal to which of the following?

A. 2   C. 4   E. 8
B. 3.4   D. 6

15. $\sqrt{23}$ is approximately equal to which of the following?

A. 4   C. 6   E. 8
B. 4.8   D. 7

16. $(\sqrt{3}+1)(2-\sqrt{3}) = ?$

A. -1 C. $-1+\sqrt{3}$ E. $1+\sqrt{3}$
B. $-1-\sqrt{3}$ D. 1

17. $\sqrt{8}+\sqrt{50} = ?$

A. $-7\sqrt{2}$ C. $\sqrt{2}$ E. 7
B. $-\sqrt{2}$ D. $7\sqrt{2}$

18. $\sqrt{(2\sqrt{3})^2 + 2^2} = ?$

A. 1   C. 3   E. 5
B. 2   D. 4

19. $\dfrac{15\sqrt{96}}{5\sqrt{2}} = ?$

A. $7\sqrt{3}$ C. $11\sqrt{3}$ E. $40\sqrt{3}$
B. $7\sqrt{12}$ D. $12\sqrt{3}$

20. Which of the following radicals is a perfect square?

A. $\sqrt{0.4}$ C. $\sqrt{0.09}$ E. $\sqrt{0.025}$
B. $\sqrt{0.9}$ D. $\sqrt{0.02}$

21. $\left(-\dfrac{1}{3}\right)^4 = ?$

A. $-\dfrac{1}{81}$ C. $-\dfrac{1}{12}$ E. $-\dfrac{1}{64}$
B. $\dfrac{1}{81}$ D. $\dfrac{1}{12}$

22. $\sqrt[12]{x^6} = ?$

A. x^6 C. x^2 E. x^{-2}
B. x^{-6} D. $x^{\frac{1}{2}}$

23. $\sqrt[k]{6^{2km}}$ MUST be a positive integer if:

A. k is a positive integer
B. k is a multiple of 3
C. $k < 0$
D. m is a non-negative common fraction
E. m is a non-negative integer

24. If n is an integer and 0.012345×10^n is greater than 10,000, what is the least possible value of n?

A. 2   C. 4   E. 6
B. 3   D. 5

ALGEBRAIC OPERATIONS

Operations of Algebraic Terms

Adding and Subtracting Algebraic Terms

Addition and subtraction are indicated in algebra, as they are in arithmetic, with the signs " $+$ " and " $-$." In arithmetic, these operations combine the numbers into a third number. For example, the addition of 2 and 3 is equivalent to combining 2 and 3 to form the number 5: $2+3=5$.

In algebra, however, only **similar (like) terms** may be combined. Similar terms are terms with the same variables having the same exponent values. Coefficients do not factor into whether or not terms are similar.

Examples:

1. $3x^2$, $40x^2$, $-2x^2$, and $\sqrt{2}x^2$ are similar terms.
2. xy, $5xy$, $-23xy$, and πxy are similar terms.
3. $10xyz$, $-xyz$, and xyz are similar terms.
4. $3x$ and $3x^2$ are NOT similar terms.
5. xy and x^2y are NOT similar terms.
6. xy, yz, and xz are NOT similar terms.

To simplify an algebraic expression, group similar terms and add/subtract the numerical coefficients of each group. Variables and exponents of combined similar terms remain unchanged.

Examples:

1. $x^2 + 2x^2 + 3x^2 = ?$

   - All three terms are similar since each includes x^2. Combine the terms by adding the coefficients: $1+2+3=6$. Thus, the result is $6x^2$.

2. $y + 2x + 3y - x = ?$

   - With two different types of terms, group the similar terms together: $(2x - x) + (y + 3y)$. Add the coefficients for each type of term. For the x terms, the combined coefficient is $2-1=1$; for the y terms, $1+3=4$. The result is $x + 4y$.

3. $x - 3x + 5x - 2x = (1 - 3 + 5 - 2)x = x$

4. $2x - y - 3x + 4y + 5x = (2x - 3x + 5x) + (4y - y) = 4x + 3y$

5. $5x^2 + 3x^3 - 2x^2 + 4x^3 = (5x^2 - 2x^2) + (3x^3 + 4x^3) = 3x^2 + 7x^3$

Notice that when you have combined all similar terms, it is not possible to carry the addition or subtraction any further.

Multiplying and Dividing Algebraic Terms

Use the arithmetic ***operations involving exponents*** (p. 607) to multiply or divide algebraic terms. Remember that $x^0 = 1$ when $x \neq 0$, and $x^1 = x$.

Operations of Algebraic Fractions

Adding and Subtracting Algebraic Fractions

Adding and subtracting algebraic fractions, like adding and subtracting numerical fractions, require common denominators. If the denominators are the same, simply add/subtract the numerators: $\frac{a}{x} \pm \frac{b}{x} = \frac{a \pm b}{x}$.

Examples:

1. $\frac{5}{x} + \frac{3}{x} = \frac{5+3}{x} = \frac{8}{x}$

2. $\frac{2x}{y} - \frac{x}{y} = \frac{2x-x}{y} = \frac{x}{y}$

3. $\frac{a}{cd} + \frac{x}{cd} = \frac{a+x}{cd}$

To add or subtract algebraic fractions with unlike denominators, you must first find a common denominator. Usually, this can be accomplished by using the same method as with numerical fractions: $\frac{a}{x} \pm \frac{b}{y} = \frac{ay}{xy} \pm \frac{bx}{xy} = \frac{ay \pm bx}{xy}$.

Example:

$$\frac{2x}{y} + \frac{3y}{x} = \frac{2x}{y} \underset{\longrightarrow}{\overset{\nwarrow\;\nearrow}{\pm}} \frac{3y}{x} = \frac{2x^2 + 3y^2}{xy}$$

Multiplying and Dividing Algebraic Fractions

To multiply algebraic fractions, follow the rule for multiplying numeric fractions. Multiply terms in the numerators to create a new numerator, and multiply terms in the denominator to create a new denominator: $\frac{a}{c} \cdot \frac{b}{d} = \frac{ab}{cd}$.

Examples:

1. $\frac{2}{x} \cdot \frac{3}{y} = \frac{6}{xy}$

2. $\frac{x^2 y^3}{z} \cdot \frac{x^3 y^2}{wz} = \frac{x^5 y^5}{wz^2}$

To divide algebraic fractions, follow the rule for dividing numeric fractions. Invert the divisor, or second fraction, and multiply: $\frac{a}{c} \div \frac{b}{d} = \frac{a}{c} \cdot \frac{d}{b} = \frac{ad}{cb}$.

Examples:

1. $\frac{2}{y} \div \frac{3}{x} = \frac{2}{y} \cdot \frac{x}{3} = \frac{2x}{3y}$

2. $\dfrac{2x^2}{y} \div \dfrac{y}{x} = \dfrac{2x^2}{y} \cdot \dfrac{x}{y} = \dfrac{2x^3}{y^2}$

FOIL Method

To multiply two binomials using the **FOIL method**, follow these steps for combining the binomial terms: (1) multiply the **F**irst terms, (2) multiply the **O**uter terms, (3) multiply the **I**nner terms, (4) multiply the **L**ast terms, and (5) combine like terms. The FOIL method is simply a mnemonic shortcut derived from the distributive property. The following diagram illustrates application of the FOIL method.

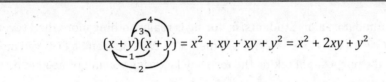

MULTIPLYING TWO BINOMIALS (FOIL: First, Outer, Inner, Last)

$$(x+y)(x+y) = x^2 + xy + xy + y^2 = x^2 + 2xy + y^2$$

Examples:

1. $(x+y)(x-y) = ?$

   - First: $(x)(x) = x^2$
     Outer: $(x)(-y) = -xy$
     Inner: $(y)(x) = xy$
     Last: $(y)(-y) = -y^2$
     Add: $x^2 - xy + xy - y^2 = x^2 - y^2$

2. $(x-y)(x-y) = ?$

   - First: $(x)(x) = x^2$
     Outer: $(x)(-y) = -xy$
     Inner: $(-y)(x) = -xy$
     Last: $(-y)(-y) = y^2$
     Add: $x^2 - xy - xy + y^2 = x^2 - 2xy + y^2$

Three situations, one in addition to the two illustrated in the previous examples, arise with such frequency that you should memorize the results to simplify the calculation.

THREE COMMON MULTIPLICATIONS INVOLVING POLYNOMIALS

1. $(x+y)^2 = (x+y)(x+y) = x^2 + 2xy + y^2$

2. $(x-y)^2 = (x-y)(x-y) = x^2 - 2xy + y^2$

3. $(x+y)(x-y) = x^2 - y^2$

You might be asked to multiply something more complex than two binomials. The process is tedious and time-consuming, but ultimately, it is executed the same way.

Example:

$$(x+y)^3 = ?$$

- Apply the FOIL method to the first two binomials, then multiply the last binomial to the resultant trinomial of the first two binomials: $(x+y)^3 = (x+y)(x+y)(x+y) = (x^2 + 2xy + y^2)(x+y) = x(x^2) + x(2xy) + x(y^2) + y(x^2) + y(2xy) + y(y^2) = x^3 + 2x^2y + xy^2 + x^2y + 2xy^2 + y^3 = x^3 + 3x^2y + 3xy^2 + y^3$.

Factoring Algebraic Expressions

Although the term ***factoring*** intimidates many students, factoring is really nothing more than reverse multiplication. For example, if $(x+y)(x+y) = x^2 + 2xy + y^2$, then $x^2 + 2xy + y^2$ can be factored into $(x+y)(x+y)$. Fortunately, for the purposes of taking the test, any factoring you might need to do will fall into one of three categories.

Finding a Common Factor

If all the terms of an algebraic expression contain a common factor, then that term can be factored out of the expression.

Examples:

1. $ab + ac + ad = a(b+c+d)$

2. $abx + aby + abz = ab(x+y+z)$

3. $x^2 + x^3 + x^4 = x^2(1 + x + x^2)$

4. $3a + 6a^2 + 9a^3 = 3a(1 + 2a + 3a^2)$

Reversing a Known Polynomial Multiplication Process

Three patterns recur with such frequency on the exam that you should memorize them. These patterns are the same as the ones you were encouraged to memorize in the discussion of the FOIL method.

THREE COMMON POLYNOMIAL MULTIPLICATION REVERSALS ✓
1. Perfect square trinomial: $x^2 + 2xy + y^2 = (x+y)(x+y)$
2. Perfect square trinomial: $x^2 - 2xy + y^2 = (x-y)(x-y)$
3. Difference of two squares: $x^2 - y^2 = (x+y)(x-y)$

Reversing an Unknown Polynomial Multiplication Process

Occasionally, you may find it necessary to factor an expression that does not fall into one of the three categories presented above. The expression will most likely have the form $ax^2 + bx + c$; e.g., $x^2 + 2x + 1$. To factor such expressions, set up a blank diagram: ( )( ). Then, fill in the diagram by answering the following series of questions.

    Step 1: What factors will produce the first term, ax^2?
    Step 2: What possible factors will produce the last term, c?
    Step 3: Which of the possible factors from step 2, when added together, will produce the middle term, bx?

Examples:

1. Factor $x^2 + 3x + 2$.

    • What factors will produce the first term, ax^2, where $a = 1$? x times x yields x^2, so the factors, in part, are $(x\ )(x\ )$. What possible factors will produce the last term? The possibilities are $\{2, 1\}$ and $\{-2, -1\}$. Which of the two sets of factors just mentioned, when added together, will produce a result of $+3x$? The answer is $\{2, 1\}$: $2 + 1 = 3$, as the FOIL method confirms: $(x + 2)(x + 1) = x^2 + x + 2x + 2 = x^2 + 3x + 2$.

2. Factor $x^2 + 4x - 12$.

    • What factors will generate ax^2? $(x\ )(x\ )$. What factors will generate -12? $\{1, -12\}$, $\{12, -1\}$, $\{2, -6\}$, $\{6, -2\}$, $\{3, -4\}$, and $\{4, -3\}$. Which factors, when added together, will produce the middle term of $+4x$? The answer is $\{6, -2\}$: $6 + (-2) = 4$. Thus, the factors are $(x + 6)$ and $(x - 2)$, as the FOIL method confirms: $(x + 6)(x - 2) = (x + 6)(x - 2) = x^2 - 2x + 6x - 12 = x^2 + 4x - 12$.

Absolute Value in Algebraic Expressions

Algebraic terms involving absolute values are treated the same way as numeric absolute values. Remember that the absolute value of any term is always a positive numerical value.

PRINCIPLES OF ABSOLUTE VALUE

1. $|x| = x$ if $x \geq 0$; $|x| = -x$ if $x < 0$

2. $|x| = |-x|$

3. $|x| \geq 0$

4. $|x - y| = |y - x|$

Examples:

1. If $w = -3$, $|w| = ?$

    • Since the value of w is less than zero, $|w| = -w = -(-3) = 3$.

2. Let x be a member of the following set: $\{-11, -10, -9, -8, -7, -6, -5, -4, -3, -2, -1, 0, 1, 2, 3, 4\}$.
$\dfrac{|2x - |x||}{3}$ is a positive integer for how many different numbers in the set?

- If $x < 0$, then $|x| = -x$: $\dfrac{\left|2x - |x|\right|}{3} = \dfrac{\left|2x - (-x)\right|}{3} = \dfrac{\left|2x + x\right|}{3} = \dfrac{\left|3x\right|}{3} = |x|$, which is always a positive. Therefore, $\dfrac{\left|2x - |x|\right|}{3}$ is a positive integer for all numbers in the set less than zero. If $x \geq 0$, then $|x| = x$: $\dfrac{\left|2x - |x|\right|}{3} = \dfrac{\left|2x - x\right|}{3} = \dfrac{|x|}{3} = \dfrac{x}{3}$. Thus, the only other number in the set that returns a positive integer is 3. The total number of values in the set that satisfy the condition is: $11 + 1 = 12$.

Algebraic Operations
Exercise 6

DIRECTIONS: Choose the correct answer to each of the following items. Answers are on page 778.

1. Which of the following is (are) like terms?

I. $34x$ and $-18x$
II. $2x$ and $2xy$
III. x^3 and $3x$

A. I only
B. II only
C. I and III only
D. II and III only
E. I, II, and III

2. $x + 2x + 3x = ?$

A. $6x^6$
B. x^6
C. $6x$
D. $x + 6$
E. $x - 6$

3. $z^2 + 2z^2 - 5z^2 = ?$

A. $-9z^2$
B. $-2z^2$
C. 0
D. $2z^2$
E. $2z^2$

4. $c^2 + 2c^2d^2 - c^2 = ?$

A. $4c^2d^2$
B. $2c^2d^2$
C. c^2d^2
D. $2cd$
E. cd

5. $3xy + 3x^2y - 2xy + y = ?$

A. $6xy - y$
B. $x + xy + y$
C. $3x^2y + xy + y$
D. $x^2y^2 + xy$
E. $3xy + x$

6. $8p + 2p^2 + pq - 4p^2 - 14p - pq = ?$

A. $-2p^2 - 6p$
B. $-p^2 + 6p$
C. $2p^2 + 6p$
D. $p^2 + 3pq$
E. $3p^2 - pq$

7. $pqr + qrs + rst + stu = ?$

A. $pqrst$
B. $pq + qr + rs + st + tu$
C. $pqr + rst$
D. $4pqrst$
E. $stu + rst + qrs + pqr$

8. $y^5 \div y^2 = ?$

A. $3y$
B. $7y$
C. $y^{\frac{5}{2}}$
D. y^3
E. y^7

9. $(abc)(a^2bc^2) = ?$

A. $4abc$
B. a^2bc^2
C. $a^3b^2c^3$
D. $a^3b^3c^3$
E. abc^6

10. $\dfrac{x^2y^4}{xy} = ?$

A. y^3
B. xy^3
C. x^2y^3
D. x^3y^5
E. xy^8

11. $\left(\dfrac{a^2}{b^3}\right)^3 = ?$

A. $\dfrac{a^5}{b}$
B. $\dfrac{a^6}{b^9}$
C. a^5b
D. a^6b
E. a^6b^9

12. $\left(\dfrac{x^2y^3}{xy}\right)\left(\dfrac{x^3y^4}{xy}\right) = ?$

A. x^2y^3
B. x^3y^4
C. x^3y^5
D. x^5y^6
E. x^6y^7

13. $\left(\dfrac{x^5y^3z^2}{x^4y^2z}\right)^2\left(\dfrac{x^2y^3z^5}{xy^2z^4}\right)^3 = ?$

A. xyz
B. $x^2y^2z^2$
C. $x^5y^5z^5$
D. $x^6y^6z^6$
E. xyz^{12}

14. $\frac{x}{y} + \frac{y}{x} = ?$

A. $\frac{xy}{x+y}$ C. $\frac{x+y}{xy}$ E. $\frac{x^2+y^2}{xy}$

B. $\frac{x+y}{y+x}$ D. $\frac{xy+yx}{xy}$

15. $\frac{x^2}{y^2} - \frac{y^3}{x^3} = ?$

A. $\frac{x^2-x^3}{y^5}$ C. $\frac{x^2-y^3}{x^2-y^2}$ E. $\frac{x^6-y^6}{x^3y^2}$

B. $\frac{x^3-x^2}{y^6}$ D. $\frac{x^5-y^5}{x^3y^2}$

16. $3a^2(ab+ac+bc) = ?$

A. $3a^3b^2c$ D. $3a^3b+3a^3c+3a^2bc$

B. $3a^3+3b^3+3c$ E. $3a^5b+3a^5c$

C. $3a^2b+3a^2c+3a^2bc$

17. $(ab+bc)(a+b) = ?$

A. $a^2b+ab^2+b^2c+abc$

B. a^2b+ab^2+abc

C. $a^2b+ab^2+a^2bc$

D. $a^2b+ab+bc+abc$

E. $a^2+b^2+c^2+abc$

18. $(a+b)(c+d) = ?$

A. $ab+bc+cd$ D. $ac+ad+bc+bd$

B. $ab+bc+cd+ad$ E. $ab+ac+ad$

C. $ac+bd$

19. $(x+y)(w+x+y) = ?$

A. $x^2+wx+wy+xy$

B. $x^2+y^2+wx+wy+2xy$

C. x^2+y^2+wxy

D. $x^2+y^2+wx^2y^2$

E. x^2y^2+wxy

20. $2x^2+4x^3+8x^4 = ?$

A. $2x^2(1+2x+4x^2)$ D. $2x^2(x+2x^2+4x^3)$

B. $2x^2(1+2x+4x^3)$ E. $2x^2(x^2+2x^3+4x^4)$

C. $2x^2(x+2x+4x^2)$

21. $abc+bcd+cde = ?$

A. $ab(c+d+e)$ D. $c(ab+bd+de)$

B. $ac(b+e)$ E. $d(a+b+c+e)$

C. $b(a+c+de)$

22. $x^2y^2+x^2y+xy^2 = ?$

A. $(x+y)^2$ D. $xy(xy+x+y)$

B. x^2+y^2 E. $xy(x+y+1)$

C. $x^2y^2(x+y)$

23. $x^2-1 = ?$

A. $(x+1)(x+1)$ D. $(x-1)^2$

B. $(x-1)(x-1)$ E. $(x+1)^2$

C. $(x+1)(x-1)$

24. $x^2+3x+2 = ?$

A. $(x+1)(x-2)$ D. $(x-2)(x-1)$

B. $(x+2)(x+1)$ E. $(x+3)(x-1)$

C. $(x+2)(x-1)$

25. $a^2-3a+2 = ?$

A. $(a-2)(a-1)$ D. $(a-3)(a+1)$

B. $(a-2)(a+1)$ E. $(a+3)(a+1)$

C. $(a+1)(a-2)$

26. $x^2+x-12 = ?$

A. $(x+6)(x+2)$ D. $(x-4)(x-3)$

B. $(x+6)(x-2)$ E. $(x+12)(x+1)$

C. $(x+4)(x-3)$

27. What number must be added to $4x^2-12x$ to make the resulting trinomial expression a perfect square?

A. 2   C. 9   E. 16

B. 4   D. 12

28. $x^2 - 9y^4 = ?$

A. $(x + 3y^2)(x - 3y^2)$ D. $(2x + 3y^2)(2x + 3y^2)$

B. $(x - 3y^2)(x - 3y^2)$ E. $(2x - 3y^2)(2x - 3y^2)$

C. $(x + 3y^2)(x + 3y^2)$

29. $\dfrac{3^{-1}x^5y^2}{2xy} = ?$

A. $\dfrac{x^2y}{6}$ C. $\dfrac{x^6y^2}{8}$ E. $\dfrac{x^6y^2}{10}$

B. $\dfrac{x^4y}{6}$ D. $\dfrac{x^6y^4}{6}$

30. If $x = -3$ and $y = 5$, then $x^2y = ?$

A. -50 C. 45 E. 55

B. -45 D. 50

31. If $x = -2$ and $y = -3$, then $x^2 - 4xy - x = ?$

A. -24 C. -18 E. -14

B. -20 D. -16

32. $\sqrt{x^2 + y^2} = ?$

A. $x + y$

B. $x - y$

C. $x^2 + y^2$

D. $x^{\frac{1}{2}} + y^{\frac{1}{2}}$

E. None of the above.

33. $\sqrt{(x + y)^2} = ?$

A. $\sqrt{x^2 + y^2}$

B. $\sqrt{x^2 + 2xy + y^2}$

C. $x^2 + y^2$

D. $x^2 + 2xy + y^2$

E. None of the above.

34. $\dfrac{x - y}{x + y} \div \dfrac{y - x}{y + x} = ?$

A. 1 C. $\dfrac{(x - y)^2}{(x + y)^2}$ E. 0

B. -1 D. $-\dfrac{(x - y)^2}{(x - y)^2}$

35. $\dfrac{1 + \frac{1}{x}}{\frac{y}{x}} = ?$

A. $\dfrac{x + 1}{y}$ C. $\dfrac{x + 1}{xy}$ E. $\dfrac{y + 1}{y}$

B. $\dfrac{x + 1}{x}$ D. $\dfrac{x^2 + 1}{xy}$

36. If $b \geq 0$, then $\dfrac{\sqrt{32b^3}}{\sqrt{8b}} = ?$

A. $2\sqrt{b}$ C. $2b$ E. $b\sqrt{2b}$

B. $\sqrt{2b}$ D. $\sqrt{2b^2}$

37. If $x \geq 0$, then $\sqrt{\dfrac{x^2}{9} + \dfrac{x^2}{16}} = ?$

A. $\dfrac{25x^2}{144}$ C. $\dfrac{5x^2}{12}$ E. $\dfrac{7x}{12}$

B. $\dfrac{5x}{12}$ D. $\dfrac{x}{7}$

38. If $y \geq 0$, then $\sqrt{\dfrac{y^2}{2} - \dfrac{y^2}{18}} = ?$

A. $\dfrac{2y}{3}$ D. $\dfrac{y\sqrt{3}}{6}$

B. $\dfrac{y\sqrt{5}}{5}$ E. None of these

C. $\dfrac{10y}{3}$

39. Given every pair (x, y) of negative numbers and resulting value $\dfrac{x}{|x|} + \dfrac{xy}{|xy|}$, what is the set of all numbers formed?

A. $\{0\}$ C. $\{2\}$ E. $\{0, 2\}$

B. $\{-2\}$ D. $\{0, -2\}$

40. When factored as completely as possible with respect to the integers, $16x^4 - 81y^{16} = ?$

A. $(4x^2 + 9y^4)(4x^2 - 9y^4)$

B. $(4x^2 + 9y^8)(4x^2 - 9y^8)$

C. $(4x^2 + 9y^4)(2x + 3y)(2x - 3y)$

D. $(4x^2 + 9y^8)(2x + 3y^4)(2x - 3y^4)$

E. $16x^4 - 81y^{16}$

ALGEBRAIC EQUATIONS AND INEQUALITIES

Solving Algebraic Formulas

An **algebraic formula** is an equation that typically involves a relationship between literal quantities. Problems that involve formulas often ask you to solve for a particular unknown (variable) using substitution. Algebraic formulas can take many different forms, including functions, scientific equations, geometric formulas, and story problems. Regardless of the format, the concept is the same: replace the variables with the values that are given and solve for the unknown variable.

Examples:

1. For all real numbers x and y, $x \oplus y = 2x + y^2$. What is the value of $3 \oplus 7$?

   - Substitute 3 for x and 7 for y in the given expression: $x \oplus y = 2x + y^2 \Rightarrow 3 \oplus 7 = 2(3) + (7)^2 = 6 + 49 = 55$.

2. The formula that relates Fahrenheit temperature to Celsius temperature is: $F = 1.8C + 32$, where F is Fahrenheit degrees (°F) and C is Celsius degrees (°C). What is the temperature, in Fahrenheit degrees, if the temperature is 25°C?

   - Substitute 25 for C in the given equation and solve for F: $F = 1.8C + 32 = 1.8(25) + 32 = 45 + 32 = 77°F$.

3. The volume of a sphere is: $V = \frac{4\pi r^3}{3}$, where r is the radius of the sphere. Find the volume of a sphere with a radius of 6.

   - Substitute 6 for r in the given formula and solve for V: $V = \frac{4\pi r^3}{3} = \frac{4\pi(6)^3}{3} = 4\pi \cdot 72 = 288\pi$.

4. If a person must pick one object from a group of x objects and then one object from a group of y objects, the number of possible combinations is xy. Jan must select 1 candy bar from 7 different candy bars and 1 pack of gum from 3 different packs of gum. What is the maximum number of combinations available to Jan?

   - Substitute 7 for x and 3 for y in the given expression: number of combinations $= xy = (7)(3) = 21$.

Formulas that represent real life situations often involve variables with units of measure, such as inches or gallons. You must ensure that all variables have similar units on both sides of the equation in order for the equality to remain true. To maintain consistency, it may be necessary to convert units using equivalent expressions (e.g., $\frac{12 \text{ inches}}{1 \text{ foot}}$, $\frac{1 \text{ foot}}{12 \text{ inches}}$, $\frac{60 \text{ minutes}}{1 \text{ hour}}$, $\frac{1 \text{ hour}}{60 \text{ minutes}}$). Thus, when dealing with quantities given in units of any type, it helps to explicitly write out the units in the expressions.

Example:

If string costs k cents per foot at the hardware store, how much will w feet and j inches of the string cost, in dollars?

- Explicitly write out the units in the expression and cancel like units in the numerator and denominator:

$$\text{Cost of string (dollars)} = \frac{k \text{ cents}}{1 \text{ ft. of string}} \cdot \text{length of string (ft.)} \cdot \frac{1 \text{ dollar}}{100 \text{ cents}}$$

$$= \frac{k \text{ cents}}{1 \text{ ft.}} \cdot \left[w \text{ ft.} + \left(j \text{ in.} \cdot \frac{1 \text{ ft.}}{12 \text{ in.}} \right) \right] \cdot \frac{1 \text{ dollar}}{100 \text{ cents}}$$

$$= \frac{k \text{ cents}}{1 \text{ ft.}} \cdot \left[w \text{ ft.} + \left(j \text{ in.} \cdot \frac{1 \text{ ft.}}{12 \text{ in.}} \right) \right] \cdot \frac{1 \text{ dollar}}{100 \text{ cents}}$$

$$= \frac{k \text{ cents}}{1 \text{ ft.}} \cdot \left(w + \frac{j}{12} \right) (\text{ft.}) \cdot \frac{1 \text{ dollar}}{100 \text{ cents}}$$

$$= k \text{ cents} \cdot \left(w + \frac{j}{12} \right) \cdot \frac{1 \text{ dollar}}{100 \text{ cents}}$$

$$= \frac{k}{100} \left(w + \frac{j}{12} \right)$$

Therefore, the cost of the string, in dollars, is: $\frac{k}{100} \left(w + \frac{j}{12} \right)$.

Basic Principle of Equations

The fundamental rule for working with any equation is: whatever you do to one side of an equation, you must do exactly the same thing to the other side of the equation. This rule implies that you can add, subtract, multiply, and divide both sides of the equality by any value without changing the statement of equality. The only exception is that you cannot divide by zero. The following example illustrates the validity of this principle using an equation containing only real numbers.

Example:

$5 = 5$

- This is obviously a true statement. You can add any value to both sides of the equation, say 10, and the statement will remain true. Add 10: $5 + 10 = 5 + 10 \Rightarrow 15 = 15$. You can also subtract the same value from both sides, e.g., 7: $15 - 7 = 15 - 7 \Rightarrow 8 = 8$. You can multiply both sides by the same value, e.g., -2: $8 \cdot -2 = 8 \cdot -2 \Rightarrow -16 = -16$. Finally, you can divide both sides by the same value (except zero); e.g., -4: $-16 \div -4 = -16 \div -4 \Rightarrow 4 = 4$.

This principle for manipulating equations applies to algebraic equations with variables, as the following example illustrates.

Example:

$5 + x = 5 + x$

- Add x: $5 + x + x = 5 + x + x \Rightarrow 5 + 2x = 5 + 2x$. Whatever x is, since it appears on both sides of the equation, both sides of the equation must still be equal. Now, subtract a value, e.g., y: $5 + 2x - y = 5 + 2x - y$. Again, since y appears on both sides of the equation, the statement that the two expressions are equal remains true.

DO NOT multiply both sides of an equation by zero if the equation contains a variable. You may lose special characteristics of the variable. For example, the equation $2x = 8$ is true only if $x = 4$. However, the equation $0(2x) = 0(8)$ is true for any value of x.

Solving Linear Equations

Equations that have only variables of the first power are called equations of the first degree or **linear equations**. While a linear equation can have any number of different variables, equations with one or two variables are most common on the exam.

The fundamental rule of equations is the key to solving linear equations. To solve for an unknown variable, identically manipulate both sides of the equation to isolate the variable on one side. Be sure to reduce the other side of the equation by combining similar terms.

> ### Examples:
>
> 1. If $2x + 3 = x + 1$, then what is the value of x?
>
>   - To solve for x, manipulate the equation to isolate x. Subtract x from both sides: $2x + 3 - x = x + 1 - x \Rightarrow$ $x + 3 = 1$. Next, subtract 3 from both sides: $x + 3 - 3 = 1 - 3 \Rightarrow x = -2$.
>
> 2. If $4x + 2 = 2x + 10$, then what is the value of x?
>
>   - Subtract $2x$ from both sides of the equation: $4x + 2 - 2x = 2x + 10 - 2x \Rightarrow 2x + 2 = 10$. Then, subtract 2 from both sides: $2x + 2 - 2 = 10 - 2 \Rightarrow 2x = 8$. Divide both sides by 2: $2x \div 2 = 8 \div 2 \Rightarrow x = 4$.
>
> 3. If $3y - 2x = 12$, then what is the value of y?
>
>   - Add $2x$ to both sides of the equation: $3y - 2x + 2x = 12 + 2x \Rightarrow 3y = 12 + 2x$. Divide both sides by 3:
>
> $y = \frac{2x}{3} + 4$.

So far, we have been very formal in following the fundamental rule for working with equations. The process is simplified using a shortcut called **transposition**. Transposing is the process of moving a term or a factor from one side of the equation to the other by changing it into its mirror image. Perform these "inverse operations" until the variable is isolated. Note that this shortcut does not change the fundamental rule or its outcome: it simply bypasses the formal steps.

To transpose a term that is added or subtracted, move it to the other side of the equation and change its sign. Thus, a term with a positive sign on one side is moved to the other side and becomes negative, and vice versa. It is imperative when using transposition that you do not forget to change signs when terms change sides.

> ### Examples:
>
> 1. $x + 5 = 10$
>
>   - Rather than going through the formal steps of subtracting 5 from both sides of the equality, simply transpose the 5: move it from the left side to the right side and change its sign from " + " to " − ": $x = 10 - 5 \Rightarrow x = 5$.
>
> 2. $x - 5 = 10 \Rightarrow x = 10 + 5 \Rightarrow x = 15$
>
> 3. $3x = 5 + 2x \Rightarrow 3x - 2x = 5 \Rightarrow x = 5$

To transpose a multiplicative factor, move the factor to the opposite side of the equation and invert it; that is, replace it with its reciprocal.

> ### Example:
>
> $\frac{2x + 5}{3} = 9$

- $2x$ and 5 are both divided by 3; in other words, they are both multiplied by $\frac{1}{3}$. Therefore, the $\frac{1}{3}$ must be transposed first. Move it to the opposite side of the equation and invert it: $2x + 5 = 9(3) = 27$. Now the 5 can be transposed: $2x = 27 - 5 = 22$. Finally, solve for x by transposing the 2: $x = 22 \cdot \frac{1}{2} = 11$.

Solving Simultaneous Equations

Ordinarily, if an equation has more than one variable, it is not possible to determine the unique numeric solution for any individual variable. For example, the equation $x + y = 10$ does not have one unique solution set for x and y: x and y could be 1 and 9, 5 and 5, −2 and 12, and so on. However, if there are as many equations as there are variables, the equations can be manipulated as a system to determine the value of each variable. This technique is called ***solving simultaneous equations*** because the equations are taken to be true at the same time, or simultaneously, in order to determine the variable value. On the exam, simultaneous equations are typically limited to two equations and two unknowns.

Example:

Given $x + y = 10$ and $x - y = 6$, solve for x and y.

- If both of the equations are treated as making true statements at the same time, then there is only one solution set for x and y, for there is only one pair of numbers that will satisfy both equations, $x = 8$ and $y = 2$.

It is easy to see the answer to the previous example, but solutions will not always be this obvious. How do you find the specific solution for a given set of equations? There are two methods for solving simultaneous equations: substitution and linear combination (elimination).

Substitution

The steps for ***substitution*** are as follows:

Step 1: Pick one of the two given equations and define one variable in terms of the other.
Step 2: Substitute the defined variable into the other equation and solve.
Step 3: Substitute the solution back into either equation and solve for the remaining variable.

Examples:

1. If $2x + y = 13$ and $x - y = 2$, what are the values of x and y?

   - Redefine one variable in terms of the other. Since y is already a single variable in both equations, define y in terms of x: $y = 13 - 2x$. Substitute $13 - 2x$ for y in the second equation and solve for x: $x - (13 - 2x) = 2 \Rightarrow x - 13 + 2x = 2 \Rightarrow 3x = 15 \Rightarrow x = 5$. Finally, solve for y by substituting 5 for x in either equation: $2x + y = 13 \Rightarrow 2(5) + y = 13 \Rightarrow y = 3$.

2. If $3x + 2y = 16$ and $2x - y = 6$, what are the values of x and y?

   - Since y is a simple term in the second equation, define y in terms of x: $2x - y = 6 \Rightarrow y = 2x - 6$. Substitute this expression for y in the first equation and solve for x: $3x + 2(2x - 6) = 16 \Rightarrow 3x + 4x - 12 = 16 \Rightarrow 7x = 28 \Rightarrow x = 4$. Finally, solve for y by substituting 4 for x in either equation: $2x - y = 6 \Rightarrow 2(4) - y = 6 \Rightarrow y = 2$.

3. If $y = 7 + x$ and $3x + 2y = 4$, what are the values of x and y?

- Substitute $7+x$ for y in the second equation and solve for x: $3x+2y=4 \Rightarrow 3x+2(7+x)=4 \Rightarrow$ $3x+14+2x=4 \Rightarrow 5x=-10 \Rightarrow x=-2$. Substitute -2 for x in the first equation and solve for y: $y=7+x=7-2=5$.

Linear Combination (Elimination)

The second method for solving simultaneous equations is **linear combination** or **elimination**. Eliminate one of the two variables by adding or subtracting the two equations. If necessary, division of one equation by another may eliminate one of two variables.

Examples:

1. If $2x+y=8$ and $x-y=1$, what are the values of x and y?

   - In this pair of simultaneous equations, there is a "$+y$" term in one equation and a "$-y$" term in the other. Since $+y$ and $-y$ added together yields zero, eliminate the y term by adding the two equations together. (Actually, you will be adding the left side of the second equation to the left side of the first equation and the right side of the second to the right side of the first, but it is easier to speak of the process as "adding equations.")

$$2x+y=8$$
$$+ (x-y=1)$$
$$\overline{\qquad 3x=9 \Rightarrow x=3}$$

   Find the value of y by substituting 3 for x in either equation: $2x+y=8 \Rightarrow 2(3)+y=8 \Rightarrow y=8-6=2$.

2. If $4x+3y=17$ and $2x+3y=13$, what are the values of x and y?

   - In this pair, each equation has a $+3y$ term, which you can eliminate by subtracting the second equation from the first.

$$4x+3y=17$$
$$- (2x+3y=13)$$
$$\overline{\qquad 2x=4 \Rightarrow x=2}$$

   Solve for y by substituting 2 for x in either equation: $4x+3y=17 \Rightarrow 4(2)+3y=17 \Rightarrow 8+3y=17 \Rightarrow 3y=9 \Rightarrow y=3$.

3. $x^5=6y$ and $x^4=2y$; x is a real number such that $x \neq 0$ and y is a real number. Solve for x.

   - The system of equations is reduced to one equation and one variable by dividing the first equation by the second equation: $\dfrac{x^5}{x^4}=\dfrac{6y}{2y} \Rightarrow x=3$.

If a system of equations has more variables than equations, then not every variable value can be determined. Instead, you will be asked to solve for one or more variables in terms of another variable.

Examples:

1. If $y=2a$ and $3x+8y=28a$, find x in terms of a.

   - Substitute $2a$ for y and solve for x: $3x+8(2a)=28a \Rightarrow 3x=28a-16a \Rightarrow 3x=12a \Rightarrow x=\dfrac{12a}{3}=4a$.

2. In terms of a, solve the following pair of equations for x and y: $3x-4y=10a$ and $5x+2y=8a$.

- First, solve for either x or y in terms of a alone. To solve for x, multiply the second equation by 2 and add the result to the first equation:

$$2(5x + 2y = 8a)$$
$$+\ 3x - 4y = 10a$$
$$\overline{\qquad 13x = 26a \Rightarrow x = 2a}$$

To find y in terms of a, substitute $2a$ for x in either equation: $5x + 2y = 8a \Rightarrow y = \dfrac{8a - 5(2a)}{2} \Rightarrow$

$y = \dfrac{-2a}{2} = -a$.

Solving Quadratic Equations

Equations that involve variables of the second power (e.g., x^2) are called **_quadratic equations_**. Unlike a linear equation with a single variable, which has a single solution, a quadratic may have two solutions. By convention, quadratic equations are written so that the right side of the equation is equal to zero. The general form is: $ax^2 + bx + c = 0$.

> **_Example:_**
>
> Solve for x: $x^2 + x - 2 = 0$.
>
> - To solve the quadratic equation, factor the left side of the equation: $x^2 + x - 2 = 0 \Rightarrow (x + 2)(x - 1) = 0$. For the equality to hold true, $x + 2$ or $x - 1$ must equal zero. Therefore, $x = -2$ or 1, so this quadratic equation has two solutions.

This last example illustrates the **_zero product property_**: if $xy = 0$, then $x = 0$ or $y = 0$.

> **_Example:_**
>
> $x^2 - 3x - 4 = 0$
>
> - Factor the left side of the equation: $(x + 1)(x - 4) = 0$. Either $x + 1 = 0$, in which case $x = -1$, or $x - 4 = 0$, in which case $x = 4$. Therefore, the solution set for this quadratic equation is $\{-1, 4\}$.

However, not every quadratic equation has two different solutions.

> **_Example:_**
>
> $x^2 + 2x + 1 = 0$
>
> - Factor the left side of the equation: $(x + 1)(x + 1) = 0$. Since the two factors are the same, the equation has one solution: -1.

For quadratic equations not in standard form, you must first group like terms and rearrange the equation into standard form.

> **_Examples:_**
>
> 1. Solve for x: $2x^2 + 12 - 3x = x^2 + 2x + 18$.
>
>   - Rewrite the equation by grouping like terms and simplifying: $2x^2 + 12 - 3x = x^2 + 2x + 18 \Rightarrow$ $(2x^2 - x^2) + (-3x - 2x) + (12 - 18) = 0 \Rightarrow x^2 - 5x - 6 = 0 \Rightarrow (x - 6)(x + 1) = 0$. Either $x - 6 = 0$ or $x + 1 = 0$. Therefore, the set of all possible values for x is $\{-1, 6\}$.

2. Solve for x: $x(8+x)=2x+36+6x$.

- Rewrite the equation by grouping like terms and simplifying: $x(8+x)=2x+36+6x \Rightarrow 8x+x^2 = 8x+36 \Rightarrow x^2 = 36$. Since squaring a negative number yields a positive and squaring a positive number yields a positive, $x=\pm 6$.

Some higher degree equations can also be solved if they can be written in quadratic form.

Example:

Solve for x: $x^4 - 13x^2 + 36 = 0$.

- Factor: $(x^2-9)(x^2-4)=0$. Factor again: $(x+3)(x-3)(x+2)(x-2)=0$. To find the four possible values of x, set each factor equal to zero and solve each for x: $x+3=0 \Rightarrow x=-3$; $x-3=0 \Rightarrow x=3$; $x+2=0 \Rightarrow x=-2$; and $x-2=0 \Rightarrow x=2$. Therefore, the solution set is: $\{-3, 3, -2, 2\}$.

Alternatively, you can use the quadratic formula, $x = \dfrac{-b \pm \sqrt{b^2-4ac}}{2a}$, to solve quadratic equations.

Example:

Solve for x: $3-x=2x^2$.

- $3-x=2x^2 \Rightarrow 2x^2+x-3=0$. $a=2, b=1, c=-3$. Substitute these values into the quadratic formula and solve for x: $x = \dfrac{-b \pm \sqrt{b^2-4ac}}{2a} = \dfrac{-1 \pm \sqrt{1^2-4(2)(-3)}}{2(2)} = \dfrac{-1 \pm \sqrt{1+24}}{4} = \dfrac{-1 \pm 5}{4}$. So, $x = \{1, -\frac{3}{2}\}$.

Solving Equations by Factoring

Factoring is an alternative short-cut method for solving some equations. Before factoring, rewrite the equation with all of the terms on one side of the equation and 0 on the other side. If the nonzero side of the equation can be factored into a product of expressions, then use the following property to yield simpler equations that can be solved: if $xy=0$, then $x=0$ or $y=0$. The solutions of the simpler equations will be solutions of the factored equation. The solutions of an equation are also called the **roots** of the equation.

Examples:

1. $\dfrac{(4x^2-1)(x+2)}{x+4}=0$

   - Either $4x^2-1=0$ or $x+2=0$. In each instance, solve for x: $4x^2-1=0 \Rightarrow x^2=\frac{1}{4} \Rightarrow x=\pm\frac{1}{2}$ and $x+2=0 \Rightarrow x=-2$. Therefore, the set of all possible values for x is $\{-2, -\frac{1}{2}, \frac{1}{2}\}$.

2. Solve for x: $x^3 + 2x^2 + x = 3(x+1)^2$.

   - Move the terms to one side and simplify by factoring like terms: $x^3 + 2x^2 + x - 3(x+1)^2 = 0 \Rightarrow x(x^2+2x+1)-3(x+1)^2 = 0 \Rightarrow x(x+1)^2 - 3(x+1)^2 = 0 \Rightarrow (x-3)(x+1)^2 = 0$. Therefore, $x-3=0$ or $x+1=0$, so $x = \{-1, 3\}$.

Algebraic Inequalities

An *inequality* is very much like an equation except, as the name implies, it is a statement that two quantities are not equal. Four different symbols are used to make statements of inequality:

- $>$ greater than
- $<$ less than
- $\geq$ greater than or equal to
- $\leq$ less than or equal to

Examples:

$5 > 1$ .... 5 is greater than 1.
$2 > -2$ .... 2 is greater than -2.
$x > 0$ .... x is greater than zero.
$x > y$ .... x is greater than y.
$8 < 9$ .... 8 is less than 9.
$-4 < -1$ .... -4 is less than -1.
$x < 0$ .... x is less than zero.
$y < x$ .... y is less than x.
$x \geq 0$ .... x is greater than or equal to zero. (x could be zero or any number larger than zero.)
$x \geq y$ .... x is greater than or equal to y. (Either x is greater than y, or x and y are equal.)
$x \leq 0$ .... x is less than or equal to zero. (x could be zero or any number less than zero.)
$x \leq y$ .... x is less than or equal to y. (Either x is less than y, or x and y are equal.)

The fundamental rule for working with inequalities is similar to that for working with equalities: Treat each side of the inequality exactly the same. You can add or subtract the same value to each side of an inequality without changing the inequality, and you can multiply or divide each side of an inequality by any *positive* value without changing the inequality.

Example:

$$5 > 2$$

Add 25 to both sides. $5 + 25 > 2 + 25$

$$30 > 27$$

Subtract 6 from both sides. $30 - 6 > 27 - 6$

$$24 > 21$$

Multiply both sides by 2. $24 \cdot 2 > 21 \cdot 2$

$$48 > 42$$

Divide both sides by 6. $48 \div 6 > 42 \div 6$

$$8 > 7$$

However, if you multiply or divide an inequality by a *negative* number, the direction of the inequality is reversed. Therefore, remember to change the direction of the inequality when multiplying or dividing by a negative number.

Example:

$$4 > 3$$

Multiply both sides by -2. $4(-2) < 3(-2)$

$$-8 < -6$$

These properties hold true for inequalities containing variables, as the following example illustrates.

> **Example:**
>
> For what values of x is $3(2-x)+7x>30$?
>
> - Solve for x: $3(2-x)+7x>30 \Rightarrow 6-3x+7x>30 \Rightarrow 6+4x>30 \Rightarrow 4x>24 \Rightarrow x>6$.

Exponents in Equations and Inequalities

Integer and Rational Exponents

Algebraic equations and inequalities can include terms with integer and rational exponents. The rules of exponents apply when manipulating these terms.

> **Examples:**
>
> 1. If $x=2$, then what is the value of $(x^{-2x})^{x^{-x}}$?
>
>   - Substitute $x=2$ into the given expression:
>
> $$(x^{-2x})^{x^{-x}} = [(2)^{-2(2)}]^{2^{-2}} = [(2)^{-4}]^{\left(\frac{1}{2}\right)^2} = 2^{(-4)\left(\frac{1}{4}\right)} = 2^{-1} = \frac{1}{2}.$$
>
> 2. Find the value of $2x^0 + x^{\frac{2}{3}} + x^{-\frac{2}{3}}$ when $x=27$.
>
>   - Substitute $x=27$: $2x^0 + x^{\frac{2}{3}} + x^{-\frac{2}{3}} = 2(27)^0 + (27)^{\frac{2}{3}} + (27)^{-\frac{2}{3}} = 2(1) + (\sqrt[3]{27})^2 + \frac{1}{27^{\frac{2}{3}}} = 2+9+\frac{1}{9} = 11\frac{1}{9}$.

Algebraic Exponentials

When solving equations that involve algebraic exponential terms, try to find a common base to use throughout the problem.

> **Example:**
>
> Solve for x: $4^{x+2} = 8^{3x-6}$
>
> - Since $4=2^2$ and $8=2^3$, the common base is 2. Thus: $4^{x+2} = 8^{3x-6} \Rightarrow (2^2)^{x+2} = (2^3)^{3x-6} \Rightarrow 2^{2x+4} = 2^{9x-18}$. Now, set the exponents equal to each other and solve for x: $2x+4=9x-18 \Rightarrow 22=7x \Rightarrow x=\frac{22}{7}$.

Exponential Growth

Items that involve exponential growth test knowledge of exponential growth sequences, also called geometric sequences. In a geometric sequence, the ***ratio***, r, of any term to its preceding term is constant. If the terms of a geometric sequence are designated by a_1, a_2, a_3, ..., a_n, then $a_n = a_1 r^{n-1}$. Sequences that involve exponential growth have real-life applications, such as determining population growth over a specific period.

> **Examples:**
>
> 1. Find the 5th term of the geometric sequence {4, 12, 36, ...}.

- In this geometric sequence, the ratio between the terms is $\frac{12}{4}=3$. The 5th term is: $a_n = a_1 r^{n-1} \Rightarrow$ $a_5 = 4(3)^{5-1} = 4(3)^4 = 4 \cdot 81 = 324$.

2. On June 1, 1990, the population of Grouenphast was 50,250. If the population is increasing at an annual rate of 8.4%, what was the approximate population of Grouenphast on June 1, 2010?

   - An annual increase of 8.4% means that each year the population will be 108.4% of the previous year's population. Thus, the ratio between terms, r, is 1.084. The population on June 1, 1990 is the starting term: $a_1 = 50{,}250$. Since June 1, 2010 is 20 years later, the population at that time is the 21st term in the sequence: $n = 21$. So the population on June 1, 2010 was: $a_n = a_1 r^{n-1} \Rightarrow a_{21} = 50{,}250(1.084)^{20} \approx 252{,}186$.

The previous example involving growth over time suggests an alternate form of the geometric sequence equation called the **exponential growth equation**: $a_t = a_0 r^{\frac{t}{T}}$. In this equation, a_t is the amount after time t; a_0 is the initial amount (i.e., the amount when $t = 0$), r is the proportionality constant, t is the total period of growth, and T is the time per cycle of growth. Note that this equation also applies to exponential decay, where the initial amount is larger than the amount after time t.

Example:

The number of rabbits in a certain population doubles every 3 months. Currently, there are 5 rabbits in the population. How many rabbits will there be 3 years from now?

- In this case, the total time of growth is 3 years. Since the population doubles every 3 months, the time per cycle of growth is one-fourth of a year. Using the formula for exponential growth: $a_t = a_0 r^{\frac{t}{T}} \Rightarrow$ $a_3 = (5)(2)^{\frac{3}{0.25}} = (5)(2)^{12} = 20{,}480$. We can verify this solution by working out the values, allowing the population to double every 3 months.

Period (months)	0	3	6	9	12	15	18	21	24	27	30	33	36
Population Size	5	10	20	40	80	160	320	640	1,280	2,560	5,120	10,240	20,480

Properties of Functions

A function is a set of ordered pairs (x, y) such that for each value of x, there is exactly one value of y. By convention, we say that "y is a function of x," which is written as: $y = f(x)$ or $y = g(x)$, etc. The set of x-values for which the set is defined is called the **domain** of the function. The set of corresponding values of y is called the **range** of the function.

Example:

What are the domain and range of the function $y = |x|$?

- The function is defined for all real values of x. Hence the domain is the set of all real numbers. Since $y = |x|$ can only be a positive number or zero, the range of the function is given by the set of all real numbers equal to or greater than zero.

When we speak of $f(a)$, we mean the value of $y = f(x)$ when $x = a$ is substituted in the expression for $f(x)$. If $z = f(y)$ and $y = g(x)$, we say that $z = f[g(x)]$. Thus, z is in turn a function of x.

This function notation is a short way of writing the result of substituting a value for a variable. Once a function $f(x)$ is defined, think of the variable x as an input and $f(x)$ as the corresponding output. In any function, there can be no more than one output for a given input. Note, however, that there may be more than one input that returns the same output.

Examples:

1. If $f(x) = 2x^x - 3x$, find the value of $f(3)$.

    *   Substitute 3 for x in the given expression: $f(x) = 2x^x - 3x \Rightarrow f(3) = 2(3)^3 - 3(3) = 2(27) - 9 = 54 - 9 = 45$.

2. If $f(x) = 2x - 9^{\frac{1}{x}}$, what is $f(-2)$?

    * $f(-2) = 2(-2) - 9^{-\frac{1}{2}} = -4 - \frac{1}{\sqrt{9}} = -4 - \frac{1}{3} = -\frac{13}{3}$.

3. If $z = f(y) = 3y + 2$ and $y = g(x) = x + 2$, then $z = ?$

    * $z = f[g(x)] = 3[g(x)] + 2 = 3(x + 2) + 2 = 3x + 6 + 2 = 3x + 8$.

Note that a geometric sequence ($a_n = a_1 r^{n-1}$) is actually a function. In general, a **sequence**, a_n, is any function $a(n)$ with a domain consisting of only the positive integers and possibly zero; that is, $n = 0, 1, 2, 3, \ldots$, or $n = 1, 2, 3, \ldots$. Note that a sequence is often written by listing its values in the order $a_1, a_2, a_3, \ldots, a_n, \ldots$. For example, $a_n = (-1)^n(n!)$ for $n = 1, 2, 3, \ldots$, is written as $-1, 2, -6, \ldots, (-1)^n(n!), \ldots$.

Example:

1. What is the fifth term of the sequence defined by $a_n = 3n^2 + 2$ for $n = 1, 2, 3, \ldots$?

    *   The fifth term of the sequence is for $n = 5$. Substitute 5 for n in the function $3n^2 + 2$: $3(5)^2 + 2 = 77$.

2. Find the fourth term of the sequence with values $-1, 2, -6, \ldots, (-1)^n(n!), \ldots$.

    *   The values of n for any sequence are consecutive integers, so determine the value of n for the fourth term of the sequence by finding the first n value. Test $n = 1$: $(-1)^1(1) = -1$. Therefore, the fourth value of n must be 4: $(-1)^4(4!) = 4 \cdot 3 \cdot 2 \cdot 1 = 24$.

Radical Equations and Inequalities

Expressions in algebraic equations and inequalities may include radicals. The same principles for working with equations and inequalities apply when manipulating radicals.

Example:

$5\sqrt{x-4} - 28 = 12$ for what value of x?

*   Solve for x: $5\sqrt{x-4} - 28 = 12 \Rightarrow 5\sqrt{x-4} = 40 \Rightarrow \sqrt{x-4} = 8 \Rightarrow (\sqrt{x-4})^2 = 8^2 \Rightarrow x - 4 = 64 \Rightarrow x = 68$.

Absolute Value in Equations and Inequalities

Expressions in algebraic equations and inequalities may include absolute values. The same principles for working with equations and inequalities apply when manipulating absolute values.

> ### *Examples:*
>
> 1. What is the sum of all different integers that can be substituted for x such that $|x| + |x - 3| = 3$?
>
>   - The absolute value of any real number, including integers, is always zero or more. Therefore, try only $-3, -2, -1, 0, 1, 2, 3$. The last four work in the equality: $|0| + |0 - 3| = 0 + 3 = 3$; $|1| + |1 - 3| = 1 + 2 = 3$; $|2| + |2 - 3| = 2 + 1 = 3$; $|3| + |3 - 3| = 3 + 0 = 3$. Thus, $0 + 1 + 2 + 3 = 6$.
>
> 2. If x represents an integer, $|x - 3| + |x + 2| < 7$ for how many different values of x?
>
>   - Absolute values are always equal to or greater than zero. Thus, if $x = -4$, $|x - 3| = |-4 - 3| = 7$; there is no need to try any integers less than -3. Similarly, if $x = 5$, $|x + 2| = |5 + 2| = 7$, there is no need to try any integers greater than 4. Therefore, test only the integers between -3 and 4. Six integers satisfy the inequality: $\{-2, -1, 0, 1, 2, 3\}$.

Algebraic Equations and Inequalities
Exercise 7

DIRECTIONS: Choose the correct answer to each of the following items. Answers are on page 779.

1. If $2x + x = 9$, then $x = ?$

A. 0   C. 3   E. 9
B. 1   D. 6

2. If $a - 8 = 10 - 2a$, then $a = ?$

A. −2   C. 2   E. 6
B. 0   D. 4

3. If $5x - 2 + 3x - 4 = 2x - 8 + x + 2$, then $x = ?$

A. −5   C. 1   E. 6
B. 0   D. 3

4. If $\frac{x}{2} + x = 3$, then $x = ?$

A. $\frac{1}{2}$ C. 1   E. 3

B. $\frac{2}{3}$ D. 2

5. If $\frac{1}{p} + \frac{2}{p} + \frac{3}{p} = 1$, then $p = ?$

A. $\frac{2}{3}$ C. 1   E. 6

B. $\frac{3}{4}$ D. 2

6. If $\frac{x}{2} + \frac{x}{3} = \frac{1}{2} + \frac{1}{3}$, then $x = ?$

A. $\frac{1}{3}$ C. 1   E. 3

B. $\frac{2}{3}$ D. 2

7. If $a + b = 5$ and $2a + 3b = 12$, then $b = ?$

A. 1   C. 3   E. 6
B. 2   D. 4

8. If $t = k - 5$ and $k + t = 11$, then $k = $

A. 2   C. 8   E. 14
B. 3   D. 11

9. If $8 + x = y$ and $2y + x = 28$, then $x = ?$

A. 2   C. 6   E. 18
B. 4   D. 12

10. If $\frac{x+y}{2} = 7$ and $\frac{x-y}{3} = 2$, then $x = ?$

A. 2   C. 8   E. 14
B. 4   D. 10

11. If $x + 2y - z = 4$ and $2x - 2y + z = 8$, then $x = ?$

A. −2   C. 4   E. 8
B. 0   D. 6

12. If $x^2 - 3x - 4 = 0$, then $x = ?$

A. −4 or 1   C. −1 or 2   E. 6 or −1
B. −2 or 2   D. 4 or −1

13. If $x^2 + 3x + 2 = 0$, then which of the following values is (are) possible for x?

I. 1
II. −1
III. −2

A. I only   D. I and II only
B. II only   E. II and III only
C. III only

14. If $x^2 = 12 - x$, then $x = ?$

A. −4 and −3   C. −3 and 4   E. 1 and 6
B. −4 and 3   D. −2 and 6

15. For what values of x is $5(3x - 2) \geq 50$?

A. $x \geq 4$ C. $x \geq 10$ E. $x > 8$
B. $x \leq 4$ D. $x \leq 10$

16. For what values of x is $8 - 3x > 35$?

A. $x > 0$ C. $x \geq 0$ E. $x \geq 9$
B. $x > -3$ D. $x < -9$

17. If $9 - 3(6 - x) = 12$, then $x = ?$

A. 4 or −2   C. 4   E. 7
B. 7 or −2   D. 6

18. If $\frac{x}{2} - \frac{x-2}{3} = 0.4$, then $x = ?$

A. −1 or 1.4   C. 2 or −1.6   E. 2.6
B. −1.6   D. 2.4

19. If $3 - 2(x - 5) = 3x + 4$, then $x = ?$

　A. $\frac{1}{2}$ or $\frac{1}{4}$ 　C. $\frac{9}{5}$ 　　E. 5

　B. $-\frac{9}{5}$ 　　D. 1 or 3

20. If $2x + 3y = 12$ and $x = -6$, then $y = ?$

　A. 2 　　C. 8 　　E. 12
　B. 4 　　D. 10

21. At what point does the line $5x + 2y = 20$ intersect the x-axis? (Hint: What must the y-coordinate be?)

　A. $(-4,0)$ 　C. $(0,0)$ 　E. $(4,2)$
　B. $(-2,0)$ 　D. $(4,0)$

22. If $8x + 16 = (x + 2)(x + 5)$, then $x = ?$

　A. 3 or -2 　C. -2 　　E. 3
　B. -3 　　D. 2 or 3

23. If $\frac{0.2 + x}{3} = \frac{\frac{5}{6}}{4}$, then $x = ?$

　A. $-\frac{40}{17}$ 　C. 0 　　E. $\frac{40}{17}$

　B. $-\frac{17}{40}$ 　D. $\frac{17}{40}$

24. If x is an integer and $6 < x < 8$, then what is the value of x?

　A. 4 　　C. 7 　　E. 10
　B. 5 　　D. 9

25. If x and y are integers, $2 < x < 4$, and $8 > y > 6$, then what is the value of xy?

　A. 12 　　C. 21 　　E. 32
　B. 16 　　D. 24

26. If $3^{8x + 4} = 27^{2x + 12}$, then $x = ?$

　A. $\frac{1}{4}$ 　　C. 4 　　E. 16

　B. $\frac{1}{9}$ 　　D. 9

27. If $|x| = 5$, then $x = ?$

　A. 5
　B. 5 or -5
　C. Any real number less than 5
　D. No real number
　E. Any real number greater than zero

28. For what value of x is $\sqrt{x} + 3 = 5$?

　A. 2 　　C. 8 　　E. 16
　B. 4 　　D. 9

29. What is the tenth term of the sequence {1, 4, 9, 16, ...}?

　A. 25 　　C. 49 　　E. 100
　B. 36 　　D. 81

30. If a sequence is defined by the rule $a_n = (a_{n-1} - 3)^2$, what is a_4 (the fourth term of the sequence) if a_1 is 1?

　A. 1 　　C. 3 　　E. 5
　B. 2 　　D. 4

31. Which of the following values for b returns two distinct real solutions to the equation $x^2 + bx + 8 = 0$?

　A. 6 　　C. 4 　　E. 1
　B. 5 　　D. $\sqrt{2}$

32. If $x^2 - 14k^2 = 5kx$, what are the 2 solutions for x in terms of k?

　A. $2k$ and $7k$ 　C. k and $5k$ 　E. k and $-5k$
　B. $-2k$ and $7k$ 　D. $-k$ and $5k$

33. An arithmetic sequence is a sequence of numbers formed by continually adding the same number; e.g., (1, 3, 5, 7, 9, 11, ...} is an arithmetic sequence formed by continually adding 2. What is the ninth term in the arithmetic sequence of {1, 4, 7, 10, 13, ...}?

　A. 16 　　C. 19 　　E. 25
　B. 17 　　D. 21

34. $\dfrac{2^{x+4} - 2(2^x)}{2(2^{x+3})} = ?$

　A. $\frac{1}{2}$ 　　C. $\frac{3}{4}$ 　　E. $\frac{7}{8}$

　B. $\frac{1}{4}$ 　　D. $\frac{5}{8}$

35. A population that starts at 16 and doubles every 30 months can be expressed as $16\left(2^{\frac{2x}{5}}\right)$, where x is the number of elapsed years. What is the approximate population size after 105 months have elapsed?

A. $11\sqrt{2}$ C. 128   E. 192

B. 27   D. $128\sqrt{2}$

36. Let n be a member of the set {5, 6, 7, 8, 9, 10, 11, 12, 13, 14, 15, 16}. For how many different values of n is the following equation true?

$$\frac{1+2+...+n}{2+4+...+2n}=\frac{1}{2}$$

A. 0   C. 6   E. 12

B. 1   D. 11

37. Let x represent a positive odd integer. The smallest value of x such that $3^{\frac{1}{4}},3^{\frac{3}{4}},3^{\frac{5}{4}},...,3^{\frac{x}{4}}$ is greater than 2^x is:

A. a multiple of 3

B. a multiple of 5 but not a multiple of 3

C. a multiple of 7 but not a multiple of either 3 or 5

D. 11

E. 13

38. The formula for determining the volume of a cone is: $V=\dfrac{\pi r^2 h}{3}$ where V is volume, h is height, and r is the radius of the base. Which of the following equations can be used to determine the height, h, of a cone with volume V and a base with radius r?

A. $h=\dfrac{\pi r^2}{3V}$ C. $h=\dfrac{\pi r^2 V}{3}$ E. $h=\dfrac{\pi r^2}{3V}$

B. $h=\dfrac{3\pi r^2}{V}$ D. $h=\dfrac{3V}{\pi r^2}$

39. If $y=3^x$, $3^{x+2}=?$

A. y^2 C. $y+3$ E. $y+9$

B. 2^y D. $9y$

40. Let x be an element of {-6, -5, -4, -3, -2, -1, 0, 2, 6, 8, 10, 12} and $x=3k$, where k is an integer. Find the sum of all different values of x such that $\sqrt{2x+8}=\sqrt{y}$ for some value of y if y is an element of {-2, 0, 2, 4, 6, 8, 10, 12, 14, 16, 18, 20, 22, 24, 26, 28}.

A. 3   C. 9   E. 15

B. 6   D. 12

41. Let $f(x)=\dfrac{x-2}{2x-13}$. If x represents a whole number, what is the largest value of x such that $f(x)<0$?

A. -1 C. 1   E. 8

B. 0   D. 6

42. If $-5<x<-1$, and $f(x)=\left|14-\left|1+2x\right|\right|$, then $f(x)$ equals:

A. $13-2x$ C. $13+2x$ E. $13+3x$

B. $15+2x$ D. $2x-13$

43. The range of the relation $\{(x,y)\big|y^2=4x\}$ is {0, 9, 16}. Which of the following is the domain?

A. {0, 20.25, 64}

B. {0, 3, 4}

C. {0, 36, 64}

D. {-4, 3, 0, 3, 4}

E. {0, 2, 25, 4}

44. If $y=2x+1$ and the domain for x is the set of all non-negative integers, then the range for y is the set of which of the following?

A. non-negative integers

B. non-negative even integers

C. odd integers

D. positive odd integers

E. real numbers equal to or greater than 1

45. $f(x)$ and $g(x)$ represent linear functions. If $f(x)=5$ for $x=1$, $g(x)=3x+8$, and $f(x)=g(x)$ for $x=2$, then what is the value of $f(4)$?

A. 12   C. 20   E. 32

B. 16   D. 24

GEOMETRY

Line and Angle Properties

For the purposes of this review and the test, the word **line** means a straight line:

The line above is designated line *l*. The portion of line *l* from point *P* to point *Q* is called "line segment *PQ*," or "$\overline{PQ}$."

When two lines intersect, they form an **angle**, and their point of intersection is called the **vertex** of that angle.

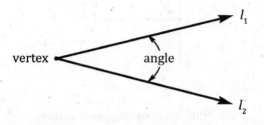

The size of an angle is measured in **degrees**. Degrees are defined in reference to a circle. By convention, a circle is divided into 360 equal parts, or degrees.

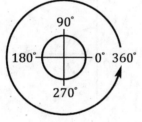

A 90° angle is also called a **right angle**. A right angle is often indicated in the following way:

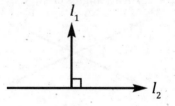

Two adjacent right angles form a straight line:

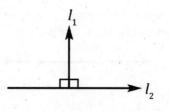

Since two adjacent right angles form a straight line, the degree measure of the angle of a straight line is $90° + 90° = 180°$:

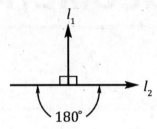

An angle that is less than 90° is called an ***acute angle***:

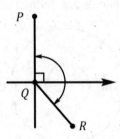

In the figure above, $\angle PQR$ is an acute angle.

An angle that is greater than 90° but less than 180° is called an ***obtuse angle***:

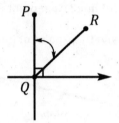

In the figure above, $\angle PQR$ is an obtuse angle.

When two lines intersect, the opposite (or vertical) angles created by their intersection are congruent, or equal:

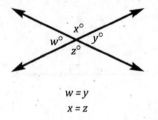

$$w = y$$
$$x = z$$

Two lines that do not intersect regardless of how far they are extended are ***parallel*** to each other. In the following figure, the symbol "||" indicates that l_1 and l_2 are parallel.

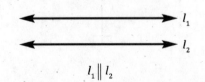

When parallel lines are intersected by a third line, a **transversal**, the following angle relationships are created:

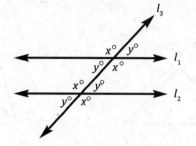

All angles labeled *x* are equal.
All angles labeled *y* are equal.
Any *x* plus any *y* totals 180.

Two lines that are **perpendicular** to the same line are parallel to each other:

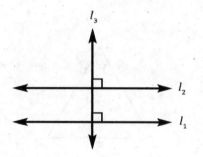

Since l_1 and l_2 are both perpendicular to l_3, we can conclude that l_1 and l_2 are parallel to each other.

Triangle Properties and Formulas

Properties of Triangles

A **triangle** is a three-sided figure. Within a given triangle, the larger an angle is, the longer the opposite side of the angle is; conversely, the longer a side is, the larger its opposite angle is.

Examples:

1. In the following figure, since $\overline{PR} > \overline{QR} > \overline{PQ}$, $\angle Q > \angle P > \angle R$.

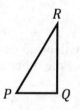

2. In the following figure, since $\angle P > \angle Q > \angle R$, $\overline{QR} > \overline{PR} > \overline{PQ}$.

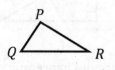

Within a given triangle, if two sides are equal, then the angles opposite the two sides are equal, and vice versa:

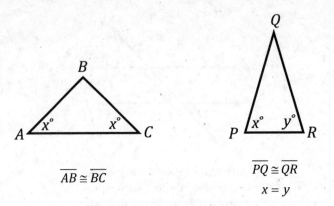

$$\overline{AB} \cong \overline{BC}$$

$$\overline{PQ} \cong \overline{QR}$$
$$x = y$$

A triangle with exactly two equal sides is called an **_isosceles triangle_**. A triangle with exactly three equal sides is called an **_equilateral triangle_**.

Example:

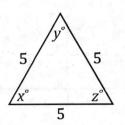

- An equilateral triangle has three equal sides and therefore three equal angles: $x = y = z$. Thus, each angle must be $60°$.

A triangle with a right angle is called a **_right triangle_**. The longest side of the right triangle, which is opposite the 90° angle, is called the **_hypotenuse_**.

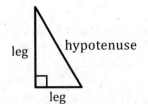

Pythagorean Theorem

The sides of every right triangle fit a special relationship called the **_Pythagorean theorem_**: the square of the hypotenuse is equal to the sum of the squares of the other two sides. This is easier to understand when it is summarized in a formula.

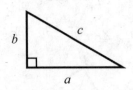

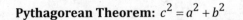

Pythagorean Theorem: $c^2 = a^2 + b^2$

Formulas of Triangles

The **perimeter** of a triangle is the sum of the lengths of the three sides:

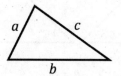

Triangle Perimeter: $P_{triangle} = a + b + c$

The **altitude** of a triangle is a line drawn from a vertex perpendicular to the opposite side. The formula for finding the **area** of a triangle is equal to one-half multiplied by the altitude and the base.

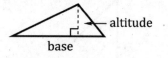

Triangle Area: $A_{triangle} = \frac{ab}{2}$

Example:

In the following figure, what is the area of the triangle?

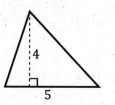

- $A_{triangle} = \frac{ab}{2} = \frac{4 \cdot 5}{2} = 10.$

Special Properties of 45°-45°-90° Triangles

The sides of **45°-45°-90° triangles** share special relationships. In a triangle with angles of 45°-45°-90°, the length of the hypotenuse is equal to the length of either side multiplied by the square root of two. Conversely, the length of each of the two sides is equal to one-half the length of the hypotenuse multiplied by the square root of two.

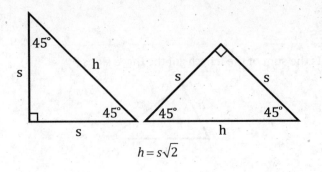

$$h = s\sqrt{2}$$

Examples:

1. In $\triangle ABC$, both $\angle A$ and $\angle C$ are $45°$. If the length of $\overline{AB}$ is 3, what is the length of $\overline{AC}$?

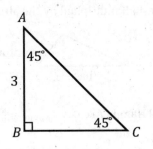

- $h = s\sqrt{2} \Rightarrow \overline{AC} = \overline{AB}(\sqrt{2}) = 3\sqrt{2}.$

2. In $\triangle LMN$, both $\angle L$ and $\angle N$ are $45°$. If the length of $\overline{LN}$ is 4, what is the length of $\overline{MN}$?

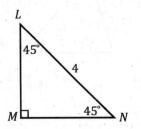

- $h = s\sqrt{2} \Rightarrow 4 = s\sqrt{2} \Rightarrow s = \dfrac{4}{\sqrt{2}} = \dfrac{4}{\sqrt{2}} \cdot \dfrac{\sqrt{2}}{\sqrt{2}} = \dfrac{4\sqrt{2}}{2} = 2\sqrt{2}.$

Special Properties of 30°-60°-90° Triangles

Similarly, the sides of **30°-60°-90° triangles** also share special relationships. In triangles with angles of 30°-60°-90°, the length of the side opposite the 30° angle is equal to one-half the length of the hypotenuse, and the length of the side opposite the 60° angle is equal to one-half the length of the hypotenuse multiplied by $\sqrt{3}$.

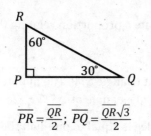

$$PR = \frac{QR}{2}; \ PQ = \frac{QR\sqrt{3}}{2}$$

Examples:

1. In $\triangle ABC$, $\angle A = 60°$ and $\angle C = 30°$. If the length of $\overline{AC}$ is 6, what are the lengths of $\overline{AB}$ and $\overline{BC}$?

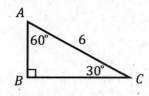

- $\overline{AB} = \frac{\overline{AC}}{2} = \frac{6}{2} = 3 \Rightarrow \overline{BC} = \frac{\overline{AC}\sqrt{3}}{2} = \frac{6\sqrt{3}}{2} = 3\sqrt{3}.$

2. In $\triangle FGH$, $\angle F = 60°$. If the length of $\overline{FH}$ is 14, what is the length of $\overline{FG}$?

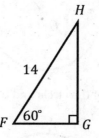

- The length of the side opposite the 30° angle, $\overline{FG}$, is equal to one-half the length of the side opposite the 90° angle, $\overline{FH}$: $\overline{FG} = \frac{\overline{FH}}{2} = \frac{14}{2} = 7.$

Similar Triangles

"Real world" items such as blueprints, scale drawings, microscopes, and photo enlargements involve similar figures. **Similar triangles** are frequently encountered on the exams. The symbol for similarity is "~." If two triangles are similar, the corresponding sides have the same ratio, and their matching angles are **congruent**; that is, they have the same number of degrees. The symbol for congruency is "≅."

Examples:

1. In the following figure, $\triangle ABC \sim \triangle DEF$. Find the length of $\overline{AC}$.

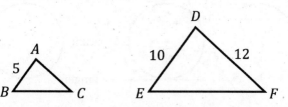

- The triangles are similar, so create a proportion relating the similar sides: $\frac{\overline{AC}}{5} = \frac{12}{10} \Rightarrow 10(\overline{AC}) = 5(12) \Rightarrow 10\overline{AC} = 60 \Rightarrow \overline{AC} = 6$.

2. Right triangle PQR is similar to right triangle STV. The hypotenuse of $\triangle PQR$ is 12 units long and one of the legs is 6 units long. Find the smallest angle of $\triangle STV$.

   - Any right triangle in which one leg is equal to one-half the hypotenuse must be a 30°-60°-90° triangle. Since the two triangles are similar, the matching angles are congruent. Therefore, the smallest angle of $\triangle STV$ is 30°.

Circle Properties and Formulas

Properties of Circles

A **circle** is a closed plane curve, all points of which are equidistant from the center. A complete circle contains 360°, and a semicircle contains 180°. The distance from the center of the circle to any point on the circle is called the **radius**.

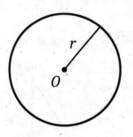

A line segment that passes through the center of the circle and that has endpoints on the circle is called the **diameter**. The diameter of a circle is twice the radius.

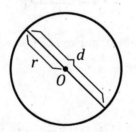

A **chord** is a line segment that connects any two points on a circle. A **secant** is a chord that extends outside the circle in either one or both directions. A **tangent** is a line that touches a circle at one and only one point. A line that is tangent to a circle is perpendicular to a radius drawn to the point of tangency. The **circumference**, or perimeter, is the curved line that bounds the circle. An **arc** of a circle is any part of the circumference. The symbol for arc is " ⌒ ."

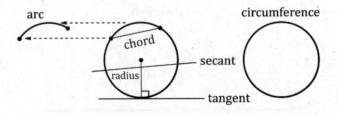

Example:

Two different circles lie in a flat plane. The circles may or may not intersect, but neither circle lies entirely within the other. What is the difference between the minimum and maximum number of lines that could be common tangents to both circles?

- Three cases are possible for the orientation of the two circles:

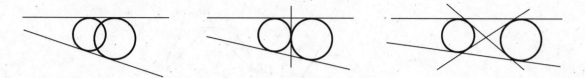

The difference between the minimum and maximum number of tangents that could be common to both circles is: $4 - 2 = 2$.

A *central angle*, such as $\angle AOB$ in the next figure, is an angle with a vertex at the center of the circle and with sides that are radii. A central angle is equal to, or has the same number of degrees as, its intercepted arc. An *inscribed angle*, such as $\angle MNP$, is an angle with a vertex on the circle and with sides that are chords. An inscribed angle has half the number of degrees of its intercepted arc. $\angle MNP$ intercepts $\overset{\frown}{MP}$ and has half the degrees of $\overset{\frown}{MP}$.

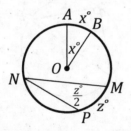

Since the number of degrees of arc in an entire circle is 360, the length of the intercepted arc of a central angle is $\frac{x}{360}$ of the circumference of the circle, where x is the degree measure of the central angle.

Example:

In the following circle with center O, if $x = 60$ and the diameter of the circle is 12, what is the length of $\overset{\frown}{MN}$?

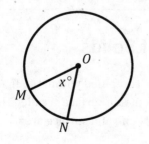

- Since the $\angle MON$ is a central angle, it has the same number of degrees as the intercepted $\overset{\frown}{MN}$. Thus, the length of $\overset{\frown}{MN}$ is: $\frac{x}{360} = \frac{60}{360} = \frac{1}{6}$ of the circumference of the circle. The circumference of the circle is:

  $C = 2\pi r = 2\pi \cdot \frac{d}{2} = \pi d = 12\pi$. Therefore, the length of $\overset{\frown}{MN}$ is: $\frac{12\pi}{6} = 2\pi$.

If each side of a polygon is tangent to a circle, the polygon is **circumscribed** about the circle and the circle is **inscribed** in the polygon. Conversely, if each vertex of a polygon lies on a circle, then the polygon is **inscribed** in the circle and the circle is **circumscribed** about the polygon.

> **Example:**
> ___
> In the following figure, $\triangle ABC$ is circumscribed about a circle and square $DEFG$ is inscribed in a circle.
>
>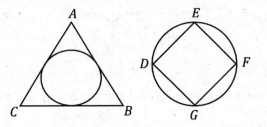

An angle inscribed in a semicircle is a right angle because the semicircle has a measure of 180°.

> **Example:**
> ___
> In the following figure, $\overgroup{NP}$ has a degree measure of 180°; therefore, the degree measure of $\angle NMP$ must be 90°.
>
>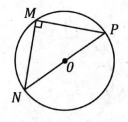

Formulas for Circles

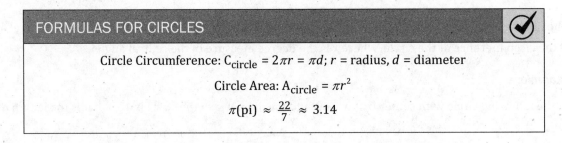

FORMULAS FOR CIRCLES

Circle Circumference: $C_{circle} = 2\pi r = \pi d$; r = radius, d = diameter

Circle Area: $A_{circle} = \pi r^2$

$\pi(\text{pi}) \approx \frac{22}{7} \approx 3.14$

Surface Area and Volume of Solids

In a three-dimensional figure, the total space contained within the figure is called the **volume**; it is expressed in **cubic denominations** (e.g., cm^3). The total outside surface is called the **surface area**; it is expressed in **square denominations** (e.g., cm^2). In computing volume and surface area, express all dimensions in the same denomination.

A **rectangular solid** is a figure of three dimensions having six rectangular faces that meet each other at right angles. The three dimensions are length, width, and height. A **cube** is a rectangular solid whose edges are equal. A **cylinder** is a solid composed of two circular, parallel planes joined at the edges by a curved surface. The centers of the circular planes both lie in a line perpendicular to both planes.

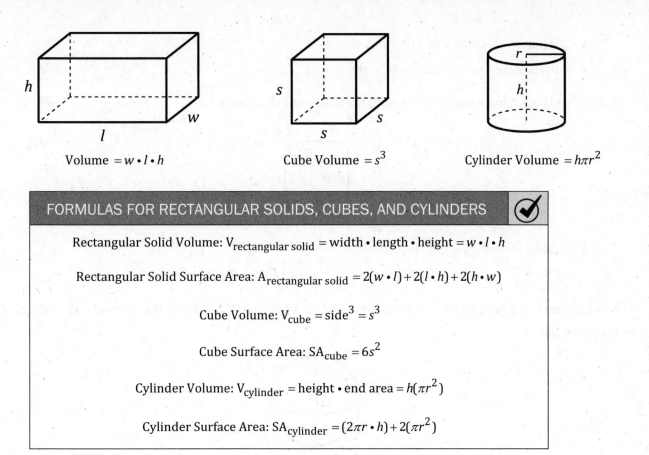

Volume $= w \cdot l \cdot h$ Cube Volume $= s^3$ Cylinder Volume $= h\pi r^2$

FORMULAS FOR RECTANGULAR SOLIDS, CUBES, AND CYLINDERS ✓

Rectangular Solid Volume: $V_{\text{rectangular solid}} = \text{width} \cdot \text{length} \cdot \text{height} = w \cdot l \cdot h$

Rectangular Solid Surface Area: $A_{\text{rectangular solid}} = 2(w \cdot l) + 2(l \cdot h) + 2(h \cdot w)$

Cube Volume: $V_{\text{cube}} = \text{side}^3 = s^3$

Cube Surface Area: $SA_{\text{cube}} = 6s^2$

Cylinder Volume: $V_{\text{cylinder}} = \text{height} \cdot \text{end area} = h(\pi r^2)$

Cylinder Surface Area: $SA_{\text{cylinder}} = (2\pi r \cdot h) + 2(\pi r^2)$

Examples:

1. What is the volume and surface area of the following rectangular solid?

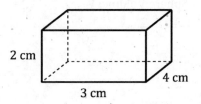

- Volume $= w \cdot l \cdot h = 3 \cdot 4 \cdot 2 = 24 \text{ cm}^3$.
- Surface Area $= 2(w \cdot l) + 2(l \cdot h) + 2(h \cdot w) = 2(3 \cdot 4) + 2(4 \cdot 2) + 2(2 \cdot 3) = 24 + 16 + 12 = 52 \text{ cm}^2$.

2. What is the volume and surface area of the following cube?

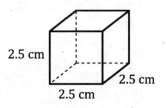

- Volume $= s^3 = (2.5)^3 = 15.625$ cm^3.
- Surface Area $= 6s^2 = 6(2.5)^2 = 37.5$ cm^2.

3. What is the volume and surface area of the following cylindrical solid?

- Volume $= h(\pi r^2) = 4(\pi \cdot 2^2) = 16\pi$ cm^3.
- Surface Area $= (2\pi r \cdot h) + 2(\pi r^2) = (2\pi \cdot 2 \cdot 4) + 2(\pi \cdot 2^2) = 16\pi + 8\pi = 24\pi$ cm^2.

The **surface area of a sphere** is 4π multiplied by the radius squared. The **volume of a sphere** is $\frac{4\pi}{3}$ multiplied by the radius cubed.

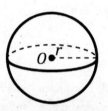

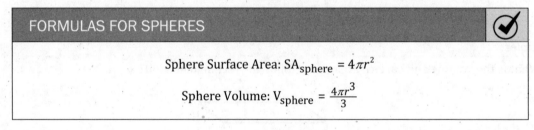

FORMULAS FOR SPHERES
Sphere Surface Area: $SA_{sphere} = 4\pi r^2$
Sphere Volume: $V_{sphere} = \frac{4\pi r^3}{3}$

Geometry
Exercise 8

1. In the figure below, $x = ?$

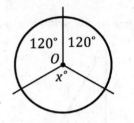

O is the center of the circle.

A. 45   C. 90   E. 150
B. 60   D. 120

2. In the figure below, $x = ?$

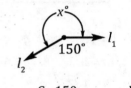

A. 210   C. 150   E. 120
B. 180   D. 135

3. In the figure below, $x = ?$

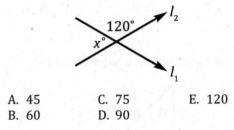

A. 45   C. 75   E. 120
B. 60   D. 90

4. Which of the following is (are) true of the figure below?

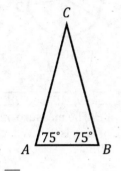

I. $\overline{AB} \cong \overline{BC}$
II. $\overline{BC} \cong \overline{AC}$
III. $\overline{AC} \cong \overline{AB}$

A. I only   D. I and III only
B. II only   E. I, II, and III
C. I and II only

5. What is the perimeter of the triangle below?

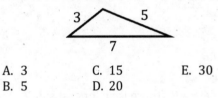

A. 3   C. 15   E. 30
B. 5   D. 20

6. What is the area of the triangle below?

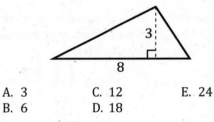

A. 3   C. 12   E. 24
B. 6   D. 18

7. In the figure below, what is the length of $\overline{PR}$?

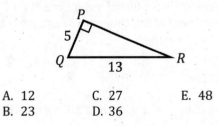

A. 12   C. 27   E. 48
B. 23   D. 36

8. In the figure below, $\overline{AC}$ and $\overline{BD}$ are diameters, and the measure of $\angle ABO$ is 70°. What is the measure of $\angle COD$?

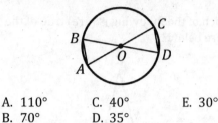

A. 110°
B. 70°
C. 40°
D. 35°
E. 30°

9. In the figure below, $\overline{AC}$ and $\overline{DE}$ bisect each other at point B. The measure of $\angle A$ is 20° and the measure of $\angle D$ is 86°. What is the measure of $\angle DBC$?

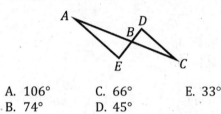

A. 106°
B. 74°
C. 66°
D. 45°
E. 33°

10. In $\triangle ABC$, the measure of $\angle A$ is 40° and the measure of $\angle B$ is 70°. What is the longest side of $\triangle ABC$?

A. $\overline{AC}$
B. $\overline{AB}$
C. $\overline{BC}$
D. $\overline{AC} \cong \overline{AB}$ (there is no longest side)
E. $\overline{AC} \cong \overline{BC}$ (there is no longest side)

11. Each side of a cube is a square with an area of 49 square centimeters. What is the volume of the cube, in cubic centimeters?

A. 49
B. 7^3
C. 7^4
D. 49^7
E. 7^{49}

12. The volume of a sphere is: $V_{sphere} = \frac{4}{3}\pi r^3$, where r is the radius of the sphere. If the surface area of the sphere is 324π , what is the sphere's volume?

A. 243π
B. 324π
C. 729π
D. 972π
E. $1{,}296\pi$

13. If the diameter of a circle is 10, what is the radius?

A. 2
B. 5
C. 8
D. 15
E. 20

14. If the diameter of a circle is 8, what is the circumference?

A. 8π
B. 6π
C. 4π
D. 2π
E. π

15. If the radius of a circle is 5, what is the area?

A. 25π
B. 21π
C. 18π
D. 2π
E. π

16. In the figure below, what are g and h?

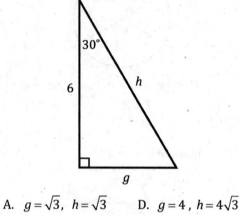

A. $g=\sqrt{3}$, $h=\sqrt{3}$
B. $g=2\sqrt{2}$, $h=2\sqrt{3}$
C. $g=2\sqrt{3}$, $h=4\sqrt{3}$
D. $g=4$, $h=4\sqrt{3}$
E. $g=6$, $h=7$

17. What is the altitude of an equilateral triangle with a perimeter of 24?

A. $2\sqrt{3}$
B. $4\sqrt{3}$
C. 6
D. $4\sqrt{5}$
E. 8

18. In the figure below, what are i and j?

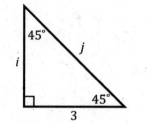

A. $i=3$, $j=3\sqrt{2}$
B. $i=3$, $j=3$
C. $i=4\sqrt{2}$, $j=4$
D. $i=5$, $j=3\sqrt{3}$
E. $i=4$, $j=5$

19. If the perimeter of a square is equal to 40, what is the length of the diagonal?

A. $10\sqrt{2}$ C. 10   E. 14

B. $5\sqrt{3}$ D. $3\sqrt{5}$

20. In the figure below, what is p equal to?

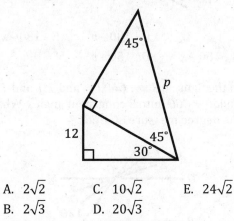

A. $2\sqrt{2}$ C. $10\sqrt{2}$ E. $24\sqrt{2}$

B. $2\sqrt{3}$ D. $20\sqrt{3}$

21. In the circle below, $\overline{RS}$ is parallel to diameter $\overline{PQ}$, and $\overline{PQ}$ has a length of 12. What is the length of minor arc $\overarc{RS}$?

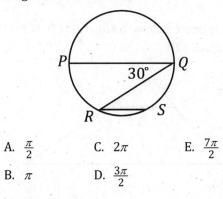

A. $\frac{\pi}{2}$ C. 2π E. $\frac{7\pi}{2}$

B. π D. $\frac{3\pi}{2}$

22. What is the radius of a circle with an area of 49?

A. 7   C. $\frac{7}{\sqrt{\pi}}$ E. π^2

B. 7π D. $\frac{7}{\pi}$

23. In the figure below, what is the area of the shaded region?

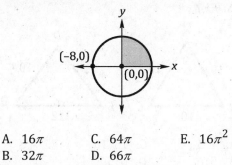

A. 16π C. 64π E. $16\pi^2$

B. 32π D. 66π

24. In the figure below, a circle with an area of 144π is inscribed in a square. What is the area of the shaded region?

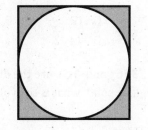

A. $576-144\pi$ D. $1,728-144\pi$

B. $216-72\pi$ E. $256-24\pi$

C. $144-24\pi$

25. What is the area of a right triangle with legs of lengths 4 and 5?

A. 6   C. 12   E. 24

B. 10   D. 20

26. At 12 cents per square foot, how much will it cost to paint the rectangular slab in the figure below?

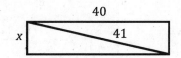

A. $43.20   C. $98.40   E. $201.50

B. $46.40   D. $196.80

27. If the diagonal of a square is $5\sqrt{2}$, what is the area of the square?

A. 10   C. 25   E. 35

B. 20   D. 30

28. In the figures below, what is the ratio of the perimeter of $\triangle ABC$ to the perimeter of $\triangle DEF$?

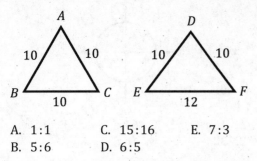

A. 1:1   C. 15:16   E. 7:3

B. 5:6   D. 6:5

29. If the hypotenuse of a right triangle is 37 and one leg is 35, what is the length of the other leg?

A. $4\sqrt{3}$ C. 12   E. 16

B. $6\sqrt{2}$ D. $14\sqrt{2}$

30. If $2\sqrt{12}$, $3\sqrt{6}$, and $4\sqrt{3}$ are the dimensions of a rectangular solid, what is the volume of the solid?

A. $216\sqrt{24}$ C. $144\sqrt{6}$ E. $\sqrt{24}$

B. $\sqrt{5{,}184}$ D. 5,184

31. In the figure below, $\triangle DEF$ is an isosceles triangle. What is the length of $\overline{DF}$?

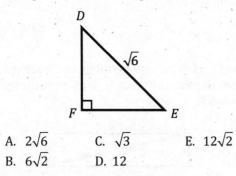

A. $2\sqrt{6}$ C. $\sqrt{3}$ E. $12\sqrt{2}$

B. $6\sqrt{2}$ D. 12

32. If the longest side of a 30°-60°-90° triangle is $2\sqrt{3}$, what is the area of the triangle?

A. 8   C. $1.5\sqrt{3}$ E. 1

B. 4   D. 2

33. In the figure below, a equals all of the following EXCEPT

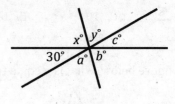

A. y C. $180 - b - c$ E. $180 - x - y$

B. $150 - x$ D. $150 - b$

34. In the figure below, $\overline{OM} \| \overline{PJ}$, and $\overline{FG}$ and $\overline{EG}$ divide $\angle CGO$ into 3 congruent angles. What is the degree measure of $\angle EGC$?

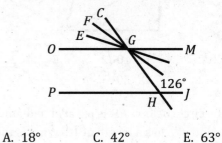

A. 18°   C. 42°   E. 63°

B. 36°   D. 54°

35. In the figure below, $\triangle ABE \sim \triangle ACD$. What is the length of $\overline{CD}$?

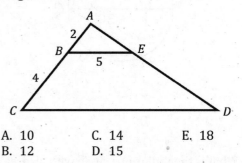

A. 10   C. 14   E. 18

B. 12   D. 15

36. A right circular cylinder has a base whose diameter is $8x$; the height of the cylinder is $3y$. What is the volume of the cylinder?

A. $24xy$ C. $48\pi xy$ E. $48\pi x^2 y$

B. $24\pi x^2 y$ D. $96\pi xy$

37. A road runs 1,200 feet from A to B, and then makes a right angle going to C, a distance of 500 feet. A new road is being built directly from A to C. How many feet shorter will the new road be than the old road?

A. 400   C. 850   E. 1,300

B. 609   D. 1,000

38. A ladder 65 feet long is leaning against a wall. Its lower end is 25 feet away from the wall. How many more feet away from the wall will the lower end of the ladder be if the upper end is moved down 8 feet?

A. 60   C. 14   E. 8
B. 52   D. 10

39. A box is 12 inches in width, 16 inches in length, and 6 inches in height. How many square inches of paper would be required to cover it on all sides?

A. 192   C. 720   E. 1,440
B. 360   D. 900

40. In the figure below, $x = ?$

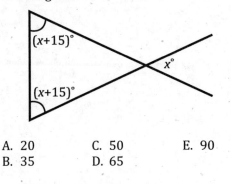

A. 20   C. 50   E. 90
B. 35   D. 65

41. In the figure below, $x = ?$

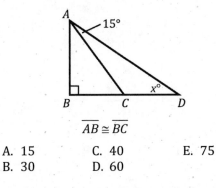

$\overline{AB} \cong \overline{BC}$

A. 15   C. 40   E. 75
B. 30   D. 60

42. In the diagram below, $\overline{AD} \cong \overline{AE}$ and $\overline{AB} \cong \overline{BF} \cong \overline{CE} \cong \overline{CF} \cong \overline{DE}$.

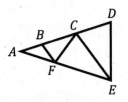

What is the degree measure of $\angle DAE$?

A. 20°   C. 25°   E. 35°
B. 24°   D. 30°

43. The figure below shows two circles lying in the same plane with respective centers at O and P. $\overline{AB}$ is a common external tangent segment to the two circles at A and B, respectively. If $\overline{OA} = 13$, $\overline{PB} = 3$, and $\overline{OP} = 26$, then what is the length of $\overline{AB}$?

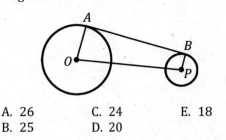

A. 26   C. 24   E. 18
B. 25   D. 20

44. The figure below shows a circle of area 144π square inches with a radius drawn to the point of tangency of the circle on the x-axis.

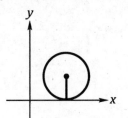

If this point of tangency is 16 inches from the origin, then the number of inches from the origin to the center of the circle is:

A. 12   C. 16   E. 20
B. $12\sqrt{2}$ D. $16\sqrt{2}$

45. In the figure below, B and E lie on $\overline{AC}$ and $\overline{AD}$, respectively, of $\triangle ACD$, such that $\overline{BE} \parallel \overline{CD}$. $\overline{BD} \perp \overline{AC}$, and $\overline{BC} \cong \overline{ED}$. If $\overline{BC} = 10$ and $\overline{CD} = 20$, what is the area of $\triangle ABE$?

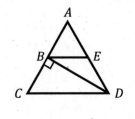

A. 100
B. $50\sqrt{3}$
C. 50
D. $25\sqrt{3}$
E. It cannot be determined from the given information.

COORDINATE GEOMETRY

Ordered Pairs

An ***ordered pair*** of coordinates has the general form (x, y). The first element refers to the ***x-coordinate***: the distance left or right of the ***origin***, or intersection of the axes. The second element gives the ***y-coordinate***: the distance up or down from the origin.

Example:

Plot $(3,2)$.

- Move to the positive 3 value on the *x*-axis. Then, from there move up two units on the *y*-axis, as illustrated by the graph on the left. The graph on the right demonstrates an alternative method: the point $(3,2)$ is located at the intersection of a line drawn through the *x*-value 3 parallel to the *y*-axis and a line drawn through the *y*-value 2 parallel to the *x*-axis.

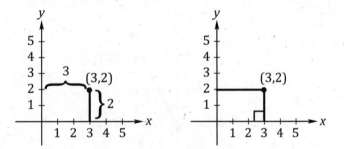

Plotting Equations

The coordinate axis system provides a framework for plotting equations. Simply plot several pairs of points for the given equation.

Examples:

1. Plot the equation $x = y$.

   - This equation has an infinite number of solutions:

x	1	2	3	5	0	−3	−5	...
y	1	2	3	5	0	−3	−5	...

   Plot these pairs of *x* and *y* on the axis system. Draw a line through them to produce a plot of the original equation. The complete picture of the equation $x = y$ is a straight line including all the real numbers such that *x* is equal to *y*.

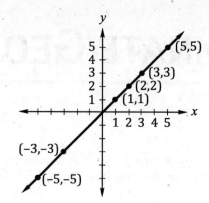

2. Plot the equation $y = 2x$.

- This equation has an infinite number of solutions:

x	−4	−2	−1	0	1	2	4	...
y	−8	−4	−2	0	2	4	8	...

After entering the points on the graph, complete the picture. It is a straight line, but it rises more rapidly than does $x = y$.

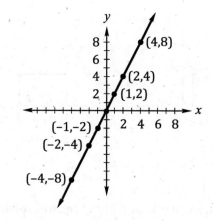

Midpoint of Line Segments

For a line segment between two points, (x_1, y_1) and (x_2, y_2), the **midpoint** $= \left(\dfrac{x_1 + x_2}{2}, \dfrac{y_1 + y_2}{2} \right)$. The x-coordinate of the midpoint is the average of the two x-axis endpoints and the y-coordinate of the midpoint is the average of the two y-axis endpoints.

Examples:

1. Find the midpoint between (−5,8) and (11,34).

- The midpoint is $\left(\dfrac{x_1 + x_2}{2}, \dfrac{y_1 + y_2}{2} \right) = \left(\dfrac{-5 + 11}{2}, \dfrac{8 + 34}{2} \right) = \left(\dfrac{6}{2}, \dfrac{42}{2} \right) = (3, 21)$.

2. One endpoint of a circle diameter is located at $(13,1)$. If the center of the circle is $(15,10)$, find the other endpoint.

- The midpoint of the diameter is $(15,10)$, so $15 = \dfrac{x_1 + x_2}{2} = \dfrac{13 + x_2}{2}$ and $10 = \dfrac{y_1 + y_2}{2} = \dfrac{1 + y_2}{2}$.

  $x_2 = (15 \cdot 2) - 13 = 17$ and $y_2 = (10 \cdot 2) - 1 = 19$. Thus, $(x_2, y_2) = (17,19)$.

Distance Between Two Points

To determine the distance between two points on a coordinate graph, consider points P and Q. For simplicity's sake, we will confine the discussion to the first quadrant, but the method works in all quadrants and even with lines covering two or more quadrants. Assign the value (x_1, y_1) to point P and (x_2, y_2) to point Q:

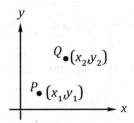

To find the distance between points P and Q, construct a triangle:

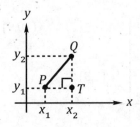

Point T now has the coordinates (x_2, y_1). To calculate the length of $\overline{PT}$, find the distance moved on the x-axis: $x_2 - x_1$ units. The y-coordinate does not change. Similarly, the length of $\overline{QT}$ will be $y_2 - y_1$ since the distance is purely vertical, moving up from y_1 to y_2, with no change in the x-value. Apply the Pythagorean theorem:

$$(PQ)^2 = (PT)^2 + (QT)^2 = (x_2 - x_1)^2 + (y_2 - y_1)^2 \Rightarrow PQ = \sqrt{(x_2 - x_1)^2 + (y_2 - y_1)^2}.$$

Example:

In the following figure, what is the length of $\overline{PQ}$?

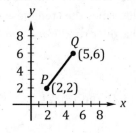

- Find the length of $\overline{PQ}$ by constructing a triangle:

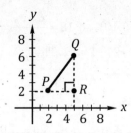

$\overline{QR}$ runs from (5,6) to (5,2), so it must be 4 units long. $\overline{PR}$ runs from (2,2) to (5,2), so it is 3 units long. Use the Pythagorean theorem: $(\overline{PQ})^2 = (\overline{QR})^2 + (\overline{PR})^2 = 4^2 + 3^2 = 16 + 9 = 25$. Therefore, $\overline{PQ} = \sqrt{25} = 5$.

Therefore, you can find the length of any line segment drawn in a coordinate axis system between points (x_1, y_1) and (x_2, y_2) using this **distance formula**: $d = \sqrt{(x_2 - x_1)^2 + (y_2 - y_1)^2}$. Notice that it does not actually matter which point is considered the start of the line and the end of the line, since the change in each coordinate is squared in the distance formula.

> **Example:**
>
> In the following figure, what is the distance between P and Q?

$$Q \bullet (10,9)$$
$$P \bullet (2,3)$$

- The distance between P and Q is: $\sqrt{(x_2 - x_1)^2 + (y_2 - y_1)^2} = \sqrt{(10-2)^2 + (9-3)^2} = \sqrt{64 + 36} = \sqrt{100} = 10$.

Linear Functions

Slope-Intercept Form

If x and y are related by a linear equation, then y is a **linear function**. Except for a vertical line, every line equation is a linear function that can be represented in **slope-intercept form**: $y = mx + b$, where m is the slope of the line and b is the y-intercept. The y-intercept is the y-coordinate of the point where the line intersects the y-axis, or where $x = 0$. The **slope**, m, of a line describes the steepness of the line. It is defined as the change in y-values divided by the change in x-values, or rise over run: $slope = m = \dfrac{y_2 - y_1}{x_2 - x_1} = \dfrac{rise}{run}$.

> **Examples:**
>
> 1. Find the slope of the line containing (3,2) and (8,22).
>
> - $m = \dfrac{y_2 - y_1}{x_2 - x_1} = \dfrac{22-2}{8-3} = \dfrac{20}{5} = 4$.
>
> 2. Find the slope of the line given by the equation $6x + 12y = 13$.
>
> - $6x + 12y = 13 \Rightarrow 12y = -6x + 13 \Rightarrow y = \dfrac{-6x + 13}{12} \Rightarrow y = -\dfrac{x}{2} + \dfrac{13}{12}$. Therefore, the slope is $-\dfrac{1}{2}$.

3. The points $(-5,12)$, $(0,7)$ and $(10,-3)$ lie on a line. What is the y-intercept of this line?

- The x-coordinate of the second point is 0. Therefore, this point's y-coordinate, 7, is the y-intercept of the line.

Parallel Lines

The equation of a line that is parallel to the x-axis is $y=k$, where k is a constant. The equation of a line that is parallel to the y-axis is $x=c$, where c is a constant. If two lines are parallel, their slopes are equal and vice versa.

Example:

Find the equation for a line that passes through the point $(0,12)$ and is parallel to the line $y=7x-15$.

- A line has slope-intercept form $y=mx+b$. If the line passes through the y-axis at $(0,12)$, then the y-intercept $b=+12$. If the two lines are parallel, then the slopes are equal and $m=+7$. Therefore, the line equation is $y=mx+b \Rightarrow y=7x+12$.

Perpendicular Lines

If two perpendicular lines have slopes m_1 and m_2, then $m_1 = -\dfrac{1}{m_2}$ and vice versa.

Example:

The equation of a line is $y=\frac{x}{4}+10$. If a second line is perpendicular to the line, what is the slope of the second line?

- If two lines are perpendicular to one another, their slopes are opposite reciprocals of one another. Thus, if a line has a slope of $\frac{1}{4}$, then the line perpendicular to it has a slope of -4.

Quadratic Functions

If y is expressed in the form $y=ax^2+bx+c$, where $a \neq 0$ and b is any real number, y is a **quadratic function**. Graphs of quadratic functions are called parabolas.

Example:

A quadratic function of the form $y=ax^2+bx+c$ includes the following ordered pairs of (x,y): $(1,17)$, $(5,61)$, and $(7,95)$. What is the value of c for this quadratic function?

- Set up the system of three simultaneous equations that are generated by the three ordered pairs:

$$17 = a(1)^2 + b(1) + c \Rightarrow 17 = a+b+c$$
$$61 = a(5)^2 + b(5) + c \Rightarrow 61 = 25a+5b+c$$
$$95 = a(7)^2 + b(7) + c \Rightarrow 95 = 49a+7b+c$$

Use the method of solving simultaneous equations to determine the values of a, b, and c. Multiply the first equation by -1, and add it to the other two equations to eliminate c:

$$-1(17 = a+b+c)$$
$$+\ \ 61 = 25a+5b+c$$
$$\overline{44 = 24a+4b}$$

$$-1(17 = a+b+c)$$
$$+\ \ 95 = 49a+7b+c$$
$$\overline{78 = 48a+6b}$$

Now, combine these new equations to eliminate a. Multiply the first equation by -2, and add it to the second equation to eliminate a:

$$-2(44 = 24a+4b)$$
$$+\ \ 78 = 48a+6b$$
$$\overline{-10 = -2b \Rightarrow b = 5}$$

Substitute 5 for b in either of the new equations and solve for a: $44 = 24a+4(5) \Rightarrow 24a = 24 \Rightarrow a = 1$.

Finally, substitute the values for a and b into any of the three original equations to solve for c. Since the first equation is simplest, we'll use that one: $17 = a+b+c \Rightarrow 17 = 1+5+c \Rightarrow c = 11$.

Identifying Graphs of Functions

You may be asked simply to identify graphs of linear and quadratic functions. The graph of a linear function is a straight line, while the graph of a quadratic function is called a parabola and always has the shape of a curve about the y-axis. The basic quadratic graph that you need to know is $f(x) = x^2$, as illustrated in the second of the following examples.

Examples:

1. The line of best fit for $y = f(x)$ for the ordered pairs $(-4,-18)$, $(1,3)$, $(2,6)$, $(3,8)$, and $(4,14)$ is best represented by which of the following graphs?

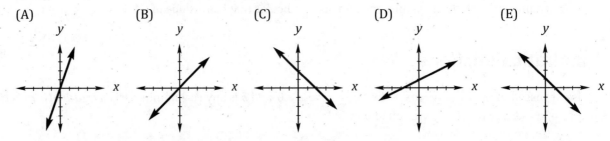

- The correct answer is (A). Both x and y increase in value for each ordered pair, so eliminate (C) and (E). You can eliminate (B) since the values of x and y in the given ordered pairs clearly indicate that $x \neq y$. Finally, eliminate (D) because when $x = 1$, $y = 3$, whereas in the graph of (D), $y < 3$ when $x = 1$.

2. Which of the following graphs depicts a quadratic function?

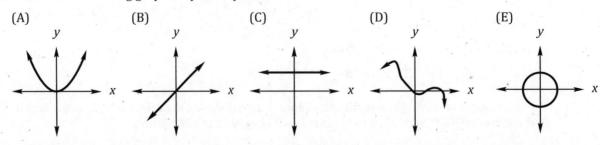

- All quadratic equations can be written in the form $y = ax^2 + bx + c$. (B) is a linear plot with the y-intercept equal to 0: $y = ax$. (C) is a constant value for y: $y = k$. (E) is a plot of a circle:

$x^2 + y^2 = k$, where k is a constant. (D) is a complicated function without a standard form of equation. Only (A) is a quadratic equation: $y = ax^2$.

Functions can be also mathematical models of real-life situations. For example, an item might present information about the projected sales of a product at various prices and ask for a mathematical model in the form of a graph or equation that represents projected sales as a function of price.

Qualitative Behavior of Graphs

You should also understand how the graphs of functions behave qualitatively. Items on the exam might show the graph of a function in the xy-coordinate plane and ask for the number of values of x for which $f(x)$ equals a particular value. Alternatively, an item may present a graph with numerical values, requiring you to recognize the form of the graphed function.

Examples:

1. The following figure shows a graph of the function $y = x^2 + 2x + 6$. The smallest possible integer value of $y = ?$

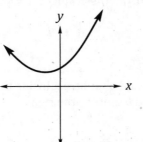

*   The lowest point on the function occurs when $x < 0$. Find the symmetry by substitution: if $x = 1$, $y = 9$; if $x = 0$, $y = 6$; if $x = -1$, $y = 5$; if $x = -2$, $y = 6$; if $x = -3$, $y = 9$. The coordinates of these points are $(-3,9)$, $(-2,6)$, $(-1,5)$, $(0,6)$, and $(1,9)$, respectively. Thus, the lowest point occurs at $(-1,5)$. Alternatively, solve for the vertex using the properties of parabolas. The standard form of a parabola is: $y = a(x-h)^2 + k$, where the vertex is at (h,k). Write the equation in standard form: $y = (x^2 + 2x + 1) + 6 - 1 = (x+1)^2 + 5 = [x-(-1)]^2 + 5$. Therefore, the vertex is at $(-1,5)$.

2. What is the sum of all distinct integer x-values for the graph of the absolute value function in the following figure?

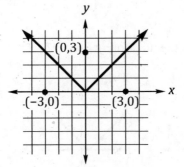

*   Each negative x-value has a canceling positive x-value. Therefore, the answer is zero.

Transformation Effects on Graphs

When you alter a graph, you transform it. If you transform a graph without changing its shape, you translate it. Vertical and horizontal transformations are translations. Items on the exam may test knowledge of the effects of simple translations of graphs of functions. For example, the graph of a function $f(x)$ could be given and you might be asked questions about the graph of the function $f(x+2)$.

Vertical Translations

To move a function up or down, you add or subtract outside the function. That is, $f(x)+b$ is $f(x)$ moved up b units, and $f(x)-b$ is $f(x)$ moved down b units.

> **Example:**
>
> In order to obtain the graph of $y=(x+2)^2+6$ from the graph of $y=x^2+4x+11$, how should the graph of $y=x^2+4x+11$ be moved?
>
> - Rewrite the original in the form $f(x)+b$: $y=x^2+4x+11 \Rightarrow y=x^2+4x+4+7=(x+2)^2+7$. Thus, to obtain the graph of $y=(x+2)^2+6$ from the graph of $y=(x+2)^2+7$, the graph must be moved one unit down.

Horizontal Translations

To shift a function to the left or to the right, add or subtract inside the function. That is, $f(x+b)$ is $f(x)$ shifted b units to the left, and $f(x-b)$ is $f(x)$ shifted b units to the right.

> **Example:**
>
> The following graph is of the function $y=|x|$.

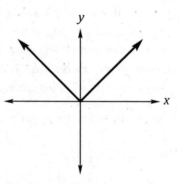

> Which of the following is a graph of the function $y=|x+3|$?

(A) (B) (C) (D) (E)

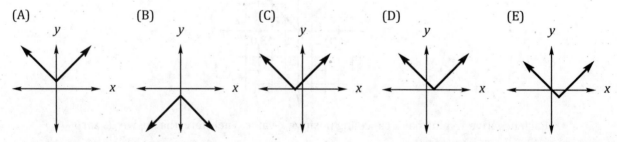

> - By translation of the original graph from $y=|x|$ to $y=|x+3|$, the original graph is moved three units to the left, (C). Alternatively, substitute values for x and y: $y=0$ for $x=-3$. (C) is the only graph that contains the point $(-3,0)$.

Graphing Geometric Figures

You can also use the coordinate system for graphing geometric figures. The following figure is a graph of a square whose vertices are at coordinates $(0,0)$, $(4,0)$, $(4,4)$, and $(0,4)$.

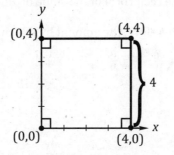

Each side of the square is equal to 4 since each side is 4 units long and parallel to either the *x*- or *y*-axis. Since every coordinate point is the perpendicular intersection of two lines, it is possible to measure distances in the coordinate system.

Examples:

1. In the following figure, what is the area of the circle?

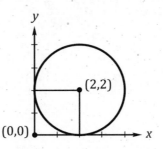

- To solve this problem, find the radius of the circle. The center of the circle is located at the intersection of $x = 2$ and $y = 2$, or the point $(2,2)$. Thus, the radius is 2 units long and the area is $r^2\pi = 2^2\pi = 4\pi$.

2. $\triangle ABC$ has coordinates A, B, and C equal to $(5,3)$, $(19,7)$ and $(17,25)$, respectively. By how much does the largest slope for any median of $\triangle ABC$ exceed the largest slope for any altitude of $\triangle ABC$?

- The largest slope occurs for the steepest ascent for increasing values of *x*. Draw a figure of the given information in the coordinate plane:

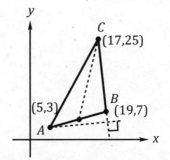

A median is drawn from one angle of a triangle to the midpoint of the opposite side. Of the three possible medians, the median that connects C to the midpoint of $\overline{AB}$ has the largest slope. The midpoint of $\overline{AB}$ is $\left(\frac{5+19}{2},\frac{7+3}{2}\right)=(12,5)$. Therefore, the slope of the median is $\frac{25-5}{17-12}=4$. An altitude is drawn from one angle of a triangle to the opposite side at a right angle. Of the three possible altitudes, the altitude that connects A to $\overline{BC}$ has the largest slope. Since this altitude is perpendicular to $\overline{BC}$, its slope is the opposite reciprocal of the slope of $\overline{BC}$. The slope of $\overline{BC}$ is $\frac{25-7}{17-19}=\frac{18}{-2}=-9$, so the slope of the altitude $\frac{1}{9}$. Therefore, the amount by which the slope of the median is larger than the slope of the altitude is: $4-\frac{1}{9}=\frac{36}{9}-\frac{1}{9}=\frac{35}{9}$.

Coordinate Geometry
Exercise 9

DIRECTIONS: Choose the correct answer to each of the following items. Answers are on page 779.

1. Which of the following graphs represents a relation of which the domain is the set of all real numbers and the range is the set of all non-negative real numbers?

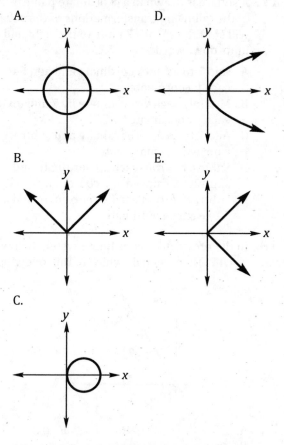

A.

D.

B.

E.

C.

2. Which of the lettered points on the number line below could represent the result when the coordinate of point *F* is divided by the coordinate of point *X*?

X A B   C D EF

(−) ←——————————→ (+)
   −4−3−2−1 0 1 2 3 4

A. A   C. C   E. E
B. B   D. D

3. $\overline{AB}$ is the diameter of a circle whose center is point *O*. If the coordinates of point *A* are $(2,6)$ and the coordinates of point *B* are $(6,2)$, find the coordinates of point *O*.

A. $(4,4)$ C. $(2,-2)$ E. $(2,2)$
B. $(4,-4)$ D. $(0,0)$

4. The vertices of a triangle are $(2,1)$, $(2,5)$, and $(5,1)$. What is the area of the triangle?

A. 12   C. 8   E. 5
B. 10   D. 6

5. The area of a circle whose center is at $(0,0)$ is 16π. The circle does NOT pass through which of the following points?

A. $(4,4)$ C. $(4,0)$ E. $(0,-4)$
B. $(0,4)$ D. $(-4,0)$

6. What is the slope of a line that passes through $(0,-5)$ and $(8,27)$?

A. 4   C. $\frac{8}{32}$ E. −4
B. 2   D. $-\frac{8}{32}$

7. The slope of a line that passes through points $(3,7)$ and $(12,y)$ is $\frac{1}{3}$. What is the value of *y*?

A. 2   C. $6\frac{2}{3}$ E. 10
B. 4   D. $7\frac{1}{3}$

8. What is the slope of the line $y = 5x + 7$?

A. 7   C. 2   E. $\frac{1}{5}$
B. 5   D. $\frac{7}{5}$

9. A line passes through points $(3,8)$ and $(w,2k)$. If $w \neq 3$, what is the slope of the line?

A. $\frac{8-2k}{3+w}$ C. $\frac{2k-8}{w-3}$ E. $\frac{3}{8}$
B. $\frac{2k+8}{w+3}$ D. $\frac{w-3}{2k-8}$

10. What is the equation of the line that passes through the point $(0,13)$ and is parallel to the line $4x + 2y = 17$?

A. $4x + 2y = 13$

B. $4x + 2y = -13$

C. $y = -2x + 13$

D. $y = 2x + 13$

E. It cannot be determined from the given information.

11. A line passes through the point $(0,-5)$ and is perpendicular to the line $y = -\frac{x}{2} + 5$. What is the equation of the line?

A. $y = -\frac{x}{2} - 5$

B. $y = 2x - 5$

C. $y = -2x - 5$

D. $y = -\frac{x}{2} + 13$

E. It cannot be determined from the given information.

12. If point P has coordinates $(-2,2)$ and point Q has coordinates $(2,0)$, what is the distance from point P to point Q?

A. -4 C. $4\sqrt{5}$ E. 6

B. $2\sqrt{5}$ D. 4

13. If point R has coordinates (x,y) and point S has coordinates $(x+1, y+1)$, what is the distance between point R and point S?

A. $\sqrt{2}$ D. $\sqrt{x^2 + y^2 + 2}$

B. 2 E. $x + y + 1$

C. $\sqrt{x^2 + y^2}$

14. Will is standing 40 yards due north of point P. Grace is standing 60 yards due west of point P. What is the shortest distance between Will and Grace?

A. 20 yards   D. 80 yards

B. $4\sqrt{13}$ yards   E. $80\sqrt{13}$ yards

C. $20\sqrt{13}$ yards

15. On a coordinate graph, what is the distance between points $(5,6)$ and $(6,7)$?

A. $\sqrt{2}$ C. 2 E. $6\sqrt{2}$

B. 1 D. 4

16. On a coordinate plane, point B is located 7 units to the left of point A. The x-coordinate of point A is x, and the y-coordinate of point A is y. What is the x-coordinate of point B?

A. $x - 7$

B. $x + 7$

C. $y + 7$

D. $y - 7$

E. It cannot be determined from the given information.

17. A square is drawn in a coordinate plane. Which of the following transformations of the square will shift the square 7 units to the right and 5 units downward?

A. Add 7 to each x-coordinate and add 5 to each y-coordinate.

B. Multiply each x-coordinate by 7 and divide each y-coordinate by 5.

C. Add 7 to each x-coordinate and subtract 5 from each y-coordinate.

D. Subtract 7 from each x-coordinate and subtract 5 from each y-coordinate.

E. Subtract 7 from each x-coordinate and add 5 to each y-coordinate.

18. In the rectangular coordinate system below, if $x = 4.2$, then y equals which of the following?

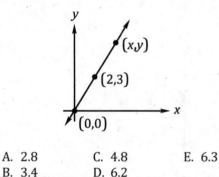

A. 2.8   C. 4.8   E. 6.3

B. 3.4   D. 6.2

19. If Sam lives 8 miles west of Jeni, and Molly lives 10 miles north of Jeni, approximately how many miles less would Molly walk if she walks directly to Sam's house, rather than first to Jeni's house and then to Sam's house?

A. 1   C. 3   E. 5

B. 2   D. 4

20. If point B (not shown in the figure below) lies below the x-axis at point $(4,-4)$, what is the area of $\triangle ABC$?

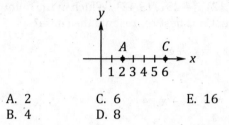

A. 2   C. 6   E. 16

B. 4   D. 8

21. On a coordinate graph, what is the distance between points $(-1,4)$ and $(2,8)$?

A. 3   C. 5   E. 8

B. 4   D. 6

22. In the figure below, $\overline{AB}$ is the base of a water ski ramp and is 18 feet long. The slope (rise divided by run) of the ramp is m. If the ramp is y feet high, then what is the value of y?

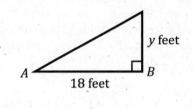

A. $\frac{m}{18}$ C. $18-m$ E. $m+18$

B. $18m$ D. $m-18$

23. What is the midpoint between $(-2,15)$ and $(8,17)$?

A. $(6,16)$ C. $(5,16)$ E. $(6,32)$

B. $(3,16)$ D. $(5,32)$

24. How many of the following graphs are graphs of functions?

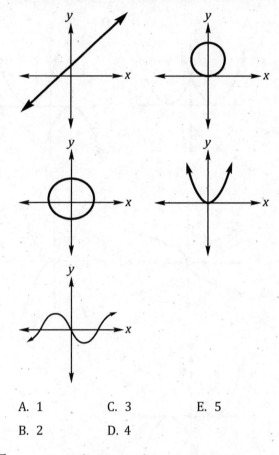

A. 1   C. 3   E. 5

B. 2   D. 4

25. In each of the following four sets, the three ordered pairs belong to a linear function. In how many of the four sets is the value of the variable x less than zero?

$\{(0,1), (-4,7), (x,0)\}$
$\{(0,2), (-5,52), (x,12)\}$
$\{(2,-5), (-2,-17), (x,13)\}$
$\{(6,17), (8,25), (x,4)\}$

A. 0   C. 2   E. 4

B. 1   D. 3

26. If $y=mx+b$, $x=5$ for $y=20$, and $x=9$ for $y=32$, then $m+b$ is:

A. 76   C. 14   E. 3

B. 52   D. 8

27. Which of the following graphs depicts the quadratic functions $y = \frac{x^2}{2}$ and $y = -\frac{x^2}{2}$?

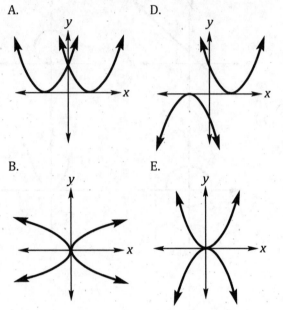

A.

D.

B.

E.

C.

28. If $y = -2x^2 + 16x - 1$, what is the largest possible value for y?

A. −1
B. 13
C. 31
D. 32
E. It cannot be determined from the given information.

29. The graph of $y = 4x^2$ intersects the graph of $y = x^2 + 3x$ at how many points?

A. 0   C. 2   E. 4
B. 1   D. 3

30. A student noted that the graph of the following ordered points for (x,y) appeared to approximate a parabolic curve: $(1,7)$, $(-1,0)$, $(2,12)$, $(4,29)$, $(5,42)$. Which of the following equations best represents the curve?

A. $y = x^2 + 6$

B. $y = x^2 + 3x + 2$

C. $y = 2x^2 + x + 4$

D. $y = x^2 - x + 8$

E. $y = 2x^2 + x + 4$

31. The graph of the following ordered pairs for (x,y) is approximately a straight line of the form $y = mx + b$: $(1,18)$, $(2,23)$, $(3,27)$, $(4,32)$, $(5,38)$. Which of the following best approximates the value of b?

A. 13   C. 20   E. 25
B. 18   D. 23

32. In the figure below, which is not necessarily drawn to scale, $ABCD$ is a square and $\angle FGH \cong \angle A$.

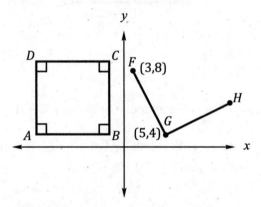

If points F and G have the coordinates as indicated in the figure, how many of the following four ordered pairs could possibly represent point H?

$(8,6), (9,6), (11,7), (13,8)$

A. 0   C. 2   E. 4
B. 1   D. 3

33. The line that passes through $(1,5)$ and $(-2,17)$ is parallel to the line that passes through $(17,6)$ and $(13,y)$. What is the value of y?

A. 10   C. 16   E. 22
B. 14   D. 18

34. The figure below shows a circle with an area of 9π.

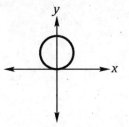

The circle is tangent to the x-axis at $(0,0)$ and the center of the circle lies on the y-axis. The constant function $y = k$ intersects the circle at exactly one point. If $k > 0$, what is the value of k?

A. 1   C. 3   E. 9
B. 2   D. 6

35. The figure below shows a graph of $y = \dfrac{12}{x^2 + 6x + 7}$. How many different integers for y are not a part of the graph of $y = \dfrac{12}{x^2 + 6x + 7}$?

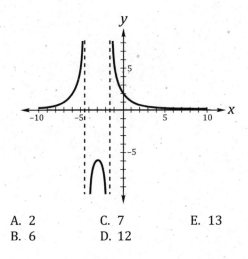

A. 2   C. 7   E. 13
B. 6   D. 12

36. The graph below shows two different parabola functions: $y = (x-1)^2 + 4$ and $y - 2 = -(x+5)^2$.

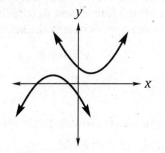

The values of y that are not on either of the parabolas are all values of y such that:

A. $-5 \le y \le 1$ C. $1 < y < 4$ E. $4 < y < 5$
B. $2 < y < 4$ D. $1 \le y \le 5$

37. The graph below is of the function $y = (x-2)^2 + 3$.

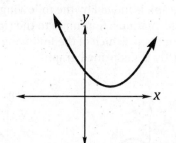

If a horizontal shift of four units to the left were performed on the original graph, at what point (x, y) would the transformed graph intersect the original graph?

A. $(2,7)$ C. $(6,3)$ E. $(0,7)$
B. $(2,-1)$ D. $(-2,3)$

38. The graph of $y = 3x^2$ can be produced from the graph of $y = x^2$ by performing a vertical stretch by a factor of three. The graph of $y = 2x^2 + 12x + 1$ can be produced from the graph of $y = x^2$ by performing a vertical stretch by a factor of two, a horizontal shift of three units to the left, and a vertical shift of:

A. 17 units down.
B. 12 units down.
C. 1 unit down.
D. 1 unit up.
E. 12 units up.

39. The following ordered pairs for (x,y) represent points on a graph: $(5,15)$, $(10,28)$, $(11,27)$, $(25,47)$, $(40,76)$, $(50,111)$, and $(60,129)$. Which of the following equations represents the line of best fit (the line that most closely approximates the set of points)?

A. $y = \frac{x}{3}$ C. $y = 3x - 6$ E. $y = 5x - 4$

B. $y = \frac{x}{3} - 2$ D. $y = 2x + 3$

40. The graph below shows a circle whose equation is $x^2 + y^2 = 16$.

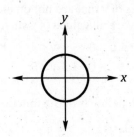

The graph is moved by the following transformations: four units to the right and two units up. Which of the following is the correctly transformed graph?

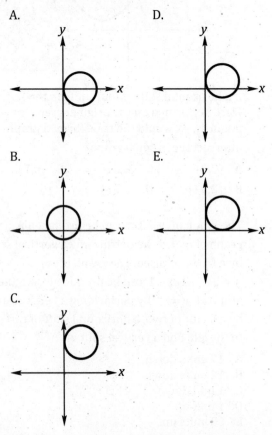

A.

D.

B.

E.

C.

STORY PROBLEMS

Story problems may test arithmetic, algebra, or geometry in the context of a "story." You should have everything you need to solve these problems. However, remember that if a math story item stumps you, you have the answer at hand. Simply work backwards from the answer choices—the right answer has to be one of the choices. Since quantitative (i.e., numerical value) choices are arranged in size order, starting with the middle answer choice will result in the fewest calculations.

In solving story problems, the most important technique is to read accurately. Be sure you clearly understand what you are asked to find. Then, evaluate the item in common sense terms to eliminate answer choices. For example, if two people are working together, their combined speed is greater than either individual speed, but not more than twice as fast as the fastest speed. Finally, be alert for the "hidden equation"—some necessary information so obvious that the item assumes that you know it.

Examples:

1. boys + girls = total class
2. imported wine + domestic wine = all wine
3. wall + floor = right angle (Pythagorean theorem)

Some of the frequently encountered types of problem-solving problems are described in this section, although not every item you may encounter will fall into one of these categories. However, thoroughly familiarizing yourself with the types of problems that follow will help you to develop the skills to translate and solve all kinds of word problems.

Number and Set Problems

Number problems can be story problems that require knowledge of the properties of numbers in order to solve the item. Typically, number problems involve *consecutive integers* or *consecutive odd/even numbers*. Consecutive integers are one number apart and can be represented by x, $x+1$, $x+2$, etc. Consecutive even or odd integers are two numbers apart and can be represented by x, $x+2$, $x+4$, etc.

Example:

Three consecutive odd integers have a sum of 33. Find the average of these integers.

- Represent the integers as x, $x+2$, and $x+4$. Write an equation indicating the sum is 33: $x+x+2+x+4=3x+6=33 \Rightarrow 3x=27 \Rightarrow x=9$. Thus, the integers are 9, 11, and 13. In the case of evenly spaced numbers such as these, the average is the middle number, 11. Since the sum of the three numbers was given originally, all we really had to do was to divide this sum by 3 to find the average, without ever knowing what the numbers were.

Set problems test understanding of relationships between different sets of numbers or *elements*. A *set* is a collection of things; e.g., the set of positive integers.

| DEFINITIONS FOR WORKING WITH SETS | ✓ |

1. The **number of elements** in set P is: $n(P)$.

2. The **union** of two sets P and Q is the set of all elements in *either* P or Q, or both: $P \cup Q$.

3. The **intersection** of two sets P and Q is the set of all elements in *both* P and Q: $P \cap Q$.

4. The **cardinal number theorem** is used to find the number of elements in a union of two sets: $n(P \cup Q) = n(P) + n(Q) - n(P \cap Q)$.

Examples:

1. Let $S = \{3, 5, x\}$. If exactly one subset of S contains two different elements whose sum is 12, what value(s) can x be?

    *   Since either $3 + x = 12$ or $5 + x = 12$, then $x = 9$ or $x = 7$.

2. In a class of 30 students, 15 students are learning French, 11 students are learning Spanish, and 7 students are learning neither French nor Spanish. How many students in the class are learning both French and Spanish?

    *   Use the cardinal number theorem: $n(F \cup S) = n(F) + n(S) - n(F \cap S) \Rightarrow 30 - 7 = 15 + 11 - n(F \cap S) \Rightarrow n(F \cap S) = 3$.

The cardinal number theorem is also known as the **addition principle for counting** and is the first of several useful methods for counting objects and sets of objects without actually listing the elements to be counted. According to the theorem, if set A contains m objects, set B contains n objects, and there are no objects common to the two sets, then the total number of objects in the two sets combined is $m + n$. However, if there are k objects common to the two sets, then the total in the combined set is $m + n - k$. In other words, you must take into account the double-counting of objects common to both sets.

Example:

Of a group of students at a campus cafe, 9 ate pizza and 5 had salad. If 3 had both pizza and salad, how many had either pizza or salad?

*   The question describes two sets: one consisting of students that ate pizza (set P: $m = 9$), and one consisting of students that had salad (set S: $n = 5$). Since the question states that 3 students had both pizza and salad, the number of students common to the two sets is 3 ($k = 3$). Therefore, the total in the combined set (number of students who had either pizza or salad) is: $m + n - k = 9 + 5 - 3 = 11$.

This kind of situation involving sets that overlap is most easily handled by displaying the given information in a **Venn diagram**.

Example:

Two circles are drawn on a floor. 20 people are standing in circle A. 15 people are standing in circle B. 9 people are standing in both circles. Find the total number of people standing in the two circles.

*   The item can be symbolized with a Venn diagram:

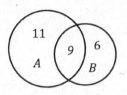

From the diagram, it can be seen that there are a total of $11+9+6$ or 26 people.

Age Problems

Age problems involve a comparison of ages at the present time, several years from now, or several years ago. A person's age x years from now is found by adding x to his present age. A person's age x years ago is found by subtracting x from his present age.

Examples:

1. Michelle was 12 years old y years ago. What is her age b years from now?

    • Michelle's present age is $12 + y$. In b years, her age will be $12 + y + b$.

2. Logan is 5 years older than Florencia. Three years ago, Logan was twice as old as Florencia. How old is Logan?

    • If you have trouble setting up the equations, use numbers. Suppose that Florencia is 11. If Logan is 5 years older than Florencia, then Logan must be $11 + 5 = 16$. Thus, if L is Logan's age and F is Florencia's age, $L = F + 5$. Three years ago, Logan was $L - 3$ and Florencia was $F - 3$. So, since 3 years ago, Logan was twice as old as Florencia, $L - 3 = 2(F - 3) \Rightarrow L - 3 = 2F - 6 \Rightarrow L = 2F - 3$. Substitute $L = F + 5 \Rightarrow F = L - 5$ for F in the equation $L = 2F - 3$ to find Logan's current age: $L = 2F - 3 = 2(L - 5) - 3 = 2L - 13 \Rightarrow L = 13$.

Mixture Problems

You should be familiar with two kinds of **mixture problems**. The first type is sometimes referred to as dry mixture, in which dry ingredients of different values, such as nuts or coffee, are mixed. For this type of problem, it is best to organize the data in a chart of three rows and three columns labeled as illustrated in the following problem.

Example:

A dealer wishes to mix 20 pounds of nuts selling for 45 cents per pound with some more expensive nuts selling for 60 cents per pound to make a mixture that will sell for 50 cents per pound. How many pounds of the more expensive nuts should he use?

• Create a table summarizing the provided information:

	# of lbs.	Price/lb.	Total Value= (# of lbs.)(Price/lb.)
Original	20	0.45	0.45(20)
Added	x	0.60	0.60(x)
Mixture	$20 + x$	0.50	0.50($20 + x$)

The value of the original nuts plus the value of the added nuts must equal the value of the mixture:

$$0.45(20)+0.60(x)=0.50(20+x)$$
$$45(20)+60(x)=50(20+x)$$
$$900+60x=1{,}000+50x$$
$$10x=100$$
$$x=10$$

Therefore, he should use 10 lbs. of 60-cent nuts.

The second type of mixture item deals with percents and amounts rather than prices and value.

Example:

How much water must be added to 20 gallons of solution that is 30 percent alcohol to dilute it to a solution that is only 25 percent alcohol?

- Create a table summarizing the provided information:

	# of gals.	% alcohol	Amount of Alcohol = (# of gals.)(% alcohol)
Original	20	0.30	0.30(20)
Added	x	0	0
Mixture	$20+x$	0.25	$0.25(20+x)$

Note that the percentage of alcohol in water is zero. Had pure alcohol been added to strengthen the solution, the percentage would have been 100 percent. Thus, the amount of alcohol added (none) plus the original amount must equal the amount of alcohol in the new solution:

$$0.30(20)=0.25(20+x)$$
$$30(20)=25(20+x)$$
$$600=500+25x$$
$$100=25x$$
$$x=4 \text{ gallons}$$

Motion Problems

The fundamental relationship in all **motion problems** is *distance = rate • time* . The problems at the level of this examination usually derive their equation from a relationship concerning distance. Most problems fall into one of three types.

Motion in Opposite Directions

When two objects moving at the same speed start at the same time and move in opposite directions, or when two objects start at points at a given distance apart and move toward each other with the same speed until they meet, then the distance the second travels will equal one-half the total distance covered. Either way, the total distance is equal to $d_1 + d_2$:

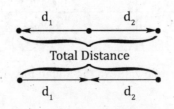

Motion in the Same Direction

This type of item is sometimes called the "catch-up" problem. Two objects leave the same place in the same direction at different times and at different rates, but one "catches up" to the other. In such a case, the two distances must be equal.

Round Trip

In this type of problem, the rate going is usually different from the rate returning. The times are also different. But if we go somewhere and then return to the starting point, the distances must be the same.

To solve any motion problem, it is helpful to organize the data in a box with columns for rate, time, and distance. A separate line should be used for each moving object. Remember that if the rate is given in *miles per hour*, the time must be in *hours* and the distance in *miles*.

Examples:

1. Two cars leave a restaurant at 1 p.m., with one car traveling east at 60 miles per hour and the other west at 40 miles per hour along a straight highway. At what time will they be 350 miles apart?

   - Create a table summarizing the provided information:

	Rate	Time	Distance = (Rate)(Time)
Eastbound	60	x	$60x$
Westbound	40	x	$40x$

   Notice that the time is unknown, since we must determine the number of hours traveled. However, since the cars start at the same time and stop when they are 350 miles apart, their times are the same: $60x + 40x = 350 \Rightarrow 100x = 350 \Rightarrow x = 3.5$. Therefore, in 3.5 hours, it will be 4:30 p.m.

2. Gloria leaves home for school, riding her bicycle at a rate of 12 miles per hour. Twenty minutes after she leaves, her mother sees Gloria's English paper on her bed and leaves to bring it to her. If her mother drives at 36 miles per hour, how far must she drive before she reaches Gloria?

   - Create a table summarizing the provided information:

	Rate	Time	Distance = (Rate)(Time)
Gloria	12	x	$12x$
Mother	36	$x - \frac{1}{3}$	$36\left(x - \frac{1}{3}\right)$

   The 20 minutes has been converted to $\frac{1}{3}$ of an hour. In this problem, the times are not equal, but the distances are: $12x = 36\left(x - \frac{1}{3}\right) = 36x - 12 \Rightarrow 12 = 24x \Rightarrow x = \frac{1}{2}$. Thus, if Gloria rode for $\frac{1}{2}$ hour at 12 miles per hour, the distance covered was 6 miles. So, Gloria's mother must drive 6 miles before she reaches her.

3. Nisha leaves home at 11 a.m. and rides to Andrea's house to return her bicycle. She travels at 12 miles per hour and arrives at 11:30 a.m. She turns right around and walks home. How fast does she walk if she returns home at 1 p.m.?

   - Create a table summarizing the provided information:

	Rate	Time	Distance = (Rate)(Time)
Going	12	$\frac{1}{2}$	6
Return	x	$1\frac{1}{2}$	$\frac{3x}{2}$

The distances are equal: $6 = \frac{3x}{2} \Rightarrow 12 = 3x \Rightarrow x = 4$ miles per hour.

Rate and Work Problems

Rate Problems

We introduced rate problems in the section above on motion problems, since distance traveled per unit time is a rate. Anytime you compare two quantities with different units, you are finding a **rate**. To find a rate, look for the different units and their corresponding numbers. Rate problems can be solved by using ratios.

Examples:

1. If Save-A-Lot Grocery advertises 2 pounds of cherries for $2.20, how much would 3 pounds of cherries costs?

   - Create two ratios corresponding to the different units and their corresponding numbers. Set the ratios equal to one another and solve for the unknown quantity. The rate in the question is quantity of cherries per price (or price per quantity of cherries), and the unknown is the cost of 3 pounds of cherries: $\frac{2 \text{ pounds}}{\$2.20} = \frac{3 \text{ pounds}}{x} \Rightarrow x = \frac{3}{2}(\$2.20) = \$3.30$.

2. During a 4-hour party, 5 adults consumed drinks costing $120. For the same drink costs per person per hour, what would be the cost of drinks consumed by 4 adults during a 3-hour party?

   - The ratio in question is drink costs per person per hour, so equate two ratios and solve for the missing value: $\frac{\$120}{5 \text{ adults}/4 \text{ hours}} = \frac{x}{4 \text{ adults}/3 \text{hours}} \Rightarrow \frac{120 \cdot 4}{5} = \frac{x \cdot 3}{4} \Rightarrow x = \frac{120 \cdot 16}{15} = 8 \cdot 16 = \$128$.

Note that the following words are frequently used in rate problems: *for, in, per, to, each*. For example: $100 *for* 5 hours of work, 3 widgets produced *in* 5 minutes, 55 miles *per* hour, 13 floors *to* a building, 7 cards *to each* person.

Work Problems

Combined rate, or **work**, problems concern the speed with which work can be accomplished and the time necessary to perform a task, if the size of the workforce is changed. Thus, work problems involve combining individual rates into a combined rate.

Example:

If Tess alone can weed a garden in 3 days and Rio can weed the same garden in 5 days, how long will it take them to weed the garden if they work together?

- Let x equal number of days required if Tess and Rio work together to weed the garden and create a table summarizing the given information:

	Tess	Rio	Together
Days to weed garden	3	5	x
Part weeded in 1 day	$\frac{1}{3}$	$\frac{1}{5}$	$\frac{1}{x}$

Since the part done by Tess in one day plus the part done by Rio in one day equals the part done by both in one day, we have: $\frac{1}{3}+\frac{1}{5}=\frac{1}{x}$. Multiply each part of the equation by $15x$ to clear the fractions:

$$\frac{1}{3}(15x)+\frac{1}{5}(15x)=\frac{1}{x}(15x)\Rightarrow 5x+3x=15\Rightarrow 8x=15\Rightarrow x=1\frac{7}{8}\text{ days.}$$

From the previous example, we can see that the basic formula for solving work problems is: $\frac{1}{a}+\frac{1}{b}=\frac{1}{c}$, where a and b are the number of minutes, days, hours, etc. that it takes the two individuals, respectively, to complete a job when working alone, and c is the number of minutes, days, hours, etc. that it takes the two individuals to do the job when working together.

Example:

When working alone, Machine X can fill a production order in 4 hours, and Machine Y can fill the same order in y hours. When the two machines operate simultaneously to fill the production order, it takes them 2.5 hours to complete the job. What is the value of y?

- $\frac{1}{4}+\frac{1}{y}=\frac{1}{2.5}\Rightarrow\frac{1}{4}(10y)+\frac{1}{y}(10y)=\frac{1}{2.5}(10y)\Rightarrow 2.5y+10=4y\Rightarrow\frac{3}{2}(y)=10\Rightarrow y=\frac{20}{3}=6\frac{2}{3}$. Thus, working alone, Machine Y can fill the production order in $6\frac{2}{3}$ hours.

Variation Problems

Variation in mathematics refers to the interrelationship of variables in such a manner that a change of value for one variable produces a corresponding change in another. There are three basic types of variation: **direct**, **inverse**, and **joint**.

Direct Variation

The expression "x varies directly with y" can be described by either of the following equations:

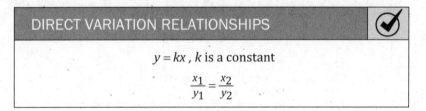

DIRECT VARIATION RELATIONSHIPS	✓
$y = kx$, k is a constant	
$\dfrac{x_1}{y_1} = \dfrac{x_2}{y_2}$	

Two quantities are said to vary directly if they change in the same direction. As one increases, the other increases and their ratio is equal to the positive constant.

For example, the amount you must pay for milk varies directly with the number of quarts of milk you buy. The amount of sugar needed in a recipe varies directly with the amount of butter used. The number of inches between two cities on a map varies directly with the number of miles between these cities.

Example:

If x varies directly as y^2, and $x=12$ when $y=2$, what is the value of x when $y=3$?

- Notice that the variation involves the square of y. Therefore, $\dfrac{x_1}{y_1^2}=\dfrac{x_2}{y_2^2}\Rightarrow\dfrac{12}{2^2}=\dfrac{x}{3^2}\Rightarrow\dfrac{12}{4}=\dfrac{x}{9}\Rightarrow x=27$.

Inverse Variation

The expression "x varies inversely as y" can be described by either of the following equations:

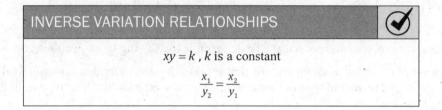

INVERSE VARIATION RELATIONSHIPS

$$xy = k \text{ , } k \text{ is a constant}$$

$$\frac{x_1}{y_2} = \frac{x_2}{y_1}$$

Two quantities vary inversely if they change in opposite directions. As one quantity increases, the other quantity decreases.

For example, the number of people hired to paint a house varies inversely with the number of days the job will take. A doctor's stock of flu vaccine varies inversely with the number of patients she injects. The number of days a given supply of cat food lasts varies inversely with the number of cats being fed.

Example:

The time t to empty a container varies inversely with the square root of the number of men m working on the job. If it takes 3 hours for 16 men to do the job, how long will it take 4 men working at the same rate to empty the container?

- $\dfrac{t_1}{\sqrt{m_2}} = \dfrac{t_2}{\sqrt{m_1}} \Rightarrow t_1\sqrt{m_1} = t_2\sqrt{m_2} \Rightarrow 3\sqrt{16} = t\sqrt{4} \Rightarrow t = 3 \cdot \dfrac{\sqrt{16}}{\sqrt{4}} = 3(\sqrt{4}) = 3 \cdot 2 = 6$.

Joint Variation

The expression "x varies jointly as y and z" can be described by any of the following equations:

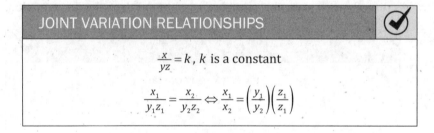

JOINT VARIATION RELATIONSHIPS

$$\frac{x}{yz} = k \text{ , } k \text{ is a constant}$$

$$\frac{x_1}{y_1 z_1} = \frac{x_2}{y_2 z_2} \Leftrightarrow \frac{x_1}{x_2} = \left(\frac{y_1}{y_2}\right)\left(\frac{z_1}{z_1}\right)$$

Example:

The area, A, of a triangle varies jointly as the base b and the height h. If $A = 20$ when $b = 10$ and $h = 4$, what is the value of A when $b = 6$ and $h = 7$?

- $\dfrac{A_1}{b_1 h_1} = \dfrac{A_2}{b_2 h_2} \Rightarrow \dfrac{20}{(10)(4)} = \dfrac{A_2}{(6)(7)} \Rightarrow A_2 = 21$.

Counting Methods

The Multiplication Principle for Counting

The **multiplication principle for counting** states that if an object is to be chosen from a set of m objects and a second object is to be chosen from a different set of n objects, then the total number of ways of choosing both object simultaneously is mn. In other words, if an operation takes two steps and the first step can be performed in m ways, and if, for each of those ways, the second step can be performed in n ways, then the total number of ways of performing the operation is mn.

Examples:

1. A litter of boxer puppies contains 4 with brindle coloring and 5 with fawn coloring. In how many ways can one choose a pair of one brindle puppy and one fawn puppy from this litter of puppies?

   - You have 4 choices for a brindle puppy and 5 choices for a fawn puppy. By the multiplication principle, the total number of possible pairs is: $4 \cdot 5 = 20$.

2. From a garden with 6 flower varieties, a bouquet of 3 different types of flowers is to be picked. How many different possible bouquets are there?

   - Extend the multiplication principle to a three-step process: there are 6 choices of flower for the first pick of the bouquet, for each of which there are 5 choices for the second flower (because one flower type has been eliminated, having been picked as the first flower in the bouquet). Furthermore, for each of these pairs, there are 4 remaining flower choices for the third pick (because two flower types have been eliminated, having been picked as the first and second flowers in the bouquet). Therefore, the total number of possible bouquets is: $6 \cdot 5 \cdot 4 = 120$.

Probability

Single-Event Probability

Probability is concerned with experiments that have a finite number of outcomes. Probabilities occur in games, sports, weather reports, etc. The probability that some particular outcome or set of outcomes (called an **event**) will occur is expressed as a ratio. The numerator of a probability ratio is the number of ways that the event of interest can occur. The denominator is the total number of outcomes that are possible. This **probability ratio** is true for experiments in which all of the individual outcomes are equally likely:

$$\text{Probability of event} = \frac{\text{number of ways that event can happen}}{\text{number of outcomes possible}}$$

Example:

If a six-sided die is tossed, what is the probability that you will get a number greater than 4?

- There are a total of six ways a die can land: 1, 2, 3, 4, 5, or 6. Each of these six events is equally likely. There are two possible outcomes that are greater than 4: 5 or 6. Therefore, the probability of the die landing with a number greater than 3 is $\frac{2}{6} = \frac{1}{3}$.

Note that the probability that an event occurs is a number between 0 and 1, inclusive. If the event has no outcomes, then it is impossible and its probability is 0. If the event is the set of all possible outcomes, then it is certain to occur and its probability is 1.

Multiple-Event Probability

Another type of probability involves finding the probability of a certain outcome after multiple events. One type of **multiple-event probability** involves individual events that must occur a certain way. For these experiments, figure out the probability for each individual event and multiply the individual probabilities together.

Example:

If two marbles are randomly chosen from a jar with three red marbles and seven black marbles, what is the probability that both marbles will be red?

- Since three out of the ten marbles are red, the probability that the first marble chosen is red is $\frac{3}{10}$. After choosing one red marble, this leaves two red marbles in the jar out of nine. Therefore, the probability that the second marble chosen will also be red is $\frac{2}{9}$. The probability that both marbles chosen will be red is: $\frac{3}{10} \cdot \frac{2}{9} = \frac{6}{90} = \frac{1}{15}$.

A second type of multiple-event probability involves individual events that can have different outcomes. For these experiments, create a probability ratio by dividing the number of desired outcomes by the total number of possible outcomes. The total number of possible outcomes is found by multiplying together the number of possible outcomes for each individual event. The number of desired outcomes can be determined by counting the possibilities.

Example:

If a dime is tossed three times, what is the probability that at least two of the three tosses will be heads up?

- There are two possible outcomes for each toss (heads or tails), so after three tosses there are a total of $2^3 = 2 \cdot 2 \cdot 2 = 8$ possible outcomes. Next, list all the possibilities where at least two of the three tosses are heads up: H, H, H; H, H, T; H, T, H; T, H, H. Thus, the total number of desired outcomes is four. Therefore, the probability that at least two of the three tosses will be heads up is: $\frac{4}{8} = \frac{1}{2}$.

Probabilities can also be determined for an experiment with two different events, A and B. The probability of A occurring is denoted by $P(A)$, and the probability of B occurring is denoted by $P(B)$. Given these two events, there are three additional events that can be defined. "Not A" is the set of outcomes that are not outcomes in A; "A or B" is the set of outcomes in A or B or both ($A \cup B$); "A and B" is the set of outcomes in both A and B ($A \cap B$). If the event "A and B" is impossible, then A and B are said to be **mutually exclusive**. If the occurrence of either event A or B does not alter the probability that the other event occurs, then A and B are said to be **independent**.

PROBABILITIES FOR MULTIPLE-EVENT EXPERIMENTS (An experiment with events A and B)	✓
1. "Not A": $P(\text{not } A) = 1 - P(A)$	
2. "A or B": $P(A \text{ or } B) = P(A) + P(B) - P(A \text{ and } B)$	
3. "A and B" (A and B are mutually exclusive): $P(A \text{ and } B) = 0$	
4. "A and B" (A and B are independent): $P(A \text{ and } B) = P(A)P(B)$	

Example:

If a six-sided die is tossed, what is the probability that you will get a prime number or an even number?

- Let A be the event that the outcome is a prime number, $\{2, 3, 5\}$, and let B be the event that the outcome is an even number, $\{2, 4, 6\}$. Since 3 outcomes are prime, $P(A) = \frac{3}{6} = \frac{1}{2}$. Similarly, $P(B) = \frac{1}{2}$. $P(A$ and $B)$, or the probability that the outcome is both even and prime, is $\frac{1}{6}$ since only 2 is both even and prime.

  Therefore, $P(A$ or $B) = \frac{1}{2} + \frac{1}{2} - \frac{1}{6} = \frac{5}{6}$. Note that this is the same as reasoning that the set of prime and even numbers on the die is $\{2, 3, 4, 5, 6\}$, so the probability of getting one of these numbers is $\frac{5}{6}$.

Data Interpretation: Tables and Graphs

You are expected to be able to interpret data displayed in tables, charts, and graphs.

Example:

The tables below show the number, type, and cost of candy bars bought in one week at two local drugstores.

Number of Candy Bars Bought						
	Type A		Type B		Type C	
	Large	Giant	Large	Giant	Large	Giant
Drugstore P	60	20	69	21	43	17
Drugstore Q	44	18	59	25	38	13

Cost per Candy Bar		
	Large	Giant
Type A	$0.45	$0.69
Type B	$0.45	$0.79
Type C	$0.55	$0.99

What is the total cost of all Type B candy bars bought at these two drugstores during the week?

- Add the cost of all Type B bars purchased: $69(0.45) + 21(0.79) + 59(0.45) + 25(0.79) = \$93.94$.

The test may also ask about the line of best fit for a scatterplot. A scatterplot is really just a plot of various data points for which a line of best fit can be drawn. For example, an item may require you to identify that a line of best fit for a scatterplot has a slope that is positive but less than 1. You are not expected to use formal methods for finding the equation of a line of best fit.

Example:

The points in the scatterplot below show the relationship between 14 students' test scores on a mid-term test and a final test. What is the approximate average (arithmetic mean) of the scores on the final test for all students who scored above 90 on the midterm test?

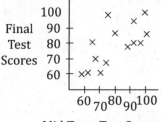

Mid-Term Test Scores

- Five students scored above 90 on the mid-term. Their marks are the five to the right on the scatterplot. The five corresponding scores on the final are approximately 80, 80, 85, 95, and 100. The average of these scores is approximately 88.

Story Problems
Exercise 10

DIRECTIONS: Choose the correct answer to each of the following items. Answers are on page 780.

1. How many ounces of pure acid must be added to 20 ounces of a solution that is 5 percent acid to strengthen it to a solution that is 24 percent acid?

A. $2\frac{1}{2}$ C. 6   E. 10

B. 5   D. $7\frac{1}{2}$

2. If x men can do a job in h days, how long would y men take to do the same job?

A. $\frac{x}{h}$ C. $\frac{hy}{x}$ E. $\frac{x}{y}$

B. $\frac{xh}{y}$ D. xyh

3. A dealer mixes a pounds of nuts that cost b cents per pound with c pounds of nuts that cost d cents per pound. At what price should he sell a pound of the mixture if he wishes to make a profit of 10 cents per pound?

A. $\frac{ab+cd}{a+c}+10$

B. $\frac{ab+cd}{a+c}+0.1$

C. $\frac{b+d}{a+c}+10$

D. $\frac{b+d}{a+c}+0.10$

E. $\frac{b+d+10}{a+c}$

4. If a furnace uses 40 gallons of oil in a week, how many gallons, to the nearest gallon, does it use in 10 days?

A. 57   C. 28   E. 4

B. 44   D. 20

5. A recipe requires 13 ounces of sugar and 18 ounces of flour. If only 10 ounces of sugar are used, how much flour, to the nearest ounce, should be used?

A. 11   C. 13   E. 15

B. 12   D. 14

6. Ivan left Austin to drive to Boxville at 6:15 p.m. and arrived at 11:45 p.m. If he averaged 30 miles per hour and stopped one hour for dinner, how many miles is Boxville from Austin?

A. 120   C. 180   E. 190

B. 135   D. 185

7. A plane traveling 600 miles per hour is 30 miles from Kennedy Airport at 4:58 p.m. At what time will it arrive at the airport?

A. 5:00 p.m.   C. 5:02 p.m.   E. 5:23 p.m.

B. 5:01 p.m.   D. 5:20 p.m.

8. A school has enough bread to last 30 children 4 days. If 10 children are added, how many days will the bread last?

A. $\frac{1}{3}$ C. $2\frac{1}{3}$ E. 3

B. $1\frac{1}{3}$ D. $2\frac{2}{3}$

9. Mr. Bridges can wash his car in 15 minutes, while his son Dave takes twice as long to do the same job. If they work together, how many minutes will the job take them?

A. 5   C. 10   E. 30

B. $7\frac{1}{2}$ D. $22\frac{1}{2}$

10. A train travels from Madison to Chicago at an average speed of 50 miles per hour and returns immediately along the same route at an average speed of 40 miles per hour. Of the following, which is closest to the average speed, in miles per hour, for the round-trip?

A. 43.0   C. 44.4   E. 45.0

B. 44.0   D. 44.5

11. If 4 workers take an hour to pave a road, how long should it take 12 workers to pave the same road?

A. $\frac{1}{4}$ hour   C. $\frac{1}{2}$ hour   E. 1 hour

B. $\frac{1}{3}$ hour   D. $\frac{3}{4}$ hour

12. At a certain printing plant, each of m machines prints 6 newspapers every s seconds. If all machines work together but independently without interruption, how many minutes will it take to print an entire run of 18,000 newspapers?

A. $\dfrac{180s}{m}$ C. $50ms$ E. $\dfrac{300m}{s}$

B. $\dfrac{50s}{m}$ D. $\dfrac{ms}{50}$

13. Gerard takes 6 hours to do a job. Leo takes 8 hours to do the same job. How many hours should it take Gerard and Leo working together to do the same job?

A. $\dfrac{7}{24}$ C. 3   E. 7

B. $2\dfrac{3}{7}$ D. $3\dfrac{3}{7}$

14. There are two drains, Drain 1 and Drain 2, in a pool. If both drains are opened, the pool is emptied in 20 minutes. If Drain 1 is closed and Drain 2 is open, the pool will be emptied in 30 minutes. If Drain 2 is closed and Drain 1 is open, how many minutes will it take to empty the pool?

A. 20   C. 50   E. 120
B. 30   D. 60

15. The variable m varies directly as the square of t. If m is 7 when $t = 1$, what is the value of m when $t = 2$?

A. 28   C. 7   E. 2
B. 14   D. $3\dfrac{1}{2}$

16. The variable m varies jointly as r and l. If m is 8 when r and l are each 1, what is the value of m when r and l are each 2?

A. 64   C. 16   E. 2
B. 32   D. 4

17. John can wax his car in 3 hours. Jim can do the same job in 5 hours. How long will it take them if they work together?

A. $\dfrac{1}{2}$ hour   C. 2 hours   E. 8 hours

B. $1\dfrac{7}{8}$ hours   D. $2\dfrac{7}{8}$ hours

18. In a run/walk marathon, Weber runs x miles in h hours, then walks the remainder of the marathon route, y miles, in the same number of hours. Which of the following represents Weber's average speed, in miles per hour, for the entire marathon?

A. $\dfrac{x-y}{h}$ C. $\dfrac{2(x+y)}{h}$ E. $\dfrac{x+y}{2h}$

B. $\dfrac{x-y}{2h}$ D. $\dfrac{2(x+y)}{2h}$

19. In the junior class at Shawnee High School, 168 students took the SAT, 175 students took the ACT, 80 students took both, and 27 students did not take either one. What is the total number of students in the junior class at Shawnee High School?

A. 440   C. 290   E. 248
B. 343   D. 282

20. Let $R = \{3, 5, 6, 7, 9\}$. How many different subsets of R with 1, 2, 3, or 4 elements contain one or more odd numbers?

A. 31   C. 29   E. 27
B. 30   D. 28

21. A survey of 51 students was conducted concerning each student's favorite flavors of ice cream. Of the 51 students, 10 students liked only vanilla, 12 students liked only strawberry, and 15 students liked only chocolate. Every student liked at least one of the three flavors. 7 students liked both vanilla and strawberry, and 9 students liked both vanilla and chocolate. The largest possible number of students who could have liked both chocolate and strawberry is:

A. 2   C. 7   E. 14
B. 3   D. 12

22. If there are 3 different roads from Seattle to Olympia and 4 different roads from Olympia to Portland, how many different routes are there from Seattle to Portland that pass through Olympia?

A. 1   C. 10   E. 24
B. 7   D. 12

23. Set X is the set of all positive integral multiples of 8: $X = \{8, 16, 24, 32, ...\}$. Set Y is the set of all positive integral multiples of 6: $Y = \{6, 12, 18, 24, ...\}$. The intersection of these two sets is the set of all positive integral multiples of:

A. 2   C. 14   E. 48
B. 4   D. 24

24. Of the 50 children in a school sports program, 40 percent will be assigned to softball, and the remaining 60 percent to baseball. However, 70 percent of the children prefer softball and 30 percent prefer baseball. What is the least possible number of children who will NOT be assigned to the sport they prefer?

A. 10   C. 20   E. 35
B. 15   D. 30

25. Each of the following choices is comprised of three equations relating x and y. Identify the set of equations that demonstrates direct variation, inverse variation, and neither direct nor inverse variation, respectively?

A. $y = 3x; x^2 + y^2 = x + 5; y = \frac{4}{x}$

B. $y = 3x; x^2 + y^2 = x + 5; y = \frac{x}{4}$

C. $x = \frac{y}{3}; xy = 7; x^2 + y^2 = \frac{x}{5}$

D. $y = 3x; y = \frac{4}{x}; x = 5y$

E. $y = \frac{2x}{3}; x = 5y; x^2 + y^2 = x + 7$

26. Let y vary directly as x, and let w vary directly as the square of x. If $y = 10$ for $x = 1.25$ and $w = 8$ for $x = \sqrt{2}$, then for what positive value of x will $y = w$?

A. 1   C. 2   E. 5
B. $1\frac{1}{2}$ D. 4

27. The perimeter of a square varies directly as the length of one side of the square with a constant of variation of 4. The circumference of a circle varies directly as the circle's radius and a constant of variation equal to:

A. π C. 1   E. $\frac{1}{\pi}$
B. 2π D. 2

28. If x and y vary inversely, then for any ordered pair (x,y), the value of xy is a constant number. The ordered pairs $(-12,-3)$ and $(6,6)$ represent an example of inverse variation for x and y. Which of the following graphs represents a possible inverse variation relationship between x and y?

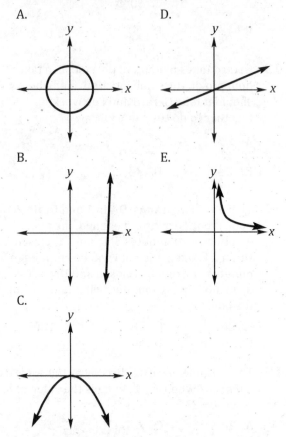

29. The probability that an event will happen can be shown by the fraction $\frac{\text{winning events}}{\text{total events}}$ or

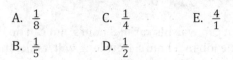

$\frac{\text{favorable events}}{\text{total events}}$. From the 8-digit number 12,344,362, Helen selects a digit at random. What is the probability that she selected 4?

A. $\frac{1}{8}$ C. $\frac{1}{4}$ E. $\frac{4}{1}$
B. $\frac{1}{5}$ D. $\frac{1}{2}$

30. Last night, Dave and Kathy both arrived at Pizza Palace at two different random times between 10:00 p.m. and midnight. They had agreed to wait exactly 15 minutes for each other to arrive before leaving. What is the probability that Dave and Kathy were together at Pizza Palace last night between 10:00 p.m. and midnight?

A. $\frac{1}{8}$ C. $\frac{15}{64}$ E. $\frac{31}{64}$

B. $\frac{1}{4}$ D. $\frac{3}{8}$

31. George must select 1 pencil from 6 different pencils and 1 pen from 5 different pens. How many different combinations can George make?

A. 5   C. 30   E. 65
B. 11   D. 56

32. One of the letters in the alphabet is selected at random. What is the probability that the letter selected is a letter found in the word "MATHEMATICS"?

A. $\frac{1}{26}$ C. $\frac{5}{13}$ E. $\frac{6}{13}$

B. $\frac{4}{13}$ D. $\frac{11}{26}$

33. Two integers are to be randomly selected from the sets below, one integer from each set. What is the probability that the sum of the two integers will equal 11?

$$X = \{2, 4, 5, 8, 9\}$$
$$Y = \{2, 3, 4, 7\}$$

A. 0.10   C. 0.20   E. 0.30
B. 0.15   D. 0.25

34. If a fair coin is to be tossed 3 times, what is the probability that on at least 1 of the tosses the coin will turn up heads?

A. $\frac{1}{8}$ C. $\frac{1}{2}$ E. $\frac{31}{64}$

B. $\frac{1}{4}$ D. $\frac{7}{8}$

35. The stronger the relationship between two variables, the more closely the points on a scatter plot will approach some linear or curvilinear pattern. Which of the scatter plots below represents the strongest relationship between the two variables?

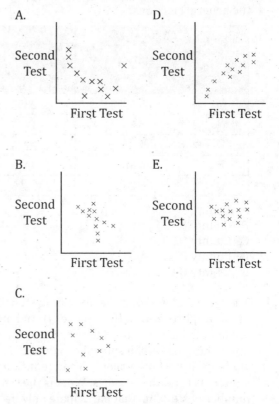

36. The table below shows the daily change in the weather temperatures for a certain city last week. What was the net change, in degrees Celsius, in the weather temperature for the week?

Day	Daily Change in Temperature (°C)
Sunday	+5.5
Monday	+1.7
Tuesday	−3.9
Wednesday	−3.3
Thursday	−0.5
Friday	+0.8
Saturday	−0.2

A. −5.7   C. 0.1   E. 5.7
B. −0.1   D. 5.3

37. The table below represents the number of voters in five counties that voted in a general election and the percent change in the number of voters from the previously held primary election. Which county had the greatest net increase in voters between the primary and the general elections?

County	Number of Voters in General Election (in millions)	Percent Change from Primary Election
M	5.67	−23%
N	2.34	+14%
O	1.25	−2%
P	4.56	+4%
Q	6.23	+8%

A. County M
B. County N
C. County O
D. County P
E. County Q

38. The table below shows the number of students in three sports at East High School. 8 students are in both basketball and tennis, 5 students are in both basketball and volleyball, and 3 students are in both volleyball and tennis. No student is in all three sports. What is the total number of students that participate only in basketball or tennis?

Sport	Number of Students
Basketball	35
Volleyball	15
Tennis	40

A. 22   C. 50   E. 75
B. 29   D. 51

Analytical Writing
Supplement

Outline

III. Revision (p. 686)

A. Proofread Your Essay (p. 686)

1. Comply with Instructions (p. 686)
2. Proofread for Structural Errors (p. 686)
3. Proofread for Mechanics/Usage Errors (p. 687)

Issue Analysis Outline—*Exercise 1* (p. 688)

Issue Analysis Essay—*Exercise 2* (p. 689)

Issue Analysis Revision—*Exercise 3* (p. 690)

Argument Analysis Outline—*Exercise 4* (p. 691)

Argument Analysis Essay—*Exercise 5* (p. 692)

Argument Analysis Revision—*Exercise 6* (p. 693)

PLANNING AN ESSAY

Understand the Assignment

Let the Prompt Be Your Topic

The essay prompt is intended to be the topic and inspiration for writing your essay. Pay careful attention to the language of the prompt, as it will help guide you in the development of your essay. Read the prompt several times until you are completely familiar with the material. Make a note of any key words or important phrases.

Consider the following sample essay prompt:

> Think carefully about the issue presented in the following excerpt and the assignment below.
>
> > Human beings are often cruel, but they also have the capacity for kindness and compassion. In my opinion, an example that demonstrates this capacity is _____.
>
> **Assignment:** Complete the statement above with an example from current events, history, literature, or your own personal experience. Then write a well-organized essay explaining why you regard that event favorably.

This topic explicitly invites you to choose an example of kindness or compassion from history, current events, literature, or even personal experience. Thus, you could write about the end of a war (history), a mission of humanitarian aid (current events), the self-sacrifice of a fictional character (literature), or even about the day that your family helped a stranded motorist (personal experience). The particulars of what you write about are not as important as how you write your essay.

Develop a Point of View

An essay prompt may invite you to present your opinion on an issue. When you encounter such prompts, you must decide whether you agree or disagree with the given statement and clearly develop this point of view in your essay.

Write Only on the Assigned Topic

While the types of prompts may differ, the directions all agree on one point: you must write only on the assigned topic and address the key points identified for discussion.

Organize Your Thoughts

Limit the Scope of Your Essay

The requirements of the writing assignment will determine the length and scope of your essay. It is important to define the scope of your essay before beginning to write, as this will improve the focus of your writing. The more defined the scope, the better able you will be to supply the specific details necessary to give depth and sophistication to your essay. This will also reduce the possibility of straying onto tangential topics or under-developing a specific claim. Consequently, your essay will be more likely to accomplish the assigned task, whether it is to defend a controversial position or to provide a definition.

Develop a Thesis

A thesis statement provides the scope, purpose, and direction of an essay in one clear and focused statement. A thesis statement usually includes your claims or assertions, as well as the reasoning and evidence you will use to support them. If possible, try to formulate the thesis of your composition into a single sentence during the pre-writing stage. When developing a thesis, keep in mind the following ideas:

DEVELOP A THESIS ✓
1. The thesis must not be too broad or too narrow.
2. The thesis must be clear to both you and the essay reader.
3. Everything in the essay must support your thesis.
4. Use specific details and examples rather than generalizations to support your thesis.

Identify Key Points

Identify the two or three (perhaps four) important points that you want to make in your essay. Then, decide the order of presentation for these points.

Write an Outline

Once you have developed your thesis and identified the key supporting points, organize your essay in a written outline. The purpose of this outline is to develop a logical structure to your arguments and streamline your essay. An outline should include your thesis statement, the key points of your argument, and the concluding statement of your essay. The following outline template summarizes this structure:

I. Introduction: Thesis Statement

II. First Key Point
   A. Sub-Point 1
   B. Sub-Point 2

III. Second Key Point
   A. Sub-Point 1
   B. Sub-Point 2

IV. Third Key Point
   A. Sub-Point 1
   B. Sub-Point 2

V. Conclusion: Restatement of Thesis

COMPOSITION

Organize Ideas into Paragraphs

A good writer uses paragraphs effectively in order to provide structure that conveys meaning. Imagine a grocery store in which items are not organized into sections: there is no fresh produce section, no canned goods section, no baked goods section, and no frozen foods section. Consequently, a single bin holds bunches of bananas, cans of beans, loaves of bread, and frozen turkeys. This lack of organization would make shopping at the store very difficult. Likewise, essays without paragraphs (or with poorly organized paragraphs) are very difficult, if not impossible, to understand.

When developing your essay, decide how many paragraphs you will write. Your essay should contain two to four important points that develop or illustrate your thesis. Each important point should be treated as its own paragraph.

Do not write excess material simply to increase word count and make it seem like you have many ideas. This approach can result in repetition and wordiness, which is a sign of disorganization and unclear thinking. Write enough to demonstrate your writing ability and to prove your thesis. Five paragraphs (an introduction paragraph, three main body paragraphs, and a concluding paragraph) are usually sufficient.

Write the Essay

Many students become frustrated before they even begin to write. They sit and stare at the blank page and complain that they are "blocked." In other words, they can't think of anything to write. The secret to successfully beginning an essay is simple: after completing the pre-writing stage, immediately start writing. You may need to go back and revise some of your work, but this is the easiest way to avoid "writer's block." As you write your essay, follow this simple essay structure:

    I. Introduction: State the thesis of your essay.
       A. State your position clearly.
       B. State the elements that you will be using to support your position.

    II. Body: Each paragraph in the body of your essay will be devoted to one of the supporting elements that are introduced in the introduction. Elaborate on the elements by using examples.

    III. Conclusion: Summarize your position and the reasons for your position.

The Introduction

During the pre-writing stage, you analyzed the topic. Now, use the introduction (the first paragraph) to write clear and concise sentences that describe the topic, your point of view on it, and what you plan to say to back up your position. In general, an introduction should let the reader know what direction your essay will take. However, don't spend too much time on an introduction. The remainder of the essay will be where you'll explain your ideas and give your examples in more detail.

When writing your introduction, keep these points in mind:

- Focus on the essay topic presented in the prompt and clearly state your point of view on this topic.

- Use a tone that is sincere, straightforward, and clear. DO NOT be cute or funny, ironic or satiric, overly emotional or too dramatic.

- DO NOT repeat the writing prompt word-for-word. Instead, paraphrase the prompt in your own words and then clearly state your point of view.

- After stating your point of view, briefly state the evidence or arguments that you will use to support your point of view.

Finally, an effective introduction will explain why the reader should care about the topic or grab the reader's attention by describing briefly an incident in real life that is related to the topic.

The Body

The heart of the essay is developed in the body paragraphs. Here, the writer must attempt, in paragraph form, to support the main idea of the essay through illustrations, details, and examples. These body or developmental paragraphs must serve as a link in the chain of ideas and contribute directly to the essay's main idea or position.

Start each body paragraph with a transitional statement or phrase that describes the relationship of the paragraph to the previous paragraphs. The length of each body paragraph can vary, but each paragraph should cover only one main idea. You may do this through a style that is descriptive, narrative, or expository. You may take a factual or an anecdotal approach. However, whatever style and approach you choose, your writing must be coherent, logical, and unified.

When writing your essay, avoid the following common mistakes:

AVOID COMPOSITIONAL ERRORS ☑

1. DO NOT use sentences with irrelevant material. In each body paragraph, only include sentences that relate specifically to the argument being made in that paragraph.

2. DO NOT use sentences that disrupt logical development. In each body paragraph, make sure each sentence logically follows from the sentence that comes before it.

Transitions

A good writer uses transitional words or phrases to connect thoughts, to provide for a logical sequence of ideas, and to link paragraphs. The following list includes some transitions and the logical relationships they indicate:

TRANSITIONAL WORDS AND PHRASES

Addition
again
also
and
besides
both...and
finally
first, second, third
furthermore
in addition
likewise
moreover
not only...but (also)
similarly

Alternation
either...or
neither...nor
nor
or
so that

Cause/Effect/Purpose
accordingly
as
as a consequence
as a result
because
consequently
for
for this purpose
hence
since
therefore
so

Conditions
as if (as though)
if
once...then
unless

Contrast
all the same
although
but
even though
however
instead
nevertheless
on the contrary
on the other hand
otherwise
still
though
yet

Space
here
in the middle
nearby
next to
opposite to
there
to the left/right
where
wherever

Support
for example
for instance
in fact
in general
such as

Summary
as shown above
in other words
in brief
in conclusion
in general
in short
in summary
to sum up

Time
after (clause)
after (noun)
as soon as
at the present time
before (clause)
before (noun)
during
eventually
finally
in (month, year)
later
meanwhile
since (clause)
then
until (clause)
when
whenever
while (clause)

The Conclusion

A good writer knows when and how to end an essay. To conclude your essay effectively, you should have a strong and clear concluding paragraph. This concluding paragraph should make a reader feel that your essay has made its point, that the thesis has been explained, and that your point of view has been supported by specific examples, ideas, or arguments. A concluding paragraph can be as short as three to six sentences. Follow these guidelines for writing a successful concluding paragraph:

- Restate your point of view on the essay topic.

- Summarize the main arguments and evidence you used to support your point of view.

- If time permits, conclude with a brief statement as to why your point of view is more defensible than a different point of view on the essay topic. What are the positive consequences of holding your point of view? What are the negative consequences of holding the opposite point of view?

And avoid these errors when writing a concluding paragraph:

- DO NOT apologize for being unable to present all possible arguments in a limited amount of time.

- DO NOT complain that the topic was uninteresting or too broad.

- DO NOT introduce new material that you won't have time to develop.

- DO NOT introduce irrelevant material.

Principles of Good Writing

The successful essay will incorporate the three principles of good composition: write grammatically, punctuate and spell correctly, and write concisely and clearly. If you follow these conventions, you will communicate your ideas clearly and effectively.

Write Grammatically

When writing an essay, observe the following principles of good grammar:

CORRECT GRAMMAR AND EFFECTIVE ESSAYS
1. Each sentence must have a conjugated (main) verb that agrees with its subject.
2. Each pronoun must have a referent (antecedent) with which it agrees.
3. Similar elements in a sentence must appear in parallel form.
4. Modifiers must agree with what they modify and be logically consistent.
5. Each sentence should use clear and concise language.

Punctuate and Spell Correctly

In addition to writing grammatically, concisely, and formally (without using slang or other low-level usage language), you must punctuate and spell correctly. Since you are in charge of writing the essay, you can choose to avoid punctuation and spelling errors. If you are unsure about how to punctuate a particular construction or spell a particular word, choose an alternative.

Write Concisely and Clearly

Use simple and direct sentences. Avoid complex and convoluted sentences. In general, the most complicated sentence you should use is one with two independent clauses that are joined by a conjunction such as "and" or "but." Of course, you can also use sentences that include one dependent clause and one independent clause joined together by a conjunction such as "while" or "although." Again, though, try to express yourself simply and directly. Also, avoid unnecessary or wordy phrases when simpler language will suffice, as the following chart illustrates.

AVOID UNNECESSARY AND WORDY PHRASES

Instead of:	Say:
In my opinion, I believe that	I believe that
In the event of an emergency	In an emergency
On the possibility that it may	Since it may
close to the point of	close to
have need for	need
with a view to	to
in view of the fact that	because
give consideration to	consider
mean to imply	imply
disappear from view	disappear
in this day and age	today
the issue in question	the issue

REVISION

Proofread Your Essay

Proofreading is an essential part of the writing process. The first draft of an essay usually will not be free of errors. This means that you will need to re-read your essay to ensure that you have followed the instructions and to correct any grammatical errors or logical inconsistencies.

Comply with Instructions

The essay prompt is very specific. It provides the topic for your essay and details what needs to be addressed. Check your essay to ensure that you've adequately addressed each component of the prompt instructions.

Proofread for Structural Errors

When proofreading your essay, first consider its structural elements. The three most important structural factors in a successful essay are unity, coherence, and support. Essays are judged by how well they meet these basic requirements. To improve your essay through revision, ask yourself the following questions:

UNITY, COHERENCE, AND SUPPORT ✓

1. Does the essay have a main thesis that is clearly stated in the introduction? What is it? What is the essay's point of view on the essay topic?

2. Does the introduction clearly state the arguments and evidence that will support the essay's point of view?

3. Does each body paragraph have a topic sentence? A topic sentence is the first sentence of a paragraph, and it summarizes what will be argued or presented in that paragraph.

4. Does each body paragraph make a different argument to support the essay's point of view?

5. Do the other sentences in each body paragraph all support the topic sentence? In other words, do the other sentences further the argument or present evidence related to the topic sentence's main point?

6. Do the body paragraphs include specific details or examples to make the argument more vivid and interesting?

7. Does the essay use transitional words or phrases that allow the reader to move easily from one idea or paragraph to the next?

8. Does the essay have a conclusion that clearly re-states the essay's point of view on the topic? Does the conclusion explain why this point of view is more defensible than a different point of view on the topic?

Proofread for Mechanics/Usage Errors

After reviewing the structures of your essay, look for mechanics/usage errors. Although less important, mechanics/usage errors can prevent the reader from focusing on the substance of your essay. Avoid these common mechanics/usage errors:

COMMON MECHANICS/USAGE ERRORS

1. Omission of words—especially "the," "a," and "an"
2. Omission of final letters in words
3. Careless spelling errors
4. Incorrect use of capital letters
5. Faulty punctuation

Issue Analysis Outline
Exercise 1

DIRECTIONS: You have 5 minutes to write an outline for the essay topic assigned below. Do not write on any other topic. Sample outlines, essays, and analyses begin on page 781.

Residents of rural areas often wonder why people would voluntarily choose to live in a large city and insist that rural life—with its open spaces, relative freedom from worries about crime, and healthful living conditions—is preferable. Conversely, residents of urban areas say that city life—with access to public transportation, cultural amenities, and many entertainment opportunities—is preferable.

Select a point of view that more closely aligns with your own position and explain your reasons for the position you take. Be sure to address both views presented.

Issue Analysis Essay
Exercise 2

DIRECTIONS: You have 20 minutes to write an essay based on the outline you created in Exercise 1. Do not write on any other topic. Sample outlines, essays, and analyses begin on page 782.

Residents of rural areas often wonder why people would voluntarily choose to live in a large city and insist that rural life—with its open spaces, relative freedom from worries about crime, and healthful living conditions—is preferable. Conversely, residents of urban areas say that city life—with access to public transportation, cultural amenities, and many entertainment opportunities—is preferable.

Select a point of view that more closely aligns with your own position and explain your reasons for the position you take. Be sure to address both views presented.

Issue Analysis Revision
Exercise 3

DIRECTIONS: Allow yourself 5 minutes to revise the essay you created in Exercise 2. Make sure you addressed each item in the Instructions. Carefully read your essay and correct any structural or mechanics/usage errors, making changes on the draft you created in Exercise 2. Sample outlines, essays, and analyses begin on page 784.

Argument Analysis Outline
Exercise 4

DIRECTIONS: You have 5 minutes to write an outline based on the topic assigned below. Do not write on any other topic. Sample outlines, essays, and analyses begin on page 784.

The lifeguards that watch the state's public beaches work from 8 a.m., when the beaches open, until 6 p.m., when they close. A 10-hour workday is much too long given the importance of the lifeguard's job. If the workday for lifeguards were shortened to only eight hours, there would be an increase in public safety.

Write an essay where you examine the stated and/or unstated assumptions of the argument. Explain how the argument depends on these assumptions and what the implications are if the assumptions prove unwarranted.

Argument Analysis Essay
Exercise 5

DIRECTIONS: You have 20 minutes to write an essay based on the outline you created in Exercise 4. Do not write on any other topic. Sample outlines, essays, and analyses begin on page 785.

The lifeguards that watch the state's public beaches work from 8 a.m., when the beaches open, until 6 p.m., when they close. A 10-hour workday is much too long given the importance of the lifeguard's job. If the workday for lifeguards were shortened to only eight hours, there would be an increase in public safety.

Write an essay where you examine the stated and/or unstated assumptions of the argument. Explain how the argument depends on these assumptions and what the implications are if the assumptions prove unwarranted.

Argument Analysis Revision
Exercise 6

DIRECTIONS: Allow yourself 5 minutes to revise the essay you created in Exercise 5. Make sure you addressed each item in the Instructions. Carefully read your essay and correct any structural or mechanics/usage errors, making changes on the draft you created in Exercise 5. Sample outlines, essays, and analyses begin on page 787.

Appendix C:
Answers and Explanations

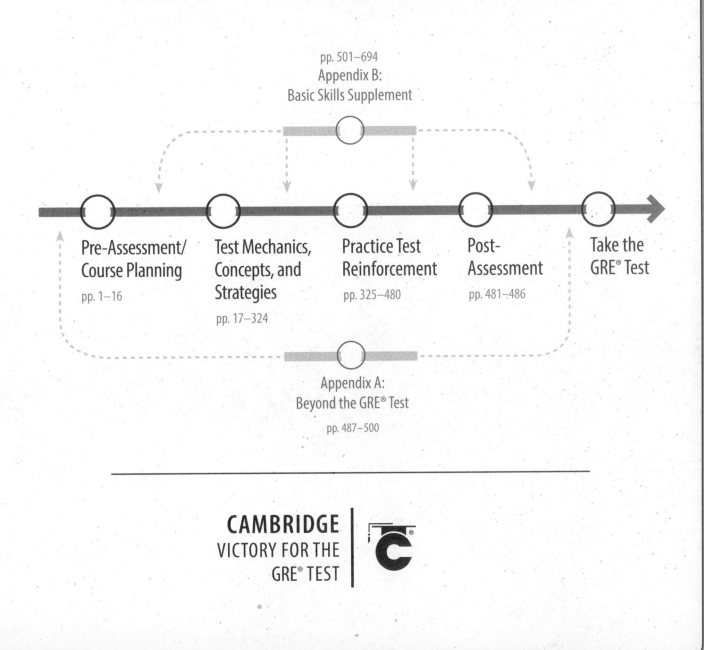

pp. 501–694
Appendix B:
Basic Skills Supplement

Pre-Assessment/
Course Planning
pp. 1–16

Test Mechanics,
Concepts, and
Strategies
pp. 17–324

Practice Test
Reinforcement
pp. 325–480

Post-
Assessment
pp. 481–486

Take the
GRE® Test

Appendix A:
Beyond the GRE® Test
pp. 487–500

CAMBRIDGE
VICTORY FOR THE
GRE® TEST

Lessons and Quizzes

Outline

VERBAL REASONING

Verbal Reasoning: Completions Time Trial (p. 26)

1. E	3. A	5. B, D	7. B, E, G	9. B, E
2. B	4. E	6. A, E	8. D, F	10. B, F

Verbal Reasoning: Completions Lesson (p. 33)

1. C	21. A	41. B	61. B	81. A, D
2. C	22. B	42. C	62. E	82. A, D
3. B	23. A	43. B	63. B	83. C, E
4. C	24. C	44. C	64. A, D	84. A, E
5. A, D	25. B	45. C	65. E	85. A, D, H
6. A, E	26. B	46. B	66. D	86. B, D
7. E	27. D	47. A, F	67. C, D	87. A, F
8. B, F	28. D	48. D	68. C, F	88. C, F
9. C	29. A	49. E	69. C	89. A, D
10. E	30. E	50. C	70. B	90. C, D
11. A	31. C	51. A	71. C, D	91. B, D
12. B, D	32. C	52. D	72. A, E	92. A, E
13. A	33. C	53. C	73. A, E, H	93. B, E
14. E	34. C	54. C, E	74. B, F, G	94. B, D
15. E	35. A	55. D	75. B, E, H	95. D, F
16. D	36. E	56. D	76. C, D, H	96. B, C
17. B	37. D	57. A, D	77. C, E	97. B, F
18. A, E	38. A	58. A	78. B, D	98. A, E
19. C	39. B	59. C	79. C, D	99. A, B
20. D	40. A	60. B, D	80. B, D	100. D, F

Verbal Reasoning: Completions Quizzes (p. 47)

Quiz I	Quiz II	Quiz III
1. C	1. D	1. B
2. B	2. D	2. C, D
3. B	3. A	3. C, E
4. A, D	4. A	4. B
5. E	5. A, D	5. A, D
6. D	6. C, E	6. C, E
7. C, E	7. C, E	7. D
8. B, E	8. B, D	8. C
9. A, F	9. A, E	9. B, F
10. B, E	10. C, D, I	10. B, E
11. B, E	11. A, D	11. C, D
12. A, B	12. A, C	12. B, C
13. B, C	13. A, B	13. B, E
14. A, C	14. B, C	14. D, F
15. B, D	15. B, C	15. C, F

Verbal Reasoning: Reading Time Trial (p. 66)

1. B	2. A	3. C	4. E

Verbal Reasoning: Reading Lesson (p. 73)

1. C	8. E	15. A	22. A	29. A
2. A	9. B	16. A	23. C	30. A
3. A	10. A	17. A	24. C	31. B
4. D	11. D	18. C	25. D	32. A
5. D	12. A	19. A, C	26. A	33. E
6. C	13. C	20. A	27. C	34. D
7. C	14. C	21. D	28. B	35. D

36. E	66. C	96. A, B	126. B	156. B
37. C	67. C	97. C	127. C	157. A
38. D	68. A, B, C	98. A	128. B	158. E
39. A	69. A	99. C	129. A	159. E
40. B	70. C	100. C	130. D	160. C
41. D	71. B	101. C	131. A	161. E
42. A, B	72. E	102. D	132. B	162. A
43. A	73. E	103. A	133. B	163. A
44. A	74. A	104. B	134. A, B	164. E
45. E	75. A	105. A	135. A	165. B
46. B	76. B	106. B	136. D	166. C
47. B	77. A	107. B	137. E	167. A
48. E	78. C	108. A	138. A	168. C
49. C	79. D	109. A	139. C	169. B
50. A, B	80. D	110. E	140. B	170. A
51. D	81. C	111. A, B, C	141. C	171. E
52. B	82. A	112. C	142. A	172. D
53. D	83. A	113. B	143. A	173. D
54. A	84. D	114. A	144. B	174. D
55. D	85. D	115. C	145. C	175. A
56. A, C	86. A, B	116. B	146. D	176. E
57. E	87. B	117. A	147. B	177. E
58. A	88. C	118. D	148. E	178. E
59. E	89. A	119. E	149. B	179. D
60. A	90. E	120. B	150. C	180. E
61. D	91. A	121. A	151. A	181. B
62. C	92. A	122. A, C	152. C	182. D
63. C	93. C	123. B	153. E	183. E
64. C	94. B	124. A	154. D	184. E
65. A	95. B	125. D	155. B	185. E

186. B	189. A	192. A	195. A	198. C
187. C	190. A	193. A	196. C	199. E
188. C	191. A	194. E	197. D	200. C

Verbal Reasoning: Reading Quizzes (p. 135)

Quiz I	Quiz II	Quiz III
1. A, C	1. D	1. A, B, C
2. E	2. B	2. A
3. B	3. D	3. C
4. E	4. A	4. D
5. A	5. A, B	5. B
6. A	6. B	6. A
7. E	7. A	7. B
8. B	8. D	8. C
9. D	9. B	9. B
10. D	10. E	10. A

QUANTITATIVE REASONING

Quantitative Reasoning: Discrete Quantitative Time Trial (p. 160)

1. C   2. C   3. C   4. E   5. A, C

Quantitative Reasoning: Discrete Quantitative Lesson (p. 165)

1. C	23. B	45. A	67. E	89. C
2. C	24. D	46. E	68. D	90. B
3. D	25. C	47. C	69. C	91. E
4. E	26. C	48. B	70. D	92. B
5. E	27. D	49. E	71. B	93. A
6. B	28. E	50. A, B, C, E	72. C	94. C
7. C	29. D	51. D	73. C	95. D
8. D	30. B	52. C	74. E	96. C
9. E	31. E	53. B	75. A	97. A
10. D	32. C	54. E	76. E	98. C
11. E	33. B	55. C	77. D	99. D
12. D	34. C	56. C	78. B	100. D
13. A, B, C	35. A	57. E	79. A	101. E
14. D	36. C	58. B	80. B	102. D
15. D	37. B	59. C	81. D	103. C
16. A	38. C	60. A	82. B	104. B
17. C	39. C	61. B	83. A	105. A
18. C	40. E	62. D	84. D	106. B
19. E	41. C	63. A	85. B	107. C
20. A, B, C	42. E	64. D	86. D	108. A
21. E	43. D	65. D	87. E	109. C
22. C	44. B	66. D	88. B, D	110. D

111. C	**119.** B	**127.** C	**135.** A	**143.** D
112. A	**120.** A, B	**128.** D	**136.** B	**144.** D
113. E	**121.** D	**129.** D	**137.** C	**145.** D
114. C	**122.** C	**130.** B	**138.** A	**146.** C
115. E	**123.** A	**131.** C	**139.** B	**147.** C
116. A	**124.** C	**132.** E	**140.** D	**148.** C
117. B	**125.** C	**133.** C	**141.** D	**149.** C
118. B	**126.** B	**134.** B	**142.** B	**150.** C

Quantitative Reasoning: Discrete Quantitative Quizzes (p. 193)

Quiz I	Quiz II	Quiz III
1. A	**1.** C	**1.** A
2. E	**2.** C	**2.** B
3. D	**3.** D	**3.** D
4. C	**4.** B	**4.** A
5. D	**5.** C	**5.** A
6. E	**6.** A	**6.** D
7. C	**7.** C	**7.** E
8. E	**8.** B	**8.** A
9. B	**9.** A	**9.** D
10. A, C, D, E	**10.** A, B, C, E	**10.** C

Quantitative Reasoning: Numeric Entry Time Trial (p. 207)

1. 18	**2.** 4800	**3.** 2	**4.** 4	**5.** $\frac{1}{4}, \frac{2}{4}, \frac{1}{2}, \frac{3}{4}$

Quantitative Reasoning: Numeric Entry Lesson (p. 209)

1. 25	**6.** 7.5	**11.** 12	**16.** 25	**21.** 6
2. 8	**7.** $\frac{1}{24}$	**12.** 8	**17.** $\frac{21}{36}, \frac{7}{12}$	**22.** 12
3. 13.6	**8.** −520	**13.** 30	**18.** 16.8	**23.** 180
4. $\frac{1}{32}$	**9.** 50	**14.** 75	**19.** 90	**24.** 2664
5. $\frac{15}{40}, \frac{3}{8}$	**10.** 2	**15.** 0.25	**20.** −10	**25.** 4

26. $\frac{24}{45}, \frac{8}{15}$	31. 1.25	36. 2	41. 8	46. 0
27. 30	32. 60	37. 13	42. 60	47. 3
28. 14	33. 45	38. 70	43. 1456	48. 8
29. 48	34. 2	39. 72	44. 5	49. 2
30. $\frac{9}{24}, \frac{3}{8}$	35. 9	40. 7	45. 3	50. 5

Quantitative Reasoning: Numeric Entry Quizzes (p. 217)

Quiz I	Quiz II	Quiz III
1. 4, 5	1. 5	1. 9
2. 2	2. 10	2. $\frac{5}{9}$
3. $\frac{6}{4}, \frac{3}{2}$	3. $\frac{3}{2}$	3. $\frac{15}{2}$
4. 30	4. 0	4. $\frac{12}{7}$
5. 5	5. 50	5. 45

Quantitative Reasoning: Comparisons Time Trial (p. 231)

1. B	3. C	5. C	7. A	9. B
2. D	4. D	6. D	8. A	10. C

Quantitative Reasoning: Comparisons Lesson (p. 235)

1. A	13. A	25. C	37. C	49. C
2. B	14. D	26. A	38. D	50. A
3. C	15. D	27. C	39. C	51. C
4. A	16. B	28. A	40. C	52. B
5. B	17. D	29. C	41. A	53. C
6. C	18. C	30. A	42. D	54. C
7. D	19. D	31. D	43. C	55. A
8. B	20. D	32. A	44. A	56. A
9. C	21. D	33. D	45. B	57. B
10. D	22. D	34. C	46. C	58. B
11. B	23. D	35. A	47. B	59. A
12. A	24. D	36. C	48. A	60. D

61. D	79. C	97. A	115. C	133. D
62. D	80. D	98. B	116. B	134. D
63. D	81. A	99. D	117. A	135. D
64. B	82. D	100. B	118. A	136. C
65. D	83. D	101. C	119. B	137. A
66. D	84. C	102. C	120. C	138. C
67. D	85. B	103. A	121. C	139. C
68. D	86. B	104. C	122. A	140. C
69. D	87. C	105. C	123. B	141. D
70. A	88. C	106. C	124. B	142. D
71. B	89. D	107. A	125. C	143. B
72. B	90. B	108. A	126. C	144. C
73. C	91. A	109. A	127. C	145. C
74. B	92. A	110. D	128. D	146. C
75. D	93. C	111. B	129. D	147. A
76. B	94. A	112. D	130. D	148. B
77. A	95. D	113. C	131. D	149. B
78. B	96. D	114. C	132. D	150. A

Quantitative Reasoning: Comparisons Quizzes (p. 251)

Quiz I		Quiz II		Quiz III	
1. B	6. C	1. A	6. D	1. D	6. D
2. C	7. D	2. D	7. A	2. C	7. A
3. C	8. B	3. D	8. B	3. D	8. A
4. B	9. A	4. B	9. A	4. C	9. D
5. B	10. D	5. D	10. C	5. B	10. C

Quantitative Reasoning: Data Interpretation Time Trial (p. 264)

1. C	2. E	3. B	4. E	5. D

Quantitative Reasoning: Data Interpretation Lesson (p. 271)

1. D	16. C	31. D	46. C	61. A
2. C	17. E	32. D	47. B	62. D
3. D	18. A	33. C	48. C	63. A, B
4. D	19. B	34. A	49. D	64. C
5. C	20. D	35. D	50. D	65. C
6. D	21. A	36. E	51. B	66. A, C
7. A	22. C	37. E	52. B	67. E
8. E	23. D	38. D	53. A	68. A
9. C	24. B	39. B	54. C	69. C
10. 2533	25. B	40. E	55. B	70. D
11. C	26. C	41. B	56. A	71. A
12. B	27. B	42. B	57. B	72. D
13. A	28. C	43. D	58. B	73. C
14. D	29. A, C	44. D	59. E	
15. C	30. D	45. A	60. E	

Quantitative Reasoning: Data Interpretation Quizzes (p. 293)

Quiz I	Quiz II	Quiz III
1. B	1. A	1. C
2. C	2. C	2. A
3. B	3. A	3. D
4. C	4. B	4. E
5. D	5. C	5. A

ANALYTICAL WRITING

Analytical Writing Lesson (p. 309)

1. A	8. D	15. C	22. A	29. D
2. A	9. B	16. C	23. D	30. D
3. B	10. C	17. D	24. D	31. B
4. A	11. D	18. C	25. B	32. B
5. A	12. C	19. A	26. A	33. C
6. A	13. C	20. B	27. B	34. A
7. C	14. D	21. B	28. A	35. A

36. On Monday, Mark received a letter of acceptance from State College. He immediately called his mother—herself a graduate of State College—to tell her about his acceptance. When he told her he had also been awarded a scholarship, she was very excited. After hanging up, Mark's mother decided to throw a surprise party for Mark. She telephoned his brother, his sister, and several of his friends. Because the party was supposed to be a surprise, she made them all promise not to say anything to Mark. Mark, however, had a similar idea: a party for his mother to celebrate his acceptance at her alma mater. He telephoned his brother, his sister, and several of his parents' friends to invite them to a party at his house on Saturday night, and he made them all promise to say nothing to his mother. On Saturday night, both Mark and his mother were surprised.

37. There is no proof presented that students are distracted by windows. Even assuming some students are distracted, many other students might find the view relaxing. A relaxed student should be a better learner than one who is tense—and learning is the goal of the classroom.

38. Even if a student is somewhat distracted, he or she may be even better able to concentrate when his or her attention returns to the teacher.

39. This distraction, which occurs in students with more limited attention spans, is easily avoided by arranging desks so that the eyes of a student are directed away from the window.

40. The easiest solution is to have the teacher order each student to keep his or her eyes directed toward the blackboard.

41. Under this seating arrangement, all of the people in the classroom, except the class monitor and the teacher, will face the blackboard, not the windows.

42. While strolling through Central Park, my companion and I were required to take shelter in the band shell due to a severe thunderstorm.

43. Down by the old mill, Paul told Mary that he would wed her.

44. When I received the notice I immediately reported to the manager's desk.

45. The chef baked the cake to please his favorite niece on her wedding day.

46. Let the kids do things their own way. It is too hard having the teacher always make them feel guilty. They might need counseling as a result. So, relax the pressure on kids and let them be themselves.

Practice Test Reinforcement

Outline

PRACTICE TEST I

Answer Keys

Section 3—Verbal Reasoning (p. 385)

1. B	6. B	11. C	16. E	21. B
2. A, B	7. B, F	12. B	17. C, D	22. A, C
3. B	8. B	13. C	18. A	23. E, F
4. A	9. A, E, G	14. C, E	19. B	24. A, E
5. B	10. C	15. C, E	20. B	25. B, D

Section 4—Verbal Reasoning (p. 393)

1. C, D	6. E	11. B, D	16. C	21. A, E
2. A, D	7. A	12. C, D	17. D	22. D
3. C, F	8. A, B, C	13. B, D, I	18. D	23. A
4. A, C	9. A	14. E	19. C, E	24. E
5. A, F	10. E	15. C	20. B, D	25. C

Section 5—Quantitative Reasoning (p. 401)

1. C	6. C	11. E	16. C	21. B
2. A	7. C	12. 50	17. B	22. E
3. B	8. D	13. A	18. D	23. A, B, D, E
4. C	9. C	14. C	19. D	24. D
5. B	10. E	15. B	20. E	25. $\frac{12}{47}$

Section 6—Quantitative Reasoning (p. 407)

1. A	6. D	11. A, B, C	16. C	21. 88
2. C	7. B	12. D	17. A	22. A, B
3. B	8. C	13. C	18. D	23. B
4. C	9. A	14. E	19. C	24. 6
5. B	10. E	15. E	20. C	25. C

Section 1—*Analytical Writing* (p. 383)

Analyze an Issue *Sample Essay Response*

Great people are always remembered for their accomplishments. Thomas Jefferson is remembered as a patriot and a profound political thinker who wrote the Declaration of Independence. Albert Einstein is remembered as the brilliant physicist who developed the Theory of Relativity. Were it not for these accomplishments, these great people would not be considered great and likely would not be remembered at all.

It is currently fashionable, however, to try to bring great people down a notch or two by parading out their shortcomings to show that they really were not so great after all. Evidence has recently become available to prove that Thomas Jefferson carried on an affair with a woman who was his slave and that he fathered a child or children by her. A popular way of scoring points in trivia is to point out that Einstein was notoriously poor at math and got Cs in high school algebra. But do these shortcomings make them any less great? Only if one has an unrealistic definition of greatness. Would Jefferson have been as deep a thinker had he been less complex? Would Einstein have grasped the fundamental intuition of relativity had he been enslaved to mathematics?

It seems likely, then, that great people will always be remembered for their shortcomings as well as their accomplishments. It is a way of making them seem human and not so distant from the rest of us. And, in a real sense, balancing a person's shortcomings with their accomplishments is appropriate. That is because a great person is also, by definition, a person. As Hegel said of Napoleon, whom he idolized but realized had faults, "No man is a hero to his valet."

Section 2—*Analytical Writing* (p. 384)

Analyze an Argument *Sample Essay Response*

The evidence provided does not support the recommendation regarding indoor facilities for three reasons. First, it is not clear that residents support the plan. Second, there is no proof that children are lacking any recreational opportunities. Third, implementing the ambitious plan could actually undermine the recreational programs.

First, it is not clear that residents think that children need other opportunities. The wording of the question includes the phrase "such as." Many of those who responded "yes" might have interpreted the question to include swimming.

Second, there is no evidence that children are denied the opportunity to play basketball or racquetball. Presumably, the City also has outdoor recreational facilities with hoops and walls. Those can certainly be used during the summer months. Plus, many other activities such as softball and soccer are available during the summer months.

Third, the attempt to keep the indoor facilities open year-round might actually undermine the quality of the City recreational programs. Obviously, there will be an attendant cost for hiring more workers to staff the additional facilities.

Money spent on indoor facilities during the summer might draw needed money away from outdoor facilities that are traditionally used only during those months. Additionally, it is logical to schedule maintenance tasks on the indoor facilities during the summer months when the weather will not interfere with work. Trying to keep the facilities open year-round could make it more difficult to keep them in top condition. Finally, some indoor facilities may not even be useable during the hot summer months due to lack of suitable ventilation.

While everyone would agree that, in principle, children should be given the widest range of recreational opportunities possible, sometimes hard decisions have to be made about what is realistic. Without further evidence that there is a real need for the indoor recreational facilities to remain open, the City should continue its policies.

Section 3—*Verbal Reasoning* (p. 385)

1. **(B)** (p. 385) *Verbal Reasoning/Reading Comprehension/Attitude-Tone*

   The statements are made in an objective and analytical way, and the author is concerned with the topic he or she has chosen, so (B) is the best choice. (A) is wrong because it is inconsistent with the topic of the passage. (C) is wrong because it overstates the case: though the author adopts the stance of a commentator, he or she is not detached or unconcerned. (D) is wrong because, while the author does seem sincere, there is nothing to warrant the description "cautious." (E) is wrong because it is inconsistent with the neutral tone of the passage.

2. **(A, B)** (p. 385) *Verbal Reasoning/Reading Comprehension/Specific Detail*

   This item includes one or more correct answers, so test each answer choice. The author describes the consequences of full-cost reimbursement at the end of the second paragraph, specifically mentioning rising costs, (A), and underused facilities, (B). Nowhere does the author mention a lack of essential services. On the contrary, the author notes excess beds and an abundance of technologies, many of which are underutilized.

3. **(B)** (p. 386) *Verbal Reasoning/Reading Comprehension/Specific Detail*

   In the beginning of the third paragraph (lines 26–27), the author states that "this pessimism derives from expecting too much." And later in that paragraph (lines 32–33), the author states that "too many patients and families are unwilling to accept such realities." Therefore, (B) is the best choice. (A) is wrong because it is contradicted by the first paragraph where the author states there have been improvements. (C), (D), and (E) are wrong because each is unresponsive to the question asked.

4. **(A)** (p. 386) *Verbal Reasoning/Reading Comprehension/Logical Structure*

   In the first paragraph, the author states that there have been disappointments that have led to pessimism. In the second paragraph, the author explains why this pessimism is, at least in part, unfounded. The author states in the third paragraph that it is not true that nothing works and then mentions the prepaid plans. The phrase "as shown by" indicates that the prepaid plans are examples of ideas that have worked, (A). (B) is wrong because this is a problem with other experiments, not the prepaid plans the author mentions by name. (C) is wrong because it is not mentioned in the passage. Finally, (D) and (E) are both wrong because the plans are examples of ideas that worked.

5. **(B)** (p. 386) *Verbal Reasoning/Critical Reading/The Inference/Ambiguity*

   The argument commits the fallacy of ambiguity: it uses the term "law" in two different senses. The first occurrence of the term in the phrase "laws of nature" implies orderly regularities that are without exceptions. In other words, a law of nature is not something that can be broken. The second occurrence refers to conventional statutes that can be broken through acts of free human choice. Therefore, (B) is the best choice. (A) is wrong because it introduces the idea of a divine being, which is never mentioned in the text. (C) is wrong because, while it could be cited as a weakness, it is not the central weakness that causes the argument to fail. (D) is wrong because, while it could also be an objection to the argument's position, it does not address the argument's conclusion that the laws of nature can be violated. Finally, (E) is wrong because it mischaracterizes the argument, which does not include any mention of the "motivations" of those who deny the existence of miracles.

6. **(B)** (p. 386) *Verbal Reasoning/Sentence Completion/Thought Reversal/Subordinate Conjunctions*

   In this item, the subordinate conjunction "although" signals a thought reversal: although something is "horrifying," something else is worse. Eliminate (A), "pervasive," and (D), "prolific," because these words speak to frequency rather than degrees of horribleness. Eliminate (C), "humane," and (E), "complacent," because these are not adjectives one would use to describe torture or dismemberment. Therefore, by the process of elimination, (B) is the correct choice. Indeed, "viler" is an adjective meaning "wretchedly worse."

7. **(B, F)** (p. 386) *Verbal Reasoning/Sentence Completion/Combined Reasoning/Subordinate Conjunctions* and *Phrases*

Two key logical signals are important to understanding the overall structure of the sentence. The subordinate conjunction "although" signals a thought reversal: what comes after the comma will be an idea that is the opposite of "maintaining good health." (B) describes a process that will prevent the maintenance of good health: inhibit the effectiveness of the vitamins. Then, the second blank is governed by a cause-and-effect continuation: _____ causes illness. An "impaired" immune system is likely to lead to illness, so (F) is the best choice for the second blank.

8. **(B)** (p. 387) *Verbal Reasoning/Sentence Completion/Thought Extension/Subordinate Conjunctions*

In this item, the word "since" signals a thought extension: because of something, something else will be true. The next important word is "few." There are only a few conservatives, so their influence must be _____. This suggests a choice such as "slight" or "insignificant." Eliminate (A) because it is not logical that only a few would have a monumental influence. Eliminate (C) because "discriminatory" does not have anything to do with the fact that there are only a few conservatives. Eliminate (D), "impractical," and (E), "cathartic," on the grounds of usage: neither of these would be used to describe the influence of a minority. Therefore, by the process of elimination, (B) is the correct choice. Indeed, it makes sense to say that the influence of a few would be "negligible."

9. **(A, E, G)** (p. 387) *Verbal Reasoning/Paragraph Completion/Thought Extension/Phrases*

The phrase "and even" sets up a relationship of degree between the first blank and "well mannered." The relationship is one of degree. The first blank should be filled by a word that refers to a characteristic that is more intense that merely "well mannered." Therefore, "staid," (A), which means "of settled character," is the best choice. As for the second blank, the word "even" signals that the missing word is a description of something more extreme than "eager." Therefore, "anxious," (E), is a better choice than "willing," (D), because "willing" is less intense than "eager." Finally, "tonic," (G), means "invigorating" or "enlivening" and completes the contrast between the characters of the two people in the third blank.

10. **(C)** (p. 387) *Verbal Reasoning/Reading Comprehension/Logical Structure*

This item asks about the overall development of the passage. The main organizational principle of the passage is the comparison and contrast of art and knowledge, (C). The author points to similarities and differences between the two. (A) is wrong because there is no refutation of anything in the passage. (B) is wrong because, while some general conclusions are offered, the author does not make any generalizations based on examples. (D) is wrong because, while the passage can be viewed as an answer to the question "What is art for?", the author does not make question and answer the organizational principle of the passage. Finally, (E) is wrong because, while the author states bold conclusions, he or she does not deduce or infer those conclusions from other premises or information.

11. **(C)** (p. 387) *Verbal Reasoning/Reading Comprehension/Attitude-Tone*

Eliminate (A) because, while the purpose of art may be an important philosophical question (and therefore related to speculation in one sense of the word), the tone of the passage is not speculative. Eliminate (B) because it goes too far: to assert with confidence is not necessarily to be argumentative. Eliminate (D) because, while poetry and art seem to go together, the author's method of presenting ideas is not poetry. Eliminate (E) because there is no hint of sarcasm in the passage. Therefore, by the process of elimination, (C) is the correct choice. Indeed, "expository" best describes the confident and neutral tone of the passage.

12. **(B)** (p. 388) *Verbal Reasoning/Critical Reading/The Assumptions* and *The Conclusion*

The conclusion of the argument is that nations will not invest money in the development projects because the tax to be imposed would make the projects unprofitable. The argument, however, rests on a very important assumption: the tax would be so great as to eliminate all potential for profit. Thus, having an answer to the question raised by (B) is very important in assessing the strength of the argument. As for (A), this question is relevant to the issue of whether the proposed tax can produce benefits, but it is not relevant to the argument's claim that the tax would halt all future development of undersea resources. As for (C), what the would-be beneficiaries of the proposed tax think of the tax will not determine whether the development projects can attract investors. Finally, (D) and (E) are both questions that one might want to ask about the proposed tax, but the answers to those questions are not nearly as critical to the feasibility of the project as the answer to the question raised by (B).

13. (C) (p. 388) *Verbal Reasoning/Critical Reading/The Conclusion*

The first sentence of the argument sets the tone for the author's conclusion. Then, the author offers two examples of deleterious effects: shortened attention spans and superficial campaigns. In the discussion of the second example, the author mentions the cost of ads as a possible explanation for why candidates do not deal with the complex issues. (C) best captures this idea. (A) is wrong because it confuses the two factors: the author does not say that one is necessarily related to the other. (B) is wrong because the author states that candidates use "emotionally evocative imagery" in order to hold the viewer's attention, not due to high costs of advertising. (D) is wrong because it reverses the causal connection: the author says that high cost undermines the democratic system, not vice versa. Finally, (E) is wrong because the author makes no logical connection between the high cost of advertising and the inability of the population to comprehend complex ideas; if anything, the author would regard the need for the former to be a result of the latter.

14. (C, E) (p. 389) *Verbal Reasoning/Sentence Completion/Thought Extension/Coordinate Conjunctions*

In this item, the "not only *this* but *that*" structure signals a thought extension: the two missing words are parallel in tone. (Note that, by itself, the coordinate conjunction "but" typically signals a thought reversal.) The first blank requires an adjective that extends the idea of a test that maims animals. Although (A) and (B) make some sense, the word "maim" provides a clue that the adjective will have a negative connotation. This leaves (C). Now, look at the second blank, which requires an adjective that summarizes what comes after: since no two people see the same thing, the test is ____. Only "unreliable," (E), works.

15. (C, E) (p. 389) *Verbal Reasoning/Sentence Completion/Combined Reasoning/Key Adjectives and Adverbs*

Two key logical signals are important to understanding the overall structure of the sentence. The first blank is an extension of the word "calmly." Eliminate (A), "ineptitude," and (B), "tempering," on the grounds of usage: neither of these would be used to extend the idea of calmness. Therefore, (C), "equanimity," which means "composure under strain," is correct. Next, the second blank should reverse the idea of "equanimity," and "rancor," (E), which means "bitter resentment," is the best choice.

16. (E) (p. 389) *Verbal Reasoning/Sentence Completion/Thought Extension/Punctuation*

In this item, the singular pronoun "this," which refers to the politician's hunger for power, signals a thought extension: the blank requires a word that describes someone who is hungry for power. Knowing that "cupidity," (E), means "eager or excessive desire" answers the question directly. Otherwise, eliminate choices containing words that cannot be correct and make a guess.

17. (C, D) (p. 389) *Verbal Reasoning/Paragraph Completion/Thought Extension/Phrases*

The key organizing principle of the paragraph is the "one, two, three" steps: worst, better, better yet. The first step is the low point, as implied by the word "industrial," so the best completion for the first blank is "nadir," (C), which means "low point." Then, the wildlife referred to have "re-emerged." The fact that they have "re-emerged" implies that they were present at a time before, so the wildlife are the original or "indigenous," (D), wildlife.

18. (A) (p. 390) *Verbal Reasoning/Reading Comprehension/Implied Idea*

The author draws an analogy between a political fable and a caricature because the political fable emphasizes certain points over others; it paints with a very broad brush, dealing in types rather than characters. Similarly, a caricature emphasizes certain personal characteristics over others. Thus, the analogy is: society is to political fable as person is to caricature, (A).

19. **(B)** (p. 390) *Verbal Reasoning/Reading Comprehension/Main Idea*

The author begins by announcing that *Nineteen Eighty-Four* is not a novel in the strict sense of that term but really a political fable. Therefore, (B) correctly echoes the author's statement of purpose. (A) is wrong because it is too narrow: the author barely mentions in passing some of the characters in the book. (C) is wrong because it is too narrow: although it is true that the author does state that one of the characteristics of a political fable is that characters are defined in relation to their society, that is but one of many points made in the passage. (D) is wrong because it is both too narrow (there are several other points made by the author) and too broad (the author takes as the focus for his discussion the particular work *Nineteen Eighty-Four*, not political fables in general). Finally, (E) is wrong because it is both too narrow (the distinction between novel and political fable is but one part of the discussion) and too broad (it fails to acknowledge that the author has chosen to focus on a particular work).

20. **(B)** (p. 391) *Verbal Reasoning/Reading Comprehension/Logical Structure*

One important feature of a political fable is that characters are reduced to mere types. They do not have the idiosyncrasies that they would have in a novel. The first sentence preempts a possible objection: Winston Smith is described in some detail. So, the author mentions this to let the audience know that he or she is aware that Winston Smith is described in some detail and to insist that this makes no difference to the overall argument. Therefore, (B) is the best choice. (A) is wrong because small details like an ulcer would not be characteristic of a type but of an individual. (C) is wrong because it is a confused reading of that section of the passage: the author implies that Winston Smith is the main character of the work. (D) and (E) are wrong because, while these echo some of the ideas developed in the passage, they are unresponsive to the question asked.

21. **(B)** (p. 391) *Verbal Reasoning/Reading Comprehension/Specific Detail*

The dilemma faced by the political fabulist is the danger of too much detail versus too little detail. In discussing this dilemma, the author says that too little detail will leave the reader without a sense of connection to life. The author proceeds to say that this is particularly true if the writer projects his or her narrative into the future. Then, the reader may conclude that the situation described by the fable is completely alien to him or herself—simply a foreign country with strange customs—meaning that the reader cannot understand why anyone does anything, so the characters' actions are not connected with the reader's own. (B) best summarizes this idea. (A) is wrong because the author does not mean that the action literally takes place in another country but that the reader feels no connection with the situation. (C) is wrong because it is the lack of detail (e.g., interacting characters) that creates the problem mentioned in this reference. (D) is wrong because it is not supported by the passage; and, indeed, the political fabulist is actually presenting his or her own political vision. Finally, (E) is wrong because it is the lack of detail, not the overabundance of detail, that creates the "foreign country" problem.

22. **(A, C)** (p. 391) *Verbal Reasoning/Sentence Equivalence/Thought Extension/Phrases*

The clarifying phrase following the comma amplifies the idea of "excluding them as viable suspects." Someone who is not a viable or possible suspect must be innocent. Both "exonerated," (A), and "absolved," (C), mean "to have found blameless or innocent."

23. **(E, F)** (p. 391) *Verbal Reasoning/Sentence Equivalence/Thought Extension/Subordinate Conjunctions*

The conjunction "as" signals that the subordinate clause identifies the root of the problem discussed. Consider changing the order of the clauses: "Growing numbers commit crimes; therefore, crime on the web is a _____ problem." According to the sentence, internet crime is a growing problem, now attracting even organized crime. The implication is that it is serious and getting worse. "Proliferating," (E), means "spreading," and "burgeoning," (F), means "growing." Interestingly, both also have overtones of plant growth, making them even closer in meaning.

24. **(A, E)** (p. 392) *Verbal Reasoning/Sentence Equivalence/Thought Extension/Phrases*

In the clarifying phrase following the comma, the behavior of the panhandlers is described as "calculated." Both "judicious," (A), and "prudent," (E), describe behavior that is planned carefully.

25. **(B, D)** (p. 392) *Verbal Reasoning/Sentence Equivalence/Thought Extension/Phrases*

The explanatory material following the comma reinforces the idea that Salinger was completely indifferent to other people, or self-centered. Both "solipsistic," (B), and "egocentric," (D), have meanings closely related to "self-centered."

Section 4—*Verbal Reasoning* (p. 393)

1. **(C, D)** (p. 393) *Verbal Reasoning/Sentence Equivalence/Thought Extension/Phrases*

In this item, the phrase "created by the new dam" indicates that the waters of the reservoir have changed the landscape, that is, no one built a church under water. Rather, the church was covered by the new water, and "inundated," (C), means "flooded," (D). Note that "bathed," (A), is wrong because it does not fully convey how covered the church was, as "flooded" does.

2. **(A, D)** (p. 393) *Verbal Reasoning/Sentence Equivalence/Thought Extension/Phrases*

The comma introduces a phrase that explains the "how" or the "why" of the collapse. Furthermore, there is the additional element of "struggles." Therefore, the blank must be completed by a word that explains how or why a practice would collapse as a result of struggles. Both "enervated," (A), and "depleted," (D), are good choices as they mean "weakened" or "exhausted." Note that "compromised," (E), is not strong enough to describe a collapse.

3. **(C, F)** (p. 393) *Verbal Reasoning/Sentence Equivalence/Thought Reversal/Coordinate Conjunctions*

The blank must be a word that suggests a work product that is made from bits and pieces drawn from various sources. "Salmagundi," (C), which roughly means "tossed salad," with the suggestion of many individual components pieced together, works in the blank, as does "miscellany," (F), though with less picturesque connotations.

4. **(A, C)** (p. 393) *Verbal Reasoning/Sentence Equivalence/Thought Extension/Key Adjectives and Adverbs*

The word "refined" suggests that the measurements needed to be more exact. Both "sensitive," (A), and "delicate," (C), are words used to describe instruments that are precise. (E) is arguably an acceptable completion, but (E) does not have a synonym match in the list of choices.

5. **(A, F)** (p. 394) *Verbal Reasoning/Sentence Equivalence/Thought Extension/Coordinate Conjunctions* and *Key Adjectives and Adverbs*

Two key logical signals are important to understanding the overall structure of the sentence. First, the "and" in the second clause signals a thought extension: exaggerated and even _____. Second, the "even" signals that the second element is a more pronounced or intense version of "exaggerated." A story even less true than if exaggerated is false. Clearly, this is the meaning of "inauthentic," (F), and "apocryphal," (A), means "of dubious origin."

6. **(E)** (p. 395) *Verbal Reasoning/Reading Comprehension/Vocabulary*

The author states that Tibetan is conservative and then supports the point by noting that a modern speaker of Tibetan can easily read texts that were written 13 centuries ago. In other words, the classical form of the language has not changed much, so one could call it "conservative." (A) is incorrect because classical Tibetan is a literary language. (B) is incorrect because the author talks about the richness of classical Tibetan, so it is not limited. (C) and (D) do not have appropriate definitions.

7. **(A)** (p. 395) *Verbal Reasoning/Reading Comprehension/Logical Structure*

The author begins the passage by preempting the possible misunderstanding that Tibetan as a language does share all of the features of English. Therefore, (A) is the best choice. The author spends the remainder of the paragraph explaining the unique characteristics of Tibetan. The second paragraph focuses on the history of Tibetan. While the remainder of the passage shares additional information readers may not know, only (A) is marked with the phrase "it is important to understand."

8. **(A, B, C)** (p. 395) *Verbal Reasoning/Reading Comprehension/Specific Detail*

The word "provide" identifies this as a Specific Detail item, and the directions ask for "all" the correct answers, so evaluate each answer choice individually. The answers to (A) and (B) are mentioned in the fourth paragraph, so (A) and (B) are both correct. The answer to (C) is mentioned in the fifth paragraph, so (C) is also correct.

9. **(A)** (p. 395) *Verbal Reasoning/Critical Reading/The Conclusion*

The author seeks to draw a distinction between the simple fact of death, which he or she argues can in no way be pleasant, and the result accomplished by that act. (A) correctly summarizes this distinction. (B) is wrong because, while it is probably true, it does not describe the distinction drawn in the argument. (C) is wrong because the author would probably deny that "sweetness" is ambiguous, even though it is used metaphorically. Instead, it seems that the author understands what is intended by the term and denies that it accurately describes the act of dying in war. Finally, (D) and (E) are both wrong because neither is a distinction made by the author.

10. **(E)** (p. 396) *Verbal Reasoning/Critical Reading/The Assumptions*

The argument is apparently aimed at people who drink brewed coffee, and it attempts to persuade them that an instant coffee has the same quality of flavor as brewed coffee. (E) considerably undermines this attempt by pointing out that those people who preferred Flash to the brewed coffee did so because they already liked the taste of instant coffee. The claim is weakened because there is no longer any evidence to support the idea that Flash can provide a better quality of flavor than brewed coffee to drinkers who prefer brewed coffee. The other choices are generally relevant to the claim, but none of them makes a very powerful attack on the claim.

11. **(B, D)** (p. 396) *Verbal Reasoning/Paragraph Completion/Combined Reasoning/Phrases* and *Key Adjectives and Adverbs*

The paragraph sets up a contrast between Verne's correct predictions, which were primarily in science and technology, and his incorrect predictions, which included almost everything else. The first blank creates a phrase that says the correct predictions were restricted to those about science and technology, and the speaker uses a literary device to make the point: "*local* to the world of", (B). Then, the second blank describes the accuracy of all the other predictions, a good example of which was the prediction that war would no longer be possible. "Mistaken," (D), is a good description of such a prediction.

12. **(C, D)** (p. 396) *Verbal Reasoning/Sentence Completion/Combined Reasoning/Key Adjectives and Adverbs* and *Phrases*

The introductory phrase modifies and describes Chambers, so the first blank will be completed by an adjective that is similar to those in the initial description. "Enigmatic," (C), echoes "cryptic," "secretive," and "opaque." Then, the phrase "at once" sets up a contrast between the second blank and "resent." And since "resent" means "dislike," "relish," (D), is a good opposite to complete the contrast.

13. **(B, D, I)** (p. 397) *Verbal Reasoning/Paragraph Completion/Combined Reasoning/Phrases*

The explanatory phrase in the second sentence (following the first comma) restates and develops the idea of being left alone by the state. And freedom from all government would be anarchy, so "anarchic," (B), is correct. Then, the clarifying phrase in the third sentence and the reference to "all power" establishes that the peasantry opposed authority in any form. And "indiscriminately," (D), is a good description of this broad resistance. Finally, the "lack of" combined with the blank in the last sentence must contrast with "better organized," so "lack of cohesion," (I), is a good choice.

14. **(E)** (p. 397) *Verbal Reasoning/Sentence Completion/Thought Extension/Phrases*

In this item, the phrase that follows the comma ("going only from his apartment to his office to his club and back to his apartment") is an extension of the word that must be used to fill in the blank. All of the material that precedes the comma (information regarding Doyle, Mycroft, and Sherlock Holmes) is unnecessary, so ignore this material and focus on what follows the comma. Knowing that "sedentary," (E), means "non-active" answers the question directly. Otherwise, eliminate as many answer choices as possible and guess.

15. **(C)** (p. 398) *Verbal Reasoning/Reading Comprehension/Main Idea*

The author of the passage begins by saying that literary critics tend to overuse the term "musical novel." Then, the author provides a conventional analysis of *Moderato Cantabile* as a "musical novel." The author goes on to say that the critics don't look deeply enough into the techniques of novelists. In the author's opinion, *Moderato Cantabile* is properly termed a musical novel because Duras' literary style enables the reader to listen to the novel. So (C) is the best description of the main idea. (A) is wrong because the passage doesn't give a definition. (B) is wrong because there is no comparison of the two named works. (D) is wrong because the author provides no such guidelines. (E) is wrong because the passage does not evaluate the effectiveness of literary techniques.

16. **(C)** (p. 398) *Verbal Reasoning/Reading Comprehension/Implied Idea*

The author explains how Duras makes use of a musical structure: the novel parallels the first movement of a sonata; it has a first, or tonic, theme and a second, or dominant, theme; the second theme is eventually merged into the first. The author indicates that Anne's structured, boring life is the first tonic theme and that Chauvin, who represents Anne's hope for escape, is the second dominant theme. Therefore, (C) is the best choice.

17. **(D)** (p. 398) *Verbal Reasoning/Reading Comprehension/Attitude-Tone*

In the last paragraph, the author clearly admires *Moderato Cantabile* and considers it a "truly musical" novel. On the other hand, the author also acknowledges that some of Duras' other works, namely the films, were not particularly successful. This admission is the qualification in the author's admiration of Duras' work, (D).

18. **(D)** (p. 398) *Verbal Reasoning/Critical Reading/The Inference/Analogy*

This argument proceeds by comparing experience with taxes to lotteries: this is an argument based on analogy, (D). (A) and (B) are wrong because the argument mentions neither authority nor statistics. (C) is wrong because, while the argument does reference two different programs, they are regarded as similar and not distinguished from one another. Finally, (E) is wrong because of the word "propose": the author is defending a proposal for a change but is not proposing the change.

19. **(C, E)** (p. 399) *Verbal Reasoning/Paragraph Completion/Thought Extension/Phrases* and *Subordinate Conjunctions*

The first blank must be filled with a word that describes fluctuation within some established limits. "Equilibrium," (C), is the best choice for the first blank. As for the second blank, the "because" signals a continuation of thought, more specifically, a causal connection. The rich are in a better position to hedge against inflation, so the rising prices hurt the non-rich more. Thus, economic inequality "intensifies," (E).

20. **(B, D)** (p. 399) *Verbal Reasoning/Paragraph Completion/Thought Extension/Phrases*

The paragraph talks about the suffering caused by left-over military ordnance. The first sentence says that the burden falls upon the innocent descendants of a particular group, and the second sentence echoes this by specifying children who play on the former battlefields. Therefore, the descendants must be the children of those to whom the battlefields belong, and those people were the ones who fought the war originally.

Therefore, "host countries," (B), is a good choice for the first blank. The second sentence uses a clarifying phrase following the comma, so the second blank should be filled by a word that describes unexploded mines, bombs, and shells. This ordnance was leftover, abandoned, or lost. Therefore, "debris" or "detritus," (D), would be an apt description.

21. **(A, E)** (p. 399) *Verbal Reasoning/Paragraph Completion/Combined Reasoning/Phrases* and *Key Adjectives and Adverbs*

The second sentence of the paragraph sets up a contrast with the first sentence. According to the second sentence, the explanation for the failure in eastern Montana was not a conspiracy to defraud but an innocent business mistake. This is the sort of honest mistake that would be made by a reputable firm. Thus, "ethical," (A), is a good choice for the first blank. Then, the third sentence should be completed in such a way as to continue the explanation offered by the speaker: conditions in the new region were not suitable. Thus, the failure would be attributable to an error in judgment or "miscalculation," (E), rather than to intent to deceive.

22. **(D)** (p. 400) *Verbal Reasoning/Reading Comprehension/Specific Detail*

This item stem includes the thought-reverser "EXCEPT," so the correct choice is NOT explicitly mentioned in the passage. (A), (B), (C), and (E) are all mentioned in the passage (lines 4–5, 8–9, 11–13, and 4–6, respectively). Only (D) is not mentioned; therefore, (D) is the correct choice.

23. **(A)** (p. 400) *Verbal Reasoning/Reading Comprehension/Logical Structure*

The author has already mentioned that liberalism has moved in two directions, so the introduction of a political philosopher as an authority is intended to support and further define the author's position, (A). (B) is wrong because the author does not refute Martin Diamond's views. (C) is wrong because the author uses the standard definition of "citizenship" throughout the passage. (D) is wrong because an author *must* be familiar with a distinction he or she writes about. Finally, (E) is wrong because the author does not suggest that Martin Diamond is a political candidate.

24. **(E)** (p. 400) *Verbal Reasoning/Reading Comprehension/Implied Idea*

In the first paragraph, the author contrasts the Greek idea of citizenship with the more modern, liberal idea. A series of parallels is set up. The liberal notion emphasizes pursuit of individual interests and limitation of government power, while the Greek notion emphasized participation in community affairs. Therefore, it is inferable that "*polis*" is the location of public life, meaning "political community," (E).

25. **(C)** (p. 400) *Verbal Reasoning/Reading Comprehension/Further Application*

In the last paragraph, the author states that majoritarians are likely to favor greater government control of the marketplace (as opposed to libertarians, who favor less government involvement). (C) best captures this idea: a majoritarian would favor legislation that provides for greater protection for consumers.

Section 5—Quantitative Reasoning (p. 401)

1. **(C)** (p. 401) *Quantitative Reasoning/Geometry Comparison/Lines and Angles* and *Triangles/Properties of Triangles*

Let the unlabeled angle of the triangle be w: $x + y + w = 180$ and $z + w = 180$, so $x + y + w = z + w \Rightarrow x + y = z$. Therefore, Quantity A is equal to Quantity B, (C).

2. **(A)** (p. 401) *Quantitative Reasoning/Arithmetic Comparison/Simple Manipulations*

The trick to solving this item quickly is to recognize that 2^4 is less than 2^5, so subtracting 2^4 from 5^7 leaves a larger quantity than subtracting 2^5 from 5^7. Therefore, Quantity A is greater than Quantity B, (A).

3. **(B)** (p. 401) *Quantitative Reasoning/Algebra Comparison/Simple Manipulations*

   Square both sides: Quantity A becomes x^2, and Quantity B becomes $x^2 + 1$. Then, subtract x^2 from both sides. The final comparison is 0 in Quantity A with 1 in Quantity B, so Quantity B is greater, (B).

4. **(C)** (p. 402) *Quantitative Reasoning/Geometry Comparison/Lines and Angles*

   Use the "big angle/little angle" theorem: $x + y = 180 \Rightarrow x = 180 - y$. Therefore, Quantity A is equal to Quantity B, (C).

5. **(B)** (p. 402) *Quantitative Reasoning/Arithmetic Comparison/Simple Manipulations*

   Do the indicated operations: Quantity A equals $\frac{15}{16}$ and Quantity B equals $2 \cdot \frac{15}{16} = \frac{30}{16}$. Therefore, Quantity B is greater than Quantity A, (B).

6. **(C)** (p. 402) *Quantitative Reasoning/Geometry Comparison/ Lines and Angles*

   Although the figures have different shapes, they are both quadrilaterals, and the sum of the measure of the interior angles of any quadrilateral is 360°. Therefore, Quantity A is equal to Quantity B, (C).

7. **(C)** (p. 402) *Quantitative Reasoning/Arithmetic Comparison/Simple Manipulations*

   Do the indicated operations: Quantity A equals $\frac{-3}{-1} = 3$ and Quantity B equals $-3 \cdot -1 = 3$. Therefore, Quantity A is equal to Quantity B, (C).

8. **(D)** (p. 402) *Quantitative Reasoning/Algebra Comparison/Manipulation of Algebraic Expressions/Evaluating Expressions*

   Multiply the centered inequality by 2: $2x > y > 0$. Does this help to make the comparison between x and y? No. The inequality asserts only that 2 times x is greater than y, but the inequality does not determine the relationship between x and y. Therefore, the relationship between Quantity A and Quantity B cannot be determined, (D).

   Alternatively, the same conclusion can be reached by substituting numbers. If $x = 2$, then y must be less than 4—but how much less? y could be 3 (in which case $y > x$) or 2 (in which case $y = x$) or 1 (in which case $y < x$). Therefore, the relationship between the two quantities cannot be determined.

9. **(C)** (p. 403) *Quantitative Reasoning/Data Analysis Comparison/Basic Descriptive Statistics/Quartiles and Interquartile Range* and *Data Interpretation/Boxplots*

   The boxplot is a visual representation of the quartiles. The first quartile is designated by the beginning of the box ($Q_1 = 3$), the second quartile is shown by the line inside the box ($Q_2 = 5$) and the third quartile is located at the end of the box ($Q_3 = 6$). The interquartile range is calculated by subtracting the first quartile from the third quartile: $Q_3 - Q_1 = 6 - 3 = 3$. Therefore, Quantity A, the first quartile, is equal to Quantity B, the interquartile range, (C).

10. **(E)** (p. 403) *Quantitative Reasoning/Algebra/Manipulation of Algebraic Expressions/Manipulating Expressions Involving Exponents* and *Solving Equations/Two Equations with Two Variables*

    Since $2^x = 16 = 2^4$, $x = 4$. Therefore, $x = \frac{y}{2} \Rightarrow 4 = \frac{y}{2} \Rightarrow y = 8$, (E).

11. **(E)** (p. 403) *Quantitative Reasoning/Geometry/Triangles/Properties of Triangles*

    There are two triangles in the given figure: the large right triangle and the smaller triangle within that triangle formed by 30°, $y°$, and $z°$. For the large right triangle, $x + 30 + 90 = 180 \Rightarrow x = 60$. Then, for the smaller triangle, since $x = y$, $y = 60$. So, $60 + 30 + z = 180 \Rightarrow z = 90$, (E).

12. (50) (p. 403) *Quantitative Reasoning/Arithmetic/Common Arithmetic Problems/Percents*

From the number of those students who attended the play, subtract the number of students who are seniors: $60\% - 20\% = 40\%$ of the student body. This 40% comes from the $100\% - 20\% = 80\%$ who are *not* seniors. So, $\frac{40}{80} = \frac{1}{2} = 50\%$ of the non-seniors must have attended the play.

13. (A) (p. 404) *Quantitative Reasoning/Algebra/Manipulation of Algebraic Expressions/Evaluating Expressions*

The least possible value for the expression $\frac{x+y}{z}$ will occur when x and y are the least and z is greatest: $\frac{6+3}{10} = \frac{9}{10}$, (A).

14. (C) (p. 404) *Quantitative Reasoning/Data Analysis/Basic Descriptive Statistics/Quartiles and Interquartile Range*

The third quartile, Q_3, is defined as the median of the upper half of the numbers. Since there are 10 teammates, the upper half consists of the five tallest teammates: 1 in the $65 < x \le 70$ interval, 3 in the $70 < x \le 75$ interval, and 1 in the $75 < x \le 80$ interval. Therefore, the median is the middle term (3rd) of the 5 terms in the upper half, which consists of an odd number of terms and occurs in the $70 < x \le 75$ interval, (C).

15. (B) (p. 404) *Quantitative Reasoning/Geometry/Triangles/Properties of Triangles*

The base of the triangle is $3k - k = 2k$, and the altitude of the triangle is $4k - k = 3k$. Therefore, the area is $\frac{(2k)(3k)}{2} = 12 \Rightarrow 3k^2 = 12 \Rightarrow k^2 = 4 \Rightarrow k = 2$, (B).

16. (C) (p. 404) *Quantitative Reasoning/Arithmetic/Complicated Manipulations/Factoring* and *Algebra/Manipulation of Algebraic Expressions/Manipulating Expressions Involving Exponents*

For this item, the trick is to rewrite the given expression: $200 = x^3 y^2 = x \cdot x \cdot x \cdot y \cdot y$. Now, factor 200: $200 = 100 \cdot 2 = 50 \cdot 2 \cdot 2 = 25 \cdot 2 \cdot 2 \cdot 2 = 5 \cdot 5 \cdot 2 \cdot 2 \cdot 2$. Compare this factorization with the rewritten algebraic expression: $y = 5$ and $x = 2$, so $xy = (2)(5) = 10$, (C).

17. (B) (p. 404) *Quantitative Reasoning/Algebra/Solving Equations/One Equation with One Variable*

Translate the information given in the item stem into an equation. Let h be the original height of the sapling: $h = \frac{9h}{10} + \frac{9}{10}$. Now, solve for h: $h = \frac{9h}{10} + \frac{9}{10} \Rightarrow 10h = 9h + 9 \Rightarrow h = 9$, (B).

18. (D) (p. 404) *Quantitative Reasoning/Algebra/Coordinate Geometry /Slope of a Line*

The given functions $f(-1) = 1$ and $f(2) = 7$ define two coordinate points included in the graph of $f(x)$: $(-1,1)$ and $(2,7)$. Therefore, the slope of the line is: $m = \frac{7-1}{2-(-1)} = \frac{6}{3} = 2$, (D).

19. (D) (p. 404) *Quantitative Reasoning/Arithmetic/Complicated Manipulations/Decimal-Fraction Equivalents*

For this item, the trick is to recognize that $\frac{2}{3}$ equals $0.66\overline{6}$. So, if the first 100 digits of the repeating decimal are all 6, the sum of the first 100 digits is $100 \cdot 6 = 600$, (D).

20. (E) (p. 405) *Quantitative Reasoning/Data Interpretation/Line Graphs* and *Circle Graphs*

According to the left-hand graph, total sales (foreign plus domestic) in 1994 were $\$10 + \$16 = \$26$ million. Therefore, foreign sales accounted for $\frac{\$10 \text{ million}}{\$26 \text{ million}} \approx 40\%$, and domestic accounted for the remaining 60%. The graph that best matches these percentages is (E).

21. **(B)** (p. 405) *Quantitative Reasoning/Data Interpretation/Line Graphs*

This item essentially asks, "Profit is what percent of total sales?" Use the "is-over-of" equation: $\frac{is}{of} = \frac{\%}{100} \Rightarrow \frac{Profit}{Sales} = \frac{\%}{100}$, where $Profit = Sales - Expenses$. Calculate the percentages for each year:

1991: $\frac{Sales - Expenses}{Sales} = \frac{14-9}{14} = \frac{5}{14} \approx 0.36 = 36\%$

1992: $\frac{Sales - Expenses}{Sales} = \frac{19-16}{19} = \frac{3}{19} \approx 0.16 = 16\%$

1993: $\frac{Sales - Expenses}{Sales} = \frac{24-21}{24} = \frac{3}{24} = 0.125 = 12.5\%$

1994: $\frac{Sales - Expenses}{Sales} = \frac{26-22}{26} = \frac{4}{26} \approx 0.15 = 15\%$

1995: $\frac{Sales - Expenses}{Sales} = \frac{30-25}{30} = \frac{5}{30} \approx 0.17 = 17\%$

So, there was only in one year, (B), in which profits more than 20% of total sales: 1991.

22. **(E)** (p. 405) *Quantitative Reasoning/Algebra/Manipulation of Algebraic Expressions/Creating Algebraic Expressions* and *Arithmetic/Common Arithmetic Problems/Rates*

Let x equal the number of minutes until the tank is empty. Set up an equation and solve for x:

$$g + mx - nx = 0 \Rightarrow g = nx - mx \Rightarrow g = x(n-m) \Rightarrow \frac{g}{n-m} = x \,.$$

Alternatively, since $n > m$, the net drain from the tank per minute will be $n - m$. So, the time required to empty the tank is $\frac{g}{n-m}$, (E).

23. **(A, B, D, E)** (p. 406) *Quantitative Reasoning/Arithmetic/Common Arithmetic Problems/Properties of Numbers*

In order for $\frac{13t}{7}$ to be an integer, the numerator must be a multiple of the denominator. Since 13 is not a multiple of 7, t must be a multiple of 7. Therefore, the correct answer choices are multiples of 7: (A), ($\frac{-49}{7} = -7$), (B), ($\frac{-7}{7} = -1$), (D), ($\frac{91}{7} = 13$), and (E), ($\frac{105}{7} = 15$).

24. **(D)** (p. 406) *Quantitative Reasoning/Algebra/Manipulation of Algebraic Expressions/Evaluating Expressions*

Solve the first equation for x and the second equation for z: $\frac{x+y}{x} = 4 \Rightarrow 4x = x + y \Rightarrow 3x = y \Rightarrow x = \frac{y}{3}$ and

$\frac{y+z}{z} = 5 \Rightarrow y + z = 5z \Rightarrow 4z = y \Rightarrow z = \frac{y}{4}$. Therefore, $\frac{x}{z} = \frac{\frac{y}{3}}{\frac{y}{4}} = \frac{y}{3}\left(\frac{4}{y}\right) = \frac{4}{3}$, (D).

25. ($\frac{12}{47}$) (p. 406) *Quantitative Reasoning/Arithmetic/Common Arithmetic Problems/Rates*

Find the time it took to drive for each of the legs, using the rate equation ($rate = \frac{distance}{time} \Rightarrow time = \frac{distance}{rate}$). So, the times for the three legs are $\frac{10 \text{ miles}}{30 \text{ miles/hour}} = \frac{1}{3}$ hour $= 20$ minutes ; $\frac{10 \text{ miles}}{40 \text{ miles/hour}} = \frac{1}{4}$ hour $= 15$ minutes, and $\frac{10 \text{ miles}}{50 \text{ miles/hour}} = \frac{1}{5}$ hour $= 12$ minutes, or $20 + 15 + 12 = 47$ minutes total. Since 12 of these 47 minutes were driven at 50 miles per hour, $\frac{12}{47}$ of the total driving time was driven at this speed.

Section 6—Quantitative Reasoning (p. 407)

1. **(A)** (p. 407) *Quantitative Reasoning/Arithmetic Comparison/Common Arithmetic Problems/Properties of Numbers*

   Write an equation using the centered information: $7(500+0+M)=3,000+500+60+N \Rightarrow 3,500+7M = 3,560+N \Rightarrow 7M=60+N$. Since there is only one digit which, when multiplied by 7, will yield a number greater than 60 but less than 70, M must be 9 and N must be 3. Therefore, Quantity A is greater than Quantity (B), (A).

   Alternatively, this item can be solved by simply reasoning that since the tens digit of $50M$ is 0, the 6 in the product had to have come from the multiplication of M and 7. The only number that M could be is 9.

2. **(C)** (p. 407) *Quantitative Reasoning/Algebra Comparison/Functions*

   Since $fg=gf$ and $f+g=g+f$, it does not matter which number is f and which is g (the commutative property). Therefore, Quantity A is equal to Quantity B, (C).

3. **(B)** (p. 407) *Quantitative Reasoning/Arithmetic Comparison/Common Arithmetic Problems/Properties of Numbers*

   Since $2x+2=2(x+1)$, $2x+2$ is a multiple of 2 and thus evenly divisible by 2. In other words, when $2x+2$ is divided by 2, the remainder is 0. Therefore, Quantity B is greater than Quantity A, (B).

4. **(C)** (p. 408) *Quantitative Reasoning/Data Analysis Comparison/Basic Descriptive Statistics/Mean*

   Do not automatically assume that (D) must be the correct choice because the item involves variables. Quantity A equals $\frac{2(x+y)}{2}=x+y$ and Quantity B equals $\frac{2x+2y}{2}=x+y$. Therefore, the two quantities are equal, (C).

5. **(B)** (p. 408) *Quantitative Reasoning/Arithmetic Comparison/Common Arithmetic Problems/Properties of Numbers*

   Redefine the two larger integers in terms of the smallest integer. Since x, y, and z are consecutive even integers, $y=x+2$ and $z=x+4$. Substitute these values for y and z in the given expressions: Quantity A equals $x+(x+2)+1=2x+3$ and Quantity B equals $(x+2)+(x+4)-1=2x+5$. Therefore, no matter the value of x, Quantity B is greater than Quantity A, (B).

6. **(D)** (p. 408) *Quantitative Reasoning/Algebra Comparison/Coordinate Geometry*

   According to the figure, x and y are both positive. (Both coordinates in the first quadrant are positive.) Furthermore, a is positive and b is negative. (In the fourth quadrant, the x-coordinate is positive and the y-coordinate is negative.) However, this information is not sufficient to determine whether the *sum* of x and y is more than the *sum* of a and b. Therefore, the relationship between Quantity A and Quantity B cannot be determined, (D).

7. **(B)** (p. 408) *Quantitative Reasoning/Algebra Comparison/Functions*

   Since $3p$ is negative, p must be negative and Quantity A is equal to 0. Since $q-3$ is positive, q must be positive, and Quantity B is equal to 1. Therefore, Quantity B is greater than Quantity A, (B).

8. **(C)** (p. 408) *Quantitative Reasoning/Algebra Comparison/Manipulation of Algebraic Expressions/Evaluating Expressions*

   The centered equation can be rewritten as $x=y$, so Quantity A is equal to 0 and Quantity B is equal to 0. Therefore, the two quantities are equal, (C).

9. **(A)** (p. 409) *Quantitative Reasoning/Geometry Comparison/Rectangles and Squares*

To calculate the volume of any rectangular solid, multiply the three dimensions. To calculate the volume of a cube (which is the special case of a rectangular solid in which all three dimensions are the same), multiply the edges: $\text{volume}_{\text{cube}} = \text{edge} \cdot \text{edge} \cdot \text{edge} \Rightarrow 8 = \text{edge}^3 \Rightarrow \text{edge} = 2$. The area of each face of a cube with an edge of 2 is $2 \cdot 2 = 4$; and since the cube has 6 faces, the total surface area of the cube is $6 \cdot 4 = 24$ square centimeters. Therefore, Quantity A is greater than Quantity B, (A).

10. **(E)** (p. 409) *Quantitative Reasoning/Algebra/Solving Equations/One Equation with One Variable*

Simply solve for x: $x + 3 = 3 + 12 \Rightarrow x = 12$, (E).

11. **(A, B, C)** (p. 409) *Quantitative Reasoning/Arithmetic/Common Arithmetic Problems/Properties of Numbers*

For this item, test each answer choice. (A), -5, (B), $-3\sqrt{2}$, and (C), -1, can all be written as the sum of two negative numbers. However, (D), 0, cannot: the sum of two negative numbers is always a negative number, so there is no way to write 0 as the sum of two negative numbers.

12. **(D)** (p. 409) *Quantitative Reasoning/Algebra/Solving Equations/Two Equations with Two Variables*

It is not possible to solve a system of two equations with two unknowns. The trick to this item is to recognize that $2x + 4y = 2(x + 2y)$ and since $x + 2y = 3$, $2x + 4y = 2(x + 2y) = 2(3) = 6$, (D).

13. **(C)** (p. 409) *Quantitative Reasoning/Data Analysis/Basic Descriptive Statistics/Mean*

Since the average of the three numbers is 6, the total of the three numbers must be 18. If the sum of two of the numbers is 11, the third number is $18 - 11 = 7$, (C).

14. **(E)** (p. 410) *Quantitative Reasoning/Data Interpretation/Bar Graphs*

From 1988 to 1992, the greatest increase in revenues occurred between 1988 and 1989: $\$7,000,000 - \$5,000,000 = \$2,000,000$, (E).

15. **(E)** (p. 410) *Quantitative Reasoning/Data Interpretation/Bar Graphs*

Divide total sales in 1993 by the number of cars sold to get the average price per car: average price $= \frac{\text{total sales}}{\text{number of cars sold}} = \frac{\$9,000,000}{750} = \$12,000$, (E).

16. **(C)** (p. 410) *Quantitative Reasoning/Data Interpretation/Bar Graphs*

This item asks for percent change, so use the "change-over-original" equation for the years given in the answer choices:

(A): 1986-1987: $\frac{450 - 400}{400} = \frac{50}{400} = 12.5\%$

(B): 1987-1988: $\frac{500 - 450}{450} = \frac{50}{450} \approx 11\%$

(C): 1988-1989: $\frac{600 - 500}{500} = \frac{100}{500} = 20\%$

(D): 1989-1990: $\frac{550 - 600}{600} = -\frac{50}{600} \approx -8\%$ (decrease)

(E): 1991-1992: $\frac{650 - 550}{550} = \frac{100}{550} \approx 18\%$

Therefore, the year with the largest increase over the previous year was 1989, (C).

17. (A) (p. 410) *Quantitative Reasoning/Algebra/Coordinate Geometry/The Coordinate System*

A point where two lines on a graph cross is called a point of intersection, which occurs when both equations are equal to each other. The question asks for the *x*-value, *m*, of the point of intersection, so set the two equations equal to one other and solve for *x*: $x^2 - 4 = -x^2 + 4 \Rightarrow 2x^2 - 8 = 0 \Rightarrow x^2 - 4 = 0 \Rightarrow x^2 = 4 \Rightarrow x = \pm 2$. If $m > 0$, then $m = 2$, (A).

Or, set one of the equations equal to 0: $(m, 0) \Rightarrow 0 = m^2 - 4 \Rightarrow m^2 = 4 \Rightarrow m = \pm 2$. Again, since $m > 0$, $m = 2$. Check that with the other equation: $y = (2)^2 - 4 = 0$.

Alternatively, "test-the-test." Substitute each answer choice for *x* to find the value for which each equation equals zero. Only (A) works: $0 = x^2 - 4 \Rightarrow 0 = (2)^2 - 4 \Rightarrow 0 = 0$ and $0 = -x^2 + 4 \Rightarrow 0 = -(2)^2 + 4 \Rightarrow 0 = 0$.

18. (D) (p. 410) *Quantitative Reasoning/Arithmetic/Simple Manipulations*

After Jerry repaid Joan $6, Joan had $9 + $6 = $15 and Jerry had $15. Therefore, before the debt was paid, Jerry had $15 + $6 = $21, (D).

19. (C) (p. 411) *Quantitative Reasoning/Data Interpretation/Boxplots* and *Data Analysis/Basic Descriptive Statistics/Median and Quartiles and Interquartile Range*

The interquartile range is the difference between the first quartile and the third quartile: $Q_3 - Q_1$. The first quartile is the median of the lower half of the numbers, 77, 79, 80, 86.5. Since the median falls between two numbers, calculate the average: $\frac{79 + 80}{2} = 79.5$. The third quartile the median of the upper half of the numbers, 86.5, 87, 94, 99. Since the median falls between two numbers, calculate the average $\frac{87 + 94}{2} = 90.5$. Therefore, the interquartile range is $90.5 - 79.5 = 11$, (C).

Alternatively, the first quartile is slightly less than 80, while the third quartile is slightly more than 90, a difference of approximately 10. Only (C) is close to 10, so (C) must be correct.

20. (C) (p. 411) *Quantitative Reasoning/Arithmetic/Simple Manipulations*

Simply count the blocks. Each of the rows has three blocks, and there are six rows. So, the total number of blocks is $3 \cdot 6 = 18$, (C).

21. (88) (p. 411) *Quantitative Reasoning/Data Analysis/Basic Descriptive Statistics/Quartiles and Interquartile Range and Median*

The second quartile is equal to the median of entire data set. First, rearrange the data values in order from least to greatest: 75, 75, 75, 76, 80, 87, 88, 88, 89, 99, 100, 100, 100, 100. Since there is an odd number of data values, the median is the middle value: 88.

22. (A, B) (p. 411) *Quantitative Reasoning/Data Analysis/Basic Descriptive Statistics/Mean* and *Standard Deviation*

For this item, test each answer choice. Since the list has a mean of 5, $\frac{2 + 4 + 5 + x + y}{5} = 5 \Rightarrow 11 + x + y = 25 \Rightarrow x + y = 14$. Test each answer choice as one of the two members that sum to 14. As for (A), if one member is 6, the remaining member is $14 - 6 = 8$, so the list is: 2, 4, 5, 6, 8. The standard deviation of this list is:

$$\sqrt{\frac{(5-2)^2 + (5-4)^2 + (5-5)^2 + (5-6)^2 + (5-8)^2}{5}} = \sqrt{\frac{3^2 + 1^2 + 1^2 + 3^2}{5}} = \sqrt{\frac{20}{5}} = \sqrt{4} = 2.$$ Therefore, 6, (A), and 8, (B), can

both be members of the list. As for (C), if one member is 9, the remaining member is $14 - 9 = 5$, so the list is

2, 4, 5, 9, 5. The standard deviation of this list is: $\sqrt{\dfrac{(5-2)^2+(5-4)^2+(5-5)^2+(5-9)^2+(5-5)^2}{5}}=\sqrt{\dfrac{3^2+1^2+4^2}{5}}=$ $\sqrt{\dfrac{26}{5}}\neq 2$, so 9, (C), cannot be a member of the list.

23. **(B)** (p. 411) *Quantitative Reasoning/Geometry/Rectangles and Squares*

    Let l represent the length and w represent the width of each card. Then, the width of the large rectangle is $l+w$, and the length of the large rectangle is equal to $5w$ or $4l$, which means that $5w=4l\Rightarrow l=\frac{5}{4}w$. So, since the area of the large rectangle is 180 (in square inches), set up an equation and solve for w:

    $5w(l+w)=180\Rightarrow 5w\left(\frac{5}{4}w+w\right)=180\Rightarrow 5w\left(\frac{9}{4}w\right)=180\Rightarrow \frac{45}{4}w^2=180\Rightarrow w^2=180\left(\frac{4}{45}\right)\Rightarrow w^2=16\Rightarrow w=4$.

    And if $w=4$, then $l=\frac{5}{4}(4)=5$. Thus, the perimeter of the large rectangle is: $2(l+w)+5w+4l=$ $2(5+4)+5(4)+4(5)=18+20+20=58$, (B).

24. **(6)** (p. 411) *Quantitative Reasoning/Algebra/Functions*

    In this item, brackets function as $f(x)$, indicating that whatever appears inside of the brackets is to be subtracted from its square. So, if $x=-2$, then $[x]=(-2)^2-(-2)=4+2=6$.

25. **(C)** (p. 411) *Quantitative Reasoning/Arithmetic/Common Arithmetic Problems/Percents*

    Given $\frac{2}{3}x=\frac{1}{10}(60)=6$, $x=6\left(\frac{3}{2}\right)=\frac{18}{2}=9$. Therefore: $\frac{1}{10}\cdot\frac{1}{3}(x)=\frac{1}{30}\cdot 9=\frac{3}{10}=0.3$, (C).

PRACTICE TEST II

Answer Keys

Section 3—Verbal Reasoning (p. 417)

1. B	6. D	11. E	16. A, E, I	21. B
2. D	7. E	12. D	17. A	22. B
3. D	8. C, E	13. C, E	18. B	23. D, F
4. C	9. E	14. B, D	19. C	24. B, F
5. A	10. B, C	15. C, E	20. D	25. D, E

Section 4—Verbal Reasoning (p. 424)

1. D, E	6. D	11. B, D	16. A	21. A
2. A, E	7. D	12. B	17. D	22. D
3. A, C	8. C	13. C	18. D	23. E
4. A, B	9. C	14. D	19. A, D	24. A
5. B	10. B, D	15. D	20. B	25. C

Section 5—Quantitative Reasoning (p. 432)

1. C	6. A	11. $\frac{9}{20}$	16. D	21. E
2. C	7. C	12. E	17. E	22. D
3. B	8. A	13. A	18. B	23. D
4. B	9. C	14. A, C	19. C	24. 20
5. D	10. B	15. B	20. E	25. C

Section 6—Quantitative Reasoning (p. 438)

1. A	6. D	11. 13.5	16. B	21. D
2. A	7. B	12. B	17. D	22. A
3. D	8. D	13. C	18. 10	23. E
4. C	9. D	14. D	19. C	24. 80
5. A	10. A	15. B	20. E	25. B

Section 1—*Analytical Writing* (p. 415)

Analyze an Issue *Sample Essay Response*

Computers are so ubiquitous that it sometimes seems as though they control every aspect of our lives. Certainly, they handle a lot of very important tasks that are literally matters of life and death. For example, large government and private computers keep track of air traffic, tracking individual airplanes, plotting safe routes, and monitoring the skies for emergencies. Or, to take another example, computers are also essential for doing advanced medical research. Whether we get a new drug or treatment seems to depend on whether a university computer concluded in a study that the therapy improved the chances for treatment of a certain disease. Computers also are responsible for a lot of small but useful tasks: they open and close doors automatically, regulate the temperature of buildings, and operate various appliances like VCRs and microwaves. And they seem to do this all behind our backs and without our asking for it or consent. Sometimes, computers are really intrusive. Who has not been interrupted during dinner by the computerized dialer of some telemarketer? Also, most of us worry that computers have so much information about us that we cannot control.

On the other hand, in spite of all of this, computers do not really control us. We control them. In the first place, computers depend on us for their very existence. We manufacture them, and then we program them. Moreover, we can always escape from them. We can go camping in the wilderness or even just take a walk in the country without the help of a computer. In the final analysis, we can always pull the plug if we want to. If you do not want to program your VCR, you do not have to.

On balance, while it may seem that computers control us, a closer look at things shows that we really control them. If there are ways that computers adversely affect us when we do not want them to, it is not really the computer's doing. It is the person behind the computer. The telemarketing computer did not tell itself to call me during dinner; the salesperson did. So, if there is any blame to be assigned, it belongs to people, not inanimate machines.

Section 2—*Analytical Writing* (p. 416)

Analyze an Argument *Sample Essay Response*

The argument to abolish the volunteer rescue squad in favor of a professional ambulance service is not persuasive for three reasons. First, the evidence cited does not prove the existence of a serious problem. Second, any problem that does exist can perhaps be solved with less drastic measures. Third, the radical plan called for might have serious side effects.

First, the six-minute difference in response time does not, in and of itself, prove the existence of a serious problem. The evidence refers simply to a review of records but says nothing more about how that review was conducted. It would be important to determine that a representative sample was taken and that representative cases were reviewed. A single difficult case, for example during a snowstorm, could skew the statistics. Additionally, the information given in the argument does not prove that the six-minute difference is an important difference. It is entirely possible that the volunteer squad responds to calls according to their survey. For example, a minor traffic accident does not call for breakneck speed.

Second, if a problem does exist, Putnam should consider ways of improving the performance of the rescue squad. At minimum, it should look at the equipment now being used. Is the squad properly equipped? Is its dispatch and radio equipment reliable? Are its vehicles in good working order? Beyond that, it should look at training procedures, perhaps compare them with those of similar rescue squads elsewhere. If improvement is needed, more training would be in order. Finally, it could even consider working more closely with Empire, calling on Empire to answer those calls when it is unable to respond.

Third, Putnam should also consider the possibility that eliminating its rescue squad may cause new problems. Of course, it has to determine what the cost of such a move would be. Additionally, it has to realize that a private company might not be as cooperative as volunteers from the community. Further, if the new plan should be a complete failure, it might be difficult to reinstate the old system. People might be reluctant to volunteer again; leadership might be lacking; equipment might not be available or available only at a prohibitive cost.

In conclusion, there are at least three good reasons why Putnam should proceed cautiously and get more information before it makes a decision.

Section 3—*Verbal Reasoning* (p. 417)

1. **(B)** (p. 417) *Verbal Reasoning/Reading Comprehension/Main Idea*

The author begins the passage by defining conventional echocardiography, stating that this technique is deficient in one respect: although it gives a picture of the structure and functioning of the heart, it does not provide any information about the quality of the heart tissue. Then, the author describes a new technique for studying the heart, one that allows researchers to make judgments about the state of the heart tissue. So, (B) is the best choice.

2. **(D)** (p. 417) *Verbal Reasoning/Reading Comprehension/Logical Structure*

In the first paragraph, after introducing the topic of conventional echocardiography, the author says that this technique is even able to measure the direction and flow of blood in the heart. The key word is "even," which suggests that the reader should be impressed with the information that follows. This idea follows the sentence in which the author states that conventional echocardiography provides highly detailed pictures of the heart. So, the author introduces the information at that point to prove how effective conventional echocardiography is. Later in the passage, the author describes a new technique that is even more impressive. Therefore, (D) is the best choice.

3. **(D)** (p. 417) *Verbal Reasoning/Reading Comprehension/Implied Idea*

The author discusses a new research technique and says that researchers *hope* it will be valuable. The fact that the new technique is still in the *research* stage and that researchers *hope* it will be useful indicates that (D) is the best choice.

4. **(C)** (p. 417) *Verbal Reasoning/Reading Comprehension/Specific Detail*

In the final paragraph, the author states that researchers hope the new technique will complement existing echocardiography techniques, (C).

5. **(A)** (p. 418) *Verbal Reasoning/Critical Reading/The Inference/Analogy*

The argument draws an analogy between patents and trade secrets, but the analogy is flawed, (A). A trade secret is just that—a secret—and if it were registered and readily available to everyone, then it would no longer be a secret. As for the remaining choices, the argument does not reverse any cause-and-effect connections, (B), make any generalizations, (C), make any logical contradictions, (D), or use circular reasoning, (E).

6. **(D)** (p. 418) *Verbal Reasoning/Sentence Completion/Thought Extension/Subordinate Conjunctions*

In this item, the subordinate conjunction "because" signals a thought extension. The sentence says that Western physicians are learning a procedure. Logically, they are doing this "because" it is desirable. Eliminate (B), "manipulation," and (E), "inflation," because neither has a positive connotation. Eliminate (A), "veracity," and (C), "liquidity," because neither creates a meaningful sentence. Therefore, by the process of elimination, (D) is the correct choice. Indeed, it makes logical sense that Western physicians would learn acupuncture based on its "effectiveness."

7. **(E)** (p. 418) *Verbal Reasoning/Sentence Completion/Thought Extension/Punctuation*

The colon signals a thought extension: what follows the colon must describe something that is "antithetical (opposite) to humor." "Macabre," (E), which is related to death and means "horrible," is the best choice.

8. (C, E) (p. 418) **Verbal Reasoning/Sentence Completion/*Thought Reversal/Phrases***

In this item, the word "rather" signals a thought reversal: the President responded with something other than "clarity and precision." Look for opposites of these words for the blanks. "Obfuscation," (C), and "vagueness," (E), are both opposites of "clarity and precision."

9. (E) (p. 419) **Verbal Reasoning/Reading Comprehension/Main Idea**

The focus of the passage is on the use of synchrotron radiation for research, (E). (A) is wrong because the discussion is not about a theory but a research instrument. (B) is wrong because the discussion about the properties of x-rays is incidental to the main point of the passage. The author mentions x-rays because synchrotron radiation is made up of x-rays, but the main point of the passage is not a discussion of the properties of x-rays per se. Finally, (C) and (D) are both wrong because, while each is mentioned in the passage as a possible research topic that might be investigated by using synchrotron radiation, neither is the main point of the passage.

10. (B, C) (p. 419) **Verbal Reasoning/Reading Comprehension/Logical Structure**

This item includes directions to select all correct answers, so evaluate each answer choice individually. The author does not mention any statistics, so (A) is wrong. The author contrasts the use of synchrotron radiation and ordinary x-ray sources, so (B) is correct. Finally, in the third paragraph, the author gives an example of the kind of research that will be improved by using with the new type of radiation, so (C) is correct.

11. (E) (p. 419) **Verbal Reasoning/Reading Comprehension/Specific Detail**

In the third paragraph, the author specifically states that concentrated samples are used to compensate for the weakness in the beam generated by conventional x-ray sources, (E). (A) is wrong because it is contradicted by the passage: the greater concentration makes conditions in the lab unlike actual conditions. (B) and (C) are both wrong because the author does not state that the technique gives a picture of larger size, nor that concentrating a sample makes an experiment run faster. Finally, (D) is wrong because it is inconsistent with what the author says about high concentrations making conditions in the lab unlike those actually found in the cell: normal function occurs at *in vivo* concentrations.

12. (D) (p. 419) **Verbal Reasoning/Reading Comprehension/Specific Detail**

This item stem includes the thought-reverser "EXCEPT," so the correct choice is NOT explicitly mentioned in the passage. (A), (B), (C), and (E) are all specifically stated in the passage (lines 7–9, 4–6, 18–22, and 1–2, respectively). Only (D) is not mentioned in the passage and, therefore, is the correct choice.

13. (C, E) (p. 420) **Verbal Reasoning/Paragraph Completion/Combined Reasoning/*Phrases* and *Key Adjectives and Adverbs***

In this item, the phrase "opposed to" creates a contrast between the phrase "ideological presupposition" and the phrase created by the second blank. A good opposite of "presupposition" is "fact" or "knowledge." Therefore, "genuine knowledge," (E), is the best choice for the second blank. Then, the first blank echoes the idea of "polarizing opinion" introduced in the first sentence, and that is consistent with "contentious assertion." Therefore, (C) is the best choice for the first blank.

14. (B, D) (p. 420) **Verbal Reasoning/Sentence Completion/Combined Reasoning/*Phrases***

The first blank requires a word to reverse the idea of grand spectacle, since the modern audience is used to the opposite of grand spectacle. (A) is wrong because "irreverence" is not the opposite of grand spectacle. (C) is wrong because "flamboyance" extends the idea of grand spectacle instead of reversing it. Therefore, (B) is the correct choice for the first blank. Indeed, the idea of "minutiae," or details, is opposite to the idea of something large or grand like opera. The second blank requires a word to extend the idea of grand spectacle. (E), "subtle," and (F), "hapless," are both wrong because neither extends the idea of grand spectacle. Therefore, (D) is the correct choice for the second blank. Indeed, "extravagant" fills the second blank nicely.

15. **(C, E)** (p. 420) *Verbal Reasoning/Paragraph Completion/Combined Reasoning/Key Adjectives and Adverbs* and *Phrases*

The first blank should parallel the word "discordant." Therefore, "cacophony," (C), which means "harsh discordance of sound," is the best choice for the first blank. The second blank reverses the thought begun in the first sentence. The correct word should convey an idea similar to unity. "Focused," (E), reverses the idea of discordance and is the best choice for the second blank.

16. **(A, E, I)** (p. 420) *Verbal Reasoning/Paragraph Completion/Combined Reasoning/Phrases* and *Key Adjectives and Adverbs*

The first blank must contrast with "vigorous intellectual skirmishes": "flaccidness," (A), which suggests a weakness that creates the needed contrast, is the best choice for the first blank. The second blank must echo "intramurally": "internecine," (E), which means "within the family or the group," is the best choice for the second blank. Note that (F) is wrong because there is no suggestion that the conflict is "unsavory." Finally, the third blank is defined by the phrase that follows the comma: "fractiousness," (I), which means "splintered or fragmented," is the best choice for the third blank.

17. **(A)** (p. 421) *Verbal Reasoning/Reading Comprehension/Implied Idea*

In the second paragraph, the author states that not even the appointment of Forrestal allayed the suspicions of Navy officers and their allies. The words "not even" imply that the appointment of Forrestal was expected to have a placating effect on those people, (A).

18. **(B)** (p. 421) *Verbal Reasoning/Reading Comprehension/Specific Detail*

In the first paragraph, the author states that Truman recommended a unified armed service. The unification plan is clarified by the parenthetical phrase, so it is understood that the president's unification plan included a separate air force, (B).

19. **(C)** (p. 422) *Verbal Reasoning/Reading Comprehension/Further Application*

In the closing paragraph, the author states that an unexpected result of the unification battle was that the military would never be able to establish itself as a power independent of and outside civilian control, (C).

20. **(D)** (p. 422) *Verbal Reasoning/Reading Comprehension/Main Idea*

Although the ideas contained in the wrong choices are mentioned in the discussion (personalities, the President, a law, and control of the military), the author views the events primarily in political terms, (D).

21. **(B)** (p. 422) *Verbal Reasoning/Critical Reading/The Inference/Generalization*

This argument is fairly simplistic and its weakness should be obvious: it oversimplifies a causal connection, (B). (A) and (D) are both wrong because, while it is true that the argument does not define the term "teacher," its meaning should be apparent. (C) is wrong because, while the argument does not rely on statistics, that is not why it is fundamentally flawed. Finally, (E) is wrong because, while the argument is weak, it does not have the structure of a circular argument.

22. **(B)** (p. 423) *Verbal Reasoning/Critical Reading/The Assumptions* and *The Inference/Cause and Effect Situation*

This item stem asks for an alternative explanation (an explanation for the result other than a flawed study). (B) provides this alternative. The findings could have been correct as reported: at the time of the survey, 36 percent of the people were committed to Green and 42 percent were committed to Green's opponent (36% + 42% = 78%); however, over the next 10 days, many of those who were previously undecided chose to vote for Green. (A) is wrong because, while it is consistent with the results and suggests that Green was picking up votes as the election date grew nearer, it does not explain what happened in the 10 days between the date of the survey and the election. (C) is wrong because it would strengthen the conclusion that the survey was inaccurate by suggesting that Green's opponent should have had even more votes than predicted by the survey. (D) is wrong because, while weather certainly could affect the outcome of the election, it is impossible to say, given the available facts, which of the candidates (if either) would have been aided by a light turnout. Therefore, this idea neither weakens nor strengthens the argument. Finally, (E) is wrong because, while it is generally related to the topic of the passage, it has no bearing on the specific issue being discussed.

23. **(D, F)** (p. 423) *Verbal Reasoning/Sentence Equivalence/Thought Extension/Phrases*

The phrase "for two generations" modifies the word that will fill the blank and indicates that no significant progress had been made during that time. Both "stymied," (D), and "confounded," (F), indicated lack of progress. Note that (E) is not correct because "retarded" refers to slowed, not blocked, progress.

24. **(B, F)** (p. 423) *Verbal Reasoning/Sentence Equivalence/Thought Extension/Key Adjectives and Adverbs*

The key to this item is the adjective "deceased." The rituals that are prescribed are for the treatment of human remains. Both "posthumous," (B), and "postmortem," (F), mean "after death."

25. **(D, E)** (p. 423) *Verbal Reasoning/Sentence Equivalence/Thought Reversal/Phrases*

The "surprise" referred to in the sentence is the contrast between the usual practice of reserving seats on the committee for senior members and the fact that the appointee was a first-term or inexperienced member. Both "novice," (D), and "neophyte," (E), are words used to describe participants who lack experience.

Section 4—*Verbal Reasoning* (p. 424)

1. **(D, E)** (p. 424) *Verbal Reasoning/Sentence Equivalence/Thought Extension/Punctuation*

The colon introduces further information about the phrase that contains the blank. The material following the colon provides evidence for the contention that dishonesty in the state house is rife: several chief executives have been convicted of crimes. Both "endemic," (D), and "prevalent," (E), mean "widespread."

2. **(A, E)** (p. 424) *Verbal Reasoning/Sentence Equivalence/Thought Extension/Coordinate Conjunctions*

In this item, the conjunction "and" signals a thought extension: the phrase completed by the blank must echo "flouting acceptable morals." "Unconventional," (A), means "contrary to convention," that is, contrary to accepted practice. And "contrarian," (E), means "acting in a manner contrary to accepted practice."

3. **(A, C)** (p. 424) *Verbal Reasoning/Sentence Equivalence/Thought Extension/Key Adjectives and Adverbs*

The sentence describes a strategy of annoying the consumer to establish brand name identification. The blank parallels the idea of advertising that is "obtrusive." Both "ubiquitous," (A), and "omnipresent," (C), mean "always present."

4. **(A, B)** (p. 424) *Verbal Reasoning/Sentence Equivalence/Thought Extension/Key Adjectives and Adverbs*

There is a parallelism in the statement between "deep-rooted," the blank, and "long-term." Both "chronic," (A), and "enduring," (B), describe conditions consistent with "deep-rooted" and "long-term." Note that (C) is wrong because, while "volatile" makes a logical statement, it is not consistent with "deep-rooted" and "long-term."

5. **(B)** (p. 425) *Verbal Reasoning/Reading Comprehension/Main Idea*

Eliminate (A) because the passage discusses geology, not scenery. Eliminate (C) because it is too narrow: though the author does mention different types of rocks, the distinctions are drawn in the service of a larger point, the history of the mountains. Eliminate (D) and (E) for the same reason: the author mentions the rhythms of the Earth's crust as part of the history, and the reference to dinosaurs is simply to give the reader a point of reference. Therefore, by the process of elimination, (B) is the correct choice.

6. **(D)** (p. 425) *Verbal Reasoning/Reading Comprehension/Specific Detail*

This item stem includes the thought-reverser "EXCEPT," so the correct choice is NOT explicitly mentioned in the passage. In the first paragraph, the author states that metamorphic rock is ancient, (C); that it is created from sedimentary rock, (B); that it is harder than sedimentary rock, (A); and that it is created by high temperatures and pressures, (E). (D), however, is a misreading of the first paragraph: granite is "later intrusive material" and not a part of the evolution of metamorphic rock.

7. **(D)** (p. 425) *Verbal Reasoning/Reading Comprehension/Further Application*

This item essentially asks for the judgment with which the author would agree. Eliminate (A) and (B) because each overstates the point (in opposite directions): scattered evidence and a good theory are not conclusive proof of anything, but neither are they total fiction. Eliminate (C) because the author cites evidence to support his or her claim. Eliminate (E) for the same reasons as (A) and (B). Therefore, by the process of elimination, (D) is the correct choice. Indeed, in the first paragraph, the author states that the story is a long one, the details of which are not clear, but that there is scattered evidence that strongly suggests a theory.

8. **(C)** (p. 425) *Verbal Reasoning/Reading Comprehension/Implied Idea*

In the first paragraph, the author says that the gneiss and schist are rocks seen today, and they "were...*once* sediments formed in the seas." The author then proceeds to explain how these sediments slowly changed over time to harder metamorphic rock. Therefore, it can be inferred that the gneiss and schist are types of metamorphic rock that formed as a result of the pressure and heat applied over time to sedimentary rock. Thus, (C) is the best choice. (A) is wrong for the same reason that (C) is correct: the gneiss and schist are not sedimentary rock but the result of pressure and heat applied to sedimentary rock. (B) is wrong because it represents a misreading of the first paragraph: granite is not a part of the evolution of metamorphic rock. (D) is wrong because, while the author does describe the rocks in the Colorado region as "crystalline," it cannot be inferred that the gneiss and schist are types of crystals. Finally, (E) is wrong because the author does not mention "igneous rock."

9. **(C)** (p. 426) *Verbal Reasoning/Critical Reading/The Assumptions* and *The Inference/Cause and Effect Situation*

This item stem asks for an alternative causal explanation for the phenomenon described. (C) provides an alternative explanation: there have been no convictions because the law has not been enforced, not because drivers have complied with the law. (A) is wrong because the fact that drivers were disciplined in the past for other reasons has no bearing on the enforcement patterns of the dress code. (B) is wrong because this idea seems to strengthen, rather than weaken, the argument by suggesting that inspectors are in a position to detect violations of the dress code. Note that (D) is an attractive distractor: it at least has the merit of suggesting that drivers are not better dressed and, therefore, that they are not complying with the new dress code. However, (D) relies on a survey of attitudes, and the attitudes might or might not be well founded. A driver might comply with a dress code and still not meet a passenger's expectation of "better dressed." Finally, (E) is wrong because, even if significantly fewer drivers are working in July and August, the decrease alone would not account for 100% compliance.

10. **(B, D)** (p. 426) *Verbal Reasoning/Paragraph Completion/Combined Reasoning/Key Adjectives and Adverbs* and *Phrases*

The first blank must assist the completion of the picture the author is describing of travel along a familiar path through familiar country. "Amble," (B), meaning "to stroll," is the best choice for the first blank. Then, the "however" introduces a contrast: the relaxed and familiar versus the difficult, embarrassing questions. Those are likely to make a person feel uncomfortable or "discomfited," (D).

11. **(B, D)** (p. 426) *Verbal Reasoning/Paragraph Completion/Combined Reasoning/Key Adjectives and Adverbs* and *Phrases*

The first blank is set up by the first sentence, and the key word there is "mocking." To "satirize," (B), is to mock something. Then, the second blank contrasts with "cleverly phrase" but also continues the idea of satirizing fashionable theories. "Meretricious," (D), which means "superficially attractive but lacking real value," is the best choice for the second blank.

12. **(B)** (p. 426) *Verbal Reasoning/Sentence Completion/Combined Reasoning/Subordinate Conjunctions* and *Key Adjectives and Adverbs*

Two key logical signals are important to understanding the overall structure of the sentence. First, the subordinate conjunction "though," combined with the comma, signals a thought reversal: the blank must be filled with a word that means the opposite of "small" and "remote." Therefore, the correct choice must express such ideas as "great in size" and "existing everywhere." Second, the word "anywhere" and the phrase "any of us" signal a thought extension. The correct choice has to describe something that could happen "anywhere" and to anyone. "Universal," (B), is the best match.

13. **(C)** (p. 426) *Verbal Reasoning/Sentence Completion/Combined Reasoning/Coordinate Conjunctions* and *Phrases*

Two key logical signals are important to understanding the overall structure of the sentence. First, the phrase "rather than" signals a thought reversal. Second, the coordinate conjunction "and" signals a thought extension. The blank must be filled with a word that means the opposite of "learned." Also, the structure of the sentence indicates that there is a relationship between the missing word and the phrase "dictated by genetic makeup." "Innate," (C), which means "inborn," is the best choice.

14. **(D)** (p. 427) *Verbal Reasoning/Reading Comprehension/Further Application*

Eliminate (A) because, in the last sentence of the passage, the author acknowledges that siting decisions can be used to achieve various goals. Eliminate (B) because the author also agrees in lines 20–23 that energy parks will have large effects. Eliminate (C) because the first paragraph indicates that the author surely would agree with this statement. Eliminate (E) because lines 38–39 indicate that the author would likely agree with (E). Therefore, by the process of elimination, (D) is the correct choice. Indeed, the author accepts the idea that siting decisions are not dictated by natural features but can be made according to the principle of created opportunity.

15. **(D)** (p. 427) *Verbal Reasoning/Reading Comprehension/Further Application*

The concluding remarks of the passage make clear that the author would most likely agree that modern society is so complex that governments must take greater responsibility for decisions such as power plant siting, (D). (A) is wrong because it is contradicted by the concluding remarks. (B) is wrong because it goes beyond the scope of the passage: such a critical judgment ("…were irresponsible") cannot be attributed to the author. In fact, the passage at least implies that decisions during the nineteenth century were made in a natural (no pun intended) way. (C) is wrong because it overstates the case: though the author believes that siting decisions for power plants need not depend on natural features, there is no support in the passage for such a broad conclusion as that given in (C). Finally, (E) is wrong because the author does not condemn the size of the Four Corners plant.

16. **(A)** (p. 428) *Verbal Reasoning/Reading Comprehension/Specific Detail*

The answer to this item is found at the beginning of the third paragraph. The most important feature of an energy park is that its location can be chosen. Therefore, unlike the harbor, a natural feature located without regard to human desires, the energy park can be located where it will serve goals other than the production of energy, (A). (B) and (D) are both wrong because each is unresponsive to the question asked. Finally, (C) and (E) are both wrong for two reasons: first, each is not supported by the passage; second, each is unresponsive to the question asked.

17. (D) (p. 428) *Verbal Reasoning/Critical Reading/The Conclusion*

The question stem asks for the general conclusion that is most supported by the information on the survey. The most striking feature of the survey results is that so many students seem to have opinions on a topic on which they could not really have an opinion. This idea is expressed in general terms by (D). (A) is wrong because it used the word "most," and those who expressed an opinion about the fictitious agency were relatively few—not most. Additionally, the survey example cannot really support a very broad conclusion about "quality education." (B) is wrong because there is no warrant for this in the information provided. The passage does not state why those who declined to answer did so. (C) is incorrect because the passage does not provide any information about the relative frequency of (1) versus (2) and (3) versus (4). Finally, (E) is perhaps the second best choice, but (E) requires a further assumption: college students lie to survey conductors. And there is no evidence for that in the information provided.

18. (D) (p. 428) *Verbal Reasoning/Critical Reading/The Assumptions*

The argument claims that psychology became a true science of mental activity only when it concentrated on observable events such as human behavior. Thus, the author must believe that behavior is tied to mental activity, (D). (A) is wrong because the author claims that psychology could become a science only when researchers abandoned the attempt to study mental impressions, so he or she evidently believes that mental impressions are wholly subjective and not observable as scientific phenomena. (B) is wrong because it is not a premise of the argument and nothing the author says suggests that it is true. The weakness of early psychology, according to the author, was that it tried to study subjective impressions rather than observable phenomena; a subjective impression is just that, regardless of whether the person describing the feeling is being candid or not. (C) is wrong because while the research participants may have altered their experiences when verbally expressing them, there is nothing to indicate that they did so intentionally. Finally, (E) is wrong because the author's remarks are specifically limited to the field of psychology.

19. (A, D) (p. 429) *Verbal Reasoning/Paragraph Completion/Thought Extension/Phrases*

The first blank echoes the idea of an "Olympian critic," someone who issues authoritative rules from on high, and "dogmatic," (A), meaning "dictatorial," is a good extension of this idea. Then, the second blank must echo the idea of things that "no longer matter." "Undistinguishable noise," (D), is suggestive of something that is mere background and unimportant.

20. (B) (p. 429) *Verbal Reasoning/Sentence Completion/Thought Extension/Phrases*

In this item, the phrase "developed into" signals a thought extension: the second part of the sentence, which describes an intensifying course of emotions (from "concern" to "despair"), must be an extension of the idea that is expressed by the missing word. Therefore, "foreboding," (B), is the best choice. The workers vague sense of worry, or "foreboding," escalated into stronger feelings of "concern" and eventually "despair."

21. (A) (p. 429) *Verbal Reasoning/Sentence Completion/Thought Extension/Key Adjectives and Adverbs*

In this item, the comma, combined with the adverb "unfairly," signals a thought extension: the blank must be filled with a negative word that parallels the idea of something being unfair. Eliminate (B) because something that is unfair could not be "objective." Eliminate (C), "suppressed," and (D), "questionable," because neither creates a meaningful sentence. Therefore, by the process of elimination, (A) is the correct choice. Indeed, "biased" is the best word to convey the idea that the book blamed the South unfairly.

22. (D) (p. 429) *Verbal Reasoning/Sentence Completion/Combined Reasoning/Phrases* and *Coordinate Conjunctions*

Two key logical signals are important in understanding the overall structure of the sentence. First, the phrase "contrary to popular opinion" signals a thought reversal: bats are going to be something that is the opposite of "aggressive" and "rabid." Second, the coordinate conjunction "and" signals a thought extension: the blank must be filled with a word that parallels "shy." Eliminate (A), "turgid," (B), "disfigured," and (C), "punctual," because none is a logical opposite for "aggressive" and "rabid." Eliminate (E) because a bat would probably not be described as "depraved." Therefore, by the process of elimination, (D) is the correct choice. Indeed, "innocuous," which means "harmless," is the opposite of "aggressive" and fits nicely with "shy."

23. **(E)** (p. 430) *Verbal Reasoning/Reading Comprehension/Vocabulary*

In the last paragraph, the author states that the drug surveillance system is made up of a lot of different pieces and that these pieces are decentralized and not coordinated. A good meaning of "disparate" in this context is "unconnected."

24. **(A)** (p. 431) *Verbal Reasoning/Reading Comprehension/Implied Idea*

The key to this item is the word "retrospective," which indicates that the study mentioned was done after the drug was already in use. Therefore, (A) is the best choice. (B) is wrong because, while the study uncovered harmful side effects, the drug was already in use. (C) is wrong because the paragraph in which this study is mentioned deals with methods of reporting adverse drug effects, not new applications for drugs. (D) is wrong for two reasons. First, the author does not mention the efficiency of the study. Second, the author is not in favor of a centralized authority. In fact, in the last paragraph, the author says that it would be inappropriate at this time to attempt to unite all of the disparate elements into a comprehensive surveillance program. Finally, (E) is wrong because, while the author mentions thromboembolism as one of the possible harmful side effects of drugs, it is not mentioned in connection with estrogen. The use of estrogen is mentioned in connection with endometrial cancer.

25. **(C)** (p. 431) *Verbal Reasoning/Reading Comprehension/Further Application*

Use the process of elimination. Eliminate (A) and (B) because, in the last paragraph, the author suggests that uniting disparate elements into a comprehensive surveillance program is inappropriate at this time. (D) is wrong because, while the author might advocate the elimination of the availability of certain drugs, this is not where the passage is leading. Finally, (E) is wrong because, while the author acknowledges that pre-approval studies are fallible, this is not where the passage is leading. Therefore, by the process of elimination, (C) is the correct choice. Indeed, the author suggests that improvements are possible in each segment of the system and urges reliance on computers to improve coordination and communication.

Section 5—Quantitative Reasoning (p. 432)

1. **(C)** (p. 432) *Quantitative Reasoning/Geometry Comparison/Lines and Angles*

The sum of the measures of the interior angles of a four-sided figure is 360, so $2x + 4x + 70 + 110 = 360 \Rightarrow 6x + 180 = 360 \Rightarrow 6x = 180 \Rightarrow x = 30$. Therefore, Quantity A is equal to Quantity B, (C).

2. **(C)** (p. 432) *Quantitative Reasoning/Arithmetic Comparison/Simple Manipulations*

Do the indicated operations: Quantity A equals $\sqrt{6} \cdot \sqrt{10} = \sqrt{60}$ and Quantity B equals $\sqrt{3} \cdot \sqrt{20} = \sqrt{60}$. Therefore, Quantity A is equal to Quantity B, (C).

3. **(B)** (p. 432) *Quantitative Reasoning/Arithmetic Comparison/Common Arithmetic Problems/Properties of Numbers*

According to the centered information, x is negative. A negative number raised to an odd power is negative while a negative number raised to an even power is positive. Therefore, Quantity B is greater than Quantity A, (B).

4. **(B)** (p. 433) *Quantitative Reasoning/Arithmetic Comparison/Simple Manipulations*

Subtract 50 from both sides: Quantity A becomes x and Quantity B becomes 50. The centered information establishes that x is less than 50, so Quantity B is greater than Quantity A, (B).

5. **(D)** (p. 433) *Quantitative Reasoning/Data Analysis Comparison/Basic Descriptive Statistics/Mean*

Create an equation that expresses the centered information algebraically: $\frac{x+y+z}{3} = y \Rightarrow x+y+z = 3y \Rightarrow x+z = 2y$. Since this is one equation with three variables, it is not possible to determine the value of any one of the variables. Therefore, a relationship between the two quantities cannot be determined, (D).

6. **(A)** (p. 433) *Quantitative Reasoning/Algebra Comparison/Coordinate Geometry*

According to the centered information, (x,z) is in Quadrant I, so x must be positive, and (z,y) is in Quadrant IV, so y must be negative. Therefore, x must be larger than y, and Quantity A is greater than Quantity B, (A).

7. **(C)** (p. 433) *Quantitative Reasoning/Arithmetic Comparison/Common Arithmetic Problems/Proportions and Direct-Inverse Variation*

Set up simultaneous equations to find the numbers of pounds of peanuts in the mixture. Let x be the number of pounds of peanuts and y the number of pounds of cashews: $x+y = 2 \Rightarrow 1.25x + 2.25y = 3.5$. (Note: The mix costs \$1.75 per pound, but there are 2 pounds, so the cost of the mix is \$3.50.) Using the first equation, express y in terms of x: $y = 2 - x$. Substitute this value for y in the second equation: $1.25x + 2.25(2-x) = 3.5 \Rightarrow 1.25x + 4.5 - 2.25x = 3.5 \Rightarrow -x = -1 \Rightarrow x = 1$. Therefore, the two quantities are equal, (C).

Alternatively, recognize that \$1.75 (the price per pound of the mix) is the average of \$1.25 and \$2.25, the price of peanuts and cashews, respectively. This means that there must be equal amounts of each in the mix.

And another alternative solution method is to work backwards. Assume that there is exactly one pound of peanuts in the mix. That would mean one pound of cashews, and the total cost of the mix would be $\$1.25 + \$2.25 = \$3.50$ for 2 pounds, or \$1.75 per pound. This proves that the mix contains one pound of peanuts.

8. **(A)** (p. 434) *Quantitative Reasoning/Arithmetic Comparison/Common Arithmetic Problems/Properties of Numbers*

Do the indicated operations: Quantity A equals $99 + 97 + 95 = 291$ and Quantity B equals $98 + 96 + 94 = 288$. Therefore, Quantity A is greater than Quantity B, (A).

Alternatively, make the comparison by reasoning that the largest odd integer less than 100, which is 99, is one more than the largest even integer less than 100, which is 98. Then, since the next less odd integer will be greater than the next less even integer and so on, the sum of the odd integers must be greater than the sum of the even integers.

9. **(C)** (p. 434) *Quantitative Reasoning/Data Analysis Comparison/Basic Descriptive Statistics/Quartiles and Interquartile Range*

The interquartile range is the difference between the first quartile and third quartile ($Q_3 - Q_1$). The first quartile is equal to the median of the lower half of the numbers. The median of the lower half of List A is the average of 0 and 4, or 2. The third quartile is equal to the median of the upper half of the numbers. The median of the upper half of List A is the average of 12 and 16, or 14. Therefore, the interquartile range is $14 - 2 = 12$. The second quartile of a list of numbers is the same number as the median of the list. For List B, the median is the middle value, or 12. Therefore, Quantity A is equal to Quantity B, (C).

10. **(B)** (p. 434) *Quantitative Reasoning/Arithmetic/Simple Manipulations*

$2 \cdot 10^4 = 20,000$, and $121,212 + 20,000 = 141,212$, (B).

11. ($\frac{9}{20}$) (p. 434) *Quantitative Reasoning/Arithmetic/Simple Manipulations*

The reciprocal of $\frac{4}{5}$ is $\frac{5}{4}$. And $\frac{5}{4} - \frac{4}{5} = \frac{25-16}{20} = \frac{9}{20}$.

12. **(E)** (p. 435) *Quantitative Reasoning/Arithmetic/Common Arithmetic Problems/Properties of Numbers*

As for (A), since k is less than l, k cannot be equal to l plus something. The same reasoning applies to (B), (C), and (D). (E), however, could be true. For example, if Jack is 5, Ken is 10, Larry is 15, and Mike is 20, then $5 + 20 = 10 + 15$.

13. **(A)** (p. 435) *Quantitative Reasoning/Algebra/Manipulation of Algebraic Expressions/Creating Algebraic Expressions* and *Geometry/Rectangles and Squares*

The perimeter is of a rectangle is the sum of the sides: $2(3a-2) + 2(2a-1) = 6a - 4 + 4a - 2 = 10a - 6$, (A).

14. **(A, C)** (p. 435) *Quantitative Reasoning/Data Analysis/Basic Descriptive Statistics/Standard Deviation*

For this item, test each answer choice independently. As for (A), since standard deviation is a measure of how far the data values are from the mean, if the standard deviation is 0, then all data values must be 0 units from the mean (they must equal the mean). Therefore, (A) must be true. As for (B), it could be true that all data values in the set are 0, but it does not have to be true. For example, a data set of {2, 2, 2, 2, 2} will have a standard deviation of 0. As for (C), the same reasoning applies to (C) as applies to (A): if the standard deviation is 0, then all data values must equal the mean.

15. **(B)** (p. 435) *Quantitative Reasoning/Arithmetic/Common Arithmetic Problems/Percents*

Since x is 80% of y, $x = 0.8y \Rightarrow y = \frac{x}{0.8} = 1.25x$. Therefore, y is 125% of x, (B).

16. **(D)** (p. 435) *Quantitative Reasoning/Algebra/Manipulation of Algebraic Expressions/Evaluating Expressions*

For this item, test each answer choice. As for (A), this proves that $m < n$, so (A) is wrong. As for (B), this proves nothing about m and n, since m and n might be either negative or positive, so (B) is wrong. The same is true of (C), which is equivalent to $m > -n$, so (C) is wrong. As for (D), rewrite $m - n > 0$ by adding n to both sides: $m > n$. So, (D) is correct. Finally, as for (E), this provides neither relative values for m and n nor their signs, so (E) is wrong.

17. **(E)** (p. 435) *Quantitative Reasoning/Algebra/Functions*

Do the indicated operation: $(-1.1)^2 = 1.21$, and the smallest integer greater than that is 2, (E).

18. **(B)** (p. 436) *Quantitative Reasoning/Data Interpretation/Table Charts*

In 1995, medical and dental care accounted for 4.0% of expenditures. Since the item specifically asks for an approximation, use $35,000 as the value of expenditures in 1995: $(0.04)(\$35,000) = \$1,400$, (B).

19. **(C)** (p. 436) *Quantitative Reasoning/Data Interpretation/Table Charts*

This item asks about percent increase, so use the "change-over-original" equation. In 1995, the expenditures were $35,000; in 1996, they were $40,000. Therefore, $\frac{\text{Change}}{\text{Original}} = \frac{\$40,000 - \$35,000}{\$35,000} = \frac{\$5,000}{\$35,000} \approx 14\%$, (C).

20. **(E)** (p. 436) *Quantitative Reasoning/Data Interpretation/Table Charts*

Rank order the categories in each year:

1995		1996	
1.	Rent	1.	Rent
2.	Food	2.	Food
3.	Clothing	3.	Clothing
4.	Automobile	4.	Automobile
5.	Utilities	5.	Utilities
6.	Savings	6.	Entertainment
7.	Entertainment	7.	Savings
8.	Medical, etc.	8.	Charity
9.	Charity	9.	Other
10.	Furnishings	10.	Medical, etc.
11.	Other	11.	Furnishings

From 1995 to 1996, six categories, (E), changed ranks: Savings, Entertainment, Medical, Charity, Furnishings, and Other.

21. **(E)** (p. 437) *Quantitative Reasoning/Geometry/Complex Figures* and *Circles*

First, find the area of the circle: $\pi r^2 = \pi(2)^2 = 4\pi$. Since the shaded area is equal to 3π, it accounts for $\frac{3\pi}{4\pi} = \frac{3}{4}$ of the circle. So, the unshaded area accounts for $\frac{1}{4}$ of the circle. This means that angle x plus the angle vertically opposite x are equal to $\frac{1}{4}(360°) = 90°$. So, $2x = 90$, and $x = 45$, (E).

22. **(D)** (p. 437) *Quantitative Reasoning/Arithmetic/Common Arithmetic Problems/Percents*

This item asks, "The tin is what percent of the whole bar?" Use the "is-over-of" equation:

$\frac{is}{of} = \frac{\%}{100} \Rightarrow \frac{100}{100+150} = \frac{x}{100} \Rightarrow x = \frac{100 \cdot 100}{250} = 40\%$, (D).

23. **(D)** (p. 437) *Quantitative Reasoning/Data Analysis/Basic Descriptive Statistics/Standard Deviation*

Standard deviation is a measure of the distance a list of data points are from the mean of that list. To calculate standard deviation, first find the mean of the data:

$$\frac{0(19) + 1(10) + 2(6) + 4(2) + 5(2) + 7(2) + 9(1) + 10(1) + 12(1)}{44} \approx 1.9$$

Then, sum the squares of the differences between each data point and the mean:

$$(19)(0-1.9)^2 + (10)(1-1.9)^2 + (6)(2-1.9)^2 + (2)(4-1.9)^2 + (2)(5-1.9)^2 + (2)(7-1.9)^2 + (9-1.9)^2 +$$
$$(10-1.9)^2 + (12-1.9)^2 = 374.84$$

Finally, divide by the total number of data points and take the square root: $\sqrt{\frac{374.84}{44}} \approx 2.9$, (D).

24. **(20)** (p. 437) *Quantitative Reasoning/Algebra/Manipulation of Algebraic Expressions/Evaluating Expressions*

Translate the item stem into an algebraic equation written in terms of the number of gallons that the fuel tank holds, x: $x - \frac{2}{5}x - 7 = \frac{1}{4}x \Rightarrow x - 7 = \frac{13}{20}x \Rightarrow \frac{7}{20}x = 7 \Rightarrow x = 20$.

25. **(C)** (p. 437) *Quantitative Reasoning/Data Analysis/Basic Descriptive Statistics/Quartiles and Interquartile Range*

The total number of commissions is 40, so there are 10 commissions in each group. The second quartile consists of the commissions from sales 11 through 20. Since Judy's sale is the second highest in the second quartile, then her commission would be 19 out of 40. If 4 more homes were sold with commissions less than the lowest commission in the second quartile, then this pushes her sale to 23 of 40. With 4 more commissions added to 40, each group now has 11 commissions. The second quartile consists of sales 12 through 22 and the third quartile consists of sales 23 through 33, so Judy's commission is now the lowest in the third quartile, (C).

Section 6—Quantitative Reasoning (p. 438)

1. **(A)** (p. 438) *Quantitative Reasoning/Geometry Comparison/Triangles/Properties of Triangles*

At first, it might seem that (D) is the correct choice because the left side of the figure is not fixed. In fact, the right part of the figure is a 3-4-5 triangle, and the area of just that part is $\frac{1}{2}(3)(4) = 6$. So, if the area of just part of the figure is equal to 6, the area of $\triangle ABC$ must be more than 6. Therefore, Quantity A is greater than Quantity B, (A).

2. **(A)** (p. 438) *Quantitative Reasoning/Arithmetic Comparison/Complicated Manipulations/Decimal-Fraction Equivalents*

0.667 is slightly larger than the repeating decimal $0.66\overline{6} = \frac{2}{3}$, and 0.166 is slightly smaller than the repeating decimal $0.16\overline{6} = \frac{1}{6}$, so Quantity A must be greater than Quantity B, (A).

3. **(D)** (p. 438) *Quantitative Reasoning/Arithmetic Comparison/Common Arithmetic Problems/Properties of Numbers*

The number of marbles in the jar is between 40 and 50, and the number is three more than a number divisible by 4. There are two numbers between 37 and 47 that are divisible by 4: 40 and 44. Therefore, the number of marbles could be either $40 + 3 = 43$ or $44 + 3 = 47$. So, the relationship between the two quantities cannot be determined, (D).

4. **(C)** (p. 439) *Quantitative Reasoning/Geometry Comparison/Circles*

Create expressions using r for radius: Quantity A equals $2(\pi r^2) = 2\pi r^2$ and Quantity B equals $\frac{\pi(2r)^2}{2} = 2\pi r^2$. Therefore, Quantity A is equal to Quantity B, (C).

5. **(A)** (p. 439) *Quantitative Reasoning/Arithmetic Comparison/Common Arithmetic Problems/Properties of Numbers*

$\overline{XY}$ is longer than $0.55 - 0.25 = 0.30$. Therefore, Quantity A is greater than Quantity B, (A).

6. **(D)** (p. 439) *Quantitative Reasoning/Data Analysis Comparison/Basic Descriptive Statistics/Mean*

The other numbers in the averages could be anything, so the comparison is indeterminate. Therefore, the relationship between the two quantities cannot be determined, (D).

7. **(B)** (p. 439) *Quantitative Reasoning/Algebra Comparison/Manipulation of Algebraic Expressions/Factoring Expressions*

The trick to solving this item is to factor the expression in Quantity A: $\frac{2x + 6y}{5} = \frac{2(x+3y)}{5} = \frac{2(6)}{5} = \frac{12}{5}$. Therefore, Quantity B is greater than Quantity A, (B).

8. **(D)** (p. 439) *Quantitative Reasoning/Algebra Comparison/Manipulation of Algebraic Expressions/ Evaluating Expressions*

   Although it is true that k might be larger than x (e.g., if $x = 2$, $y = 3$, and $k = 6$), it is also true that y might be 1, in which case x and k are equal: $x(1) = k$. Therefore, the relationship between the two quantities cannot be determined, (D).

9. **(D)** (p. 439) *Quantitative Reasoning/Geometry Comparison/Triangles/Properties of Triangles*

   While it is inferable that $x + y = 90$ and that $w + z = 90$, this is not sufficient to find a value for $x - y$ and $w - z$. Additionally, note that distortion of the figure causes the sizes of the angles change—x might be larger than y (in which case $x - y$ is positive), equal to y (in which case $x - y = 0$), or smaller than y (in which case $x - y$ is negative). Therefore, the relationship between the two quantities cannot be determined, (D).

10. **(A)** (p. 440) *Quantitative Reasoning/Geometry/Lines and Angles*

    According to the figure, $60 + x = 130$, so $x = 130 - 60 = 70$, (A).

11. **(13.5)** (p. 440) *Quantitative Reasoning/Data Analysis/Basic Descriptive Statistics/Quartiles and Interquartile Range*

    First, rearrange the numbers in order from least to greatest: 12, 13.5, 14, 15.5, 16, 17.5. The first quartile is equal to the median of the lower half of the numbers (12, 13.5, 14): 13.5.

12. **(B)** (p. 440) *Quantitative Reasoning/Arithmetic/Complicated Arithmetic Application Problems*

    There are a total of $5 + 12 + 13 = 30$ roles in the play, and 10 actors play two of these roles each. This leaves $30 - 2(10) = 10$ roles that must each be played by a different actor. Therefore, there are $10 + 10 = 20$ actors in the play, (B).

13. **(C)** (p. 440) *Quantitative Reasoning/Algebra/Manipulation of Algebraic Expressions/Evaluating Expressions*

    Substitute 10 for k in the given expression and evaluate it: $\frac{k^2}{20} + k = \frac{10^2}{20} + 10 = \frac{100}{20} + 10 = 15$, (C).

14. **(D)** (p. 441) *Quantitative Reasoning/Data Interpretation/Line Graphs*

    This item asks for percent increase, so use the "change-over-original" equation. In 1995, the earnings were $1.5 million, and in 1986, they were $0.3 million. Therefore, $\frac{\text{Change}}{\text{Original}} = \frac{\$1.5\text{ million} - \$0.3\text{ million}}{\$0.3\text{ million}} = 4$, or 400%, (D).

15. **(B)** (p. 441) *Quantitative Reasoning/Data Interpretation/Line Graphs*

    The trick to solving this item quickly is to notice that the y-axis of the right-hand "Earnings" graph is 10% of the y-axis of the left-hand "Sales" graph ($\frac{\$2.0\text{ million}}{\$20\text{ million}} = \frac{1}{10} = 10\%$). Therefore, every year that has earnings of at least 10% of sales will have a data point on the "Earnings" graph at the same point or higher than the corresponding point on the "Sales" graph. This is true for the following years: 1989, 1990, 1991, and 1994. Therefore, earnings were at least 10% of sales for 4 years, (B).

16. **(B)** (p. 441) *Quantitative Reasoning/Arithmetic/Common Arithmetic Problems/Properties of Numbers* and *Algebra/Solving Equations/One Equation with One Variable*

    Solve the given equation for x: $n = \frac{x}{12} + \frac{x}{12} + \frac{x}{12} + \frac{x}{12} \Rightarrow n = \frac{4x}{12} \Rightarrow n = \frac{x}{3} \Rightarrow x = 3n$. The item stem asks for the *least* possible value of x, so n must be its least possible value as well. Since n is a positive integer, its least possible value is 1. Therefore, the least possible value of x is $3(1) = 3$, (B).

17. (D) (p. 441) *Quantitative Reasoning/Arithmetic/Complicated Manipulations/Factoring*

The trick to solving this item quickly is to recognize that the expression is simplified by factoring:

$$\frac{10^3(10^5+10^5)}{10^4}=\frac{10^5+10^5}{10}=\frac{2(10^5)}{10}=\frac{2(10)(10^4)}{10}=2(10^4)\text{, (D)}.$$

18. (10) (p. 441) *Quantitative Reasoning/Arithmetic/Common Arithmetic Problems/Ratios* and *Algebra/Solving Equations/One Equation with One Variable*

Create an equation expressing the ratio as described in the item stem: $\frac{1}{100}=\frac{0.1}{x}$. Now, solve for x:

$$\frac{1}{100}=\frac{0.1}{x}\Rightarrow x=(0.1)(100)=10.$$

19. (C) (p. 442) *Quantitative Reasoning/Arithmetic/Simple Manipulations*

Notice that the directions for items #19-20 specifically state that the letters on the number line represent a series of consecutive integers. Therefore, $y-w$ is the difference between two numbers 2 units apart on the number line, that is, 2, (C).

20. (E) (p. 442) *Quantitative Reasoning/Algebra/Manipulation of Algebraic Expressions/Evaluating Expressions*

Rewrite x and z in the given expression in terms of v. Since the letters represent consecutive integers, $x=v+2$ and $z=v+4$. Therefore, $v+x+z=v+(v+2)+(v+4)=3v+6$, (E).

21. (D) (p. 442) *Quantitative Reasoning/Data Analysis/Basic Descriptive Statistics/Standard Deviation*

Determine which segments of the graph corresponds to a score range of 80-88. A standard deviation of 0 corresponds to the mean, which is 75.4. Each increment on the chart corresponds to 0.5 units of standard deviation, or $\frac{8.2}{2}=4.1$. A score of 80 corresponds to $80-75.4=4.6$, or slightly more than 0.5 standard deviation above the mean. A score of 88 corresponds to $88-75.4=12.6$, or slightly more than 1.5 standard deviations above the mean. Therefore, the percentage of students expected to receive a score between 80 and 88 falls between 0.5 standard deviation from the mean to 1.5 standard deviations from the mean. Add the percentages from those ranges on the chart: $15.0\%+9.2\%=24.2\%$. There are 273 students in total, so $(0.242)(273)=66.066\approx66$ students, (D), can expect to receive a score between 80 and 88.

22. (A) (p. 442) *Quantitative Reasoning/Algebra/Functions*

Since $7+1=8$, which is an even number, use the first defined function: $\clubsuit(x)=x^2\Rightarrow\clubsuit(8)=(8)^2=64$, (A).

23. (E) (p. 443) *Quantitative Reasoning/Arithmetic/Common Arithmetic Problems/Proportions and Direct-Inverse Variation*

The more eggs that are used, the more servings that are produced, so use a direct proportion:

$$\frac{2\text{ eggs}}{x\text{ eggs}}=\frac{8\text{ servings}}{12\text{ servings}}\Rightarrow x=\frac{2\text{ eggs}\cdot12\text{ servings}}{8\text{ servings}}=\frac{24\text{ eggs}}{8}=3\text{ eggs},\text{ (E)}.$$

24. **(80)** (p. 443) *Quantitative Reasoning/Geometry/Lines and Angles* and *Triangles/Properties of Triangles*

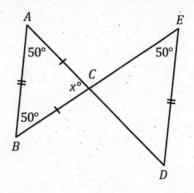

Since $\overline{ED} \parallel \overline{AB}$, $\angle E = \angle B = 50°$ (alternate interior angles). Since $\overline{AC} = \overline{BC}$, $\angle A = \angle B = 50°$. (In a triangle opposite equal sides are equal angles.) In $\triangle ABC$, $50 + 50 + x = 180 \Rightarrow x = 80$.

25. **(B)** (p. 443) *Quantitative Reasoning/Arithmetic/Common Arithmetic Problems/Percents*

Since S is 150% of T, $S = 1.5T$. Therefore, $\dfrac{T}{S+T} = \dfrac{T}{1.5T + T} = \dfrac{T}{2.5T} = \dfrac{1}{\frac{5}{2}} = \dfrac{2}{5} = 40\%$, (B).

PRACTICE TEST III

Answer Keys

Section 3—Verbal Reasoning (p. 449)

1. E	6. B, E	11. D	16. A, E	21. B
2. C	7. D	12. D	17. A	22. C, D
3. A	8. A, E	13. A, C	18. E	23. A, D
4. A	9. C	14. A, D	19. B	24. B, D
5. A, F	10. A	15. E	20. A	25. B, D

Section 4—Verbal Reasoning (p. 457)

1. A, F	6. E	11. B, D	16. A	21. C
2. C, E	7. A, C	12. C	17. B	22. B
3. D, F	8. C	13. B	18. C, D, G	23. B
4. B, D	9. A	14. A	19. C, D	24. A
5. A, F	10. E	15. C	20. D	25. C

Section 5—Quantitative Reasoning (p. 465)

1. C	6. D	11. B	16. D	21. C
2. C	7. C	12. E	17. E	22. C
3. A	8. D	13. B	18. E	23. 1800
4. A	9. A	14. A	19. B	24. D
5. D	10. D	15. 27	20. E	25. D

Section 6—Quantitative Reasoning (p. 473)

1. C	6. C	11. B	16. B	21. 72
2. D	7. B	12. 9	17. E	22. C
3. D	8. C	13. A	18. C	23. C
4. B	9. B	14. C	19. C	24. B
5. B	10. C	15. 150	20. E	25. A

Section 1—Analytical Writing (p. 447)

Analyze an Issue **Sample Essay Response**

Providing a public school education to children is one of the most important functions of government because most children (except those in private schools) have to attend public school until they are at least 16 years old. Children are in school several hours every day, so the content of the curriculum influences them in some important ways. But what should be the limits of a public school curriculum in a democracy where freedom of conscience is so important?

On the one hand, it might be thought that the sole function of public schools should be to teach academic and practical skills and to avoid ethical issues altogether. Certainly, government through public education should avoid dictating religious views. It is no business of the schools to tell children that they should be Protestant, Catholic, Jewish, Muslim, or any other religion. And related issues such as abortion and sexual activity should be left to parents.

On the other hand, it seems impossible to avoid such issues altogether. While it might be possible to teach pure math without ethical overtones, history and even literature are about human activities. It is impossible to teach about the Holocaust without saying that it was morally wrong. Teaching the history of western expansion would be one-sided if it did not raise questions about the actions of the white settlers. Hamlet would not be Hamlet without the dilemma of "to be or not to be." And even in the so-called *hard* sciences, questions about the environment and the appropriate use of and conservation of resources raise ethical issues that just cannot be avoided. Biology and human reproduction are legitimate academic subjects that also start to raise ethical questions including evolution.

It is easy in theory to say that government should not be in the business of teaching ethics in the public schools. But in practice, the ethical issues are impossible to avoid. Instead of pretending that schools can avoid morality altogether, we should insist that when such issues come up, they are presented from a variety of perspectives so that children are exposed to different viewpoints but not told what to believe.

Section 2—Analytical Writing (p. 448)

Analyze an Argument **Sample Essay Response**

The argument is interesting but not entirely persuasive. It will obviously appeal to many people who uncritically accept the idea that *computers* are a silver bullet for all of our educational woes. A closer look, however, shows that much more would be needed to support the conclusion.

First, it is necessary to determine in what respects, if any, the education at Hudson Falls School is deficient. The argument does not say that students at Hudson Falls are prevented from going to college because they do not learn about computers. For all we know, Hudson Falls already has all of the computer equipment that it needs and gives its students instruction in computers. Additionally, the number of students who go to college is not the only measure of a school's effectiveness. Not every student wants to go to college. It would also be important to learn whether Hudson Falls effectively serves the needs of students who want vocational training using computers.

Second, it would be important to ask whether or not the computers used at Fort Ann School made the difference in the number of college-bound students. Perhaps Fort Ann already had enough computers to begin with, and the twelve new computers were really just extra resources that did not have a real impact. And what was taught during the two hours of computer instruction? Word processing, graphics, bookkeeping, internet research? Some computer skills are more relevant to college preparation than others. Nothing in the argument draws a causal connection between the computer instruction and the number of students going to college.

Third, it is necessary to consider what would be the overall effect of investing in new computer equipment and requiring computer study. We do not know anything about the size of the student body at Hudson Falls School, but new computer equipment may mean a substantial investment compared to the overall budget. That could mean money not available for texts, library books, newspaper subscriptions, field trips, and even sports. Additionally, time spent in a computer lab is time not spent learning a second language or working in the chemistry lab. These other activities may be even more important for college preparation than learning a little about computers.

In summary, the argument fails to prove the conclusion. It does not establish that there is a problem at Hudson Falls; it does not identify the real cause of the supposed problem; and it does not consider the overall effect of spending more money on computers. The word "computers" has a nice ring to it; but a lot more research would have to be done before it could be concluded that new computers and required courses are needed at Hudson Falls School.

Section 3—Verbal Reasoning (p. 449)

1. **(E)** (p. 449) *Verbal Reasoning/Reading Comprehension/Specific Detail*

   This item stem includes the thought-reverser "EXCEPT," so the correct choice is NOT explicitly mentioned in the passage. Although the word "galaxy" is used in the passage, the author does not say that supernovas are caused by colliding galaxies, (E).

2. **(C)** (p. 449) *Verbal Reasoning/Reading Comprehension/Implied Idea*

   The key word in line 33 is "anomalous." The author states that the unexpected makeup of the meteorites is evidence that a supernova helped form our solar system. However, this evidence supports the conclusion only if the strange content is foreign to our solar system, (C). None of the other choices explains the connection between the theory of the origin of our solar system and the strange makeup of the meteorites.

3. **(A)** (p. 450) *Verbal Reasoning/Critical Reading/The Inference/Either-Or Situation*

   Eliminate (D) and (E) because the argument is not based on analogy, nor does it include a generalization. The remaining choices, (A), "dilemma," (B), "contradiction," and (C), "paradox," are close in meaning and share a common logical feature: each involves a pair of ideas. "Dilemma," (A), is the best description because the argument describes two possible courses of action, neither of which is a satisfactory choice. On the one hand, the university cannot suppress ideas without failing in its function. On the other hand, the university does not want to encourage the expression of totalitarian ideas that are opposed to its function. This "damned if you do, and damned if you don't" situation is the defining characteristic of a dilemma. A contradiction, on the other hand, is simply the conjunction of two statements, one of which is the negative of the other: "I will go, but I will not go." A paradox is a special logical form, a statement that is seemingly contradictory or opposed to common sense. The most famous example of which is the Liar's Paradox: "The sentence you are now reading is false."

4. **(A)** (p. 450) *Verbal Reasoning/Critical Reading/The Assumptions* and *The Inference/Analogy*

   The conclusion of this argument is based on the analogy between watching television at school and at home; the assumption is that the two situations are analogous. The argument addresses a concern voiced by some parents and teachers about commercial television in schools and states that students already understand the difference between commercials and programming. However, this argument depends on the unsupported assumption that the student will be able to apply that distinction in the classroom situation. It might be argued on the other side that students have been taught to accept information provided in a classroom setting and that they will not be able to draw the distinction as easily. So, the argument is logically committed to the idea expressed by (A). (B) is wrong because the argument assumes that indoctrination will not be a necessary consequence of the news program (not that educators are willing to accept the indoctrination). (C) is wrong because the argument is not committed to any comparison between print and television advertising. (D) and (E) are both wrong because the argument is not committed to one viewpoint or the other on the effectiveness of the program.

5. **(A, F)** (p. 450) *Verbal Reasoning/Sentence Completion/Combined Reasoning/Punctuation* and *Phrases*

The sentence starts with the thought reverser "Despite," so the correct choice for the first blank will describe something unexpected given the amount of money invested. Eliminate (B), "bombastic," and (C), "suspicious," because neither creates a meaningful phrase when substituted into the first blank. Therefore, (A), "primitive," is the correct choice for the first blank. The second blank will be a logical continuation of "inconvenience." Eliminate (D) and (E) because neither creates a meaningful phrase when substituted into the second blank. Therefore, (F), "retards," is the correct choice for the second blank.

6. **(B, E)** (p. 450) *Verbal Reasoning/Sentence Completion/Combined Reasoning/Key Adjectives and Adverbs* and *Phrases*

Two key logical signals are important to understanding the overall structure of the sentence. The first blank needs a word that extends the idea of vagueness. The second blank is "unlike" the first and must therefore be something close to an opposite. "Extraneous," (A), "obscure," (B), and "trivial," (C), could all be used to describe images, but only "obscure," (B), parallels "vague." For the second blank, "concrete," (E), is an opposite of "obscure" and completes the sentence logically. "Virulent," (D), and "pallid," (F), do not create meaningful descriptions of images.

7. **(D)** (p. 451) *Verbal Reasoning/Sentence Completion/Combined Reasoning/Key Adjectives and Adverbs*

The correct choice for the blank will be something that extends the idea of "personal," and reverses the idea of "godless." Eliminate (A) because it is illogical to say that people need a personal sense of "morbidity." Eliminate (B), (C), and (E) because it is counterintuitive to say that people would need a personal sense of "despair," "guilt," or "alienation" in a godless universe—in fact, these feelings are exactly what the sentence suggests people are trying to avoid. Therefore, by the process of elimination, (D), "spirituality," is the correct choice. Indeed, it makes sense to say, "people need to feel a personal sense of spirituality in a godless universe."

8. **(A, E)** (p. 451) *Verbal Reasoning/Paragraph Completion/Combined Reasoning/Phrases*

The sentence is discussing the wisdom of making predictions about the future of China. The first sentence states that there are two equally likely outcomes. A fifty-fifty outcome is not readily predictable; it could go either way. "Prognostication," (A), which means "forecasting" or "predicting," is therefore the best choice for the first blank. The second blank must be filled by a word that describes the outcome of being proved wrong. (D) and (E) do not create meaningful statements when substituted in the second blank. "Embarrassed," (E), is the best choice for the second blank.

9. **(C)** (p. 451) *Logical Reasoning/Inductive Argument/The Assumptions/Attacking Arguments*

The conclusion of the argument implies that student will eat more healthy foods. The evidence, however, proves only that students will buy more healthy foods. There is obviously a large gap between "buying" and "eating." (C) correctly points out this hidden assumption and undermines it. (A) is wrong because, while it is probably true that some people will not eat broccoli but will eat cauliflower, and others will not eat the cauliflower but will eat broccoli, this fact does not undermine the evidence (in general, students will buy more good foods) nor the conclusion. (B) is wrong because, if anything, it strengthens the argument by neutralizing a possible objection to the plan: too costly. (D) is wrong because it merely repeats something that is explicitly stated by the behaviorist; the lack of greater precision does not mean that the increases within that range were not realized. Finally, (E) is a minor objection, tantamount to saying, "We can't create a perfect plan, so we shouldn't do anything at all."

10. **(A)** (p. 452) *Verbal Reasoning/Reading Comprehension/Logical Structure*

In the third paragraph, the author cites the ICC to make the point that antitrust policy, because it is not direct government intervention, does not require a large bureaucracy. Then, the author mentions that the ICC does have a large bureaucracy. This example helps prove the point that antitrust policy does not require as large a bureaucracy. Therefore, (A) is the best choice. (B), (C), and (D) are all wrong because, while each is an idea found at various points in the passage, these choices are unresponsive to the question asked.

Finally, (E) is wrong because, while the ICC is an example of a government agency that intervenes directly, this is not the author's main point in citing the ICC example. (A) better explains why the author mentions the ICC.

11. (D) (p. 452) *Verbal Reasoning/Reading Comprehension/Attitude-Tone*

In the first paragraph, the author outlines the basic philosophy of antitrust policy and notes that it avoids the "politically hazardous thicket" of direct intervention. This is a positive attitude. In the third paragraph, the author discusses advantages of antitrust policy (it is not a large bureaucracy) and some disadvantages (antitrust policy is not an exact science). Therefore, it is inferable that the author's attitude is a positive one tempered by the realization that antitrust policy is not perfect. (D) best describes this attitude.

12. (D) (p. 452) *Verbal Reasoning/Reading Comprehension/Specific Detail*

This item stem includes the thought-reverser "EXCEPT," so the correct choice is NOT explicitly mentioned in the passage. The author never mentions high industry profits, (D), as desirable from a public policy standpoint. The remaining choices are all mentioned in the first sentence of the passage as desirable qualities of economic performance.

13. (A, C) (p. 453) *Verbal Reasoning/Reading Comprehension/Specific Detail*

This item includes directions to select all correct answers, so evaluate each answer choice individually. In the second paragraph, the author mentions both price-fixing agreements, (A), and predatory pricing practices, (C), as behavior that compromises performance. The author does not mention "outsourcing," (B).

14. (A, D) (p. 453) *Verbal Reasoning/Paragraph Completion/Combined Reasoning/Phrases*

The first sentence explains that modernism was a response to the exigencies of the Great Depression. People purchased less costly products. The best description offered for this "spirit" is "frugal," (A), which means "thrifty." The third sentence contrasts the "undecorated movement" with any established school of design. The "undecorated movement" opposes formality and is therefore a democratic sort of design movement. Democracy, of course, refers to the people, and so "populist," (D), is a good description of the "undecorated movement."

15. (E) (p. 453) *Verbal Reasoning/Sentence Completion/Combined Reasoning/Phrases*

The phrase "in fact" in the second part of the sentence signals that the theory of the breakup of the continents has somehow changed. Look for the opposite of "occurring in stages" or something close to it. Therefore, "cataclysmically," (E), is the best choice because it reverses the idea that the continents broke up in stages.

16. (A, E) (p. 453) *Verbal Reasoning/Sentence Completion/Combined Reasoning/Phrases*

Two key logical signals are important to understanding the overall structure of the sentence. The sentence says that the lawyer argues only what is central, eliminating something. Logically, what is eliminated is what is not central, so look for a word that means not central. "Extraneous," (A), which means "irrelevant," best communicates this idea. As for the second blank, eliminate (D) and (F) because it doesn't make sense to say that the lawyer would not want to "amuse" or "initiate" her client. Therefore, (E) is the correct choice for the second blank. Indeed, it is logical to say that the lawyer would not want to "jeopardize" her client.

17. (A) (p. 454) *Verbal Reasoning/Reading Comprehension/Main Idea*

The author begins by citing the NICB study. The study found correlations between concentration and productivity and between size and productivity. This prompted the NICB and the magazine to conclude that concentration and size equal efficiency. In the second paragraph, the author attacks the study's claim that concentration is correlated with productivity; and in the third paragraph, the author attacks the study's claim that size is correlated with productivity. In the final paragraph, the author directly contradicts the claim that size means efficiency. (A) best describes this development. (B) and (C) are both wrong because each overstates a point made by the author. Even if they weren't overstated, neither could be considered the overall theme of the passage. Finally, (D) and (E) are both wrong because each is only a small point made in the passage.

18. **(E)** (p. 454) *Verbal Reasoning/Reading Comprehension/Implied Idea*

The author mentions (A), (B), (C), and (D) in the second paragraph. Lines 24–26 state that entry barriers are low because the industries are labor intensive, (A). Lines 22–24 convey that many of the "low-productivity" industries are unconcentrated and have low capital requirements for entry, (B) and (D). Lines 27–32 mention textiles and apparel as examples of industries with low productivity as defined by the study, that is, low shipments per employee, (C). Thus, by process of elimination, (E) is correct.

19. **(B)** (p. 455) *Verbal Reasoning/Reading Comprehension/Specific Detail*

This item includes directions to select all correct answers, so evaluate each answer choice individually. In the third paragraph, the author objects that the study included smaller firms that should not have been taken into account. (Those firms really should be classified as belonging to a different industry.) Thus, (B) is specifically mentioned in the selection. As for (A), the author does single out the consumer goods industries, but he does not say the study failed to include those industries. As for (C), it is the author of this selection (not the study) that compares large firms with medium-sized firms.

20. **(A)** *Verbal Reasoning/Reading Comprehension/Specific Detail*

The last two sentences of the second paragraph specifically make the point suggested by (A). The other choices make statements that are to be found in the selection (made by the author or by the study), but those choices are not responsive to this question.

21. **(B)** (p. 455) *Verbal Reasoning/Reading Comprehension/Attitude-Tone*

Eliminate (A) and (E) because, in the last paragraph, the author offers evidence that he or she believes deals the deathblow to the idea that size equals efficiency. Eliminate (C) and (D) because the author disagrees with both the methodology and the conclusion of the study. Therefore, by the process of elimination, (B) is the correct choice. Indeed, "conclusively disproved" best describes the author's attitude regarding the NICB study's conclusions.

22. **(C, D)** (p. 455) *Verbal Reasoning/Sentence Equivalence/Thought Extension/Phrases*

The phrase following the comma adds further description of the word that will fill the blank: erased and overwritten. A "palimpsest," (C), is a writing surface (like parchment) that is used repeatedly. And "superimposition," (D), conveys the idea of overlaying. Note that (A), "tournament," is wrong because it has no equivalent answer choice.

23. **(A, D)** (p. 455) *Verbal Reasoning/Sentence Equivalence/Thought Extension/Phrases*

The phrasing following the comma defines the word to complete the blank as "balance." "Equipoise," (A), means in a state of balance, and "stasis," (D), is a state of balance or equilibrium.

24. **(B, D)** (p. 456) *Verbal Reasoning/Sentence Equivalence/Thought Reversal/Key Adjectives and Adverbs*

The sentence creates a contrast between the supremely confident version of the professor and some other characteristic. "Diffidence," (B), means lacking confidence. Similarly, "modesty," (D), meaning a lack of boastfulness, contrasts with the exhibition of supreme confidence.

25. **(B, D)** (p. 456) *Verbal Reasoning/Sentence Equivalence/Thought Extension/Phrases*

The phrase "excessive moderation" indicates that the military leaders did not give Bismarck unqualified support. Both "suspicion," (B), and "skepticism," (D), convey the idea that support was tempered by concern. Note that "admiration," (A), and "respect," (E), while close in meaning, do not best describe someone seen as "excessive."

Section 4—Verbal Reasoning (p. 457)

1. **(A, F)** (p. 457) *Verbal Reasoning/Sentence Equivalence/Thought Reversal/Coordinate Conjunctions*

   The sentence creates a contrast between the results of a system that is productive and economically efficient and a system that is more oriented toward human needs and concerns. "Devoid," (A), and "bereft," (F), both mean "lacking."

2. **(C, E)** (p. 457) *Verbal Reasoning/Sentence Equivalence/Thought Extension/Phrases*

   The key to this sentence is "formidable temper." Both "irascible," (C), and "choleric," (E), describe someone with a temper. Note that while "garrulous," (A), and "loquacious," (B), are close in meaning, they do not describe someone with a "formidable temper."

3. **(D, F)** (p. 457) *Verbal Reasoning/Sentence Equivalence/Combined Reasoning/Coordinate Conjunctions* and *Phrases*

   The sentence sets up a parallel between economic and political activities, and the word that fills the blank must refer to economic activities that are similar to political activities. "Analog," (D), and "counterpart," (F), refer to activities that are similar in function though belong to a different sphere.

4. **(B, D)** (p. 457) *Verbal Reasoning/Sentence Equivalence/Thought Extension/Key Adjectives and Adverbs*

   "Tribulation," (B), and "travail," (D), have the advantage of suggesting illness, suffering, and death. And "tribulation" and "travail" are close in meaning. Note that "encounter," (C), is wrong because it lacks the dire overtones.

5. **(A, F)** (p. 458) *Verbal Reasoning/Sentence Equivalence/Thought Reversal/Phrases*

   The sentence sets up a contrast between the common experience of the African countries, which would support generalizations, and a limit on the commonality of that experience. The opposite of "common" and "general" would be something "unusual," unique," or "special." "Divergent," (A), and "disparate," (F), are appropriate substitutes.

6. **(E)** (p. 458) *Verbal Reasoning/Reading Comprehension/Specific Detail*

   In the first paragraph, the author specifically states that the founders regarded education as a political necessity, not as a means to gain knowledge or a skill. So you can eliminate all choices but (E). The obligation was political, not religious, (A), and was therefore a public obligation, not a private matter, (B). As an obligation, it was a matter of necessity, not a luxury, (C), and not a matter of choice, (D).

7. **(A, C)** (p. 458) *Verbal Reasoning/Reading Comprehension/Further Application*

   There is ample support for (A), patriotic and civic virtues, and (C), principles of American government, in the first two paragraphs. As for (B), the first paragraph specifically states that at that time education would not have included occupational training. Therefore, only (A) and (C) are correct.

8. **(C)** (p. 459) *Verbal Reasoning/Reading Comprehension/Specific Detail*

   In the middle of the last paragraph, the author states that textbooks did not change during the first half of the nineteenth century. So you can eliminate (A). As for (D) and (E), these ideas are not specifically mentioned, so neither can be the correct answer to a Specific Detail question. Finally, (B) represents a confused reading of the last paragraph. The author says that liberty was even more revered in later books, not that it was first mentioned in later books.

9. **(A)** (p. 459) *Verbal Reasoning/Reading Comprehension/Implied Idea*

   In the second paragraph, the author states that the textbook writers, most of whom were Puritans, believed that political virtue rests upon moral and religious precepts. Therefore, it is inferable that other Puritans would agree that moral and religious values are the foundation of civic virtue, (A). The remaining choices are wrong because they are not supported by the passage.

10. **(E)** (p. 459) *Verbal Reasoning/Critical Reading/The Assumptions* and *The Inference/Cause and Effect Situation*

Hawkins explains the structure at Stonehenge by reference to the intentions of the builders. (E) most seriously weakens the argument by suggesting a different explanation: the viewing lines are merely a coincidence. As for (A), it is a weak attack on the argument: people might construct something with astronomical significance even if they did not worship heavenly bodies. (B) is not much of an attack on the argument, for even if true, it does not mean that Hawkins is wrong. (C) is wrong because the passage states that Hawkins used the "positions of the stars, planets, and the sun at the time the structure was built," rather than their positions in the present day. Thus, Hawkins accounted for the fact that their positions have changed over time. Finally, (D) is wrong for the same reason as (B).

11. **(B, D)** (p. 460) *Verbal Reasoning/Paragraph Completion/Combined Reasoning/Phrases* and *Key Adjectives and Adverbs*

The paragraph describes the founding of the Socialist International. The author refers to the organization as "peaceable" and notes that it hoped to use international cooperation to overcome the rancor of nationalism. "Parochial," (B), the secondary meaning of which is "very limited or narrow in scope or outlook," suggests a contrast to the idea of an international movement. As for the second blank, the author refers to the ideas advanced as "ambitious schemes," so a good description would be "extravagant," (D).

12. **(C)** (p. 460) *Verbal Reasoning/Sentence Completion/Thought Extension/Subordinate Conjunctions*

In this item, the subordinate conjunction "because" signals a thought extension: the missing word must extend the first half of the sentence by explaining why hot milk has been a cure for insomnia. Since "soporific," (C), means "tending to induce sleep," it is clearly the right answer.

13. **(B)** (p. 460) *Verbal Reasoning/Sentence Completion/Thought Extension/Phrases*

In this item, the phrase "due to" signals a thought extension: first, they said it was due to this; then, later, they said it was due to that. The blank must be filled with a word that results in a phrase that means something similar to "due to." "Ascribed," (B), is the only choice that creates a phrase that functions similarly to "due to."

14. **(A)** (p. 461) *Verbal Reasoning/Reading Comprehension/Implied Idea*

The word *inferred* signals that this is an Implied Idea question, so the correct conclusion will not have been specifically stated in the passage, but it will be deducible from the information provided by the author. The correct answer is (A). In the third paragraph, the author states that the physical effects of tardive dyskinesia are slight, but patients are bothered by the effects and the abnormal movements may hinder social adjustment. We may infer, therefore, that the most serious problem is psychological. Given this, we can easily eliminate (D), the only other likely choice. As for (B), long-term use is the cause of tardive dyskinesia, not one of its effects. As for (C), tardive dyskinesia results from dopamine hypersensitivity, not addiction. (E) is incorrect since an inability to remain in therapy is not mentioned as an effect of tardive dyskinesia.

15. **(C)** (p. 461) *Verbal Reasoning/Reading Comprehension/Implied Idea*

The author does not specifically describe the mechanism by which neuroleptic drugs have their effect, but a conclusion about that mechanism can be deduced. The second paragraph describes the functioning of neuroleptic drugs: they interfere with the action of dopamine by binding to the dopamine receptors. It is inferable that this means the drugs block the receptors so the dopamine cannot be absorbed, (C). (A) is wrong because the passage does not state that less dopamine is produced, only that the existing dopamine is rendered relatively ineffective. (B) is wrong because neuroleptic drugs block the absorption of dopamine by the nerve cells, not the impulses going to the muscles. (D) is wrong because hypersensitivity to dopamine is an unwanted side effect of the drugs, not the method by which psychosis is controlled. Finally,

(E) is wrong because the passage describes the operation of the drugs in terms of dopamine, a chemical produced by the brain itself, not another drug introduced from outside the body.

16. **(A)** (p. 461) *Verbal Reasoning/Reading Comprehension/Attitude-Tone*

In the final paragraph the author suggests that a new drug, sulpiride, might be effective in controlling tardive dyskinesia, but he notes that it is not yet clear whether it will be effective over the long run. (A) is the best description of this treatment of the topic.

17. **(B)** (p. 461) *Verbal Reasoning/Reading Comprehension/Logical Structure*

The second paragraph begins with a discussion of the effect of neuroleptic drugs. At the end of the first sentence, the author states that dopamine is considered a likely cause of schizophrenia. Then, in the second sentence, the author says that large doses of amphetamines cause the secretion of dopamine and are associated with psychosis. It is inferable that the author mentions the effect of amphetamines in order to show that dopamine is related to schizophrenia. Note that lines 20–22 are sufficient to establish that dopamine release is a factor in the development of schizophrenia, so (B) is the best choice.

18. **(C, D, G)** (p. 462) *Verbal Reasoning/Paragraph Completion/Combined Reasoning/Phrases*

The paragraph describes a cycle of musical invention. The first version of a style is "pure" and vital. Then, it is watered down to create the second version; to create the third version, a new group takes over. The first blank must be filled with a word that suggests that the music is watered down. "Adulterate," (C), meaning "dilute," is the best choice for the first blank. The second blank is governed by a contrast: this rather than that. The best contrast to "edification," which means "instruction" or "enlightenment," is "diversion," (D). As for the third blank, the new group takes over, and they are "upstarts." Of the three choices, "rebellious," (G), is the best way to describe "upstarts."

19. **(C, D)** (p. 462) *Verbal Reasoning/Sentence Completion/Combined Reasoning/Subordinate Conjunctions* and *Key Adjectives and Adverbs*

Two key logical signals are important to understanding the overall structure of the sentence. First, the subordinate conjunction "although" signals a thought reversal: the first part of the sentence contrasts with the second part of the sentence. Second, the coordinate conjunction "and" (two instances) signals a thought extension: the first blank must be filled with a word that parallels the idea of "seriousness." Eliminate (A), "levity," and (B), "fragility," because neither provides such parallels. The second blank must be filled with a word that parallels the idea of "naïve." Eliminate (E), "grave," and (F), "macabre," because neither relates to being naïve. Therefore, by the process of elimination, (C) and (D) are the correct choices. Indeed, Mozart's musical "sophistication" contrasts with his being "uncouth."

20. **(D)** (p. 462) *Verbal Reasoning/Sentence Completion/Combined Reasoning/Coordinate Conjunctions*

This item is characterized by both a thought-reverser clue and a thought-extender clue. First, the "but" signals a contrast between "benefits" and the word to be put in the blank to describe the side-effects. "Adverse," (D), is a good opposite to "beneficial." Second, the relative clause introduced by "that" explains that the side-effects are ones that pose risks. Again, "adverse" nicely describes the sort of outcome.

21. **(C)** (p. 462) *Verbal Reasoning/Critical Reading/The Assumptions* and *The Inference/Analogy*

The argument is saying that "earn your age" is the standard in England and concludes on that basis that MBAs are paid less in England. The fallacy is that there is a big difference between earning 26,000 dollars and 26,000 pounds—as (C) correctly points out.

22. **(B)** (p. 463) *Verbal Reasoning/Critical Reading/The Conclusion*

The argument points out that United States forces were approximately equal to those of the Soviet Union but goes on to note that total United States and NATO forces were superior to total Soviet Union and Warsaw Pact forces. For this to be true, it must be the case that non-U.S. NATO forces were greater than non-Soviet Warsaw Pact Forces, (B). (A) is wrong because simple military superiority may not be sufficient to win a war. (C) is wrong because it misconstrues the comparison. (D) is wrong because it goes beyond the scope of the argument. Finally, (E) is wrong because it is only inferable from the premise that one group of countries was militarily superior to another group, not that the first group was numerically superior to the second.

23. **(B)** (p. 463) *Verbal Reasoning/Reading Comprehension/Implied Idea*

In the first and second paragraphs, the author discusses the effect of drunk driving laws. He or she states that after the implementation of the Road Safety Act in Britain, motor vehicle fatalities fell considerably. On this basis, we infer that the RSA was a law aimed at drunk driving. We can eliminate (D) and (E) on this ground. (C) can be eliminated since it is not clear whether the number of arrests increased. Equally consistent with the passage is the conclusion that the number of arrests dropped because people were no longer driving while intoxicated. (B) and (A) are fairly close since both describe the RSA as a law aimed at drunk driving. But the last sentence of the first paragraph calls for (B) over (A). As people learned that they would not get caught for drunk driving, the law became less effective. This suggests that the RSA made drunk driving illegal, not that it lowered the BAC required for conviction. This makes sense of the sentence "they could drink and not be stopped." If (A) were correct, this sentence would have to read, "they could drink the same amount and not be convicted."

24. **(A)** (p. 464) *Verbal Reasoning/Reading Comprehension/Further Application*

In the third paragraph, the author states that increased taxation on alcohol would tax the heaviest drinkers most, but the author notes that it would also penalize the moderate and light drinker. In other words, the remedy is not sufficiently focused on the problem. In the second paragraph, the author notes that drunk driving laws are aimed at the specific problem drivers. It is inferable from this that the author would likely advocate drunk driving laws over taxation because the former is aimed only at those who abuse alcohol, (A). (B) is wrong because the author never suggests that taxation is likely to be more effective in solving the problem. (C) is wrong because the author never raises the issue of personal liberty in conjunction with the breath alcohol test. (D) is wrong because the author does not discount entirely the effectiveness of measures against drunk driving. Even the British example gives some support to the conclusion that such laws have an effect. Finally, (E) is wrong because the author never mentions the expense or administrative feasibility of breath alcohol tests.

25. **(C)** (p. 464) *Verbal Reasoning/Reading Comprehension/Logical Structure*

The author argues that although criminalizing driving while alcohol impaired may make philosophical sense, it isn't as effective as people would hope. This is supported with the British experience. Once people realize that the chances of being caught are relatively small, they will drink and drive, (C). (A) is wrong because the passage does not support the conclusion that the problem is any worse or any better in one country or the other. (B) is wrong because this statement is the conclusion the author is arguing against. (D) is wrong because the author is not discussing the effectiveness of taxation in citing the British example. Finally, (E) is wrong because, while the author would likely accept this statement, it is not the reason for the author's introduction of the British example.

Section 5—*Quantitative Reasoning* (p. 465)

1. **(C)** (p. 465) *Quantitative Reasoning/Arithmetic Comparison/Common Arithmetic Problems/Percents*

You can, if you need to, work out the math to find p:

$AV = p\%$ of FMV
$6,000 = p\%$ of $240,000$
$p = 0.025 = 2.5\%$

So the assessed value of a property with a fair market value of \$300,000 is:

$0.025 \cdot 300,000 = 7,500$

Or you could reason that 300,000 is 125% of 240,000, and 125% of 6,000 is 7,500. In no case should you pick (D), as there is sufficient information for a calculation.

2. **(C)** (p. 466) *Quantitative Reasoning/Geometry Comparison/Triangles/45°-45°-90° Triangles*

The hypotenuse of the right triangle is the diameter of the circle, and the diameter's length measures:

$C = \pi d$
$4\pi = \pi d$
$d = 4$

Since ABC is an isosceles right triangle, AB and BC each have a length of $\frac{1}{2} \cdot 4 \cdot \sqrt{2} = 2\sqrt{2}$. And the area of the triangle is:

$$A = \frac{1}{2} \cdot 2\sqrt{2} \cdot 2\sqrt{2} = 4$$

Or you might construct an altitude for the triangle from B:

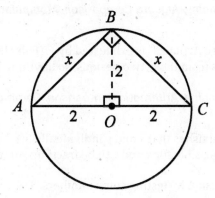

The area of ABC is $A = \frac{1}{2} \cdot 2 \cdot 4 = 4$.

3. **(D)** (p. 466) *Quantitative Reasoning/Algebra Comparison/Solving Equations/One Equation with One Variable*

Just solve for x:

$$\frac{4}{5}x - 7 = 3 \Rightarrow \frac{4}{5}x = 10 \Rightarrow x = 12.5.$$

4. **(A)** (p. 466) *Quantitative Reasoning/Geometry Comparison/Triangles/30°-60°-90° Triangles*

In a 30°-60°-90° triangle, the length of the side opposite the 60° angle is equal to one-half the length of the hypotenuse multiplied by $\sqrt{3}$. Therefore, Quantity A equals $D = \left(\frac{1}{2}\right)(13)(\sqrt{3}) \approx 11$ and is greater than Quantity B, (A).

5. **(D)** (p. 467) *Quantitative Reasoning/Arithmetic Comparison/Common Arithmetic Problems/Properties of Numbers*

Begin with the Quantity B. The largest fraction in S occurs when $n = 9$: $\frac{9}{9+1} = \frac{9}{10}$. And half of $\frac{9}{10}$ is $\frac{9}{20}$. As for Quantity A, the largest product of any two fractions in S is: $\left(\frac{9}{10}\right)\left(\frac{8}{9}\right) = \frac{8}{10}$, which is larger than Quantity B. The smallest product is: $\left(\frac{1}{2}\right)\left(\frac{1}{3}\right) = \frac{1}{6}$, which is smaller than Quantity B, so the correct answer is (D).

6. **(D)** (p. 467) *Quantitative Reasoning/Arithmetic Comparison/Common Arithmetic Problems/Properties of Numbers*

x, y, and z are negative integers, so both the product of the three and their sum will be negative. But that conclusion is not sufficient to answer the question. The sum of $-3, -2$, and -1 is -6, and the product of the three numbers is -6. In that case, the two quantities are equal. But x, y, and z could also be $-4, -3$, and -1. In that case, the sum is -8 and the product is -12, so the two quantities are not always equal. Since the quantities are equal in one case and unequal in another, the problem does not provide sufficient information to determine a relationship, and the correct answer is (D).

7. **(C)** (p. 467) *Quantitative Reasoning/Algebra Comparison/Manipulation of Algebraic Expressions/Evaluating Expressions*

The logical space for "Stone Age Artifacts" is exhausted by P (Paleolithic), N (Neolithic), and C (Chalcolithic). $P + C$ is the number of artifacts from those two periods, so anything left over is from the N period.

8. **(D)** (p. 467) *Quantitative Reasoning/Arithmetic Comparison/Common Arithmetic Problems/Properties of Numbers*

The centered information establishes that x and y individually are both negative, so the quantities in each column are positive. But it is possible for x and y to be fractions, in which case xy is greater than $(xy)^2$.

You can reach the same conclusion by testing some numbers. Try $x = -1$ and $y = -2$. On that assumption, Quantity A is greater—and you eliminate (B) and (C). Next try $x = -\frac{1}{2}$ and $y = -\frac{3}{4}$, and Quantity B is greater, thus proving that the relationship is indeterminate, (D).

9. **(A)** (p. 468) *Quantitative Reasoning/Coordinate Geometry Comparison/Slope of a Line*

This item contains a "gotcha" feature. The pitch of l_2 is clearly steeper that the pitch of l_1, so the unwary student will choose (B) for this item. But the slope of each line is <u>negative</u>, so the greater pitch of l_2 means that the slope of l_2, defined as $(y_2 - y_1)/(x_2 - x_1)$, is less than that of l_1.

10. **(D)** (p. 469) *Quantitative Reasoning/Arithmetic/Common Arithmetic Items/Percents*

This item is easily solved using the "Change Over Original" formula:

$$\frac{15,000 - 12,500}{12,500} = \frac{2,500}{12,500} = \frac{1}{5} = 20\%.$$

11. **(B)** (p. 469) *Quantitative Reasoning/Algebra/Manipulation of Algebraic Expressions/Evaluating Expressions* and *Arithmetic/Common Arithmetic Problems/Properties of Numbers*

The sum of $3k, 4k, 5k, 6k$, and $7k$ is $25k$, a number that will be divisible by 7 only if k is divisible by 7. If, however, the coefficient of k were divisible by 7, then that number would be divisible by 7 regardless of the value of k. If the term $4k$ were dropped from the group, the sum of the remaining terms is $21k$. Since 21 is divisible by 7, $21k$ will be divisible by 7 regardless of the value of k. Assume a value for k, say $k = 1$. Then, the total of the five terms is $3+4+5+6+7=25$. Eliminating which term will yield a sum that is divisible by 7? The answer is to get rid of the 4, (B), because 21 is divisible by 7.

12. **(E)** (p. 469) *Quantitative Reasoning/Arithmetic/Common Arithmetic Problems/Properties of Numbers*

Adding 1 to any integer will result in either an odd or even integer, depending on the original integer. Therefore, (A), (B), and (D) are not necessarily even integers. As for (C), adding 2 to $3n$ will result in an even integer if n is even, but will result in an odd number if n is odd. Therefore, (E) is the correct choice. Indeed, if n is even, then n^2 is even and n^2+n is also even, and if n is odd, then n^2 is odd, but n^2+n is still even.

13. **(B)** (p. 469) *Quantitative Reasoning/Algebra/Manipulation of Algebraic Expressions/Creating Algebraic Expressions*

Just translate the information into "algebrese:"

$T = x + (x-3) + ((x-3)+4) = x + (x-3) + (x+1) = 3x - 2$

Or you could assume a value for x, say 30:

$A = 30$
$H = 30 - 3 = 27$
$B = 27 + 4 = 31$
Total $= 88$

Then substitute 30 for x in the expressions provided by the choices, evaluate, and find the one that returns the value 88:

(A) $x + 1 = 30 + 1 = 31$ ✗
(B) $3x - 2 = 90 - 2 = 88$ ✓
(C) $3x + 1 = 90 + 1 = 91$ ✗
(D) $3x + 3 = 90 + 3 = 93$ ✗
(E) $\dfrac{x}{3} = \dfrac{30}{3} = 10$ ✗

14. **(A)** (p. 470) *Quantitative Reasoning/Arithmetic/Common Arithmetic Problems/Proportions and Direct-Inverse Variation*

To drive 300 kilometers, Motorcycle X uses $\dfrac{1 \text{ liter}}{x \text{ liters}} = \dfrac{40 \text{ kilometers}}{300 \text{ kilometers}} \Rightarrow x = \dfrac{300}{40} = 7.5 \text{ liters}$, and Motorcycle Y uses $\dfrac{1 \text{ liter}}{y \text{ liters}} = \dfrac{50 \text{ kilometers}}{300 \text{ kilometers}} \Rightarrow y = \dfrac{300}{50} = 6 \text{ liters}$. Therefore, the difference in the cost of the trips for the two motorcycles is $(7.5 - 6)(\$2) = \$3$, (A).

15. **(27)** (p. 470) *Quantitative Reasoning/Geometry/Complex Figures*

A cube has six faces, so each face of the cube described has an area of $\dfrac{54}{6} = 9$. The face of a cube is a square, so the edge of the cube has length of $\sqrt{9} = 3$. And the volume of the cube is $3 \cdot 3 \cdot 3 = 27$.

16. **(D)** (p. 470) *Quantitative Reasoning/Algebra/Manipulation of Algebraic Expressions/Factoring Expressions*

Let T be the total capacity of each tank, so that $\dfrac{T}{4}$ is the rate at which the content drains out. Since capacity and rate are equal for both Tank A and Tank B, units are irrelevant. We are interested in the time when $T - x\left(\dfrac{T}{4}\right) = \dfrac{1}{2}\left(T - (x-1)\dfrac{T}{4}\right)$ where x is the elapsed time in hours. Solve for x: $T - x\left(\dfrac{T}{4}\right) = \dfrac{1}{2}\left(T - (x-1)\dfrac{T}{4}\right) \Rightarrow$

$T - \dfrac{Tx}{4} = \dfrac{1}{2}\left(T - \dfrac{Tx}{4} + \dfrac{T}{4}\right) \Rightarrow 2T - \dfrac{Tx}{2} = T - \dfrac{Tx}{4} + \dfrac{T}{4} \Rightarrow 8T - 2Tx = 4T - Tx + T \Rightarrow 3T = Tx \Rightarrow 3 = x$, so the correct answer is (D), $t + 3$ hours.

Alternatively, set up a table:

	Tank A	Tank B
t $(x = 0)$	$\dfrac{4}{4}T$	$\dfrac{4}{4}T$
$t + 1$ $(x = 1)$	$\dfrac{3}{4}T$	$\dfrac{4}{4}T$
$t + 2$ $(x = 2)$	$\dfrac{2}{4}T$	$\dfrac{3}{4}T$
$t + 3$ $(x = 3)$	$\dfrac{1}{4}T$	$\dfrac{2}{4}T$
$t + 4$ $(x = 4)$	0	$\dfrac{1}{4}T$

17. **(E)** (p. 470) *Quantitative Reasoning/Data Analysis/Basic Descriptive Statistics/Mean*

Translate the information given into the formula for calculating an average:

$m = \dfrac{5 + 7 + c}{3}$

$3m = 12 + c$

$c = 3m - 12$

It is also possible to assume a value for c, say 3 (so that the average will be an integer). On that assumption, the average of 5, 7, and 3 is 5. Then substitute 5 for m in each choice until you find the one that returns 3.

18. **(E)** (p. 471) *Quantitative Reasoning/Data Interpretation/Bar Graphs* and *Line Graphs*

Use a ratio to relate applications not approved to total applications. Then turn the resulting decimal into a percent. In 1993, the total number of applications was 180,000 and the number of "not approved" applications was $180,000 - 60,000 = 120,000$. Therefore, $\dfrac{120,000}{180,000} = .66666\overline{6} = 66\dfrac{2}{3}\%$, (E).

19. **(B)** (p. 471) *Quantitative Reasoning/Data Interpretation/Bar Graphs* and *Line Graphs*

During the period 1993 through 1996, inclusive, total deaths increased for two years: 1995 and 1996. During that period, applications for permits increased for one year: 1995. So, both measures increased for only one year (1995), (B).

20. **(E)** (p. 472) *Quantitative Reasoning/Algebra/Manipulation of Algebraic Expressions/Creating Algebraic Expressions*

Devise an expression to express the cost for the first ounce, x, plus the additional postage for weight over 1 ounce. The postage for the additional weight is y cents per ounce, and the additional weight is w minus the first ounce, or $w - 1$. So, the additional postage is $y(w - 1)$, and the total postage is $x + y(w - 1)$, (E).

21. **(C)** (p. 472) *Quantitative Reasoning/Geometry/Complex Figures* and *Circles* and *Rectangles and Squares*

Note that the side of the square is also the radius of the circle. Since the square has an area of 2, its side is: $s \cdot s = 2 \Rightarrow s^2 = 2 \Rightarrow s = \sqrt{2}$. $\sqrt{2}$ is the radius of the circle, so the area of the circle is $\pi r^2 = \pi(\sqrt{2})^2 = 2\pi$, (C).

22. (C) (p. 472) *Quantitative Reasoning/Arithmetic/Common Arithmetic Problems/Properties of Numbers*

The quickest approach to this item is to count the eligible numbers. The first such number is 3 ($3 \cdot 1 = 3$). The next eligible number is 9 ($3 \cdot 3 = 9$). The next is 15 ($3 \cdot 5 = 15$). The next is 21 ($3 \cdot 7 = 21$). The last is 27 ($3 \cdot 9 = 27$). So, there are 5 such positive integers, (C).

23. (1800) (p. 472) *Quantitative Reasoning/Arithmetic/ Complicated Arithmetic Application Problems*

Let p equal the school's population. Then, translate the information given in the item stem into an equation: $p = \frac{p}{4} + \frac{p}{5} + \frac{p}{3} + 390$. And solve for p: $p - \frac{p}{4} - \frac{p}{5} - \frac{p}{3} = 390 \Rightarrow \frac{60p}{60} - \frac{15p}{60} - \frac{12p}{60} - \frac{20p}{60} = 390 \Rightarrow \frac{13p}{60} = 390 \Rightarrow p = \frac{390 \cdot 60}{13} = 1,800$.

24. (D) (p. 472) *Quantitative Reasoning/Algebra/Manipulation of Algebraic Expressions/Creating Algebraic Expressions*

Just translate the description given into "algabrese." The cost per gallon is $\frac{d}{100}$ dollars per g gallons: $\frac{d}{100g}$. Multiply the per gallon cost by 10,000 to get the cost of 10,000 gallons: $10,000 \cdot \frac{d}{100g} = \frac{100d}{g}$.

You could also assume some numbers here. Say that $d = 100$ and $g = 5$. In other words, 5 gallons cost $1 or $1/5 gal. Multiply that cost by 10,000 to get the cost of 10,000 gallons: $10,000 \text{ gal.} \cdot \frac{\$1}{5 \text{ gal.}} = \$2,000$. Now substitute your assumed values into the expressions in the answer choices to find the one that returns the value 2,000:

(A) $\frac{gd}{1,000} = \frac{5(100)}{1,000} = 0.5$ ✗

(B) $\frac{gd}{10,000} = \frac{5(100)}{10,000} = 0.05$ ✗

(C) $100gd = 100(5)(100) = 50,000$ ✗

(D) $\frac{100d}{g} = \frac{100(100)}{5} = 2,000$ ✓

(E) $\frac{d}{100g} = \frac{100}{(100)(5)} = 0.2$ ✗

25. (D) (p. 472) *Quantitative Reasoning/Data Analysis/Basic Descriptive Statistics/Standard Deviation*

The standard deviation is a measure of the distance data points are from the mean. If additional numbers equivalent to the mean are added, the standard deviation must become smaller. Any data points not equal to the mean may change the standard deviation, larger or smaller. Since x is not defined, adding only data points equal to the mean (5) are certain to lower the value of the standard deviation. Therefore, (D) is the correct choice.

Section 6—*Quantitative Reasoning* (p. 473)

1. (C) (p. 473) *Quantitative Reasoning/Arithmetic Comparison/Simple Manipulations*

The trick to this item is to multiply both sides of the comparison by $\sqrt{2}$ (a positive number, so the relationship doesn't change): Quantity A equals $\sqrt{2} \cdot \sqrt{2} = 2$ and Quantity B equals $\frac{2}{\sqrt{2}} \cdot \sqrt{2} = 2$. Therefore, the two quantities are equal, (C).

2. (D) (p. 473) *Quantitative Reasoning/Algebra Comparison/Manipulation of Algebraic Expressions/Evaluating Expressions*

Begin by performing the operation indicated in Quantity A: $\frac{1}{x} + \frac{1}{y} = \frac{y+x}{xy}$. However, without knowing the signs of x and y, it would be a mistake to multiply or divide by x or y across the comparison, so it is not possible to simplify the comparison any further. Therefore, the relationship between the two quantities cannot be determined, (D).

Alternatively, assume some numbers and "plug-and-chug." Start with $x = 1$ and $y = 1$. (Nothing says that x and y are different numbers.) On this assumption, the two quantities are equal. Next, try $x = 2$ and $y = 2$. On this assumption, Quantity A is 1 and Quantity B is 4, which proves that the relationship is indeterminate.

3. (D) (p. 473) *Quantitative Reasoning/Geometry Comparison/Complex Figures* and *Circles*

Distort the figures:

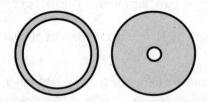

In the first distorted figure, the area of the smaller circle appears to be larger than the area of the shaded part of the figure; however, in the other distorted figure, the area of the smaller circle appears to be less than the area of the shaded part of the figure. Therefore, the relationship between the two quantities cannot be determined, (D).

4. (B) (p. 474) *Quantitative Reasoning/Arithmetic Comparison/Common Arithmetic Problems/Percents*

75% of 32 is 24, so $32 - 24 = 8$ red marbles remain in the jar. 50% of 16 is 8, so $16 - 8 = 8$ blue marbles remain in the jar. $8 + 8 = 16$ marbles out of an original total of $32 + 16 = 48$ marbles remain in the jar. So, the fraction of the number of marbles originally in the jar that remain in the jar is $\frac{16}{48} = \frac{1}{3}$. Therefore, Quantity B is greater than Quantity A, (B).

Alternatively, reason that if 75% of one type of marble and 50% of the other type are removed then only 25% of the one type and 50% of the other remain in the jar. So, fewer than $\frac{1}{2}$ of the original number of marbles remain.

5. (B) (p. 474) *Quantitative Reasoning/Algebra Comparison/Solving Equations/Two Equations with Two Variables*

Set up simultaneous equations to find how many pens and pencils were purchased. If x is the number of pens purchased, and y is the number of pencils purchased, then $x + y = 17$ and $0.35x + 0.20y = 4.60$. Use the first equation to redefine x in terms of y: $x = 17 - y$. Substitute this value for x in the second equation: $0.35(17 - y) + 0.20y = 4.60$. Solve for y: $5.95 - 0.35y + 0.20y = 4.60 \Rightarrow 0.15y = 1.35 \Rightarrow y = 9$. Substitute this value for y back into the first equation: $x + 9 = 17 \Rightarrow x = 8$. Therefore, the student bought 9 pencils and 8 pens. Therefore, Quantity B is greater than Quantity A, (B).

Alternatively, solve the comparison by working backwards. For example, assume that 8 pencils were purchased and 9 pens. On that assumption, the student spent: $8(\$0.20) + 9(\$0.35) = \$1.60 + \$3.15 = \$4.75$, which is too much money. Therefore, since the assumption generates a total cost of more than $4.60, too many pens were purchased. (The pens are more expensive.) So, invert the assumption so that the number of pens is 8 and the number of pencils is 9. But at this point, the comparison is already made. It is already established that the student purchased at *least* 9 pencils, which means she purchased more pencils than pens.

6. **(C)** (p. 474) *Quantitative Reasoning/Geometry Comparison/Slope of a Line*

The equation is given in slope-intercept form, and a is the slope of the line. Therefore:

$$a = \frac{y_2 - y_1}{x_2 - x_1}$$

$$a = \frac{0 - b}{c - 0} = -\frac{b}{c}$$

7. **(B)** (p. 475) *Quantitative Reasoning/Data Analysis Comparison/Basic Descriptive Statistics/Mean*

You can analyze this item as a "weighted average" problem. If the number of males equaled the number of females, the percentage of the entire population infected is the average of 12% and 16%, or 14%. But the actual percentage of the entire population infected is 14.1%, which means that the number of females in the population is greater than the number of males.

8. **(C)** (p. 475) *Quantitative Reasoning/Coordinate Geometry Comparison/Distance Formula*

This problem can be solved with the Distance Formula:

$$d^2 = (x_2 - x_1)^2 + (y_2 - y_1)^2$$
$$d = \sqrt{(x_2 - x_1)^2 + (y_2 - y_1)^2}$$

$$AB = \sqrt{(5-1)^2 + (4-7)^2} = \sqrt{16+9} = \sqrt{25} = 5$$

$$AC = \sqrt{(1-6)^2 + (7-7)^2} = \sqrt{25+0} = \sqrt{25} = 5$$

Or you could sketch the coordinate system and plot the points:

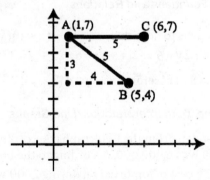

9. **(B)** (p. 475) *Quantitative Reasoning/Arithmetic Comparison/Complicated Manipulations/Factoring*

You can solve this item by taking advantage of the QC structure. Multiply both sides by x (x is positive).

Quantity A: $\left(\dfrac{x^{23} - x^{22}}{x} \right) x = x^{23} - x^{22}$. And Quantity B: $(x^{22})(x) = x^{23}$. Now subtract x^{23} from both sides.

Quantity A: $x^{23} - x^{22} - x^{23} = -x^{22}$. And Quantity B: $x^{23} - x^{23} = 0$. Since Quantity A is a negative number, Quantity B is greater.

10. **(C)** (p. 476) *Quantitative Reasoning/Arithmetic/Common Arithmetic Problems/Properties of Numbers*

The easiest way to approach this item is to see that the squares, and therefore the integers, must be fairly small, no greater than 6 ($7^2 > 41$). Then just combine integers to test possibilities:

(A) $10 = 3^2 + 1^2$ ✗
(B) $13 = 3^2 + 2^2$ ✗
(C) 18 is not equal to the sum of the squares of two different integers. ✓
(D) $34 = 3^2 + 5^2$ ✗
(E) $41 = 4^2 + 5^2$ ✗

11. **(B)** (p. 476) *Quantitative Reasoning/Arithmetic/Common Arithmetic Problems/Ratios*

You can create a series of equations:

$$A = \frac{B}{2}$$

$$C = \frac{A+B}{2}$$

Manipulate the first equation to define B in terms of A:

$$B = 2A$$

Then substitute $2A$ for B in the second equation:

$$C = \frac{A+2A}{2} \Rightarrow C = \frac{3A}{2} \Rightarrow 2C = 3A \Rightarrow \frac{C}{A} = \frac{3}{2}$$

Or you could, if you like, assume a concrete number to work with. Say B is 4 grams (or ounces or whatever you prefer). If $B = 4$, then $A = 2$, and $C = 3$. The ratio of $C : A$ is 3:2.

12. **(9)** (p. 476) *Quantitative Reasoning/Algebra/Manipulation of Algebraic Expressions/Factoring Expressions* and *Solving Equations/Quadratic Equations and Relations*

The trick to solving this item quickly is to note that $x^2 - y^2 = (x+y)(x-y)$. Therefore, solve the two given equations for $x+y$ and $x-y$: $2x + 2y = 6 \Rightarrow 2(x+y) = 6 \Rightarrow x+y = 3$ and

$3x - 3y = 9 \Rightarrow 3(x-y) = 9 \Rightarrow x-y = 3$. Therefore, $x^2 - y^2 = (x+y)(x-y) = (3)(3) = 9$.

13. **(A)** (p. 477) *Quantitative Reasoning/Data Interpretation/Line Graphs*

This item requires coordination of data from the two graphs. According to the top graph, the number of barrels imported each day in 2000 was 6,000,000. According to the bottom graph, the price per barrel in 2000 was $30. So, the average daily cost of imported oil during 2000 was 6,000,000 barrels $\cdot \frac{\$30}{\text{barrel}} =$ $180,000,000, (A).

14. **(C)** (p. 477) *Quantitative Reasoning/Data Interpretation/Line Graphs*

This item requires coordination of data from the two graphs. From 1991 through 2000, the quantity of imported oil increased over the previous year (positive slope for the solid line in top graph) in 1991, 1992, 1993, 1994, 1995, 1997, and 1998. From 1991 through 2000, the price of imported oil increased over the previous year (positive slope in bottom graph) in 1991, 1992, 1993, 1994, 1995, 1996, 1997, 1999, and 2000. Therefore, both the quantity and price of imported oil increased in 1991, 1992, 1993, 1994, 1995 and 1997, or a total of 6 years, (C).

15. **(150)** (p. 477) *Quantitative Reasoning/Data Analysis/Counting Methods/Combinations*

Use the formula for combinations, $\dfrac{n!}{(n-k)!\,k!}$, where n is the total number of candidates and k is the number of positions available. Determine the total for each group.

Juniors: $\dfrac{5!}{(5-3)!\,3!} = \dfrac{5\cdot4\cdot3\cdot2\cdot1}{(2\cdot1)(3\cdot2\cdot1)} = \dfrac{5\cdot4}{2\cdot1} = 10$

Seniors: $\dfrac{6!}{(6-2)!\,2!} = \dfrac{6\cdot5\cdot4\cdot3\cdot2\cdot1}{(4\cdot3\cdot2\cdot1)(2\cdot1)} = \dfrac{6\cdot5}{2\cdot1} = 15$

And the total number of combinations when the two subgroups are combined is: $10\cdot15 = 150$.

16. **(B)** (p. 478) *Quantitative Reasoning/Data Analysis/Basic Descriptive Statistics/Quartiles and Interquartile Range*

The interquartile range is defined as the difference between the third quartile and the first quartile, $Q_3 - Q_1$. The first quartile is the median of the lower half of the data and the third quartile is the median of the upper half of the data. Since List X is the set of all integers between and including 101 and 500, it can be divided into four equal groups: 101–200, 201–300, 301–400, and 401–500. The first quartile, Q_1 , or median, of the lower half of the numbers is 200.5 (the average of 200 and 201). The third quartile, Q_3 , is the median of the upper half of the numbers, 400.5 (the average of 400 and 401). Therefore, the interquartile range is $400.5 - 200.5 = 200$, (B).

17. **(E)** (p. 478) *Quantitative Reasoning/Arithmetic/Complicated Manipulations/Simplifying*

Simplify and do the indicated operations: $\sqrt{1+2+3+4+1+2+3+4+1+2+3+4+1+2+3} =$
$\sqrt{(1+2+3+4)+(1+2+3+4)+(1+2+3+4)+(1+2+3)} = \sqrt{10+10+10+6} = \sqrt{36} = 6$, (E).

18. **(C)** (p. 478) *Quantitative Reasoning/Data Analysis/Basic Descriptive Statistics/Mean*

The trick to solving this item quickly is to note that the average of 6 and 15 is 10.5, the average of 7 and 14 is 10.5, the average of 8 and 13 is 10.5, and so on. Therefore, the average of all integers 6 through 15 inclusive must be 10.5, (C).

Alternatively, calculate the average: $\dfrac{6+7+8+9+10+11+12+13+14+15}{10} = \dfrac{105}{10} = 10.5$.

19. **(C)** (p. 478) *Quantitative Reasoning/Geometry/Lines and Angles* and *Triangles/Properties of Triangles*

Label the missing angle in the left-side triangle:

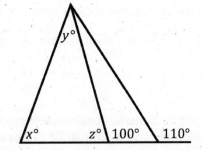

Therefore, $100 + z = 180 \Rightarrow z = 80$. And $x + y + z = 180 \Rightarrow 50 + y + 80 = 180 \Rightarrow y = 50$, (C).

20. **(E)** (p. 478) *Quantitative Reasoning/Geometry/Rectangles and Squares* and *Algebra/Manipulation of Algebraic Expressions/Creating Algebraic Expressions* and *Solving Equations/Quadratic Equations*

Create an expression for the area of the rectangle and solve for x: area = (length)(width) $\Rightarrow 72 =$ $(x+3)(x-3) \Rightarrow 72 = x^2 - 3x + 3x - 9 \Rightarrow x^2 - 81 = 0 \Rightarrow (x+9)(x-9) = 0 \Rightarrow x = \pm 9$. Since distances must be positive, x must be 9, (E).

Alternatively, "test-the-test," starting with (C). If $x = 6$, then the area of the rectangle is $(6+3)(6-3) = 27$, which is too small. The area is 72, so x must be bigger than 6. Next, test (D): $(8+3)(8-3) = 55$. Again, too small, so (E) must be the correct choice.

21. **(72)** (p. 478) *Quantitative Reasoning/Arithmetic/Common Arithmetic Problems/Proportions and Direct-Inverse Variation*

The more candies that are bought, the more money it costs, so use a direct proportion: $\frac{12 \text{ candies}}{x \text{ candies}} = \frac{\$1.70}{\$10.20} \Rightarrow$ $x = \frac{\$10.20(12 \text{ candies})}{\$1.70} = 72 \text{ candies}$.

22. **(C)** (p. 478) *Quantitative Reasoning/Geometry/Lines and Angles*

$\overline{PQ} \| \overline{RS}$, so if the line between $\angle x$ and $\angle y$ is extended below $\overline{RS}$, the following is true:

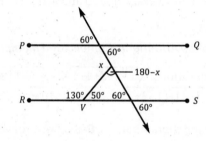

Therefore, $180 = 60 + 50 + (180 - x) \Rightarrow x = 110$, (C).

23. **(C)** (p. 479) *Quantitative Reasoning/Data Analysis/Counting Methods/Venn Diagrams*

All 56 of the 30 and below group could theoretically be first termers.

24. **(B)** (p. 479) *Quantitative Reasoning/Arithmetic/Common Arithmetic Problems/Rates*

Use the "rate" equation: rate $= \frac{\text{distance}}{\text{time}} \Rightarrow$ time $= \frac{\text{distance}}{\text{rate}}$. Note that because the answer choices include fractions, rather than decimals, keep the arithmetic in fractions. The time it takes the driver to arrive at her destination is $\frac{60 \text{ miles}}{40 \text{ miles/hour}} = 1\frac{1}{2}$ hours; the time it takes to return is $\frac{60 \text{ miles}}{30 \text{ miles/hour}} = 2$ hours; the total time for the 120 mile trip is $1\frac{1}{2} + 2 = 3\frac{1}{2}$ hours. Therefore, the average speed for the entire trip is $\frac{120 \text{ miles}}{3\frac{1}{2} \text{ hours}} =$ $\frac{120 \text{ miles}}{\frac{7}{2} \text{ hours}} = \frac{240}{7}$ mph $= 34\frac{2}{7}$ mph, (B).

25. **(A)** (p. 479) *Quantitative Reasoning/Arithmetic/Common Arithmetic Problems/Properties of Numbers* and *Algebra/Manipulation of Algebraic Expressions/Evaluating Expressions*

The product of the terms $x+1$ and $x-2$ is positive if both terms are negative or both are positive. First, consider the case when both are positive: $x+1$ is positive for $x > -1$ and $x-2$ is positive for $x > 2$, so for both $x+1$ and $x-2$ to be positive, $x > 2$. Next, consider the case when both are negative: $x+1$ is negative for $x < -1$ and $x-2$ is negative for $x < 2$, so for both $x+1$ and $x-2$ to be negative, $x < -1$. Thus, for $(x+1)(x-2)$ to be positive, $x < -1$ or $x > 2$, (A).

Basic Skills Supplement

Outline

VERBAL REASONING SUPPLEMENT

Vocabulary in Context (p. 506)
Exercise 1

1. D	10. B	19. C	28. D	37. D
2. C	11. D	20. D	29. A	38. C
3. E	12. B	21. B	30. A	39. B
4. B	13. C	22. D	31. C	40. A
5. A	14. A	23. B	32. D	41. D
6. D	15. C	24. C	33. E	42. B
7. B	16. E	25. A	34. C	43. B
8. C	17. B	26. C	35. D	44. C
9. A	18. B	27. D	36. A	45. C

Vocabulary Completions (p. 513)
Exercise 2

1. C	4. D	7. C	10. C
2. B	5. A	8. D	11. A
3. E	6. B	9. D	12. B

13. exceed, surpass

14. climax, high point, zenith

15. boring, dull, uninspiring

16. serious, severe, large-scale

17. complete, comprehensive, exhaustive

18. complete, total, authoritarian

19. hides, camouflages, conceals

20. wanted, infamous, notorious

21. dazed, confused, disoriented

22. generate, spark, increase

23. The survivors had been drifting for days in the lifeboat, and in their weakness, they appeared to be ____ rather than living beings.

    The blank must be filled with a word that means the opposite of something that is alive. "Dead," "spirits," and "ghosts" are possible completions. Notice that the missing word can either be an adjective (e.g., "dead"), modifying the noun "beings," or a noun (e.g., "spirits"), paralleling the phrase "living beings."

24. The guillotine was introduced during the French Revolution as a reformatory measure, an alternative to other _____ means of execution.

    The blank must be filled with a word or phrase that answers the following question: an "alternative to" what type of execution would be considered a "reformatory measure"? "Less humane" and "more painful" are possible completions.

25. Because of the ____ nature of the chemical, it cannot be used near an open flame.

    The blank must be filled with an adjective that extends the idea of a chemical that "cannot be used near an open flame." "Flammable," which means "easily capable of burning," is one obvious completion.

26. The Mayor's proposal for a new subway line, although a(n) ____, is not a final solution to the city's transportation needs.

    The blank must be filled with a noun that both extends the idea of something that is "new" and reverses the idea of something that is "final." "Start" and "beginning" are possible completions.

27. In a pluralistic society, policies are the result of compromise, so political leaders must be ____ and must accommodate the views of others.

    The blank must be filled with an adjective that extends the idea of a "compromise" and parallels the idea of accommodation. "Tolerant" and "understanding" are possible completions.

28. The committee report vigorously expounded the bill's strengths but also acknowledged its ____.

    The blank must be filled with a plural noun that means the opposite of "strengths." "Weaknesses" and "shortcomings" are possible completions.

29. Because there is always the danger of a power failure and disruption of elevator service, high-rise buildings, while suitable for younger persons, are not recommended for ____.

    The sentence suggests that high-rise buildings are suitable for "younger persons" but not for a different group of people. So, the blank must be filled with a word or phrase that means the opposite of "younger persons." "The elderly" and "senior citizens" are possible completions.

30. For a child to be happy, his day must be very structured; when his routine is ____, he becomes nervous and irritable.

    The "if-then" logical structure of the sentence indicates that if the child is to be happy, his day must be structured. However, the word clue, nervous and irritable, after the semicolon suggests that the parallel structure in the second clause of the sentence must be the reverse of the first. If "structured" activity makes a child "happy," then unstructured activity would make a child "nervous and irritable." So, the blank must be filled with a verb that suggests the idea of unstructured activity. "Disrupted" and "interrupted" are possible completions.

31. The current spirit of ____ among different religions <u>has led to</u> a number of meetings that their leaders hope will lead to better <u>understanding</u>.

The blank must be filled with a noun that satisfies the following construction: The spirit of ____ has led to understanding. "Cooperation" and "accord" are possible completions.

32. Our modern industrialized societies have been responsible for the greatest <u>destruction of nature and life</u>; indeed, it seems that more civilization <u>results in greater</u> ____.

The blank must be filled with a noun that describes something that has led to understanding. "Cooperation" and "accord" are possible completions.

Identify Parts of Arguments (p. 537)
Exercise 3

1. E	**3.** C	**5.** E
2. A	**4.** D	**6.** B

7. Every winter for the past ten years, I have caught at least one cold. <u>This winter, I will probably catch one or more colds.</u>

8. All members of the Board of Trustees are graduates of the college. <u>Irving</u>, who is a trustee, <u>is a graduate of the college</u>.

9. The company rules require a supervisor to discipline a habitually tardy employee either by docking his pay or by firing him. Since Smith has been late every day this week, <u>either his pay will be docked or he will be fired</u>.

10. <u>The student protest proved very effective.</u> The day after the students first occupied the administration building, the president of the college announced that he would reverse the longstanding policy of requiring certain courses.

11. <u>It is possible to reduce our reliance on foreign energy sources</u> because, despite the fact that the United States relies heavily on imported oil as an energy source, we have a considerable nuclear energy capacity that remains idle.

12. The tuition and other costs of getting a college education continue to soar, and recent cutbacks in government aid for students have made it even more difficult for families of even moderate means to finance their children's education. <u>We may soon see the day when a college education is once again the prerogative of only the very rich.</u>

13. <u>The Federal Reserve Board must have moved last month to slow the growth of the money supply.</u> Following a month in which prices rose more than they did the month before, interest rates rose noticeably and, in similar situations in the past, the Board has moved to counteract inflation.

14. Protectionists argue that an excess of exports over imports is essential to maintaining a favorable balance of trade. The excess can then be "cashed in" as precious metals. This means, however, that the most favorable of all trade balances will occur when a country exports its entire national product and, in turn, imports only gold and silver. Since one cannot eat gold and silver, <u>the protectionists must surely be wrong</u>.

| 15. C | 17. B | 19. F |
| 16. A | 18. E | 20. D |

Determine the Main Idea (p. 541)
Exercise 4

| 1. C | 3. D | 5. B |
| 2. B | 4. A | |

Outline Passages (p. 543)
Exercise 5

Passage 1 Outline
   I. A tremendous electrostatic charge builds up within a cloud.
  II. Lightning occurs within the cloud itself.
 III. Negative charges called stepped leaders emerge from the bottom of the cloud, moving toward the Earth and creating an ionized channel.
 IV. A strong electric field causes streamers of positively charged ions to develop and flow upward.
  V. A return stroke moves through the object from which the streamer emanated and up the ionized channel to the charge center within the cloud.
 VI. An ionized channel remains in the air, and dart leaders will quickly move down this path, resulting in further return strokes.
VII. The return stroke's extremely high temperature creates the visible lightning and produces thunder.

Passage 2 Outline
   I. The efforts of the Convention on International Trade in Endangered Species
     A. An international moratorium was enacted on the buying and selling of ivory.
     B. The moratorium prompted significant declines in ivory trading and in the rate of elephant poaching.
  II. The cooperative effort of the U.S. with the Central African Republic and the World Wildlife Fund
     A. A reserve has been established in the southeastern portion of that country.
     B. Anti-poaching patrols were established using funds provided by the U.S.
 III. The efforts of Senegal's anti-poaching program
     A. An African elephant conservation fund grant has provided protection for the elephant population.
     B. Similar protection projects have begun in Cameroon, Congo, Eritrea, Gabon, Mali, Tanzania, Zambia, and Zimbabwe.

Locate Verbal Signs (p. 545)
Exercise 6

    A <u>flood is an overflow of water that covers lands that are normally not covered by water</u> (***defining***). A <u>flood occurs, for example, when a stream or river overflows its banks</u> (***example***). Small streams are subject to <u>flash floods—that is, the very rapid increases in water that may last only a few minutes</u> (***defining***). In larger streams, floods usually last from several hours to a few days, and a series of storms might keep a river above flood stage for several weeks.

    Floods can occur at any time, but weather patterns have a strong influence on when and where floods happen. Cyclones—<u>similar in structure to tornadoes</u> (***similarity***)—bring moisture inland from the ocean, causing floods in the spring in the western United States. Thunderstorms are relatively small but intense storms that cause flash floods in smaller streams during the summer in the Southwest. Frontal storms at the edge of large, moist air masses moving across the country cause floods in the northern and eastern parts of the United States during the winter.

The <u>magnitude of a flood is described by a term called the recurrence interval,</u> (***defining***) which is based upon long-term study of flow records for a stream. A <u>five-year flood is one that would occur, on the average, once every five years</u> (***defining***). Although <u>a 100-year flood is expected to happen only once in a century</u> (***defining***), it is <u>important to remember</u> (***prompting***) that there is a one percent chance that a flood of that size could happen during any given year.

Of course, the frequency and magnitude of floods can be altered if changes are made in the drainage basin of a stream or river. <u>Significantly, harvesting timber or changing land use from farms to housing can cause the runoff to increase</u> (***prompting***), resulting in an increase in the magnitude of flooding. <u>On the other hand, dams can protect against flooding</u> (***contrast***) by storing storm runoff. Although the same volume of water must eventually move downstream, the peak flow can be reduced by temporarily storing water and then releasing it when water levels have fallen.

Locate Specific Details (p. 546)
Exercise 7

1. C	**3.** D	**5.** C	**7.** A	**9.** C
2. A	**4.** B	**6.** A	**8.** B	**10.** D

Analyze the Arguments (p. 548)
Exercise 8

1. D	**3.** D	**5.** C	**7.** D	**9.** A
2. B	**4.** A	**6.** B	**8.** B	**10.** C

Consider the Author's Point of View (p. 551)
Exercise 9

1. The author claims to be both a physician and a professor at a prestigious medical school.

2. One could assume that the author, as a physician, has a working knowledge of the field of medicine. One could also assume that the author, as a professor at a prestigious medical school, is well-versed in the needs of the medical community and the status of students entering medical school.

3. The author most certainly has the highest respect for the application of the Hippocratic method of reason and observation within the medical practice. The author dislikes, or holds in contempt, medical students who pursue medical careers for the reasons of fame and fortune.

4. The author is attempting to change what he or she perceives as problems in the attitudes and perceptions of medical students.

5. The author wants you to believe that the Hippocratic method of observation and reason is essential for medical students. He or she also wants you to believe that this perspective must be acquired prior to being admitted into medical school.

6. The passage discusses the origins of modern medicine; specifically, the passage is about Hippocrates in the role of father (or founder) of modern medicine.

7. The author has spent 30 years in the American banking industry, was one of the first female members of Congress, and wrote legislation regarding banking.

8. The author has 30 years of banking experience and knowledge regarding banking laws.

9. The author writes to make a strong case for the government not to get involved in banking bailouts.

10. The author wants you to believe that government bailouts of banks have detrimental results to the economy as a whole.

Probe the Mood of the Passage (p. 553)
Exercise 10

1. The mood of the passage is quite depressing and bleak. The passage might be described as somber or dark.

2. The author uses the terms "melancholy" (line 1), "deplorable" (line 18), and "helpless infants" (lines 9–10). He verbally paints a picture of begging mothers and children in need of charity.

Bonus Passages (p. 554)
Exercise 11

1. D	8. C	15. B	22. C	29. D
2. B	9. A	16. A	23. D	30. D
3. A	10. D	17. C	24. B	31. A
4. C	11. A	18. B	25. A	32. C
5. B	12. D	19. C	26. A	33. C
6. D	13. D	20. D	27. A	34. B
7. A	14. C	21. B	28. B	

QUANTITATIVE REASONING SUPPLEMENT

Numbers (p. 574)
Exercise 1

1. B	10. D	19. A	28. C	37. D
2. C	11. D	20. D	29. C	38. C
3. C	12. E	21. D	30. B	39. A
4. C	13. B	22. B	31. D	40. E
5. C	14. B	23. B	32. A	41. B
6. C	15. B	24. A	33. D	42. E
7. B	16. C	25. E	34. C	
8. B	17. C	26. C	35. D	
9. C	18. A	27. A	36. B	

Percents (p. 582)
Exercise 2

1. C	9. A	17. B	25. A	33. E
2. A	10. A	18. C	26. E	34. D
3. A	11. C	19. C	27. D	35. E
4. C	12. C	20. C	28. D	36. A
5. C	13. B	21. C	29. C	37. D
6. D	14. C	22. A	30. B	38. A
7. E	15. D	23. C	31. A	39. A
8. D	16. B	24. E	32. D	40. C

Statistical Measures (p. 589)
Exercise 3

1. B	3. E	5. C	7. A	9. B
2. C	4. A	6. E	8. E	10. A

11. C	17. B	23. D	29. D	35. C
12. D	18. B	24. D	30. A	36. C
13. A	19. C	25. A	31. B	37. E
14. D	20. E	26. C	32. E	38. C
15. E	21. B	27. C	33. D	39. B
16. E	22. B	28. B	34. B	40. D

Ratios and Proportions (p. 595)
Exercise 4

1. B	6. D	11. B	16. C	21. D
2. A	7. D	12. C	17. D	22. E
3. D	8. E	13. A	18. B	
4. D	9. D	14. D	19. B	
5. C	10. E	15. B	20. C	

Exponents and Radicals (p. 599)
Exercise 5

1. D	6. B	11. A	16. C	21. B
2. C	7. D	12. C	17. D	22. D
3. A	8. C	13. A	18. D	23. E
4. A	9. C	14. B	19. D	24. E
5. C	10. A	15. B	20. C	

Algebraic Operations (p. 607)
Exercise 6

1. A	9. C	17. A	25. A	33. B
2. C	10. B	18. D	26. C	34. B
3. B	11. B	19. B	27. C	35. A
4. B	12. C	20. A	28. A	36. C
5. C	13. C	21. D	29. B	37. B
6. A	14. E	22. D	30. C	38. A
7. E	15. D	23. C	31. C	39. A
8. D	16. D	24. B	32. E	40. D

Algebraic Equations and Inequalities (p. 623)
Exercise 7

1. C	10. D	19. C	28. B	37. A
2. E	11. C	20. C	29. E	38. D
3. B	12. D	21. D	30. D	39. D
4. D	13. E	22. A	31. A	40. A
5. E	14. B	23. D	32. B	41. D
6. C	15. A	24. C	33. E	42. B
7. B	16. D	25. C	34. E	43. A
8. C	17. E	26. E	35. D	44. D
9. B	18. B	27. B	36. E	45. E

Geometry (p. 639)
Exercise 8

1. D	10. D	19. A	28. C	37. A
2. A	11. B	20. E	29. C	38. C
3. B	12. D	21. C	30. C	39. C
4. B	13. B	22. C	31. C	40. C
5. C	14. A	23. A	32. C	41. B
6. C	15. A	24. A	33. E	42. A
7. A	16. C	25. B	34. B	43. C
8. C	17. B	26. A	35. D	44. E
9. B	18. A	27. C	36. E	45. D

Coordinate Geometry (p. 655)
Exercise 9

1. B	7. E	13. A	19. E	25. C
2. A	8. B	14. C	20. D	26. D
3. A	9. C	15. A	21. C	27. E
4. D	10. C	16. A	22. B	28. C
5. A	11. B	17. C	23. B	29. C
6. A	12. B	18. E	24. C	30. B

31. A	**33.** E	**35.** B	**37.** E	**39.** D
32. D	**34.** D	**36.** B	**38.** A	**40.** D

Story Problems (p. 672)
Exercise 10

1. B	**9.** C	**17.** B	**25.** C	**33.** B
2. B	**10.** C	**18.** E	**26.** C	**34.** D
3. A	**11.** B	**19.** C	**27.** B	**35.** D
4. A	**12.** B	**20.** C	**28.** E	**36.** C
5. D	**13.** D	**21.** D	**29.** C	**37.** E
6. B	**14.** D	**22.** D	**30.** C	**38.** D
7. B	**15.** A	**23.** D	**31.** C	
8. E	**16.** B	**24.** B	**32.** B	

ANALYTICAL WRITING SUPPLEMENT

Issue Analysis Outline (p. 688)
Exercise 1

Above Average Response

I. Prefer rural life for better emotional health, better community involvement opportunities, and better use of my time

II. Emotional health
   A. Less stress
   B. Less noise
   C. Less traffic

III. Community involvement and opportunity
   A. Community-wide issues
   B. Be known and make a difference
   C. Challenges of entering a smaller community

IV. Best use of my time
   A. Not stuck in traffic
   B. Less demand for services leads to shorter wait times
   C. Results in extra time to follow my own interests

V. Prefer the rural life (the conveniences of cities available in rural areas without drawbacks of city living)

Below Average Response

I. Prefer city life because of convenience, entertainment opportunities, and good health care

II. Convenience
   A. Good roads
   B. Everything is close together

III. Entertainment opportunities

IV. Good health care

V. Like city life

Issue Analysis Essay (p. 689)
Exercise 2

Above Average Response

The question of the quality of the rural life versus the life of a city dweller is an interesting one that faces each adult making a decision about their life activities. Plainly, United States citizens "voted with their feet" and have flocked to the cities in the 20th century. But recently there has been some movement back to rural areas and the "simple life" that they represent. I feel that a more rural area offers the best quality of life in the beginning of the 21st century. This opinion is based on the issues of emotional health, community involvement and opportunity, and best usage of my time.

Life in urban areas can be very stressful and difficult. Noise and traffic go on 24 hours a day. "Street people" who may need intervention may be outside your door in a downtown area. Traffic may make your voyage to work or entertainment difficult and lengthy. In rural areas the noise level is lessened, the roads less crowded, and more humane contact is likely.

In a more rural area, each person can have more of an impact within the community. The problems and challenges may be shared community wide and not just in your own neighborhood as in a large city. You can more easily be known and make a difference in a rural area. A contrary view contends that newcomers are sometimes not part of the "community family" in a small town. Gaining acceptance can be harder than in cities used to an influx of new people.

A rural area places less demands on my personal time: less traffic, less commuting, and fewer lines of people waiting to get services. I could get home faster from work and pursue my own interests.

In conclusion, I prefer rural areas. Keeping in communication and accessing healthcare used to be a problem there. But the Internet and satellite dishes helped alleviate the first concern. Regional health centers and rapid transportation have helped make "big city" healthcare available to rural areas.

Writing skill and position on issue: This essay shows good facility with written English, clear organization, and mostly consistent writing skills. The writer's position on the issue is presented clearly and the thesis is well developed. In the third paragraph, the writer presents a contrary viewpoint, which is a strong and persuasive technique. However, he or she fails to refute this opposing viewpoint, which is important when presenting evidence that is contrary to the thesis.

Development of ideas and organization of essay: The initial paragraph effectively details both sides of the issue. Reference to social trends gives the writer a voice of authority. Examples are well presented and elaborated upon with sufficient detail. The arguments are laid out in a logical order and structured closely after the thesis statement. Each supporting paragraph begins with an organizing topic sentence and continues with an in-depth discussion of the writer's major points.

Structure of essay, paragraphs, and transitions: In the introduction, the writer previews the evidence that will be used to support his or her thesis, and the structural set-up in the opening paragraph is closely followed throughout the essay. The supporting paragraphs are appropriate, and each deals with an argument or position of the writer. The transition that is used to move from the second paragraph to the third paragraph ("In a more rural area") is very effective; however, transition usage in general is low. For example, "In conclusion" is a low-level usage transitional phrase.

Language usage, sentence structure, and punctuation: The analogy "voted with their feet" is effective in this essay, and the supporting details hold the reader's interest. Minor errors in grammar and mechanics do not distract the reader from understanding the essay and are likely present due to the time restrictions placed on the writer.

Summary and conclusions: The essay is clearly written and demonstrates a firm command of the language. It would likely receive a reader's score of average to above average (4–6).

Below Average Response

Residents of rural areas insist that their life is better. People living in urban city areas prefer the lively life that they lead. Each has a viewpoint, but I feel that the city life is much better. Urban areas have good streets and roads and many things to do.

A city is closer together than rural areas. Everything can be reached pretty quickly by car, bus, or even bicycle. The streets are maintained by the city in winter and summer. My Aunt in the mountains is snowed in each winter for days at a time. Sometimes traffic is a problem in urban areas, but that's the price you pay.

The urban areas have so many activities to do. Lots of movies, concerts, and sports events are always going on. Because the urban areas have more people and money, more famous artists visit and perform there.

Some really important things in cities include good hospitals and healthcare. With lots of people there is a need for specialist doctors and great hospitals, even for children. I feel that I can find people in the city that share my interests whatever I decide on.

In conclusion, urban areas are the best places to live. Americans, and people around the world are moving from rural areas more each day to get to the excitement and opportunity of urban areas.

Writing skill and position on issue: This essay demonstrates developing writing skills. Although the writer's position on the issue is clear, he or she fails to provide an adequate introduction to the issue. The writer does discuss both sides of the argument, but he or she is unsuccessful in describing the relationship between the two sides. The writer's thesis is not broad enough to sufficiently cover the point raised in the fourth paragraph regarding "hospitals and healthcare."

Development of ideas and organization of essay: The ideas presented are good but lack sufficient elaboration. The writer does not include clear topic sentences in any of the three body paragraphs, and there are random statements that are not organized in any coherent pattern throughout the essay. This lack of coherence distracts the reader from obtaining a clear understanding of the argument. For example, the writer mentions that he or she "can find people in the city that share my interests" in the same paragraph (fourth) that he or she discusses "hospitals and healthcare"; however, no logical connection is made between these two ideas. Since the essay prompt asks the writer to compare two living conditions, the development of such an essay would require the use of comparisons and contrasts. However, the writer does not adequately use either of these tools to support his or her thesis. Overall, the writer presents a list of the qualities that he or she prefers in cities but does not explain why this list adds up to a higher quality of life.

Structure of essay, paragraphs, and transitions: The writer has a grasp of the basic structure of an essay: an introduction, a body, and a conclusion. However, the paragraphs are too short; they are not supported or expanded sufficiently; and they become unfocused. The essay also lacks transitions; its content is presented in a choppy fashion, with random introductions of the writer's main points. The only transitional phrase ("In conclusion"), which appears in the last paragraph, is contrived and low-level usage.

Language usage, sentence structure, and punctuation: The essay is understandable, but it contains many errors in grammar and mechanics that distract the reader from its content. In the first paragraph, for example, the writer states that "Urban areas have…many things to do." However, "areas" cannot "have things to do." The proper phrase would be "There are many things to do in urban areas." Also, in the second paragraph, the writer omits the word "living" from the sentence "My Aunt in the mountains…." Overall, an excess of low-level language (e.g., "pretty quickly," "that's the price you pay", and "Lots of") mars the quality of the essay. In the last paragraph, the comma after "Americans" is unnecessary. Stylistically, the writer does not vary the sentence structure and resorts to simple sentences and lists.

Summary and conclusions: The essay would likely receive a reader's score of below average (2–3).

Issue Analysis Revision (p. 690)
Exercise 3

Above Average Response

The writer should revise the Issue Analysis essay to:

- refute the opposing viewpoint presented in the third paragraph;

- improve transitions between paragraphs and main ideas; and

- correct minor grammatical errors.

Below Average Response

The writer should revise the Issue Analysis essay to:

- provide an adequate introduction to the issue;

- describe the relationship between the two points of view;

- expand the thesis to cover sufficiently the point raised in the fourth paragraph regarding "hospitals and healthcare";

- expand paragraphs and elaborate on ideas;

- add clear topic sentences to each paragraph;

- add transitions between paragraphs;

- move random statements to appropriate locations or remove them from the essay; and

- address grammar, punctuation, and mechanics errors.

Argument Analysis Outline (p. 691)
Exercise 4

Above Average Response

    I. Lifeguard argument is flawed

   II. Assumes there is a link between length of life guard shifts and a danger to public safety
      A. Does not establish the extent of danger
      B. Does not identify other sources of public safety issues

  III. Assumes there are no other alternatives
      A. Reduced swimmer capacity at beaches
      B. Decrease the amount of time in the water allowed per swimmer

    C.   Increased breaks for life guards or overlapping shifts

IV. Fails to address unintended consequences of hiring additional lifeguards
    A.   Less qualified candidates could be hired
    B.   Insufficient training
    C.   Less experienced staff

V. Assumes the costs may outweigh benefits
    A.   Additional costs of hiring and training more life guards
    B.   Cost overruns for state
    C.   Possible closure of beaches

VI. Conclude the argument is flawed
    A.   Assumes the current system results in decreased public safety
    B.   Assumes there are no simpler solutions
    C.   Assumes the costs are worth the benefits

Below Average Response

I. Argument lacks information
    A.   Most injuries happen due to crowded beaches

II. No link between life guard shifts and decreased public safety

III. Offer alternatives
    A.   Limit number of swimmers
    B.   Hire additional life guards
    C.   Take additional breaks

IV. More information is needed

Argument Analysis Essay (p. 692)
Exercise 5

Above Average Response

The argument that the workday of lifeguards must be decreased from ten hours to eight hours in order to increase public safety is flawed for four reasons. First, it assumes that there is currently a serious danger to public safety as a result of longer lifeguard shifts. Second, the argument assumes that less drastic alternatives are not available. Third, it assumes that the proposed plan would result in increased public safety. And finally, it assumes that the costs associated with longer lifeguard shifts may outweigh any benefit to public safety.

In the first place, the argument fails to prove the assumption that the public is currently unsafe. Not only is the extent of the danger to the public not established, but we are given no information about how the longer shifts are the cause of this alleged danger. It may seem plausible that the public is in greater danger because lifeguards are increasingly tired towards the end of their shifts, but an assumed increase in public endangerment may equally be due to other causes, such as beach crowding or swimmer fatigue. It would important to know both the current degree of public endangerment as well as how it is a function of the length of lifeguard shifts.

Second, it assumes that simpler means cannot solve any problem with public safety that does exist. Rules could be enforced that would have the impact of increasing safety at the public beaches. For example, decreasing the swimmer capacity of beaches would increase safety as the available lifeguards would better be able to monitor swim activity. Another simple safety measure would be to decrease the amount of time each swimmer is allowed in the water, thereby decreasing swimmer fatigue and the probability of accidents. Finally, simpler alternative changes could be made to the lifeguard shifts, such as increased break frequency or overlapping existing shifts. Such effortless actions should be pursued before the more complicated measure of decreasing lifeguard shifts.

Third, it assumes that changing the length of lifeguard shifts would positively impact public safety. In fact, there is the chance that this could have the opposite effect. Shortening lifeguard shifts would mean hiring more lifeguards, and as the available pool of applicants is exhausted, lifeguards may be hired who are not sufficiently trained or experienced, resulting in the public being less protected. Therefore, before implementing changes to the length of lifeguard shifts, we must be ensured that said changes will not negatively impact public safety.

Finally, it assumes that the cost of the plan to decrease the lifeguard shifts outweighs any existing endangerment to public safety. Changing the shift lengths from ten hours to eight hours will necessarily require training and hiring additional lifeguards. This increase in costs for maintaining a lifeguard staff may have the negative consequence of cost overruns for the state's public beaches. Obviously, having to close beaches because they are too costly to maintain is an outcome that nobody benefits from.

In conclusion, the argument for decreasing lifeguard shifts is not persuasive. Before such a plan is pursued, we must be convinced that the current system of longer shifts is the cause for decreased public safety at our beaches. In addition, we must be sure that simpler solutions are not possible and if so, the proposal for shorter shifts is subjected to vigorous cost-benefit analysis. It's not a question of wanting safer beaches—obviously this is the desired result. Rather, we must be diligent in the process for achieving these means.

Position on issue: This essay competently cites a number of deficiencies in the argument presented: the information presented about public safety doesn't warrant the conclusion, simpler means may exist, and nothing is presented to suggest the proposal would be effective or without unwanted side effects.

Topic development and essay organization: The essay then goes on to clearly discuss each flaw in a logical and sensible manner. Each point discussed is clearly introduced and developed within a separate paragraph, supported by thoughtful insight into alternative solutions and necessary evidence. The essay ends with a concluding paragraph that nicely reiterates the points of the essay without being repetitive.

Language usage, sentence structure, and punctuation: Overall, the writer demonstrates good control of language, including diction and syntactic variety, though some phrases are repeated several times. Minor errors in language ("It would important to know") exist, but are to be expected.

Summary and conclusions: This essay would score a "5" or possibly a "6." The analysis of the proposal is clearly developed with insightful reasons and examples, though it is sometimes weakened by needless repetition of the same language.

Below Average Response

The argument has no information about the threat to public safety at the state's public beaches. I think most cases of injury to swimmers happens because the beaches are so crowded. Irregardless, there is no reason to think of decreasing the length of the lifeguard shifts would solve the problem.

I think this argument is not logically reasonable. It's assumption is that decreased public safety at the state's public beaches are caused by long lifeguard shifts. If the beaches are so crowded the lifeguards can't even see what is happening, it will matter how short or long the lifeguards' shifts are.

If the argument was providing evidence that the problem of decreased public safety at the state's public beaches is in fact due to the length of the lifeguard shifts, this would not be a much more unconvincing argument.

Therefore, unless it is proved that the public was at risk because the lifeguard shifts are going too long, other things can be done. For example, limit the number of swimmers at the beaches. Or, hire additional lifeguards. Finally, whether the decreased public safety is really because of the long lifeguard shifts, other solutions exist. For example, lifeguards could take breaks so not getting tired.

Therefore, more information about the threat to public safety at the state's public beaches is needed before the issue can be adequately addressed.

Position on issue: The essay does present a critique based on analysis of the argument's flaws, but the problems with language confuse this analysis. For example, the second paragraph begins by stating the argument is not reasonable, but then due to confusion of language ends by stating the proposal would be effective.

Topic development and essay organization: The essay doesn't develop clearly and basically reiterates the same point several times. While the essay attempt to introduce some examples of other solutions in the second to last paragraph, they are not properly developed nor appear to be logically placed due to problems with language.

Language usage, sentence structure, and punctuation: The essay contains numerous errors in grammar ("injury to swimmers happens," "argument was providing," "breaks so not getting tired"), usage ("Irregardless," "to think of decreasing the length of," "whether the decreased...other solutions exist"), and mechanics ("It's assumption"). Furthermore, several sentences contain language that confuses the meaning intended (last sentence of second paragraph, entire third paragraph).

Summary and conclusions: This essay would probably score a "2." It is seriously flawed mainly due to numerous errors in grammar, usage, and mechanics that interfere with its meaning. These problems with language further cause problems in the development of the ideas, making the essay disorganized and illogical.

Argument Analysis Revision (p. 693)
Exercise 6

Above Average Response

The writer should:

- avoid needless repetition of the same phrases; and

- fix minor errors in language.

Below Average Response

The writer should:

- fix errors in grammar, usage, and mechanics;

- clearly introduce and expand on each point before transitioning to the next point;

- avoid restating the same point; and

- reorganize text so that examples appear in with the point they are supporting.

ITEM INDEX

In the following index, all of the numeric references are designed as follows: **Page #/Item #**. The parenthetical information beside each item category refers to the subject–area in which that item category appears.

ITEM INDEX • 795

Graphs of Linear Equations (Coordinate Geometry)

Discrete Quantitative Lesson: **179**/93; **182**/108

Graphs of Quadratic Equations and Relations (Coordinate Geometry)

Discrete Quantitative Lesson: **180**/95–96

Implied Idea (Reading Comprehension)

Lesson: **75**/8–10; **78**/23–24; **81**/37, 39; **82**/40; **83**/46, 48; **85**/55–56; **87**/60, 62–63; **89**/69–70, 72; **90**/75; **92**/84; **93**/86; **94**/90; **95**/94; **99**/104; **101**/110; **104**/119; **105**/122; **107**/127, 130; **109**/134; **110**/138–139; **111**/143; **113**/149
Quiz I: **135**/2; **137**/5
Quiz II: **139**/1–3; **140**/4
Quiz III: **144**/6–7
Directed Study Practice Test, Section 3: **335**/4; **338**/9; **339**/12
Directed Study Practice Test, Section 4: **354**/15; **356**/19
Practice Test I, Section 3: **390**/18
Practice Test I, Section 4: **395**/6; **398**/16; **400**/24
Practice Test II, Section 3: **417**/3; **421**/17
Practice Test II, Section 4: **425**/8; **431**/24
Practice Test III, Section 3: **449**/2; **454**/18
Practice Test III, Section 4: **459**/9; **461**/14–15; **464**/23

The Inference (Critical Reading)

Lesson: **122–129**/172–190; **130–133**/192–200
Quiz II: **142**/9–10
Directed Study Practice Test, Section 3: **340**/13
Directed Study Practice Test, Section 4: **360**/25
Practice Test I, Section 3: **386**/5
Practice Test I, Section 4: **398**/18
Practice Test II, Section 3: **418**/5; **422**/21; **423**/22
Practice Test II, Section 4: **426**/9
Practice Test III, Section 3: **450**/3–4
Practice Test III, Section 4: **459**/10; **462**/21

Key Adjectives and Adverbs (Combined Reasoning)

Lesson: **40**/60, 65; **41**/72; **42**/74
Quiz III: **52**/3
Directed Study Practice Test, Section 3: **336**/6
Practice Test I, Section 3: **389**/15–16
Practice Test I, Section 4: **396**/11–12; **399**/21
Practice Test II, Section 3: **420**/13, 16
Practice Test II, Section 4: **426**/10–12
Practice Test III, Section 3: **450**/6; **451**/7

Practice Test III, Section 4: **460**/11; **462**/19

Key Adjectives and Adverbs (Thought Extension)

Lesson: **34**/12–15; **35**/16; **40**/62
Directed Study Practice Test, Section 3: **345**/21
Directed Study Practice Test, Section 4: **347**/1; **348**/4
Practice Test I, Section 4: **393**/4; **394**/5
Practice Test II, Section 3: **423**/24
Practice Test II, Section 4: **424**/3–4; **429**/21
Practice Test III, Section 4: **457**/4

Key Adjectives and Adverbs (Thought Reversal)

Lesson: **38**/47–48, 50; **41**/69
Practice Test III, Section 3: **456**/24

Line Graphs (Data Interpretation)

Lesson: **277**/25–29; **278**/30–32; **279**/34–35; **280**/36–38
Quiz I: **293**/1–2; **294**/3–5
Quiz III: **296**/1–5
Practice Test I, Section 5: **405**/20–21
Practice Test II, Section 6: **441**/14–15
Practice Test III, Section 5: **471**/18–19
Practice Test III, Section 6: **477**/13–14

Lines and Angles (Geometry and Geometry Comparison)

Discrete Quantitative Lesson: **166**/10; **167**/11–12; **170**/34; **185**/120, 124; **186**/127
Discrete Quantitative Quiz I: **194**/10
Discrete Quantitative Quiz III: **197**/4
Numeric Entry Lesson: **212**/23; **214**/38, 42
Numeric Entry Quiz I: **217**/4
Numeric Entry Quiz II: **219**/1
Comparisons Lesson: **240**/59; **243**/101; **247**/128–129; **248**/132
Comparisons Quiz I: **251**/2
Comparisons Quiz II: **253**/8
Comparisons Quiz III: **254**/4
Directed Study Practice Test, Section 5: **362**/5; **365**/12–13
Directed Study Practice Test, Section 6: **376**/15
Practice Test I, Section 5: **401**/1; **402**/4, 6
Practice Test II, Section 5: **432**/1
Practice Test II, Section 6: **440**/10; **443**/24
Practice Test III, Section 6: **478**/19, 22

Cambridge *Victory for the GRE® Test, 10th Edition*
Error Correction and Suggestion Form

Name/Location:_____ Day Phone:_____ E-mail Address:_____

Part of Materials: ☐ Student Text, Specify Subject:_____ Page:_____ Item:_____
☐ Teacher's Guide, Specify Subject:_____ Page:_____ Item:_____

Error/Suggestion:_____
_____
_____

Part of Materials: ☐ Student Text, Specify Subject:_____ Page:_____ Item:_____
☐ Teacher's Guide, Specify Subject:_____ Page:_____ Item:_____

Error/Suggestion:_____
_____
_____

Part of Materials: ☐ Student Text, Specify Subject:_____ Page:_____ Item:_____
☐ Teacher's Guide, Specify Subject:_____ Page:_____ Item:_____

Error/Suggestion:_____
_____
_____

Part of Materials: ☐ Student Text, Specify Subject:_____ Page:_____ Item:_____
☐ Teacher's Guide, Specify Subject:_____ Page:_____ Item:_____

Error/Suggestion:_____
_____
_____

Part of Materials: ☐ Student Text, Specify Subject:_____ Page:_____ Item:_____
☐ Teacher's Guide, Specify Subject:_____ Page:_____ Item:_____

Error/Suggestion:_____
_____
_____

Part of Materials: ☐ Student Text, Specify Subject:_____ Page:_____ Item:_____
☐ Teacher's Guide, Specify Subject:_____ Page:_____ Item:_____

Error/Suggestion:_____
_____
_____

Mail form to Cambridge Educational Services, Inc., O'Hare Atrium Office Center, 2860 S. River Road, Des Plaines, IL 60018, or fax form to 1-847-299-2933. Visit our Web site at www.CambridgeEd.com.